THE PSALMS

The Psalms

Translated and Interpreted in the
Light of Hebrew Life and Worship

ELMER A. LESLIE

ABINGDON PRESS
New York • *Nashville*

THE PSALMS

Copyright MCMXLIX by Pierce & Smith

Library of Congress Catalog Card Number: 49-8204

D

SET UP, PRINTED, AND BOUND BY THE
PARTHENON PRESS, AT NASHVILLE,
TENNESSEE, UNITED STATES OF AMERICA

To
my brother
WILLIAM ROBERT LESLIE
in admiration, gratitude, and deep affection

PREFACE

This volume has one major aim, to make the reading of the psalms an intelligible, interesting, and inspiring experience. Its appeal is to ministers, thoughtful laymen, and students, who know that the Psalter contains untold spiritual wealth, yet feel themselves to be in possession of but a small part of it. Its intent is to bring to the average reader of the Bible, in nontechnical terms, the sifted results of the most reliable scholarly study of these lyric expressions of Hebrew life and worship.

Acknowledgment of indebtedness to particular interpreters of the Psalms is due, and I record it here gratefully. Those who are familiar with Dr. Hermann Gunkel's commentary *Die Psalmen übersetzt und erklärt* and his introduction *Einleitung in den Psalmen* will recognize his influence along three lines: The first is the placing of the psalms of Israel side by side with the psalms of Egypt and Babylonia, both in similarity and in contrast. The second is the distinguishing of numerous literary types among the psalms, which owe their origin to the variety of functions the psalms had in the living worship of the Hebrews (*Sitz im Leben*). The third is his masterful guidance at points where the Hebrew text of the Psalter is manifestly imperfect. He gives a clear analysis of the difficulties. He surveys and weighs the value of the reconstructions suggested by the most capable scholars, then presents his own tentative solution. His suggestions, often starting from his classification of the psalm as to literary type, give evidence of an intellectual and spiritual intuition comparable to that of Martin Luther.

Those familiar with the six stimulating *Psalmenstudien* by Dr. Sigmund Mowinckel of Norway will likewise recognize the great indebtedness to him. His work has given a new insight into the meaning of the cult, the organized public worship of ancient Israel, and along with this a deepened appreciation of the primitive force of the covenantal religion which unfolds before us in the Psalms.

In Chapter X and the first part of Chapter XI there is great indebtedness to a careful study by Dr. Hans Schmidt of "The Prayer of the Accused in the Psalms." Likewise the influence of his commentary *Die Psalmen,* with its sensitive knowledge of the folk life of Palestine, will be evident at many points.

Three features characterize this volume. First, there is a fresh translation of every psalm in the Psalter, on the basis of the third edition of Dr. Rudolf Kittel's *Biblia Hebraica* (1937), with careful heed to the critical notes, in which are concentrated the sifted findings of textual study on the part of generations of Old Testament scholars. Students of the Hebrew text will readily recognize this in the translation, although the earnest desire to make the fruits of such study available to the nontechnical reader has necessitated the reduction of explanatory

7

notes to the minimum. The translations embody much of the color and flavor suggested by the root meanings of the Hebrew words. They also retain, wherever possible, the rhythmical stresses characteristic of the lines of Hebrew poetry. Because of the religious quality of the content it has seemed wise to use "the Lord" instead of "Yahweh" for the name of Israel's God. While I have always proceeded from the Hebrew text, the numbering of the verses is in accord with the English versions. No knotty problem of interpretation has consciously been evaded. I have tried to give as clearly as possible the meaning most likely intended by each particular psalmist.

Second, a title has been given to each psalm, and in the case of Ps. 119 one in addition to each of its twenty-two sections. In every case I have sought a phrase or a sentence to suggest the very heart of the psalm. The nature of the treatment has made it seem wise to ignore the present order of the psalms and to interpret them in groups in accordance with the various types of worship setting in Hebrew religion which they represent. Each psalm is dealt with as a separate unit as well as in relation to its group. Such a treatment naturally involves some repetition. Occasionally, as in the Prayers of the Falsely Accused, there is much similarity between the separate psalms in the group. Yet even in such cases the reader will be enabled to see all the more clearly the remarkable variety that is there also. The Table of Contents on the following pages will show the various groups and the psalms assigned to each. To facilitate locating quickly a particular psalm which one may desire to consult, an index of every psalm in numerical order, along with its title, has been provided immediately following the Table of Contents.

Third, the psalm itself and its interpretation are in each case so interwoven that the experience which the psalm embodies unfolds before one's eyes. One is prepared for the clear understanding of each portion of the psalm in turn, then is led through it so that section by section he knows what he is reading, understands its allusions, and feels the relation it bears, both in form and content, to the total experience which the psalm represents. Thus he is kept face to face with the great words of the psalmists themselves. At the same time the footnotes will guide him to the Bibliography, where other sources of background and interpretation are available.

The most important introductory questions as regards the book of Psalms are not handled here because I have already discussed these matters in the article "Introduction to Psalms" in the *Abingdon Bible Commentary*. The questions concerning the psalm superscriptions and the significance of certain technical terms in them are there dealt with, and I have utilized some of that material in this volume. Since the superscriptions did not form part of the original psalms, the translations here presented begin in each case with the psalms themselves.

Into this volume have gone many hundreds of hours of earnest and conscientious toil. I have really lived with these outpourings of the heart of Israel. They are to me the priceless classics of the soul's quest for God—the soul of the congregation and the soul of the individual. It is my hope that this book may help the Psalms to become that for others.

I am greatly indebted to my graduate student assistant, the Rev. Willard A. Page, pastor of the Community Church, West Dennis, Massachusetts, and his wife. Their keen interest in the material, her skill in typing, and his ready assistance in innumerable ways I here gratefully acknowledge.

Most of all I am indebted to my wife, without whose sacrificial co-operation through the years the book could never have been written. Her generous devotion, unfailing interest, and constructive criticism of content and form have been of inestimable value. She carefully read the entire manuscript and typed the greater part of it in its final form.

ELMER A. LESLIE

CONTENTS

INDEX TO THE PSALMS

Chapter I

THE PSALMS IN LIVING WORSHIP

IN THE PSALMS WE CONFRONT THE RELIGION OF ISRAEL IN ALL ITS RANGES AND reaches, in its vast variety of tempers and moods. Here is to be found religion so pure, so deeply spiritual, that without the least sense of obtrusion we can place it alongside the profoundest ideas and the loftiest heights of aspiration in the words of Jesus or Paul. Yet in the psalms we are frequently face to face with tempers of harsh national exclusiveness, and of sharp and passionate vindictiveness which even a mediocre moral standard would vehemently condemn. Often these two ranges of religious expression appear in the same psalm, and both of them are genuine in the experience of the particular psalmist.

As we immerse ourselves in this literature, however, and as we set ourselves sympathetically at the point of view of the psalmists themselves—seeing with their eyes, feeling with their souls, and thinking from their outlook in time— we gradually lay hold of a very helpful and emancipating thought. The piety that is uncovered so vividly in the Psalter is not static but dynamic. It is a growing piety. In that religious experience, the spiritual fountain that created the psalms, there is something alive. And just as life, particularly under discipline, rejects as it grows, so the piety of the Psalter corrects itself. To be sure, this is not often apparent within the limits of an individual psalm, which is the creature of a particular time and mood, but in the psalms taken as a whole it is perfectly evident. If it were possible to arrange the material chronologically with some degree of certainty, this growing religious life of the Psalter and its self-corrective power would become plain.

At the same time it is well to remember that chronological order does not necessarily mean the order of ethical and spiritual progress. Knowledge of our own times, with waves of idealism followed by waves of reaction, helps us to be sensitive to this. In Israel's history the broad universalism of Deutero-Isaiah with his concept of one God for all the world was followed by a flinthearted nationalism which would make a fetish of the chosen-people idea and lose out of Israelite religion that breadth and tolerance which gave it world vision and world mission.

Of central importance for an adequate appreciation of the Psalter is the germinal and self-corrective power of the piety that is here unveiled. For in the psalms we meet religious experience in its primitive heart-outpouring. It is permeated with the consciousness of a vital, personal relationship to a living God. Here is something dynamic, instinct with life, and therefore growing. If we keep this in mind as we read the psalms, we will not close our eyes to the primitive tempers—far lower than Christian, and indeed far lower than normative Hebrew, spirit—which we shall frequently meet. We will not gloss them over, mini-

17

mize them, or apologize for them. Rather we will look at them frankly, with fear-
less eyes, seeing in them revelations of mental and spiritual attitudes which were
very real in the particular psalmist's day, and which, we must admit, still persist
in our time even within sincerely religious circles. And we will view such tempers
with no pharisaical superiority, constantly thinking, "We have got beyond this."
Rather we will see more of ourselves in these pained and stirred lives. In the
striking words of H. Scott Holland we will say:

> There am I. I see myself in all these tribes: I am one with all these poor sufferers. They
> work for me; our souls run together; we are one. The whole teeming life is my life; I
> fling myself into all these efforts—its hopes, its labors, its weariness, its pain. . . . I grow
> with its growth; I feel myself alive in it: and therefore I am utterly committed to it. [1]

One who immerses himself in the psalms and makes an earnest effort to understand what the psalmists were trying to say finds himself bridging the chasm
of centuries between the present and past. He feels himself very close to the living,
breathing, suffering, and rejoicing psalmist. And the most profound impression
left upon him is the amazing reality of the psalmist's sense of relationship with
God. Whatever there is in the psalmist's experience which may seem temporarily
to befog this relationship vanishes before it like a cloud before the burning sun.
Here is thought; here is emotion; here is the poetic rhythm of spiritual exaltation. But deepest of all is this sense of relationship. God is a Being, not of
whom, but unto whom the psalmist speaks. The words of the Psalter are alive
with the awareness of an Other. The religion of the psalms is a communion,
a sharing between the human and the divine. And the thing that lifts this
communion, great as it is in itself, to something yet nobler and more potent is
that it is communion with God *in fellowship with other men.* For always behind the experience of the psalmist, undergirding it and buoying it up, is the
social fellowship of the congregation.

There may be a few instances where the influence of the congregation was
not a present fact in the psalm's creation or rendition. A distinction is sometimes made between "spiritual songs," sung at home or elsewhere entirely
away from the organized public worship and never intended for it, and cultic
songs, belonging in the public congregation and intended to be rendered there.
Even if this distinction be granted, it was worship in the congregation—in the
worshiping fellowship—that had created the very vocabulary of the soul's communion. What the author of the "spiritual song" derived from the public congregation is inestimably great. The fellowship of public worship is the spiritual
mother of individual religious utterance. Moreover, Sigmund Mowinckel's brilliant and extraordinarily suggestive studies in the psalms have made it appear
most likely that practically every psalm in the Psalter was intended for rendition
in the regular and officially constituted worship of the Temple and is rightly

---

[1] Quoted in Wade Crawford Barclay, *A Book of Worship,* p. 187.

understood as a part of that worship. This point of view makes clear how the public worship of the Temple with its strong congregational consciousness fed the springs of personal piety. Equally important, it helps us see how the depth and intensity of personal piety—illustrated, for instance, in the songs of individual thanksgiving—stimulated, purified, and deepened the corporate religious values of the Temple worship.

A new epoch of insight as to the interpretation of the psalms began with the work of Hermann Gunkel. He was keenly aware that the Israelite psalms were a distinctive part of the psalmody of the Middle East. Indeed, in all his work on the Old Testament he has insisted on viewing the literature of Israel in its total ancient East context in order rightly to interpret it. He did not isolate Israel from its world, but saw Israel and what came from Israel's soul in this more extensive association. It is inevitable that the highly developed national religions of Egypt and Babylonia, each with its elaborate public cult, would influence the worship of Israel, particularly after the Temple had been built. Both Egypt and Babylonia influenced the hymns of the Psalter in style and in content. Babylonian psalms profoundly influenced the individual laments. Immersion in the psalmody of Egypt and of Babylonia, however, only sends us back to the psalmody of Israel with a sense of its immeasurably greater spiritual power and with the certainty that whatever Israel may have derived from these sources, it was no passive spiritual recipient.

But more distinctive than this linkage of Israelite psalmody with that of the ancient East, although greatly helped by it, is Gunkel's insistence on penetrating behind the literature to the life that created it. For every part of Old Testament literature, for each separate piece of it, he insists that we must ask how this individual, originally independent fragment of literature came into being. In ancient Israel very little was written. The earliest portions of literature in the Old Testament probably do not date before 1200 B.C., and few indeed had their origin before 1000 B.C. We must go back to the time when literature was not yet written, but was a part of the folk life; when it was sung poetry or recited poetry; and when, to the accompaniment of music and dance, it was *lived* by the folk soul of Israel. Every type of song which we meet in the Old Testament had its own distinctive place in the diversified life of the people. There were the work songs sung by laborers in the field as they toiled. There were the joyous harvest songs and the songs of the vineyard. At night there were the songs of the watchman from his watchtower. There were wedding songs for commoners in Israel and other songs which celebrated the marriage of kings. There were love songs rendered in the prolonged celebrations of weddings, which praised the charms of the bride or the bravery of her spouse. There were public laments at fasts, and there were private personal laments. There were triumph songs, national and personal, to celebrate great victories. There were songs of satire wherein, for example, Israel revealed just how it felt about Moab, or in which popular judgment upon an individual might be voiced with unforgettable incisiveness. Each of these songs had its own mood, its distinctive gestures, and its characteristic accompaniment of action. All of these types of songs were sung long before words, notes, or music were written. Each had its own differentiating marks and its own unique place in the people's life. To use a phrase which Gunkel has coined, each had its own *Sitz im Leben*, its own "seat in the life" of Israel. Here is literature while it is still in the mouth of Israel. Such songs were passed on from person to person and from group to group and so from generation to generation, largely, as with folk songs today, by means of oral transmission. These songs with their accompanying music and action created the forms which developed into what Gunkel calls *Gattungen*, or literary types. Each literary type had its own particular setting in the life of the people. Who wrote it and when it was written become relatively unimportant questions. But the kind of utterance it was, how it was expressed, where it was spoken or sung, and the function it had—such questions are all-important.

Thus far we have been thinking of secular life. But from its very foundation as a people with a germinal national consciousness, which was the achievement of Moses, Israel was a religious nation, and its literature had largely a religious character. It is a striking fact that almost all existing literature of Israel which dates from before the Exile is included in the Old Testament. As was the case in Egypt and Babylonia, only to a greater degree, from the very beginning of Israel's life the religious literature predominated over the secular.

To the psalms, accordingly, we must make this same kind of approach through their life setting. Fundamental to Gunkel's understanding of the psalms is the recognition that their origin is to be found in the organized public worship, the cult. We move imperceptibly in Israel from the life situation which created secular songs to the cultic or worship situation which created Temple psalms. For each psalm we should ask: What is its real origin and purpose? What is it intended to do? We must look for the characteristic marks of its setting in Hebrew worship. In some psalms to discern this is a simple matter. To ask the question as to its life or worship setting is to answer it. But in many a psalm this is not so plain because it is not all of one type. Different literary types and worship settings are combined in it to form a richer but more complex whole. When this is the case, the psalm dates from a period when the different literary types had begun to meet, mingle, and influence each other. This period set in at approximately 500 B.C.

When that life setting in worship which gives the psalm its most distinctive character has been discovered for every psalm of the Psalter, we can readily arrange the psalms in major groups. We have then learned where to take hold of a psalm, because we know its most distinctive mark.

In such an approach to the psalms we become sensitive to form, not merely of literary beauty, but of cultic expression. Yet always we must go behind the form to the life it embodied and expressed. To get at the forms of religious expression and the exact nature of the worship settings of the psalms through literary marks must be a major aim.

The result of interpreting the psalms in accordance with their setting in Hebrew worship is threefold. In the first place, one is surprised by the rich diversity in the Psalter. A famous American scholar, whose work is in an entirely different area from this, once confessed to me that he got very little out of the psalms, for they all seemed to be so much alike. However, a mere glance through the Table of Contents of this volume will suggest the rich diversity embraced by 150 psalms. Here is variety in the personalities of the psalmists, in their religious outlook, in their literary skill and poetic power. Here is rich diversity of the social background of the psalmists, their psychological mood in worship, and their physical condition as they sing and pray. Here is great difference in the bodily attitudes of the psalmists and even in the garments of the worshipers, both described and implied. Whether speaking for themselves as individuals or on behalf of the worshiping congregational fellowship, the psalmists had one major concern—to lay hold upon the power of God. Yet how manifold were the ways by which they sought His presence and help!

A second result is a new sense of the significance of public worship, past, present, and future. There is drama in public worship. Indeed, one may say that public worship is creative drama, both in its intention and in its spiritual results. The study of the types of worship situation in the psalms gives one a new feeling about the importance of every separate part in the order of contemporary worship. The organ voluntary takes the place of trumpet, lyre, harp, flute, and cymbals. The processional of choir and ministers is historically linked to the processionals of ancient Israel into the sanctuary. The call to worship is a congregational summons to praise. Note the expressed or implied gesture accompanying the invocation whereby the officiating minister—acting as priest—invokes the divine presence. The hymns sung by choir, congregation, and ministers are chosen—with a spiritual sensitiveness attuned to the church season or to the particular mood and need of the hour—from the rich repertoire of congregational psalms, hymns, and spiritual songs. That such was the case in the worship of the Jerusalem Temple the following interpretations will make clear. These hymns in turn have been gathered and selected by the felt needs of the living Church across the centuries. As did the Levitical choirs of the Temple, so the church choir lifts the anthem, and a single clear tenor voice sings a psalm of personal thanksgiving. Then comes that remarkable group of worship themes concentrated in the ritual of the offering. Here is unique connection with the thank offering of ancient Israel. First is the invitation to give, then the (priestly) blessing upon the givers and the gathering of the offering by the laymen ushers, acting as Temple servants. Then follows that high moment in this ritual when the congregation rise to sing their doxology as the offering is presented and placed upon the altar in their behalf. The prayer of dedication to the work of God in its world-wide extent closes this varied worship ritual. Then comes a solemn hush in the worship when the minister, as priest, bears the needs of his people to God in a comprehensive yet brief intercession, at the close of which minister and congregation in unison recite the Church's most beloved prayer. A hymn that inspires in the congregation the mood of quiet receptivity is followed by that climactic moment when the minister, now as prophet, brings the living word of "thus saith the Lord" to his people. This corresponds to the prophetic oracle in the psalms. The final hymn with its note of spiritual commitment follows, and toward its close comes the recessional of choir and ministers—how greatly beloved were such ceremonies in Israel— bringing the ministers to the rear of the sanctuary. There, with hands extended over the congregation, the presiding minister, again as priest, pronounces the benediction, the "good words" of the Lord's blessing, succeeded by the choir's "Amen." There follow the hushed moments of silent prayer, with the congregation standing, sitting, or kneeling before the organ peals the glad music of spiritual encouragement and challenge to divine enterprise. Every element is richly present in the "seat in life" approach to the psalms. To the worshiper made sensitive to this approach will come suggestions, new trails yet untrod to the throne of grace, new forms for expressing modern moods and tempers and for stimulating contemporary commitments of active faith.

A third result is that we shall learn to view a psalm first as the soul utterance of the unknown psalmist who created it, and then as a vehicle of the soul utterance, whether congregational or individual, of others. There was a time when that which a particular psalm tells us was unwritten, unreported, living experience. In early Israel when the psalms were in the making, many a gifted individual sang forth in the Temple what God had done for his soul. The experience itself preceded its telling. The telling often preceded its literary formulation. The written psalm followed the living Temple witness. There must have been many instances in Israel when a religious-minded priest encouraged a gifted worshiper to put his own vital experience in literary form. Thus his blessing at God's hands might be used to encourage other worshipers yet to come. And it is reasonable to believe, with Mowinckel, that many a psalm owes its origin to the Temple singers who knew music, who knew the needs of worshipers, and who knew God.

There was a particular moment for each psalm when for the first time it was sung in the Jerusalem Temple. However much the congregation might have shared in creating it, in the final analysis it came from one individual's hand. The worshiper who created it, however, speaks not merely for himself. There is little of the purely personal in what he says, for his ego is merged in the "we," "our," and "us" which mark his psalm. He writes what will be a medium of expression for the greater social unit of the congregation. The Temple repertoire thus gradually grew, and there were many collections of psalms across the centuries, as the present discernible collections imply.

The psalms of the Psalter represent the survival of the fittest. Out of more than six centuries of life during which national or congregational worship was carried on in the Temple at Jerusalem, only 150 psalms survive, plus a few now in other parts of the Bible, in the Apocrypha, and in the Pseudepigrapha. We can be reasonably sure that whatever the editorial process out of which the psalms of the Psalter were finally chosen, the desire of the editors was to produce the best collection possible. Those which the Psalter contains have met the test of value both to the congregation as a whole and to its participating members. The remarkable popularity of the psalms across more than twenty centuries is witness that the editors did their work well.

Chapter II

THE HYMN IN HEBREW WORSHIP

THE HYMN IS A SONG GLORIFYING GOD SUNG AT THE SANCTUARY ON A HOLY DAY before the assembled congregation. It was sung by the choir or by a gifted individual singer and occupied a place of prime importance in the public worship of Israel from the earliest historical era of Israelite religion to the late years of the Temple worship at Jerusalem.

One of the earliest of Israelite hymns is the Song of Miriam (Exod. 15:21), and an early hymn sung by an individual singer is the Song of Deborah (Judg. 5), both dating before 1000 B.C. The Wisdom of Jesus son of Sirach (*ca.* 180 B.C.) presents us with a picture of the living worship of the latest Temple services of Judaism. There appear singers before the altar making sweet melody by their music, participating in the orderly worship of the Temple year, glorifying the name of the Lord, and making the sanctuary resound from early morning with His praise (Ecclus. 47:8-10).

The roots of the hymn are not national or political, but psychological and universal. The hymn gives utterance to the deepest and most instinctive spiritual need of man, "to kneel in the dust, and worship that which is higher than himself." [1] Consequently the hymn is not unique to Israel but is the earliest discernible form of religious utterance in the whole cultural milieu of Egypt, Babylonia, and Canaan. It was in close relationship with this cultural area that Israel lived, moved, and had its being throughout the Old Testament period. Let us then note the cultural environment of the Hebrew hymn and, to some extent, of Hebrew psalmody as a whole.

1. THE CULTURAL ENVIRONMENT OF HEBREW HYMNODY

Egypt presents religious hymns from the age of the pyramids (2890-2470 B.C.). The literary feature of parallelism of lines is already present in these hymns, a feature which dates from the fourth millennium B.C. [2] This same literary element is destined to become the most characteristic feature of Hebrew poetry, and there is no question that it played its part in the latter's development. In the New Kingdom of Egypt (1580-1150 B.C.) hymns were sung by women singers "before the beautiful countenance of the god, . . . to the accompaniment of the sistrum." [3] Among the most beautiful examples of world poetry are the hymns to Aton, the sun god, which come from around 1400 B.C., the epoch of Amenhotep IV (Ikhnaton), and reveal a high standard of psalmody.

[1] Gunkel, *What Remains of the Old Testament*, p. 74.
[2] See Breasted, *The Development of Religion and Thought in Ancient Egypt*, p. 97.
[3] Erman, *Handbook of Egyptian Religion*, p. 72.

In Babylonia, long before Israel had entered Canaan, hymns were sung in the literary form of parallelism to the accompaniment of stringed instruments "to rejoice the heart of the gods." [4] Among the most beautiful and characteristic of these are the hymns to Marduk and to Sarpanitum that are part of the ritual of the Babylonian New Year festival (*Akitu*) [5] and were among the best known in Babylonian psalmody. However, as Stummer points out, [6] in the Babylonian hymns the congregation, as such, played no role. The contrast to this in Israel is an indication of the towering superiority of the Hebrew hymns to the Babylonian in national importance and influence. They are full of the consciousness of the worshiping congregation, and in the rendering of them there was a large extent of congregational participation.

After 597 B.C., the date when the first phase of the Chaldean captivity of the Judeans took place, the influence of Babylonia upon Hebrew life and worship was direct and very great. But before that date whatever influence may have come upon Hebrew hymnody from both Egypt and Babylonia was for the most part indirect. This, however, was not the case so far as the influence of Canaan is concerned. To a great extent Canaan was simply the cultural medium through which both Egyptian and Babylonian influences reached Israel. But in 1928 occurred the discovery of a number of mythological-religious texts from ancient Ugarit, now called the Ras esh-Shamra, situated on the Mediterranean coast in North Canaan. From these texts we can now see that Canaan in her own right had a rich religious poetry to which in language, grammar, the literary feature of parallelism of lines, and a meter of word stresses the psalmody of Israel has marked similarity. Only one hymn is in this group of texts. They are, for the most part, epic poems with mythological themes. But at many points they explain allusions in the psalms, and they set the psalms of the Old Testament in a new light.[7]

Many years before the discovery of these texts from ancient Canaan, Dr. Franz Böhl had already called attention to the "rich treasure of hymn literature which pre-Israelite Canaan must have possessed, which Israel received from Canaan as an inheritance." He had uncovered the "psalm fragments" embodied in the Tell el-Amarna letters, written by Canaanite chieftains to the Egyptian Pharaohs Amenhotep III and IV (1411-1375 B.C.). [8] From early Old Testament evidence (Judg. 9:27) we know that Canaanite worshipers sang "songs of jubilation" [9] in the temple of Baal-Berith of Shechem in the period before the Israelite mon-

---

[4] Meissner, *Babylonien und Assyrien*, I, 331-32.

[5] Thureau-Dangin, "Le ritual des fêtes du nouvel an à Babylone," in *Rituels Accadiens*, pp. 127-48.

[6] *Sumerisch-akkadische Parallelen zum Aufbau alttestamentlicher Psalmen*, p. 26.

[7] See Patton, *Canaanite Parallels in the Book of Psalms*, esp. pp. v, 1, 4 ff., 13-14, 47-48.

[8] For a full discussion with concrete examples of this Canaanite psalmody and contacts of Israelite psalmody with it see Leslie, *Old Testament Religion, in the Light of Its Canaanite Background*, pp. 134-38.

[9] The descriptive words are *wayya'asû hillûlîm*; see Gunkel, *Einleitung*, p. 59.

archy. Such Canaanite hymns of praise to the deity probably began to be in-fluential in Hebrew psalmody at least as early as the establishment of the Solomonic Temple. By the eighth century B.C., as we know from the prophet Amos' trenchant words, hymns were sung to Israel's God to the accompaniment of the harp at the famed sanctuary of Bethel.[10]

2. THE SPIRIT AND THE VARIETY OF HEBREW HYMNS

The hymns all belong to the regularly established public worship of the sanctuary. First and foremost the hymn was rendered in close relation to the act of sacrifice and belongs to it.[11] The Chronicler, Judaism's chief historian of the official Temple cultus in Jerusalem informs us: "And when the burnt offering began, then the song of the Lord began, and the trumpets together with the instruments of David, king of Israel. Then all the congregation prostrated themselves, and the singers sang, and the trumpeters sounded; all this continued until the whole burnt offering was finished." (II Chr. 29:27-28.)

There are two elements which characterize the hymn: one has to do with its mood, the other with its content. The native mood of the hymn is thrilling gladness, heartfelt appreciation, and overflowing joy. Its spirit is that of enthusiastic and adoring praise. The characteristic verbs of the hymn are "praise," "laud," and "exalt." The hymn has a native form of expression. It is built upon a simple pattern. Yet its spirit is never bound by established literary forms. We are impressed by its note of spontaneity. Praise wells up from the psalmists' hearts in humble recognition of God. He is to them of such worth that they can but praise Him, and to summon others to praise is no duty but the inevitable impulse of a glad heart. Consequently there is awakening influence in this exalted and sincere enthusiasm. The hymns have power to kindle the heart of a whole congregation and lift it into inspired moments. The church and synagogue are keenly aware of this today. In the hymn persons sing together; and as they sing, they summon their neighbors to sing: "Oh come, let us sing!" Such is the spirit of a hymn. Augustine has profoundly said, "One loving spirit sets another on fire." The hymns of the Psalter illustrate the truth of this in congregational worship, for they kindle praise. A lonely sadness often merges into a congregational gladness.

In content the hymns lay emphasis upon the objective side of religion. About the intricate problems of the individual they are largely silent. The abysmal depth of the soul in its desperate need does not appear. The social situation out of which or for which a hymn was composed has little place in the poet's concern. The hymns have to do supremely with God Himself. They deal with His various attributes. They glorify His mighty deeds. The soul of the psalmist moves out of self toward God in emancipating objectivity.

---

[10] "The sound of your songs, . . . the melody of your harps" (Amos 5:23).
[11] See Gunkel, *Einleitung,* p. 61.

In the hymn the experience of public worship becomes articulate with meaning. The exalted moods of awe and fealty which congregational worship awakens
do not evaporate in vague feeling; the hymns give them intelligible thought content. The hymns gather up and express in clear ideas just what the worship
experience of the congregation means. Immersion in the thoughts of Hebrew
hymnody soon reveals to us that here is to be found the concentrated essence
of the prophetic teaching about God, His relation to Israel and to the world.
If we lost the words of the prophets, we would still have the essentials of their
teaching about God in the hymns. Moreover, in the hymns these teachings are not
merely stated; they are sung. The God of whom the prophets taught is comprehended and felt in them. They have served a unique function in bringing the
lofty, pioneering insights of prophecy down into the common life of men where
they can be concretely understood, felt, and applied.

One of the most magnificent scenes of a hymn's rendition and its effect is given
by the Chronicler in II Chr. 5:11-14. He is describing imaginatively a scene of
Temple worship at that great moment—some six centuries before his own day—
when the ark of the Lord was installed in the most holy place of the newly
erected Temple of Solomon. But he portrays it in terms that were to him perfectly familiar and authentic as great moments of the Temple worship as he knew
it in his day (ca. 300 B.C.). He pictures all the priests garbed in their priestly
robes. He brings before us the three famous Temple choirs arrayed in fine linen,
with musicians carrying cymbals, harps, and lyres, and with them 120 priests
bearing their ram's-horn trumpets. There they stand at the east end of the altar.
We hear the trumpets, cymbals, harps, and lyres playing "as one" in glorious
harmony. Then the choir lifts its voice in a song, "praising and thanking the
Lord." And we hear the glad response of the great congregation, in the beloved
cultic words:

> For He is good;
> For His lovingkindness endures forever!

The Chronicler here becomes poet and says: "Then the house was filled with
a cloud, even the house of the Lord, . . . for the glory of the Lord filled the
house of God!"

The hymns constitute a greatly diversified classification in the Psalter. A very
few of these hymns had their origin in northern Israel and were at home in
the sanctuary at Bethel. After the fall of the northern kingdom in 721 B.C. they
found their way into the Jerusalem Temple worship, and we can discern in them
no essential difference in spirit from the psalms that had their origin in Judah.
There are general hymns of praise that have no distinctive setting in Hebrew
worship but would be appropriate at various occasions. Hymns were a prominent
part of all Hebrew festivals, such as Passover (and Unleavened Bread), Weeks
(or Harvest), and Ingathering (or Tabernacles, Booths). There are hymns of
Zion which praise Jerusalem as the spiritual mother of the Lord's worshipers,

and as the place where God dwells, the center of His rule over His people and of His ultimate rule over the world. Several of the hymns grew out of the greatly beloved rite of pilgrimage to the sanctuary. Some hymns were composed and sung in the public worship by gifted and inspired individuals. Certain hymns trace God's objective revelation of Himself in nature. Others find His presence in the great normative moments of Hebrew history. Still others focus attention upon the revelation of His will for His people in the gift of the law. The great New Year festival, which embraced eight days of celebration, was observed with hymns in the Temple that gave fitting emphasis to a remarkable variety of themes. The hymn played a significant role in the psalm liturgies of the Temple; and when the various literary types began to meet and mingle, the hymn became related to practically every other literary form to be found in the Psalter.

3. GENERAL HYMNS OF PRAISE

Two hymns of the Psalter have no apparent indication of any distinctive setting in Hebrew worship—Pss. 117 and 150. The former emphasizes God's character as worthy of praise. The latter concentrates attention upon the rendering of the praise and has an informed musical interest in the instruments to be employed for that sacred purpose.

Because of their excellence and brevity they were no doubt sung at many types of worship service in the Temple. In the terminology of Judaism, Ps. 117 was one of a group called "the Egyptian Hallel" (Pss. 113-118).[12] Ps. 150 with its tenfold "hallelujah" suggests to Hebrew thought the complete, rounded, and perfect praise. We may designate these psalms as general hymns of praise.

Ps. 117. THE OUTFLOW OF MAN'S SOUL TO GOD

Ps. 117 is a general congregational hymn of praise. It is the briefest of the psalms and the shortest chapter in the Bible, but it contains the essentials of a hymn—a summons to praise and a basis for praise. Simple as it is, it is a little gem of the Psalter.

The hymn opens with a summons to praise, which is expressed in the plural imperative. Such a call to praise appears in the hymns of the Psalter about two hundred times.[13] The psalmist calls all nations to the praise of the Lord. "Laud" is an Aramaic word and is an indication of a quite late date for the hymn.

> 1   Praise the Lord, all ye nations;
>   Laud Him, all ye peoples.

The theme of praise—the basis for it—is the elements in God's character which flow out toward Israel in abundant streams. The theme is always the chief

---

[12] So called from reference to Egypt in Ps. 114:1 to distinguish it from "the Hallel" (Ps. 136).
[13] See Gunkel, *Einleitung*, p. 34.

part of a hymn and is introduced by the word "for" (*kî*). This introductory word appears in such a connection over one hundred times in the psalms and thus is a characteristic mark of the hymn. The first element emphasized is God's lovingkindness. This word expresses His innermost essence. "Toward us" means toward the congregation of the Lord's worshipers, of whom the psalmist is one. At first it strikes us as strange that the pslamist calls upon the nations to praise God because of what He has done on behalf of Israel. But the "for" here is to be conceived not as objective but as subjective. The spirit of the congregation is so moved with wonder at the grace of God to Israel that the whole world is called upon to praise Him.

The second element in God's character which calls forth praise to Him is His never-ending faithfulness—His trustworthiness—which the psalmist does not limit to Israel. Thus he presents his theme of praise:

> 2 For His lovingkindness is great toward us;
>   And the faithfulness of the Lord endures forever.

At the close of this brief hymn comes a renewed summons to praise, addressed directly to the congregation. Such a renewed call at the end is frequently present in the hymns. It always expresses a deepened mood, for it is enriched by the whole thought and feeling content of all that precedes it.

> Praise ye the Lord!

This was almost certainly part of the hymn sung by Jesus and his disciples at the Passover meal, [14] after the closing prayer and after the drinking of the third cup, just before they went out to the Mount of Olives (Matt. 26:30). However, from its general nature and its brevity we may assume that it was sung upon many types of occasion when the assembled congregation praised God for what He is and does.

Ps. 150. A PAEAN OF PRAISE

This psalm is a general congregational hymn. It is a veritable paean of praise, most appropriate for the closing psalm of the Psalter, and no doubt created or chosen with that in mind by the final editor of the Psalms. In the body of the psalm "Praise ye" (*hallelû*) appears exactly ten times, an arrangement which was most likely intentional with the poet. Such a general hymn might be sung on many occasions but would be particularly appropriate for great hours of the festal year, when the Temple courts would be thronged with worshipers and the worship would be the richest and most inspiring. The psalmist answers four implicit questions: Where, why, and how is God to be praised, and who are to praise Him?

Where is God to be praised? Both in His earthly Temple and in the high firmament of heaven:

---

[14] See Strack and Billerbeck, *Kommentar zum Neuen Testament aus Talmud und Midrasch*, IV, 69.

1 Praise God in His sanctuary;
Praise Him in His majestic firmament.

Why is God to be praised? Because of the deeds He has done and because of what He is in His own being:

2 Praise Him because of His mighty deeds;
Praise Him because of His supreme magnificence.

How is God to be praised? The writers of hymns of praise take delight in enumerating the musical instruments which are to accompany the words of the psalm. In this section of the poem we get in a single passage the most complete summary we possess of the musical instruments used in the Temple worship. The Lord is to be praised with the blast of the trumpet (*shôphār*), an instrument made from the horn of the ram or goat. It is one of the most ancient musical instruments, used to give signals and to announce the reign of a new king (II Sam. 15:10). It is significant that this is the instrument named to be used particularly "at the new moon," for the reference (Ps. 81:3) is to the New Year festival, when the congregation proclaimed the Lord as King.[15] But the *shôphār* was not by any means limited to these ceremonies. It was used particularly by the priests for calling the congregation together (Num. 10:2).

The harp (*nehbel*) had more strings than its kindred instrument, the lyre (*kinnôr*). The term *nehbel* was the regular word for skin bottle, and possibly gave its name to the harp because it was shaped like a skin bottle. The lyre (*kinnôr*), called cithara by the Greeks and Romans, was an instrument for joy and mirth. It was introduced into the Egyptian Old Kingdom (before 2000 B.C.) by Semites from Palestine. Purely instrumental music on the lyre would be performed with the hand, just as David played (I Sam. 16:23). In accompanying a song the player used a plectrum or pick.

The hand drum (*tôph*) was played both by women (Exod. 15:20; Ps. 68:25) and men (I Sam. 10:5). It was made from a hoop of wood and two skins, without any jingling device, and it was beaten by hand to accentuate the rhythm. As was the case here, it often accompanied the dance, giving expression to the mood of joy and praise. "Stringed instruments" (*minnîm*) meant the whole family of such instruments, not any particular one. The flute (*ûgābh*) was the Mesopotamian *ti-gi,* a simple reed tube held vertically, and was highly esteemed in the temple ritual of Mesopotamia as well as Israel. The clanging cymbals (*çilçelê shāma'*) are the harsh, noisy, heavy ones which were struck vertically. The Hebrew term itself, as pronounced, imitates the sound made by the instruments. The clear cymbals (*çilçelê terû'āh*) were lighter than those and were struck horizontally. Their handles were leather thongs.[16]

[15] See Oesterley, *The Psalms,* II, 590.
[16] See Sellers, "Musical Instruments of Israel," *The Biblical Archaeologist,* IV, 33-47.

So the question, How praise the Lord? is thus answered:

3 **Praise Him with the blast of the trumpet;**
Praise Him with the harp and lyre.
4 **Praise Him with the hand drum and dance;**
Praise Him with stringed instruments and flute.
5 **Praise Him with clanging cymbals;**
Praise Him with clear cymbals.

While the trumpet was the particular instrument of the priest (I Chr. 15:24), the harp, lyre, and cymbals were the instruments of the Levites (I Chr. 15:16 ff.). The other instruments would be played by any of the participants in the festal dance.

There is implied a final question in the psalm: *Who* are to praise the Lord? At the end, as is often the case in the Psalter, there stands out intentionally from the rest of the psalm a half line which answers that question. It would be sung by all participants in the festival with great joy.[17] It is a fitting sentence for the close of the psalm, which from beginning to end is a summons to praise.

6 **Let everything that has breath praise the Lord!**

The first and last sentences, "Praise ye the Lord," are not part of the original psalm. The first is a superscription to it, and the last is a doxology placed at the end of the entire Psalter by the final editor. It sums up appropriately a pre-eminent note in the book which the Hebrew Bible suggestively calls "Praises" (*tehillim*).

Praise ye the Lord!

4. Hymns of Zion

"Sing us one of the songs of Zion" was the request of the Chaldean captors to their Judean captives. The "songs of Zion" may well have been in their mouths an over-all designation of the Judean psalms. Or it may have been true that, because of the well-known affection of the Jews for Zion and their consequent love of the Zion hymns, the captors were using a specific phrase and were asking them to sing one of those psalms which glorified Zion as the seat of the Temple and the dwelling place of the Lord.

Zion emerges into historical record in the era of David. It was a Jebusite stronghold when David captured it from the Canaanites and made it his capital, "the city of David" (II Sam. 5:7). To it he brought the ark of the Lord, the most ancient symbol of His presence, and set it there "in its place" in the sacred tent which he had pitched for it (II Sam. 6:17). When Solomon's Temple was built, the ark was brought up in festal procession from the sacred tent and was housed permanently in the "most holy place" (I Kings 8:1-6). Zion gradually comes to be the designation for the Hebrew center of worship up until the Exile,

[17] See Gunkel, *Die Psalmen*, p. 622.

and after the Exile represents the rallying center of Judaism, always with a religious connotation.[18] It is then viewed as the capital of Judaism and stands for the Temple worship and worshipers conceived as a social entity.

The hymns of Zion are Pss. 48, 87, 46, and 76. The last two are eschatological; that is, they deal with the final triumph of the Lord over the pagan powers of the world. They have a unique grandeur of their own and contribute richly to the basic optimism of the prophetic religion of Israel, which the poets who composed these psalms have imbibed and have here expressed.

Ps. 48. THE DIARY OF A ZION PILGRIM

This Zion hymn may suggestively be viewed as the diary of a Zion pilgrim, for much of it offers us vivid glimpses of how pilgrims celebrated their great festivals. It begins with the praise of Zion as the citadel of the Lord's rule. Through such praise of Zion, however, there always pulsates the yet deeper praise of the Lord who dwells in Zion.

As the pilgrim approaches Jerusalem from the east over the hump of Mount Olivet, suddenly, towering beautifully before him, he sees Mount Zion. When this psalmist wrote, Semitic mythology had already begun to lend its own color to history so that actual Zion and mythological Zion merge. For the alabaster throne of the Lord was mythologically conceived as being set upon the summit of the loftiest of seven holy mountains.[19] The assembly of the gods was viewed as taking place in the extreme parts of the north (Isa. 14:13-14). Yet to the psalmist this holy residence of his great God was in Mount Zion, where the Lord had demonstrated His protective presence and power. We feel the psalmist's overflowing love and reverence for Jerusalem as he sings:

> 1   Great is the Lord and very worthy of praise,
>   In the city of our God.
> 2   His holy mountain, beautiful in elevation,
>   Is the exultation of all the earth.
>   Mount Zion, in the uttermost parts of the north,
>   Is the city of the great King.
> 3   God, in her palaces,
>   Has made Himself known as a secure high retreat.

All this is introductory to the concrete experiences which the psalmist pilgrim now describes. First, in an open space—probably within the outer court of the Temple—he *sees* a dramatic portrayal of the Lord's triumph over the pagan powers of the world, a theme very popular at the festivals. There are four simple episodes to the drama: (*a*) kings, representing the pagan rulers of the world, assemble by appointment; (*b*) they ally themselves against Zion; (*c*) they see Zion, become confused, amazed, terrified, and are set into precipitate flight; (*d*)

[18] An excellent illustration is in Isa. 62:1, which dates *ca.* 450-350 B.C.

[19] Cf. Enoch 18:8; 25:3; 70:3; 77:3. Cf. also "the mountain of the Lord's House . . . on the top of the mountains" and "exalted above the hills" (Isa. 2:2; Mic. 4:1).

these pagan rulers are defeated and destroyed by the mysterious spiritual power of the Lord who dwells in Zion, just as a sudden and severe storm on the Mediterranean may wreck the strong merchant ships bound for the Phoenician commercial colony of Tarshish in southern Spain. The psalmist has heard that over and over again the Lord has protected Zion. No doubt he has often been told how God wondrously preserved Zion from capture by Sennacherib of Assyria in the days of Hezekiah and Isaiah (Isa. 36–37). Now he has not only heard but in drama has seen that Zion is the immovable city of God, which the Lord has taken under His own protection. Thus the psalmist describes what he has seen:

> 4 For lo, the kings of the earth assembled by appointment;
>   They allied themselves together.
> 5 They saw; then they were dumbfounded;
>   They were terrified; they were hurried away in alarm.
> 6 Trembling seized them there,
>   Pangs as of a woman in labor.
> 7 As does an east wind, Thou shatterest [20]
>   The ships bound for Tarshish.
> 8 Even as we had heard, so have we seen,
>   In the city of our God;
>   God will establish it forever.

The next activity of the pilgrim takes place in the Temple—the most sacred place in the world to him—where he *thinks* the great thoughts of his faith. First, he ponders the lovingkindness of God. It is that quality in God, His *ḥesedh*, which Hosea illumined so clearly. Second, he meditates upon the extent of the Lord's influence—how the knowledge of Him has reached to the ends of the earth—and in imagination he hears the praise songs ascending to the Lord from His loyal ones, some of whom live in its distant places. Indeed, in the worshiping assembly itself he probably sees not only Jews but proselytes who have come up to the feast from many corners of the then-known world (cf. Acts 2:5-11). Third, he broods upon the righteous acts of God, which across the centuries of history the Lord has wrought for His people, and which now inspire the congregation of Zion to rejoice. Thus his festal celebration has at its heart a rich and deep thought content.

> 9 We have thought of thy lovingkindness, O God,
>   In the midst of Thy Temple.
> 10 As is the report of Thee, so is the praise of Thee,
>   Unto the ends of the earth:
>   Thy hand is filled with righteousness.
> 11a   Let Mount Zion be glad!

Then the pilgrim *celebrates* joyously in the mood which is astir in the holy city. He observes with sympathetic eyes the festive gladness of the young women of Jerusalem—"the daughters of Judah"—whose joy is not secular but sacred

---

[20] Cf. Ezek. 27:26.

as they glory in the righteous judgments of God. He joins a thanksgiving procession that makes a circuit of the walled city. He observes with pride the ramparts, the walls, the towers. Inside the walls he visits the famous palaces where noble leaders of Judah have lived and still live. He makes a mental note of each thrilling experience, for when he gets home, his children—"the generation following" —will sit enthralled as he tells them of his interesting experiences. But it will not be merely a narrative of sight-seeing, for it will be permeated with appreciation of the Lord and of His meaning for His people. Then the children too will love Him and, claiming Him as their God, will follow Him forever!

> 11b Let the daughters of Judah rejoice,
>   On account of Thy judgments.
> 12 Go around Zion and make a circuit of her;
>   Count her towers;
> 13 Set your mind on her ramparts;
>   Visit her palaces;
>   In order that you may tell the coming generation
> 14   That such the Lord is,
>   Our God forever and aye:
>   He will lead us on.

Ps. 87. "O MOTHER DEAR, JERUSALEM"

This is one of the hymns of Zion that had its origin in the Diaspora and probably dates from the early postexilic period. The theme of the psalm is "O mother dear, Jerusalem."

It opens with the praise of Zion as being, in a unique degree, the city of God for all Israelites who live in "the dwellings of Jacob." It has its foundations in the holy mountains. The sanctity of Zion began when King David brought the ark of the Lord to his fortress capital. As we have seen, the holiness of Zion was greatly augmented when Solomon built the Temple there and placed the ark in the most holy place. Isaiah's teaching as to Zion's inviolability (37:33-35) gave this further impetus, and the centralization of all legitimate public worship there by the Deuteronomic law (Deut. 12), published in 621 B.C., brought it to a great climax. After the fall of the Jewish state, with the Diaspora spreading apace into all parts of the world, Zion, the seat of the restored Temple, became the spiritual focus of Judaism.

So sings the psalmist his praise of Zion, addressing her directly in verse 3.

> 1 Her foundation is in the holy mountains,
> 5c And the Most High will establish her.
> 2 The Lord loves the gates of Zion
>   More than all the dwellings of Jacob.
> 3 Glorious things are spoken of thee,
>   O city of God!

The psalmist then thinks of all the places where the Lord's people now live, according to the careful record of the sons and daughters of Zion which He keeps in His "book." He mentions Rahab, prophetic name for Egypt (Isa. 30:7), Babylon, Philistia, Tyre, and Ethiopia (Cush), regions which extend from south of the first cataract of the Nile in the southwest to Babylon in the northeast. The great spread of the Diaspora which had been achieved in the early New Testament times is vividly portrayed in Acts 2:9-11. This dispersion had already begun at the time of this psalm. So the Lord calls the roll of the lands where His scattered people dwell, and thinks of His individual worshipers born in each place. But, continues the psalmist, God calls Zion the place of their spiritual birth and the religious mother of His people who dwell in these lands. Spiritually speaking, each one considers her the mother of his soul.

> 4   I can enumerate as those who know me, Rahab and Babylon;
>   Lo, Philistia, and Tyre along with Cush:
>   This one was born there.
> 5   But Zion I call mother,
>   And each one has been born in her!

Then he pictures the Lord making a list of His loyal ones—whether Jews or proselytes to Judaism—now residing in all the nations of the world. It is indeed a wonderful record, veritably "a book of nations." We feel the glowing pride of the psalmist as he thinks of the Lord's worshipers as now to be found among all the peoples of the world. Yet—and this is his main point—wherever they may have been born physically, they have been born spiritually in Zion. She is their great mother. And the Lord counts them not as so many Egyptians or Babylonians, Philistines, Tyrians, or Ethiopians, but as sons and daughters of Zion. In the closing sentence the psalmist thinks of the glad worship in the Temple, the singing and the dancing of the sons and daughters of Zion, all of it worship of the Lord, yet of the Lord whose dwelling is in Zion, for verse 7, like verse 3, is spoken not of, but to, Zion:

> 6   The Lord counts, in the register of peoples,
>   This one was born there!
> 7   Singers and dancers alike—
>   All of them sing unto thee!

We are here at the Old Testament roots of that conception of the new birth which plays so great a part in the New Testament in Pauline and Johannine thought.

Ps. 46. CONFIDENCE IN THE PRESENT HELP OF GOD

This hymn of Zion is saturated with faith in God such as Isaiah had taught and proclaimed to Kings Ahaz and Hezekiah. Kittel has truly said, "It is the most magnificent song of faith that has ever been sung." Upon it in 1529 Martin Luther founded his majestic hymn "A Mighty Fortress Is Our God" when the Protestant cause was wavering in the balance.[21] Four thoughts are uniquely

---

[21] Ker, *The Psalms in History and Biography*, p. 78.

intertwined in the psalm: One is that Zion is the seat and dwelling place of God. A second is the doctrine of God's real presence there in the very midst of His people. A third is that God is King over the nations, speaking a word of command to them from His throne. And a fourth is the mystical atmosphere of the ultimate in the psalmist's faith. He moves not only in the sphere of the present. His thought embraces finalities. For our psalmist has drunk not only at the fountains of Isaiah's thought of the eighth century but also at those "streams in the desert" opened up by the great poet-prophet of the Exile, who had represented the Lord as saying:

> Truth hath gone forth from my mouth,
> A word which shall not return,
> That to me every knee shall bow,
> Every tongue shall swear. (Isa. 45:23.)

The theme that runs through the whole psalm, and which has lent it urgency and influence in crisis hours generation after generation, is confidence *now* in the presence and help of God. The psalm must have been sung by the pilgrims to Zion at the great annual festivals of postexilic Israel, especially in the periods when international crises stirred the Middle East.

It opens with a hymnic expression of confidence in the protection of God in the face of the destructive outbreak of cosmic power. Here are forces which mankind cannot control: the melting of the earth in volcanic eruption (cf. Mic. 1:3-4), the tottering of mountains in earthquake and the tumbling of great eroded masses of rock into the sea, the angry roaring of the sea, "the child of chaos." We see shimmering through the words (vs. 3) the myth of Tiamat, powerful dragon of disorder (cf. Job 38:8; Pss. 89:9; 104:5-9) whose overflowing floods (Jer. 47:2) made the mountains tremble at their roots. We are conscious of that peculiar terror felt in common by all mankind when in the presence of such cosmic power. This the poet suggests by the vagueness and vastness of his conceptions.

But let those powers break with all their fury, says the psalmist. We will not fear, for God is here, "exceedingly found," giving His people His sheltering strength. He is their secure high retreat to which they may flee.

> 1 God is our shelter and strength,
>   A help powerfully experienced in distress.
> 2 Therefore we will not fear at the melting of the earth.
>   Or at the tottering of the mountains into the heart of the seas.
> 3 Let the sea roar! Let its waters foam!
>   Let the mountains quake at its arrogance!

Across the centuries these eruptions of cosmic nature have been the symbols of sudden, dreadful, and inexplicable calamity when catastrophe, vast and overwhelming, shakes us to the recesses of our being. We are caught in life's terrific storms and tossed about ruthlessly in its perilous deeps "amid the flood of mortal ills."

Then comes the refrain (vss. 7, 11), which according to most modern interpreters should be restored here. The psalmist is imbued with a sense of history, for he calls Israel by the name of its great ancestor Jacob, and he likewise makes use of Isaiah's favorite name for God, the "Lord of hosts." God is a present refuge, a secure, high retreat!

> The Lord of hosts is with us;
> A secure height for us is the God of Jacob.

From the mysterious manifestations of vast cosmic energy the psalmist moves into the realm of history. Violent nations, storming pagan world kingdoms take the place of cosmic forces, and the psalmist utters his confidence in God's protection in the very face of raging antagonistic world powers (vss. 4-7). In the background is the implicit suggestion of Assyria, whose brutal force Judah has most tragically experienced (cf. Isa. 17:12-14). But the poet is also thinking of the hour when pagan power—however embodied in widespread national presumption—will come to its ultimate clash with the Lord, whose glory fills the earth. His mind is moving in the realm of finalities such as Ezekiel had in view when he pictured Gog of Magog and his hordes coming against the Lord's restored people in an ultimate struggle which will decide finally and for all time who is master (Ezek. 38–39). Is might or is God the Lord?

But before he describes the raging nations, in striking contrast to the roaring of the stormy sea with which the first part ended, the psalmist paints a vivid scene in word pictures of poetic beauty. We see a quiet, beautiful river, with canal tributaries distributing streams of life- and health-bringing water to Zion and its environment. It is Ezekiel's vision of the Temple stream (47:1-12; cf. Isa. 33:21; Joel 3:18; Zech. 14:8) to which the poet is indebted. This river represents the quiet, creative, gladdening, saving presence of God, who is present in His Temple on Mount Zion. It stands for the steadying presence of God that will keep Zion from swerving aside in impotent defeat when the world powers of "darkness grim" are arrayed against her. It depicts the intervening presence of God breaking in upon Israel at its darkest hour, even as the break of day defeats all the cohorts of darkness, hurling them into abject surrender to the lordship of the rising sun. We must sense with him this quiet river, too full for sound but strong with the strength of God. And we must feel the emptiness of those storming pagan forces, their power only seeming, not real. When the struggle is finally drawn and the righteousness of Zion stands opposed by the onslaught of all heathendom, the commanding voice of God splits the air. Paganism in its might has found its Master and dissolves in fear before its Lord. Exclaims the psalmist:

4 A river! Its canals gladden the city,
  Which the Lord has consecrated as His dwelling.
5 The Most High is in her midst;
  She shall not swerve;
      God will help her at the dawning of the morning.
6 Nations raged; kingdoms surged!
  He gave forth His voice; the earth melted!

The refrain now deepens in effectiveness. With us—the Lord's people—is God, protecting us against "the rage of the people pressing to hurtful measures" or against "the aspect of a threatening tyrant"! [22] In the ultimate struggle with pagan world powers the Lord will win!

7 The Lord of hosts is with us;
  A secure height for us is the God of Jacob!

The third part of the psalm (vss. 8-11) expresses confidence in the world dominion of God, enthroned as King over all the earth. It was as King that He uttered His voice (vs. 6b). It is as King that He is yet again to speak from His throne in accents of command (vs. 10). In imagination the psalmist takes his fellow worshipers in Zion to some high point from which they can view that battlefield where the spiritual power of the Lord has put to utter, final, and decisive defeat the pagan enemies of Zion and all for which Zion stands. We see the shattered bows, the spears cut to pieces, the burning shields, never to be recovered and never to be replaced. For now as a result of His triumph—here conceived of as already having been accomplished—wars throughout the earth have ceased. It is a pledge and an ultimate hope that springs from the psalmist's deep faith. As Oesterley well says, the psalmist "encouraged and heartened his people during a present emergency by reminding them of the ultimate victory of the Lord." [23]

8 Come, see the deeds of the Lord,
  What ruin He has wrought in the earth.
9 He makes wars to cease unto the end of the earth;
  He shatters the bow; He cuts in pieces the spear;
  The shields He burns in the fire.

Then God, "the high and lofty one that inhabiteth eternity, whose name is holy" (Isa. 57:15), King of all nations of the world, speaks from His exalted throne His word of universal command:

10 Desist, and perceive that I am God:
   High among the nations, exalted in the earth!

The Lord is here speaking to all those forces in the universe that are opposed to Him. The words used in this divine command carry rich spiritual suggestions: "desist," cease from what you are doing; "refrain," withhold yourself from

---

[22] Horace, "Justem et tenacem."   [23] *The Psalms*, I, 255.

antagonistic rebellious assertion; "relax," let the reins of your life fall into God's hands; "be still," be receptive of the power of God. To perceive that the Lord is God means to be certain of His presence, His help, and His blessing. Realize what it means to have God in your midst. The closing refrain sounds like a mighty shout of ultimate triumph. How it must have thrilled the Zion pilgrims!

> 11 The Lord of hosts is with us;
>   A secure height for us is the God of Jacob!

Ps. 76. THE LORD, MIGHTY JUDGE AND SAVIOUR

This Zion hymn has as its theme: the Lord, who dwells in Zion, is the mighty Judge of the earth. It has closest relationship with Pss. 46 and 48. The most distinctive thing in the psalm—which is rightly inferred from verse 3—is the symbolic pantomime, a type of dramatic portrayal.

The beginning (vss. 1-3) emphasizes the presence of the Lord in awful power in Zion. It is as Israel's God that the Lord's repute is known, and particularly in Judah has He been revealed unto men. For there in Jerusalem, Judah's political and religious capital, stands the Temple, here poetically called the Lord's "booth" (ṣukkāh); the Lord's "lair," where the majestic and awesome Being rests; and the Lord's "dwelling," where He abides. There it was that God shattered the weapons of the pagan powers which opposed Him. We note the same "there" in a similar context in Ps. 48:6.

> 1 Because of Judah, God is known:
>   Because of Israel, great is His name.
> 2 His booth is in Shalem [Jerusalem],
>   And His lair is in Zion.
> 3 There He shattered to pieces quiver and bow,
>   Shield and sword and spear.

In verse 3—as in Ps. 48:4-7—we have implicit reference to a bit of symbolic pantomime. This was a representation in some simple kind of dramatic form of the triumph of the Lord over advancing pagan enemies. As Mowinckel suggests, possibly bows and arrows actually were broken and shields burned, the attention of the worshipers being thus focused upon the inner spiritual meaning of these symbolic acts—God's destruction of all weapons of pagan aggression.

The next section of the psalm (vss. 4-6) has the same import and looks far ahead to God's ultimate triumph. The Lord, the God of terrifying majesty, has defeated for all time the pagan forces of evil. The stouthearted, ungodly powers lie vanquished and plundered by Him, the majestic and dread-inspiring Being. The once war-skilled cavalry by the rebuke of God have been drugged to sleep and made utterly impotent. There is an implicit reference here to the cup which the wicked of the earth are to drink from the Lord's hand (cf. Jer. 25:15; Ps. 75:7-8). The words resound with the victorious note of the ultimate triumph of right over pagan might, as the choir glorifies the Lord:

4 Dreadful art Thou, O Lord,
    More majestic than the ancient hills.
5 Plundered are the stouthearted;
    They sleep their sleep;
    And the warriors cannot find their hands.
6 At Thy rebuke, O God of Jacob,
    The riders of horses fell into deep sleep.

The third part of the psalm (vss. 7-9) portrays the Lord as the awesome Judge of the earth. From heaven—just as in Ps. 46:6—the Lord pronounces the divine sentence of judgment upon all the godless powers in the earth. The psalmist paints a magnificent picture of the Lord rising up, taking upon Himself the cause of the meek of the whole earth who are helpless before the terrible onslaught of the godless forces. Suddenly we hear His divine voice pronouncing judgment, and the earth, hearing it, is terrified into silence. Such words speak to our day:

7 Fearful art Thou, and who can stand
    Before Thee, before the strength of Thine anger?
8 From heaven Thou wilt make judgment heard;
    The earth will fear and become silent,
9 When Thou wilt arise, O God, for judgment,
    To save all the meek of the earth.

This impressive psalm ends in a hymn of thanksgiving (vss. 10-12), already anticipated in verse 7. Those exempt from the destructive judgment because they had hold upon God—those who are the true "remnant" in the whole world—see this ultimate triumph of the Lord, behold His intervention in behalf of the meek of the earth, and accordingly speak of Him with thanksgiving. The psalmist summons the neighboring peoples around Israel to vow and pay their vows along with Israel in awed gratitude to God, who humbles the pagan rulers and brings into subjection the kings of the earth.

10 For the earth beheld it, thanks Thee;
    The remnant beheld it, utters Thy praise.
11 Vow, and pay to your God:
    Let all around Him bear a gift to the One feared.
12 He humbles the spirit of rulers;
    He is awesome to the kings of the earth.

5. HYMNS OF PILGRIMAGE

It was a moment fraught with significant consequences for the Temple worship when, in 621 B.C., under King Josiah of Judah, the reform code of Deuteronomy became the law of the land. It lifted tremendously the prestige of the Jerusalem Temple, making it the only legitimate sanctuary for the public worship of Judah. In accordance with the requirements of the Deuteronomic law, three times in the year—the Festival of Unleavened Bread (with which Passover was merged),

the Festival of Weeks, and the Festival of Booths—all the males of Judah must
worship at the Temple (Deut. 16:16). The already age-old practice of pilgrimage
to the sanctuaries was now narrowed down to the Temple of Jerusalem. In the
far more exhaustive and effective priestly law—promulgated around 397 B.C.
by Ezra—these three festivals became the "fixed festivals of the Lord" (Lev. 23:4).
They were to continue in effect until the seventh decade of the Christian era. This
practice gave rise to two small groups of psalms: one, the hymns of Zion, we have
already considered; the other group may be entitled hymns of pilgrimage. All the
hymns of pilgrimage are also Zion hymns, because Zion is the pilgrimage goal. But
not all Zion hymns are pilgrimage hymns. Two of the psalms are pre-eminently
hymns of pilgrimage—Pss. 84 and 122. They would be appropriately sung in the
Temple ceremonies of any of the great pilgrimage festivals.

Ps. 84. THE SUPREME PSALM OF THE SANCTUARY

This is a hymn of pilgrimage to the Temple in Zion, sung at its first rendition
by the individual pilgrim [24] who had created it. It is the artistic utterance of one
of Israel's greatest representative minds [25] and, as Fleming James has said, "will
remain forever the supreme psalm of the sanctuary." [26] As it opens, the pilgrim
psalmist is inwardly stirred by the sweep of the whole Temple area with its
various buildings and its dwellings—the loveliness of it all. His words remind
us of a similar impression which the whole complex of the Temple buildings in
a later century made upon one of Jesus' disciples who exclaimed as Jesus and
the twelve went forth out of the Temple, "Look, Teacher, what wonderful
stones and what wonderful buildings!" (Mark 13:1).

Yet it is not primarily the buildings that attracted the pilgrim—much as he
loved the whole Temple area—but the Person who dwelt there, not conceived
of merely as a historical memory or as a tangible but lifeless idol, but as a living
Presence. He thinks back upon the time when with almost consuming longing
he was homesick for the Temple courts. Such heartsick memories of the past
heighten his present joy as his whole being now cries out to God:

> 1 How lovely are Thy dwellings,
>   O Lord of hosts!
> 2 My soul longed, yes, it pined away
>   For the courts of the Lord.
>   My heart and my flesh cry out
>   To the living God!

The theme of the next verse is summed up in the phrase "at home." As the
psalmist stands in the Temple court, he sees a sparrow darting to her nest. Having
hunted for a place to build it, she at length "found her a house" in the Temple.

---

[24] For the likelihood of such solo hymns in the Temple in late pre-exilic times see Gunkel,
Einleitung, p. 150.

[25] See Buttenwieser, *The Psalms*, p. 776.   [26] *Thirty Psalmists*, p. 72.

He sees a mother swallow flying to her brood in another corner of the Temple court, a worm for her young in her bill. How very much at home seem these wild things of the air! What a wonderful sanctuary [27] they have found in this sacred place! He whose house means home to the birds also has a place in His house that means home to the psalmist's soul—the Temple altars.

> 3 Even the sparrow has found a house,
> And the swallow a nest for herself,
> Where she has laid her young.

And so his thought continues, "As for me, I too have a home—"

> Thine altars, O Lord of hosts,
> My King, and my God!

The next two verses are a blessing, not such as a priest would utter, but in a formula familiar on the lips of a layman. It is a blessing both upon the permanent residents in the Temple area and upon those who are there only temporarily as pilgrims. What a privilege have the priests and Levitical servants who dwell in the Lord's house, who—as Ben Sirach informs us for his time (ca. 180 B.C.)— "sang praise every day continually" (Ecclus. 47:8) in connection with the daily whole burnt offering morning and evening (cf. I Chr. 23:30-32; II Chr. 29:27-28). Yet those also are blessed who, like himself, are but pilgrims to Zion. Only occasionally do they move up the paved processional street [28] which leads to the city of David and the Temple mount; yet they ever have the inclination thus to go as pilgrims to Zion—a holy and blessed desire. Such have the very strength of God in their life, and they treasure the sacred processional way (vs. 5b) [29] in their hearts. So through indirect praise of God the psalmist pours out words of blessing upon both these continuous and occasional Temple worshipers.

> 4 Oh the happiness of those who dwell in Thy house;
> They praise Thee forever!
> 5 Oh the happiness of the man whose strength is in Thee!
> Pilgrimage is in their heart!

The psalmist is a poet, one of the noblest we encounter in the Psalter. His thought moves easily from the material to the spiritual realm, for he sees in the one symbols of the other. Pilgrimage to Zion entailed hardship. Says Walker: "This sanctuary . . . could only be reached by a long and wearisome journey. Palestine is a mountainous and thirsty land, and doubtless there was real suffering attendant upon the journeys up to the annual religious festivals." [30] The psalmist starts with the actual physical journey to Zion; then in swift transition

[27] See Oesterley, The Psalms, II, 379-80.
[28] Called hamma'alôth, the paved processional way referred to at the New Year festival in Neh. 3:15; 12:37. This way was discovered by Schick and Guthe. See Guthe, in Zeitschrift des Deutschen Palästina-Vereins, p. 315.
[29] The term is meṣillôth, "an amplified plural poetic style," which the Septuagint understands as the processional way (hamma'alôth) up which pilgrims walk to the Temple.
[30] The Modern Message of the Psalms, pp. 61-62.

he thinks of the Zion traveler walking as a pilgrim on the way of life, passing through its desolate valley areas and wastes. Into those low hours when the human spirit is parched and dried up, God pours His spiritual blessings, comparable to the Palestinian rains of October to December which drench the parched soil and make it fertile. And what lifting, festival joy the Zion pilgrims experience as they move on from station to station! Truly it is the joy of the Lord (Neh. 8:10), and at length they appear at their goal in the presence of God! So it is in life, for God gives His pilgrims on life's way strength sufficient for each stage. They move from one blessing of divinely proffered strength to another.

> 6 Passing through the desolate valley, [31]
>   They make it a fountain;
>   Yes, the early rain
>   Envelops it with blessings.
> 7 They go from strength to strength.
>   Every one of them appears before God in Zion.

Buttenwieser sensitively remarks: "The psalm tells what enabled Israel to carry on in those dark centuries. . . . Suffering may be transmuted into spiritual triumph." [32]

The closing verses (10-12) teach us the life-creating power of the Temple worship as the psalmist experienced it. In pictures arresting and tender this sensitive spiritual poet tells us what that worship meant to his soul. One single day spent at the Temple is more to him than a thousand in his own chamber at home. And the spiritual joys of worship are of inexpressibly greater worth to him than feasting on the abundant hospitality of the wealthy. He would rather haunt the threshold of the Temple, where beggars were accustomed to gather to receive the alms doled out to them by entering worshipers (Acts 3:2-3), than be a guest in tents of wealth. For in his Temple he finds God. And from Him, as water from a fountain, stream light, protection, a consciousness of gracious acceptance, a sense of dignity, and indeed all that is truly good. He ends his psalm (vss. 8-9 follow vs. 12) in a formula of blessing (vs. 12) similar to verses 5-6, yet a blessing which is also an implied exhortation to his fellow pilgrims.

> 10 For better is a day in Thy courts
>   Than a thousand in my chamber;
>   I had rather haunt the threshold [33] of the house of my God,
>   Than to be guest in the tents of riches.
> 11 For a sun and a shield is the Lord;
>   Favor and glory He gives;
>   The Lord holds back nothing good
>   From those who walk in integrity.
> 12 O Lord of hosts,
>   Oh the happiness of the man who keeps trusting in Thee!

[31] Cf. Schmidt, *Die Psalmen*, p. 159.   [32] *Op. cit.*, p. 776.
[33] Cf. the suggestive rendering of Oesterley, *The Psalms*, II, 379, literally "stand at the threshold."

It is most likely that the festival celebrated by the pilgrim who created this psalm was Tabernacles, with which the New Year festival coincided. The emphasis upon the Lord as King (vs. 3) enthroned in Zion (vs. 7) would suggest this. Moreover, inserted into this psalm between verses 7 and 10—at a point which somewhat disturbs the logical connection—is a prayer of intercession for the reigning king. Such a feature is also present in the ritual of the Babylonian New Year festival. In that festival, in the liturgy for the fifth day of the month Nisan (March-April), prayer is offered for the good fortune of the king as the sacramental representative of the community, as the embodiment in his own person of the welfare of the people.[34] Similarly in ancient Israel the king was viewed in some sense as the channel for the blessing of God to the Judean state. This prayer, later inserted into the psalm, presupposes the presence of the reigning Judean king in the Temple worship, and it would be sung by the choir, which thus lifts an intercession for their monarch, their "shield" and divinely "anointed" one.

8   Lord God of hosts,
        Hear my prayer;
            Give ear, O God of Jacob.
9   Behold, O God, our shield,
        And show regard to the face of thine anointed.

Ps. 122. WHAT JERUSALEM MEANS TO THE PILGRIM

This is a psalm of pilgrimage to the Temple. It is a pilgrim's parting salutation to Jerusalem. For seven memorable days—in accordance with the regulations of the Deuteronomic law (Deut. 16:13-15) —he has celebrated the Festival of Tabernacles, as his purpose of thanksgiving implies (vs. 4). By the whole experience he has been deeply stirred, and this psalm has its origin in that hour when he turns to go back to his home. As he recalls that earlier joy which filled his soul when a group from his community invited him to go up with them to the feast, he sings:

1   I was glad when they said to me,
        "Let us go to the house of the Lord."

So they came, and now the experience is at an end. We can sense awe in the tones of his voice, the awe of deep and moving recall. Thinking of what those precious days have meant to him and his fellow pilgrims, he speaks to the personified soul of what is to him the dearest city in the world:

2   Our feet have been standing
        Within thy gates, O Jerusalem!

We feel here a spiritual kinship between this ancient pilgrim and the greatest Soul that ever entered that city as a pilgrim, who, several centuries later, like him, but with a sob in his heart, spoke unforgettable words to Jerusalem (Luke 13:34).

[34] Cf. Mowinckel, *Psalmenstudien*, II, 177-78, 327-28.

What does Jerusalem mean to our psalmist pilgrim? First of all, in new degree it has become to him the unifying bond that joins him with all Judeans. Regardless of where he lives, whether in some little town in Judah or at a pagan oriental court, with his window open to the holy city, this sense of oneness with his Judean comrades will ever be real and precious. Again, Jerusalem is the pilgrimage goal of the several tribes of Israel. It is the great city to which all Israelites, whatever their ancient tribal connection—whether with Benjamin or Judah, Zebulun or Napthali, Ephraim or Issachar—"go up" as pilgrims to their one great unifying center. Again, it is the seat of the rule of a long line of great Judean kings, like David and Solomon, Asa, Jehoshaphat, Joash, Hezekiah, and Josiah, who from their thrones have administered justice to their people. So to Jerusalem he sings:

> 3 Jerusalem, built as a city
>   That unites us together,
> 4 Thither the tribes go up,
>   The tribes of the Lord,
>   A solemn charge for Israel,
>   To give thanks to the name of the Lord.
> 5 For there are set for judgment
>   The thrones of the house of David.

Then he gathers his fellow pilgrims about him and in a bidding prayer leads them in intercession on behalf of Jerusalem. Thus he summons them to prayer:

> 6 Pray for the peace of Jerusalem.

The original words of this simple prayer, *Sha'alû shelôm Yerûshālāyim*, are poetically beautiful. There is in them a striking alliteration built upon the name Shalem (Jerusalem). From this feature Staerk makes the beautiful suggestion that "'Jerusalem' is the peal of the bell which accompanies this devout song with its gentle vibrations." [35] The pilgrim's prayer is a fourfold wish, uttered in the mood of eager intercession but spoken directly to Jerusalem, and at its very close it rises to a vow. His prayer embraces the very humble homes of the rank and file of its people, Jerusalem's "tents." He sees proudly her bulwarks where the harsh clang and clamor of battle has often been heard. His thought includes her palaces, residences of the king and the princes, but so often beset with wranglings and plots within. So on behalf of his fellow pilgrims who need to have someone give voice to their eager aspiration and love he prays that in that beloved city all may be well. His prayer rises to its loftiest dedication in a vow that, so far as he himself is concerned, he must seek to be and do what will strengthen Jerusalem, because the Temple is there. Thus the psalm, which begins in invitation to the house of the Lord, ends in the precious spiritual awareness of that for which the Temple stands, and the pledge of his soul to seek in daily

[35] *Die Schriften des Alten Testaments, III (Lyrik)* , 247; note vss. 2, 3, and 6.

life all that will further its deepest meaning. Thus his intercessory wish and his vow:

> 6b May thy tents prosper.
> 7 May there be peace within thy bulwarks.
>   May tranquility reign in thy palaces.
> 8 For the sake of my brothers and companions
>   Let me say, "May it go well with thee!"
> 9 For the sake of the house of the Lord our **God**
>   I will seek what is good for thee.

Suggestively Fleming James remarks that this psalmist "stands out in the Psalter as perhaps the man who had Jerusalem most in his heart." [36]

6. Hymns of Great Individuals

Most of the hymns in the Psalter were in origin and in rendition the affair of the worshiping congregation. In them the social consciousness is strong, and the predominant pronouns are "we," "our," and "us." But there are several psalms which both in their creation and in their rendition were the hymnic utterance of individual souls. They were not intended to be merely religious poems but presuppose the presence of the congregation and were sung before the worshiping throng. It is likely that the composer of such a psalm put into it the spiritual, intellectual, and aesthetic quality of his own soul, and in many instances the poet who created the hymn was the one who first rendered it.

One such hymn—Ps. 103—has unique spirituality and reaches a religious depth far profounder than that of the normal corporate utterance of the Temple congregation in any period of its history. Two others—Pss. 111 and 145—are marked by a planned artistry, both being acrostic poems. While they are, accordingly, artificial rather than spontaneous, still they reach a remarkably high level of poetic utterance. They are filled with the conviction of their authors that in them they are presenting to God praise songs of abiding worth. Such psalms help us see how ancient Israel took account in the public worship of the needs both of the group and of the individual, and the psalms thrill social worship with the vitality of individual piety. The Temple worship of the great annual festivals is the setting in which such psalms would be appropriately rendered.

Ps. 103. A HEART'S CRY OF PRAISE

This is a hymn sung in the public worship of Israel, not by the choir or the congregation as a whole, but by an individual. It is one of the deepest spiritual utterances of individual piety in the psalms and moves in a religious atmosphere that is closely akin to the spirit of the New Testament.

The psalmist begins with a summons to praise. But his summons is unique

[36] *Op. cit.,* p. 76.

in that it is directed not to his fellow worshipers but to his own soul—and that at its deepest depths, his innermost being. The term "bless" in such a context means "adore with bended knees."

> 1 Bless the Lord, O my soul,
>   And all my inner being, [bless] His holy name.

The subject of the praise thus to be uttered from his very heart is stated in verse 2b—the gracious dealings of God, which are now to be called to mind lest they be forgotten.

> 2 Bless the Lord, O my soul,
>   And forget not all His dealings:

In his classic recall of what God has "dealt out" to him in his lot in life, the psalmist thinks of the divine Providence in ever-widening concentric circles. He begins with his own life (vss. 3-5) and addresses his own soul as though it were a separate person. Then he broadens his thought to include God's dealings with Israel, His people as a whole (vss. 6-14). Finally, taking a still greater sweep of God's benefits into his survey, he includes all mankind (vss. 15-18), the key word here being "man" (vs. 15).

The first area is the circle of the psalmist's own personal experience—God's dealings with his own life (vss. 3-5). With swift strokes of his pen and in the mood of awe he tells of his blessings—the forgiveness of sins, the healing of his bodily ills, even his restoration from dangerous illness. He uses the vivid figure of God's buying him back, "redeeming" him as something precious from the possessive hands of the grave—the pit of the underworld—reaching out to seize him. He feels like a king crowned by the hand of God, not, however, with a crown of gold, but with the richest of spiritual values. All that his life really needs God provides, giving to his soul new life force, just as He does to the molting eagle which casts off the old feathers and puts forth new pinions. We perceive here that the physical, spiritual, and psychological energies of the psalmist's life have felt upon them the creative touch of God. So, addressing his own soul, he summons it to praise Him:

> 3 Who forgives all your iniquities;
>   Who heals all your diseases;
> 4 Who redeems your life from the pit;
>   Who crowns you with kindness and mercy;
> 5 Who satisfies your longing with good;
>   Your youth renews itself like the eagle.

His survey of God's provision now broadens as it sweeps within its circle of interest the Lord's dealings with Israel, His people (vss. 6-14). Central to his thought in this range is the Lord as the God of righteous action on behalf of His people. God takes the side of those oppressed, raising up for them leaders like Moses, who interpreted to Israel the Lord's everlasting mercy (vs. 8) as the fountain source of His deeds. The psalmist here recalls the high moment on Mount Sinai when God revealed to Moses His nature of grace and compassion, as told by the great Yahwist narrator in Exod. 34:1-7. Moreover, deep and classic words of prophecy are in this psalmist's soul as he writes of God's mercy (vs. 9) — words from Jeremiah:

> Will He keep His anger forever;
> Will He retain it to the end? (3:5.)

> "For I am full of kindness," is the oracle of the Lord;
> "I will not keep angry forever." (3:12.)

And the thoughts of that prophet, called Trito-Isaiah, who was a disciple of the great poet-theologian of the Exile (Isa. 40–55), were also in his mind:

> For I will not contend forever,
> Nor be angry for all time. (Isa. 57:16.)

Indeed this mercy is so essential in God's being that He deals with Israel, not as their sins would seem to warrant and justify, but as His own boundless mercy impels Him to do.

And how can we conceive the amazing reach of this mercy? Look up to the heavens as high as the eye can reach—that is one dimension that suggests its scope. Or think of the vast distance from the eastern to the western horizon. God's merciful forgiveness thus distances Israel's sins from His heart. For He deals with His people as a compassionate father deals with his children.

6 The Lord is one who carries out righteous acts,
  And judgments for all oppressed.
7 He made known His ways to Moses,
  His deeds to the children of Israel.
8 Gracious and merciful is the Lord,
  Slow to get angry and great in mercy.
9 For not perpetually will He contend;
  And not forever will He keep angry.
10 He has not dealt with us as our sins deserve,
   Nor has He paid us back in proportion to our guilt.
11 But as high as are the heavens above the earth,
   So high is His mercy toward those who fear Him.
12 As the distance of east from west,
   So He has distanced from Himself our sins.
13 Like the compassion of a father for his children,
   Is the compassion of the Lord to those who fear Him.
14 For He knows our form,
   Mindful that we are dust.

From himself to his people, from his people to mankind—in such direction the psalmist's thought moves as he now shows how all humanity in its generations-embracing life is related to the dealings of God (vss. 15-18). He proceeds indirectly here and emphasizes first the weakness and the temporal nature of man ('*ādhām*). Here is implied the cultural-philosophical viewpoint of the South or Seir document in the book of Genesis [37] as regards the origin of man: "And the Lord formed man out of the dust of the ground" (Gen. 2:7). Made thus of mere dust, man is fragile and as transient as grass, and just as doomed to extinction. Yet while he lives, he is as brilliant as an anemone—a touch of beauty which mitigates the psalmist's pessimism.

But now we see that this emphasis upon humanity's frailty is but a foil against which the psalmist portrays the eternity of God. The Lord undergirds this time-bound creature, upholding with His mercy and righteousness man's brief life and that of his children and their descendants. We are aware here (vss. 15-16) of the influence of Deutero-Isaiah, the great exilic poet-prophet, with his keen sense of the transiency of all "flesh" as over against the eternity of God (Isa. 40:6-8). Yet such eternal care is not given indiscriminately to all mankind, but only to those who listen to God's word and are obedient to His commands. Here the psalmist, again under the influence of the same great prophet, thinks of God's "word" in universal terms—"His word" not merely to Israel but to the world (cf. Isa. 55:11).

> 15   As for man, his days are like grass;
>   Like the flower of the field, so he sparkles.
> 16   But the wind passes over it, and it is not;
>   And its place no longer recognizes it.
> 17   But the mercy of the Lord endures forever,
>   And His righteousness unto children's children;
> 18   To such as listen to the voice of His word,
>   And to those who remember His commandments to do them.

The psalm ends in a yet vaster universalism that embraces not merely all mankind but even the heavens and the earth (vss. 19-22). There is nothing that lies outside God's dominion. He is King and now sits enthroned in the heavens. From that loftiest point in the world the King of the world sees all, knows all, and rules over all. The psalmist summons all His subjects to praise their exalted Monarch—the mighty angels who are His messengers; the heavenly host, sun, moon, and stars, who are His servants; and His whole creation in His universal domain. We thrill to the great rolling anthem of praise, augmented in volume as each new section of the chorus is thus summoned to sing. Then we hear the psalmist call upon his own voice to join in with glad fealty, for the great anthem is not complete until he himself is also swelling it by his own heart's cry of praise.

> 19   The Lord has established His throne in the heavens;
>   And His kingdom rules over all.
> 20   Bless the Lord, His messengers,
>   Mighty in strength, who perform His word.

[37] See Pfeiffer, *Introduction to the Old Testament*, pp. 159-67.

21 Bless the Lord, all His host,
    His servants who do His will.
22 Bless the Lord, all His works,
    In all places of His dominion:
    Bless the Lord, O my soul!

Of this poet Kittel has said, "He is one of the most eloquent preachers of the Father love of God in the Old Testament, and the New Testament teaching that 'God is love' has already found in him an inspired proclamation which has its source in the depths of personal experience." [38] His hymn, so rich in this experiential knowledge of the healing, disciplining, and forgiving expressions of God's grace, has its roots in the deepest thoughts of prophecy. It is the heart utterance of a man of profound piety, to whom, as Staerk has finely said, "we Christians must look up with reverence." The portrayal of God as King with His throne in heaven (vs. 19) would suggest that an appropriate setting in worship for the psalm would be at the festival of the Lord's enthronement at the New Year. The longing for the turn from discipline to mercy (vs. 9) is also in harmony with the prayer for the turn of fortunes, which is another theme of that festival.

Ps. 111. AN ARTISTIC PRAISE SONG FOR GOD'S WONDERFUL DEEDS

Ps. 111 is an alphabetic hymn, the hymn of an individual sung before the worshiping fellowship—as the psalmist himself says—"in the assembly of the upright and of the congregation." So far as the creation of the psalm is concerned, we have here the private expression of personal piety, an artistic exercise of a deeply devoted soul. But its rendition was in the public congregation.

We hear a clear, beautiful voice giving a hymnic introduction in the first person:

א 1 I will praise the Lord with all my heart,
ב   In the assembly of the upright and of the congregation.

The subject of the hymn is the deeds of the Lord, a theme which is ever appropriate for the great festal days of Israel. In a unique sense the festival of Passover was the "memorial" of the release of Israel from Egyptian bondage. The specifications for the observance of this festival state: "This day shall be unto you for a memorial, and ye shall keep it a feast to the Lord" (Exod. 12:14). It was to be forever a memorial that God, with a strong hand, had brought His people out of Egypt (Exod. 13:8-9). A proper setting for this psalm in the worship life of Israel would accordingly be the Passover festival, which took place on the first day of the Feast of Unleavened Bread (Deut. 16:1-3). Yet the respective themes of God's giving of the law (vs. 9bc) and of His provision of food (vs. 5a) would make it also appropriate, respectively, for the Festival of Weeks or of Tabernacles.

[38] *Die Psalmen*, p. 331.

To the psalmist the Lord is a supremely active God, and His great works, splendid and majestic, are a challenge to investigation and exploration. They are all the expression of His righteousness. So the psalmist sings from a full heart:

> ג 2 Great are the works of the Lord,
> ד   Worthy of study by all who take pleasure in them.
> ה 3 Splendor and majesty are His work;
> ו   And His righteousness stands forever.

The psalmist now becomes more concrete. These mighty acts of the Lord on behalf of His people are the practical outflow of His graciousness and compassion (vs. 4b) and of His truth, uprightness, and justice (vss. 7a, 8b), but they are also the fulfillment of His covenant obligations to them (vss. 5b, 9b). Even now, as in the presence of the congregation the soloist sings this artistic utterance of praise, these covenant acts of the holy and awesome God (vs. 9c) are being recalled in memorial tribute. And what are these mighty acts? They are the ransom of His people from Egyptian bondage (vs. 9a), the giving to them at Sinai of His forever-authoritative law (vss. 7b, 8a), the provision of food for them in the wilderness (vs. 5a), and, the climax of all, the giving to them of the land of Canaan, once possessed by other nations (vs. 6). Appropriate is such recall for Passover inspiration:

> ז 4 A memorial He hath appointed for His wonderful works.
> ח   Gracious and compassionate is the Lord.
> ט 5 Food He gave to those who feared Him:
> י   He remembers His covenant forever.
> כ 6 The power of his acts He has declared to His people,
> ל   In giving them the property of the nations.
> מ 7 The works of His hands are truth and justice;
> נ   Faithful are all His precepts,
> ס 8 Unshakable forever and ever.
> ע   They are done in truth and uprightness.
> פ 9 Ransom He sent to His people;
> צ   He has commanded His covenant forever;
> ק   Holy and awesome is His name.

The psalm closes with a strong sentence (vs. 10c) which views a song that praises God as sharing in God's own eternity. But just before this final word is spoken, the psalmist gives a beautiful utterance of Hebrew wisdom (vs. 10a), which clearly marks the psalm as dating from the late centuries of classical Judaism. The object aimed at by wisdom, and at the same time its noblest content, is the fear of the Lord. This utterance is one of the very finest proverbs in the Old Testament and gives an insight from the poet's own experience (vs. 10b).

> ר 10 The goal [39] of wisdom is the fear of the Lord,
> ש   An insight that is wholesome to all who exercise it.
> ת   His praise song stands forever.

[39] Cf. Quell, *Das kultische Problem der Psalmen*, p. 135.

Ps. 145. AN ARTISTIC PORTRAYAL OF GOD'S ETERNAL KINGDOM

This is a hymn of an individual which is rendered in the worshiping congregation as a solo.[40] Like Ps. 111 it is an acrostic, and because of the limitations thus set upon the poet it is somewhat artificial in nature. Yet here are uttered deep spiritual thoughts which have entered into the classic language of faith. It comes from the latest period of Hebrew psalmody, as two indications imply—the Aramaic elements [41] and the emphasis placed upon the kingdom of God (vs. 13).

An extended introduction opens this individual hymn. God is addressed as "my God, the King," and the psalmist expresses his purpose to praise the Lord's name—that is, His nature, His very being—forever. The reason for his praise follows and expresses in a summary fashion the theme of the whole hymn— the unfathomable greatness of God.

> א 1 I will extol Thee, my God, the King;
>   And I will bless Thy name forever.
> ב 2 Every day will I bless Thee;
>   And I will praise Thy name forever and ever.
> ג 3 Great is the Lord and very worthy of praise;
>   Yes, as for His greatness—it is unsearchable.

The psalmist starts anew, with a more elaborate and detailed introduction. He expresses the wish that successive generations may bear witness to God's might, His glorious majesty, His wonderful acts, His great goodness, and His righteousness:

> ד 4 May one generation laud Thy deeds to another,
>   And may they declare Thy might.
> ה 5 May they utter the splendor of Thy glory; [42]
>   May they sing of Thy wondrous deeds;
> ו 6 May they speak of the might of Thine awe-inspiring acts;
>   And may they recount Thy greatness.
> ז 7 May they pour forth the memory of Thy great goodness,
>   And may they sing of Thy righteousness.

Then he gives as his second theme the graciousness, compassion, forbearance, mercy, and goodness of the Lord. In verse 8 he has in mind God's revelation of His nature to Moses (Exod. 34:6):

> ח 8 Gracious and compassionate is the Lord;
>   Slow to get angry and of great mercy.
> ט 9 The goodness of the Lord is for all;
>   And His compassion is upon all His works.

Once again (vs. 10) the psalmist starts anew. We now become aware, however, that each new beginning moves up to a nobler level, that each theme of

---

[40] For the hymn of an individual see Gunkel, *Einleitung*, p. 38.

[41] This is apparent in vs. 14: *wezôqēph*, "raises up," *hakkephûphîm*, "bowed down"; and vs. 16: *ûmashpia‛*, "bestow lavishly."

[42] Following Gunkel and Cheyne.

praise is loftier than the preceding. First, it was God's nature, conceived in general terms (vs. 3); second, it was God's wonderful deeds, expressive of His innermost character as Moses and the greatest prophets had expounded it (vss. 8-9). Finally, it is the eternal kingdom of God, conceived especially in its manward and deeply spiritual aspects (vss. 13-20). And this rich and profoundly spiritual theme for God's praise is introduced by the wish that all His works and worshipers may praise Him so as to make known to all humanity His kingdom in its majesty and power:

> י 10 Let all Thy works praise Thee, O Lord;
>   And let all Thy loyal ones bless Thee.
> כ 11 Let them tell of Thy glorious kingdom;
>   Of Thy might let them speak.
> ל 12 So as to make known to humanity Thy strength,
>   And the glorious majesty of Thy kingdom.

In the last two verses of this final introduction we encounter a subject which developed late in Judaism and was destined to be the central theme of Jesus' teaching—the kingdom of God. In verse 13 it clearly becomes, in the intention of the psalmist, the theme par excellence of his whole psalm. The description of this eternal kingdom of God, as here given, was taken up almost verbatim in the Aramaic section of the book of Daniel, where it is quoted as sacred scripture. Furthermore, this is an indication that our psalm was already in existence and was viewed as sacred scripture before 165 B.C.

> מ 13 Thy kingdom is a kingdom of all eternity,
>   And His dominion endures generation after generation.[43]
> נ   Trustworthy is the Lord in all His words,
>   And kind in all His deeds.[44]

It is God's kingdom in its gracious and tender expression toward men that absorbs the attention of the psalmist, and God as the sustainer and provider for all His creatures.

> ס 14 The Lord upholds all who are about to fall,
>   And raises up all who are bowed down [in distress].
> ע 15 The eyes of all wait for Thee;
>   And Thou dost give their food at the proper time.
> פ 16 Thou openest Thy hands,
>   And dost bestow lavishly upon every living thing what it desires.

Then he describes the Lord as the righteous, kind, and available God, who is responsive to those who in their need call upon Him in trustful sincerity:

---

[43] Dan. 4:3: "His kingdom is an everlasting kingdom, and His dominion endures generation after generation." Daniel 4:34: "His dominion is an everlasting dominion, and His kingdom endures generation after generation."

[44] The נ section is not in the Hebrew text but is in one manuscript and in the Septuagint, Vulgate, and Syriac.

ש 17 Righteous is the Lord in all His ways,
And kind in all His deeds.

ק 18 Near is the Lord to all who call upon Him,
To all who call upon Him in good faith.[45]

ר 19 What they who fear Him desire, He does;
And their cry for help He hears, and saves them.

Finally he portrays God as the keeper of those loyal to Him and, in accord with the retribution dogma of Judaism, as the exterminator of the wicked:

ש 20 The Lord keeps all who love Him;
But all the sinners He exterminates.

The psalmist closes as he begins, in the first person. It is the expression of his sincere personal wish that in this solo, created by his own mind and sung from the depths of his soul, his mouth may give such utterance to God's praise as will move future generations to praise Him. And we are convinced that his eager hope has been fulfilled.

ת 21 May my mouth speak a praise song of the Lord;
So that all flesh may bless His holy name!

[45] Cf. Judg. 9:15 for "good faith."

Chapter III

THE NEW YEAR FESTIVAL IN ISRAEL

ONE OF THE GREAT FESTIVALS—AND ONE OF THE MOST PERSISTENTLY OBSERVED IN the religious history of Israel—was that of the New Year. The celebration of this festival in some form goes back to a time long before the monarchy. In its origin it was a Canaanite festival, and it is the earliest of which we hear in the Israelite records. In an authentic source which gives an illuminating glimpse of the old Canaanite festival as observed in Shechem at the temple of Baal-Berith, we learn that the worshipers "went out into the field, and gathered their vineyards, and trod the grapes, and held festival, and went into the house of their god, and ate and drank." (Judg. 9:27.) It was a joyous festival, with the vegetation idea at the center of all its ceremonies and rites.[1] The earliest name for it in the Israelite records is the Feast of Ingathering. This is found in the original nucleus of the Code of the Covenant, the origins of which must be sought outside of Israel among the population which the Israelites found in Canaan,[2] and it was held "at the going out" (Exod. 23:16) or "at the turn" (Exod. 34:22) of the year. The present renderings of these two terms, respectively, in the American Standard Version of the Old Testament as "at the end of the year" and "at the year's end" (margin: "revolution") are, as G. Buchanan Gray [3] has shown, mistranslations. From the analogy of the Accadian (*ṣit shamshi*), the rendering should be "at the going out" of the year, in the same sense as the sun is said to "go out" of his chamber (Ps. 19:6).

In a careful historical study of the development of the Hebrew New Year celebration Fiebig agrees with Volz [4] that Tabernacles (Ingathering) was the old New Year festival of Israel, and that the celebration of the New Year in the autumn goes back to oldest times. The entire seventh month (Tishri) was celebrated as a sacred festal month of the turn of the year. After the Exile, the Day of Atonement (on the tenth of Tishri) put the Festival of Tabernacles somewhat in the shade. In the Priestly Code in two classical passages (Num. 29:1; Lev. 23:24) prominence is given, alongside of Tabernacles and the Day of Atonement, to "the holy convocation," which was "a memorial of blowing of trumpets" on the first day of the seventh month, although it is not spoken of or emphasized as the beginning of the year. It is not until the Seleucid era

---

[1] See Leslie, *op. cit.*, pp. 42-43.

[2] Alt, *Die Ursprünge des israelitischen Rechts*, pp. 24-25; and Pfeiffer, *Introduction to Old Testament*, p. 211.

[3] *Sacrifice in the Old Testament*, pp. 300-301. Also, in the Gezer Calendar (Macalister, *Excavations at Gezer*, II, 24-28), the month of "ingathering" is the first of the series.

[4] *Das Neujahrfest (Laubhüttenfest)*.

(*ca.* 200 B.C.) that New Year's Day was separated from Tabernacles and definitely fixed on the first of Tishri.[5]

This festival of the New Year, thus evidenced in sources which date from before 1200 B.C., was adopted by the Israelites from the Canaanites after their invasion of the land but before the establishment of the Israelite monarchy under King Saul. It has vital points of contact with the *Akitu* festival, that of the Babylonian New Year. From 3000 B.C. this Babylonian festival held a central place in the community life of the various city-states of Mesopotamia, and its significance was primarily agricultural.[6] When, under Hammurabi (1792-1750 B.C.) ,[7] Babylon rose to political supremacy, there took place a unification of the older forms which had earlier characterized the festival. It lost something of its agricultural nature, and it became an urban spring ceremony, the king having a central place in it. The festival was very popular, the place it held in Babylonian life being comparable to that of the Feast of Tabernacles in Israel. Indeed, the Feast of Tabernacles (Ingathering) , which was the New Year festival in Israel, represented an independent development of the central New Year ritual of the East, such as took place on the soil of Canaan. The earliest form of this was the Tammuz ritual, and the latest the *Akitu* ceremonies of Babylon.[8]

The Hebrew New Year festival had significant points of contact with the Babylonian *Akitu* celebration.[9] On the evening of the fourth day in the Babylonian festival the high priest entered into the most holy place—before the statue of Marduk—and recited from beginning to end the Babylonian epic of creation. One of the most important episodes in this epic was the combat which took place between Marduk, king of the gods and men, and Tiamat, the mighty dragon of chaos. Marduk, entering into combat with Tiamat and her monstrous consort, Kingu, slew them and out of their bodies created the universe and man. The gods in their gratitude made him their king and cried, "Marduk is become king." [10] Similarly in the Hebrew account of creation the Lord (Yahweh) entered into combat with the deep *(tehôm)*, the vast primeval watery chaos, overcame it, and then created the universe and man. Elements of the Hebrew version of this combat are most clearly discernible in Gen. 1; Pss. 74:12-17; 89:9-12; Isa. 51:9-10; and Job 9:13. Here the Lord (Yahweh) replaces Marduk.

[5] Fiebig, "Rosch ha-schana," in Beer and Holtzmann, *Die Mischna, Seder II, Traktat 8,* pp. 31-35.

[6] Langdon, *Babylonian Menologies and the Semitic Calendars,* p. 69.

[7] For Hammurabi's dates, see Albright, *From the Stone Age to Christianity,* pp. 111, 319.

[8] See Hooke, *The Origins of Early Semitic Ritual,* pp. 6, 57, and his essay "Traces of the Myth and Ritual Pattern in Canaan" in *Myth and Ritual,* p. 70.

[9] The primary sources for this description of the *Akitu* festival in Babylon are the following: Thureau-Dangin, "Le rituel des fêtes du nouvel an à Babylone," in his *Rituels Accadiens,* pp. 127-48; Zimmern, "Das babylonische Neujahrfest," in *Der alte Orient,* XXV, 3; Zimmern, "Über Alter und Herkunftsort des babylonischen Neujahrsfestrituals," in *Zeitschrift für Assyriologie,* XXXIV (1922) , 190 ff.; Langdon, *The Babylonian Epic of Creation;* Meissner, *Babylonien und Assyrien,* II, 95-99; Pallis, *The Babylonian Akitu Festival.*

[10] Langdon, *The Babylonian Epic of Creation,* IV, 28.

Tehôm, "the deep," is the Hebrew counterpart of Tiamat. The terms "the sea," "the raging sea," "heads of the dragon," "the heads of Leviathan," "fountain," "flood," "the roaring waves," "Rahab," "the monster," are synonyms for the abysmal chaotic deep which Tiamat with her consort and helpers represent.

It is likely that the annual Hebrew ceremonies of the New Year with a major emphasis upon the combat that issued in creation are responsible for that familiarity with these originally Babylonian elements now so discernible in the priestly, lyric, and prophetic literature of Israel. And the presence in Hebrew cultic poetry (note especially Pss. 74, 89, and 93) of this myth about the Lord's conquering the dragon, in closest connection with the account of creation (especially Pss. 74:16; 89:11; Gen. 1), is exactly what we have in the Babylonian epic of creation. This was recited in full at the New Year ceremony in Babylon. Humbert, in a recent investigation of the relation the priestly account of creation (Gen. 1) bears to the liturgy of the Israelite New Year, has arrived at the conclusion that the liturgical form of this creation story points to its use by the Israelite priests as a chant in a manner similar to what was the practice in Babylon.[11]

On the fifth day of the celebration of the Babylonian New Year occurs an important rite in which the reigning Babylonian king plays the chief role. On that day the king is brought into Esagila, the temple of Bel Marduk. He washes his hands, then comes before Marduk. The high priest now takes from him his scepter, ring, and scimitar—all his insignia of royalty—and lays these down on a chair in the chapel before Marduk. For the time being, the king is thus as a commoner before the god. The high priest then smites the king upon both cheeks and leads him before Marduk. Then he pulls the king's ears and causes him to kneel before the god. The king prays to Marduk in a prayer which solemnly maintains his faithfulness as a ruler, and declares his loyalty, using the following words:

> I have not sinned, O lord of the lands; I have not been negligent unto thy divinity.
> Babylon I have not ruined, nor commanded its dispersion.
> I have not . . . Esagila, nor forgotten its rites,
> I have not smitten the cheeks of my subjects, . . . nor caused their humiliation.
> I have paid attention to Babylon, and have not destroyed its walls.[12]

The priest answers, giving to the king the content of a favoring oracle from Marduk:

> Fear not; Bel has spoken;
> He will magnify thy kingdom;
> He will make thy dominion great;
> He will destroy thy enemy and overthrow thine opponent.

[11] "La relation de Genèse 1 et du Psaume 104 avec la liturgie du nouvel-an israëlite" in *Revue d'histoire et de philosophie religieuses.*

[12] Thureau-Dangin, *op. cit.,* ll. 423-27; cf. Langdon, *Semitic Mythology.*

He then gives back to the king his scepter, ring, and scimitar. He is monarch again. The high priest once more smites the king's cheek. If this brings tears to the king's eyes, it is an omen that Bel Marduk is gracious to him. If tears do not flow, it is an omen that the god is angry.

We see in this rite an annual re-enthronement of the reigning king of Babylon over his people each New Year's Day. It is probable that in Judah likewise an annual ceremony of the official enthronement of the Judean monarch took place on New Year's Day, the date of his reign being reckoned from the first New Year's Day after the death of his predecessor, just as was the case in Babylon.[13] This would account for the presence of so many hymns of the king in the Psalter, as a number of them have a unique fitness for such a ceremony where the king would be accepted annually as the legitimate ruler. He would affirm his loyalty to his covenant with God and with his people and would become anew the channel of the divine blessing from God to Judah.

On the sixth day of the Babylonian celebration the god Nebo came from Borsippa to visit his father Marduk in Babylon and was placed in his own chapel in Esagila, the temple of Marduk. On that same day came also the great gods of the various sanctuaries in Babylonia—i.e., their images were brought— and they were arranged in the temple in correct order of rank and in such a way as to give honor to Marduk. On the eighth and eleventh days there occurred a most important ceremony in the assembly room in the part of Esagila which was sacred to Nebo. On those days Nebo, as the scribe of the gods, "fixed the fates" whereby a new fate of supremacy was decreed to Marduk for the new year and—as Gadd suggests—by a parallel acceptation to the king of Babylon as his earthly vicegerent.[14] This ceremony is reflected in the Babylonian epic. Marduk, upon his defeat of Tiamat and her spouse Kingu took from Kingu the tablets of fate, sealed them, and fastened them to his breast.[15] Henceforth, enthroned in his temple Esagila, he is "lord of the gods of heaven and earth," [16] "the help of his land and of his people," [17] "the creator of grain and plants, causing the grass to spring up," [18] and "the administrator of justice." [19]

Certain psalms, as we shall see, which have their worship setting in the ceremonies of the Hebrew New Year emphasize the Lord's judgment of the earth, of the world, and of the nations. This is in harmony with what has ever been, and still is, the central emphasis of the Hebrew New Year celebration—the idea of the kingdom of God. Moreover, this concept rests upon the deepest element in the religion of Israel, which goes back to Sinai and to Moses—the covenant which the Lord made with Israel, out of which, as Pedersen main-

[13] Cf. Mowinckel, *op. cit.*, II, 7-8, 114.
[14] Cf. Gadd in Hooke, ed., *Myth and Ritual*, p. 56.
[15] Langdon, *The Babylonian Epic of Creation*, Tablet IV, ll. 120-22.
[16] *Ibid.*, Tablet VI, l. 117.   [17] *Ibid.*, Tablet VI, l. 113.
[18] *Ibid.*, Tablet VI, l. 2.   [19] *Ibid.*, Tablet VII, l. 39.

tains, "grew the whole fabric of their existence." [20] The New Year is the time when the covenant is annually renewed, when a new series of God's dealings with His covenant people begins. "On New Year's Day," says Elbogen, "the recognition of the lordship of God over humanity has its religious expression. God as King unites all humanity in one covenant. He judges mankind, is mindful of their deeds and determines their fate; and if the kingship of God has not yet been realized in the present, in the future He will extend His dominion over the whole world, and one day it will be acknowledged by all creation." [21] But, as Fiebig has discerned, the idea of judgment as emphasized by the Babylonian epic expresses not primarily the concepts of pronouncing unfavorably upon and condemning to punishment. It embodies a deeper element, that of decreeing what shall happen, that of fixing or determining of fate or fortune, whether good or bad.[22] When the gods gather in the assembly room for the fixing of the fates and to Marduk is decreed supremacy for the coming year, the decisions or judgments having to do with the different men, lands, things, and conditions are written down and sealed.[23] This is true in a yet more profound sense in the Israelite concept of judgment—the determining of fortunes which God is thought to administer to His people and to the peoples of the world on New Year's Day. A very significant expression of this very early conception of judgment is given in the Mishnah.[24] Here it is maintained that the world is judged at four times in the year: at Passover, as manifested through grain; at Pentecost (or Weeks), as shown through fruits of trees; at Tabernacles, as revealed through water; and on New Year's Day, when "all that come into the world pass before Him like flocks of sheep." [25] Mankind He then divides into three classes—the entirely righteous, the entirely wicked, and those in between. New Year's Day is a call to repentance to this third group. They have until the Day of Atonement to repent, for the judgment passed on New Year's Day is sealed on the Day of Atonement.

In the Babylonian festival on the same day (the eighth), and immediately following the extremely important ceremony of the fixing of the fates, came the famous New Year procession. For the great mass of the people this was the chief rite of the entire festival and was participated in by thousands and even tens of thousands. It was started by the king of Babylon, as every monarch, in order to be accepted as rightful ruler, was required to participate in this ceremony. As Thureau-Dangin says, "the most important of all the rites of the New Year was that which was the privilege of the king, 'to take the hand' of the god, in order to call upon him to leave his temple and to conduct him to

---

[20] *Israel, Its Life and Culture,* p. 18.
[21] *Der jüdische Gottesdienst in seiner geschichtlichen Entwicklung,* p. 141.
[22] *Op. cit.,* p. 43.   [23] Cf. Mowinckel, *op. cit.,* II, 75.   [24] Fiebig, *op. cit.,* I, 2.
[25] The Mishnah here quotes from Ps. 33:15, one of the psalms which I discuss under "New Songs for the Newly Enthroned King": "As it is said, 'He who fashions the hearts of all, who scrutinizes all their doings.' "

the *Akitu*." [26] The king took the hand of the image of Marduk to lead him out, which was the signal for the start of the procession. This opening ceremony was of intense interest. Every slightest movement of the king was observed. Any trembling of the king's hand was viewed as a bad omen. Likewise, any mishap to the horse or wagon or ship upon which the image of Marduk was borne was viewed as having dire consequences. This reminds us forcibly of the Hebrew story of the sudden death that was visited upon Uzzah at that moment when he put forth his hand to steady the ark of the Lord, the oxen having jostled it (II Sam. 6:6-10). The New Year procession moved out through the north gate, "the holy gate," the image of Marduk being borne upon a wagon. It passed through the splendid Ishtar gate to the processional street and along the sacred way to the Euphrates, followed by the throng of people. From this point it continued by ship to the street which led to the prayer chapel in the Festival House, the goal of the procession. Hymns accompanied the progress of the procession. From the eighth to the eleventh days Marduk and the other gods remained at the Festival House, where certain dramatic re-enactments took place, among which was the combat between Marduk and Tiamat. In this connection it is instructive to note that similarly in Egypt an ancient drama was annually performed at the New Year festival in the temple of Ptah, at Memphis, which re-enacted the death of Osiris and the accession of Horus. This drama was in the form of a narrative, which a reader recited and which was interspersed with dramatic interludes. At the end of the play there was a remarkable account of the creation of the world by Ptah.

On the eleventh day of the feast the return of the gods to the temple of Marduk took place. Probably the procession proceeded on the Euphrates as far as the bridge with the stone pillars, where the plastered processional street to the temple begins. When the image of Marduk was again in its proper place in Esagila, the high priest chanted a festal hymn, a prayer for the peace of the temple, the city, and its people, and the festival was at an end.

The Hebrews likewise, as we have seen, had a processional street—a sacred way leading up to the Temple. Mowinckel believes this began at the house of Obed-Edom, a Levite in Jerusalem (I Chron. 13:14), in the western city, and that it led from there to the Temple hill. He thinks the title of each psalm in the collection Pss. 120–134, *shîr hamma'alôth,* a "processional song," marks the group as belonging to a collection of songs of wide variety, which forms a songbook for the procession ascending Mount Zion.[27]

One cannot immerse oneself in these well-authenticated sources for the Babylonian New Year celebration without sensing overtones from it in the rites of the Hebrew New Year. And indeed, considering the vast extent and strength of the cultural influence of Babylonia, this is to be expected. Gadd reminds us that

---

[26] *Op. cit.,* p. 46.   [27] Cf. Mowinckel, *op. cit.,* II, 128-30.

"since Babylonia was at once the creator of one of the world's oldest civilizations and the general mentor of Western Asia, both in religion and in the arts, it is only natural that its influence upon the Hebrews, both before and particularly after the exile, would be the most distinguishable of all." [28]

The New Year festival in Israel coincided with the Feast of Tabernacles, and in the psalms which had their worship setting in this festival we can discern six major themes. These single out the primary emphases in the rituals of the festival, illumine its thought and teaching content, and help us to understand the amazing spiritual hold which it has retained upon Israel across the centuries: (a) There was for the occasion a preparatory night festival. In such a ceremony the night hymn (Ps. 134) had its rightful setting. (b) The festival celebrated the annual enthronement of the Lord as King over His people. The psalms which have their setting in this feature of the celebration are Pss. 47, 68, 95, 96, 97, 98, and 99. (c) It summoned the congregation to sing "new songs" for the New Year and in recognition of the newly enthroned king. Such "new songs" are Pss. 33, 149, and—also under (b) above—Pss. 96 and 98. (d) The festival included a ceremony in which the reigning Judean king would annually be accepted as the legitimate monarch of his people and as the unique channel of the Lord's blessing unto them. The psalms that are at home in such a worship setting are Pss. 2, 21, 72, 101, 110, and 132. (e) Coming at the "finished circuit" of the year (Exod. 34:22), the festival looked back over the past year in thanksgiving for the blessings experienced. Coming as it did at the end of the year's harvests (Deut. 16:13-17), it was the festival of national thanksgiving in Israel, and Pss. 65, 67, 118, and 124 have their appropriate setting in it. (f) Coming at the going forth of the year (Exod. 23:16), at the point when a new circuit begins, the festival looked forward in anticipation and hope to the new year that was just dawning. Hooke, calling attention to this point where the year "goes out," says, "It is not the end of the year but its beginning, the magical point when, the cycle being completed, the powers of nature begin anew to re-create the world."[29] Thus this festival looked forward in persistently recurring optimism and faith to the blessing of God upon the coming year, its harvests and its fortunes. It was felt that both good fortune and ill fortune came from God. He was the Sovereign who fixed the fates and who continued the good fortunes of His people. Or if times had been hard and misfortunes severe, He had it in His power to turn their fortunes. He was the Judge of His covenant people and of all mankind. Ps. 53 (with which Ps. 14 is identical), 85, 123, 125, 126, and 129 are prayers for *die Wendung des Schicksals* (the turning of the fortunes) of Israel. And one (Ps. 82) presents God as Judge, giving sentence.

---

[28] *Op. cit.,* p. 66. [29] *Origins of Early Semitic Ritual,* p. 51.

Chapter IV

HYMNS, SONGS, AND PRAYERS FOR THE HEBREW NEW YEAR

WE HAVE DISTINGUISHED SIX MAJOR THEMES OF THE HEBREW NEW YEAR CELEBRATION. These themes represent the thought content of the festival. They are closely related one to the other and often merge into one another. In some of the hymns, songs, and prayers of the New Year several of these themes appear. But almost always there is one theme of pre-eminent importance which is our guide to the psalm's particular classification. Not all the psalms whose distinctive worship setting is a phase of the New Year will be found here. This is because the literary type of a psalm, or the nature of its make-up, may be more distinctive for its classification than its seasonal setting in worship.

In this chapter I shall interpret the psalms that give primary expression to the six major themes of the Hebrew New Year. This represents one of the richest areas in Hebrew psalmody.

1. A PREPARATORY NIGHT HYMN

There were nocturnal festivals in Israel, and the Levitical singers were on duty in them. These singers are described as "set free" from other service, dwelling "in the chambers" of the Temple, "employed in their work day and night" (I Chr. 9:33). Josephus informs us that the priests spent nights and days in the sanctuary observing certain sacred celebrations.[1] From the Mishnah we learn that on the eve of each of the seven days of the Feast of Tabernacles there was held in the Temple a nightly preparation which lasted until dawn.[2]

Ps. 134. A NIGHT HYMN OF PRIESTLY PREPARATION

This is a vigil liturgy, a night hymn of spiritual preparation for the Festival of Tabernacles. The priests addressed in Ps. 134 are evidently on duty, not for a single night, as would be the case on the eve of the Passover, but for several nights. At such a service this psalm has its setting. It was a vigil liturgy, a ceremony of preparation primarily for the officiating priests.

We are to picture the whole festal congregation assembled in the great inner court of the Temple. The mood is that of solemn joy. Boys from the priestly families light the great lamps standing in the court. Torches are also lit, so that the court is ablaze with light. The priestly choir stands to the right and left of the great altar. The high priest, as Josephus informs us, is present at the

---

[1] *Contra Apionem* I. 22.
[2] Sukkah II. 4, 9; cf. Ps. 46:5, "at the dawning of the morning."

festivals, [3] and it is he who chants the call to the ministering priests to perform their priestly prerogative, for they alone are permitted to pronounce the blessing of the Lord (Deut. 10:8; 21:5).

> 1 Bless the Lord, all ye servants of the Lord,
>   Who are ministering in the house of the Lord by night.
> 2 Lift up your hands toward the sanctuary,
>   And bless the Lord.

The priestly choir responds to the high priestly summons by pronouncing a blessing upon the high priest. It contains two themes which characterize the ceremonies of the New Year—the Lord's seat of rule in Zion and the Lord as Creator:

> 3 May the Lord bless thee from Zion,
>   Who made heaven and earth.

2. HYMNS OF THE ENTHRONEMENT OF THE LORD

A striking contribution made by Mowinckel, and one of great significance for our understanding of the psalms, is his demonstration of the existence in Israel of an annual ceremony, the opening rite of the New Year festival, in which the Lord was enthroned anew as King over his people and over the nations of the earth.[4] The prototype of this festal rite in Israel was "the feast in the month Ethanim," the seventh month (Tishri), in which was celebrated the entrance of the ark into the newly built Temple (I Kings 8:2-9). In pre-exilic times the coming of the Lord as King over His people was annually enacted by a festal procession of "the Lord of hosts, . . . the King of glory."

The concept of the Lord as King, which is the basic idea of this festal celebration, receives marked emphasis in the psalms. In ten of them the title of "King" is applied to God (Pss. 5:2; 10:16; 24:7-10; 29:10; 48:2; 74:12; 84:3; 95:3; 98:6; 149:2). Eight more contain references to the "throne" of the Lord (Pss. 9:4; 9:7; 11:4; 47:8; 89:14; 93:2; 97:2; 103:19). But in five psalms we encounter a unique and distinctive exclamation which should probably be rendered "The Lord is become King!" (Pss. 47:8, reading originally "the Lord"; 93:1; 96:10; 97:1; 99:1). These psalms, along with Pss. 98 and 68, form a special group in the Psalter and were composed for and rendered in the ceremonial rite of the Lord's enthronement.

The concept of the Lord's throne or of the Lord as King is very old in Israel. In one of the earliest sources, of which the editor of the book of Kings availed himself and which had its origin in the sons of the prophets, the Lord is represented as "sitting on His throne, with all the host of heaven standing by Him on

---

[3] *Jewish Wars* V. 230; cf. Oesterley, *The Psalms,* II, 537.
[4] *Op. cit.,* II, 7, 40, 81; called "New Year's Day" (Rosh Hashana), "the day of festivity" (yôm terûʻāh), "the day of the blast of the trumpet" (yôm shōphār) in Num. 29:1.

His right hand and on His left" (I Kings 22:19). In the inaugural vision of Isaiah the Lord is seen "sitting upon a throne high and lifted up." And Jeremiah in a lament to the Lord cries, "Do not disgrace the throne of Thy glory" (Jer. 14:21). The concept of the Lord as King is accordingly clearly pre-exilic and certainly as early as the eighth century B.C.

But how did the title "King" come to be applied to the Lord? We have already seen that the Babylonian New Year festival—with the enthronement of Marduk as king and the ceremonial enthronement cry, "Marduk is become king"—most likely had its influence upon Israel, although indirectly through the environmental culture of Canaan. But upon this subject important new light has come from the Ras esh-Shamra cuneiform tablets of North Canaan, which belong to the fourteenth century B.C., a time contemporaneous with the Tell el-Amarna documents.[5] These give us rich information as to Canaanite myths and rituals in the period when there was a strong interpenetration of culture between Canaan and Israel. In these sources El is the highest god of the pantheon. He is supreme in power, the father of the lesser gods and of mankind. He is "the creator of creatures." Moreover, he is the eternal king. Of him it is said, "Thy wisdom is eternity; . . . with eternity thou dost live; . . . thou shalt take thy eternal kingdom, thy kingdom which is of the ages." He is called "the king, father of years." Such conceptions as are here applied to El are applied in the psalms to the Lord. It is more than likely that this Canaanite view of El as king and ruler influenced to some extent the Israelite concept of God. Moreover, the concept of God as taking His seat on His throne, which thrills these psalms of the Lord's enthronement, is quite at home in the Ugaritic literature.[6]

The most central and important feature in these psalms of enthronement, however, is not that the Lord is viewed as King. Rather it is to be found in the unique exclamation which is a distinctive feature of most of the enthronement psalms—"The Lord is become King!"—an exclamation filled with profound and stirring emotion, and which implies that the enthronement has just taken place. We have here a striking use of the perfect tense in Hebrew, which expresses the act of enthronement as having happened in the immediate past—in the sense that the Lord has just now been enthroned—but the effects of the act continue on in the present.[7] The words are manifestly a cultic exclamation which embodies something similar in mood to that of the ancient Easter cry still rendered in the Easter sunrise celebration in Budaun, India. At the close of this service the officiating minister comes out to the open court before the church, where the

---

[5] See above, p. 25. Also cf. Muilenburg, "Psalm 47," in *Journal of Biblical Literature*, LXIII (1944), p. 236.

[6] Cf. Patton, *op. cit.*, pp. 15-19; cf. also in Leslie, *Old Testament Religion*, the discussion under Ras Shamra.

[7] Cf. Driver, *Hebrew Tenses*, p. 10 (4); and Davidson, *Hebrew Syntax*, sec. 39b.

worshipers who have filed out stand awaiting him, and cries, "The Lord is risen!" And they respond, "The Lord is risen indeed!"

The model for the psalms of the enthronement of the Lord was given by the ceremonies incidental to the enthronement of an earthly monarch in Israel and Judah. We get vivid features of these ceremonies in the historical sources of Israel. The one who was to be anointed king rode on the royal mule to the Spring of Gihon, where he was anointed by the chief priest assisted by the court prophet (I Kings 1:38-39, 45). The trumpet was blown, and all the people clapped their hands (II Kings 11:12) and shouted, "Long live the king!" (I Kings 1:39). The king then rode in royal procession to the capitol, followed by the people generally who "went up after him playing upon flutes and rejoicing with such great outburst that the earth was rent with their noise" (I Kings 1:40). The day was celebrated by the inhabitants of Jerusalem (I Kings 1:45) and presumably by the whole nation (I Sam. 11:15; II Kings 11:19-20).

In the enthronement psalms there is, of course, no anointing of the invisible, spiritual King. His throne is the most holy place; His palace is the Temple of Jerusalem, for He dwells on Mount Zion, which is at once His dwelling and His fortress. However, they imaginatively describe the King as robed in majesty. They tell of the jubilation and rejoicing of His loyal subjects and especially the members of His congregation. They imply an annual procession with the ark— the sacred symbol of the real presence of the Lord—borne by the priests. That famous palladium, the Lord's processional sanctuary, having been taken out from its permanent resting place in the holy of holies for the purpose of the celebration, is carried by the priests in procession, followed by the celebrating throng as they go up the sacred way to the Temple. Placing the ark anew in its resting place, they thus enthrone Him anew as King.

The psalms refer to the blast of the trumpet, the enthronement cry, the jubilation of Jerusalem, of Zion, of the Temple congregation, of the nations, and even of nature, with shouts, hand clapping, playing, and singing. They call upon all other gods and their idols to bow before Him as Lord, who has come anew to judge the world and to rule the world. The psalms of the Lord's enthronement are Pss. 47, 68, 93, 97, 98, and 99.

Ps. 47. THE ENTHRONEMENT OF THE KING OF KINGS

The first of this special group of hymns of the enthronement of the Lord is Ps. 47. According to the Talmud (Sopherim 19:2) it was the special psalm for the New Year festival and is still spoken at the New Year service of Judaism, before the sounding of the horn in the synagogue.[8] The psalm opens with a general summons to the jubilant praise of God on the part of the nations.

> 1   Clap your hands, all nations;
>   Raise a shout to God with the sound of a ringing cry.

[8] Keet, *A Liturgical Study of the Psalter*, p. 88.

The familiar "for" now introduces the theme of the praise. It all centers in God, and He is seen from three points of view: the exalted and awe-inspiring Lord, the great King who rules the earth, and the God who opened the way for His people to gain expanding mastery of the land of Canaan and who put Israel in dominant control of the surrounding nations.

> 2 For the Lord most high is awe-inspiring,
>   The great King over all the earth,
> 3 Subduing nations under us,
>   Yes, peoples under our feet.
> 4 He enlarges our territory for us, [9]
>   Jacob's glory, which He loves.

Then the ceremony of enthronement unfolds before our eyes. It is the most distinctive part of the psalm. It begins with the holy procession of the Lord, the King. The ark of the Lord, the most ancient symbol of His living presence, is borne up the processional way to the Temple by the priests (I Kings 8:3), accompanied by the King's loyal subjects—worshipers. In verse 5 "gone up" refers to the royal procession of the Lord. We hear the shout of the popular acclaim. We hear the "blast" of the trumpet. The words in verse 5—"is gone up" ('ālāh), "shout" (terû'āh), and "blast of a trumpet" (qôl shôphār) —are not secular expressions but definitely ritual terms that have to do with the cult. This hymn, which focuses attention upon particular motifs in the festal celebration, was sung in the Temple when the ark of the Lord, "the King of glory," had been installed anew in "its place . . . in the holy of holies, under the wings of the cherubim" (I Kings 8:6). At verse 6 we are in the midst of the worshiping congregation, and the command is to the Temple musicians.[10] The climactic moment of the festal celebration—up to which all else leads—comes when the ark is at length installed and the Lord's enthronement is affirmed. Let us picture the living scene as the choir sings:

> 5 God is gone up with a shout,
>   The Lord with the blast of a trumpet.
> 6 Sing to our God, sing!
>   Sing to our King, sing!
> 7 For the Lord is become King over all the earth.
>   Sing a song of spiritual power.[11]

Then there bursts forth the enthronement cry, and we realize that the Lord has taken His seat upon His throne.

> 8 The Lord is become King over the nations:
>   He has taken His seat upon His holy throne!

[9] So reading with Stade.   [10] So, rightly, Schmidt.
[11] The term *maskil* means "a song powerfully effective in its spiritual influence," says Schmidt, *Die Psalmen,* p. 59; it is a song containing a wisdom, not theoretical but which comes from divine revelation, says Mowinckel, *op. cit.,* IV, 5-7.

The nations of the earth, the pagan peoples, recognize the superiority of Israel's God. So they gather about "the God of Abraham." They remain, however, in the psalmist's thought, vassals of Israel. In order to share in the blessings of Israel, they join themselves to Abraham's God.[12] There is an implicit reference here to Gen. 12:3: "In Thee shall all the families of the earth bless themselves."

We do not have here the noble, practical universalism of Deutero-Isaiah. "We must not overestimate such universalism as the psalmist here suggests. Rather it follows naturally from the work of the Lord as Creator." [13] As Creator of all He is Lord of all. We do have here, however, under the limitation of a political nationalism, the first step toward that deep universalism of Deutero-Isaiah, with his sense of the world-embracing mission of reconciliation and spiritual illumination on the part of the Lord's servant, Israel. Sings the psalmist:

> 9 The princes of the peoples assemble.
>   Along with the people of the God of Abraham.
> For to God belong the rulers of the earth:
>   He is highly exalted.

Ps. 68. A HYMNBOOK OF ENTHRONEMENT SONGS

Ps. 68, as Schmidt has maintained and brilliantly argued, is best understood as a small liturgical textbook for the festival of the Lord's enthronement. It is composed of a number of brief songs originally independent, touching upon the various motifs of the festival. The unity of the psalm is accordingly to be sought, not in its subject matter, but in the great occasion for which its constituent parts were assembled and at which they were sung.[14] Yet the resultant liturgy viewed as a whole is magnificent, as Ker has likewise noted. He calls it "a psalm of wonderful power and compass, of living fire and dramatic picturesqueness, ranging from the remote past with its triumphs, onward to a final and irreversible victory in the future."

It opens with a processional hymn (vss. 1-3) in the form of a war song, taken from the ancient ritual of the ark when that famous palladium was borne forth into battle (Num. 10:35). The summons to God to "arise" is here changed into an imaginative description of His arising and the consequent rout of His enemies. In verse 3 the reference is to the exultant rejoicing of those accompanying the ark as the Lord comes in triumphant procession to His people.

> 1 God arises! His enemies are dispersed;
>   And those who hate Him flee from His presence.
> 2 As a cloud which the wind pursues is driven about,
>   As wax dissolves before the fire,
>   So the wicked perish before the presence of God.

---

[12] *Ibid.*, II, 182-85.   [13] *Ibid.*, II, 182.

[14] *Die Psalmen*, pp. 127-28. Schmidt finds sixteen separate songs. I consider them fifteen, believing that 7-10 make up but one song and that vss. 28-31 also belong together. I have closely followed Schmidt's lead in the interpretation of this psalm.

3 But the righteous are joyful before God;
   They rejoice and exult in gladness.

The second (vs. 4) is another hymn, a processional sung by the worshipers
as they joyously participate in the sacred procession wherein the Lord "comes,"
even as in ancient times He "came" from Sinai (Deut. 33:2) to the help of His
people in their need. Every festival of the Lord's enthronement was, in a sense,
a *re-enactment of that majestic coming* of God "riding through the steppes"
between Sinai and Canaan.

4 Sing to God; sing praise to His name.
   Extol Him who comes riding through the steppes.
   The Lord is His name; exult before Him!

A third song (vss. 5-6) glorifies the Lord, now installed in His holy residence,
because of His helpful, saving provision on behalf of the powerlessness of His
people. Only the stubborn who reject His protection remain in hard circumstances.

5 A Father to orphans and a Judge of widows
   Is God in His holy habitation.
6 God gives to the solitary a home:
   He brings prisoners into prosperity;
   Only the stubborn remain in arid land.

The fourth song (vss. 7-8) is dependent upon the ancient Song of Deborah
(Judg. 5:4-5) and celebrates the Lord's manifestation of Himself in storm and
in beneficent, life-giving rain. It pictures God as going forth at the head of His
people, and is thus appropriate to be sung in connection with the sacred procession to the sanctuary. When He "came" across the wilderness from Sinai to
Canaan, He manifested Himself in earthquake and storm, and in the downpour
of the rains upon which all life depends. The song is thus appropriate for the
autumnal New Year's festival, which came just before the longed-for rains set in.
What God has done He will do again.

7 O God, when thou wentest forth before Thy people,
   When Thou didst march through the wilderness,
8 The earth shook; yes, the heavens dropped rain;
   Sinai quaked before God, the God of Israel.
9 Thou dost liberally sprinkle rain, O God;
   Thou raisest up the sick and weary.
10 They are satisfied from Thy sustenance,
   Which Thou in Thy goodness dost provide for the poor, O God.

A fifth song follows (vss. 11-12, 13bc), a brief ancient war song. It is probably
but a fragment of the original. It is introduced by God's "word" to the dancing,
rejoicing women (cf. Exod. 15:20-21), which commanded the procession to begin.
In words of exultant joy the dancing maidens proclaim the defeat of the enemy
(cf. I Sam. 18:7). They exalt the most beautiful woman of the victorious clan,

who divides the booty, the spoils of war. Special attention is focused upon an exquisite ornament, perhaps upon a captive king's helmet.

> 11 The Lord gives the word:
> The women who proclaim the tidings are a great army.
> 12 The kings of the armies, they flee, they flee;
> And the beautiful one in the house divides the booty—
> 13b The wings of a dove, covered with silver,
> 13c And its pinions with pale green gold.

The next two songs (vss. 13a, 14) are likewise but fragments, yet are sufficient to recall the whole to the mind of the singers. At verse 13a (which should follow vs. 13bc) is inserted a taunt song, a satire on the shepherds' love of peace. It is the opening line of a song which was borrowed from the ancient paean of Deborah (Judg. 5:16):

> 13a Wouldst thou lie among the sheepfolds?

Verse 14 is the first line of a war song which celebrates a famed victory on Mount Salmon, in the vicinity of Shechem (Judg. 9:48), during a snowstorm, which was a great and memorable rarity in Palestine.

> 14 When the Almighty scattered the kings,
> Then it snowed in Salmon.

The eighth song (vss. 15-16) glorifies Mount Zion as the place of the Lord's permanent dwelling. With passionate love in his heart the psalmist compares Zion, which God has chosen as His abiding place, with the far more majestic, many-peaked Mount Hermon, which he designates by the region where it is located, "Mount Bashan." Imaginatively he pictures the great Mount Hermon looking with envious eyes at the far smaller Mount Zion, which has the distinction of being the Lord's dwelling place forever.

> 15 A mountain of God is Mount Bashan;
> A mountain with peaks is Mount Bashan;
> 16 Why looked ye with envy, ye mountains, ye peaks,
> At the mountain which God desired for His dwelling,
> Aye, where the Lord will dwell forever?

It is a song of the Lord's entry into Zion.

The ninth section (vss. 17-18) is another song accompanying the procession of the Lord into His sanctuary. The imaginative description is based on a militant type of procession in which a victorious monarch, amid enthusiastic popular acclaim, rides in triumph into his capital. So the Lord, who "has come from Sinai" (Deut. 33:2), rides majestically in His chariot into His sanctuary, accompanied by the march of vast numbers of warriors, and followed by captive prisoners and by tribute received from the conquered. These pictures are but inadequate attempts to portray the deep spiritual reality that stirs the psalmist's soul as "the horses and chariots of fire" of the Lord of hosts, the invisible God, enter in solemn procession into His holy place:

> 17 The chariot of God is amidst myriads of companies of Israel: [15]
> The Lord hath come from Sinai into His sanctuary.

Suddenly the psalmist turns from description to direct address and speaks to the majestic King:

> 18 Thou hast ascended on high;
> Thou hast taken prisoners captive;
> Thou hast received gifts from men; [16]
> Yes, even the rebellious must bow before Thee, O God.

The tenth song (vss. 19-20), similar to the second (vss. 5-6), celebrates the merciful acts of God as the ruler of infinite resourcefulness and the deliverer of His people:

> 19 Blessed is the Lord day after day!
> He carries us, the God of our help.
> 20 God is for us a God of saving acts;
> God, the Lord, has ways out in the presence of death.

The eleventh and twelfth portions are war songs, primitive and sanguinary. They express the motif of judgment in the form of triumph over the Lord's enemies, a theme characteristic of the psalms of enthronement, and one which follows upon the ritual enthronement act.[17] The eleventh is a single verse:

> 21 Surely God will smash the head of His enemies,
> The hairy scalp of him who struts about in his guilt.

The twelfth (vss. 22-23) likewise has the theme of the judgment of the Lord, but in verse 23 it is clear that an individual is addressed. This can be only the king as the representative of the nation. It seems to presuppose a prayer of lamentation by the king on behalf of his people, and this portion is an oracle of a priest or prophet of the cult to the king promising him victory. This is similar to the case in Babylonian psalmody, where a lament by the king on behalf of his people beseeching divine deliverance is followed by the pronouncement of a priestly oracle promising victory over the enemy.[18] The judgment of the Lord, thus pledged to the king, will pursue and take captive his enemies, though they flee for safety to the heights of Bashan (Mount Hermon) or hide in the depths of the sea—a metaphorical way (cf. Amos 9:3) of expressing certainty of the inexorable judgment of God (cf. I Kings 21:23; II Kings 9:37; also Isa. 34:6; Isa. 63:2-6).

---

[15] Cf. Num. 10:36; cf. Schmidt, *Die Psalmen*, p. 126.
[16] Reading, with Gunkel, *mēʾādhām*.   [17] Cf. Mowinckel, *op. cit.*, II, 65-66.
[18] Cf. Quell, *op. cit.*, p. 73; Balla, *Das Ich der Psalmen*, pp. 109-10, where a good illustration is given from a lamentation by Nebuchadrezzar for his people.

22 The Lord hath said, I will take enemies captive from Bashan;
    I will take them from the depths of the sea;
23 So that thy foot may bathe itself in blood;
    The tongue of thy dogs may lick it up.

The next song, the thirteenth (vss. 24-26) is one of the finest in the entire
psalm. It is a song for the festal procession of the Lord and His worshipers into
the temple, a feature which remained the most popular rite of the entire celebration and emphasized the central idea in all the enthronement psalms, the *coming*
of the Lord anew to the help of His people. The song itself pictures such a procession with vividness and detail unequaled in the Old Testament.

24 See the festal procession, O God,
    Thy procession, O my King, [19] into the sanctuary.
25 In front are the singers; behind are the players;
    In the midst are maidens beating tambourines.
26 In choirs [20] they praise [21] God,
    The Lord, who from the spring appears. [22]

The brilliant scene unfolds before our eyes. It is the New Year's procession
of the Lord into His sanctuary on His enthronement day with the ark, the processional symbol of His presence in the lead. The procession starts at the "spring"
of Gihon (vs. 26) at the foot of the Temple mount. Up in front are the singers.
Behind them are the musicians with harp and zither. In the midst of the singers
and players are the maidens beating tambourines and dancing. The description
continues: following those in the lead comes the entire festal congregation arranged in order according to tribal rootage [23] and thus forming several "choirs."
Only two of the southern and two of the northern tribes are mentioned, but all
others would be included, for this was the New Year festival of all Israel. The one
unifying bond, embracing all in a rich sense of fellowship, is the Lord, Israel's
divine King.

27 There is Benjamin, few in men; [24]
    The chiefs of Judah, great in men; [25]
    The chiefs of Zebulun, the chiefs of Naphtali.

How colorful, how rich in patriotic and religious feeling was such a procession!
How great a part it must have played in the ceremonies of the New Year!

An important feature of the festival of the Lord's enthronement was the

---

[19] Omitting *ʾēlî*.

[20] So render *maqehēlôth*, choirs of individual tribes of Israel; similarly separate choirs,
maqehēlim, in Ps. 26:12; cf. Gunkel, *Einleitung*, p. 66.

[21] Reading *bĕrekhû*.

[22] Reading, with Schmidt, *Die Psalmen*, p. 130: *yĕrāʾeh* for Israel. The spring is Gihon.

[23] Cf. Ps. 122:4, "whither the tribes go up, the tribes of the Lord," *wohin die Stämme pilgern*,
so Schmidt. I have heard three similar tribal choirs in a church service at Elisabethville, in the
Belgian Congo.

[24] *Çʿîr ʾādhām*.   [25] Reading, with Gunkel, *rabh methîm*.

dramatic portrayal [26] of the Lord's triumph over the pagan national powers that
challenged His lordship. We have recounted how at creation God mastered the
monstrous dragon of chaos with her gang of mighty helpers. Here, as is characteristic of Israelite thought, the great enemy pagan powers replace the monstrous
beasts of primitive story. The psalmist, as in psalms of lament, appeals to God
to intervene now on behalf of His people, who so sorely need protection, even
as He has done in primeval times. May the Lord render powerless these pagan
enemies, some of them as far distant as extreme Upper Egypt—Egypt, Pathros,
and Cush (cf. Isa. 11:11) —and so transform them that these very nations may
pay obeisance to Him. Accompanying this dramatic portrayal, which re-enacts
the defeat of these pagan powers and their consequent obeisance to the Lord,
the fourteenth song was sung: [27]

> 28   Command, O God, Thy protection,
>   Like the divine protection Thou didst [once] accomplish for us.
> 30a Rebuke the beast in the reeds,
>   The gang of the mighty, the lords of the nations.
> 30c Scatter the nations who delight in battles;
> 29   Let them hasten to Thee, to Jerusalem;
>   Let the kings bear along gifts to Thee;
> 31a Let them bring bronze [28] from Egypt,
> 30b From Pathros, gold and silver.
> 31b May Cush lift up [29] her hands to God.

The psalm ends in a majestic processional hymn (vss. 32-35), the fifteenth
song, in which the psalmist summons the kingdoms of the earth to praise the Lord.
He glorifies God as one who comes to His people riding in stateliness across
the ancient heavens. The clouds, heavy with rain, are an expression of His
majesty and power. The winter rains that mean strength and blessing to the
Lord's people are at hand. Schmidt says, "For in the final analysis all ideas connected with this festival are directed toward the return of the rainy season, the
essential gift of the God who in the autumn ascends his throne." [30] The thunder
peals forth, a welcome sound after the long, dry season. It is the "voice" of God.
The psalmist summons his people to the reverent and awesome acknowledgment
of God's might and power which He exerts (vs. 34a) on behalf of His congregation. We feel the similarity of ideas in this section with Ps. 29, and the exalted
mood of reverent awe is alike in both.

> 32   Ye kingdoms of the earth, sing to God;
>   Sing praises to the Lord; lift a song

---

[26] Such dramatic portrayals were performed, as we have noted, at the Babylonian and Egyptian
New Year celebration. Likewise for Israel (cf. Ps. 48:4-8).

[27] The original order of the lines has been restored by Schmidt.

[28] Reading, with Gunkel, *hashmal*.

[29] Reading *tārēm*, with Hitzig and Graetz.   [30] *Die Psalmen*, p. 130.

33a To Him who rides in the heavens, the heavens of old.
   Hark! He gives forth His voice, His mighty voice;
     His majesty and strength are in the clouds.
34 Ascribe might unto God, people of Israel;
   Awesome is God in His sanctuary:
35 It is the God of Israel who gives strength and power to His people.
   Blessed be the Lord, Israel's God!

This psalm is thus a veritable corpus of enthronement themes. Predominant are the songs of procession, because the sacred procession was the most popular of all the New Year ceremonies of Israel. In that rite universal participation was possible, and the rank and file as well as the cultured and spiritually sensitive found in it drama, color, and deep and joyous emotion. One song, as we have seen, accompanied a dramatic re-enactment such as is known both in Babylon and Egypt. Five are war songs—some primitive and bloody—yet there never fails the motif of judgment wherein human triumph is viewed as the result of God's fixing of the fortunes of His people and of their enemies. Strong in the psalm is the theme of the gracious provision of God through rainfall and through the saving acts of the enthroned King for the helpless and oppressed. Similarity to the thoughts of Deutero-Isaiah, as Schmidt rightly points out, is not due to any dependence upon the prophet on the part of the psalmist, but grows rather out of the fact that Deutero-Isaiah himself describes the Lord's return to Zion in colors of a sacred procession of God (Isa. 40:9-11; 52:7-10). Schmidt is right in maintaining for this psalm that "the entire world of [its] ideas and of [its] cultic transactions have place only in old pre-exilic times." [31]

Ps. 93. THE LORD'S COMBAT WITH THE FLOODS OF CHAOS

Another hymn of the enthronement of the Lord is Ps. 93—brief but majestic. In this psalm we see quite clearly the chief point at which the Babylonian New Year rites and concepts influenced the ritual of the Israelite New Year: in the combat between the Lord and the storming, chaotic floods which issued in God's triumph and the creation of the world. Shimmering through the Hebrew psalm we see the combat of Marduk with Tiamat, the dragon goddess of chaos. It will be well, however, to preface the discussion of this psalm with two similar passages in other psalms where the themes of combat and the resulting creation are more complete and explicit—Ps. 74:12-17 and Ps. 89:9-11.

The first of these passages—Ps. 74:12-17—is in a psalm of national lament. In it the psalmist strives to hearten the Lord's impotent people when they are in despair. Their plight was probably due to the ruthless assaults of the Persian Artaxerxes III (Ochus) in 344 B.C.[32] He recalls the power God had manifested in primeval days when He had shown Himself victor over the awful forces of

[31] *Die Psalmen*, p. 131.
[32] Buttenwieser, *op. cit.*, p. 555. He cites Eusebius *Chronicon* (Schoene) II. 112-13.

chaotic disorder and had created the cosmos. Marduk's place is taken by the Lord. Tiamat, mighty dragon of the deep, her spouse Kingu and their helpers are absent from this account, but the terms the psalmist uses—"sea," "heads of the dragon," the "heads of [the monster] Leviath?n"—take their places and represent them. Cries the psalmist:

> But Thou, O God, art our King of old,
> Achieving victory in the midst of the earth.
> Thou didst split the sea in Thy strength;
> Thou didst break the heads of the dragon upon the waters;
> Thou didst crush in pieces the heads of Leviathan;
> Thou didst give him as food, as grub for the jackals.[33] (Vss. 12-14.)

In such words he utters his faith that God is still King, as He was at primeval creation when He defeated the chaotic forces of the deep. The "sea," "the heads of the dragon," the monster "Leviathan" were mastered and destroyed by the Lord, just as Marduk defeated and destroyed the dragon of chaos, her monstrous consort, and their helpers. We must feel the shame and disgrace thus cast upon the dragon and her helpers, as the carcass of the feared and hated sea monster becomes food for land demons, the jackals of the desert.

It is the dragon, whose reign has represented vast chaos, that is defeated. Now God, the victor, establishes the orderly universe. The frightful, destructive torrents are in His mastery, and He transforms them into fountains. Dry land appears when the floods that submerged it are bound. So the psalmist says:

> Thou didst cleave out fountain and torrent:
> Thou didst dry up inexhaustible streams. (Vs. 15.)

We are reminded of the similar account of the transformation of the chaotic waters into the waters of the sky and of the nether springs, and the gathering of the chaotic deep below the sky into seas so as to let the dry land appear. This is described in the priestly narrative of creation.[34]

Then God creates the luminaries which divide day from night, and differentiates the zones of the earth—regions where it is hot and where it is cold—and He establishes the seasons, summer and winter. Says the psalmist:

> Thine is the day, Thine also the night:
> Thou didst establish the moon and the sun;
> Thou didst fix all the zones of the earth;
> Winter and summer, Thou didst devise them. (Vss. 16-17.)

The other passage—Ps. 89:9-11—comes from a king's psalm. A Judean monarch, in a desperate, humiliating hour when he and his people have lost face

---

[33] Reading with Wellhausen, la'am çiyyîm, so Gunkel.
[34] Gen. 1:6-9. "Then God said, 'Let there be a firmament in the midst of the waters and let it permanently divide the waters in two.' And it was so [LXX]. God made the firmament and divided the waters which were under the firmament from the waters which were above the firmament. And God called the firmament heaven. . . . And God said, 'Let the waters below heaven be collected into one mass and let the dry land appear.'" Cf. also Isa. 51:10a.

among the nations, appeals to God to intervene. He utilizes a hymn that glorifies God's wondrous deeds at creation when He had broken the power of the dragon of chaos—here called Rahab—and then had created the orderly world:

> Thou abidest Ruler over the raging of the sea:
> The roaring of its billows, Thou stillest them.[35]
> Thou didst crush Rahab like one pierced;[36]
> With Thy strong right arm Thou didst scatter Thine enemies.
>
> (Vss. 9-10.)

Clearly Rahab is here the name of a primeval sea monster, the dragon of the deep, whose presumptuous arrogance manifested itself in the storming billows of the raging sea, and whose aim was to take the land into possession and thereby defy the dominion of the Lord. And in this decisive struggle with the Lord, Rahab, like Tiamat, had mighty helpers, [37] enemies of God. But God's superior power stilled the angry waves, pierced the monster, and destroyed its cohorts.

From the psalmist's point of view this monster of the primeval deep is the epitome of evil, and its arrogant intent to flood the land is a dangerous threat to all life. But now the Lord is in control. Let the sea rage; it is in God's power; He sets for it its bounds. So completely is the primeval deep in the Lord's mastery that He can plant islands in it (see Ecclus. 43:23). So He, who is now in supreme control, creates the heavens and the earth. The psalmist says:

> Thine are the heavens, yes, Thine the earth:
> The world and that which fills it,
> Thou hast established them. (Vs. 11.)

These illustrations from Pss. 74 and 89, which tell how the Lord conquered the dragon, both have as their immediate context the Lord as King (Pss. 74:12; 89:9) and as Creator of the world (Pss. 74:16-17; 89:11). This is exactly the case in the Babylonian epic of creation, which, as we have seen, was recited in full on the fourth day of the New Year celebration in Babylon. Marduk is enthroned,[38] then comes his victorious combat with the dragon,[39] after which he creates the heavens and the earth.[40]

We are now prepared to interpret the compact and powerful Ps. 93, the shortest of the enthronement psalms. It opens with the enthronement cry, the enthusiastic acclaim of God's festal congregation as the Lord is enthroned anew.

1a The Lord is become King!

---

[35] Cf. Ecclus. 43:23:
> By His counsel He hath stilled the deep,
> And planted islands therein.

[36] Cf. Isa. 51:9: "Was it not Thou that didst hew Rahab in pieces, that didst pierce the dragon?" Also cf. Job 26:12: "Through his power the sea was stilled, and by his skill he smote through Rahab."

[37] Job 9:13: "The helpers of Rahab bowed down under him."

[38] Langdon, *The Babylonian Epic of Creation*, IV, 28.

[39] *Ibid.*, IV, 69-122.   [40] *Ibid.*, IV, 128-46.

Imaginatively the psalmist pictures the Lord's splendor at the moment of His enthronement. Behind his word is the recall of the royal splendor of a Judean monarch whom he had seen enthroned:

> He has clothed Himself in majesty;
> 1b The Lord has clothed Himself with strength,
> And has girded Himself.

Then comes the distinctive thing in this psalm (vss. 1c-4): the Lord's combat with the destructive, primeval floods of chaos (vs. 3), His triumph over them, and then His creation of the world (vs. 2). In primeval times—so runs the Hebrew version of the Babylonian myth—what was eventually to become the cosmos was formlessness and waste; what was to be an orderly universe—earth and sky, land and sea, day and night—was then a vast chaos, a dark watery abyss with floods, frightful and powerful, defying control, the enemy of all order. Nothing was established; nothing secure; nothing stable. Such was the state of things when the Lord entered into combat with this chaotic deep. He drove back this threatening, arrogant, defying enemy—the storming floods of chaos— mastered and bound them, then proceeded to create the world and take it under His almighty control. For the moment the psalmist merely implies the combat but emphasizes the outcome.

> 1c Yes, He has regulated the earth, so it cannot be shaken!

In his words there is the background of tension—a keen awareness of the vast and awful struggle the Lord had experienced with these stupendous, antagonistic forces which issued in the decisive and abiding triumph of God. Ever since that primeval victory He has been—and in the psalmist's thought is now become anew—King of the inhabited world. So in reverent acclaim he acknowledges God's lordship.

> 2 Thy throne is established from remote times:
> From eternity Thou art God.

Having already anticipated the outcome, now the psalmist pictures the combat in toneful, poetically descriptive words. On the one hand are the storming, destruction-threatening floods. We see them foaming in angry violence. We hear the surging, seething roar of the waters as the mighty billows boom and crash. On the other hand, and opposed to them in the conflict, is God. There He sits upon His throne, high above the mad beat of the angry waves—more majestic than they, more powerful than they, and their Lord!

> 3 The floods lift up, O Lord;
> The floods lift up their voice;
> The floods lift up their roar.
> 4 Greater than the thunder of mighty waters,
> More powerful than the breakers of the sea,
> Is the Lord, majestic on high!

Staerk suggestively says, "The psalmist knew how to give his song, through the suppressed notes of the theme of Marduk's battle with Tiamat, a wonderful tonal quality. His final word, 'the Lord, majestic on high,' sounds above the uproar of the waves of the sea like a reverberating shout of joy." [41]

The psalmist has thus far presented three pictures: the first, the Lord newly enthroned; the second, the Lord the Creator; the third, the Lord in combat and triumph. Now comes a forth, the Lord as Judge, the fixer of the fortunes of His people. What He certifies—His laws—can be depended upon. They are reliable and adequate. And with the Lord now enthroned anew in His "house," the Temple, the psalmist calls down a heavenly blessing upon the Temple from the holy King.

> 5 Thy laws [42] are very reliable:
>   May the beauty [43] of holiness be upon thy house,
>   O Lord, forevermore!

Ps. 96. THE KING WHO HAS COME TO JUDGE THE WORLD

Among the most complete of the psalms created for the annual festival of the enthronement of the Lord is Ps. 96. It was inevitable that the annual ceremony which year after year exalted the Lord as King would be a stimulus for the creation of new hymns: a new hymn for the New Year, a new hymn for the newly enthroned Lord. The creators of these hymns had the same desire that present-day leaders of worship have with regard to the recurring festal days in the church calendar—to make them meaningful, to fill them with significant spiritual teaching, to save them from mere pageantry and display. Among the Temple priests there were poets who put their feeling for the day's deeper meaning into hymns that would mediate it to the rank and file of worshipers.

This psalm opens with a summons to praise which is directed to "all the earth" (vss. 1-3). Let all the earth blaze a new trail of praise to God. But what is to be the content of the praise song? (a) It is to bear daily tidings of God's salvation, which includes deliverance from external evils as well as spiritual help. (b) It is to tell the nations about His majesty. (c) It is to declare the wonderful deeds that He has accomplished, especially the creation of the world. The psalmist calls the people of the earth to bless the nature of God, that is, to adore Him on bended knee. For the main thing which the enthronement always set in new perspective was God as the active being, working on behalf of His people.

> 1 Sing to the Lord a new song:
>   Sing to the Lord, all the earth.

---

[41] *Op. cit.*, III, 52. [42] The term means literally "testimonies."
[43] Reading *newēh*, from *nāwāh*, "beautify"; cf. Mowinckel, *op. cit.*, V, 27. The line should be rendered as a wish for the blessing of the newly enthroned King upon the Temple.

2 Sing to the Lord; bless His name;
    Bear tidings from day to day of His salvation;
3 Relate among the nations His glory,
    Among all peoples His wonderful acts.

The psalmist grounds his summons to praise (vss. 5-6) in what God essentially is. His greatness of character sets Him above all divine beings in the deserved praise of humanity. He is the Creator. He made the heavens. This it is which makes Him worthy of praise. And this exalts Him above all idols, who cannot make anything but are themselves made (cf. Deutero-Isaiah, in Isa. 44:10-20). We feel the appropriateness of this theme of the Lord as Creator when we recall that each New Year's Day when God ascends His throne brings a renewal of creation. The psalmist is moving in the concepts of the great Prophet of the Exile as he thinks of the new things the Creator King is about to do in the new year. Said the prophet:

I am the Lord, your Holy One, the Creator of Israel, your King. . . .
Behold I will do a new thing; now shall it spring forth. . . . (Isa. 43:15, 19.)

Verse 6 takes on the quality of vividness when we place it in the setting of the procession of the Lord to His sanctuary. Moving before Him are majesty and splendor. In the sanctuary, where His worshipers are, is strength and beauty.

5 For all the gods of the peoples are idols,
    But the Lord made the heavens.
6 Majesty and splendor are before Him;
    Strength and beauty are in His sanctuary.

The scene of verses 7-9 is the open space before the gates of the Temple area. At the enthronement of an earthly monarch those paying him allegiance rejoice before him in festal array. And just as the celestial beings, imaginatively conceived, bow "in holy adornment" before their King (cf. Ps. 29:1-2), so here the nations, "the clans of the peoples," are summoned to enter the Temple courts bearing their gifts of fealty. The psalmist is under the influence of late prophetic thoughts which portray the glory and the international drawing power of the new Jerusalem (cf. Isa. 60:10-14).

7 Ascribe to the Lord, ye clans of the peoples;
    Ascribe to the Lord glory and strength.
8 Ascribe to the Lord the glory of His name;
    Bear a gift and enter His courts.
9 Bow down before the Lord in holy adornment;
    Entreat His favor, all the earth.

Oesterley has drawn attention to what might be called the order of service [44] at the ceremony of the Lord's enthronement, which is here suggested. First comes the act of homage—the recognition by the nations of God's supreme lord-

[44] *The Psalms*, II, 423-24.

ship. Second is the act of praise, wherein the worshipers would laud those qualities in God—"the glory of His name"—which characterize Him. Third is the act of offering, in which the worshipers would enter the inner court of the Temple, bearing on their shoulders their sacrificial gifts. They would be received by the Levites, who would prepare the sacrifices to be offered upon the altar, then deliver them to the priests, who would perform the sacrificial rite. Finally would come the act of prayer, the entreating of the Lord's favor, prostrate before Him.

The climax of the psalm is the enthronement ceremony itself. All other rites lead up to this. The enthronement cry is to be heralded among the nations. We feel again the background of the Lord's struggle with the primeval chaos and His triumphant establishment of the orderly world. We hear, imaginatively, the exultant acclaim of the newly enthroned King—the heavens, sea, and land, and the trees of the forest all raising their voice before the Lord, who has come as King of the world and, more particularly, as Judge of the world:

> 10 Say among the nations, "The Lord is become King!"
>   He has established the world so it cannot be shaken.
> 11 Let the heavens be glad, and let the earth rejoice;
>   Let the sea roar, and that which fills it;
> 12 Let the field exult, and all that is in it;
>   Yes, let all the trees of the woods raise a ringing cry
> 13 Before the Lord; for He has come,
>   For He has come to judge the earth:
>   He will judge the world in accordance with righteousness,
>   And peoples in accordance with His truth.

In the closing words of the psalm we feel the intense passion of late Judaism as it looked forward in the certainty of faith to the ultimate lordship of God over the world. Yet the Lord's judgment of the world—which includes both vindication and punishment—does not belong merely to the far-off days of eschatology. These psalms emphasize that the Lord *is come*. His lordship has already been introduced. The time of salvation has already begun. It begins anew today! [45] There is a glad recognition of the power of this righteous Judge, who "has come" to rule the world, or of this righteous King, who "has come" to judge the world. God comes afresh in power to His people and to the world. We are reminded of Jesus' words: "The Kingdom of God is among you."

Ps. 97. THE AWESOME KING OF ZION

A psalm of indescribable majesty, likewise sung at the festival of the Lord's enthronement, is Ps. 97. It opens with the enthronement cry, which resounds through the whole earth and even to the distant islands of the Mediterranean. It summons all the earth to festal joy.

[45] Cf. Mowinckel, *op. cit.*, II, 70.

1 The Lord is become King. Let the earth rejoice!
  Let the many islands be glad!

The next part of the psalm (vss. 2-6) is highly imaginative. The newly enthroned King appears, manifesting Himself to the rejoicing world and arousing vast commotion in the realms of nature and of men. In vivid, descriptive poetry, richly colored from the ancient classical accounts of the Lord's primeval self-disclosure to His people at Sinai in volcanic fire, storm, and earthquake (Judg. 5:4-5; Deut. 33:2; Mic. 1:3-4; Hab.: 3:3-6), the psalmist tells how the newly enthroned monarch manifests Himself to the world.

The Lord, seated upon His throne, is enveloped in the deep darkness of a storm cloud, as was likewise the case in Ezekiel's vision of the divine glory (Ezek. 1). But that awful darkness is lit up from within by blazing fire and great flashes of lightning. We are permitted to see how secure and dependable is the reign of this world King, just now enthroned; for the foundations upon which His throne stands are such as make even an earthly throne secure—righteousness and justice. What happens when the awesome God thus manifests Himself and takes His seat on His majestic throne? His enemies are consumed as by fire. Flashes of lightning illumine the world. The earth trembles in volcanic earthquake; mountains erupt; the heavens, the Lord's swift heralds, bear the news to all the lands that the righteous God is become King. And all peoples look and behold.

2 Clouds and darkness surround Him;
  Righteousness and justice are the foundation of His throne.
3 Fire goes before Him
  And sets ablaze His enemies round about.
4 His lightning flashes light up the world;
  The earth sees and writhes;
5 Mountains dissolve like wax
  Before the Lord of all the earth.
6 The heavens make known His righteousness;
  And all the peoples behold His glory.

In the next section (vss. 7-9) the psalmist abandons the world of fantasy and comes down to earth. How does the enthronement affect the non-Judean world, the idolaters, the image worshipers? How does it affect the Lord's own loyal worshipers? The proud idolaters, the worshipers of God's rivals among the gods (nonentities), stand before the enthroned King in humiliation and shame. In keen irony the psalmist calls upon their gods to worship God! Then in vivid contrast he turns from the disillusioned idolaters to the devout festal congregation in Zion. When Zion, the religious community of the Lord's loyal worshipers, hears the enthronement cry, "The Lord is become King," there is only joy. In ancient Israel women greeted the Lord's mighty act of Israel's rescue from Egyptian bondage with timbrel, song, and dance. Now their descendants rejoice in the Lord's enthronement as the righteous Judge, and the King of gods and men.

> 7   All the image worshipers are ashamed,
>   Who pride themselves in their idols.
>   Bow to Him, all ye gods!
> 8   Zion hears and is glad;
>   And the daughters of Judah rejoice
>   On account of thy judgments, O Lord.
> 9   For Thou art most high over all the earth:
>   Thou art exalted over all gods.

The psalm closes with words of encouragement, counsel, and warning to the celebrating congregation. If you hate evil, you are in the love and care of the King. You may now be in darkness and sadness; but if you live in fealty to the newly enthroned Lord, light and gladness will break upon you. So the psalmist brings his words to a climax by a renewed summons to joy and gratitude because of the character of the Lord:

> 10   The Lord loves those who hate evil:
>   He preserves the life of His loyal ones;
>   He rescues them from the hand of evildoers.
> 11   Light breaks forth upon the righteous,
>   And gladness upon the upright in heart.
> 12   Be glad, ye righteous, in the Lord;
>   And give thanks at the remembrance of His holiness.

Ps. 98. THE WORLD ACCLAIM OF THE KING

Ps. 98 is a hymn of the enthronement of the Lord, intended for the great enthronement festival of the New Year. It begins with a summons to praise. The psalmist's spirit is alive with the sense of the immediacy of God's presence now, anew with His People. Hence old songs will not suffice. A new song must greet the newly enthroned King. And that new song is now being lifted by the choir in a call to the congregation:

> 1a   Sing to the Lord a new song!

The psalmist makes clear what the theme of this "new song" is and introduces it by the familiar "for." The theme is the wonderful acts which the Lord's mighty right arm has wrought. These are threefold: (a) He has achieved victory over the chaotic forces, cosmic and historical, that have hindered His dominion. (b) He has wrought the salvation of His people Israel. Their rescue and blessing at His hands have brought about the vindication of His own character, along with that of His people, before the nations to the far ends of the earth. (c) He has granted to the Israel of the present the renewal of the spiritual blessings of His covenant of lovingkindness and faithfulness, first made in the days of the Hebrew fathers. So the psalmist continues:

1*b* For He has done wonderful things:
1*c* His right hand has given Him victory;
       Yes, His holy right arm has helped Him.
2   The Lord has made known His salvation:
       He has revealed His righteousness before the eyes of the nations.
3   He has remembered His lovingkindness to Jacob,
       And His faithfulness to the house of Israel.
       All the ends of the earth have seen
       The salvation of our God.

The next part of the psalm (vss. 4-9*a*) takes us into the ritual of the enthronement ceremonies but also includes imaginative poetic elements which are aglow with deep feeling. The ground features are supplied by the ceremonies incidental to the enthronement of an earthly monarch. We hear, in imagination, the pent-up enthusiasm now breaking forth in glad fealty from all parts of the earth, thundering forth praise to the enthroned King from the inhabitants of the whole world. We hear the glad enthronement shouts and the lively music of lyre and clarion. We hear the ritual blasts of the priests on the ram's horns. The sea, which in the primeval epoch was a storming, antagonistic enemy, now thunders its loyal acclaim. The floods that had once lifted up their voice in opposition to the Lord (Ps. 93:3) now in devout fealty, applaud Him. The towering mountains in united chorus utter ringing cries of joy to their Creator and King.

4   Raise a shout to the Lord, all the earth:
       Break forth, give a ringing cry, and sing.
5   Play to the Lord with a lyre,
       With a lyre's melodious sound.
6   With clarions and the blast of the ram's horn
       Raise a shout to the King, the Lord.
7   Let the sea and its fullness thunder,
       The world and those who dwell in it;
8   Let the floods clap their hands;
       Let the mountains together give ringing cries of joy
9   Before the Lord!

God is now King, installed anew over His people, yet how much still remains to be brought under His dominion! And here our psalmist, out of profound hope and optimism inspired by the prophets, dreams of God's ultimate lordship over the world and all its peoples. Ultimately His sway, bringing justice and equity to mankind, will be a fact. Ultimately He will be Lord of all.

9*b* For He has come
       To judge the earth:
       He will judge the world with righteousness,
       And the peoples with equity.

Ps. 99. THE CHALLENGE TO THE PRIESTHOOD OF THE LORD'S RIGHTEOUS RULE

Ps. 99 opens with the enthronement cry and portrays the Lord at the moment of enthronement when the ark—the throne of the invisible God, whose seat is above the cherubim [46]—is placed in the most holy place. The pagan nations of the world may well tremble when the Lord mounts His throne! Earthquake occurs at His self-manifestation.

> 1   The Lord is become King! Let the peoples tremble!
>   He has taken His seat above the cherubim; let the earth quake!

Zion, where the Lord, the great King, is now enthroned, is the center of His reign. From there His rule extends throughout the world. Let the trembling peoples praise their holy and rigorous King.

> 2   The Lord is great in Zion; He is exalted over all the peoples.
> 3   Let them praise His name as One great and awesome!
>   Holy is He, and a rigorous King. [47]

Then the psalmist sounds the note which makes this psalm of the Lord's enthronement distinct from all others. It is the righteousness and justice of His rule. We feel here the rich contribution of the prophets to the conception of God. From the thought of the Lord's rigorous domination of the pagan nations the psalmist turns to what His righteous rule means for "Jacob," His own people, and he speaks directly to the Lord. Then in a stirring refrain (vs. 5) which divides the psalm into two parts (cf. vs. 9) he gives a renewed summons to the nations and to Israel to exalt their holy King.

> 4   Thou hast established uprightness in Jacob;
>   Thou hast effected justice and righteousness.
> 5   Extol the Lord our God:
>   Fall prostrate at the footstool of His feet;
>   For the Lord our God is holy. [48]

The day of the Lord's enthronement emphasizes the renewal of His covenant which He made with His people in the days of Moses. The Lord heeded the prayers of Moses, Aaron, and Samuel in the days of yore. He manifested His gracious leadership of them at Sinai and in the wilderness by the pillar of cloud, the symbol of His active presence. So may He renew His covenant and show Himself gracious to their successors, the present priests of Israel. Verses 6-8 are thus a prayer to the covenant-renewing God. We feel the solidarity of the generations in the psalmist's thought. Let God deal with today's priests as at Sinai and in the wilderness he dealt with their great priestly ancestor Aaron. May He answer their prayers as he answered the prayers of the great intercessors on behalf of the people of that mighty past, Moses and Samuel (see Exod. 32:30-33,

---

[46] See I Sam. 4:4; II Sam. 6:2; II Kings 19:15; also the classical description of the ark in Exod. 25:8-22, especially vs. 22.
[47] Following Gunkel and Duhm.   [48] Restoring the last line of the refrain, as in vs. 9.

Moses; I Sam. 12:19-23, Samuel; also Jer. 15:1). May He deal with them, not in vengeance but in forgiveness. We feel also the indirect appeal of the psalmist to the priesthood of his day—the challenge which those earlier generations give to the present—to keep the ordinances and the statutes of God. And his words are also a warning against corrupt spiritual leadership. The psalmist is in a mood similar to that of Malachi as he pleads for a righteous and responsible priesthood (Mal. 2:1-9), and he gives them implicit caution that the vengeance of God continues to be visited upon evildoers. Only faithfulness to their priestly calling is acceptable to the Ruler, who brings justice and equity.

> 6 Moses and Aaron are among His priests,
>   And Samuel with those who call upon His name;
>   They cried to the Lord, and He answered them.
> 7 In the pillar of cloud He spoke to them;
>   They kept His charges and the law which He gave to them.
> 8 O Lord our God, Thou didst answer them:
>   A God who forgave, Thou wast to them,
>   But who took vengeance upon their evil deeds.

The psalm closes with the refrain, a renewed summons to the Lord's worshipers in the Temple:

> 9 Extol the Lord our God;
>   Fall prostrate at His holy hill:
>   For the Lord our God is holy.

3. "New Songs" for the Newly Enthroned King

An outstanding theme of the New Year celebration in Israel, as the name itself suggests, is the emphasis upon the new. The re-enthronement of the Lord, year by year, represents, as Hooke expresses it, the renewal of creation, the be-ginning—at the strategic mystical turn of the year—of a new, potent, and beneficent series of God's dealings with His people. Indeed, the origin of ritual in general lies in the attempt to control in the interests of the good life the new span of time that now begins. And the singing of these songs in worship is viewed as the congregation's co-operation with the energies of God, or their effective appeal to God to open in the face of great crisis a new series of divine blessings, sensitively fitted to the congregation's material and spiritual needs.[49] We have already interpreted two such "new songs," Pss. 96 and 98, but their central feature is their emphasis upon the enthronement itself.

Ps. 33. WAITING IN CONFIDENCE FOR THE RENEWAL OF CREATION

Ps. 33 is sung by the Temple choir. It opens with a summons to the wor-shipers to sing a new song of praise, to play to the Lord with harp and lute—

---

[49] Cf. Hooke, ed., *Myth and Ritual*, pp. 4, 8.

the players are the Levites—and to honor Him with the festal clamor of those singing and playing worshipers, and especially with the blasts of the trumpets by the priests. The designations "righteous" and "upright" are simply names of honor for the Lord's worshiping congregation. The words present a vivid, normal picture of congregational worship.

> 1 Raise a ringing cry, O ye righteous, because of the Lord;
>   A praise song is fitting for the upright.
> 2 Give thanks to the Lord with the harp:
>   Play to Him with the lute of ten strings.
> 3 Sing to Him a new song;
>   Play skillfully with a shout of joy.

The theme of the hymn of praise opens in verses 4-5 and is introduced by the familiar "for." It is the Lord's word at creation. But the needs of the hour have led the psalmist to single out a particular aspect of creation. It is the "word" by which God created the heavens (Gen. 1:6) so that the firmament of heaven permanently separated the waters of the clouds that bring rain, from the waters of the springs, the rivers, and the sea. The need for water is in the psalm, as we shall soon see (vss. 6-7). But first the psalmist thinks in a quite general way of God's creative word as being addressed to man. It is His truthful word, faithful to His people. It is the expression of God's innermost being in its manward reach, His righteousness, justice, and kindness.

> 4 For the word of the Lord is truthful,
>   And all His work is [done] in faithfulness.
> 5 He loves righteousness and justice:
>   The earth is full of His kindness.

Then the psalmist becomes more explicit. When the Lord created the heavens and the starry hosts by His divine fiat (Gen. 1), He was the Creator in control, for He had conquered all that had challenged and hindered His creative might. The storming waters, once a threat to all life, are now subject to the Creator's will. Even now those waters, completely in His power, are held by Him in reserve in His "bottle," in His store chambers—note the charm of these childlike pictures—until His people's needs lead Him to send them down in life-restoring and life-saving rain. So, says the psalmist, let Israel remember the kind of Lord it has, this God who has but to speak and it is done. Yes, let all human beings in the world revere Him. For He, who once by a word commanded the world into being, can re-create the world! We feel the psalmist's implicit summons: "Let the congregation on this New Year's day trust in the provision of God. For the Creator God is a God of resource." Schmidt with sensitive insight says, "There must have been a famine when this song arose." [50]

---

[50] *Die Psalmen,* p. 63.

6 By His word the heavens were made,
      Yes, all their host by the breath of His mouth.
7 He collects, as in a bottle, the waters of the sea;
      He puts the deeps in storehouses.
8 Let all the earth be in fear before the Lord;
      Let all who dwell in the world stand in awe of Him.
9 For He spoke, and it was:
      He commanded, and it came into being.

A second theme is developed in verses 10-12, one familiar in the prophetic thought of Israel. This theme was taught by word of instruction for the ear and by drama for the eye. It is the power of the Lord to frustrate the plots of the nations which are directed against God and His people. Just as He defeated the destructive power of the storming waters of chaos and set up a world in order, so will He annul the godless plots of pagan peoples and set up His constructive kingdom of blessing. For God is a Being of purpose. He is the dependable Ruler, moved by no caprice. And just as His word at creation stands confirmed, so what He counsels has hold upon the real world. It *stands*. His reign is the consistent expression across the generations of the deep purposes of His heart. Almost certainly Isa. 14:24 is in the psalmist's mind. There God speaks: "As I have purposed, so shall it stand." Let Israel remember that this mighty Lord is Israel's God. And let Israel choose Him as Lord, who chose Israel as His people. The New Year was ever a call to Israelites to renew the covenant that God had made with Israel and Israel with Him.

10   The Lord annuls the designs of the nations;
      He frustrates the plots of the peoples.
11   His counsel stands forever,
      The purposes of His heart from generation to generation.
12   Oh the happiness of the nation whose God is the Lord!
      The people whom He chose as His property!

The third theme likewise stems from the thoughts of God as King, enthroned in the heavens; and of God as the Creator of all human beings, and so comprehending utterly their deeds, thoughts, and motives. God looks down upon all humanity, searching their innermost being. What is in men's hearts? Where do they look for security? The times are hard; the problems are great; the issues are critical.

13   From the heavens the Lord looks forth;
      He sees all the sons of men.
14   From where He is enthroned He looks down
      Upon all the inhabitants of the earth;
15   He who alone shaped their heart,
      Who understands all their deeds.

His all-seeing eyes miss nothing. He sees, above all, that upon which mankind truly depends. He sees kings counting themselves secure because of the size and equipment of their armies. He sees skillful warriors armed to the teeth. He sees the horses, symbols of military might. Is it material strength that makes a people strong? To the psalmist such strength is but a show of strength. To depend upon it means collapse and disillusionment.

> 16 No king is saved by the greatness of his army:
>   A warrior is not saved by great efficiency.
> 17 A horse is a disappointment for victory;
>   And one does not escape by his great strength.

The eyes of God, how they intrigue this psalmist! He sees them looking at mankind, and not at all pleased with what they see as His look searches men's hearts for some evidence of dependence upon a power other than themselves. Then His searching eyes behold His worshipers, those who fear Him, gathered even now in the Temple, waiting in humility, dependence, and desperate physical need upon Him. And the psalmist, sensitive to a vivid contrast, sings:

> 18 Lo, His eyes rest on those who fear Him,
>   On those who wait for His kindness,
> 19 To deliver their life from death,
>   And in hunger to keep them alive.

The close of the psalm paints a vivid picture of the New Year congregation as it worships in His Temple in this critical time. Three attitudes steady the souls of the Lord's worshipers: first, the attitude of humble waiting upon the Lord for His help and protection; second, joyful confidence in the character of God and in the certainty of His response to their cry of great need; and third, unquenchable hope that He will manifest Himself to them in mercy. The congregation is as one soul.

> 20 Our soul waits for the Lord;
>   Our help and our shield is He.
> 21 For our heart rejoices in Him,
>   And we trust in His holy name.
> 22 Let Thy mercy, O Lord, be upon us,
>   Even as we hope in Thee.

Ps. 149. MILITANT AGENTS OF THE JUDGMENT OF GOD

This psalm is a "new song," and it belongs in the circle of ideas and rites associated with the enthronement of the Lord. A central idea in the psalm is God's judgment upon the enemy powers. That judgment has already been decreed. But now with the enthronement of God as King consummated anew, the Israelites are inspired to the faith that this decreed sentence may through them be carried into effect. The occasion is significant and unites the spiritual and the military aspects of the congregation of the Lord in a unique synthesis. The needs of the hour call for a "new song." The mood is ecstatic joy; the whirling dance, the music of the harp, and the rhythmic beat of the timbrel accompany the song.

The psalm opens with a summons to the congregation of the devout sons of Zion to exult in their newly enthroned King.

> 1 Sing to the Lord a new song;
> Sing His praise in the congregation of the devout.
> 2 Let Israel rejoice in his maker;
> Let the sons of Zion exult in their King.
> 3 Let them praise His name in the dance:
> Let them sing to Him with timbrel and harp.

This summons to praise is based on the experience of Israel that God accepts His people and is Himself the source of the victory that comes to their arms. Here we see the first indication of the military quality of the psalm.

> 4 For the Lord accepts His people favorably:
> He glorifies the humble with victory.

In verses 5-6 a vivid setting for the psalm is painted. The worshipers have come armed to the festal celebration. They are reclining upon their cushions as they partake of the sacrificial meal. They sing hymns and join in the festal dance. They are in the mood of exultant joy, and the call to praise is renewed:

> 5 Let the devout exult at the glory that has come: [51]
> Let them sing upon their cushions; [52]
> 6 With songs of praise to God in their mouth,
> And a two-edged sword in their hand. [53]

This militant exultation not only looks back to past experience, but it looks forward into the immediate future with special enthusiasm. For the Lord, newly enthroned as King (vs. 2), is in the midst of His people, bringing power to His militant worshipers. Judgment has been divinely decreed upon the pagan nations which threaten and hamper God's rule. This is a persistent theme of the New Year ceremony. These militant worshipers are viewed by the psalmist as being God's agents, empowered by Him to put into vigorous effect God's divinely decreed judgment within the coming year. They are viewed as the exponents of God's purpose.

> 7 To wreak vengeance upon the pagans,
> Rebuke upon the nations;
> 8 To bind their kings with manacles,
> Their distinguished men with iron foot chains,
> 9 To execute the decreed judgment:
> He is a power [54] for all his loyal ones.

[51] I follow in this line the rendering of Buttenwieser, *op. cit.*, p. 690.

[52] Cf. Mowinckel, *op. cit.*, II, 66; cf. also I Sam. 1:4 and Deut. 15:20 for allusions to the festive meal.

[53] Cf. Judith 15:12-13.

[54] Mowinckel, *op. cit.*, II, 158, note 2, suggestively interprets this word *hādhār* as supermundane power.

This psalm at first thought seems utterly pagan in its spirit. There is an intense note of vengeance in it. Not to excuse but to understand this spirit of vengeance, however, we must realize that the pagans—the nations—represented all that kind of dominating material might to which the Lord's will and power were unalterably opposed. Over against such power Israel stood helpless. But the annual New Year festival, with its emphasis upon the coming of the King afresh to His people, gave Israel hope of triumph over all such throttling and persecuting powers. This helped keep faith alive in the ultimate triumph of God's worshipers over all that opposed His will.

4. NEW YEAR SONGS AND PRAYERS FOR THE REIGNING MONARCH

The date of reign of a Judean king was reckoned from the first New Year's Day after the death of his predecessor. This was likewise the case in Babylonia. The prominence of the king in the Babylonian ceremonies of the New Year—in the light of other points of contact they had with the Hebrew festival—makes it a reasonable presumption that the Judean king would occupy a place of similar importance in the Hebrew New Year. There are thirteen psalms in the Psalter which are primarily concerned with the Hebrew king. Seven of these have no connection whatever with the New Year ceremonies, and will be interpreted in Chapter VIII under the topic "Psalms Concerning the King." The other six, when viewed in the light of a distinctive worship setting in the New Year rites, seem to fit into that background with unique pertinency, and therein achieve dignity and force. They are Pss. 2, 21, 72, 101, 110, and 132.

The New Year emphasizes the renewal of God's covenant with Israel. The anointing of a king was a religious act and was performed by a priest (I Kings 1:39) or a prophet (II Kings 9:6). In Solomon's prayer of the dedication of the Temple, as reported by the Deuteronomic historian (I Kings 8:22-26), the king renews the covenant (vs. 23) which through Nathan the prophet the Lord had made with King David (II Sam. 7:5-17). This service of dedication of the Temple was planned and carried out at "the Feast" of the seventh month, which means the Festival of Tabernacles, with which the New Year coincides. It is reasonable to expect that such a rite of renewal of the covenant on the part of the king would become normative in Israel. It would be viewed as a matter of first importance for the nation that their monarch should annually recognize and affirm his covenant with Him "who keeps the covenant and the lovingkindness with His servant who walks before Him with all his heart" (I Kings 8:23, following codices Vaticanus and Alexandrinus of the Septuagint). For the Hebrew king was viewed as the unique channel through which God poured His blessing upon His people. In that part of the Babylonian ritual wherein the king was the chief participant, it was clearly intended that he should experience through its performance a heart-searching challenge. This was assuredly true likewise, and even to a deeper degree, for the king's part of the Hebrew New Year rites. The rich spiritual content of these psalms, even when somewhat compromised by unattractive nationalistic and political coloring, argues for their effectiveness as a safeguard against royal oppression and as an inspiration to beneficent rule.

How are we to account for the extravagant international hopes often confronting us in these psalms, especially hopes of the domination of foreign nations by the Hebrew monarch? They have their rise partly in the superlative grandeur of the occasions for which these psalms were created and in which they were rendered. But they were also influenced by the grandiose court style of utterance which was prevalent in nations such as Babylonia and Egypt, nations which actually did exercise sway over other nations, sometimes even comparable to world dominion.

Ps. 2. THE CHALLENGE OF WORLD DOMINION

Ps. 2 is a king's psalm, spoken in part by a Judean monarch himself at the moment when he is anointed king. We are to think of some scene such as is given in the report of the anointing of the young prince Jehoash. We must presuppose that the preliminary and private ceremonies—ritual bathings and so on— have preceded this high moment. The king appears before his people in the inner court of the Temple and stands beside one of the two great pillars of the Temple porch at the entrance to the Temple, "as was the custom" (II Kings 11:14). The life setting of such a psalm is the part of the ceremony of his enthronement in which the king is anointed and clothed with the insignia of his office.

The anointing of a king in Israel was ever viewed as a religious act. It was a sacrament designed to call into expression the latent energies that slumbered in the depths of his soul, such as his aptitudes and talents for rule.[55] The ceremony had its own definite liturgical form and was accompanied by ritual words.[56] We should view the setting of this psalm in Israel's life, not as a political manifesto, but as a religious utterance which presents the king as the spokesman of those ideal values for which Judah at its best stands.

The psalm opens with the nations in commotion. This was often the case in Babylonia, Assyria, and Egypt at the accession of a new ruler. We feel the influence of these great world empires upon the court style of Israel in this psalm, for the concept of world dominion came to Israel quite early and from without. The pagan kings and their peoples are in revolt, not only against the Lord's king, but also against the Lord Himself. They are now in angry uproar and are conspiring secretly against the Judean monarch, the Lord's anointed, to throw off the Judean yoke.

The psalmist's soul is imbued with the conviction that Israel is the Lord's covenant people and is under His protection. Accordingly, the rebellion of the

---

[55] Cf. *ibid.*, III, 82, and Pedersen, *op. cit.*, p. 157.
[56] Performed by a prophet: I Sam. 10:1; II Kings 9:6; performed by a priest: I Kings 1:39.

pagan powers against Judean sovereignty is, in the last analysis, rebellion against God. His question, "Why are the pagans in uproar?" is a rhetorical way of saying that such rebellious plotting is futile.

> 1 Why are the pagans in uproar,
>   And the nations in futile commotion?
> 2 The kings of the earth conspire,
>   And the potentates plot secretly together,
>   Against the Lord and against His anointed one [saying],
> 3 "Let us tear off their shackles,
>   And let us throw off from us their yoke!"

The Judean king then pictures—in sharp contrast to the puny little pagan lords in revolt—the Lord, the mighty Ruler of the world, in whose hand are all the nations of the earth. God looks down from His heavenly throne and laughs in keen ridicule at their futile conspiracy. The time will come when the Lord will rebuke and punish them, for the Judean king has the inner consciousness that he sits upon his throne in Zion, where God rules from His Temple, as one installed there by the will and hand of God. However these pagan kings may rage, says the king, as for me, the Lord has made me king.

> 4 He who dwells in the heavens laughs;
>   Yes the Lord God ridicules them.
> 5 Some day He will speak to them in His anger,
>   And dismay them in His flaming wrath.
> 6 But as for me, I have been installed as His king
>   Upon Zion, His holy mountain.

But how are we to account for this serene conviction on the king's part that his hold upon his throne and his sovereignty are secure? Upon what is such assurance based? The king continues speaking, and tells now of an oracle, a divine revelation, that has come to him in those hours during which he was being prepared for his installation. Whether directly, as in the case of Solomon (I Kings 3:1-14), or indirectly through the mediation of a priest or prophet, God has by decree accepted the Judean king as his "son." The form of expression here used is the ancient formula of the Babylonian law of adoption. We are again conscious, in such words, of the strong influence of the court style of Babylonia, Assyria, and Egypt. The conception that the king is the son of God is quite familiar in these world empires where the reigning king is likewise occasionally even called "god." [57] In this decree we are reminded of the oracle that had come through the prophet Nathan to David: "I will be his father, and he shall be my son" (II Sam. 7:14). It is pertinent to recall that in the holy hour of the baptismal experience of Jesus this ancient decree of God to the Judean king helped mediate to our Lord a sense of his unique sonship to God: "Thou art my beloved Son" (Mark 1:11). In addition to the decree

---

[57] Cf. Gunkel, *Einleitung*, pp. 163-64.

of sonship to God there came to the king in those high preparatory hours God's pledge of world sovereignty. It is his adoption as God's son that entitles him to world rule. As the "son" of God he has claim to participation in the rule of One whose glory fills the whole earth. Mowinckel has rightly seen that while Oriental court style of utterance has here influenced the psalmist, "it is more than court style. The claim of the Israelite kings to world dominion, even as the claim of Jerusalem to be the world metropolis, is not political-historical reality but religious-ideal challenge." [58] The king is the head of a covenant nation, but not every Judean king ruled as the exponent of a God-commissioned people. The pledge of God to the king is uttered in the form of a summons, and we must feel the realism of challenge in the Lord's pledge to the monarch of His people, "Ask, and I will give!" Yet the concept of world sovereignty as here expressed is still tinged with an unattractive Jewish nationalism. In all candor, it is not world dominion but world domination that is here pictured. We feel in the words the intelligible but tragic backwash of centuries of experience of Israelite and Judean oppression at the ruthless hands of Assyrian kings. So the king bears witness to God's decree and pledge.

> 7b He said to me, "Thou art my son;
> 7c   I, this day, have begotten thee.
> 7a   I will take thee up into my bosom.
> 8 Ask, and I will give thee nations for thy inheritance,
>   And for thy possession the extreme limits of the earth!
> 9 Thou shalt smash them with a club of iron;
>   As though they were potter's vessels shalt thou shatter them!"

The nobler conceptions of the great exilic prophet—that Israel was to be a light to the nations and the bearer of the Lord's salvation to the ends of the earth (Isa. 49:6)—had not yet tempered this passionate nationalism of pre-exilic days.

So in dramatic imagination the ruler addresses himself to the revolting, plotting kings, in the form of a proclamation. He feels in his own soul the claims to world sovereignty, yet there is One to whom his soul bows in reverent allegiance. And it is not to himself but to the Lord that he challenges their prudent and humble submission.

> 10 So now, O kings, act prudently:
>   Be admonished, O judges of the earth.
> 11 Submit yourselves to the Lord in obeisance;
>   In fear kiss His feet
> 12 Lest He be angry and you get lost as to the way,[59]
>   For His anger will soon burn.
>   Happy are all who seek refuge in Him.

[58] *Op. cit.*, III, 84.
[59] Accusative of place: see Gesenius-Kautzsch, *Hebrew Grammar*, 118 g.

This psalm, which originated in the experiences of a king incidental to his anointment as monarch, would thereafter have a fitting worship setting in the ceremonies that prepare the king annually to become the unique channel of the Lord's blessing to his people. The oracle to the king reminds us forcefully of the priestly oracle to the Babylonian ruler as he kneels, stripped of all his symbols of royalty, an ordinary human being, before Marduk, his divine lord.

> He will magnify thy kingdom;
> He will make thy dominion great;
> He will destroy the enemy and overthrow thine opponents.

In this psalm we are in the atmosphere of vast struggle between the pagan rulers of the world and the Lord of nations and men, a strong New Year theme which we have already encountered in the Zion hymns (Pss. 46:6; 48:4-8; 76:5-6), where it had been a vital element in prophetic thought since Isaiah (Isa. 17:12-14).

Ps. 21. ARISE AND CLAIM THE PROTECTION OF GOD

Ps. 21 is a king's song, sung by the royal choir in the Temple in the presence of the reigning monarch of Judah. The occasion is the anniversary of his enthronement. We feel the background of popular enthusiasm for the reigning monarch. But great as is the psalmist's enthusiasm for his ruler, it is yet greater for his ruler's God.

The psalm begins with a glad recognition of the blessings of God which have been poured upon the person of His monarch. The king is there, glad and rejoicing, in the very presence of the Lord (vs. 7). Upon him God has bestowed His protection and His help, the fulfillment of his heart's desires and the answer to his prayers. Everywhere he is confronted with God, who has crowned him as king and granted him material blessings, long life, splendor, and undying repute. And why have all these blessings come to him? Because the king is securely rooted in the mercy of God, in whom he trusts. We feel the thrill of love for the monarch as the royal choir sings:

1 O Lord, in Thy protection the king is glad;
   And in Thy help how greatly he rejoices!
2 The desire of his heart Thou hast given him,
   And the request of his lips Thou hast not withheld.
3 For Thou dost meet him with blessings of prosperity:
   Thou dost place on his head a golden crown.
4 Life he asked; Thou gavest it to him,
   Length of days for ever and aye.
5 Great is his renown through Thy help:
   Splendor and majesty Thou dost place upon him.
6 For Thou dost make him an abundant blessing forever;
   Thou dost cheer him with gladness from Thy very presence.
7 For the king trusteth in the Lord;
   And of the lovingkindness of the Most High he has no doubt.[60]

[60] So Ehrlich.

The second part of the psalm is a longing wish for the king that he may be victorious over his enemies, that he may consume them so that they will have no descendants. The poet pictures the enemy who had "turned evil" upon his monarch as "turning the back" in humiliating rout before the arrows of the king. The army of the king comes not at all into the picture. The king is the center of attention. As a mighty, majestic warrior armed with sword and with arrow and bow may he come upon the enemy, turn them back, and shatter them utterly.

8 May thy hand come upon [61] all thy enemies;
  May thy right hand shatter those who hate thee.
9 Mayest thou burn them like a furnace in the hour of thine anger.
  Mayest thou swallow and devour them like fire; [62]
10 May their progeny perish from the earth,
  Their descendants from the children of men.
11 Since they have turned evil against thee,
  Have hatched a plot they could not carry out,
12 So mayest thou make them turn their back with thy sword; [63]
  Mayest thou aim thy bowstrings at their back. [64]

The psalm reaches its climax in the closing verse. In verse 1 the Lord's protection of the king is acknowledged. But in verse 13 the king is challenged by the choir to act upon that protection, to arise in his valor and claim it. In the last line of the psalm a vow is uttered by the choir that if he heeds the challenge and conquers his enemies, they will glorify him with a song of victory.

13 Arise in the protection of the Lord!
  We will sing and praise thy valor!

This psalm is sensitively appropriate for the annually repeated New Year ceremony, wherein the divine blessing upon the king fits him anew to become a channel of blessing to his people (vs. 6). The wish of verses 8-12 is spoken directly to the king, but it has almost the intensity of a prayer of intercession for him. It closes with a challenge to divine enterprise under the newly, acknowledged protection of the Lord. We feel in the background the strong congregational longing to see the king rise to meet this challenge.

Ps. 72. THE KING AS THE CHANNEL OF GOD'S BLESSING

Ps. 72 is a prayer for the king, probably for any Judean king in connection with the religious celebration of his anointing and official enthronement. [65] The reference has nothing to do with the messianic ruler but is concerned solely with the earthly monarch. It opens with a petition to God that He may grant to the king the Lord's own "judgments" or "decisions," and His own righteous character

[61] Cf. Brown, Driver, Briggs, *Hebrew Lexicon*, p. 593, 3a.
[62] Following Gunkel's careful reconstruction of the text.
[63] Adding, with Budde, *beharbekhā*.
[64] Reading, with Gunkel, *gabbām*.
[65] So Mowinckel, *op. cit.*, II, 178; cf. Hos. 7:5, "On the day of our king."

to the prince who stands next to the king in royal succession. The petition implies a deep sense of social responsibility—the very heart of social religion—and centers in the covenant which Israel made with the Lord under Moses, who was "the creator of the whole Israelitic type of life" and from whom "everything that is essential to the life of the people is derived." [66] God's covenant with Israel "makes it a duty of honor for Him to uphold all who do not break the conditions of the covenant." To "judge," accordingly, means far more than its legal sense. God's judgments are his acts which uphold the covenant, i.e., the whole common life of the community.[67] Accordingly the prayer asks him to whom the Lord's judgments have been given to deal with the people so as to advance the community life as a whole. He is to give particular attention to the poor, the weak, and the needy of the people, who stand in pre-eminent need of the rights granted under the covenant. When this kind of rule prevails, peace and righteousness will clothe the mountains and the hills of Israel like spring foliage.

The prayer that the king may live as long as the sun and moon, i.e., forever, is a familiar one in the entire Orient (Neh. 2:3; Dan. 2:4) and must be understood from the Israelite psychological standpoint: "The soul may live, even though the ego disappears. . . . The king is to have the blessing that his soul may never die." As long as sun and moon shine, "his name is to send forth shoots." [68] His rule is to be to Israel what rain which prepares the crop for the second mowing is upon mown land. His reign is to be as gentle showers that sprinkle the earth, causing it to sprout righteousness and abiding peace.

1   O God, grant Thy judgments to the king,
    And Thy righteousness to the king's son,
2   That he may judge Thy people in righteousness,
    And Thy poor with justice.
3   So may the mountains
      Bear peace for the people,
      And the hills righteousness.
4   May he judge the weak of the people;
      May he deliver the poor
      And crush the oppressors.
5   May he live as long as the sun
      And as long as the moon,
      To future generations.
6   May he come down like the rain upon mown land,
      Like copious showers which sprinkle the earth.
7   May righteousness sprout in his days,
      Abundance of peace, until the moon is no more.

In the next section (vss. 8-11) the petition is for the king's world sovereignty. May his dominion extend from the Persian Gulf to the Mediterranean—that is, from one end of the world to the other—from the Euphrates unto the world's

[66] Pedersen, *op. cit.*, p. 18.   [67] *Ibid.*, p. 349.   [68] *Ibid.*, p. 255.

end. May he reduce his enemies to abject humiliation, with their monarchs
acknowledging him as their overlord, serving him, and paying him tribute.
So may treasure pour in to the king's coffers from the native rulers of Tarshish,
the Phoenician commercial metropolis in southern Spain at the western end of
the Mediterranean, and from the Mediterranean's other distant islands and coast
lands, from Sheba in southern Arabia, and from Seba,[69] royal city of Ethiopia,
south of Egypt.

> 8 And may he have dominion from sea to sea,
>   And from the river to the ends of the earth.
> 9 Before him may his adversaries bow down,
>   And may his enemies lick the dust.
> 10 May the kings of Tarshish and the coastal regions
>   Pay an offering as tribute;
>   May kings of Sheba and Seba
>   Present a gift;
> 11 And may all the kings pay him obeisance;
>   May all nations serve him.

We feel in this world sovereignty theme how strongly the political in the
psalm outweighs the religious and spiritual. We note, moreover, the contrast
between the extravagant wishes by which the king is glorified and the actual
conditions and situation of his kingdom. Gunkel reminds us that in such a
psalm it is the court singer and not the nation speaking. A king thus exalted by
the hopes and imaginations of the court singer might at the same time be plotted
against by conspirators or thundered against deservedly by prophets. And particularly in such passages the high-flown Oriental court style of thought and
expression of Egypt, and especially of Babylonia, have been very influential
upon the Israelite royal psalms.[70]

Upon what basis does the singer rest his extravagant hopes for the world
sovereignty of his monarch? The word "for," which in a hymn so often introduces
the theme of the praise, here introduces the grounds upon which the singer
prays the Lord to grant the king world rule. He conceives of world sovereignty
as God's reward to the king because of his righteousness, because he protects
and delivers the poor and needy from the ruthlessness and violence of wealthy
men, deeming the life of the common men of his realm as something of costly
value. Accordingly may the needy, for whom the king shows such consideration,
live and receive alms from his hand, even gold of Sheba. Thus blessed by the
king's beneficence will the poor man lift to the Lord intercession for his monarch
every day. Gunkel thinks it likely that in verse 15 the poet—a poor man, although
modest and reserved—speaks indirectly for himself, hoping that the king may
reward his singer with a bit of gold. Then he would sing such songs to his king
every day.

[69] Afterward named Meroë by Cambyses, after his own sister (Josephus *Antiquities* II. 249).
[70] Cf. Gunkel *Einleitung*, secs. 5:5, 12, 13, pp. 144, 154-55.

12 For he delivers the needy from the rich,
     And the poor who has no one to help him.
13 He looks with pity upon the poor and needy,
     And the lives of those in want he saves.
14 He redeems their life from injury,
     And their blood is costly in his eyes.
15 So may he [the poor man] live and be given Sheban gold;
     Then he will intercede on his [the king's] behalf continually,
     And will bless him every day.

A characteristic prayer for an abundant harvest follows, a theme never lacking in such a psalm and particularly at home in the New Year. In imagination the singer sees that for which he prays—mountainsides hitherto lying fallow now planted to their summits with corn, the beautiful ripe fruit sparkling in the sun like the Lebanon cedars famed for their summer glory of blossoms (Ecclus. 50:8), then the sheaves of ripened grain covering the ground like the grass.

16 Let there be an increase of corn in the land,
     To the top of the hills may it abound;
     May its fruit blossom like the Lebanon,
     And its sheaves be as the grass of the earth.

Such thoughts take on peculiar pertinency when we realize the unique place which the king occupied in early Israelite thought in respect to the material welfare of his people. He was the called and the anointed representative of the people. The concern of the king was the concern of the nation. The wholeness and health of the nation had its kernel in the wholeness of the king. Through the monarch God imparted Himself to His people. The power of the king was viewed as being more than human. "He was the channel through which the divine blessing flowed to the people." [71]

The psalm closes in a prayer for the lasting fame of the king. May his name live in the grateful memory of his people as long as the sun shines. Recalling the famous blessing of God to Abraham, with which the oldest epic narrative in the Old Testament begins (Gen. 12:1-3b), he prays that all the nations of the earth by considering Israel's king a blessing to the world may bless themselves in him.

17 May his name be blessed forever;
     As long as the sun endures, may his renown be increased.
     And may all the nations of the earth bless themselves in him;
     And may all the families of the earth call him blessed!

This psalm is strongly imbued with prophetic thought as to what a ruler should mean to his people as the exponent of the righteousness and justice of God. It must have been written originally with a king in mind who was a good man and keenly interested in his people's welfare. The prayer for an abundant harvest

[71] Cf. the suggestive words of Mowinckel, *op. cit.*, II, 299-302.

is a characteristic feature of the New Year, and here the king is viewed as the channel of that material blessing to the Lord's people (vss. 6-7, 16).

Verses 18-19 are not part of Ps. 72, but form the doxology of the second book of the Psalter, Pss. 42–72.

> 18 Blessed be the Lord, God of Israel,
> Who in His uniqueness does wonderful acts:
> 19 And blessed be His glorious name forever·
> Yes, may His glory fill all the earth.
> Amen! Amen!

Ps. 101. A KING'S SENSE OF SOCIAL RESPONSIBILITY

Ps. 101 is a king's psalm. It is the vow of a king and was probably rendered in connection with the religious ceremonies incidental to the anointing and official enthronement of a Judean monarch. It is likely that this vow of a monarch to walk in the paths of the Lord may have been a part of the annually recurring festal liturgy of the autumnal New Year. In this case it would be the vow of a king who enters anew into the covenant with the Lord as he is again sanctioned and accepted as the legitimate ruler of his people. There is for this a parallel in the affirmation of guiltlessness on the part of the monarch in the Babylonian New Year ritual.[72] Such a vow may have been written by the monarch himself, or it may have been composed by a court singer.

The psalm moves in prophetic thoughts where its author is thoroughly at home, and it probably dates from the late years of the Judean kingdom, close to the time when Deuteronomy became the official law code of Judah. The content reminds us of a royal proclamation of a kindly monarch to his people. It presents the ideal treasured in the hearts of Judeans as to what a king ought to be, and the spirit and the temper of his rule. There were times when the purpose of such words would be to tame the impetuous lion blood of a Davidic prince.[73] Always there would be the desire to set high the standards for the king's reign.

The king's vow reveals how he will proceed in the rule of his people, and it states the great ideals that his reign will embody. In giving utterance to this he uses the form of Hebrew tense which expresses his intention or desire. We are aware in these opening words of the great deposit of moral ideals which the prophets had left in Israelite life, especially Hosea (mercy), Amos (justice), and Isaiah (truth).

> 1 Mercy and justice will I practice:
> To the Lord will I pay heed.[74]
> 2 I will give attention to the blameless way:
> May truth come before me.

---

[72] Cf. Thureau-Dangin, *op. cit.*, Mowinckel, *op. cit.*, II, 178, and especially 328-29.
[73] Gunkel, *Die Psalmen*, pp. 433-34. [74] Reading ᵓ*eshmōrāh*, with Gunkel.

The king then proclaims how he plans to rule. The tense changes to that which indicates principles in operation. We feel how intense will be the interest of his subjects as he mentions in the presence of the congregation the great principles that will characterize his reign, both in the administration of his palace and in the moral quality which he will bring to all his official acts. No shameful deeds such as are vividly retained in the memory of the royal court will be a model for his acts, and any hint of disloyalty or unfaithfulness he abominates. He is simple and sincere, with a heart that harbors no evil.

> 2b I will go about in the soundness of my heart
> In the midst of my house.
> 3 I will not hold before me as a model
> Wicked deeds:
> To act unfaithfully I hate;
> It shall not cling to me.
> 4 A perverted heart is removed from me:
> Of evil I know nothing.

Then he tells what he purposes to do. We sense the problems of the royal court—the clash of personalities, the enmities, the secret intrigues with which every monarch must reckon. Three sins as real today as in the psalmist's time he mentions—secret slander, haughty pride, and unseemly ambition. These he will not tolerate. Scandal he will stop. With the proud and the immoderately ambitious he will have no fellowship.

> 5 Whoever slanders his friend in secret,
> I will bring him to silence:
> Whoever has haughty eyes and an unseemly ambitious heart,[75]
> With him I will not eat! [76]

He thinks now of his people throughout the realm, the kind of people upon whom his eyes rest with approval. They are to him not only his subjects but his fellow inhabitants of Judah. Not obsequious personal service does this monarch desire of his fellow citizens, but loyalty, integrity of character and of conduct. Persons with these qualities truly serve their king. One is instinctively reminded of Jesus' words in Matt. 25:40, where practical, social goodness lived among men is exalted as true ministry.

> 6 My eyes rest upon the faithful in the land,
> That they may dwell with me:
> Whoever walks in the upright way,
> He ministers to me.

Already twice has the psalm touched upon the king's life in his palace (vss. 2b, 5), and once again the poet returns to it. But now he thinks of what takes place in the innermost part [77] of his palace where counsels are given and

---

[75] Ehrlich rightly perceives the force of this word (*Die Psalmen*, p. 237) ; cf. Prov. 21:4.
[76] Following the vivid and expressive rendering of the Septuagint.
[77] So, rightly, Ehrlich, *op. cit.*, p. 237.

received and where decisions of state are made. For that inner area and all that
goes on there he has one shining ideal, loyalty. There treachery, breach of
trust or faith is the great sin. No liar will last long in the king's presence.

> 7 He cannot dwell in the inner part of my house,
>   Who practices treachery;
>   He who lies will not be secure
>   Before my eyes.

The closing verse of this brief psalm helps us picture the king as one who
is deeply concerned about the moral welfare of his people. When he knows of
any evil in his realm, he feels it his responsibility to destroy the evildoers, for
evil wherever found is the enemy of his righteous rule and a threat to the
security of his kingdom. The familiar Israelite proverb expresses this viewpoint
pertinently.

> Take away the wicked from before the king,
>   And his throne shall be established in righteousness.
>   (Prov. 25:5)

So daily he purges the wicked from his kingdom. Especially is he concerned
about ridding Jerusalem, his capital, of all evildoers. And it is significant as an
indication of his own spiritual attitude that he calls Jerusalem, not "my royal
city," but the city of the Lord, where He rules and dwells.

> 8 Every morning I annihilate
>   All the wicked in the land;
>   So as to wipe out from the city of the Lord
>   All evildoers.

There moves in this psalm a deep sincerity and a consciousness of community
responsibility that makes it quite likely that in this case the person who created
the psalm was himself the king.

Ps. 110. AN ENTHRONEMENT ORACLE TO A PRIEST KING

Ps. 110 is a king's psalm. It was rendered in a festal assembly in the Temple,
with the king and court present, at the celebration of the official enthronement
of the monarch. The psalm was no doubt used in connection with various
celebrations of this sort across the centuries. Gunkel fittingly calls attention to
the "powerful freshness" and moving elevation of the style of the psalm and
says, "To the brilliant splendor of the royal celebration correspond the wonderful words with which the song adorns the festival." [78]

The psalm opens with a divine oracle, a message to the king from the King,
whose glory fills the earth. It is "the whisper of God" which the poet has received
from the Lord, for the singer is evidently the court poet in the service of his
king, whom he calls "my lord." The oracle to the earthly king gives him the

[78] *Die Psalmen*, p. 481.

seat of honor at the right hand of the throne of the King of glory. And it pictures the time in his reign when he is to be seated on his throne with his feet resting upon the necks of his enemies, just as did the feet of the army commanders in the Israelite conquest of Canaan (Josh. 10:24). It is an Oriental picture here painted to us, unattractive but thoroughly understandable in the primitive times from which the psalm comes.

> 1 The whisper of the Lord to my lord:
> "Sit at my right hand,
> Until I make thy enemies
> The stool for thy foot."

The oracle continues and reveals to the king what is to be the nature of his rule. He is described as though he were a mighty giant. There he sits upon his throne in Zion like a god. In his hand is his strong scepter, the symbol of world rule. At the approach of the enemy he is to extend that scepter. There is to be no question as to who is king. His alone is the right to rule. We must feel the splendor of the occasion and take account of the exaggeration of the Oriental court style of the enraptured utterance of the poet. For his words move not in the realm of actuality—no Israelite king ever exercised world sovereignty— but in the world of fancy, longing hope, and adoration. For in this psalm lingers a primitive conception familiar in the Orient, the divinity of the king.[79]

> 2 "Thy strong scepter extend,
> Thou divine one, from Zion;
> Rule when Thine enemies approach!
> Thine is the eminence."

The enthusiasm of the singer is yet more deeply stirred as he goes back long behind this day, the day of enthronement, to the day of the king's birth. Then was he glorified. From the very womb of his mother he was holy and so uniquely under God's protection. The poet also applies to him a legendary conception of a life-giving, youth-bringing dew flowing from the clouds upon men, a conception familiar to Israel as "the dew of light" which God sends, and which brings even the dead to life (Isa. 26:19). From the dawn—always a phenomenon of mysterious, developing, vitalizing power—streams forth upon the king this divine dew, which will make him eternally young.

> 3 "In the day when thou wast born, thou wast glorified,
> Holy from the womb!
> Out of the dawn flows
> The dew of thy youth."

The oracle comes to its dramatic and unexpected climax in the proclamation to the king of the Lord's solemn oath as regards him, the substance of which is guaranteed by the very essence of God's nature, which is to call back no word

---

[79] Mowinckel, *op. cit.*, II, 304; cf. also Ps. 45:7.

He has uttered. What is the oracle now to proclaim to the king who is thus so solemnly introduced, to whom He has already pledged world sovereignty? It is that he is to be priest forever. The priest stands more especially under the guardianship of God. In ancient Israel the king exercised on occasion the office of priest, as was the case especially with David (II Sam. 6:18) and Solomon (I Kings 8:14, 55-56). David well knew what he was doing when he appointed his own sons priests and thus laid his strong hand on the priesthood. In Egypt and Babylon, as well as in Israel, the monarch combined in his own person the office of leader of the army, judge, and king. Says Gunkel, "How great significance must the king have imputed to priestly dignity when he has it conferred upon him through an irrevocable oath of the Lord! He does not feel himself securely established on his throne until he is not only a sovereign but also a priest." [80]

Moreover, the oracle announces that this king who reigns in Jerusalem as king and priest has a famous predecessor, Melchizedek. Even before King David captured Canaanite Zion and made it his fortified capital, Melchizedek had ruled in Salem (Jerusalem) as "king of Salem" and priest of El Elyon, the chief deity of ancient Canaan (Gen. 14:18-20). There is at the heart of this late Jewish legend an element of historicity, and Melchizedek (my king, i.e., god, is righteous) is a good Canaanite name like Adonizedek (Josh. 10:1), who was king of Jerusalem at the time of the Israelite invasion of Canaan. Thus Melchizedek in this oracle is a famous personage in the pre-Israelite past, possibly, as Gunkel suggests, himself the ancestor of a royal house. And since Judean kings of Jerusalem ruled over the conquered and absorbed Canaanites as well as Israelites, Melchizedek was the most illustrious and most ancient forerunner of the Judean priest king that could be conceived.

The message to the king thus comes to its most important revelation:

> 4 The Lord hath sworn,
>   And will not repent:
> "Thou art a priest forever
>   After the order of Melchizedek."

The oracle is ended, and the closing verses are in the third person. They describe a mighty expedition of war led by the priest king. The poet speaks, not to, but of the king.

With courage and confidence awakened by the oracle the king lifts up his head. He enters upon his campaign against his enemies, strengthened by the active presence of the Lord. With terrible blows on "the day" of the Lord he shatters and judges the kings of the earth until the valleys are covered with dead bodies, and the extensive battlefield is sodden red, its streams being likewise swollen with blood.

[80] *Die Psalmen*, p. 483.

7b Therefore he lifts up his head:
5   The Lord is at his right hand.
     In the day of his anger he shatters,
        He requites kings;
6   He fills up the valley with corpses;
     He makes the summits red with blood upon a wide area;
7   He waters streams with their blood.[81]

The attempt to see in the psalm a reference to Simon the Maccabean, because the beginning consonants in the first four verses spell the name Simeon, [82] fails when we see that this violates the meter, as these letters do not appear at the beginning of the Hebrew long line. Moreover, in the Maccabean period it is expressly said that oracles ceased (see I Macc. 14:41-42; cf. I Macc. 4:46; 9:27-28). The psalm has also a primitive, archaic quality which seems to take us into the earlier period of the Judean monarchy. The interpretation of this psalm as referring to the future messianic king rather than to the reigning monarch takes no account of the clear reference in verse 1, not to a future, but to a present king.

The oracle to the king reminds us of the priestly oracle to the Babylonian king, as given in the liturgy of the New Year, with its emphasis upon the overthrow and destruction of the king's enemies. The grandeur of the occasion fits well the unique importance of the Hebrew New Year in those rites where the king is the center of attention.

Ps. 132. THE ENTHRONEMENT OF THE KING AND OF THE LORD

Ps. 132 is a king's psalm. It is a dramatic processional psalm with the ark of the Lord, the symbol of His real and living presence, as an important feature in the procession. The reigning Judean king of the house and lineage of David plays a significant role in the ceremonies in which the psalm was rendered. But deeper than the interest in the David of the past and in the reigning Davidic king of the present, deeper even than the enthusiasm for the ark itself which plays so great a part in the psalm, is the interest in Zion, which the Lord has chosen as His dwelling place.

In a truly remarkable manner this unique psalm intertwines these distinctive themes. Mowinckel, with fine sensitiveness to the drama in Judean worship, rightly views it as "the dramatic processional liturgy of a festival which repeats the first entry of the ark of the Lord into Zion." [83] Thus it is part of the annually celebrated ceremony of the enthronement of the Lord which took place on New Year's Day. But it is probable that, as was the case in Babylonia, an annual ceremony of the official enthronement of the Judean king took place also on New Year's Day, the date of his reign being reckoned from the first New Year's

---

[81] I am here indebted to the brilliant reconstruction of the text achieved by Gunkel.
[82] Cf. Pfeiffer, *Introduction to the Old Testament*, p. 630.
[83] *Op. cit*, II, 112; see II Sam. 6:12b-19.

Day after the death of his predecessor.[84] This would account for the unusual prominence of the Judean king in the content and in the actual rendering of the psalm.

The rendering of this processional liturgy sets in at the point on the western hill of the Holy City, which is the beginning of the processional way, the *via sacra* in Jerusalem, comparable to the famous processional street in Babylon between Esagila, the temple of Marduk, and the chamber for the fixing of fates for the coming year. The Lord's people in great numbers are present, along with His priests and the reigning king.

The first part of the psalm (vss. 1-10) has to do primarily with the annual enthronement of the Lord. It opens with an intercession for the present Davidic king, "David, Thy servant" (vss. 1-5). The subject matter of this intercession evidently made use of a source which dealt with the life of David and his concern for the ark of the Lord, and which we do not now possess. The intercession recalls before God the passion of David that the ark of the Lord might be appropriately housed. It describes how in deep humiliation of soul he had ascetically castigated himself, solemnly swearing unto the Lord and vowing before Him that he would not enter his own palace, nor enjoy the luxury of sleep upon his own bed, until he had found a dwelling place for the ark, the sacred symbol of the living presence of the Lord, the Mighty One of Jacob. The reigning king is of the house of David, and here he plays the role of David, for in him the God-beloved ancestor of the Davidic house lives on. The reigning king is here viewed as "the point of union of God and the nation," as "the channel of the divine grace and power." [85]

1 Remember, O Lord, David Thy servant for good,
    All his self-affliction;
2 How he swore to the Lord,
    How he vowed to the Mighty One of Jacob:
3 "I will not enter into the tent, my house;
    I will not go up to the couch, my bed;
4 I will not permit sleep to my eyes,
    Nor slumber to my eyelids;
5 Until I have found a place for the Lord,
    A dwelling place for the Mighty One of Jacob."

At this point in the dramatic liturgy we are transported from past to present— from this ancient episode in David's life to something which once occurred and is now about to be dramatically re-enacted so as to be seen and felt. We note the change to the first person plural. The singers in this section (vss. 6-7) are the choir. But they represent David and his men, who after searching have found the long-missing ark of the Lord. They tell how rumor of it reached Ephrathah, the region where David's home town Bethlehem was located (I Sam.

[84] *Op. cit.*, II, 7-8.   [85] Cf. *Ibid.*, II, 113-14.

17:12). They tell how they tracked it down until they came to the region of Jaar, a poetic play upon the name of the famous town Kiriath-Jearim, also called Baalah (Josh. 15:10) and Baale-Judah (II Sam. 6:2), the place where the ark was situated when David first started to bring it to his newly captured capital Zion. So in the form of a summons, familiar in the hymns, the choir invites the Lord's worshipers to bring the ark of the Lord to its rightful seat in the most holy place of the Temple, just as David once brought up the ark ultimately from Kiriath-Jearim to Zion (II Sam. 6:2-17). The ark itself is called by the Chronicler, as here by the psalmist, "the footstool of the feet of our God" (I Chr. 28:2). They sing:

> 6 Lo, we heard of it in Ephrathah;
>   We found it in the field of Jaar.
> 7 Let us bring it to its dwelling place;
>   Let us bow down at the footstool of His feet.

The procession now sets in motion.

The ark, which is the very center of the procession, has been brought out of the Temple for the annual celebration of the Lord's entrance into His sanctuary.[86] At the time of the first processional of the ark into Zion in David's reign, it had been situated in the house of Obed-Edom the Gittite (II Sam. 6:6-12), so far David had brought it from Kiriath-Jearim. Obed-Edom was a priestly family of the Levitical guild (I Chr. 26:4). The "Gittite Obed-Edom" is in all likelihood no historical person but the legendary projection of the Levitical priestly guild back into the time of David. [87] According to the context, the house of Obed-Edom was in Jerusalem but outside the city of David, most likely in the west city. The ark would be brought out from the Temple before the festival to a building to be found there. It was from that point that the procession started.

The procession represents the annual re-enactment of the great event when King David, both as king and as priest, properly clothed for this priestly ministry in a linen ephod (tunic), with "all the house of Israel brought up the ark of the Lord from the house of Obed-Edom with shouting and the sound of the trumpet" to the city of David. David "whirled with all his might" in a sacred dance before it and set it "in its place" within the "tent" he had prepared for it. Since the building of Solomon's Temple the most holy place was the goal of the procession and the place where the ark permanently resided. All this is to be realized afresh and re-enacted in the festal rites.

All is now ready for the sacred procession to start. We note how central a place the ark occupies in it, and we feel the deep religious enthusiasm of the Lord's congregation for this symbol of His real presence. Wherever the ark is there in real potency is the Lord. Its regular and distinctive place is in connection with

---

[86] Cf. the Mishnah tradition for Mosa, where the green branches for the crowning of the altar were assembled, Sukkah 4:5.

[87] Cf. Mowinckel, *op. cit.*, II, 128 ff.

the festal religious ceremonies. The cry that greets the ark is a cultic cry, "a great shout" (*terû'āh*) on the part of the congregation (I Sam. 4:5). Ritual words are spoken by the priests when the ark sets forth, that is, is taken out— "Arise, O Lord"—and when it is returned to its resting place—"Return, O Lord"—and these ritual words (Num. 10:35-36) in the first instance belong to the rites connected with the holy processions with the ark and especially with the ceremonies of the Lord's enthronement.[88] The priests bearing the ark are clothed in the garments appropriate to their office as mediators of the divine blessing to the Lord's people. We hear the glad worship cries of the enthusiastic and deeply stirred people of the Lord as they greet it in awe and in fear with a sense of its mighty importance.[89] The choir sings:

> 8 Arise, O Lord, to Thy resting place,
>   Thou and Thy mighty ark!
> 9 Let Thy priests be clothed in due order;[90]
>   Let Thy godly ones exult for joy.

The priests in response to the choir's summons take up the ark, the king dancing before it as they bear it up the processional way toward the Temple.

Before the ark is installed in the most holy place, there is a halt which probably takes place within the inner court of the Temple before the Temple proper. Here the king, acting as priest, presides at the great sacrifice of burnt offerings and of peace offerings in which the throngs of worshipers participate. Because of the greatness of the occasion the bronze altar is probably inadequate and ampler space in the inner court will be consecrated for the purpose.[91] The climax of the first major part of the psalm is the prayer for the reigning monarch, which fittingly accompanies the sacrifice presided over by the king. It is uttered, as was the case with the opening prayer, by the king himself, and before his actual enthronement. By the words, "for the sake of David," it gathers up and completes the earlier intercession and applies it definitely to the Lord's "anointed," the present Judean king. Taken in connection with that earlier prayer, it asks for the Lord's blessing upon the sanctuary, dynasty, and throne.[92]

> 10 For the sake of David Thy Servant,
>   Reject not Thine anointed.

The sacrifice has now been completed. This we may suppose from the order of events in the normative ceremonies in which David (II Sam. 6:13-15) and Solomon (I Kings 8:1-11) occupy the role here taken by the reigning king. The ark of the Lord is re-enthroned in its place in the innermost sanctuary of the Temple.

[88] Cf. *Ibid.*, II, 332.   [89] Cf. Schmidt, *Die Psalmen*, p. 235.
[90] With Schmidt, rendering *çedheq* as here meaning *nach der Ordnung*.
[91] See Gray, *Sacrifice in the Old Testament* on I Kings 8:64, which is instructive for what took place at great sacrificial occasions.
[92] Cf. Gunkel, *Die Psalmen*, p. 565.

The second major part of the psalm (vss. 11-18) is a prophetically inspired message, an oracle to the king. This is the most distinctive thing in this royal psalm. There were official prophets connected with the public cult, and the utterance of such oracles was part of the regular agenda of worship, elements of a fixed and regularly repeated liturgy. While in primitive times the oracular word or message was obtained by technical means, such as by sacred lots, in more advanced times, as here, prophets seized by the spirit of the Lord gave free utterance to their "thus saith the Lord" in connection with the public ritual worship. At such a moment it would be the expected thing that a prophetic utterance from a prophet be here delivered. Usually, no doubt, the form the oracle took would be left to the inspiration of the moment. But gradually in many cases the wording would become fixed, and such oracles would be retained intact in the Temple repertoire under priestly supervision. Thus certain oracles could be used in differing contexts, as is the case with a single prophetic oracle now found in two different psalms, 60 and 108.

The first part of this royal oracle (vss. 11-12) is concerned with the Judean kings who were successors to David and were of his house and lineage. We feel the appropriateness of such a message to a king at the time of his enthronement. In it the prophetic oracle spoken by Nathan to David (II Sam. 7:2-17) is recalled and its essence brought anew to the present king as a searching challenge. He is so to reign in his high office that he will observe the statutes of God and thus keep operative and directive God's covenant with His people and pass it on to his successors undiminished.

> 11   The Lord hath sworn to David;
>   In faithfulness He will not swerve from it:
>   "Of the offspring of thy body, I will raise up
>   Kings upon Thy throne.
> 12   If thy sons observe my covenant,
>   And my charges which I shall teach them,
>   Their sons, also, forever
>   Shall sit upon thy throne."

The oracle continues, but in its second part the theme changes from the Davidic "house," the dynasty, to the Lord's "house," the Temple (vss. 13-18). Not Zion as the seat of the reign of the Davidic king, but Zion as the place where the Lord dwells is what stirs the psalmist's soul. This is in harmony with the two-fold theme of this psalm—the annual enthronement of the Judean monarch and the annual enthronement of the ark of the Lord on its seat in Zion as the symbol of the Lord's presence. It represents the fulfillment of the choir's summons in verse 8, which started the Lord's procession to Zion. Now the Lord dwells, installed anew in his dwelling, the Temple. His presence there guarantees the adequate supply of grain, grapes, and figs to Zion's people generally, but especially to Zion's needy ones. Zion's priests will abound in spiritual blessings, and the members of the Lord's loyal congregation will be gloriously happy. There in Jerusalem the Davidic line will flourish, and from that royal house, conceived as the "lamp" of Judah, will stream forth light upon each reigning monarch and his subjects. The closing verse portrays the Lord's king among his defeated enemies, proudly wearing as the gift of the Lord his shining crown.

13 "For the Lord has chosen Zion;
 He desires it for his dwelling.
14 This is my resting place forever:
 Here I will dwell, for I desire it.
15 Its food supply I will bless in superabundance,
 And its needy ones I will satisfy with bread.
16 Its priests I will clothe with salvation,
 And its godly ones will exult for joy,
17 There I will cause a horn to sprout for David:
 I will supply a lamp for my anointed.
18 His enemies I will clothe with shame,
 But upon him shall his crown sparkle."

5. HYMNS OF NATIONAL THANKSGIVING

The first obligation of the Israelite in the New Year, as the Deuteronomic and Priestly law unite in stating (Deut. 16:15; Lev. 23:40), was to be "altogether joyful, . . . to rejoice before the Lord," because over and over the Lord blesses him in all his agricultural labor. To give expression to this joyous recognition of the Lord's blessings there were created in Israel psalms of national or congregational thanksgiving. This festival (Tabernacles) came when the year had finished its circuit, so the blessings of God experienced during the past year were acknowledged with gratitude. The New Year came at the end of the agricultural year, when the barley and wheat, the grapes and olives had all been gathered in. So the bountiful harvests were a beloved thanksgiving theme. There were other themes as well, such as the repeated deliverance of Israel across the centuries wherein God had brought His people from distress to freedom, and the help He had granted them in times of fierce persecution. The hymns of national thanksgiving are Pss. 65, 67, 118, and 124.

Ps. 65. THANKSGIVING FOR THE GOOD EARTH OF PALESTINE

Ps. 65 celebrates God as the giver of fruitfulness (vss. 9-12) and as Creator (vss. 6-8), themes which are stressed in the Israelite New Year. Attracted by the vivid pictures of early growth following the winter rains (vss. 10-14), Gunkel calls the psalm "a spring song." But he fails to see the significance of the psalmist's reference to the "crowning of the year" with God's goodness in verse 11. The psalmist looks back over the total yield of the year in a mood characteristic of the New Year celebration in the autumn. Mowinckel, calling attention to this same verse, states that the presupposition of verse 11*b* is that the Lord has come on His wagon—a means of conveyance for the ark in the annual ceremony (II Sam. 6:3-5) —and is now enthroned in Zion.

This community utterance of thanksgiving is viewed as the payment of vows which were made by the Israelite farmer at sowing time. If the Lord gives a fruitful and prosperous year, then he will pay his vows at the sanctuary. The psalm opens with the view of Zion as the great national center where the vows of all men (i.e., Israelites) are to be paid:

1   Praise is appropriate for Thee, O God, in Zion;
    And to Thee shall vows be performed.
2   O Thou who hearest prayer,
    Unto Thee all flesh, oppressed by guilt, come.
3   When our sins overpower us,
    Thou wilt forgive us them.

In threatening conditions whenever crops seem imperiled, and when Israelites feel that their sins have turned aside God's help, they come to God in His Temple. Now that He has blessed His people with a bountiful harvest, it is to them a clear token of His forgiveness.

Every Israelite of the rank and file thinks of himself as belonging to the people whom God has chosen out of all peoples that are upon the face of the earth (Deut. 7:6). Accordingly, he draws near to God in worship as one entitled so to do and experiences His forgiving grace. And he is likewise invigorated by the material blessings which originate in God's holiness and stream forth from His Temple upon His people. The psalmist implies that through the worship of God's people in the Temple contact with the divine sources of power is effectively made. So he sings:

4   Oh the happiness of those whom Thou dost choose to draw near,
    To dwell in Thy courts!
    They are satisfied by the goodness of Thy house,
    With the holiness of Thy Temple.

Again and again when God's people have thus come to Him in need, He has answered them. But He is the basis of confidence not only for His own people, but for those who dwell in the far distant islands of the Mediterranean as well. Such words place us in the period when the dispersion has already begun.

5   With wonderful deeds Thou dost answer us in faithfulness,
    O God of our salvation,
    The confidence of all the ends of the earth,
    And of isles far away.

Most wonderful of all the "deeds" of God was that wrought when He brought the world into being. So the psalmist moves into his first great thanksgiving theme, God the Creator of the world. The emphasis upon this theme in the

New Year celebration grows out of the thought that "there is a new creation year by year." By these very ceremonies primeval creation was re-enacted. "By their rites was secured the due functioning of all things, sun, moon, stars, and seasons in their appointed order, the removal of the guilt and defilement of the old year, and the ensuring of security and prosperity for the coming year." [93] This is the meaning in the Babylonian New Year celebration of the annual ritual combat of Marduk with Tiamat. And it is the meaning of the annual focusing of attention in the Israelite ceremony upon that primeval creative deed of God, which was ever to Israel the basic ground of their confidence in Him. Girded with His own unshared might as Creator, He firmly established the mountains and stilled the roaring of the storming sea. He brought into terror even those fearful monsters, such as the helpers of Rahab, which inhabited the sea that lay around the yet unformed earth. Then He created the orderly world, with morning followed by evening, day by night.

6 Who establisheth the mountains by His strength,
   Girded with might;
7 Who stilleth the roaring of the seas,
   The storming of their waves.
8 So that those [beings] who dwell at the [world's] ends [94] are afraid
   Because of Thy wonders:
   The going forth of morning and of evening
   Thou dost cause to sing for joy.

With the words that are to follow there is a close connection with what has just been said. For our psalmist, with his eyes on the rich harvest that crowns the year with God's goodness, sees a repetition of God's creation, a repetition and a continuation. For just as in the primeval beginning He mastered the monstrous forces that opposed an orderly universe, conquered them and eliminated them, so He has conquered the persistent enemies to harvest—dearth, locusts, sirocco, and blight. And likewise in the deeper life of the people He has eliminated all that is evil—malefactors, sin, and impurity—and as of old has made the land of His people like a paradise.[95] In the verses that immediately follow, God is the Creator, renewing and continuing His creation. And we must keep in mind that to this ancient Hebrew the acts of worship themselves, this act of thanksgiving among them, meant the making of a New Year. As the result of these very ceremonies "there is a new creation year by year." [96] Worship was thus, as Mowinckel suggestively says, "creative drama." The acts of cult were not merely symbolic, but creative. They effected something. They accomplished something. They laid hold upon the creative, energy-producing God.

[93] Hooke, *The Origins of Early Semitic Ritual*, p. 19.
[94] The reference, as Mowinckel has seen (*op. cit.*, II, 139 ff.), is to the fearful monsters such as "the helpers of Rahab" (Job 9:13).
[95] Cf. Mowinckel, *op. cit.*, II, 140.
[96] Cf. Hooke, *The Origins of Early Semitic Ritual*, p. 19.

Such thoughts issue in one of the loveliest word pictures to be found in the psalms. We see the good earth of Palestine. We are alive to the miracle and mystery of growth. We note the reverent acknowledgment of God as the bountiful provider. The passage is athrill with creative life. Nature sings its praise to its Creator. For to this psalmist the very center of his thought is not the earth, but God, not "it," but "Thou."

> 9 Thou dost visit the earth and dost water it;
>   Thou dost greatly enrich it.
>   The channel of God is full of rain;
>   Thou dost provide for its [the earth's] grain, for so Thou dost get
>   it ready.
> 10 Its furrows saturated, its clods pressed down,
>   With copious showers Thou dost soften it; Thou dost bless its
>   sprouting.
> 11 Thou dost crown the year with Thy goodness;
>   Thy wagon tracks drip with blessings.
> 12 The pastures of the steppe shout:
>   And the hills gird themselves with rejoicing.
>   The mountains are clothed with sheep;
>   And the valleys enwrap themselves with corn;
>   They shout for joy; they sing!

Exclaims Kittel, "What a poet who could utter such words; what a folk soul which could thus imagine!"

Ps 67. THANKSGIVING FOR A BOUNTIFUL HARVEST

The most persistent occasion for psalms of national thanksgiving was thanksgiving for a good harvest. Ps. 67 is an excellent example of such a hymn, as verse 6 clearly shows. We must picture a great celebration in the Temple. Whole burnt offerings were presented unto the Lord (I Macc. 5:52-54). Peace offerings likewise were offered, for the occasion was one of resounding joy (Jer. 33:11; Neh. 12:43). One of the rites which seem to have preceded the singing of the hymn of thanks, at least in later Judaism, was that of drawing water from "the fountains of salvation" (Isa. 12:3), for at this season, as the Mishnah tells us, judgment was passed by God concerning the rains of the coming year.[97] Water was brought from the spring of Gihon and poured out as a libation before the Lord. Originally this was a magical rite.

The psalm proclaims in quite general terms what God has done which has occasioned the hymn of thanksgiving. This is sung by the priestly choir:

> 1 God has been gracious to us and blessed us,
>   And has caused His face to shine upon us,
> 2 So that His ways may be known,
>   His salvation among all nations.

[97] Cf. Danby, *The Mishnah*, "Rosh Hashana," I, 2.

Through the way God deals with Israel He is revealing His salvation to the whole world (Isa. 49:6). The psalmist is indebted both to Deutero-Isaiah's universal outlook and to the beloved priestly benediction (Num. 6:24-26). But he changes the benediction from a blessing to an assertion of what has now happened. God's blessing has come upon Israel. But just what that blessing is the psalm does not yet say.

The congregation lifts the refrain, an invitation to the nations of the world to praise the God who deals so graciously with His people:

> 3 Let peoples give Thee thanks, O God;
>   Let the peoples, all of them, give Thee thanks.

The choir then renders a little hymn complete in itself. It contains a summons to praise, and with the word "for" introduces the chief element in the psalm, the general theme of the praise, God as the righteous judge of the world and leader of the nations. The psalmist still withholds, however, the particular theme of the thanksgiving.

> 4 Let peoples rejoice and sing,
>   For Thou dost judge the world in righteousness.
>   Thou dost judge the nations in uprightness,
>   And as for the peoples, Thou dost lead them in the earth.

We feel here the pertinence of the New Year's theme of the Lord as judge of mankind, "mindful of their deeds" and shaper of their fortunes. Again the congregation lifts the refrain:

> 5 Let peoples give Thee thanks, O God;
>   Let the peoples, all of them, give Thee thanks.

Then at last comes that which up to now has been withheld, the particular reason for thanksgiving. Verse 6 makes it perfectly clear that the hymn is one of thanksgiving for a bountiful harvest. The choir sings its gratitude for the yield of the earth during the past year.

> 6 The earth has yielded its produce:
>   God, our God, has blessed us;
> 7 God blesses us,
>   And all the ends of the earth
>   Shall fear Him.

Originally the refrain, again chanted by the congregation, brought the psalm to a close:

> Let peoples give Thee thanks, O God.
> Let the peoples, all of them, give Thee thanks.

Ps. 118. THANKSGIVING FOR GOD'S REPEATED DELIVERANCE

Ps. 118 is a unique liturgy of national thanksgiving which celebrated God's repeated deliverance of Israel across the centuries. It is a processional psalm in which we can discern the worshiping throngs on New Year's Day moving through the Temple gates and, as a climax of the worship, surrounding the altar. The procession forms at the beginning of the processional way with the choir in the lead and the worshipers following. The leader of the procession summons the choir to praise:

> 1 **Oh give thanks to the Lord, for He is good;**

Then the whole choir joins in the beloved response, just as in Ps. 136:

> **For His mercy endures forever.**

The leader summons each of the classes of participants in the processional in turn to praise the Lord: the Israelite laity, "House of Israel"; the priests, "House of Aaron"; and the proselytes, [98] "those who fear the Lord." Each of these classes, who stood together in the worship,[99] in turn responds in the same way, raising the beloved cultic cry.

> 2 **Let the house of Israel say,**
>   **For His mercy endures forever.**
> 3 **Let the house of Aaron say,**
>   **For His mercy endures forever.**
> 4 **Let those who fear the Lord say,**
>   **For His mercy endures forever.**

The song of thanksgiving follows (vss. 5-19), sung most likely by the choir in the name of the congregation, for the first person is clearly to be interpreted here as representing the corporate whole of the worshiping fellowship. The theme of the whole song of thanksgiving is given in verse 5. The experience of Israel across the centuries is here concentrated into a single sentence: distress, cry to the Lord, and the Lord's answer.

> 5 **Out of distress I cried to the Lord:**
>   **The Lord answered me with freedom.**

Influenced by the regular form of the song of individual thanksgiving, this corporate psalm of thanks now gives acknowledgment to God that it is He and He alone who time and time again has helped His people (vss. 6-9). It is at once an acknowledgment and a glad confession of faith that He and He only is worthy of trust.

> 6 **The Lord is for me; I fear not;**
>   **What can mere man do to me?**
> 7 **The Lord is for me, helping me:**
>   **So I—I will gloat over those who hate me.**
> 8 **Better is it to seek shelter in the Lord**
>   **Than to trust in men.**
> 9 **Better is it to seek shelter in the Lord**
>   **Than to trust in nobles.**

[98] Cf. Gunkel, *Die Psalmen*, p. 506.   [99] *Ibid.*, p. 498.

There follows the total experience of Israel's history represented in one situation. The surrounding peoples—such as Edom, Moab, Ammon, and Syria—have attacked Israel, have surrounded her like swarming bees. As men drive bees from the honeycomb by fire and smoke, those enemies have been driven off by God's help. In this section, as Duhm has rightly seen, four times the leader speaks, and each time the choir responds with a refrain:

> 10 All the nations have surrounded me:
>   In the name of the Lord I mow them down.
> 11 They have surrounded me; yea, they have encompassed me:
>   In the name of the Lord I mow them down.
> 12 They have surrounded me like bees:
>   In the name of the Lord I mow them down.
>   They have been extinguished in the fire of thorns: [100]
>   In the name of the Lord I mow them down.

As the outcome of these many experiences of rescue and assistance across the centuries there has been built up in the soul of Israel a confidence in God's saving help. Consequently, in just such a service as this, Israel in festal joy can praise the Lord as a God of effective power, who works on behalf of His people. Imaginatively the psalmist hears the joyous shouts of deliverance in the tents of Israel wherever His people are. They feel confident that in spite of all they have suffered and yet will suffer as a people, they will not die. Rather does Israel interpret that suffering as having been set by God Himself for His people. Yet this has been done, not in order to destroy them, but as a severe discipline for them, so as to make their life worth the living and to fill their mouth with praise. How pertinent still today are such words on the lips of Judaism!

> 13 I have been thrown down violently so as to fall,
>   But the Lord has helped me up.
> 14 My strength and my song is the Lord,
>   And He has become my salvation.
> 15 Hark! a ringing cry and victory
>   In the tents of the righteous!
>   The right hand of the Lord exerts strength:
> 16 The right hand of the Lord exalts.
> 17 I shall not die but live,
>   And recount the deeds of the Lord.
> 18 The Lord has severely disciplined me,
>   But has not given me up to death.

The procession has all the time been moving and has arrived at the Temple. There now takes place a beloved ritual similar to that which we meet in Ps. 24:7-10, the opening of the Temple gates. The choir sings to the keeper of the Temple gates the call to open:

[100] Cf. Mowinckel, *op. cit.*, II, 333, who rightly interprets this passage.

19 Open to me the gates of righteousness:
    That I may enter through them to thank the Lord.

From within the keeper of the gates answers:

20 This is the gate of the Lord;
    The righteous may enter through it.

The gates are then opened, and the procession enters. As the procession passes through the arch, the choir in the name of the congregation sings a beautiful little hymn, one of the loveliest of the Psalter. Israel praises God for the severe discipline through which he has passed. There were times in his history when he seemed worthless as a stone which a builder would refuse to use because it was not good enough. But now through the very discipline which God has made His people undergo, present Israel—purged and refined by that centuries-long suffering—has become worthy to be a foundation stone, even the cornerstone of the new Israel. It is basically the same thought as the doctrine of the righteous remnant as taught by Isaiah, who speaks of this sifted, disciplined remnant as a nucleus of the new Israel:

Behold I am laying in Zion a stone, a well-tested stone,
A precious stone, as the cornerstone of a sure foundation.
                                                    (Isa. 28:16.)

How wonderful it all seems now on this great festal day, the day holy to Him and the day when under His mighty hand a new cycle begins! So sings the choir:

21 I will praise Thee that Thou didst humble me,
    And didst become my salvation.
22 The stone which the builders rejected
    Has become the cornerstone.
23 This has come from the Lord!
    It is extraordinary in our eyes!
24 This is the day which the Lord has made;
    Let us rejoice and be glad in it!

The festal procession has now reached the inner court of the Temple. It is New Year's Day, and verse 25 is the New Year's prayer of the congregation, a prayer for God's help and for a successful new year:

25 Ah now, O Lord, we entreat Thee, help!
    Ah now, O Lord, give success!

The answer which comes is chanted by the priests. It is the priestly blessing upon the processional worshipers:

26 Blessed be he who comes in the name of the Lord:
    We bless you from the house of the Lord.

At the close of the psalm there are two bits of the ritual which can best be explained by references in the Mishnah from late Jewish times. One is the ritual of light (vs. 27a). The Festival of Tabernacles opened with the illumination of the Temple by lamps and torches. The ultimate primitive purpose of this ritual was the creative renewal of light in the universe. As the magical element in the ceremony faded into the background, the symbolical increased, and it came to suggest not merely the beginning of creation (Gen. 1:3), a constant New Year theme, but also a reference to the pillar of fire by night by which Israel was led through the wilderness. It is likely that some such thoughts lie behind this prayer:

> 27   The Lord is God; may He give us light.[101]

The other ritual was the climax of the whole celebration by those taking part in the procession. It was a ceremony near the altar. The participants joined themselves into a procession, carrying palm branches with which they touched the horns of the altar, always considered the most potent part of that sacred object. The Mishnah describes a procession with palm branches around the altar which took place each day of the Festival of Tabernacles, and which was repeated seven times on the last day of the feast (Sukkah 4:5-7). The primitive purpose of this rite seems to have been to gain through contact the purification and the holiness for which the altar stood. It is probably in this realm of ideas and practice that verse 27b is to be understood. It is sung as a bit of self-direction to the participants.

> 27b   Join yourselves into a procession with palm branches
> Unto the horns of the altar.

The psalm ends with a small hymn of thanksgiving which follows upon the ritual of the altar and gathers the central note of the psalm into a fine conclusion:

> 28   My God art Thou, and I praise Thee:
> My God, I exalt Thee.

Just as at the beginning, now at the end the leader of the procession summons the celebrants to praise:

> 29   Praise the Lord, for He is good.

And the worshipers respond with their beloved cry,

> For His lovingkindness endures forever!

Ps. 124. OUR SOUL HAS ESCAPED!

Ps. 124 is a hymn of national thanksgiving sung by the congregation in gratitude to God for His help in time of fierce persecution. It is likely that the wave of persecution of the Jews in the provinces referred to in Joel 3:19 forms the sordid background for this thrilling song of escape. It took place in the Persian period at the hands of Edomites and Egyptians, and it was responsible for the destruction of the Jewish Temple in the island of Elephantine.[102]

---

[101] *Ibid.*, II, 99-100.
[102] Cf. Oesterley and Robinson, *History of Israel*, II, 163.

It is likely that the sentence in verse 1*b* (cf. Ps. 129:1*b*) is a kind of liturgical direction, yet belongs as an authentic part of the psalm. The priest sings the opening words, which give the keynote of the psalm; then the worshiping congregation take up the same words and sing the psalm through to the end.

In vivid figures of speech the psalmist portrays the fierceness of the persecution that he and his people have experienced. Israel's enemies were like a cruel, angry monster about to swallow up his prey. They were like a raging torrent of engulfing waters. They were like a fowler's trap which has caught birds.

1 If it had not been the Lord [who] was on our side,
  Let Israel say;
2 If it had not been the Lord who was for us
  When men rose up against me,
3 Then they would have swallowed us up alive
  When their anger flamed against us:
4 Then the waters would have overflowed us;
  The torrent would have passed over our soul;
5 Then the raging waters would have passed over our soul.

But the Lord has saved them. Their souls athrill with the joy of release, the worshipers sing their thanksgiving to God, who has helped them in the grave crisis:

6 Blessed be the Lord,
  Who has not given us up
    As prey to their teeth!
7 Our soul has escaped like a bird
  From the trap of the fowlers!
  For lo, the trap is broken,
  And we have escaped!

The psalm ends with a creed of faith of a more general sort, yet rising out of the experience just described. This is frequently the case also with the psalms of individual thanksgiving.

8 Our help is in the name of the Lord,
  Who made heaven and earth.

6. Hymns to the Lord as Judge and Prayers for the Turn of Fortunes

The New Year festival as one of the central emphases celebrates the Lord as Judge. In one highly imaginative psalm, grand in conception, the newly enthroned King as Judge of the whole earth pronounces a death sentence upon the gods who had hitherto enthralled the earth in chaos (Ps. 82). Other psalms which present the Lord as Judge think of Him, not as sentencing the gods and men, but rather as determining the fortunes and fixing the fates of mankind.

Such a determination of fortunes, as Pallis says, "is a positive creation of fruit-fulness and plenty, peace and happiness for the coming year."[103] This is a pro-founder concept of judgment and has already been repeatedly expressed in other New Year hymns in the psalms of the Lord's enthronement—Pss. 93:5; 96:13; 97:8; 98:9; 99:4—and in the new songs for the newly enthroned King—Ps. 33: 13-15. It rests back upon the power of God, His covenant with His people, and His relation to the world. In Pss. 53 (=14), 85, 123, 125, 126, and 129 this concept is expressed in prayers of longing for a turn of fortunes as the New Year starts upon its new circuit. Two other New Year psalms also celebrate the Lord as Judge: one, Ps. 149, emphasizes Him as having already decreed His judgment of defeat upon enemy powers. But this psalm is also "a new song," its mood is that of exalted, emotion-filled joy mingled with the militant enthusiasm of a holy war; and we have classified it as a new song for the New Year. The other is Ps. 50, where the Lord judges His people, sifting and disciplining them. But this psalm, at home in the New Year, is in form of expression and content of thought one of the finest examples of a prophetic liturgy and accordingly is interpreted under that head in Chapter VI.

Ps. 53 (=14). TOWARD A NOBLER PRIESTHOOD

There were times when the Judean community became unspeakably corrupt and when Zion, its spiritual center, was destitute of any responsible, directive influence because its priesthood was degenerate. Malachi's criticism of the priest-hood of his day (Mal. 1:6–2:9) is a case in point. Then the New Year prayer for the change of fortunes was concentrated on the priesthood, the spiritual leadership of the worshiping congregation of the Temple. Such a liturgy is this psalm, with which Ps. 14 was originally identical.

The first five verses are an oracle of God uttered by a prophet. It opens with a description of the wicked in all their corruption.

> 1 The senseless man says in his heart,
>   "There is no God."
>   They act corruptly and abominably.
>   There is none who does good.

The prophet vividly pictures the Lord from His exalted heavenly throne looking down upon Israel to convince Himself that the situation of His people is sufficiently serious to demand His interference. Is Israel as bad as all this?

> 2 The Lord looked down from heaven
>   Upon the sons of men
>   To see whether there was one acting prudently,
>   Even one seeking God.

[103] *The Babylonian Akitu Festival*, p. 196.

The situation is indeed desperate, and the verdict is given as though through the prophet God Himself were speaking:

> 3 All of them have backslidden together.
>   They are corrupt, and not one does good,
>   Not even one!

The psalmist moves from divine diagnosis to divine rebuke. Who is responsible for this degenerate condition in Israel? Why this low moral ebb? He lays it definitely at the door of the corrupt and irresponsible priesthood. His words remind us vividly of Hosea's penetrating criticism of the priesthood of pre-exilic Israel, who had "forgotten the teaching of God" and "set their heart on their iniquity" (4:6, 8). It likewise recalls Malachi's charge that the priesthood of the fifth century B.C. had corrupted the Levitical (priestly) covenant (2:8). The psalmist points out the faults of the priests. They are themselves iniquitous men, and their conduct puts stumbling blocks in the path of the common people who look to them for spiritual leadership. They secure their livelihood from the sacrificial offerings, "the bread of God," presented at the Temple by the people, but they actually are profane men and godless. And they will be rejected, humiliated, and destroyed by the Lord. This divine judgment upon the corrupt priests is spoken in a rhetorical question:

> 4 Do they not know, those who do iniquity,
>   Who cause my people to stumble?
>   They eat the bread of God,
>   [But] do not call on His name.
> 5 Will there not be terror [for them]?
>   For God will scatter their bones.
>   The profane will be put to shame,
>   For God has rejected them.

The words of the prophet are at an end and are followed by a brief pause. Then comes the prayer sung by the choir. It is the most distinctive thing in the psalm and is uttered in the form of a lament. It is an intense, passionate prayer for a change of fortunes for the people. The psalmist is convinced that God alone can bring about such a turn in Israel's lot, by which the now backslidden community will become a righteous people. And he thinks that this turn in fortunes must originate in Zion, where the Lord dwells. The implication is that a transformed Temple priesthood, calling upon God's name, teaching the people the true knowledge of God (Mal. 2:6), and turning them from iniquity, can prepare the ground spiritually for this great consummation. Thus sings the choir:

> 6 Oh that the salvation of Israel might come out of Zion
>   By the Lord's turning the fortunes of His people!
>   Jacob would rejoice; Israel would be glad!

Ps. 82. THE LORD IN THE ASSEMBLY OF THE GODS

This is a New Year hymn which celebrates the Lord as Judge. The ceremony of His enthronement has just taken place. The spiritual level of Israel has been low. Unrighteousness and injustice are rampant. To the psalmist who created this hymn for the Lord's worshiping congregation it seems that the cohorts of heathendom are in the ascendancy. We sense it best when we contemplate the worship of the gods of pagan power, which has made our own day tremble before the forces of materialistic military might. This psalmist could say: "Truth forever on the scaffold, Wrong forever on the throne." But now the Lord has just been enthroned. This is the presupposition of the psalm as into the congregation of the gods now comes God the Lord, supreme over gods and men! In a manner awe-inspiring and with terrifying effect upon the hitherto seemingly powerful deities He stands up as Judge in the assembly of the gods:

> 1 God takes His stand in the assembly of the gods;
>   In the midst of the gods He holds court.

In a form of speech characteristic of the prophetic lament and which imaginatively represents the existence of the gods as being taken for granted, the Lord utters against these divine beings His sharp accusation of their unrighteous dealing with His poor and needy people. Then in the imaginative presence of these divine beings the psalmist, in the tones of a prophet and speaking for God, utters what the Lord demands from "whatever gods may be" on behalf of men.

> 2 How long will you judge corruptly
>   And show partiality to the wicked?
> 3 Protect the oppressed and the orphan;
>   Defend the poor and destitute;
> 4 Rescue the helpless and needy;
>   Snatch them from the power of the wicked.

As yet these divine beings have not been displaced or dethroned. In imagination we are back in the primeval chaos, and the earth is in their power and at their mercy. They have not yet been sentenced by the Judge of all the world. But they have now heard his moral demands. What will these gods now assembled say in self-defense to the sharp charges of the Lord as He takes the side of His harried and distressed people? We feel the dramatic suspense as the Lord awaiting their answer, is met by only their impotent silence. In an aside God gives His estimate of these pagan divinities and of the results of their hitherto unchallenged sway:

> 5 They have neither knowledge nor understanding;
>   They grope about in darkness;
>   So all the foundations of the earth are shaken.

Then comes the climax of the psalm. The Lord, the righteous Judge, has just been enthroned. And now from His throne He speaks directly to these pagan divinities in a vein of irony, then pronounces upon them His solemn sentence of death:

> 6 As for me, I had thought you were gods!
>   Yes, sons of the Most High, all of you!
> 7 But in fact you shall die like men;
>   You shall fall like one of the princes.

The Lord, enthroned as King, is now in sole control of the whole earth. The pagan gods whose reign had hitherto kept the earth in chaos and its foundations insecure [104] have been thrown out of power, and upon them the sentence of death [105] has been laid. But God's activity, in the mind of the psalmist, is something far more positive than this. The Lord active as Judge means God exercising His righteousness, establishing His justice, fulfilling for His people His covenant obligation of rescue and protection. So the psalm closes in the mood of intense longing, eager faith, and mighty hope uttered by the congregation:

> 8 Arise, O God, judge the earth;
>   For Thou shalt rule over all the nations.

The psalm comes from a period when, under vigorous and determined leadership, the community of the Lord's worshipers had for a time shown a tolerance toward other gods, in whose existence perhaps even their leader had believed. The times were desperate. Such a situation as is reflected in Jer. 44:15-19 and as is implied in the Deuteronomic Decalogue (Deut. 5:7-8) suggests its background. It was a sincere and reasoned attempt to achieve better and greater economic security by a more cosmopolitan and less nationalistic religion.

A member of the Lord's congregation who had possibly been sympathetic with this trend (vs. 6) now turned with all his heart to the Lord. The desperately unstable and oppressive times which such cosmopolitanism had brought on had rudely disillusioned him. Now he is thoroughly convinced that the Lord is the sole divine Being in the universe. He had brilliant imaginative and literary power, so he created this psalm for the New Year to awaken his disillusioned fellow worshipers to a like faith in God as the enthroned Judge of all the earth.

Ps. 85. REVIVE US AGAIN

We have seen that the first duty of the Israelite at the New Year was to thank the Lord for bringing to fruition the past year's agricultural labors, and that this theme is expressed in the psalms of national thanksgiving. Not always, however, were harvests bountiful in Israel. Often did the New Year come when the material fortunes of the community were at low ebb. The future was viewed with anxious foreboding. The memory of many disappointed hopes and frus-

---

[104] We feel here the Babylonian background of the time before Marduk was enthroned.
[105] Cf. the death of Tyre viewed as a god in Ezek. 28, and especially vs. 8, "Thou shalt die the death of them that are slain in the heart of the seas."

trated longings was poignant in the hearts of the Temple worshipers. The longing for a turn of fortunes, for the beginning, as it were, of a new period in God's dealings with His people, became intense and strong. And not merely was there longing, but *faith* and *hope* as well, that God would change the fortunes of His people and start for them a new series of experiences, thus renewing with them His covenant and revealing to them afresh His mercy.

Such was the psychological origin of Ps. 85. It is a New Year prayer for the change of fortunes. The Lord's people feel themselves to be under a divine interdict. He does not look with favor upon them. They are in difficult straits. They have fallen upon hard times. And they are ready to confess that this is the result of their sins. They are experiencing the fury of God's wrath. Yet often in the past in just such circumstances God turned the fortunes of the people. He made all things new and different for them. So the choir on behalf of the congregation sings a theme of confidence in God. What He has often [106] done He may do again.

1 Thou hast been favorable to Thy land, O Lord;
　　Thou hast [oft] turned the fortunes [107] of Jacob.
2 Thou hast pardoned the iniquity of Thy people;
　　Thou hast forgiven all their sin.
3 Thou hast removed all outbursts of Thy fury;
　　Thou hast stopped the heat of Thine anger.

This expression of confidence prepares the way for the most distinctive part of the psalm (vss. 4-7), a passionate prayer that now at the revolution of the year the Lord may turn the fortunes of His people. The choir rises to the note of urgency as it sings:

4 Restore us, O God of our help,
　　And remove Thy vexation against us.
5 Wilt Thou be angry with us forever?
　　Wilt Thou prolong Thine anger for generations?
6 Wilt not Thou revive us again,
　　That Thy people may rejoice in Thee?
7 Show us, O Lord, Thy lovingkindness,
　　And grant us Thy help.

At this point a significant act in the worship takes place. A professional prophet, one who in his own self-consciousness and in the view of others is prophetically gifted, and who is possibly a permanently appointed cultic official,[108] steps forward and gives God's answer to the prayer of the congregation for a change in fortunes. Says this prophet:

[106] For the perfects in these verses, see Gesenius-Kautzsch, *op. cit.*, sec. 106k: "They express facts which have formerly taken place and are still of constant recurrence, and hence are matters of common experience."

[107] Reading the consonantal text, *shebhûth.*

[108] So Mowinckel, *op. cit.*, III, 3; Johnson, "The Prophet in Israelite Worship," *Expository Times*, XLVII (1936), 312-19. Cf. also Johnson, *The Cultic Prophet in Ancient Israel.*

8 I will listen to what the Lord speaks within me;
    Will He not speak of salvation
    To His people, aye to His loyal ones,
    And confidence to those who turn to Him? [109]
9 Surely near is His help to those who fear Him,
    That His glory may dwell in our land.

The prophet's words bring confidence for the future. Help from God is near. Let His people turn to Him and be loyal to Him. Salvation, confidence, help, glory—all this God is about to bring to them.

The prophetic oracle continues in pictures of material and spiritual beauty, every one of them suggesting the change in fortunes which the Lord is about to effect. God's anger is over; guilt and punishment are past. God's heavenly grace and righteousness will be responded to by men in truthfulness and in the temper of peace. Moreover, to truth expressed in men's lives God from heaven will graciously respond, providing the dew which makes the soil productive. We see how this prophet is convinced that a productive and prosperous New Year is directly dependent upon the spiritual life of the community.

10 Kindness and truth meet each other:
    Righteousness and peace kiss each other.
11 Truth sprouts from the ground;
    And righteousness looks down from heaven.
12 Yes, the Lord gives the dew,
    And our land gives its yield.

The prophetic words rise to a climax which implies the concept of the Lord as King of His people. This conception linked with material productivity is characteristic of the Hebrew New Year. Just as a king comes to his people preceded by heralds and followed by guardsmen, so comes the Lord to His people heralded by "righteousness" and followed by "peace."

13 Righteousness goes before Him,
    And peace in the way of His steps.

Ps. 123. OUR EYES LOOK TO THEE

Ps. 123 is a psalm of lamentation of the congregation which dates from the Persian period, when Judaism was under foreign masters. As Gunkel says, "It is conceivable that the distinguished men of the foreign kingdom had scarcely a shrug of the shoulders for such an insignificant little people as the Jews: an attitude on the other hand which embittered honor-loving, even vainglorious Judaism in its deepest soul." [110] This congregational lament has been profoundly influenced in ideas and in style by the individual lament, as the opening part of the psalm (vss. 1-2) shows. Yet the "I" of verse 1 is not the utterance of a single pious soul for himself, which was later taken up and made the expression

[109] So reading with Gunkel.   [110] *Die Psalmen*, p. 545.

of the congregation. Rather it is the utterance of a precentor or some other cultic representative of the congregation. He feels the deep spiritual experience in his own individual soul, yet speaks it forth as representative of the greater "I," the worshiping community of which he is but the leader.[111] Thus seen, the "I" and "my" of verse 1 pass naturally into the "our," "us," and "we" of verses 2-4. This lament is a prayer for the turning of the fortunes of the congregation.

Thus the leader, speaking in a genuinely Semitic manner on behalf of the congregation, lifts his eyes to the heavenly throne of God. The picture of a Palestinian household is in his mind. He sees the lord of the household as the responsible dispenser of all good to the entire retinue of servants; and, wholly dependent upon his mood and act, they look to him in reverence, in conscious need, and with expectancy. The psalmist likewise sees the personal maid of the mistress of the household, utterly dependent upon her mood or whim, looking in eager and confident hope toward her mistress' slightest act. All these servants have no rights of their own but rely absolutely upon lord or mistress. These are pictures of the attitudes of souls on the part of the Lord's congregation as they look in conscious need to God hopeful that He will show Himself merciful and gracious toward them. The psalmist's sensitive painting of this simple and pertinent picture for the expression of the congregation's spiritual mood shows him to be a true poet. In utterance of humble trust the individual voice begins:

> 1 To Thee I lift my eyes,
>   Who sittest enthroned in heaven.
> 2 Lo, as the eyes of servants
>   Look to their lords,
>   As the eyes of a maid
>   Look to the hand of her mistress,
> So our eyes look to the Lord our God
> Until He have mercy upon us.

Suddenly the mood of calm, trustful waiting is interrupted by a passionate petition sung by the whole choir that surprises us in its imploring eagerness.

> 3a Have mercy upon us, O Lord, have mercy upon us!

Fast upon the petition the congregation pours forth its lament, which, as we now see, comes from the deeply troubled heart of the congregation, whose members are surfeited with the contempt felt for them and which already for a long time had been poured upon them by the dominant Persians. They still occupy and rule the land, derisive, arrogant, and contemptuous toward the weak yet proud-spirited worshipers of the Lord. The lament pours forth from the hurt souls of God's humiliated people as an urgent basis for His merciful intervention.

---

[111] Mowinckel, *op. cit.*, II, 132-33. This is an interpretation which the work of Smend on the psalms has strongly emphasized, although he has applied it far too stringently.

3b For we are surfeited with contempt.
4 All too long hath our soul been sated
With the derision of the arrogant,
With the contempt of the proud.

This psalm has its rightful setting in the ceremonies of the New Year in connection with the enthronement of the Lord. In the opening part of the psalm
is expressed the longing for the hour of the Lord's coming. The festival of the
Lord's enthronement is "the festival of the great arrival." So it is athrill with the
note of expectancy. The purpose of the cultic festival among primitive men is to
bring in the new time, to turn the fortunes of the congregation of the Lord.[112]

Ps. 125. FROM NOW ON NEW HOPE

This psalm is a prayer liturgy which was sung in Zion in connection with
the annually recurring ceremonies of the Israelite New Year. It contains several
themes which are at home in those rites: the Lord enthroned in Zion from now
on forevermore, the immovable city of Zion, and God's protection of Zion against
all enemy powers. This last reminds us of the repeated prayers in the Babylonian
ritual of the New Year for the protection of Babylon and its inhabitants, and
for Esagila, the temple of Marduk. There is in the psalm a unique note of trust
in the Lord. It is one of a group of psalms (Pss. 120-134) which taken together
are among the most tender and fervent in the entire Psalter.[113] But its distinctive
setting in worship is with those psalms that believe in and plead for a turn in the
fortunes of Israel. That unique note of confidence is sounded with classical beauty
in the psalm's opening words—the security of the Lord's loyal worshipers in Zion,
where God dwells. There "sits" Jerusalem, under the protection of surrounding
mountains and just as secure are those who put their trust in God.

1 Those who trust in the Lord
Are like Mount Zion, which never swerves;
2 Jerusalem sits surrounded by mountains;
So the Lord will surround His people from now on forever.

But whence comes such confidence that the Lord "from now on forever" will
protect His people? The present situation gives no inkling of such hope, for now
God's "righteous" people are suffering under the heel of foreign occupation. That
they are "righteous" is Judaism's self-estimate of that for which they stand in
contrast to the world. They are smarting under the oppressive scepter which lies
heavily upon Palestine, that very land which the Lord has allotted to His people
(Josh. 13-20). But the Lord has just come to Zion. This is the presupposition
of what the psalmist has just said and of what immediately follows. This is the
meaning of "from now on forever." *Now* He dwells as King in the Temple.
Such confidence and expectancy, even in the darkest days of Israel, are awakened

---

[112] Cf. *Ibid.*, II, 79, 132-33.   [113] Cf. *Ibid.*, II, 170, 175-76, 180, 327.

by this festival which celebrates the Lord's coming to His people in their need and His presence with them in power. However dark the hour, it arouses new hope and keeps faith alive.

It is our psalmist's certain faith that such a state of affairs as exists in Palestine will not be permitted by the Lord to continue. But to this ground of his confidence he adds a certain practical appeal to God for His immediate intervention. If relief from the harsh oppression of foreign occupation does not soon come, so he argues, the Lord's people will be provoked beyond endurance to overt resistance; they will lose their faith and resort to violence. So the psalmist gives expression to his faith that God will put an end to the foreign occupation of Palestine.

> 3 For He will not let the godless scepter
>   Remain upon the allotted land of the righteous,
>   Lest the righteous stretch out their hands in violence.

Such thoughts lead him to pour out an eager, ardent petition to the Lord that He deal well with His "upright" people, and his petition issues in the passionate wish that God will destroy those who now "in their crooked ways" are oppressing them.

> 4 Deal well, O Lord, with the good,
>   And with the upright in heart.
> 5 But as for those who turn aside in their crooked ways—
>   Let the Lord destroy them!

The closing words of the psalm, which stand outside its metrical arrangement, form a refrain, a prayer sung by the congregation in longing and with intensity of feeling:

> Peace be upon Israel!

Ps. 126. TURN OUR FORTUNES, O LORD

This psalm is a fervent New Year prayer that God will turn the fortunes of His people. In common with humanity, whenever Israel stood at the dawn of another year, there awakened a deep confidence that God would open a new series of dealings with His people. In part it was simply an utterance of hope which "springs eternal in the human breast." But a profounder origin of it was the conviction that only God could change the lot of Israel. How often at the turn of the year the Israelite congregation looked back over a time of adversity and distress. And their wretchedness had been heightened by the proud contempt of pagan political overlords who scoffed and mocked at the apparent impotence and indifference of the Jewish God. But as New Year's Day dawned, the hope that their fortunes would turn became an expression of their faith.

The psalm opens in reminiscence of the past (vss. 1-3). Year after year this festival, with its emphasis upon the Lord's coming anew in power to His people, filled Israel's soul with hopeful expectation. Nor had that expectation been disappointed. Time after time their lot had turned. Laughter had succeeded tears. They felt almost as though they were walking in a dream. Even the scoffing pagan overlords were impressed by the comeback of Israel and gave grudging acknowledgment that their God must have wrought amazingly for them, because upon no other basis could they account for the betterment of their fortunes. How joyful they were in the improvement of their condition.

> 1 When the Lord turns the fortunes of Zion,
>   We are like those in a dream!
> 2 Then was our mouth full of laughter
>   And our tongue full of cries of joy.[114]
>   Then it was said by the nations:
> 3 "The Lord has done great things for them!"
>   The Lord *had* done great things for us.
>   We were joyful!

Now once more Israel stands at the New Year. Again the sharp contrast between Israel's lot and her longing is poignantly evident to every eye. The desolate appearance of the land, the dry water beds (wadies) of the parched steppes of southern Judah (the *negebh*) are to the psalmist a striking indication of the severity of the dearth and likewise suggestive of that psychological dryness of soul upon which the community has fallen.

But the New Year is at hand. It is within the power of God to fill those thirsty water beds of Palestine with the abundant winter rains. Those wadies, now without a trickle of water, may become brooks, life-restoring and hope-bringing. The Lord can revive the total life of His people and open unto them a new series of blessings, both material and spiritual. The turn of the year may mean for God's disappointed, disillusioned, dispirited people a radical change in fortunes. So in a prayer that brings to a pitch of great longing the congregation's passionate lament the psalmist prays on behalf of his people that the Lord will transform their lot even as the now dried-up water channels of the Judean steppes south of Hebron are in the winter transformed into lifegiving streams:

> 4 Turn our fortunes, O Lord,
>   Like the water courses of the South country.

In the worship of ancient Israel the lament of the congregation was often immediately followed by the prophetic or priestly oracle. Scarcely had the lament died away when the voice of the priest or the man of God was lifted to utter to the submissive people the answer of the Lord.[115] So here, under the influence of this practice and in imitation of it, the psalmist speaks to his people an oracle of comfort in the form of a familiar proverb.[116]

---

[114] Gesenius-Kautzsch, *op. cit.*, sec. 107*b*, *e*; and Driver, *Hebrew Tenses*, sec. 27 (1) *a*, for frequentative imperfect.

[115] Cf. Gunkel, *Einleitung*, pp. 137-38; note as an illustration Joel 2:19.

[116] The proverbial nature of the utterance was first pointed out by Duhm.

5 They who sow with tears
    Shall reap with ringing shouts of joy.

The proverb is directed to the Lord's dejected yet repentant and hopeful people. Times are now hard, but better days are destined for Israel. In ancient Egypt, where the ordinary practices of agriculture were linked in popular conception with the rites of religion, the sowing of the seed and the covering of it with the soil was like the burying of the god Osiris. To this ritual were attached ceremonies of weeping and lamentation, intended to resuscitate the deity into vital power. Primitive people whose very life is dependent upon the yield of the soil believe that "one must not laugh when he sows, lest he weep when he harvests." [117] And indeed the Palestinian farmer well knew as he wrestled with the stubborn stony soil of Palestine how great was the hazard that all his sowing would issue in but a crop failure. Our psalmist was a poet alert to such primitive customs and feelings and at home in the seedtime and harvest of Palestine. Sowing is difficult business. It takes blood, sweat, and tears to make a farmer. But to the psalmist sowing is the ground of hope. If Israel would reap, Israel must sow. The psalmist possibly had in mind the great words of his Israelite pioneer Hosea:

Sow to yourselves in righteousness;
Harvest in proportion to kindness. (10:12.)

If Israel sows, Israel will reap—not merely the harvests of grain for the New Year, but harvests of national character, stability, and advancement. With such positive and practical thoughts the psalmist closes his oracle of comfort in the high assurance of faith.

6 Though one goes along weeping,
    Sowing the seed,
    He will surely come in with shouts of joy,
    Carrying his sheaves.

Ps. 129. YET THEY HAVE NOT PREVAILED AGAINST ME

Ps. 129 is a lament of the congregation which seems to be connected with the autumnal festival [118] of the New Year. It is composed of a song of national thanksgiving (vss. 1-4) and a national lament (vss. 5-8). The one glides easily into the other. Yet clearly the major impression left upon the reader is the solemn mood of lament. The song of thanksgiving in its present connection serves as a kind of ultimate basis for confidence. The implied hope of the psalmist is that the Lord will come to His people and turn their fortunes by frustrating those who hate Zion. To him Zion represents the community of the faithful and all for which the worshiping fellowship stands.

The first part of the psalm, the song of national thanksgiving (vss. 1-4), looks

[117] Cf. Gunkel, *Die Psalmen,* p. 552, citing Maack.   [118] Cf. Mowinckel, *op. cit.,* VI, 31, 35.

back upon the long centuries of suffering which the nation has experienced. The "me" and "my" of these verses represent the personification of Israel. It is the nation as a whole which the poet here represents as speaking. The indefinite "they" deals with no one particular group but includes the historic national enemies of Israel. The Israelites suffered at the hands of the Egyptians, Philistines, Syrians, Assyrians, Chaldeans, and Persians. These were the great powers. But they suffered also at the hands of the smaller peoples who surrounded them and took advantage of their exposed situation—the Ammonites, Moabites, and Edomites. From the time when Israel was a "child" in Egypt until now, he has known such harsh hostility. But he has not gone under. The enemy did not destroy Israel. The psalmist feels what we today sense all the more remarkably— the marvelous hold upon life which across centuries of enmity and persecution Judaism has demonstrated.

> 1 **Long enough have they harassed me from my youth,**
>   **So let Israel say;**
> 2 **Long enough have they harassed me from my youth;**
>   **Yet they have not prevailed against me.**

The picture changes, and the suffering of Israel across the ages of history is presented more poignantly. Israel has been like a beast of burden, a draft animal. Great welts are on his back as the result of the blows of the driver's stick. Again the psalmist's figure swiftly changes. It is as though Israel's back has been cruelly treated, as though it were a field to be ploughed, as though every welt that there appears were a furrow cut long and deep by the ruthless ploughman. Yet once more the figure changes, and Israel is not the land being ploughed. He is himself the beast of burden. But those wicked ropes, the tugs that held Israel to his forced burden, the righteous God has cut and has set His people free.

> 3 **Upon my back ploughmen have ploughed;**
>   **They have made their furrows long.**
> 4 **The Lord, the righteous One, has cut in two**
>   **The ropes of the ungodly.**

We feel the thrill of joy and thanksgiving, not for any one experience, but for all the experiences of release which Israel has enjoyed from time to time across the centuries of his existence.

But now the nation Israel is no more. What once was the political people has now become merely the religious community of Zion. But just as formerly the nation experienced the constant antagonism of enemies, so it still is the case with Zion, for she now is surrounded by the small peoples who hate her. Yet Zion still remains! The psalm moves into the mood of lament. A passionate petition is uttered in the form of a strong wish for the humiliation and destruction of Zion's enemies. May their onslaughts be turned back.

The psalmist compares this destruction of Zion's enemies, for which he so passionately longs, to the withering of the green grass upon the roof of a Palestinian home. In springtime it shoots up from the shallow soil that gathers there, but swiftly dries up under the hot east wind from the desert. No harvest comes from such growth. No reaper will ever hold its yield in one hand while he sickles it with the other. No binder coming along behind will gather it up into his bosom and tie it with twine into sheaves. No joyous exchange of friendly harvest-time greetings with mutual good wishes for the Lord's blessing upon the yield will there be heard. May all who hate Zion meet a fate comparable to such doomed grass! So may the Zion of the psalmist's day, now surrounded by small nations that hate her, still be protected and her foes destroyed.

5 May they be put to shame and turned back,
  All who hate Zion.
6 May they be like the grass on the roofs,
  Which the east wind scorches,
7 With which the reaper fills not his hand,
  Nor a binder his bosom;
8 With those passing by not saying,
  "May the blessing of the Lord be upon you!
  We bless you in the Lord's name!"

The ceremonies of the New Year with emphasis upon the coming of the Lord anew in salvation to Zion, deliverance against her foes both outer and inner, and their destruction by His mighty power seem the fitting worship setting for the rendering of this psalm. Its general nature and lack of any specific historical reference strengthen the likelihood of such use of it.

Chapter V

HYMNS OF THE REVELATION OF GOD

THE PSALMS COME FLAMINGLY FROM THE SOUL OF AN EXPERIENCING PEOPLE. THE ancient Israelites were uniquely gifted in the capacity to feel. And in no aspect of their life is this quality so evident or so rich in contribution to humanity as in the lyrical expression of their religious experience.

The psalmists found God most of all in the world within, that inner realm of immediate awareness wherein they felt themselves confronted by an Other, searching, comprehending, condemning, rebuking, challenging, and comforting. But they also found Him in the world without. In physical nature they saw His glory. In their national history they felt His presence. In their law they heard His voice.

In the present section we are concerned only with the first of these realms of the outer world in which the psalmist found God, and more especially with those psalms which have the best right to be called hymns of nature. They are Pss. 8; 19:1-6; 29; 104; 147; 148.

1. HYMNS OF THE REVELATION OF GOD IN NATURE

Ps. 8. THE SYMPHONY OF THE HEAVENS

Ps. 8 is a hymn of the night. The psalmist has an awed appreciation of what every nature lover in Palestine felt, the living beauty of an Oriental night. There is a universal quality in the psalm, for there are no national limits to the God whose glory fills heaven and earth. And when the psalmist deals with "man" as he does in verse 4, it is not man as Israelite that he has in mind, but man as man, a universal.

The most distinctive thing in this psalm is the revelation of God in nature, and it is this which determines its classification. At the same time it heightens the importance of the psalm when we note that it has a most appropriate worship setting in the Festival of Tabernacles. This is implied by its central theme, the creation of the world. The Festival of Tabernacles, with which Israel's New Year coincides, is the festival of the renewal of creation. The psalm, like Ps. 134, is a vigil liturgy,[1] appropriate for a night service in connection with that festival par excellence of Israel. Just such a night service in the Temple, participated in by the pilgrims to the Festival of Tabernacles[2] with gladness of heart, is described in the book of Isaiah:

> Ye shall have a song in the night
> As when a holy feast is observed. (30:29.)

---

[1] Cf. also Quell, *op. cit.*, p. 78; Josephus *Contra Apionem* I. 22.
[2] Vs. 30, which describes the storm-bringing winter rains, implies that it is Tabernacles.

Although Ps. 8 appears to be dependent upon the priestly account of creation (Gen. 1:1–2:4a; note especially 1:26), it is really pre-exilic, for Gen. 1 rests upon very ancient foundations, to which the creation of man belongs. The fundamental tone of the psalm is antique, and the quotation of verse 4 in one of the king psalms (Ps. 144:1-11, especially vs. 3) argues strongly for a date when the Judean kingdom was still in existence.

The chief part of the psalm was rendered as a solo (vss. 3-8)—note change of person—and this is set into the framework of the hymn of the congregation (vss. 1-2, 9).

The hymn opens with a congregational outcry of reverent awe over the majesty of God:

1   O Lord, our Lord,
         How majestic is Thy name!
     Thy glory is in the earth! [3]
     Thy splendor is upon the heavens!

The psalmist is under the spell of the night. The wide expanse of the night sky, the brilliant beauty of the stars shining "upon" the dark firmament like precious jewels upon the background of black velvet—all this stirs him to praise on behalf of the worshiping throng. Similar thoughts moved Longfellow when he wrote:

I heard the trailing garments of the Night
     Sweep through her marble halls!
I saw her sable skirts all fringed with light
     From the celestial walls!

I felt her presence, by its spell of might,
     Stoop o'er me from above;
The calm, majestic presence of the Night,
     As of the one I love. [4]

The psalmist, awed by the glory of God as seen in the nocturnal beauty of the oriental sky, is keenly aware of his own inadequacy to give expression to it. Humble in the presence of vast majesty, he feels words well up in his soul to utter it. Yet his words must seem to God as inadequate as the prattle of babes. Then comes a consideration that gives voice to his emotions and words to his thoughts. It has ever been God's way to use as his potent instruments the low, the despised, and the humble to bring to defeat those opposed to Him. The sincere and simple words of mere babes often deliver a reprimand to God's fierce and powerful opponents. Such thoughts free his words from self-con-sciousness as he says:

[3] So read with Gunkel, *Die Psalmen*, p. 29, following Grimme and Schlögl. As in Ps. 57:5, 11, heaven and earth are placed along side of one another.
[4] From "Hymn to the Night."

2 Out of the mouth of babes
   Thou dost reprimand the fierce,
So as to put to shame
   The enemy and opponent.

Then from the priestly choir soars a solo voice which gives classic expression to the chief thought content of the hymn (vss. 3-8). The singer is under the spell of the heavens, which were fashioned by the strong, sensitive, and skilled fingers of the supreme Artist. How orderly the motions of those distant planets moving according to the ordinance of God! Amid such majestic movement of the spheres how strange that God should take any notice whatever of mere man!

3 When I behold the heavens,
   The work of Thy fingers,
     The moon and the stars,
      Which Thou hast ordained,
       [I have to cry out] [5]
4 What is man that Thou dost remember him,
   Aye, mortal man that Thou dost pay attention to him?

However, vast as are the heavens, brilliant as are those radiant luminaries in the night sky, man, this *seemingly* insignificant creature, is himself grander, more brilliant even than they. For God made him but little lower than Himself and granted him a share in dominion, which is the sole prerogative of God. Welch suggestively points out that from the angle of the psalmist "man's dignity does not belong to him by nature but as a direct gift from God. So sharing in God's mind he becomes the world's master." [6]

5 Yet Thou mad'st him lack but little of God,
   And didst crown him with majesty and dignity.
6 Yes, Thou hast given him dominion over the works of thy hands;
   Everything hast Thou put under his feet:
7 Sheep and cattle, all of them,
   And likewise the beasts of the field,
8 The birds of the heaven and fish of the sea,
   Whatever passes through the paths of the waters.

Man, truly mortal and of the earth earthy, yet man like a king, majestic and full of dignity from the will and power of God the Creator—this is at once the realism and the idealism of the psalmist. *Thou* mad'st him; *Thou* dost crown him; *Thou* dost give him dominion—thus does this hymn temper the brilliance of human achievement by the sense of ultimate dependence. May it not have been this very psalm that awakened in the soul of the masterful thinker Immanuel Kant this famous dictum: "Two things there are which, the oftener and more steadfastly we consider them, fill the mind with an ever new and ever

---

[5] Thus supply in thought this suppressed clause of conditional sentence; cf. Gesenius-Kautzsch, *op. cit.,* 159dd.
[6] *The Psalter,* p. 19.

rising admiration and reverence: the starry heavens above, the moral law within." And it is in that mood of awe that the worshiping congregation sings the omega, as it had the alpha, of its praise.

> 9 O Lord, our Lord,
> How majestic is Thy name in all the earth!

Ps. 19:1-6. THE ANTHEM OF THE HEAVENS

This psalm fragment was originally an independent psalm, as both change of meter and of theme at verse 7 imply. The theme of the psalm, the subject of the psalmist's praise, is God's "work" at creation. It is most likely the New Year festival wherein this psalm had its original setting in the life of ancient Israel, for the hailing of God as Creator was a prominent theme in the celebration of this annually recurring feast. Yet it would be appropriate as a morning hymn for any day, for with each new day there is a new creation, and the cycle of the day with the sun moving across the vault of the heavens is but the cycle of the year written small.

The psalmist opens with the perpetual anthem of the heavens:

> 1 The heavens keep recounting the glory of God,
> And the firmament keeps declaring the work of His hands.
> 2 Day pours forth speech unto day,
> And night declares knowledge unto night.

The poetic fantasy of the psalmist takes us back to the primeval beginnings of creation when the amazed heavens saw the knowledge of God in action, that mysterious and secret wisdom by which He fastened the foundations of the earth, laid its cornerstone, and confined behind gates and bars the chaotic, tempestuous sea. That was

> When the morning stars sang together,
> And all the divine beings shouted for joy! (Job 38:7.)

This was the mighty "work" wrought by His hands. It was God's power in creating that displayed "His glory."

What the astonished heavens thus saw at the beginning of time from that primeval epoch unto the present they have kept recounting and will keep recounting until the end. The theme of this perpetual anthem of the heavens is "God is our Creator." By day the heavens are alight. The firmament is dark by night. But be it day or night the anthem never ceases. The story of this unique and unshared skill of the Creator has been passed down from primeval times to the present by an unending chain of transmission, one day like a bubbling fountain pouring forth its speech in glad ecstasy to the next, each night declaring to its successor this mysterious and secret knowledge of God.

Yet, says the psalmist, this anthem of the heavens is rendered not in words:

> 3   There is no utterance, and no words;
>   Their voice is not heard.

For the anthem of the heavens is more universal than any speech. It suffers no restricting limitations of human language. Israelite or Gentile receive and understand it. Educated and uneducated alike comprehend it. Wheresoever light penetrates, wheresoever darkness falls, there is experienced and understood the wordless speech of the heavens. Says Kittel: "Here is a language which speaks to the heart and therefore is understood over all the earth." [7] Purposively the psalmist used not Yahweh (the Lord), although he clearly means the God of Israel, but El, the more general word "God," as though to emphasize the unbounded extent of the Creator's sway.

> 4a   Yet into all the earth their voice goes forth,
> 4b   And their speech to the end of the world.

In the closing part of the psalm (vss. 4c-6) our attention is focused upon the sun. The psalmist writes with a knowledge of, and under the influence of, Babylonian mythology, in which Shamash, the sun god, was a bridegroom whose tabernacle was in the sea, wherein his bride Aya dwelt. And Shamash was a hero, a champion running his race and overcoming demons with whom he fights as he pursues his course across the dome of the sky. Sing Babylonian psalmists:

> O Shamash, on the horizon of the heavens hast thou risen ablaze;
> The bolt of the glorious heavens hast thou unlocked;
> The gates of the heavens hast thou opened!
> O Shamash, thine head hast thou raised o'er the land;
> O Shamash, with the glory of the heavens, thou coverest the lands:
> Light hast thou granted to the face of the land!
> Life's course on the earth dost thou guide;
> All creatures that live, thou dost quicken.
>
> .   .   .   .
>
> O'er the wide earth is thy daily course,
> O'er sea and ocean, mountains, earth and heaven.[8]

Yet while in Babylonian thought Shamash, the sun, was a god, in the Hebrew psalmist's conception *shemesh,* the "sun" in all its glory, was but one of the majestic created works of God and but fulfills its Creator's will. And while the psalmist still speaks of the sun as though it were a god, the Babylonian mythology has surrendered to the Hebrew psalmist's monotheism.

> 4c   The sun has there a tent in the sea,
> 5   And he is like a bridegroom who comes forth from his chamber;
>   He exults like a hero to run his course.

[7] *Die Psalmen,* p. 70.
[8] Gressmann, *Altorientalische Texte zum Alten Testament,* pp. 243, 245; cf. Oesterley, *The Psalms,* I, 169.

6   From the end of the heavens he goes forth,[9]
     And unto their extremities is his circuit;
     And nothing is hidden from his heat.

What does the psalmist see in the heavens while his ear listens to the silent anthem? He sees the brilliant, clear blue of the sky in the daytime and its glorious, bejeweled darkness at night. He beholds the splendor of the ball of fire, first peeping out of the eastern horizon, then making its daily course across the circuit of the heavens, rising overhead to its zenith, and at length sinking to its rest in the sea amid the flaming glory of the western horizon. He feels the warmth and life-giving power of the sun's rays. All that he sees and feels in the heavens are proclaiming in wordless reality, "The hand that made us is divine!" Appropriately Gunkel says that this psalm "belongs to the sublimest creations of the Old Testament and towers above many hymns by virtue of its primitive force and archaic beauty." [10]

Ps. 29. THE HYMN OF THE SEVEN THUNDERS

This psalm, while its setting in Hebrew worship is in the ritual of the Hebrew New Year, has its unique distinction as a hymn of God's revelation in nature. It glorifies the Lord as the storm God, and more specifically as the God who gives forth His "voice" in the thunder. The underlying elements in it that link it to the New Year, however, lift into greater importance God's revelation in nature and set the psalm in its proper perspective. Let us first see what these underlying elements are.

According to the superscription of the psalm as given in the Septuagint (ἐξοδίου σκηνῆς) it was the special psalm for the eighth or final day of the Festival of Tabernacles. Such evidence of its association with the ritual of this festival, while not earlier than about 250 B.C., probably preserves some authentic reminiscence that the psalm was created for it. Schmidt [11] has argued convincingly that it was created for "the festival of the turn of the year [*Jahreswende*]," which coincided with the Festival of Tabernacles, originally called the Festival of Ingathering. This was celebrated "at the going forth" (*beçē'th*, Exod. 23:16), or "at the turn" (*tequphath*, Exod. 34:22) of the year, that is, at the autumnal equinox when the new year begins. Hence Ps. 29 is a hymn of the New Year, which was celebrated in ancient Israel on the first day of the Festival of Tabernacles.[12] It came after the wheat and vintage harvest had been gathered in and the six dry months were at an end. Then it was that the thundering voice of the Lord in storm heralded the downpour of the winter rains, upon which the life of men, beasts, and plants depended in the dawning new year.[13]

The psalm unfolds dramatically in three scenes. The first scene (vss. 1-2) is

---

[9] Literally, "is his issue."   [10] *Die Psalmen,* p. 76.   [11] *Die Psalmen,* p. 55.
[12] Cf. Oesterley, "Early Hebrew Festival Rituals," in Hooke, ed., *Myth and Ritual,* p. 124.
[13] Cf. also Mowinckel, *op. cit.,* II, 4.

set in the Lord's heavenly court. God is not described, but His presence is clearly assumed. About Him in orderly stations are the divine beings of second rank—less than God, but greater than men. Accordingly they are not called "gods" but "sons of the gods" (*benê 'ēlim*). They are the "celestial beings," the heavenly powers, which the Deuteronomist designates as "all the host of the heavens, the sun, moon, and stars" (4:19), and they are personified in our psalmist's thought. He calls upon these "celestial beings" to praise their Lord, acknowledging His lordship and imputing to Him His "glory," that is, His character in its innermost being.[14] He summons these heavenly powers, clothed in the beauty of holiness as is due Him, to bow before their Lord.

> 1 Ascribe unto the Lord, ye celestial beings,
>   Ascribe unto the Lord glory and strength!
> 2 Ascribe unto the Lord the glory due His name!
>   Make obeisance to the Lord
>   In holy adornment!

Such a summons of lesser deities to praise the highest deity is familiar in Babylonian and Egyptian hymns, but our psalmist has already in principle acknowledged the triumph of monotheism over polytheism.

The second scene (vss. 3-9*ab*) is set in the world of nature. We have left the rarified spiritual atmosphere of supermundane worship where celestial beings bring their tribute of praise and prostrate themselves before the Lord. We are transported to the earthly realm. We are in the awesome majesty of a storm, stupendous in its proportions. The theme of this scene is "the voice of the Lord." To our scientific ear it is simply the thunder of a rainstorm that the psalmist hears, a phenomenon which we understand as "the detonation of the air as it comes together after being split by the lightning, and the lightning itself caused by the meeting of two clouds charged with positive and negative electricity." [15] However, our psalmist is no scientist, but a great poet. He may have known of Teshub, storm god of the Hittites, or of Ramman of Babylonia, or of Hadad of the Canaanites. He certainly knew that marvelous picture of Israel's Lord which the great poet of Isa. 30:27-30 had painted:

> And the Lord will cause to be heard
>   His glorious voice,
>   And will cause the descent of His arm to be seen,
>   In raging anger,
>   And in flame of devouring fire,
>   In cloudburst, and downpour, and hail. (30:30.)

Such religious conceptions had been his tutelage, and it is in such terms that he describes the seven peals of thunder as issuing from the very lips of God. They are "the voice of the Lord."

---

[14] The glory of God is the essence of His revealed character; see Exod. 33:18-23; 34:6.
[15] Walker, *The Modern Message of the Psalms*, p. 31.

Our poet knows where storms arise in the Levant and how they eventually reach Judah and the wilderness. He himself is in Jerusalem, but with vivid imagination he describes the course of the storm. He hears the first distant peal of thunder over the troubled waters of the Mediterranean, which warns that a storm is brewing. It is moving eastward. A second powerful peal, then a third reaches his ear as the storm is sweeping inland over the narrow Phoenician coastline. Hark! A terrific peal resounds and re-echoes among the peaks of Mount Lebanon.

> From peak to peak, the rattling crags among
> Leaps the live thunder![16]

Accompanying that mighty peal he hears the crack and crash of majestic cedars as the whole Lebanon range trembles under the lightning's vicious stroke, and he sees beautiful snow-capped Mount Hermon[17] shake under its electric impact.[18] Another peal sends flaming streaks of forked lightning darting out from the blackened sky, as though caused by the hot breath from the mouth of the Lord. Down across the whole of Palestine the storm pursues its now southerly course. A sharp peal breaks the peace of the Judean wilderness. It hurls into violent agitation the whole arid south country (the *negebh*) of Judah, which stretches from the hills below Hebron far down to ancient Kadesh.[19] The poet describes this agitation through the vivid metaphor of birth pangs. Then (vs. 9*ab*) comes the climax of his description. It is the one verse in the second scene that has any reference to the animal world. We are stirred to swift sympathy with the wild things of the steppe as the frightened hinds and mountain goats that are with young writhe as they give premature birth.

This section of the psalm is rendered antiphonally. Every one of the seven "voice of the Lord" sentences is sung as a solo in its first rendering in the Temple, probably by the psalmist himself. To his solo voice at three points there are choir responses [20] (vss. 3*c*, 5*b*-6, 8*b*), which not only make for variety in the rendition but enrich the more general features with vivid geographical and historical detail. The first response calls attention to the vastness of the Mediterranean waters; the second vividly pictures the great mountain ranges of Lebanon and Hermon atremble at the voice of their Maker; and the third takes us to ancient Kadesh Barnea, of ineradicable historical importance in the annals of the beginnings of Israel.

How alive with the suggestion of thunder is that sevenfold phrase "the voice of the Lord" when we hear it pronounced in the Hebrew mother tongue of our

---

[16] Byron, *Childe Harold's Pilgrimage.*

[17] Sirion is the Sidonian name for Mount Hermon (Deut. 3:9).

[18] These words were written in Lebanon. I well remember the Lebanon range as it rises out of the sea, and a visit to the great cedars of Lebanon in a snow-storm, and a view from Nebatiyeh of the whole range of Mount Hermon, covered with snow. One feels the note of reality in the poet's description.

[19] Cf. Brown, Driver, Briggs, *op. cit.,* p. 616.   [20] See Schmidt for this insight.

psalmist—*Qôl Yahwéh!* How colorless is our phrase "the voice of the Lord" in comparison! The Hebrew consonant with which it begins is a "sound starting deep in the throat, pronounced with a strong articulation and a compression of the larynx." [21] Followed by the long-drawn-out *o* sound and sustained by the liquid letter *l*, its strong pronunciation vividly suggests a sharp peal of thunder, with the sound lingering on in reverberation until it ends in the two staccato syllables of Yahweh with accent on the last, *Qô-o-o-o-l-l-l Yah-wéh!*

Let us put ourselves under the spell of the psalmist singer and the Temple choir as they portray to the worshiping congregation the majesty of God in storm. Let us listen to "the voice of the Lord." [22]

> 3a **The voice of the Lord is over the waters;**
> 3b   **The glorious God thunders!**
>
> *Choir response:*
> 3c **The Lord over the great waters!**
>
> 4a **The voice of the Lord is powerful!**
> 4b **The voice of the Lord is majestic!**
> 5a **The voice of the Lord shatters the cedars!**
>
> *Choir response:*
> 5b **Yes, the Lord breaks the cedars of Lebanon;**
> 6a   **He makes Lebanon skip like a calf,**
> 6b   **And Sirion like a young wild ox.**
>
> 7 **The voice of the Lord hews out flames of fire!**
> 8a **The voice of the Lord causes the wilderness to writhe!**
>
> *Choir response:*
> 8b **The Lord makes to writhe the wilderness of Kadesh.**
>
> 9a **The voice of the Lord sets the hinds in labor,**
> 9b   **And causes the mountain goats to give speedy birth!**

While in the rendering of the psalm all three scenes were sung in the Temple, only the third scene has its imaginative dramatic setting there. Scene one is set in the heavenly court. Scene two is in the outer world of nature. But scene three is set in the Temple. By a transition even more striking than that from scene one to scene two, scene three transports us from the outer world of nature to the inner world of worship. We move from the area of description to the spiritual world of recognition and appreciation. Whence comes this voice of the Lord? The Lord who has thus "caused His glorious voice to be heard" is

[21] Gesenius-Kautzsch, *op. cit.*, sec. 6*m*.
[22] It is suggested to the reader that for the phrase "the voice of the Lord" he substitute in reading the colorful Hebrew phrase *Qô-o-o-l-l Yah-wéh*, hurling himself into it with imagination and abandon.

that holy Being who has His seat in Jerusalem. Amos himself said that it comes from the Temple:

> The Lord roars from Zion,
> And from Jerusalem gives forth His voice. (1:2.)

But the worshiping congregation in the Temple do not "mourn" like "the pastures of the shepherds" at that voice, nor do they "wither" like "the top of Carmel." Before that voice they do not cower in terror. They know that the seeming fierceness of God in storm is but the reverse side of blessing. Schmidt has finely said, "For the inhabitants of Palestine in October or November, the voice of the Lord is extraordinarily impressive. It means joy—not only vast majesty but also grace and love." [23] For that "voice" heralds release from drought and barrenness. It means for Israel, as the Deuteronomist says (28:12), that "the Lord will open unto thee His good treasure, the heavens, to give the rain of thy land in its season, and to bless all the work of thy hand." The Lord's voice is the promise of that autumnal rain called by the prophet Joel "the former rain in normal measure" (2:23). So the worshipers who are gathered in the Temple to celebrate the New Year—along with all else in the Temple, which vibrates in sympathy with their thankful recognition and trustful hope—now utter a glad exclamation:

9c **And in His Temple, everything saith, "Glory!"**

Then comes a pause, which the space between verses 9 and 10 in the printing of the psalm in the modern versions fittingly suggests. Often in a thunderstorm there comes a terrific peal of thunder, then after a few seconds of utter silence a veritable downpour of rain. So it is here. A pause, then comes a "flood" of rain. It is not the destructive deluge of primeval Hebrew story. Nor is it the heavenly ocean as Gunkel and Schmidt maintain. Rather is it the primeval deep, the storming chaotic flood which was opposed to the rule of the Lord, and which He had to master before He could create the world. But master it He did; then He created the world; and bringing those waters under His control, He made them serve His ends. As Oesterley has suggestively said, "The New Year festival was, as it were, a repetition of creation." That "flood," now in the Lord's control, will be poured down upon His people and their land in the winter rains. It will make the soil fertile and its yield adequate. Over that flood now sits the Lord enthroned forever! So the choir sings in triumph:

> 10   **The Lord hath been enthroned over [24] the flood.**
>   **Yes, the Lord is enthroned as king [25] forever.**

[23] Lecture on the Psalms, June 11, 1929, at Halle.
[24] Reading, with Duhm and Mowinckel, $m\bar{e}{}^{\iota}al\ lammabbúl$.
[25] So Gesenius-Kautzsch, *op. cit.*, sec. 111r.

11   The Lord will give strength to His people;
      The Lord will bless His people with peace.[26]

Delitzsch suggestively calls attention to the fact that this psalm, which begins with "glory in the highest," ends with "peace on earth."

Ps. 104. THE CREATOR, CONTROLLER, PROVIDER, AND SUSTAINER

Ps. 104 is a hymn of an individual, yet unlike Ps. 103, with which its opening is identical, it does not have its rise in a purely individual experience. The psalmist, as Kittel says, is "a genuine and great poet." He knows the ancient Babylonian myth of creation, in which is told how Marduk, the state god of Babylon, mastered and destroyed Tiamat, the dragon of the deep and the powerful enemy of constructive order in the world, and then brought into being an orderly world (vss. 2b-9). He has thoughts which remind us of the Greek concept of cosmos—an order which runs through the inanimate world and the world of animals and men. Yet his ideas are still intensely Hebraic, for this order and purpose, this life principle, is to him the expression of the "spirit" of God (vss. 27-30). This poet has his roots in the cultic life of the Israelite congregation and uses the language of public worship to express the feeling of his fellow worshipers and of himself.[27] "I will sing to the Lord," he cries. "I will make melody to my God." On behalf of the whole worshiping community he is expressing praise to God as the wise creator, as the governing and sustaining Lord of nature. But the psalmist is also distinctly a Palestinian. Not of the realm of nature in general does he sing, but of nature as his sensitive discerning eye sees it in his own mother country. It is a land of valleys and hills, a land of wooded mountains and of rocks untrod by human feet, and on its western border the mysterious sea.

The psalmist in the opening line calls his own soul to praise, then suddenly (vs. 1b) addresses God, acknowledging His greatness and majesty:

1   Bless the Lord, O my soul!
      My God, Thou art very great;
2a With splendor and majesty Thou art clothed;
      Thou envelopest Thyself with light like a mantle.

Then he speaks of God as creator of the heaven (vss. 2b-4) and the earth (vss. 5-9), and pictures Him stretching out the heavens like a tent cover, laying deep below in the waters—the cosmology is Babylonian [28]—the great foundation beams of His heavenly dwelling. The chariot in which He rides is furnished by the clouds speeding along on the wings of the wind. His messengers are the winds; His servants are fire and flame. These elemental forces of nature—wind and fire—which are aids both to fruitfulness and destruction have no inde-

---

[26] The term is *shālôm* and means "completeness, soundness, welfare," as well as the most frequently found translation "peace."

[27] Cf. Quell, *op. cit.* pp. 104-5.   [28] Meissner, *op. cit.,* II, 108.

pendent will of their own. As the Lord's servants they obey their Master and are themselves a revelation of the kind of God He is:

2b Who stretches out the heavens like a curtain;
3 Who lays the beams of their roof chambers in the waters;
Who makes dark clouds his chariot;
Who marches upon the wings of the wind,
4 Making winds his messengers,
His ministers, flames of fire.

But all this is only preliminary to the psalmist's major interest, which is the creation of the earth and the sustaining of it and all that is therein in life. In a single verse, still in the third person, he tells in summary fashion how in primeval times the Lord created and sustained the earth:

5 Who established the earth on its pillars,
So that it cannot forever and aye be moved.

But how did so great an achievement come about? Here we catch echoes of the Babylonian epic of creation, which vitally influenced Israelite thought. The time was when that which is now the earth was covered by a vast watery deep extending above what now are the mountains.

6 The deep covered it [i.e., the earth] like a garment;
Above the mountains the waters were standing.

These waters were the mighty and terrifying floods of chaos. The deep was an abysmal monster of disorder. It sought to resist the control of God. It was the enemy of all order. Such was the situation when the Lord, like a mighty warrior with His thundering war cry, rebuked the rebellious floods so that they fled in terrified alarm and submitted finally to the bounds their Lord set for them. Speaking now to God, the psalmist cries in exultation:

7 At Thy rebuke they fled;
At the peal of Thy thunder they hurried away.
8 They had [once] risen up upon the mountains; they [now] receded into the valleys,
To the place which Thou didst ordain for them.
9 Thou didst set a boundary over which they must not pass,
So that they may never again cover the earth.

The psalmist in primitive fashion exalts the wisdom of God as a creative principle of order, yet deals with it not abstractly, but with vivid concreteness. Wisdom is not personified, as in a similar description of creation in Prov. 8:25, 27, 29, but what God *does* is the expression of what He *is*.

Then the great drama of creation with its thrilling note of the Lord's triumph, a theme which has never failed to stir enthusiasm in Israelite hearts, is left behind. The second major part of the Psalm (vss. 10-30) begins by explaining how God controls and makes provision for His creation. Verses 10-18, the

opening part of this section, tell how God constructively utilizes the once destructive waters that are now in His control. He deals first with fountains and
brooks. We are transported to Palestine on a spring morning. The person
changes from "Thou" to "He," and the poet celebrates the Lord,

> 10 Who sendeth forth springs into the wadies;
>   Waters flow down between the mountains.
> 11 They give drink to all the beasts of the field;
>   The zebras quench their thirst.
> 12 Beside them [i.e., the springs] dwell the birds of heaven;
>   From amidst the foliage they give forth their voice.

We note that the psalmist's interest in God's orderly control over nature is now
supplemented by his thought of divine purpose. The fountains and streams
give drink to the wild animals. He mentions especially the zebra, the shy animal
of the desert. And from among the rich foliage where the birds have built their
nests we hear pouring forth the lovely songs of these glad beings who have
experienced their Maker's bountiful provision.

Then the psalmist deals with God's provision of rain, which waters the mountains and the valleys. From His roof chambers God waters the mountains; from
the clouds, His storehouses of moisture, He saturates the earth. And now we
see how all of this makes the earth yield grass for grazing animals and food for
man. And God provides not merely for man's necessities, but also, touching his
life with beauty—so it seems to the psalmist!—provides wine to ease his hard
lot and oil for healing and perfume. Lebanon's famed cedars, gigantic holy trees
which are not planted by man as are fruit trees, but by God (see Num. 24:6),
also get their fill. And this makes them in turn useful to the birds who nest in
them and to the storks who build their nests in the treetops. And those lofty
mountains and rocks, too high for the tread of human feet, provide refuge for
the mountain goats and the rock badgers. Here is a remarkable consciousness of
the interrelatedness in God's creation between inanimate life and the life of
beasts, birds, and men. Let us see with the psalmist's eyes as he describes the
orderly Provider,

> 13 Who waters the mountains from his roof chambers;
>   From the drink of Thy storehouses the earth is sated.
> 14 Who causes the green grass to sprout for the cattle,
>   And herbage for the animals of men,
>   So as to bring forth the natural vigor of the earth,
> 15   And wine that rejoices the heart of man,
>   So his face may shine from oil,
>   And bread may sustain his energies.
> 16 The trees of the Lord get their fill,
>   The cedars of Lebanon which He planted,
> 17 Where the birds make their nest,
>   The stork who has his house in the top of them.

18   **The high mountains are for the mountain goats;**
     The rocks are a refuge for the rock badgers.

The succeeding verses of the psalm (19-23) appear to be connected with the famous Hymn to the Sun by Amenhotep IV (Ikhnaton, 1375–1358 B.C.). It was written on the wall reliefs of the chapels of the cliff tombs at his capital city Akhetaton (Tell el-Amarna) and comes from a time in Egyptian history and culture which Breasted describes as "the most interesting and picturesque chapter in the story of the early East." The young king introduced into Egypt a type of monotheism. In the god Aton, whose symbol was the sun disk, "from which diverging beams radiated downward, each ray terminating in a human hand," he sought to discern the universal God as the God of all men "in the illimitable sweep of his power." [29] It seems most likely that our psalmist was familiar with this hymn and was influenced by it.

In the religion of Aton there was nothing dogmatic or theological, but the genuine love of deity whose activity man could both see and feel in the daily processes of nature. To Ikhnaton and his followers in the new faith the sun disk represented the life-giving goodness of God. The true content of the religion is presented in the hymns and prayers such as this great hymn to Aton.[30]

The excavated ruins of Akhetaton (Horizon of Aton) I visited in November, 1947. This unique capital is situated on a site of wonderful beauty on the east bank of the Nile in the middle of its course. The ruins of the palace and of the temple of Aton were fascinating. I entered a number of the brown sandstone rock tombs in the cliffs that rise to a height of 150 feet above the plain, where the great men of Ikhnaton's court were buried. Everywhere engraved on the walls appears the characteristic disk with its radiating beams—in one chamber alone, five times. It is little wonder that this brilliant although brief period of genuine vitality of Egyptian religion left its mark upon Israelite religious poetry. The present psalm is our best indication of this, and is itself the work of one of the greatest of Israelite poets.

Ikhnaton, speaking to Aton, says,

> When thou goest down in the western horizon,
> The earth is in darkness as if it were dead.
> Every lion cometh forth from his den,
> And all snakes that bite.

Similarly our psalmist in a vigorous new movement of thought turns to the celestial bodies, the moon and the sun. The moon is like a great clock calling out the periods of time, marking out the months, designating the sacred seasons to be sure (see Ecclus. 43:7, as also probably in Gen. 1:14), but in far wider order than this and with larger interest in mind God has taught moon and sun

---

[29] See Breasted, *op. cit.*, pp. 320 ff.
[30] For the most penetrating insight into the significance of this religious movement, see Erman, *Die Religion der Ägypter*, ch. 8, pp. 110-24.

to serve both men and beasts. Night belongs to the beasts. Says the psalmist of God,

> 19   Who made the moon for set times;
>   The sun He made know its setting.
> 20   Thou dost make it dark so it is night;
>   In it all the beasts of the forest prowl about,
> 21   The young lions roaring after prey
>   To ask from God their food.

Far deeper is the Hebrew hymn than the Egyptian. To our psalmist the sun is no god but is itself taught of God. The hungry roar of the young lions is an unconscious prayer to God, and God provides the night for the beast to seek its food.[31]

Then with the day comes man's turn. To the sun speaks Ikhnaton:

> When it is dawn, and thou risest in the horizon and shinest as the sun, it is day;
> Thou dispellest the darkness and sheddest thy beams.
> The two lands [Upper and Lower Egypt] keep festival, awake, and stand on
>   their feet;
> For thou hast raised them up.
> They wash their bodies;
> They take their clothes;
> Their hands [are uplifted] in adoration to thy rising;
> The whole land doeth its work.

And the Hebrew psalmist sings:

> 22   Thou makest the sun to rise; they betake themselves off,
>   And stretch out in their lairs.
> 23   Man goes forth to his work,
>   And to his labor until evening.

There seems to be a yet closer Egyptian parallel to the opening verse of the next section of the Hebrew psalm (vss. 24-26), which begins,

> 24   How manifold are Thy works, O Lord!
>   All of them Thou hast made in wisdom;
>   Thy creation fills the earth.

The Egyptian hymn similarly cries out in wonder to Aton:

> How manifold are thy works;
> They are hidden from me,
> O sole God, to whom none is to be likened.

The Hebrew psalmist continuing, as with an afterthought, deals with the sea. He knows that it is great and expansive. He knows that it teems with creeping things and with sea monsters. Here, however, his language is vague and rests, not upon what his own experience as a landsman in southern Judah has taught him, but upon hearsay:

[31] Cf. Welch, *op. cit.*, p. 24-25.

25 There is the sea, great and broad,[32]
    Where are crawling things innumerable.
26 There go the terrible monsters,[33]
    Leviathan [i.e., the dragon] whom Thou didst make to play with.

The only end that Leviathan, the famed dragon of the deep, serves is to be a plaything for God!

The Egyptian psalmist has a remarkable passage which expresses the absolute dependence of all created life upon God. Says he to Aton:

> The earth is in thy hand,
> For thou hast made them.
> When thou arisest, they live;
> When thou settest, they die.
> Thou art life in thyself;
> Men live through thee.
> The eyes look on thy beauty
> Until thou settest.

Similarly our psalmist is struck with the utter dependence of all created life upon God. God did not create and then leave the universe to go its own way. He remains in constant touch with His creation. He is its sustainer. His creative "breath," His Spirit, enlivens it all. And this divine sustenance of animals and men expresses itself in timeliness (vs. 27b) as well as in orderliness.

27 All of them wait upon Thee
    To give them their food at its right time.
28 [When] Thou givest to them, they gather it up;
    [When] Thou openest Thy hand, they are sated with what is good.
29 [When] Thou hidest Thy face, they are terrified;
    [If] Thou withdrawest Thy breath, they expire
    And return to their dust;
30 [When] Thou sendest forth Thy breath, they are created,
    And Thou renewest the face of the earth.

The wisdom that fashioned the world is never for a moment withdrawn from it. In Him all created life lives and moves and has its being.

The first major section of this psalm (vss. 1-9) deals, as we have seen, with the past and takes us far back to the primeval epoch when God created the world. The second section (vss. 10-30), as has just been noted, has to do with the present and describes how God sustains His creation. The third section (vss. 31-35) is concerned with the future, first expressing wishes for the majestic God— that He whose mere glance upon the earth makes it tremble, and whose touch upon the moutains makes them erupt, may rejoice in all His created works:

31 May the Lord's glory be forever;
    May the Lord rejoice in His works;

---

[32] Literally "broad of [on] both hands," i.e., in both directions; cf. Brown, Driver, Briggs, op. cit., p. 390, 3d; the suggestion is vastness.
[33] Read with Gunkel, *ēmôth;* "ships" is inconsistent with vs. 27.

32 He who [but] looks upon the earth, and it trembles,
   Who [but] touches the mountains, and they smoke.

Then the psalmist speaks for himself. It is the most personal part of the psalm, and in it we feel how his contemplation of nature in the fashioning and sustaining hands of God has lifted his very soul into genuine and exalted emotion. He ceases any representative capacity for the congregation, in which up to now he has been speaking, and pours out his words from his own heart of pure devotion. No soul should live who cares not for so great a Being. And "with such words," says Gunkel, "the psalmist lays down his poem before the throne of the Highest." [34]

33 I will sing to the Lord while I live:
   I will make melody to my God while I have my being.
34 May my poem be pleasing unto Him!
   I will rejoice in the Lord.
35 May sinners be destroyed from the earth.
   And may the wicked not continue.
   Bless the Lord, O my soul!

And the throng of the worshipers cry in response,

   Hallelujah!

Ps. 147. THE GOD OF NATURE AND THE SUSTAINER OF HIS PEOPLE

Ps. 147 is a congregational hymn created for the Temple in Jerusalem (vs. 12). It has two major themes—God the Creator, who manifests Himself in nature, and God the merciful Sustainer of His people. The most distinctive feature in it is the psalmist's sensitive, vivid, and imaginative view of nature, and the psalm is accordingly classified as a hymn of God's revelation in nature. There are verses in the psalm that would make it appropriate for congregational worship in the spring (vss. 8, 18). Likewise there is a section that would make it fitting for worship in the freezing cold of winter (vss. 15-17). Moreover, the poet has manifestly been inspired by the love of the stars which characterized the great poet-prophet-theologian of the Chaldean exile (cf. vss. 4-5 with Isa. 40:26, 28).

The psalm dates from a period not before the early fourth century B.C. This is clear, first, from its reference to the restoration of the Lord's people from exile and the refortification of the gathered postexilic community (vss. 13-14). Second, the term rendered "laud" (shabbeḥi) in verse 12 is a late Aramaic word. Third, the enthusiastic appreciation of God's gift to His people of the priestly law (vss. 19-20), which was introduced by Ezra about 397 B.C., is the most certain indication as to date which the psalm gives.

There is a striking feature which is present in every one of its three parts. It is the arresting way in which the poet throughout the psalm binds together his

[34] *Die Psalmen,* p. 452.

two major themes. We shall note this as we proceed in the interpretation of each part of the psalm. It moves in three cycles.

In the first cycle (vss. 1-6) the psalmist summons the congregation to praise the good God in an appropriate song of praise. Then in four vivid pictures he gives specific content to this good God. First, God is the rebuilder of destroyed Jerusalem. The psalmist has Isa. 56:8 in mind as he thinks of the Lord as the one who "gathers" those who in the Chaldean exile of 597 and 587 B.C., were "banished" from Jerusalem and Judah. Second, the Lord is the physician of His people. The psalmist has the noble words of Isa. 61:1 in view as he pictures the Lord healing His people's broken hearts and bandaging their wounds. Third comes the first swift and unexpected transition—from God as the gracious helper of His people to God the mighty Creator of the stars. The Lord's unsearchable understanding shows the same kind of individualizing knowledge of the innumerable stars of the heavens that His love does for His banished and broken people. Then in similar swift transition comes his fourth picture, which brings us back from vast nature to man, for God is here the reliever of the oppressed and the humiliator of their godless oppressors. We are vividly conscious of the psalmist's own deep sympathy with the destitute and lowly of his people. His heart is with these who are the socially, economically, and politically helpless, and he is convinced that the Lord is with them too. So the choir sings:

1   Praise the Lord, for He is good.
       Sing to our God, for a praise song is fitting.
2   The Lord is the builder of Jerusalem;
       He gathers the banished of Israel.
3   He heals the broken in heart,
       And binds up their hurts.
4   He counts the number of the stars;
       To all of them He gives names.
5   Great is our Lord and strong in might;
       His understanding none can plumb.
6   The Lord relieves the afflicted;
       He abases the ungodly to the ground.

The second cycle (vss. 7-11) opens with a new summons to praise:

7   Sing to the Lord with thanksgiving;
       Sing praises to our God with a harp.

The theme of praise which predominates in this cycle is the creative activity of God in spring and summer. Suddenly we are aware that the picture of God, who is with His afflicted people, has vanished. (*a*) We are in the vast spaces of the heavens where the majestic Lord of nature is preparing those mysterious processes that provide rain for watering the earth. Then we see the rolling Palestinian hills sprouting grass to feed man's beasts of burden, the domestic cattle, and the wild and hungry young ravens. Yet—note again the vivid transition—this God of the vast heavens and of amazing material provision, the controller of the vigorous physical energies of His creation, takes no delight in mere material strength, whether in nature, animals, or men. (b) Rather what pleases Him is the reverent recognition on the part of His loyal ones of their trustful dependence upon His kindness and love. It is a glorious spring song which is thus lifted to God,

8 Who covers the heavens with clouds,
   Who prepares rain for the earth,
   Who causes the mountains to sprout grass
   And herbage for the animal servants of man, [85]
9 Who gives to the beast its food,
   To the young ravens that for which they cry.
10 Not in the strength of the horse does He delight;
   Nor does He take pleasure in the thighs of a man.
11 The Lord is pleased with those who fear Him,
   With those who wait for His lovingkindness.

In the third cycle (vss. 12-20) the choir sings a new summons to the congregation to praise the Lord. And now we see for the first time clearly that the setting of the psalm is in Zion, in the Temple at Jerusalem.

12 Laud, O Jerusalem, the Lord!
   Praise thy God, O Zion!

The theme of the praise is threefold. First, the Lord is conceived as the restorer of peace and prosperity to Zion, the worshiping community of Jerusalem. The times are favorable, and the city walls have already been rebuilt by Nehemiah (444 B.C.). The yield of the soil is good in quality, "the finest of the wheat," and abundant in quantity. Then comes another startling transition. Suddenly we are in winter, and again we are in the mysterious processes of nature. The second theme of this cycle is God conceived as the Lord of the winter. He sends forth His word to the earth, personified as a "winter spirit," through whose agency God creates the snow, fashioning it into billowy white piles, like mounds of clean wool. Through this same "winter spirit" He scatters everywhere a gray-white film of hoarfrost. He hurls down hail. He congeals running streams into ice. The world is frozen in dead winter. Then comes the third theme—God as the awakener of frozen nature in the springtime. Again God's word is His messenger, but now it is "the spirit of spring." Through this spirit God melts the frozen waters, sets the warm winds to blowing, and the streams to pouring down the wadies. The fourth theme introduces us to our final surprise. Suddenly we have left the universal world of nature and are again in the human world. Indeed we are in the particular world of *Israel!* The psalmist uses the double designation for God's people, Jacob and Israel—Jacob, whose name was changed to Israel. So the fourth theme is God's word, not now as a nature spirit, but as

---

[85] So supply with Duhm, partly on the basis of the Septuagint (*Die Psalmen*, p. 298).

the revealer of His charges and His decisions for His people, His word of the law. The psalmist is writing very shortly after that law was brought to Israel by Ezra the scribe about 397 B.C. The intention of the law was to make Israel a holy people of God. It came, in the wonderful providence of God, to Israel! We feel the deep, surging emotion of the psalmist's heart as he clasps to his breast this revelation of God's will—God's unique gift to His people, unshared by any other nation, and the climactic expression of His covenant with His own.

Thus the choir calls Zion to the fourfold praise of God.

13 For He has strengthened the bars of your gates;
   He has blessed your sons in your midst.
14 He bestows peace upon your borders;
   He satisfies you with the finest of the wheat.
15 He sends out His word to the earth;
   Speedily His word runs.
16 He dispenses snow like wool;
   He scatters hoarfrost like ashes.
17 He hurls down His ice as hail;
   Before His cold, waters congeal.
18 He sends out His word and melts them;
   He makes His wind blow and the waters flow.
19 He declares His word to Jacob,
   His charges and His judgments to Israel.
20 He has not done so to every nation,
   Nor has He taught them His judgments!

And the congregation lift the glad cultic cry of praise to the Lord:

Hallelujah!

Ps. 148. ALL NATURE SINGS THE MUSIC OF THE SPHERES

This is the third of the last five psalms of the Psalter, which are designated by the superscription "Hallelujah," meaning "praise ye the Lord." It is a hymn of praise to God. Indeed the psalmist himself accurately describes the nature of his psalm. The psalm ends at verse 14a with the thought that the Lord has restored His people's dignity and courage. Then the psalmist adds a sort of subscript to indicate the nature of his psalm and the use for which he intended it. It is "a praise song for all His godly ones, for the sons of Israel, a people [composed] of those who are near to Him." The hymn would be rendered by the processional choir. It is likely that in verse 12 there is a reference to groups composing the choir—young men, young women, old men, and boys.[36] At the close of the hymn the whole congregation would raise the beloved worship cry, "Hallelujah!"

But the unique and most distinctive feature in the psalm is its sensitive and highly imaginative view of nature. The psalmist is a poet. To him all nature

[36] Cf. Quell, *op. cit.*, p. 71.

sings—physical nature, animal nature, and human nature. There is a native grandeur in his words and an exalted rapture in his soul as he summons all three to the praise of the Lord.

The psalm begins with an exalted summons to praise the Lord, whose unapproachable and unshared dwelling is the loftiest conceivable point "in the heights." Underneath Him are "the waters which are above the heavens" (vs. 4b), such as are referred to in the priestly account of creation in Gen. 1:7. Through this reference glimmers the ancient Babylonian myth of creation. Below these waters is "the heaven of heavens" (vs. 4a) or the highest heaven; yet below this is the realm where dwell the Lord's messengers, His host of angels. And still below this is the heaven where the sun, moon, and stars have their courses. The psalmist summons the supercelestial waters, the highest heaven, the angelic host, and the heavenly bodies to praise the name of the Lord:

> 1 Praise ye the Lord from the heavens:
> 　Praise Him in the heights.
> 2 Praise Him, all His messengers:
> 　Praise Him, all His host.
> 3 Praise Him, sun and moon:
> 　Praise Him, all stars of light.
> 4 Praise Him, heaven of heavens,
> 　And the waters which are above the heavens.
> 5a Praise ye the name of the Lord.

The basis of the praise (vss. 5b-6) emphasizes a central theme of the New Year and of the Festival of Tabernacles—the Lord as Creator. The great supercelestial reservoir which provides rain for the earth, the highest heaven, the celestial beings, and the heavenly luminaries were created by His word of command. They move at His charge and in the eternal order established by Him. That charge they do not disobey. They are constantly sustained by Him.

> 5b　For He commanded, and they were created.
> 6 He established them forever and aye:
> 　A charge He gave so they do not trespass.

We are very close here to the abstract concepts of universal law and the regularity of nature.

From the heavens the psalmist turns to the earth and issues a new summons to praise. Again he makes implicit reference to the Babylonian myth of creation, wherein Tiamat, the dragon of chaos, the mythical monster of the abyss, was subjected by Marduk. In the Israelite version the mighty dragon and the awful abyss, always in the Old Testament symbols of vast evil, are summoned to praise Him who is now their Master, the Lord. The psalmist moves on to the mysterious phenomena of nature—hail, snow, mist, and storm wind—all of which move at God's law. He comes then to the nearer-at-hand elements of nature, where there is less mystery and more familiarity—the mountains and hills, the fruit trees and majestic cedars, the wild animals, domesticated beasts, insects, and birds. At length he comes to man—man in his high dignity—composing the population of the nations of the earth, their kings, their princes, and their judges. And in moving climax he comes finally to the true center of his interest and the object of his direct appeal—the young men and women, the old men and boys, of the Lord's worshiping fellowship, who are now moving in processional choir in the Temple worship. Let all of these praise the Lord!

> 7 Praise the Lord from the earth.
>   Dragons and all deeps;
> 8 Fire and hail, snow and mist;
>   Storm wind, which fulfills His word;
> 9 The mountains and all hills;
>   Fruit trees and all cedars;
> 10 The wild animals and all tame beasts;
>   Creeping things and winged birds;
> 11 Kings of the earth and all peoples;
>   Princes and all judges of the earth;
> 12 Young men and virgins also;
>   Old men together with youths:
> 13a Let them praise the name of the Lord;

And a new basis of praise is now given, a new theme that includes both earth and heaven in its sweep. The keynote is exaltation. For over all creation, heaven and earth, is the name of the Lord, the exalted Lord of all. But again we feel the close-to-life appeal to God's living congregation, now present in worship. God lifts up His loyal people. And through the ceremonies of this very festival of thanksgiving and renewal He quickens their spirit with courage and hope!

> 13b For His name alone is exalted;
> 14 His splendor goes over earth and heaven,
>   And He has lifted up the dignity of His people.

2. Hymns of the Revelation of God in History

The most distinctive characteristic in God as the Israelites understood and interpreted Him is action. He is from everlasting to everlasting, not merely as an existing, but as a working Being. The psalmists never tire of glorifying and glorying in the majestic and marvelous works of God. The supreme point at which they see in God fundamental contrast with the gods or divine beings of the nations is that He is the living God (Pss. 42:2; 84:2).

The supreme work of God as viewed by the psalmists was the creation of the world. One cannot immerse oneself in the psalms long without grasping with heightened awe and sensitive appreciation the vast meaning of such a classic phrase as "the Creator of the ends of the earth." But next to God's work at primeval creation, in the appreciation of the psalmists, is His work in history and more particularly in Israel's history.

It is clear that the psalmists who deal with this theme were familiar in varying degrees with the great epic stories of Israel's past as written by the Yahwist and Elohist in the tenth and eighth centuries B.C. respectively. And the more miraculous account as told by the writer of the Priestly Code, published in the early fourth century B.C., is likewise to them a treasured possession. But they use these stories quite freely and give relatively little detail.

In the bare facts of Israel's history as such the psalmists have no interest. They see history solely as the revelation of the hand of God. The religious meaning of history is their theme, and the Lord of history is their God. The psalmists use history to teach, to warn, to convict, to arouse, to encourage, and to inspire. Basic in their thought is that the God of Israel is a covenant God who Himself took the initiative in drawing near Israel, and who has never, nor will He ever, let go of His people.

These psalms came from scholarly minds who were interested in three things. They wanted to pass on to the younger generation the major facts of their history as seen in the light of faith. The oppression in Egypt, the exodus from Egypt, Israel at Sinai and Kadesh, the invasion and conquest of Trans-Jordan and of Canaan, the monarchy and the reign of David, and the division of the kingdom— these are the great events. But a second interest was to make sure that these facts would not be grasped merely as secular events. Individuals—even great ones like Moses, Joshua, Samuel, and David—enter extremely little into the record. The great actor in the drama of Israel's development is God. A third interest was evangelistic. It was that through familiarity with such psalms youth "might set their hope in God."

The historical psalms are Pss. 78, 105, 106, and 114. They have their distinctive worship setting at the great pilgrimage festivals and especially at Passover, where the story of Israel's great release is retold (Exod. 13:14-16), and at Tabernacles, where the covenant of the Lord with Israel is annually renewed.

Ps. 78. THE RIDDLING STORY OF THE PAST

This is a historical psalm which emphasizes the revelation of God in the history of Israel. The purpose of such a psalm is the spiritual upbuilding of the congregation. The setting in which it would be most at home would be in services associated with the festival of the Passover, where the story of the past with special reference to the Exodus was told. To Israel this story of the Passover with Israel's release from Egyptian bondage was the most significant event in the nation's entire history. The only individual who comes into the story by name in this psalm is David. The events of Exodus, conquest, the establishment of the monarchy, the division of the kingdom, and the building of the Temple are told without reference to a single human being. In the psalmist's thought God is the great doer. He is the Lord (vs. 65). It is not history that is the poet's theme, but history as the revelation of God. Even David is but an instrument of God.

The psalm opens with a summons to attention. The psalmist has created a didactic poem that tells the classic story of Israel's past history, embracing the centuries from the epoch of Moses to the fall of Samaria (721 B.C.), capital of the northern kingdom, Israel. To many in the congregation of Israel to which the psalmist addresses himself that past, embracing close to five centuries of time, is an enigma, a puzzling, baffling mystery, truly a riddle. Yet its story has been passed down by the fathers from generation to generation as a praise song to the Lord for all His marvelous deeds on behalf of Israel, His people. The kind of appeal for attention which the psalmist uses is that familiarly employed by the sages of Israel in their summons to their students:

> 1 Give ear, my people, to my instruction:
>   Incline your ears to the words of my mouth.
> 2 I will open my mouth in a poem;
>   I will pour forth riddles from the past,
> 3 Which we have heard and known,
>   And our fathers have recounted to us.
> 4 And we will not conceal them from our children,
>   Telling to the generations following
> The praises of the Lord and His might,
> And the wonderful things He has done.

The poet then calls to mind the classic Israelite summons to religious instruction (Deut. 6:7), in which is enjoined the obligation to pass down from generation to generation the mighty deeds of God. The purpose of this religious teaching of one generation by the other is that through faithful recall of what God has wrought the congregation might be kept from stubborn rebellion and an unruly spirit toward God such as had characterized their fathers, and might be made truly faithful to Him.

> 5 He raised up a regulation in Jacob,
>   And established a law in Israel,
> Which He commanded our fathers
>   To make known to their sons,
> 6 So that the generation following might know them:
>   That the children yet to be born
> Might arise and recount them to their sons,
> 7   That they may put their confidence in God,
> And not forget the deeds of God,
>   But keep His commandments,
> 8 And not be like their fathers,
>   A generation stubborn and rebellious,
> A generation which did not direct its heart aright,
> And whose spirit was not faithful to God;

9 Unruly sons who played false,
   Like a warped bow in the day of battle; [37]
10 Who kept not the covenant of God,
   And refused to walk in His law;
11 Who forgot His deeds,
   And His marvelous acts which He showed them.

The psalmist then in two great cycles rehearses the story of Israel from the standpoint of God's sovereign lordship of history and Israel's response to His mighty hand.

The first cycle (vss. 12-42) traces the history from the exodus from Egypt to the sojourn in the wilderness; the second (vss. 43-72) from the plagues of Egypt to the reign of David, yet clearly implying the fall of Samaria.

There were repeatedly times when the Lord's mercy and salvation had come in a great beneficent wave of divine grace, sweeping Israel from the spirit of doubt and rebellion to that of faith and obedience. Yet the Israelites did not long ride the crest of the wave, but oftener than not sank into its trough of doubt and rebellion where they were overwhelmed by the Lord's punishment. But God was not the destroyer of His people. Moved by their desperate need, over and over again and in wave after wave of mercy He forgave them and saved them. In this unique story Israel's trust in God's mercy often grew presumptuous, and doubt of His salvation always led to sin. We can observe these waves of God's mercy and salvation toward Israel, and one negative response of Israel after another in doubt and rebellion. We can also see wave after wave of God's judgment and punishment, each awakening a characteristic response from Israel in obedience and faith. Thus we can follow the movement in the heart of the living God as the psalmist interprets it, and likewise the ebb and flow of obedience on the part of Israel, His people.

First comes the divine initiative, God's mighty deliverance of Israel. Its scene is the ancient northern capital of Egypt, a city whose existence goes back to the early Semitic occupancy of Egypt in Hyksos times, here designated "the field of Zoan." [38] Israel's crossing of the Sea of Reeds, the leadership through the wilderness by cloud and by fire, the provision of water from the rock while they were at Kadesh-Barnea—all precious elements in the classical historical pattern—are here viewed as the Lord's wonderful acts.

12 In sight of their eyes He did wonders,
   In the land of Egypt, the field of Zoan.
13 He divided the sea and let them cross,
   And made the waters stand like a heap.

---

[37] I follow here Gunkel's restoration of the text.

[38] The Hyksos capital Avaris, Raamses (Exod. 1:11), Zoan, or Tanis (Greek)—successive names for the same capital city—is mentioned in Num. 13:22 as having been built seven years later than Hebron. See Isa. 19:11-13; 30:4; Ezek. 30:14. See also p. 211.

14 And He led them in a cloud by day,
 And all the night by the light of fire.
15 He broke open rocks in the wilderness,
 And watered the steppe like the deeps.
16 And he brought forth streams from the rock,
 And caused the water to flow down like rivers.

But Israel none the less doubted that the God who had bountifully provided them with water in the wilderness could also supply bread and meat for His people.

17 But yet again they went on to sin against Him.
 To rebel against the Most High in the desert.
18 And they put God to the test in their heart
 By asking food for their appetite.
19 They said, "Is God able
 To provide a table in the wilderness?
20 Lo, He struck the rock and there gushed out
 Water, and the torrents began to flow;
 But is He able to give bread also,
 Or provide flesh for His people?"

Because they did not trust Him, because they did not think Him able, the Lord's anger at them was aroused, and He proved before them His power by raining down upon them "bread of heaven," the manna, and the quails.

21 The Lord heard and grew furious,
 And fire was kindled in Jacob;
22 For they believed not in God,
 Nor did they trust in His salvation.
23 So He commanded clouds from above,
 And opened the doors of heaven;
24 And He rained manna upon them,
 And grain of heaven He gave them.
25 Bread of angels man ate:
 He sent supplies to satiety;
26 He caused an east wind to spring up in heaven,
 And guided on the south wind in its strength.
27 Then He rained down flesh as dust,
 And winged birds as the sand of the sea,
28 And they fell in the midst of their camp,
 Round about their dwellings.

The Israelites accepted to their full physical satisfaction this merciful provision, which God in response to their great need had made:

29 So they ate and were fully sated;
 Yes, that for which they lusted He brought them.

But even before their lust for food had been satiated, the judgment of God came upon them in the form of a plague that struck them down in vast numbers.

30 Not even had their lust become loathsome;
       Their food was yet in their mouth
31   When God's anger went up against them;
       He slew the most robust among them,
       And made the choice youth of Israel bow down in death.

Yet in spite of such stern discipline the Israelites heeded it not but persisted in sin and unbelief, spending their days empty of meaning and living out their years barren of results.

32 In spite of all this they kept on sinning,
       And did not believe in His wonders.
33 So they brought their days to an end for no purpose,
       And all their years in dismay.

God's severe judgment upon them made Israel repentant. So, remembering that He was their protector and champion, they sought fellowship with Him. But their eagerness for Him degenerated into deception, flattery, and insincerity. Their loyalty wavered; they lost faith in the covenant He had made with them. Yet the Lord is a God of compassion and forgiveness. He did not destroy them in anger but turned from anger to mercy. Remembering their weak human nature, He showed them consideration. How often in those wilderness days had they brought pain to God's heart, utterly forgetting what He had done for them!

34 When He slew them, then they sought Him,
       And turned and looked eagerly for Him.
35 Yes, they remembered that God was their rock,
       And God Most High their Redeemer.
36 But they deceived Him with their mouth,
       And lied to Him with their tongue.
37 Their heart was not steadfast with Him,
       Nor did they trust in His covenant.
38 But He is compassionate;
       He forgives iniquity
          And does not destroy,
       But repeatedly turns away His anger,
       And does not stir up all His wrath.
39 So He remembered that they were but flesh,
       A breath which, passing along, returns not.
40 How oft they showed rebelliousness in the wilderness,
       Caused Him pain in the desert,
41 And turned, putting God to the test,
       Yes, pained the Holy One of Israel!
42 They remembered not His hand,
       Nor the day when He redeemed them from distress—

This last line forms the transition to the new cycle (vss. 43-72). It recalls the great day when at the Exodus the Lord had redeemed Israel from Egyptian bondage. The new cycle takes up the story just before that event, starting with the ten plagues which, as the Israelite legend tells us, the Lord sent against the Egyptians to compel them to let the Israelites go. These plagues in Egypt are the Lord's signs. The events of the Exodus which took place in the region that centered in Zoan are His wonders. The psalmist starts with an enumeration of the plagues: streams changed to blood, mosquitoes, frogs, caterpillars, locusts, hail, frost, and lightning. All are viewed as manifestations of God's hot anger. The climax of them all is the destructive pestilence through which the Lord's angel of death smites Egypt's first-born.

43 When He gave His signs in Egypt,
    And His wonders in the field of Zoan,
44 And turned their streams into blood,
    Their rivers so that they could not drink,
45 He sent among them mosquitoes which consumed them,
    And frogs which destroyed them.
46 And He gave their produce to the caterpillar,
    And all the fruit of their toil to the locust.
47 He ruined their vines with hail,
    And their sycamores with frost.
48 He delivered up their beasts to hail,
    And their cattle to bolts of fire.
49 He sent upon them the heat of His anger;
    He commanded fury and indignation.
    He caused His angel to pass through for destruction; [39]
50   He smoothed out a path for His anger.
    He withheld not their soul from death,
    But delivered over their life to the pestilence.
51 And He smote all the first-born of Egypt,
    The best part of their strength, in the tents of Ham. [40]

Although the Egyptians, the oppressors of the Lord's people, were thus severely dealt with, God the Shepherd, the Herdsman of Israel, led His flock out of Egypt safely, and without fear, and guided His herd into the wilderness, while the pursuing Egyptians were drowned in the Sea of Reeds. At the border of Canaan, the holy land, from the hills of Moab the Lord apportioned to the tribes the land of Canaan. Then driving out the pre-Israelite inhabitants, He gave the tribes of Israel a home.

52 But He led out His people like a flock,
    And guided them like a herd in the wilderness.
53 And He led them into security so they feared not;
    But the sea overwhelmed their enemies.
54 So He brought them to the border of His sanctuary, [41]
    The mountain which His right hand acquired. [42]

[39] So read with Graetz; cf. "for destruction," Exod. 12:13, 23.
[40] In the late psalms a collective name for Egyptians.   [41] That is, the land of Canaan.
[42] By this the poet means, not Sinai (so Oesterley), but Canaan itself; note parallelism. It was the highlands that the Israelites first acquired.

55 And He drove out nations from before them,
And assigned them their territory by allotment,
And He caused the tribes of Israel to dwell in their tents.

But still the root of rebellion remained in Israel. The poet writes under the influence of the Deuteronomic interpretation of history expressed in Judg. 2:11-19. They failed to keep the charges of the Lord; and, just as a treacherous bow swerves from hitting the mark, so they swerved from the trail of faithfulness, following the bad example of their ancestors. They fell away from the true worship of God and absorbed the Canaanite idolatry of the high places, thus stirring the Lord to fury, who as a jealous God would brook no rivals.

56 Still they put to the test and rebelled against God;
They heeded not the Most High and His charges.
57 But they turned back and dealt treacherously like their fathers;
They swerved aside like a treacherous bow,
58 And they provoked Him to anger by their high places,
And by their idols made Him jealous.

None of this disloyalty was hidden to God, and because of it He abhorred His people. He let Shiloh, the sacred city which housed the ark of God, and the ark itself, the Lord's "strength," His "glory," be captured by the Philistines, and He gave Israel over to utter defeat at their hands. In that awful war the blood of Israel's choice youth flowed freely, and even priests were killed. The Israelites, caught unawares, were so stunned and stupefied by such unprecedented blows that even all private lamentation for the dead was neglected because of the yet greater disaster, the loss of the ark.

59 God heard [of this] and became furious
And greatly abhorred Israel;
60 So He abandoned His sanctuary [in] Shiloh,
The tent where He dwelt among men,
61 And gave up His strength to captivity,
Yes, His glory into the hand of the enemy.
62 He delivered up His people to the sword,
And became furious with His inheritance.
63 Fire consumed their choice youth, [48]
But their virgins made no lament.
64 Their priests fell by the sword,
But their widows did not weep.

Then the Lord, as though from a drugged sleep, awoke. The picture is vigorous and vivid. It is the Almighty now stimulated beyond His customary power, like a warrior excited by wine. It is the Lord protecting His own and smiting the enemies of His people. It is God rejecting the Joseph section of Israel, Ephraim, the northern kingdom, and Shiloh, "the tent of Joseph," its

[48] I follow the Septuagint here. Gunkel has shown that the poet has I Sam. 4:19-22 in mind.

most famous sanctuary where the ark has been. The rejection of Ephraim reflects the fall of Israel, which to the poet, in whose soul lives the Deuteronomic interpretation of history (II Kings 17:7-23), was the result of the sin of disloyalty on the part of the northern kingdom. And it is God actively choosing Judah and Mount Zion as the objects of His peculiar affection, and there building His eternal sanctuary. The poet ignores the fact that it was really Solomon, David's successor, who built the Temple.

65 Then like one who had been asleep the Lord awoke,
   Like a hero exhilarated with wine!
66 And He smote His enemies in the rear;
   He laid on them perpetual disgrace.
67 He rejected the tent of Joseph,
   And chose not the tribe of Ephraim;
68 But he chose the tribe of Judah,
   Mount Zion which He loves.
69 And He built His sanctuary like the heights of heaven;
   Like the earth He established it forever.

The poet is a Judean and writes with a bias toward Judah, and especially toward David. He refers implicitly to Samuel's choice of David (I Sam. 16:11), the lad whom the Lord took, as Nathan's famed oracle said, "from following the sheep" (II Sam. 7:8) and at length made the skilled shepherd of the people Israel.

70 And chose David His servant,
   And took him from the sheepfolds.
71 From following the ewes He brought him
   To shepherd Jacob, His people.
72 And he fed them in the integrity of his heart,
   And by his skilled hands he led them.

Ps. 105. THE GOD WHO REMEMBERS

Ps. 105 is a historical hymn and deals with God's revelation of Himself to Israel through her history. The psalmist covers the period from Abraham to the settlement of Canaan, a sweep of at least five hundred years. He does not deal with events of his time, but only with the ancient past, which has come to have for him the luster of the sacred. The thing that makes such a hymn truly distinctive when it is compared with the hymns of Babylonia and Egypt is the entrance of the sacred legend into the Israelite hymn. In this the Israelite hymns are unique. To the psalmist the history of Israel is a living together with, a comradeship of, the Lord and His people.[44]

The psalm opens with an elaborate introduction, which indicates the overwhelming rapture of the Hebrew poet.[45] In his call to praise he addresses the congregation of the Lord as the "descendants of Abraham, . . . sons of Jacob,

44 Cf. Gunkel, *Einleitung*, p. 78.   45 *Ibid.*, p. 37.

His chosen" people—classic phrases from the burning center of Israel's spiritual self-consciousness. He invites the congregation to bear glad and thankful witness, even to the nations, of what the Lord has done for Israel. The joyful melody of the congregation's praise is to be saturated with brooding recall and glorying recognition of what God has wrought in their behalf. And this is to be the joy of seeking and inquiring worshipers whose hearts are desirous of the fellowship of His presence even while they recall in song His mighty acts and His dependable decrees.

1 Give thanks to the Lord; call out His name;
    Make known among the peoples His deeds.
2 Sing to the Lord; make melody to Him;
    Muse on all His wonderful acts.
3 Glory in His holy name:
    Let the heart of those who seek the Lord rejoice.
4 Inquire after the Lord and His strength;
    Seek His face continually.
5 Sing of His marvelous deeds which He has done,
    His wonders and the decrees of His mouth,
6 O descendants of Abraham,
    O sons of Jacob, His chosen ones.

The chief part of the psalm now begins—that which thrills the poet's heart. It celebrates the Lord as He who *remembered,* who did not forget the covenant made long centuries before with Abraham, Isaac, and Jacob, pledging that He would give them Canaan as their land (Gen. 15:18-21, Abraham; 26:2-5, Isaac; 28:13-15, Jacob). As Gunkel says, "this is the great word which runs like a red thread throughout Genesis." We feel the note of awed wonder in the psalmist's soul as he realizes that this God who did not forget has now become the righteous Judge of all the earth, yet still is uniquely Israel's God.

7 He is the Lord our God:
    His judgments are in all the earth.
8 He remembers forever His covenant,
    The word He enjoined upon a thousand generations,
9 Which He covenanted with Abraham,
    And [by] His oath to Isaac,
10 And established with Jacob as a decree,
    With Israel as an eternal covenant:
11 "To you will I give the land of Canaan
    As your assigned possession."

In dealing with the Lord's hand in Israel's history the psalmist takes as his starting point the nomadic period of the Hebrew fathers, when, few in number and with no settled home, they wandered from Ur to Canaan, then to Egypt, but ever under the protecting care of God. The Lord put terror of them upon the cities of Canaan (Gen. 35:5) and in dreams reproved Abimelech, Canaanite king of Gerar, for laying hands on Sarah, wife of Abraham, and warned him against thus harming one of His "prophets" (Gen. 20:1-7; see also the parallel in the Isaac cycle, Gen. 26:6-11).

> 12 When they were but few in number,
>   Yes, very few and but strangers in it,
> 13 Then they wandered from nation to nation,
>   From one kingdom to another people.
> 14 He did not allow men to oppress them,
>   But reproved kings on account of them,
> 15 "Touch not My anointed,
>   And to My prophets do no harm."

Then the psalm moves on into the Joseph history. From occasional phrases such as "He sent before them" (vs. 17) we see that the poet had a knowledge of the legends themselves (see Gen. 45:5). He tells of the famine that arose in Canaan, and how Joseph was sold as a slave (Gen. 37:28) and carried to Egypt, where he was unjustly thrown into prison (Gen. 39:20). There he lay, the iron manacles entering even into his sensitive soul. But God's word that had been communicated to Joseph in a dream (Gen. 37:5-7) was confirmed. The Pharaoh ("a king") sent for him, put him in charge of his palace (Gen. 41: 40-41), and made him ruler over all his land (Gen. 45:8). Joseph introduced food control into Egypt, storing the grain in granaries over seven productive years (Gen. 41:46-49). Although Egypt was famous for its wisdom (Isa. 19:11), Joseph was wise enough to teach the Egyptian elders. At length Jacob himself took up his residence in Egypt (Gen. 46:6-7).

The poetic narrative is brief. Joseph is mentioned by name only once. Jacob is called by his name of honor, "Israel." We feel that the psalmist's recall of the whole Joseph legend is in order that the congregation of Israel, a people now humbled under a foreign power and fettered in spirit if not in iron, may feel that God has not forgotten His covenant. They too, like Joseph, will be released!

> 16 When He called a famine upon the land,
>   He broke all the staff of bread.
> 17 He sent before them a man;
>   Joseph was sold as a slave:
> 18 They humbled his feet in fetters;
>   Iron went into his soul,
> 19 Until the time when his word was fulfilled,
>   The promise of the Lord was confirmed.
> 20 A king sent and loosed his bonds,
>   A ruler of peoples, and he set him free.
> 21 He made him lord over his house,
>   And ruler over all his property,
> 22 So as to direct his officials as he desired,
>   And teach his elders wisdom.
> 23 Then Israel entered into Egypt,
>   And Jacob sojourned in the land of Ham.

The psalmist now comes to the major theme of the legend of Israel, the exodus from Egypt and the oppression which preceded it. This chapter of Israel's story sets in at the time when, having become numerous and powerful in Egypt, the Hebrews began to be hated by the Egyptians and to be dealt with in guile and deceitful cunning (Exod. 1:9-16), so that the increase in their population was forcibly stopped. Then the Lord sent to His people Moses and Aaron. He sent the plagues upon the Egyptians—natural features of familiar experience they were to the Egyptians, but exaggerated to fearful proportions and climaxing in the death of Egypt's first-born. Then the Lord brought out His people, leading them safely through the deep without stumbling, and to Egypt's great relief, for the Israelites had terrified them (Exod. 12:33).

24 Then He made His people very fruitful,
   And made them stronger than Egypt.
25 Their [the Egyptians'] hearts turned to hate His people,
   So they dealt craftily with His servants.
26 He sent Moses, His servant,
   Aaron, whom He had chosen.
27 He performed upon Egypt His signs,
   And His wonders in the land of Ham.
28 He sent darkness so that it became black, [46]
   Yet they paid no heed to His words.
29 He turned their waters to blood, [47]
   And all their fish He let die.
30 Their land swarmed with frogs; [48]
   They were even in the chambers of the king.
31 He spoke, and there came a swarm of gnats, [49]
   Mosquitoes [50] in all their territory.
32 He turned their rain into hail; [51]
   Flames of fire were in their land.
33 And he struck their vines and fig trees,
   And stripped the trees of their yield.
34 He commanded, and a swarm of locusts came, [52]
   Yes, locusts without number.
35 So they ate up all the herbage in their land,
   And consumed the fruit of their ground.
36 Then He struck all the first-born of Egypt, [53]
   The first issue of all their manly vigor.
37 And He brought them out with silver and gold, [54]
   And not a stumbler was in their tribes.
38 Egypt rejoiced when they went out; [55]
   For terror at them had fallen upon them.

[46] Exod. 10:21-23. [47] Exod. 7:19-21. [48] Exod. 8:5-6.
[49] Exod. 8:21-24. [50] Exod. 8:16-17. [51] Exod. 9:22-25.
[52] Exod. 10:12-15. [53] Exod. 12:29-31. [54] Exod. 3:21-22; 11:2; 12:35-36.
[55] Exod. 12:33.

The next part of the psalm (vss. 39-41) deals with the Lord's protection of His people from the pursuing Egyptians (Exod. 14:19-20). God's presence was always with them, symbolized by a column of cloud to guide them by day and a column of fire to guide them by night, as they marched both day and night (Exod. 13:21-22). In the wilderness they asked for food, and the Lord sent them quails and manna (Exod. 16:3-16; Num. 11). They asked for water, and the Lord gave them water in the desert from the rock (Exod. 17:2-7; Num. 20:5-11).

> 39 He spread a cloud for a covering,
>   And a fire to illumine the night.
> 40 They asked, and He brought in quails,
>   And with bread from heaven He satisfied them.
> 41 He opened up the rock, and waters gushed forth;
>   They flowed as a river in the desert.

The psalm ends as it began, with reference to God's primal promise to Abraham. The great classic and holy period of Israel for this psalmist—and normative for all future development—is the time from Abraham to the conquest of Canaan, a period which saw the fulfillment of His holy covenant word to Abraham. So the psalmist summarizes the story. God brought His people into Canaan with such songs of exultant joy as Miriam and the women sang when the Sea of Reeds was crossed and Israel was at last free (Exod. 15:1). The lands of the seven nations, greater and stronger than Israel, at the conquest of Canaan (Deut. 7:1) were acquired by Israel as the gift of God because of Israel's obedience to His commands. We sense here the psalmist's implicit appeal to the congregation for such faith as had characterized Israel in the greatest moments of its historic past.

> 42 For He remembered His holy word
>   To Abraham His servant.
> 43 And He brought out His people in exultation,
>   His chosen ones with singing.
> 44 He gave them the lands of the nations;
>   And they took possession of what the peoples had acquired,
> 45 In order that they might keep His statutes
>   And observe His laws.

The congregation then lifts the glad cultic cry:

> Hallelujah!

Ps. 106. A GENERAL CONFESSION FOR THE DIASPORA

Ps. 106 is a congregational lament. It is in the form of a general confession for Israel. But the main feature of the psalm is a narrative of Israel's history. Accordingly, we classify it as a hymn of God's revelation in history. The psalmist singles out those episodes which reveal the sins of the past and the amazing mercy and forgiveness of God. We move from Israel's sin to God's anger, then to His forgiving mercy. The theme of the whole psalm is the confession expressed in verse 6, which gives a remarkable statement of Israel's sense of solidarity with the past, "We have sinned along with our fathers." The psalm is a public liturgy which begins with a brief hymn of praise (vss. 1-3), the closing verse of which is a beatitude, an indirect way of praising God.[56] This leads to a petition (vss. 4-5), of which the closing verse of the psalm is the climax, that the Lord's people, now in exile, may share ultimately in the prosperity of the Palestinian community. Distinctive for this psalm is that it was rendered in a congregation of the Diaspora. The author made use of the narrative of the Hexateuch inclusive of the priestly document. The Chronicler, who wrote around 300 B.C., had this psalm before him along with the doxology (vs. 48) which closes the fourth book of the Psalter (I Chr. 16:34-36=Pss. 106:1, 47, 48).

The life setting for the rendering of such a psalm is portrayed in I Kings 8:46-53. A congregation of the Diaspora "bethink themselves in the land whither they are carried captive, . . . saying 'We have sinned and have done perversely; we have dealt wickedly.'" They return unto God with all their heart and with all their soul in the land of their enemies who carried them captive, and pray unto the Lord toward their land and toward the Temple.

The brief hymn which introduces the liturgy praises the Lord for His merciful goodness and, in the form of a rhetorical question, for His mighty deeds. It lauds Him indirectly through the pronouncement of a beatitude upon His just and righteous worshipers.

> 1 Give thanks to the Lord, for He is good,
>   For his lovingkindness endures forever.
> 2 Who can utter the mighty deeds of the Lord;
>   Who can sound aloud all his praise?
> 3 Oh the happiness of those who observe justice,
>   Who do righteousness at all times!

The present suppliants are clearly far away from the community of the Lord's worshipers in the Palestinian homeland. They are of those who are now among the nations (vs. 47), yet they definitely feel themselves to be part of Israel, and they pray that they may not be forgotten, that the Lord may take thought for them as well as for His Jerusalem community. They beseech Him that they too may experience His help, and that in some future day they may not merely learn from hearsay but see with their own eyes and glory in the prosperity yet to come to His people in the homeland. Tenderly they call the Palestinian community His "property"! So they pray:

> 4 Remember us when acceptance comes [57] to Thy people;
>   Be mindful of us when Thy salvation comes,

---

[56] Gunkel, *Einleitung*, p. 55.

[57] Cf. Ehrlich, *op. cit.*, pp. 261-62, who maintains that the clause refers to the time of God's favor which His people will experience.

5 So that we may see the prosperity of Thy chosen ones,
  So we may rejoice in the gladness of Thy people,
  So we may triumph, along with Thy property.

Now for the first time there sounds forth the central note which we hear as a solemn undertone throughout the psalm. From the days of exile on into latest Judaism this was the characteristic temper of its deepest religious spirit, the acknowledgment and confession of sin. Distinctive here, however, and likewise remarkable is the thought that we, the present generation, share in the sin and in the guilt of our fathers. The psalmist here acknowledges the solidarity of God's people across the generations. The depth of the penitence felt is revealed in the three differing terms employed for sin.

6 We have sinned along with our fathers;
  We have committed iniquity; yes, we have acted wickedly.

This general confession of sin now is particularized in the wonderful story of her past, of which Israel never tired. It is now told, partly to teach the present Israel about the rock from which they were hewn, but more particularly to lay hold upon the energies of God and move Him to save His people. The psalmist takes for granted the general familiarity of the worshipers with the episodes to which reference is made. In every historical reference there is the implication that the ancient sin is still a perilous factor in the Israel of the psalmist's day.

The first period of history touched upon opens in Egypt with the wonderful events of the Exodus. But, alas, Israel took these mighty events for granted, not accepting them as the expression of God's lovingkindness, but even rebelling against Him at the Sea of Reeds when they doubted His power to save them (Exod. 14:10-14). The psalmist uses the ancient name *Elyon* for his God, which had its origin in Canaan. It is the sin of forgetting what the Lord did that is here recalled. Yet God, moved by regard for His own repute, even as He had once dealt with the chaotic waters at creation, rebuked the sea so that His people could pass through on dry ground (Exod. 14:21-22), just as though it were wilderness. So the Lord rescued His people from the pursuing Egyptians by causing the waters to return and destroy them. Consequently Israel believed in God's presence and power and sang praises to Him (Exod. 14:21–15:1).

7 Our fathers in Egypt
  Did not reflect on Thy wonders:
  They did not remember the abundance of Thy lovingkindness;
  They rebelled against the Most High at the Sea of Reeds.
8 But He saved them for His name's sake,
  In order to make known His strength.
9 And He rebuked the Sea of Reeds, and it dried up;
  Then [He] led them through the waters as through the wilderness,
10 And delivered them from the hand of the foe,
  And redeemed them from the power of the enemy.

11 Then He covered the sea with their foes;
      Not one of them was left.
12 So they believed His words;
      Then they sang His praise.

The next period dealt with is that of the wilderness wanderings, and the sins to which attention is directed are the doubt of God's provision and the intemperate use of His blessings. All too quickly Israel forgot what God had done in their behalf. In their impatience they did not wait for Him to supply their needs but lusted for food and doubted that He would provide. Yet, answering their request he sent them quails. Their reprehensible lust for these, however, brought on a flesh-diminishing sickness, a wasting of the larynx (Num. 11:18-20, 31-34).

13 Quickly they forgot His deeds
      And did not wait for His counsel.
14 But they surrendered themselves to unseemly lust in the wilderness,
      And put God to the test in the desert.
15 So he gave to them that which they asked,
      And he sent a wasting disease into their bodies.

The next sin of which the people were guilty was rebellion against their appointed leaders. Dathan and Abiram rose up against the authority of Moses as leader and sheik of the community. They had charged him with self-importance, self-seeking, and with favoritism toward the priestly guild of Levi, of which Aaron, according to the Priestly Code, was the head. The rebellion was put down, and the ancient story tells that an earthquake consumed the two leaders of it, and fire devoured their followers (Num. 16). So the psalmist says:

16 Now they were envious of Moses in the camp,
      Of Aaron, the holy one of the Lord.
17 The earth opened up and swallowed Dathan,
      And it covered up the clique of Abiram.
18 Then the fire consumed their company;
      Flame set the wicked ablaze.

The next historical episode has to do with the sin of idolatry, the worship at Horeb of the golden calf in place of the Lord; thus, as Jeremiah says, they "changed their glory for that which is useless" (2:11) and so forgot Him, who in the land of Ham (the poetic name for Egypt) had saved them from bondage. But when the Lord threatened to destroy them (Deut. 9:25; Exod. 32:10), Moses interceded with Him on their behalf (Exod. 32:30-32), standing between them and destruction, even as a brave soldier might take his stand in the breach made in a city wall by a foe.

19 They made a calf in Horeb,
      And they worshiped a molten image.
20 And they exchanged their Glory
      For an image of an ox that eats grass.

21 They forgot God, their Saviour,
      Who did great things in Egypt,
22 Wonders in the land of Ham,
      Awesome things at the Sea of Reeds.
23 And He said He would destroy them
      If Moses were not His chosen one.
    He stood in the breach before Him,
      To turn back His wrath so it could not destroy them.

The next episode that the psalmist interprets is Israel's faithless rejection of the advice of the spies Joshua and Caleb to conquer the desirable land of Canaan (Num. 14:4-10). It was the sin of failing to show the spirit of venture. They criticized the plan to invade the land, grumbling in their tents (Deut. 1:27) and disobeying the command to take possession. So the Lord swore that He would overthrow them even while they were still in the wilderness (Num. 14:29) and scatter their descendants among the nations (Deut. 4:27; Lev. 26:33).

24 But they rejected the desirable land
      And did not believe His word.
25 And they grumbled in their tents
      And did not listen to the voice of the Lord.
26 So He lifted His hand against them
      To overthrow them in the wilderness,
27 To scatter their descendants among the nations,
      To disperse them among the lands.

The next section (vss. 28-31) has to with the sin of easy surrender to an immoral environment and deals with the first contact the Israelites had with the type of cultic immorality which was characteristic of the worship of *Baal Peor* in the old Amorite region of southern Canaan. This happened at Shittim, opposite Jericho, just before their crossing the Jordan into Canaan. The psalmist views this cult as the worship of the dead, to the Jews especially despicable and abhorrent to the Lord. As a consequence a plague broke out among the Israelites. Phinehas, grandson of Aaron, with courageous initiative put an end to a particularly bold and flagrant pair of idolaters, and the plague was stopped (Num. 25:1-9). Phinehas' righteous deed redounds to his priestly descendants in perpetual honor (Num. 25:11-13).

28 And they attached themselves to Baal Peor,
      And ate sacrifices to the dead.
29 So they provoked Him to anger by their deeds,
      And a plague broke out among them.
30 Then Phinehas stood up and interposed,
      And the plague was restrained.
31 So it was ascribed to him as righteousness
      From generation to generation forever.

The next episode is that which occurred at Meribah, near Kadesh. Because there was no water, Moses' followers rose up in grumbling revolt against him. The sin of the people was doubt of the provision of God for their needs. But the sin of Moses, with which the psalmist is here more concerned, was that which withheld him from entering the promised land (Num. 20:12; Deut. 3:26-27) — that is, his lack of faith in the divine omnipotence (Num. 20:10). This led him to utter to the people indiscreet words (Num. 27:14; Deut. 32:51). And by the obstinancy of the people (Num. 20:3-10) the spirit of Moses was embittered.

> 32 They provoked Him to wrath by the waters of Meribah,
>   And it went ill with Moses on their account;
> 33 For they had embittered his spirit,
>   So he had spoken rashly with his lips.

The next section (vss. 34-39) has to do with sins committed in Canaan, the root sin being that of unholy compromise. According to all the ancient traditions of J, E, D, and P, respectively, the Israelites were not to make treaties with the Canaanites, but were to drive them out so that they would not be influenced by the Canaanite civilization (Exod. 34:11; Exod. 23:32-33; Deut. 7:1-3; Josh. 23:12). But this command the Israelites disobeyed and intermingled with the Canaanites, absorbing their ways, their idols, and cultic practices. Child sacrifice, the blood purge of innocent men (II Kings 21:16), and immorality rooting in idolatrous religious rites are especially mentioned.

> 34 They did not exterminate the peoples
>   As the Lord had commanded them.
> 35 But they mingled with the nations
>   And learned their deeds.
> 36 They served their idols,
>   So they became a snare to them.
> 37 They sacrificed their sons
>   And their daughters to demons.
> 38 They poured out innocent blood,
>   So the land was polluted with blood.
> 39 And they became unclean in their deeds,
>   Committing fornication in their practices.

Then comes a section (vss. 40-43) which deals with the Lord's anger against His people as evidenced in their defeat and exile. Although He often delivered them, this was only to be met again by their rebellion. This section is permeated with the Deuteronomic conception of Israel's history, which is given in its earliest summary in Judg. 2:11-23. It is a conception which is profoundly influenced by prophetic religion, and which views Israel's history as being indissolubly linked with issues of morality and religion.

> 40 So the anger of the Lord burned against His people,
>   And He abhorred His property.

41 Then He gave them over to the power of the nations,
    And those who hated them ruled over them.
42 So their enemies oppressed them,
    And they were subdued under their hand.
43 Many times He saved them,
    But they repeatedly rebelled against His counsel.

Then as the psalmist approaches the end of his work, he comes closer home. We catch his implicit appeal to the present generation. We feel the purpose and the power of such hymns of God's revelation in history. So he deals (vss. 44-46) with the alleviation of the situation in which the exiles now find themselves. The Lord sees and hears their cry of entreaty in their present need (I Kings 8:28). There is here an implied appeal to them to pray; then the Lord, aware of their covenant rights (Lev. 26:42), will hear, and those who are now in the presence of their captors will be recipients of His redemptive mercy. The words of I Kings 8:48-53 finely portray the psychological situation.

44 When He saw their distress,
    When He heard their cry of entreaty,
45 He remembered His covenant with them
    And was sorry in accordance with the greatness of His mercy;
46 So He made them objects of His compassion
    In the presence of all their captors.

The psalm comes to its end in a petition which turns from the present (vss. 4-5) to the future and longs for the restoration of the scattered Diaspora to Jerusalem, where they may praise Him in His sanctuary. Verse 48 is a doxology which closes the entire fourth book of the Psalter.

47 Save us, O Lord our God,
    And gather us together out of the nations
    To give thanks to Thy holy name,
    To boast in Thy glory.

48 Blessed be the Lord, the God of Israel,
    From everlasting to everlasting,
    And let all the people say: "Amen!"
    Hallelujah!

Ps. 114. TREMBLE AT THE PRESENCE OF THE LORD

Ps. 114 is one of the "Hallel" (Pss. 113–118), which were treated in Jewish liturgy as one psalm and were known by heart. The whole group was sung at the great festivals in the Temple, a practice which was taken over from the Temple into the synagogue. But originally it is most likely that this psalm was intended for rendering at the Festival of Passover, inasmuch as its major theme is the revelation of the Lord at the exodus of Israel from Egypt.

It is, accordingly, a hymn of God's revelation in history. No historical character is mentioned. Neither Moses nor Joshua comes into the poet's pictures. There is but one great actor in Israel's drama, the Lord Himself. For behind all human history, and uniquely behind Israel's history, is God. The author is a poet, one of the finest in the Psalter. There is an unstudied naïveté in his work. With sensitive, awestruck eyes he views the mighty moments of his people's past. Nature is personified: the Sea of Reeds flees; the river Jordan turns back; the mountainous range and the foothills of Sinai skip like rams and lambs of the flock, trembling in response to God's voice. With light, deft touch, yet with insight born of brooding, he makes use of the sacred legends of Israel's mighty past. Yet in mere history as such he has little interest. It is history as it reveals God that moves him to write.

Moreover, without saying much about it he paints a Palestinian springtime with skipping lambs among the rocky, green-clad fields. Suggestively Welch says, "The psalmist was a Jew steeped in the ideals of his people; he was also a man with his feet among the springing grass of a Passover morning." [58] Yet here again it is not nature primarily that interests him, but nature sensitively responding to the reality of the divine Presence. In his psalm "awestruck nature recognized and obeyed its Master's will." His poem shows great individuality and independence.

The opening section sets in at the point of the exodus of Israel, the house of Jacob, from the barbarous-tongued Egyptians. In a great sweep of centuries he pictures Israel as having now become two kingdoms. Judah is spoken of first, because the author is himself a Judean, and because it contains the Lord's sanctuary—and Israel is called the Lord's realm," the dominion over which He exercises rule. It was at the Exodus that God chose Israel (Hos. 11:1), later to become the kingdoms of Judah and Israel. So the psalmist sings in rhythmic parallel lines:

> 1 When Israel went forth out of Egypt,
>   The house of Jacob from a people of barbarous tongue,
> 2 Judah became His sanctuary;
>   Israel became His realm.

In the next portion the psalmist refers to the legend of Exod. 14:21, which tells how the Lord caused the sea to go back by a strong east wind all night and made the sea dry land, and the waters were divided. He likewise makes implicit reference to the legend of Josh. 3:14-17, which tells how the waters of the Jordan were driven back, that is, they "stood, rising up in one heap." He also has in mind the legend of the giving of the law on Mount Sinai, with the consequent earthquake that took place when God descended upon it in fire (Exod. 19:18). He compares the quaking ranges and their foothills to the skipping of rams and lambs. Thus he portrays nature's reaction to the mighty events of the Exodus and of the giving of the law:

[58] *Op. cit.,* p. 88.

3 The sea saw and fled;
  The Jordan turned about backwards.
4 The mountains skipped like rams,
  The little hills like lambs.

With charming, childlike naïveté the psalmist imaginatively addresses the Sea of Reeds, the River Jordan, the mountains and foothills of Sinai, and asks, "What was it in these epochal events that so set you into commotion?"

5 What happened to you, O sea, that you fled;
  O Jordan, that you turned back;
6 You mountains, that you skipped like rams;
  You little hills like lambs?

And the psalmist answers his own question. Sea, river, mountains, and hills were all set atremble because God was there—the mighty God who at Rephidim provided for His people water from the rock. The reference is to the story of Exod. 17:1-6; Num. 20:1-11; and Deut. 8:15.

So the psalmist, speaking to the assembled congregation, says to the worshipers: God is *now* here, still able in power, mighty in provision. He can still bring a fountain out of flint! The theme of this historical hymn is verse 7, and the stress is on the real and potent presence of the Lord, Jacob's (Israel's) God. Thus the most important part of the hymn is withheld until the last two verses, and the effect is extraordinarily impressive.

7 Before the presence of the Lord tremble, O earth,
  Before the presence of the God of Jacob,
8 Who turns the rock into a pool of water,
  The flint into a spring of water.

The note of release is strong in this psalm, and Dante's interpretation of it is spiritually suggestive when he says:

Now if we regard the letter alone, it signifies the going out from Egypt of the children of Israel in the time of Moses; if the allegory, it signifies our redemption by Christ; if the moral meaning, it signifies the conversion of the soul from the grief and misery of sin to the state of grace; if the anagogical,[59] it signifies the departure of the holy soul from the servitude of this corruption to the freedom of eternal glory.[60]

3. Hymns of the Revelation of God in the Law

The hymns of the revelation of God in the law likewise came from scholarly minds in Israel. The priests, among whom the scholars were to be found, had as their sphere of activity, responsibility, and interest the knowledge of God (see Hos. 4:6; Mal. 2:7a). They functioned as imparters and administrators of that knowledge primarily through the Torah, which means direction, instruc-

[59] That is, mystical, secondary, spiritual meaning.
[60] *Purgatorio,* Canto II, lines 45 ff.

tion, teaching, and thus comes to mean law, which is the embodiment of that priestly counsel in codes, rituals, and procedures. The law was primarily the instrument through which the priest functioned (Jer. 18:18; Mal. 2:7b).

While the origin of Israelite law goes back to around 1200 B.C., the earliest law representing an accepted and authoritative body of divine requirements for the nation is that of Deuteronomy. It dates in origin from around 650 B.C. and was inaugurated as the basis of Judean life in 621 B.C., when the kernel of the book of Deuteronomy served as the documentary basis of a reform carried out by King Josiah. This was a prophetic law book which attempted to restate the social and religious ideals of the eighth-century prophets in terms of legal requirements upon Judah. From this time on Judah was "the people of the book."

A yet more significant step in this direction was taken in 397 B.C., when Ezra the scribe, coming from Babylon, introduced the Priestly Code and made it binding upon the people of Israel. It had no political aim, for such would have been interpreted by the dominant Persians as political revolt. But including as it did the noble Code of Holiness (Lev. 17–26), which dates from shortly after Ezekiel's time and was largely inspired by him, its aim through both its moral and ceremonial requirements was to make of Israel a holy people. Israel was thus to become a church within an empire, rallying the people of God around the Temple, its priests, and its rituals.

Legalism as we know it from the Judaism of the first century A.D. does not appear in its best light in the criticisms of Jesus and Paul. The psalms of God's revelation through the law are an illuminating corrective to this. They help us to see the true beauty and the lofty spiritual values of life under the law as the religious leaders of Judaism envisioned it.

The zeal for the law that characterized the Judaism which produced these psalms has been sensitively grasped and accurately expounded by Moore in his interpretation of the "cornerstone of Judaism." Says he:

> The cornerstone of Judaism is the idea of revealed religion. God has not only made himself known to men, but has declared to them his will for man's whole life. This revelation the Jews possess in their Holy Scriptures and in its complement, the unwritten Law. There is no duty towards God or man which is not either expressly or by plain implication contained in this twofold revelation. The study of God's law is therefore the first duty of every Jew, for upon knowledge of God's will the keeping of it depends.[61]

The worship setting in ancient Israel in which such psalms were at home would be chiefly the Festival of Weeks, or Harvest, which came to be associated in Judaism with the giving of the law. They would likewise be appropriate at the Festival of Tabernacles, which emphasized the annual renewal of God's covenant with Israel. They are Pss. 19:7-14 and 119.

---

[61] *History of Religions*, II, 68-69.

Ps. 19:7-14. LIFE UNDER THE LAW

Ps. 19:7-14, probably originally an independent psalm, is a hymn of the Lord's revelation in the law. In this psalm and in Ps. 119 we have excellent illustrations of that most characteristic emphasis of postexilic Judaism as it developed in the fourth and third centuries B.C., following the introduction of the priestly law by Ezra about 397 B.C.—the zeal for the law.

A notable feature of the psalm is the sevenfold appearance of the name of Israel's God (i.e., Yahweh), which is intended to suggest the perfection of His revelation. The psalmist has carefully and with purposive artistry created this poem and views it as the devout musing of his own heart toward God. As such he prays that the words and thoughts that have issued in his psalm may be acceptable to God as his offering, his sacrifice.

The psalm opens with the praise of the law (vss. 7-9). It is also an indirect praise of God, for that which gives the law distinction is that it gives expression to the divine will. For each line of his poem the psalmist has a characterizing word for the law and tells how the law, seen from that particular point of view, may be described. In the first four lines he also tells what the law, viewed respectively from each of those pertinent angles, accomplishes in the life of him who thus studies, loves, and observes it. The six terms used for the law are: (a) law, (b) testimony, (c) precepts, that is, things appointed, (d) commandments, (e) word, and (f) ordinances. The law thus conceived is described respectively as: (a) sound, entire, complete; (b) trustworthy, reliable, verified; (c) just; (d) clean, clear, pure; (e) declaring (ceremonially) pure and (vs. 9a) being forever valid; and (f) true and (vs. 9b), viewed as a whole, righteous. The law so conceived and described respectively (a) refreshes the spirit, (b) gives wisdom to the teachable, (c) brings joy to the heart, (d) brings illumination to the eyes of the mind, and (e and f) brings a sense of abiding, dependable effectiveness in life.

7 The law of the Lord is sound, refreshing the soul;
   The testimony of the Lord is trustworthy, making the open-minded wise.
8 The precepts of the Lord are just, rejoicing the heart:
   The commandment of the Lord is clean, illuminating the eyes.
9 The word of the Lord is pure, forever valid:
   The ordinances of the Lord are true [and], taken all together, are righteous.

After this objective praise of the law the poet, addressing himself directly to God (see vs. 11), acknowledges what the law means to him personally. We feel here the sincere note of precious experience. In material comparisons—such as the value of refined gold and the sweetness of honey as it exudes fresh from the honeycomb—he expresses his sense of its value to him. Then, leaving figures of

speech behind, he tells of admonition he has received from the Lord's commandments and reward won in consequence of obeying them.

> 10 They are more desirable than gold,
>   Yes, more than much refined gold;
>   And sweeter are they than honey,
>   Yes, honey exuding from the comb.
> 11 Moreover, Thy servant is admonished by them;
>   The consequence of observing them is great reward.

In verses 12-13, still addressing himself to God, the psalmist opens to us yet
more frankly his experience in trying to live a life of obedience to the law. He
knows that he goes astray from the path God would have him take. There are
errors in his life, mistakes not of intent; guilt is also there, hidden even from
himself, yet needing the forgiveness of God. But far more serious than this, he
knows in his own heart the boiling up of a rebellious will which often leads him
to take the reins of his life presumptuously into his own hands. And he knows
of times when the rule of his own evil will has displaced the divine dominion.
If God would but withhold him from such presumption, then he would be guilty
of no great sin.

> 12 As to errors, who can discern [them]?
>   Free me from guilt of hidden sins.
> 13 Also hold back Thy servant from overweening self-confidence;
>   Let it not have dominion over me:
>   Then I shall be unimpaired and innocent
>   Of great transgression.

The psalmist brings his hymn to a close in one of the classic prayers of the
Psalter. He uses a term familiar in the priestly ritual, the word "acceptable." To
be made acceptable to God, he is told by his law that he must bring the properly
prescribed offering (Lev. 1:3), which will then be acceptable, pleasing unto God
(Isa. 56:7). So the psalmist lifts up to God, his Rock, his Redeemer, this very
psalm that he has written, the product of his pen, the sincere utterance of his
mouth, the honest, meditative brooding of his heart. This is his sacrifice, his
offering unto God. May God receive both it and him!

> 14 May the words of my mouth and the meditation of my heart
>   Be acceptable before Thee, O Lord, my Rock and my Redeemer!

Ps. 119. THE LAW AS A LIGHT AND A LIFT

This psalm is the most extensive poem of the Psalter. It is an acrostic of 176
verses. In form it is a perfect creation of artistry, for it is composed of twenty-two
stanzas, a stanza for each of the twenty-two letters of the Hebrew alphabet, taken
in accurate order. But instead of merely each stanza's beginning with the appropriate letter of the alphabet, every one of the eight lines composing each stanza
begins with the proper letter.

One single theme binds the psalm's 176 verses together—praise of the law. The psalmist feels not in the least the burden of the law. He loves it; it inspires him beyond words. It is his joy, his recreation, his diversion. In the midst of persecution, misunderstanding, and trouble of every kind it is his study of the law that holds him steady and brings him through.

He is a student of the psalms. Moreover, he makes use of almost every type of literary form to be found in the Psalter, but he turns each toward the law. He writes probably from the late Persian period, approximately in the first half of the fourth century B.C. His words reveal that there are two major parties in Judaism—the devout, loyal worshipers of the Lord and the arrogant, wicked evildoers. He is himself a representative of and a spokesman for the godly, who are few; certainly they are in the minority. Writing in the period when the priestly law introduced by Ezra in 397 B.C. was gaining steadily in recognition and authority for the community, still he does not turn his back on the religious lyric as a medium of expression. As Gunkel discerningly says, "He did not wish to break with tradition but to extend it. He did not feel himself to be in opposition to the religion of the psalmists but rather their loyal student. He lived in the religious lyrics of his people, and out of their fullness he created with joy." [62] He utilizes the psalm themes as the foundation for his own poem, but turns them all to the glorification of the law. Thus he opens to the religious lyric a new sphere of use. He uses ten different terms for law: law, testimonies, ways, precepts, statutes, commandments, judgment, word (words), ordinances, fear.

Since there is considerable repetition of ideas and sameness of thought in this psalm, a complete translation of each portion will be given, then a brief discussion of what seems most characteristic or most striking in each, and each section will be entitled accordingly.

LIVING WITHOUT SHAME

א 1 Oh the happiness of the blameless in life who walk in the law of the Lord!
2 Oh the happiness of those who keep His solemn charges, who seek Him with all their heart!
3 Who also do no injustice, who walk in His ways.
4 Thou hast commanded Thy charges to be diligently kept.
5 Oh that my conduct were fixed so as to keep Thy statutes!
6 Then I would not be ashamed when I look at all Thy commandments.
7 I will thank Thee in uprightness of heart when I learn Thy righteous judgments.
8 Thy word will I faithfully keep; do not forsake me!

Verses 5-6: The psalmist longs that his conduct may steadily be consistent with God's law. Then whenever he looks squarely at the requirements of God, his moral nature will feel no sense of shame.

[62] *Die Psalmen,* p. 514.

KEEPING LIFE CLEAN

ב 9 How can a young man keep his life clean? By keeping in accord with Thy word.

10 With my whole heart I have sought thee; let me not swerve from Thy commands.

11 I have treasured up Thy words in my heart so as not to sin against Thee.

12 Blessed art Thou, O Lord, for Thou dost teach me Thy prescriptions.

13 With my lips I recount all the decisions of Thy mouth.

14 I exult in the way of Thy charges more than over all riches.

15 I will meditate upon Thy charges, and I will look unto Thy paths.

16 I take delight in Thy law; I will not forget Thy word.

Verse 11: He has learned by heart great words of the law and has treasured them in the chambers of his memory. His reason for doing this is that by positive commitment to such standards he may be safeguarded from sinning against God and may thus keep his life clean.

ILLUMINATION

ג 17 Deal well with Thy servant that I may live, and I will keep Thy word.

18 Open my eyes that I may see wonders from Thy law.

19 A pilgrim am I in the earth; hide not Thy words from me.

20 My soul is crushed with longing for Thy judgments at all times.

21 Thou dost rebuke the presumptuous; cursed are those who go astray from Thy commandments.

22 Roll off from me insult and contempt, for I have observed Thy charges.

23 Although even princes sit and speak against me, Thy servant meditates on Thy prescriptions.

24 Yes, Thy charges are my delight; Thy statutes are my counselors.

Verse 18: Over against blindness of moral vision the psalmist prays for that inner illumination of soul that will make clear to him the true meaning of the ideas, aims, and bearings of the law.

RUNNING IN THE MARKED PATH

ד 25 My body cleaves to the dust; restore me according to Thy word.

26 I recounted my ways, and Thou didst answer me; teach me Thy statutes.

27 Instruct me about the mode of life of Thy precepts, and I will muse upon Thy wonders.

28 My soul weeps itself away because of grief; raise me up in accordance with Thy promise.

29 Turn aside from me the way of falsehood, and point out to me Thy law.

30 I have chosen the way of faithfulness; I long for Thy ordinances.

31 I cling to Thy solemn charges; O Lord, let me not be ashamed.

32 I run the way of Thy commandments, for Thou hast enlarged my heart.

Verse 32: The Lord has granted the psalmist a broad, mind-expanding insight as regards God's requirements. Accordingly the psalmist follows that path.

The Reward of the Good Way

ה 33 Teach me, O Lord, the way of Thy statutes; if I keep it I shall have
reward.

34 Instruct me that I may keep Thy law and wholeheartedly observe it.

35 Lead me in the path of Thy commandments; for I delight in it.

36 Incline my heart to Thy injunctions and not to unjust gain.

37 Turn away my eyes from seeing frivolity; revive me by Thy word.

38 Carry out for Thy servant Thy word, which belongs to those who fear
Thee.

39 Take away my reproach, which I fear, for Thy judgments are good.

40 Lo, I long for Thy precepts; revive me by Thy righteousness.

Verse 33: The psalmist is motivated, as is often the case in psalms of the law,
by the hope for reward. But his reward is dependent upon his obedience to the
way of life to which God's statutes point. Accordingly he prays that the Lord
may teach him that way.

Liberty Through Law

ו 41 Let Thy grace come upon me, O Lord, Thy salvation according to Thy
promises,

42 That I may respond to him who taunts me with an answer; for I trust
in Thy word.

43 Let not the word of truth be withdrawn from my mouth, for I wait for
Thy judgment.

44 Then will I observe Thy law continuously for ever and ever.

45 Then I will walk about at liberty, for I follow Thy statutes.

46 And I will utter Thy solemn charges before kings and will not be
ashamed.

47 And I will delight myself in Thy commandments, which I love greatly.

48 And I will lift up my hands to Thee and will muse on Thy enactments.

Verse 45: The psalmist thinks of the law of God, not as something that re-
strains him or hems him in, but as something which, when observed, sets him
free and opens to him a larger, fuller life.

Singing Where You Live

ז 49 Remember Thy word to Thy servant, because of which I have waited.

50 This is my comfort in my affliction, that Thy word has revived me.

51 The presumptuous have scorned me greatly; from Thy commandments
I have not turned aside.

52 I remember Thy judgments from of old, O Lord, and I am comforted.

53 Raging took hold of me because of the wicked, those who have forsaken Thy law.

54 Thy statutes were songs to me in the house where I sojourn.

55 I remember at night Thy name, O Lord, and Thy law in the night
watch.

56 This is my experience, that I have kept Thy precepts.

Verse 54: The psalmist feels the brevity of time. He is but a sojourner in life and has no permanent dwelling. But wherever he dwells he sings! And the theme content of his songs centers in the priceless boon to himself and his people—God's law. Here is an interesting indication that such songs as make up this psalm were thus often sung by private individuals in their homes.[63]

Considering, Then Taking God's Ways

נ 57 The Lord is my possession; I have promised to keep Thy word.

58 I have entreated Thy favor with my whole heart; be gracious to me according to Thy word.   .

59 I have considered Thy ways, and I turn my feet toward Thy charges.

60 I have hastened and have not delayed to keep Thy commandments.

61 The cords of wicked men have surrounded me, but Thy law I have not forgotten.

62 In the middle of the night I arise to praise Thee because of Thy righteous judgments.

63 I am a comrade of all who fear Thee, and who keep Thy commandments.

64 The earth is full of Thy mercy, O Lord; teach me Thy statutes.

Verse 59: The psalmist has submitted the Lord's ways, as outlined in His laws, to careful study, to earnest consideration. But he goes further than mere consideration of God's ways, for he sets his feet toward them and starts to follow them.

Learning Through Affliction

ט 65 Rightly hast Thou dealt with Thy servant, O Lord, according to Thy word.

66 Teach me discernment and knowledge, for I trust in Thy commandments.

67 Before I was afflicted I was in error, but now I keep Thy word.

68 Good art Thou and doest rightly; teach me Thy statutes.

69 Presumptuous men have plastered me over with falsehood, but as for me, with all my heart I keep Thy charges.

70 Their heart is dense like fat, but as for me, I take delight in Thy charges.

71 It is good for me that I have been afflicted, in order that I might learn Thy judgments.

72 The law of Thy mouth is more valuable for me than thousands of gold and silver.

Verses 67 and 71: The psalmist has lived in error. Affliction of some kind has come upon him, and through it he has become aware of God's laws, so now he lives a life of faithful obedience to the divine requirements. God, who has thus disciplined and taught him, he acknowledges to be good (vs. 68), and he accepts the discipline itself as something good.

[63] Cf. Gunkel, *Einleitung*, p. 67.

Divine Discipline Through Affliction

, 73 Thy hands have made me and established me: teach me Thy commandments.

74 Those who fear Thee see me and rejoice because I wait for Thy word.

75 I know, O Lord, that Thy judgments are righteous, and that Thou dost afflict me in faithfulness.

76 Pray, let Thy kindness comfort me, according to Thy word to Thy servant.

77 Let Thy mercies come upon me that I may live; for Thy law is my delight.

78 May the presumptuous be ashamed, for by fraud they have deprived me of justice, but as for me, I muse on Thy charges.

79 May those who fear Thee turn to me, even those who know Thy laws.

80 Let my heart be perfect in Thy statutes, in order that I may not be ashamed.

Verse 75: The psalmist feels himself under severe affliction, which he humbly and resignedly accepts as proceeding from the righteous God, who only in this severe way can express to him His loyalty and faithfulness.

Persecuted but Faithful

כ 81 My soul pines away for Thy salvation; for Thy word I wait.

82 My eyes long for Thy promise, saying, "How long till Thou wilt comfort me?"

83 Although I have been like a wineskin in the smoke, I have not forgotten Thy statutes.

84 How many will be the days of Thy servant? How long ere Thou wilt execute judgment upon those persecuting me?

85 The presumptuous have dug pits for me, those who do not live according to Thy law.

86 All Thy commandments are truth; they pursue me wrongfully; help me!

87 They have almost exterminated me from the earth, yet I have not abandoned Thy charges.

88 Revive me in accordance with Thy mercy, and I will keep the charges of Thy mouth.

Verse 87: The psalmist is under fierce persecution and goes about covered with ashes and wearing dark garments. He fears extermination at the hands of his persecutors. Yet in the face of all this he is faithful to the requirements of God.

Kept Alive by the Law

ל 89 Thy word, O Lord endures forever, established like the heavens.

90 Thy promise lasts unto generation after generation; as Thou didst establish the earth, so it stands.

91 They stand until today according to Thy laws, for all are Thy servants.

92 Had not Thy law been my delight, I would have perished in my affliction.

93 Never will I forget Thy charges, for Thou didst preserve me alive by them.

94 Thine am I; save me! For I follow Thy statutes.

95 The godless lie in wait for me to destroy me, but I show myself attentive to Thy charges.

96 To all else I have seen an end, but Thy commandment has no limits at all.

Verses 92-93: The psalmist has been in great affliction at the hands of the godless and desperate men. But in his severe distress and grave peril he has remained obedient to the law, not driven by compulsion, but led by delight. It is God's beloved law that really kept him alive in those dark hours, and now in better times he declares that he will never forget it but will always attend to what it requires of him.

WISDOM OR KNOWLEDGE

ם 97 Oh how I love Thy law! All the day it is my meditation.

98 Thy commandment makes me wiser than my enemies, for it is mine forever.

99 I have more insight than all my teachers, for Thy charges are the subject of my study.

100 I have more discernment than the elderly, for I keep Thy statutes.

101 I restrain my feet from every evil way in order that I may keep Thy word.

102 I have not turned aside from Thy judgments, for Thou givest me direction.

103 How smooth are Thy words to my palate: sweeter than honey to my mouth!

104 I get understanding from Thy statutes, therefore I hate every deceitful way.

Verses 98-100: The psalmist has teachers whose instruction informs him, but in God's law he finds a teaching that gives him wisdom, insight, discernment. And this law not only is to him a subject for study, but it tells him what God's will is and inspires him to do it. How much greater is such wisdom than mere knowledge!

THE LAW AS ILLUMINATION

נ 105 Thy word is a lamp to my feet and a light to my pathway.

106 I have sworn, and I will fulfill it to keep Thy righteous judgments.

107 I am severely afflicted, O Lord; revive me according to Thy word.

108 Pray accept, O Lord, the offerings of my mouth, and teach me Thy commandments.

109 My life is continually in my hand, but I do not forget Thy law.

110 The godless have set a trap for me, but from Thy charges I do not stray.

111 Thy laws are my inheritance forever, for they are the joy of my heart.

112 Incline my heart to perform Thy statutes; the reward lasts forever.

Verse 105: The psalmist finds in his law illumination for life. It lights up the dark pathway ahead. But it is yet more practical. It lights up the near-at-hand

decision where the next step has to be taken. It is a light to the feet as well as to
the whole path.

The Righteous Appraiser of Conduct

ם 113 I hate high-sounding ideas,[64] but Thy law I love.

114 My shelter and my shield art Thou; I wait for Thy word.

115 Turn aside from me, evildoers; I intend to keep the commands of my
God.

116 Sustain me according to Thy promise that I may live, and let me not
be ashamed because of my hope.

117 Uphold me that I may be saved, and I will delight myself continually
in Thy statutes.

118 Thou dost rightly appraise all who go astray from Thy charges, for in
vain is their disguise.[65]

119 Thou dost regard all the wicked of the earth as dross; therefore I love
Thy charges.

120 My flesh bristles up from fear of Thee, but I stand in awe of Thy
judgments.

Verse 118: The psalmist has learned in experience that any attempt to disguise
our conduct before God is utterly in vain. The Lord sees through our every
make-believe and values us for what we truly are.

The Hatred of the False

ע 121 I have done justice and righteousness; abandon me not to those oppressing me.

122 Give Thy word in pledge for the good. Let not the presumptuous
wrong me.

123 My eyes pine with longing for Thy salvation and for Thy righteous
promise.

124 Deal with Thy servant in accordance with Thy mercy, and teach me
Thy statutes.

125 Thy servant am I; teach me, that I may know Thy solemn charges.

126 It is time for the Lord to act; they have broken Thy law.

127 Above everything I love Thy commandments, more than gold, yes,
than fine gold.

128 Therefore I have walked straight along in accordance with all Thy
charges; I hate every deceitful path.

Verses 127-28: The psalmist prizes the laws of God above any material value
and has put them to practice in his life, walking straight along in obedience to
them. There has resulted in his life a basic sincerity, a hatred of anything that
smacks of insincerity, which appears to be something other than it truly is.

Light from Exposition of God's Word

פ 129 Thy solemn charges are wonderful; therefore my soul keeps them.

130 The opening up of Thy word gives light, teaching the open-minded.

[64] So Ehrlich, *op. cit.*   [65] *Ibid.,* p. 318.

131   I have opened my mouth wide, and I pant, because I long for Thy commandments.

132   Turn to me and be gracious to me according to the law of Thy being toward those who love Thy name.

133   Establish my steps in accordance with Thy promise; and let not any iniquity get the mastery of me.

134   Ransom me from oppression of man, that I may keep Thy charges.

135   Make Thy face shine upon Thy servant, and teach me Thy statutes.

136   My eyes overflow with streams of tears because they do not keep Thy law.

Verse 130: To the psalmist the word of the law, the scripture, is God's word of revelation. Hence when the law is opened up, interpreted, and applied, light breaks upon the pathway of life, making God's will clear to every open-minded person who is seeking to know and do it.

The Eternal Rightness of God

137   Righteous art Thou, O Lord, and Thy judgments are just.

138   Thou dost command Thy statutes in righteousness and in deep faithfulness.

139   My zeal puts an end to me, because my adversaries forget Thy words.

140   Thoroughly purified is Thy word, and Thy servant loves it.

141   I am insignificant and despised, but I do not forget Thy charges.

142   Thy righteousness is eternal rightness, and Thy law is truth.

143   Distress and hardship have befallen me, but Thy commandments are my delight.

144   Righteous are Thy solemn charges forever: teach me that I may live.

Verse 142: The psalmist here gives a penetrating and striking statement of the truth that the righteous statutes, laws, requirements of God are not His arbitrary demands subject to whim, but they are the expression of His innermost moral character, His eternal rightness. We are reminded of Abraham's great interceding question in Gen. 18:25, "Shall not the Judge of all the earth do right?"

Before Dawn and Before Night—God

145   I cry with all my heart, answer me: I will keep Thy statutes.

146   I cry to Thee, "Save me! And I will observe Thy charges."

147   I arise in the morning twilight and cry for help; I wait for Thy word.

148   My eyes anticipate the night watches to meditate on Thy promises.

149   In Thy mercy, O Lord, hear my voice; according to the law of Thy being, revive me.

150   Those pursuing me draw near with craftiness; they are far from Thy law.

151   Thou art near by, O Lord: and all Thy commandments are true.

152   Long have I known from Thy charges that Thou dost establish them forever.

Verses 147-48: The psalmist here refers to his practices in the contemporary worship—the early morning prayer in the Temple, his cry for help, and the private prayer of meditation in the night watches. He starts in before the night begins, so eager is his spirit for God and the things of God. Here is tender heart religion, a sincere hunger for God alongside zeal for the law.

HARASSED BUT SWERVING NOT

ר 153 See my affliction and deliver me! for I have not forgotten Thy law.

154 Plead my cause and vindicate me: revive me according to Thy word.

155 Help is far distant from the wicked, for they inquire not about Thy statutes.

156 Thy mercies are great, O Lord: revive me according to the law of Thy being.

157 Those pursuing me and harassing me are many, but from Thy charges I do not swerve.

158 I have seen those who deal treacherously, and I loathe them, because they do not keep Thy commandments.

159 See that I love Thy statutes: O Lord, revive me according to Thy mercy.

160 The sum of Thy words is truth; and Thy righteous judgments last forever.

Verse 157: The psalmist is in deep distress. He has been falsely accused by godless enemies who are treacherously pursuing and harassing him. He is ill and afflicted. Yet he is loyal to God, obedient to His law, and he prays eagerly and confidently for restoration to health and for vindication at the hands of a faithful God.

A CONSTRUCTIVE ESCAPE

ש 161 Princes have persecuted me without cause, but my heart stands in awe of Thy words.

162 I exult over Thy word, as one who brings in great spoil.

163 I abhor and hate falsehood, but Thy statutes I love.

164 Seven times in the day do I praise Thee, because of Thy righteous judgments.

165 Great peace have they who love Thy law; they have no occasion for stumbling.

166 I have waited for Thy salvation, O Lord, and I have done Thy commands.

167 My soul has kept Thy solemn charges, and I love them very much.

168 I have kept Thy charges and regulations, for all my ways are before Thee.

Verses 161-62: The psalmist is suffering unmerited persecution at the hands of princes. But in his deep distress he has resorted to the study of the law; and as he reads it, his heart is filled with awe. Here is a constructive escape. He thrills to what he discovers in his study. The findings of those hours he compares to the plunder taken by a victorious warrior.

The Heart's Bubbling Fountain

ה 169 Let my cry come before Thy face, O Lord; revive me according to Thy word.

170 Let my supplication come before Thy face; save me in accordance with Thy promise.

171 My lips will pour forth a song of praise, for Thou dost teach me Thy statutes.

172 My tongue shall sing of Thy truth, for all Thy charges are righteous.

173 Let Thy hand come to help me, for I have chosen Thy statutes.

174 I long for Thy salvation, O Lord, and I delight in Thy law.

175 Let my soul live and praise Thee, and let Thy judgments help me.

176 I have erred like a lost sheep; seek for Thy servant, for I have not forgotten Thy commandments.

Verses 171-72: The psalmist's heart is a fountain of praise that bubbles forth through his lips in joy. It becomes articulate in words which give expression to God's truth, treasured in his soul. For he has been taught of God the divine will and hails God's requirements as altogether righteous.

Chapter VI

PSALM LITURGIES

LITURGY IN ITS ORIGINAL GREEK FORM MEANT PUBLIC SERVICE IN GENERAL, AND later public worship in particular. However, the term has come to suggest particularly those forms of public worship wherein there is an interchange of speakers or singers. This chapter is by no means exhaustive of the liturgical expression in the Psalter. Some psalms which were rendered liturgically may best be dealt with from the angle of their predominant thought content. But there are four types of liturgical rendition which are here interpreted: (1) liturgies of entrance, (2) liturgies of praise and thanksgiving, (3) prophetic liturgies, and (4) liturgies of supplication.

1. LITURGIES OF ENTRANCE

The liturgies of entrance have to do with the moment when the worshipers are entering the holy place. Ps. 15 is a torah (law) liturgy, which gives ten requirements, somewhat in the form of laws, which are obligatory upon the genuine worshiper of God. Such a psalm has real effectiveness as a dramatic device for religious instruction. Ps. 24 is similar to this in its central part (vss. 3-6), although its "laws" penetrate through conduct to the underlying motives. But the most distinctive thing in it is the ceremony wherein the ark of the Lord enters the sanctuary as a feature of the Hebrew New Year celebration. The question as to who should enter as worshiper, a query universally present when worship has become self-conscious, here changes to who may enter to be worshiped, an inquiry that arrestingly focuses attention upon God. Ps. 100 has in common with Ps. 24 (vss. 7-10) an emphasis upon the Temple gates. The gateway to the Temple introduces the worshiper in ancient Israel to that numinous world where in unique reality he makes contact with the presence of the living God.

Ps. 15. WHO CAN DWELL IN GOD'S HOLY HILL?

This psalm is a Temple liturgy which was used at the moment when a company of pilgrims was on the point of entering the holy place. "Tent" stands for the Temple. The term itself is a precious reminiscence reaching back to the days before Solomon. The "holy hill" is the Temple mount.

One of the most penetrating of biblical questions, next in importance to the question as to the nature of God, is, What does God require of His worshipers? The prophets raised it and answered it. For instance, Micah represented the worshiper as asking it:

> Wherewith shall I come before the Lord,
> And bow myself before the high God? (6:6.)

And a prophet, with the numinous awe of worship in his soul, asks a rhetorical question, before he answers it:

> Who among us can abide with the devouring fire?
> Who among us can dwell with everlasting burnings? [1] (Isa. 33:14.)

Such questions became pertinent and an adequate answer timely when a group of worshipers stood before the outer gate of the Temple area ready to enter, first through the outer, and thence into the inner court. It was such moments that created these Temple liturgies.

The priests of the Temple were most likely the authors of such liturgies, which were constituent parts of a beloved Temple ritual. Some of the liturgies employed the romantic motif of the ancient Temple gates (Ps. 24:7-10; Ps. 100:4; Isa. 26:2). Others laid the emphasis upon entering into the holy, awe-inspiring presence of the Judge of men (Isa. 33:14). Two of them (Pss. 15 and 24:3-6) emphasize the Temple worshiper as the *gēr* (guest) of God and remind us of a *gar Allah* in Islam, one who dwells at Mecca and has thus placed himself under the protection of Allah.[2] And we feel the intimate human background of Oriental hospitality that makes the question tender and warm as the ⁝ ⁚ʋers intone it:

> 1   Lord, who can sojourn in Thy tent?
>   And who can dwell in Thy holy hill?

From within the gates came the answer of the priests, created by them and sung by them. The question gave them just that opportunity of ethical religious instruction which the best of the priests coveted, and which was distinctly within their province, even as Malachi had said:

> The priest's lips should keep knowledge,
> And they should seek the law at his mouth. (2:7.)

In ten concentrated statements (vss. 2-5*b*) which reflect both prophetic teaching and the three great codes of law—Covenant (*ca.* 950 B.C.), Deuteronomic (*ca.* 650 B.C.), and Priestly (*ca.* 400 B.C.)—the answer is intoned by the officiating priest or the priestly choir:

> 2   He who walks in integrity and does righteousness,
>   And who speaks truth in his heart,
> 3   Who does not go about taking slander on his tongue,
>   Who does not do evil to his fellow
>   Or utter an insult against his neighbor,
> 4*b* Who honors those who fear the Lord,[3]

---

[1] Figuratively used as the judgment of God.

[2] Cf. also from Phoenician religion the personal names Ger-Melkarth, Ger-Sakun, Ger-Ashtart—"guest" of the respective deities Melkarth, Sakun, and Ashtart; see Cooke, *A Textbook of North Semitic Inscriptions*, p. 63.

[3] Transposing 4*b* and 4*a*, with Buhl.

4a But who rejects the despised in His eyes,
  Who if he has sworn does not change [it] for what is worse; [4]
5 Who does not put out his money at interest,
  And who will not take a bribe against the innocent.

It is suggestive and instructive to observe that these ten requirements may be appropriately restated as a Temple decalogue, somewhat as follows:

Thou shalt walk uprightly and do what is right.
Thou shalt speak in truthfulness of heart.
Thou shalt refrain from slanderous gossip.
Thou shalt do no evil to thy neighbor.
Thou shalt not insult thy nearest kin.
Thou shalt honor those who fear the Lord.
Thou shalt reject those whom the Lord despises.
Thou shalt not change what thou hast sworn for something worse.
Thou shalt not lend out thy money at interest.[5]
Thou shalt not accept a bribe against the innocent man.[6]

We note at once that the psalmist in every instance emphasizes, not ceremonial or ritual, but ethical requirements, and we feel the influence of the great prophets in each command. Ker, speaking of the pattern of conduct here featured, says: "It is a description of a class of men who for centuries and in every rank of life have been an honor and strength to their church and country." [7]

The worshipers, thus examined in mind and heart, now enter the inner court, and as they move forward, the officiating priest pronounces upon them the Lord's blessing of stability.

5c He who does these things shall never waver.

Ps. 24. THE ENTRANCE OF THE KING OF GLORY

This psalm is a liturgy of entrance into the sanctuary. It has three parts: verses 1-2 form a hymn of the Lord's world dominion; verses 3-6, a compact liturgy of entrance; and verses 7-10, likewise a thrilling liturgy of entrance, in which the ark of the Lord plays a significant part, especially in the ceremonies of the New Year in Israel. The noble liturgical hymn created by the fusion of these three parts is one of the most exalted and majestic in the Psalter and has fittingly found rich entrance into the anthems and solos of Judaism and Christianity.

The first part (vss. 1-2) is a hymn of praise to the Lord and in its first line celebrates Him as the owner of the physical earth and all that it includes—"its store of wonders untold"—as well as the habitable world and all who live in it. But why does God own it? Here again we see gleaming through the Hebrew

---

[4] See Lev. 27:10, 33; Mal. 1:14. Cf. Gunkel, *Die Psalmen*, p. 49.

[5] Note the striking unanimity of the great law codes on this point: the Code of the Covenant (Exod. 22:25), the Deuteronomic Code (Deut. 23:19-20), and the Priestly Code (Lev. 25:36-37).

[6] Cf. Exod. 23:8 and Deut. 27:25.   [7] *Op. cit.*, p. 29.

thoughts of creation features of primitive Semitic cosmology. Starting with the primeval watery chaos, the seas, God reduced it to order and firmly founded the earth upon that order. Once there existed floods, "the fountains of the great deep" (Gen. 7:11), "the waters under the earth" (Exod. 20:4), sometimes viewed as a crouching dragon controlling the springs (Gen. 49:25; Deut. 33:13). But upon those vast chaotic floods the Lord imposed His own mighty control and "established" the earth (vs. 2). We sense here features of the combat between these seas and floods and the Lord, which we have seen finely portrayed in Ps. 93. That combat forms the background of this brief hymn. But ethical theism has triumphed over Semitic mythology. Thus the hymn of the Lord's world dominion:

> 1 To the Lord belongs the earth and what fills it,
>   The inhabited world and those who dwell in it.
> 2 For He founded it upon the seas
>   And established it upon the floods.

The liturgy of entrance (vss. 3-6) is very similar to Ps. 15. The pilgrims stand at the entrance to the Temple. They intone the question as to who may be permitted to enter the sacred area.

> 3 Who may go up into the mountain of the Lord,
>   And who may stand in His holy place?

From within the sanctuary the priestly choir chants the answer and states the requirements of the true worshiper (v. 4). He must be morally clean in conduct and pure in heart. He must not desire to possess anything which God hates and pronounces evil. When he takes an oath he must swear in sincerity with no deceit in his heart. We are reminded of a very ancient inscription on the walls of a tomb from the Old Kingdom of Egypt: "He who enters here must be pure, and he must purify himself as one purifies himself for the temple of the great God." [8] Says the psalmist:

> 4 He that is clean in hands and pure in heart,
>   Who does not long after what is worthless,
>   And has not taken an oath in deceit.

Accepting the priestly challenge, they enter; and as they move into the inner court, the priests pronounce a blessing upon the entering worshipers, who have come to the sanctuary where the Lord, Jacob's (Israel's) God, dwells. As for the person who meets these requirements:

> 5 He shall receive a blessing from the Lord,
>   And righteousness from the God who helps him.
> 6 Such is the lot of those who seek the Lord,
>   Who seek the face of the God of Jacob.

[8] Erman, *Die Religion der Ägypter*, p. 190.

Then comes the most exalted and colorful part of the psalm, which glorifies the Lord as war God (Exod. 15:3) and "is a strain from primitive times in Israel." [9] It presents vividly a greatly beloved ritual that had a distinctive place in ceremonies connected with the annual enthronement of the Lord at the Hebrew New Year. The ark was taken from the most holy place to the foot of Mount Zion, where the procession formed. It was the most sacred symbol of the presence of the Lord, the throne of the invisible King. The ark was the glory of Israel (I Sam. 4:21-22). The King of glory was the Lord, Israel's spiritual monarch, enthroned above the cherubim (Ps. 80:1). The ceremony about to be enacted was one such as was performed as an integral part of many festivals in ancient Babylon, the ceremony of the opening of the gate by which entrance into the Temple was granted to the people.[10] That the same was true for Israel we may be confident (see Pss. 100:4; 118:19-20; Isa. 26:2). The prototype of this procession with the ark may be seen in II Sam. 6:12b-17, and especially in I Kings 8:1-7 (cf. Josh. 3:14).

The ark is borne by the priests, and the worshiping throngs follow in glad mood and in festal array, for in such a ceremony, as was the case in ancient Babylon, the populace participates with tremendous enthusiasm. The procession reaches the ancient Temple gates; already the marks of the centuries since the days of Solomon are upon these. The throngs of worshipers who are seeking entrance call out their appeal to the gates. The gates, as in Isa. 14:31, are addressed. They must lift their heads high because "the high and lofty One, . . . whose name is Holy" (Isa. 57:15), and whose "glorious throne was set on high from the beginning" (Jer. 17:12), is about to enter! The pilgrims cry:

> 7 Lift up your heads, O ye gates;
>   And be ye lifted up, ye ancient doors,
>   That the King of glory may enter!

There is a pause; then from within the Temple resounds the challenge of the priestly choir:

> 8a Who, now, is the King of glory?

The throng without, with exultant enthusiasm, thunder forth the answer:

> 8b The Lord, powerful and mighty;
> 8c   The Lord, mighty in battle!

Then again comes a pause, and in a moment the appeal is renewed by the seeking pilgrims:

> 9 Lift up your heads, O ye gates,
>   And be ye lifted up, ye ancient doors,
>   That the King of glory may enter!

---

[9] Gunkel, *Die Psalmen*, p. 103.   [10] Cf. Meissner, *op. cit.*, II, 95.

The challenge comes anew from the priestly choir within:

> 10a   **Who, then, is the King of glory?**

When the response comes, the ancient name of God, already current in Judah at least as early as the eighth century B.C. (Isa. 6:3), is thundered out by the entrance-seeking throng. It is a strain out of Israel's ancient militant faith:

> 10b   **The Lord of hosts,**
> 10c   **He is the King of glory.**

And at the first mention of this distinctive name of Israel's God the Temple gates swing open, and the worshipers enter, led by the sacred symbol of His presence.

Ps. 100. ENTER HIS GATES SINGING

This beloved psalm is a liturgy of entrance for the procession of pilgrims into the sanctuary bringing their thank offerings to the Lord. The psalm is in the form of a liturgical hymn and is rendered antiphonally by the procession of pilgrims and the priestly choir. As the pilgrims enter the outer court of the Temple, they sing a summons to praise. It is a summons to the worshipers themselves, but also a summons to all the citizens of Israel, conceived of as the Lord's land. They are to raise the glad cultic shout unto God, worshiping Him in the mood of rejoicing and with the resounding cry of singing voices:

> 1   **Shout to the Lord, all the land.**
> 2   **Serve the Lord with gladness;**
>   **Come before Him with singing.**

The theme of their glad song is threefold: (a) the Lord conceived of as one, the clearly implied belief in monotheism; (b) the Lord as Creator of His people, who accordingly belong to Him; and (c) the Lord as the Shepherd of His people, who provides for them pasture. These three themes are all characteristic thoughts of the great Prophet of the Exile, Deutero-Isaiah (ca. 540 B.C.), and the psalmist is probably indebted to him for these ideas: monotheism (Isa. 45:22), God as Creator (Isa. 42:5), and as Shepherd (Isa. 40:11).

The theme is introduced, as is frequently the case, by the imperative "know ye," and is sung by the entering pilgrims:

> 3   **Know ye that the Lord alone is God:**
>   **He has made us, and we belong to Him;**
>   **His people [are we], and the sheep of His pasturage.**

From within the sanctuary responds the priestly choir with invitation to the pilgrims to enter through the gates which lead to the inner court of the Temple. We note the three acts of worship which the pilgrims are invited to perform: to enter, to present their thank offerings, and to "adore with bended knee."[11]

---

[11] Such is the rich meaning of the familiar term "bless" when the Lord is its object. Cf. Brown, Driver, Briggs, *op. cit.*, p. 138.

Thus the priestly invitation:

> 4 Enter into His gates with a thank offering,
>   Into His courts with praise.
>   Give thanks to Him, bless His name!

Just as there is a second summons to praise in the psalm, so there is a second and profounder theme of praise—the character of God. Both are sung by the priestly choir from within the sanctuary and express the deepest elements in the character of God. The first is His goodness and reminds us of the great conclusion with which Ps. 73 opens, and of the great words of Whittier:

> Yet, in the maddening maze of things,
>   And tossed by storm and flood,
> To one fixed trust my spirit clings;
>   I know that God is good.[12]

The second is the quality in God that Hosea puts at the center of the divine nature—His lovingkindness. The third is that dependableness of character that leads men to trust Him utterly—His continuing faithfulness.

> 5 For good is the Lord; His lovingkindness endures forever,
>   And His faithfulness lasts from generation to generation.

2. Liturgies of Praise and Thanksgiving

The praise of God is one of the deepest human impulses in worship. Humanity is at its best when it honestly evaluates, prizes, and celebrates the being of God. In these psalms the keynote is praise, now of the God to whom men look up, now of the God who in mercy looks down (Ps. 113). There is antiphonal singing in them between Levitical choirs (Ps. 113), or between the Levitical choir on the one hand and the laity, priests, and proselytes who have become worshipers of the Lord on the other (Pss. 115; 135). The simplest of these is Ps. 136. There the whole psalm is a liturgical hymn by the priestly choir and the throng of the Israelite congregation, who answer every priestly strain with the universally known and beloved cultic cry. These liturgies all have a strong monotheistic note and a clear knowledge of and interest in Israel's history. They were accordingly popular and were used at all the great seasonal pilgrimage festivals.

Ps. 113. THE UPWARD AND THE DOWNWARD LOOK

This psalm is a liturgical choir hymn which was sung antiphonally by two Levitical choirs. In Jewish practice Pss. 113–118 are called the Hallel (Praise) and are designated to be sung at the pilgrimage festivals of Passover, Weeks, and Tabernacles, and at the feast of dedication of the Temple. At Passover, Pss. 113–114 were sung before, and Pss. 115–118 after, the Passover meal. It is

---

[12] From "The Eternal Goodness."

interesting to recall that probably just as Jesus and the disciples sang a hymn after they had eaten the Passover meal (Matt. 26:30) —almost certainly Pss. 115–118—so most likely before the meal they had sung Pss. 113–114.

In the Temple rendition the officiating priest addressing the two Levitical choirs intones to them the invitation to praise:

> 1　Praise, ye servants of the Lord,
> 　　Praise the name of the Lord.

The first choir answers this invitation by pronouncing a blessing upon the Lord's name, with the strong wish that it be effective from now on, even forever. It summons to praise peoples of all regions, from east to west. Their resounding praise will roll up to God where He sits in His divine glory exalted above all nations, yes, even above the heavens.

> 2　Let the name of the Lord be blessed
> 　　From now, even forever.
> 3　From the rising of the sun to its setting,
> 　　Let the name of the Lord be praised.
> 4　Exalted above all nations is the Lord;
> 　　Above the heavens is His glory.

The second Levitical choir now takes up the praise with the rhetorical question, Who in heaven or in earth can compare with the Lord? But just as the first choir had sung of their upward look at the exalted and glorious Lord, now the second choir follows the loving, searching downward look of God Himself into the deeps of the earth. It is a manward look, the exalted Lord hunting out the poorest, neediest, most humble of people, and with eyes of solicitude and love in order to lift them from their misery into honor. The Lord looks down into the deep. How pertinent are these words today, as with unwonted poignancy we hear men out of the deeps of unbelievable national, racial, and personal suffering crying unto God. Sings the choir:

> 5a　Who is like the Lord our God,
> 6b　　In heaven or in earth?
> 5b　Who sits enthroned on high,
> 6a　　Who looks down into the deep,
> 7　Who raises the poor from the dust,
> 　　Who lifts up the needy from the dunghill
> 8　To let him sit with nobles,
> 　　With the nobles of his people,
> 9　Who gives the childless a dwelling,
> 　　And makes her glad [as the] mother of children.
> 　　Hallelujah!

As they sing of the poor, the needy, and the childless, they think of their own sad lot as a people, and glory in a God able to lift them up and place them again in honor.

Ps. 115. NOT UNTO US THE GLORY

This psalm is a prayer liturgy probably originally intended for rendering at the great autumnal festival of the New Year. It is the first of a group of psalms sung in Judaism after the Passover meal, and it also was almost certainly sung by Jesus and the disciples (Matt. 26:30).

The people of postexilic Israel stand dishonored among the nations. Their consequent humiliation becomes most poignant when pagans, who know of Israel's historic pride in their God, ask in scoffing, taunting tones, "Where is your God?" Israel's petition, which originally made up the third line of verse 1, has fallen out, but it must have been some such prayer as "Save us from our enemies," and it was based upon a quality in God to which Ezekiel had taught his people to appeal: God's regard for His own holy name, that is, His own nature—merciful, compassionate, and faithful (Ezek. 36:22-23). The worshipers eschew any desire for honor to themselves, but they will have the Lord so act on behalf of His people that His fame among those now-scoffing nations may become great. The Lord's regard for His own reputation is thus made the basis of appeal for His help. So the congregation opens with an ascription of praise to God, followed by a lamenting petition:

> 1 **Not unto us, O Lord, not unto us,**
> **But unto Thy name give glory.**
> **[Save us from our enemies,]** [13]
> **Because of Thy mercy and Thy faithfulness.**
> 2 **Why do the nations say,**
> **"Where is their God?"**

This scornful question of the nations is now answered (vss. 3-8) in a choir hymn which glorifies the Lord through contrasting "our God," the God of the worshiping congregation, with "their idols," the gods of the nations. We feel the psalmist's conviction of the great superiority of the invisible God in heaven, the active Being who does what He wills, over the man-made idols. These, though existing in human form, are lifeless, having none of the senses of human beings. Such derision cast upon idolatry is but the reverse side of the praise of the Lord and accordingly belongs specifically to the hymn. [14] This portion of the psalm closes with the wish that those who make and worship idols may become like what they worship:

> 3 **But our God is in the heavens above:**
> **All in which He delights He does.**
> 4 **Their idols are silver and gold,**
> **The work of the hands of men.**
> 5 **Mouths have they, but cannot speak;**
> **Eyes have they, but cannot see;**

[13] So Briggs tentatively supplies the missing portion of ʋs. 1.
[14] Gunkel, *Einleitung*, p. 73.

6 Ears they have, but cannot hear;
   Noses they have, but cannot smell;
7 Their hands—they cannot feel;
   Their feet—they cannot walk;
   They cannot speak with their throats.
8 May those who make them become like them,
   Everyone who trusts in them!

In contrast with such trust in idols, which is so strong among the nations other than Israel, the psalm now moves into an exhortation to all the worshipers of the Lord to trust in Him. He distinguishes three groups of these: the rank and file of the Israelite laity ("house of Israel"), the priesthood ("house of Aaron") and the proselytes ("those who fear the Lord").[15] This part of the psalm is rendered antiphonally, the choir singing the first line, and each group mentioned in turn singing the response, thus securing a greatly heightened effectiveness. The use of the third person in the reference—"their" instead of "our"—implies humility and an awed sense of distance between God and man.[16]

Choir:
9 O house of Israel, trust in the Lord:

Laity:
   Their help and their shield is He.

Choir:
10 O house of Aaron, trust in the Lord:

Priests:
   Their help and their shield is He.

Choir:
11 O you who fear the Lord, trust in the Lord:

Proselytes:
   Their help and their shield is He.

From the theme of exhortation the psalm moves into that of blessing. This part is sung by the priests, whose prerogative it is to pronounce the divine blessing. Here again, as though in response to the congregation's trust in God, the blessing is pronounced, first upon all—the "us" including the entire congregation—then upon each of the three groups in turn, the laity, the priests, and the proselytes. At verse 14 it moves from the general blessing to the earnest wish that the Lord's blessing may manifest itself in the greatly needed increase of numbers in the postexilic community, which has now been restored after the devastating and dispersing catastrophe of exile. And in verse 15 the priests

---

[15] Cf. I Kings 8:41-43; Isa. 56:6-7; Acts 10:2 (Cornelius); Acts 13:16 (in Antioch of Pisidia); Acts 16:14 (Lydia). Cf. also Gunkel, *Die Psalmen,* p. 498; and Pss. 135:19-20; 118:2-4.
[16] See Schmidt, *Die Psalmen,* p. 209.

pronounce the general blessing, but emphasize that He, who thus blesses His congregation, is the mighty Creator:

12 May the Lord remember us and bless us:
      May He bless the house of Israel;
        May He bless the house of Aaron;
13 May He bless those who fear the Lord,
      The obscure along with the distinguished.
14 May the Lord increase you,
      Both you and your sons.
15 Blessed may you be of the Lord,
      Maker of heaven and earth.

The liturgy closes with a hymnic portion sung by the whole congregation, which gives itself up to joyous praise of the Lord. The psalmist thinks of three realms of existence—the highest, or heaven; the lowest, or Sheol, the realm of silence; and the inhabited world of the living. The heavens belong to the Lord; human beings have nothing to do with what takes place there; yet the heavens continually declare God's glory (see Ps. 19:1). What praise of the Lord goes up from the earth depends solely upon humanity, for God has placed that sphere under the dominion of men (Gen. 1:26-28). From the vast home of the dead, the land of silence, no praise of God can come—a thought frequently expressed in the psalms (Pss. 6:5; 30:9; 88:10-12; cf. Isa. 38:18). But we the living can praise the Lord, and the congregation vows as it peals forth the climax of the liturgy, we "the living" [17] will praise Him evermore.

16 The heavens are the heavens of the Lord,
      But the earth He has given to the sons of men.
17 It is not dead men who can praise the Lord,
      Not any who go down to silence;
18 But we the living will praise the Lord,
      From now on even forever!
Hallelujah!

Ps. 135. A PAEAN OF PRAISE TO THE LORD

This psalm is a liturgical hymn prepared for rendition at one of the great festivals of Israel. Its aim is to provide congregational utterance for the praise of God as Lord of nature and of history. The former is evidenced by His creation of the world, and the latter is revealed in the great events of release from Egyptian bondage and the invasion and settlement of Canaan.

The psalm opens with an exhortation to praise which was probably sung by the high priest, who was present in the Temple at the festivals.[18] It is addressed to clergy and laity respectively—the Levites, who were set apart (Deut. 10:8) "to stand before the Lord, to minister unto Him, and to bless in His name" (vs. 1b), and the body of lay worshipers standing in the courts of the Temple

---

[17] So rightly, the Septuagint.   [18] So Josephus *Jewish Wars* V. 5, 7.

(vs. 2*b*). The goodness of the Lord and the greatness of His repute are reasons for praise, but most of all is the Lord's choice of Jacob, i.e., Israel, as His own peculiarly cherished treasure. This central idea in Judaism is a climax of this part of the psalm. So sings the high priest:

1 Hallelujah!
   Praise ye the name of the Lord!
   Praise the Lord, ye servants
2 Who are standing in the Lord's house,
   Who are in the courts of the house of our God.
3 Praise the Lord, for He is good!
   Sing to His name, for it is pleasant.
4 For Jacob the Lord has chosen for Himself,
   Israel as His especial treasure.

Suddenly a clear, beautiful tenor voice is heard singing a solo based upon a beloved theme, the greatness of the Lord and His superiority over all divine beings.

5 For I know that the Lord is great;
   Yes, our Lord is greater than all gods.

The choir then pronounces the first major theme of the praise hymn (vss. 6-7), the Lord as the Creator. Whatever He wishes to do He accomplishes, whether in heaven or in earth, whether in the sea or in the deeps. The psalmist pictures the mists rising out of the distant Mediterranean. He sees the rain pouring down, lit up by vivid flashes of lightning, and describes the pent-up wind as it issues, released at the Lord's will, from His storehouses (cf. Jer. 10:13) where He keeps the rain, hail, and snow also. Sings the choir:

6 All that pleases the Lord
   He does in heaven and in earth,
      In the seas and in all deeps,
7 Who makes mists ascend from the end of the earth,
   Who makes lightning flashes for the rain,
   And brings out wind from His storehouses.

The choir now moves on to the second major theme of the liturgy (vss. 8-12), the praise of God as the Lord of Israel's history, the One who accomplished the mighty deeds connected with the release of Israel from Egyptian bondage (vss. 8-9), and who at Israel's invasion and conquest of Canaan gave His people a land. It deals generally with the plagues of Egypt, singling out for particular mention the tenth and final one, the plague upon the first-born, both of men and animals (Exod. 12:29-36). The choir glorifies God,

8 Who struck the first-born of Egypt,
   From men even unto beasts;
9 Who sent signs and wonders
   Against Pharaoh and all his servants.

Of the invasion and conquest as told in the heroic legend of Joshua (3:10) tne choir now sings. It recites how the Lord prepared the way for Israel's mastery of Canaan by driving out from before them the Canaanites, Amorites, Hittites, and Hurrians; [19] how He empowered His people to smite Sihon, king of the little Amorite kingdom in southern Trans-Jordan, likewise Og, king of Bashan, in northern Trans-Jordan, and so all the kings of Canaan. They are enumerated in Josh. 12:7-24. Thus the choir sings the fame of the Lord,

> 10   Who struck great nations,
>   And killed powerful kings;
> 11   Sihon, king of the Amorites,
>   And Og, king of Bashan,
>   And all the kings of Canaan,
> 12   And gave their land as an inheritance,
>   An inheritance to Israel, His people.

Again we hear a clear solo voice, its deep bass singing forth the glorious implications of the name of the Lord. There is here an implicit reference to the classic yet enigmatic passage, Exod. 3:14, which suggests the meaning of Yahweh (the Lord), the name of Israel's God. He interprets that enigmatic name in the light of this past history as signifying a pledge of God's unspeakable helpfulness to His people: "I will be what I will be." Forever He will judge them in righteousness and deal with them in compassion. Thus the soloist sings to his God:

> 13   O Lord, Thy name lasts forever;
>   O Lord, Thy title is for generation after generation.
> 14   For God judges His people
>   And has compassion upon His servants.

The third theme of the liturgy is the implied superiority of the Lord, the living God of Israel, to idols. This is a favorite theme in the psalms and rests back in origin upon the vivid description of how idols are made as given first in Jeremiah (10:6-10) and more fully in Deutero-Isaiah (44:12-20). The latter wrote in Babylon, where idols were numerous and had great national prestige. Though made in human form, idols lack all the senses. And the idolaters who manufacture them, and who worship them, are as void of real worth as the images they make.

> 15   The idols of the nations are silver and gold,
>   The work of human hands.
> 16   They have mouths, but cannot speak;
>   Eyes, but they cannot see;
> 17   Ears, but they cannot hear;
>   Furthermore there is no smelling in their nostrils.

[19] The Hivites as Horites (Hurrians); cf. Speiser, *Mesopotamian Origins*. On the Hurrians, cf. also Albright, *From the Stone Age to Christianity*, p. 9; and his *Archaeology and the Religion of Israel*, p. 55.

18 **Like them are those who make them,**
   And all who trust in them.

The liturgy comes to a climax in a paean of antiphonal praise of the Lord (vss. 19-21). The priests, the sons of Aaron, as the Priestly Code classifies them, summon the lay worshipers, the house of Israel, to praise; and the lay congregation in turn respond, similarly calling the priests to praise. The priests call the Levitical servants; and the Levitical servants in turn summon the lowest Temple servants, called the Nethinim (I Chr. 9:2), the other worshipers of the Lord, to praise Him. These latter were of heathen origin and at the time and long after formed a class by themselves, the members of which could marry only among themselves.[20] The closing verse is uttered by all four groups of worshipers in Zion—priests, lay worshipers, Levites, and Nethinim—in a mighty burst of unison praise.

Priests:
19 **O house of Israel, bless the Lord;**

Israel:
   O house of Aaron, bless the Lord;

Priests:
20 **O house of Levi, bless the Lord;**

Levites:
   You other worshipers of the Lord, bless the Lord.

Unison:
21 **Blessed be the Lord, in Zion,**
   Who dwells in Jerusalem!
   Hallelujah!

Ps. 136. FOR HIS LOVINGKINDNESS ENDURES FOREVER

Viewed from the standpoint of thought content, Ps. 136 is a psalm of the revelation of God in nature (vss. 4-9) and in history (vss. 10-24). The predominance is given to history, to which thirteen verses (10-22) are specifically, and two (23-24) generally, devoted. Looked at from the viewpoint of appropriateness for Hebrew worship, it would be fitting for the great seasonal festivals. In Jewish liturgy it is called "the Great Hallel," in distinction from the Hallel of Egypt (Pss. 113–118), and has been sung by Judaism at the festival of Passover,[21] to which verses 10-15 are especially pertinent. However, its opening emphasis upon God as Creator (vss. 4-8), its closing stress upon God's provision of food for all

---

[20] Cf. Ehrlich, *op. cit.*, p. 352, who renders the phrase in vs. 20*b*, "you other worshipers of the Lord." See interpretation of Ps. 115:11*a* for an alternative view as to those addressed.

[21] Cf. Oesterley, *The Psalms*, I, 100. Hallel comes from *hallēl*, the piel stem of the verb *hālal* (to praise). The phrase Hallel of Egypt originates from Ps. 114:1.

flesh, and the major tone of thanksgiving throughout the psalm make it particularly appropriate in ancient Israel for the festival of the New Year, which, as we have seen, coincides with the opening day of the Festival of Tabernacles and is the festival of national thanksgiving in Israel.[22] With the Exile, under the influence of Babylonian practice, the festival of the New Year was celebrated in both spring and autumn. This is made clear in Ezekiel's blueprint for the worship of the postexilic Temple as he envisioned it in 573 B.C. (Ezek. 45:21-25).

But the unique element in this psalm is its liturgical form; it is the one psalm in the Psalter that is purely liturgical throughout. Every verse of it is rendered antiphonally, the first line of each being chanted by the priestly choir, the second line by the congregation. This congregational response is a part of the beloved cultic cry which often is heard in the Old Testament literature (see Pss. 107:1; 118:1-4; I Chr. 16:34; Jer. 33:10-11). The Chronicler, writing in the third century B.C., painted a vivid picture of the congregational utterance of such a response. The Temple was filled with the glory of the Lord. The congregation bowed themselves upon the pavement of the inner court with their faces to the ground as they cried out (see II Chr. 7:1-3, 6),

> For He is good,
> For His lovingkindness endures forever.

Accordingly, we classify it as a liturgy of national thanksgiving.

The psalm opens with an elaborate summons to the worshiping congregation to give thanks unto the Lord, whose outstanding characteristic is His goodness, and who is at the same time the awesome God of gods and Lord of lords. The phraseology of Deut. 10:17 is here employed. Each summons to thanksgiving and all that follows these verses, each specific act of God which inspires thanksgiving, is grounded in the deepest quality of His nature, his *ḥeṣedh*, best rendered as "lovingkindness," which endures forever. First, then, comes the elaborate introduction which for each verse includes both priestly summons and congregational response.

> 1 Give thanks to the Lord, for He is good,
>   For His lovingkindness endures forever.
> 2 Give thanks to the God of gods,
>   For his lovingkindness endures forever.
> 3 Give thanks to the Lord of lords,
>   For His lovingkindness endures forever.

The psalmist centers upon five themes as he guides the heart of the Israelite congregation in its utterance of thanksgiving: creation, exodus, entrance, deliverance, and provision. First comes the pre-eminent theme of creation (vss. 4-9). Again we see shimmering through this account of the wonder-working Lord the

---

[22] In late Judaism the New Year festival became one of solemnity. The Mishnah informs us that the Hallel was sung on all festival days except the New Year; cf. Rosh Hashana 4:7.

Babylonian epic of creation. It was God's deep insight by which He created the heavens and spread out the earth upon the once-chaotic waters. Then, creating the sun and the moon, He made each lord, respectively, over day and night.

> 4 To Him, who alone does great wonders,
>   For his lovingkindness endures forever.
> 5 Who with insight made the heavens,
>   For His lovingkindness endures forever;
> 6 Who spread out the earth upon the waters,
>   For His lovingkindness endures forever;
> 7 Who made great luminaries,
>   For His lovingkindness endures forever;
> 8 The sun for dominion over the day,
>   For His lovingkindness endures forever;
> 9 The moon for dominion over the night,
>   For His lovingkindness endures forever.

The second theme is the exodus from Egypt. He begins with the last plague, the destruction of the first born of Egypt (Exod. 12:29), then tells of the Exodus itself (Exod. 14:22), made possible by God's strong hand (Exod. 13:3), and describes the passing of Israel through the Sea of Reeds (Exod. 14:22) and the shaking off into the sea of the pursuing Egyptian army (Exod. 14:27). The psalmist glorifies the Lord,

> 10 Who smote the Egyptians in their first-born,
>   For His lovingkindness endures forever;
> 11 And brought out Israel from their midst,
>   For His lovingkindness endures forever;
> 12 With a strong hand and outstretched arm,
>   For His lovingkindness endures forever;
> 13 Who divided the Sea of Reeds into parts,
>   For His lovingkindness endures forever;
> 14 And let Israel cross in the midst of it,
>   For His lovingkindness endures forever;
> 15 And shook off Pharaoh and his army into the Sea of Reeds,
>   For His lovingkindness endures forever.

The third theme is the entrance of Israel into Canaan. This includes God's leadership of His people through the wilderness (Exod. 13:18; 15:22; Deut. 8:15), His defeat of the pre-Israelite inhabitants of Canaan on Israel's behalf, and His grant of Palestine to His servant, Israel. Two classic episodes are here singled out, just as they are in Ps. 135:10-12, where there is virtual identity with this account: the defeat of the Amorite king Sihon in central Trans-Jordan and the defeat of Og of Bashan in northern Trans-Jordan (Num. 21:21-26, 33-35). Thus the psalmist continues his glorification of the Lord of history,

> 16 Who led His people through the wilderness,
>   For His lovingkindness endures forever;

17 Who struck great peoples,
      For His lovingkindness endures forever;
18 And killed majestic kings,
      For His lovingkindness endures forever;
19 Sihon, king of the Amorites,
      For His lovingkindness endures forever;
20 And Og, king of Bashan,
      For His lovingkindness endures forever;
21 And gave their land as an inheritance,
      For His lovingkindness endures forever;
22 An inheritance :ᴏ Israel, His servant,
      For His lovingkindness endures forever;

The fourth theme is deliverance. Israel was not always loyal to God. Their frequent rebellions were punished through foreign dominion. Yet, to their repentance, which their debasement awakened, the Lord had repeatedly responded by snatching them from the power of the enemy. Over and over this had taken place. Behind the psalmist's words is the fine statement of Nehemiah (9:26-28), which is a bit of prophetic-priestly philosophy of history such as our poet himself held. Feeling himself one with his people, he praises the Lord,

23 Who in our debasement remembered us,
      For His lovingkindness endures forever;
24 And snatched us from our enemies,
      For His lovingkindness endures forever.

The final theme is in particular degree a New Year emphasis, God's provision of food for both men and animals. For just a moment the psalmist lifts us into the atmosphere of universality, "all flesh." Then he closes with a final call to thanksgiving, designating the Lord by "God of heaven," a title which is prevalent only in the late Persian period. It is God

25 Who gives food to all flesh,
      For His lovingkindness endures forever.
26 Give thanks to the God of heaven,
      For His lovingkindness endures forever.

Such a psalm, because of its simplicity of congregational response, the clear pattern of its historical allusions, and its implied ethical appeal in verses 23-24, would fill well the need for religious instruction in the celebration of the festival, even while it gave definite direction for the impulses of thanksgiving in Israelite hearts.

3. Prophetic Liturgies

The feature which characterized the prophetic liturgy is the utterance of a single voice imbued with the spirit of prophecy in direct and immediate relationship with the rendering of a hymn. To grasp the ultimate origin of such a liturgy let us set ourselves imaginatively in the king's sanctuary at Bethel about the middle of the eighth century B.C. There was no other sanctuary in the northern kingdom of Israel where worship would be conducted with greater decorum than there, for it had been established as the chief of two national centers of worship nearly two centuries earlier by Jeroboam, and it was "the king's sanctuary" (Amos 7:13). When Jeroboam had inaugurated there the worship of the golden bull, Bethel was already a famous Hebrew sanctuary dating back to the epoch of the Hebrew fathers, and behind that had a Canaanite cultic history still more ancient. Into that sumptuous sanctuary, with its great traditions, feasts, highly developed system of sacrifices, and cultic music and songs, came the herdsman-prophet one festal day to utter in the name of the Lord his sharp condemnation of the worship and to call the worshipers to a righteousness expressed in terms of moral conduct. Said Amos:

> I hate, I despise your feasts,
>   And I take no delight in your sacred assemblies.
> Though you offer up to me burnt offerings . . . ,
>   And your meal offerings, I do not accept;
>   Nor do I have regard for the peace offerings of your fat beasts.
> Take away from me the noise of your songs;
>   I will not hear the melody of your harps:
> But let justice roll along like the waters,
>   And righteousness as a perpetual stream. (5:21-24.)

Such words had never before been heard by worshiping Israel!

Similar to this situation, in which the prophet criticizes the living worship at the sanctuary, is that wherein Isa. 1:10-17 was spoken. It was in the southern kingdom of Judah at the Temple of Jerusalem, in the presence of the worshiping rulers and people, that the prophet Isaiah in the name of the Lord heaped scorn upon the cultic rites and ceremonies of the worshipers, then impinged upon them the ethical call of God:

> Cease to do evil; learn to do well;
>   Seek justice; relieve the oppressed;
> Deliver the orphan; plead the cause of the widow. (1:16b-17.)

Such pioneer, prophetic appearances and spoken criticisms right where the worship was going on gave the initial stimulus to the creation of liturgical forms in postexilic days. In these the prophetic voice was no more considered to be an intrusion in the worship, but a constituent and expected part of it. The prophetic speaker would then not be an interloper, but an authoritative cultic official, a cult prophet. He would speak in the first person on God's behalf, in the firm conviction that God was speaking through him to the worshiping congregation.[23]

[23] On the whole question of the cultic prophet cf. Johnson, *The Cultic Prophet in Ancient Israel*; and "The Prophet in Israelite Worship," *The Expository Times*, XLVII (1936), 312-19.

In such a case the prophetic oracle might be free and uttered spontaneously by a prophet or by a priest of prophetic temper who felt empowered of the spirit of God to speak. An illustration of such spontaneity on the part of a cult prophet is given in II Chr. 20:1-19. Men, women, and children are present at a great service of lamentation wherein the king, acting as priest, has just uttered to the Lord a great lament on his people's behalf. At the end of this congregational lament, while the worshipers stand before the Lord, in the new court of the Temple, suddenly the spirit of the Lord comes upon Jahaziel, an Asaphite Levite "in the midst of the congregation," and he speaks to them the oracle which God gives him to say:

> Thus saith the Lord to you,
> "Fear ye not, and be not scared before this great number,
> Because the battle is not yours but God's." (Vs. 15.)

Not always, however, was the utterance of the prophetic voice spontaneous. There gradually developed such oracles in the liturgical repertoire of the Temple,[24] and an already existing oracle which was deemed appropriate to a worship situation would be used. The prophets thus not only influenced the ideas of the liturgies and so of the Temple worship as a whole, but they also gave to psalm poetry the stimulus for the creation of new liturgical forms.[25] The prophetic liturgies are Pss. 50, 75, 81, and 95.

Ps. 50. WHAT DOES GOD REQUIRE?

This psalm is a prophetic liturgy which emphasizes the theme of the Lord as Judge of His people. He is not Judge in the sense that He pronounces the sentence of destruction upon the congregation, but rather in the sense of sifting and disciplining His people. He distinguishes their superficial worship by animal sacrifice from the profounder worship of the heart, and separates for blessing those in the worshiping congregation who are truly obedient to the ethical demands of the law from those who know the law but do not observe it. Consequently its worship setting, as we have noted above (p. 118), is in the celebration of the Lord's enthronement when He comes annually to judge His people. Its literary type, however, is clearly that of a prophetic liturgy. This, together with the fact that in content it is one of the most prophetic psalms of the Psalter, determines this psalm's primary classification. It dates from a time after the introduction of the priestly law (*ca.* 397 B.C.) when the trend which set the law at the center had become strong in Judaism, but before the minute study of it characteristic of legalism had begun.

The psalm begins, like Ps. 97, with a majestic theophany, an imaginative description of the self-manifestation of God (vss. 1-6). The Lord has come to

[24] Cf. under Ps. 108, and Mowinckel, *op. cit.*, II, 117, note 1.
[25] Cf. Gunkel, *Einleitung*, p. 413.

His people in beloved and beautiful Zion, and from there (cf. the similar thought of Amos 1:2) He calls to the whole earth, His voice carrying from the rising of the sun to its setting. The Lord comes, as portrayed in the classical ancient poems of Israel, manifesting Himself in volcanic eruption and in storm (Hab. 3:3-6; Deut. 33:2; Judg. 5:4-5). The psalmist pictures God's presence as being preceded by devouring fire and encompassed by tempest. Just as the prophet Micah portrays God as calling the mountains to be witnesses to His charges against Judah (Mic. 6:1), so the psalmist represents Him as summoning heaven and earth to be witnesses as He judges His people. He calls unto Himself His godly ones, the congregation of His covenant people, who have consistently renewed their covenant with Him by the sacrifices as stipulated in the law. The witnessing heavens proclaim the righteousness of the Judge and thus guarantee the justice of His decisions as He opens His case against them.

1 The Lord speaks and calls to the earth
   From the rising of the sun to its setting.
2 From Zion, the perfection of beauty,
   God shines forth!
3 Our God comes and cannot keep silent!
   Fire devours before Him,
      And roundabout Him it is exceedingly tempestuous.
4 He calls to the heavens above
   And to the earth, to judge His people:
5 "Assemble to Me, My godly ones,
   Who have made a covenant with Me by sacrifice."
6 Let the heavens declare His righteousness,
   That He is a God of judgment.

Then suddenly God speaks to His people. In the whole section (vss. 8-23) the voice of a cultic prophet uters a prophetic oracle in the Lord's name. The first part of the utterance (vss. 8-15) has as its theme, sacrifice; the second part (vss. 16-23) is concerned with a sharp criticism of the religious life of the time, certainly dating from a period after the priestly law has become authoritative in the Jewish community, for it is legalism without ethics that is here condemned.

We turn to the first section that deals with sacrifices (vss. 8-15) and note that in verses 8-13 the cult prophet censures the congregation for placing exaggerated emphasis upon sacrifice as though it were the major requirement of God. The speaker, who was likewise probably the author of the psalm, was himself a prophetic spirit who had drunk deeply at the springs of the great prophets of pre-exilic Israel (Amos 5:21-24; Hos. 6:6; Isa. 1:10-17; Mic. 6:6-8). This oracle clearly shows us that the prophetic message of that earlier day had not been merely a voice crying in the wilderness, unheard and unheeded. It did get hold of men in Israel, not in quite the exclusive manner that the prophets had themselves hoped, in the outrooting of sacrifice. But this psalm distinctly shows that gradually the ethical and the moral note characteristic of prophecy had come to outweigh in importance the ritualistic and ceremonial requirements of the law. Sacrifice remained in the worship, the offerings being viewed more as tangible, symbolic gifts to the Lord. But the weightier parts of the law, emphasized especially in such a psalm as this, were the moral requirements of God.

Sacrifice has been viewed by Israel as the act through which the covenant with Israel was ever repeatedly renewed. In this prophetic oracle, however, a more advanced conception of the nature of this covenant bond, uniquely renewed at the New Year, is interpreted. It represents a forward step both in religious thought and in worship. The argument implied in the prophetic utterance of verses 8-13 is that it is not through sacrifice that the covenant bond with God is renewed. The Lord's congregation is not pleasing Him by its scrupulous observance of the sacrificial system of Judaism. God, the Creator of all animals in deep forest or upon unscalable mountains, of all birds of heaven, and of all life of the field, needs no such food as is thus presented to Him. He drinks no blood such as Israel pours out to Him. Thus God, through His spokesman, the cultic prophet, remonstrates with His people:

> 7a "Hear, My people, and I will speak:
> 7b   [Hear] O Israel, and I will testify against you.
> 21c I will reprove you and set it in order before your face:
> 7c   I am the Lord your God.
> 8 Not about your sacrifices do I chide you.
>   For your burnt offerings are continually before Me.
> 9 I would not take from your house a young bull,
>   Or he-goats from your folds:
> 10 For all the beasts of the forest are Mine,
>   And the cattle on the mountains of God.
> 11 I know all the birds of heaven,
>   And the moving beings of the field belong to Me.
> 12 If I were hungry, I would not tell you,
>   For the world and what fills it are Mine.
> 13 Will I eat the flesh of bulls,
>   Or drink the blood of he-goats?"

Thus far the Lord's word is negative. How then is His covenant bond with His people to be renewed? This question the prophetic voice now answers. God states in positive terms what He does require of His worshipers. The real offering which God desires is not that His worshiper slaughter for Him such a bloody sacrifice, but that he offer to Him a song of thanksgiving and therewith pay his vows.[26] In such words the sacrificial system, while still retained in the worship, has been in fact superseded. It has thus become the purely symbolic or sacramental and tangible expression of a receptive and grateful heart. Indeed, in the next verse the psalmist goes farther in this same direction. When His worshiper

---

[26] The word for "slaughter," *zebhaḥ,* is used for "offer," thus boldly suggesting the contrast. Cf. vs. 23.

is in distress, the thing that God most values, and to which He most sensitively and potently responds, is the earnest cry to Him for help. In other words, just as He desires a song of thanksgiving, so He values and wants to hear a song of lamentation, a sincere appeal to Him from a needy heart. Thus the prophetic voice states God's positive requirements:

> 14 "Offer unto Me a song of thanksgiving,
>   And so pay your vows to the Most High.
> 15 Yes, call upon Me in the day of trouble,
>   And I will rescue you and honor you."

Gunkel suggestively says: "Into this word the poet briefly and powerfully compresses the entire life of the godly: It is distress and appeal, rescue and thanksgiving." [27]

The second part of the prophetic oracle (vss. 16b-23 [28]) deals particularly with the spirit of the times in which the psalmist himself lived. It is a penetrating criticism of the superficial piety of those who lived under the priestly law, who knew its statutes by heart and loved to repeat them, but obeyed them not and hated the very correction of life which was intended by them.

> 16b "What means it to you to recount My statutes
>   And take My covenant upon your mouth?
> 17 Yes, you hate correction
>   And put my words behind you."

They knew the Decalogue by heart—the psalmist himself follows its order in verses 18-20—yet they resorted habitually with thieves and adulterers, utterly unconcerned about their corrupt conduct, yes, even attracted by it. They let fall slanderous words against their neighbors, falsely attributing wrong where in all honesty none existed. God could no longer keep silent, else His people would consider Him as indifferent to sin as they themselves were.

> 18 "If you see a thief, you are pleased with him,
>   And your companionship is with adulterers.
> 19 You let loose your mouth against your neighbor,
>   And you couple your tongue with deceit.
> 20 Lies you speak against your brother,
>   Against the son of your mother you [falsely] allege something as
>   blameworthy.
> 21 These things you have done, but I kept silent.
>   You have thought that I am like you."

The last two verses of the psalm gather up both parts of the prophetic address and introduce the psalmist's conclusion with a form of utterance very common in prophetic speech, a ferocious threat. Still addressing the congregation of the Lord, he singles out those who truly revere God and will be rewarded by Him.

---

[27] *Die Psalmen*, p. 216.
[28] Vs. 16a disturbs the meter and thought, and is a later insertion.

They are the ones who honor Him by offering Him a sincere song of thanksgiving, and who consistently live upright lives.

> 22 "Pray discern this, you who are forgetting God,
>   Lest I rend you and there be none to rescue you.
> 23 He who offers a song of thanksgiving honors Me:
>   And I will let the upright of life experience My salvation."

Ps. 75. IT IS GOD WHO JUDGES

This psalm is a hymn in the form of a prophetic liturgy. It opens with a
description of jubilation, a feature which appears in the hymn far less often
than the summons to praise, but which forms a very effective beginning of the
psalm and gives an impression of confident trust.[29] It is the congregation singing
their thankful praise to the Lord because of the wonderful deeds He has done.

> 1 We give thanks to Thee, O God; we give thanks,
>   And those who call upon Thy name recount Thy wonderful deeds.

Then suddenly comes a characteristic element in the psalm, the utterance of
a prophetic oracle by a single voice. The times are, like our own, unsteady,
shaken, and insecure. Enormous disorder is in the earth, and unrest is felt in
the whole populated world. This prophetic utterance comes without warning
or introduction, which adds greatly to its effectiveness. Says the prophet, speaking
in the name of God:

> 2 When I seize the appointed time,
>   I judge with rectitude.
> 3 Though the earth and all who inhabit it be agitated,
>   I will firmly establish its pillars.

This prophetic oracle gives expression to the prophet's faith, not in another
temporary political stability based on such a thing as the balance of power, but
in the divine spiritual order of God. Here is a faith in that ideal world of
spiritual reality which awaits the initiative of God. Only He can establish such
an order of righteousness, and no world disorder can be so overwhelming as to
sweep God into its chaos. The singer does not mean to say that God does not
use human personalities to bring about such an order, as reference to verse 10
will show, but "the appointed time" is God's, not man's.

This prophetic oracle is now answered by the hymn of an individual (vss. 4-
10). We hear a clear, single voice uttering a message of warning against the
proudly defiant godless in the community (vss. 4-5); then it emphasizes that
it is God alone who judges with righteousness, exalting one and humiliating
another (vss. 6-8). To this psalmist, faced by the responsible perpetrators of
monstrous world disorder from which the Israelite society is suffering, God's
judgment is serious business (vs. 8). He here makes use of gruesome prophetic

---

[29] Cf. Gunkel, *Einleitung*, p. 39.

pictures in which Jeremiah had pioneered (25:15-29). They express the wrath of God meted out as His judgment upon the evil enemies and hinderers of His righteous rule. The Lord hands the cup of His wrath to those who oppose Him, and no one upon whom His verdict falls can escape. He must drink it to the dregs. But it is the righteous Judge who decides who must drink it. So sings the individual voice this warning-permeated hymn:

> 4 I say to the boastful, "Boast not,"
>   And to the wicked, "Lift not up the horn."
> 5 Lift not up your horn on high;
>   Speak not impudently against the Rock.
> 6 For not from East or West [comes judgment],
>   And not from steppe or from mountains;
> 7 But God it is who judges;
>   One He abases, and another He exalts.
> 8 For a cup is in the hand of the Lord,
>   Foaming wine full of intoxicating mixture,
>   And He pours out from one to the other.
>   Even its dregs they must sip up.[30]

This individual hymn closes with a song of thanks (vss. 9-10). It is sung in anticipation of this righteous judgment of God, which will undo the power of the wicked and both vindicate and exalt the righteous. Moreover, it suggests more closely here than in any other part of the psalm the psalmist's own participation in the destruction of evil.

> 9 But as for me, I will rejoice forever;
>   I will sing to the God of Jacob.
> 10 And the horns of the wicked I will hew off;
>   But the horns [31] of the righteous shall be lifted up.

Ps. 81. A CALL TO EXCLUSIVE ALLEGIANCE

Ps. 81 is a prophetic liturgy. Its most distinctive element is the prophetic oracle which begins at verse 5b. It is one of the few psalms of the Psalter that had their origin in northern Israel, as the identifying of Joseph with Israel in verse 5 suggests. After the fall of the northern kingdom in 721 B.C., the psalm found its way into the psalms of the Temple at Jerusalem.

The first part of the psalm (vss. 1-5a) is a festal hymn. It opens with an elaborate introduction in the form of a joyous summons to praise the mighty God of Jacob with vocal and instrumental music (vss. 1-3). Gunkel reminds us that the words are a secondary matter. Primary in importance in Israel is the performance of the worship itself in the festally arrayed sanctuary, the many musi-

---

[30] Omit with Mowinckel, *op. cit.*, III, 48, the last clause of the verse, as a gloss.
[31] Horns are a symbol of presumptuous strength. The verse means: "And I will reduce all the might of the wicked; but the dignity of the righteous shall be increased."

cal instruments playing in harmony and sounding forth the praise of the vast
congregation to the Lord.

1 Ring out a cry of joy to God our strength;
   Raise a shout to the God of Jacob.
2 Lift a song, and play the timbrel,
   The sweetly sounding lyre along with the harp.
3 Blow the trumpet at the new moon,
   At the full moon on the day of our feast.

The theme of the praise, introduced by the familiar "for," is given in verse 4.
The praise which Israel is challenged to express is viewed as the fulfillment of a
divine command given to Israel in the law, most likely that of the Code of the
Covenant (Exod. 23:15), since our psalm dates before 721 B.C. It is the festival
of Passover, which opens the seven-day Festival of Unleavened Bread. It celebrates the Exodus, the wonderful release of Israel from Egyptian bondage.

4 For it is a statute for Israel,
   A command to the tents of Jacob.
5 A law He made it in Joseph,
   When he went forth from the land of Egypt.

Suddenly after a pause we hear the single voice of the inspired cultic prophet,
who speaks to the people in the Lord's name. We are not to think here of a
spontaneous utterance by a momentarily inspired prophet, but rather of a
regular and expected part of the order of worship. It is a feature greatly loved
by Israel and has come to be waited for as one of the richest contributions
of public worship. The oracle begins and ends with a confession of "how to the
singer comes the song," of how the Lord spoke to the prophet in his innermost
soul:

5b A language I did not know, I kept hearing:
10b "Open thy mouth, and I will fill it."

In the early part of this oracle the speaker has in mind the great release of
Israel from the Egyptian bondage of forced labor upon the store cities of Pithom
and Raamses, built by the pharaoh of the oppression, Ramses II (Exod. 1:11).
The "shoulders" of these Israelite slaves had then known such burdens as had
made them sigh, groan, and cry out (Exod. 2:23). And how many thousands of
heavy baskets had their weary hands carried! At Palestinian excavations one
can see the long lines of Arab laborers carrying their familiar baskets, the male
workmen bearing them at their side, the women carrying them on their heads,
the baskets being laden with dirt for the dump. The vast extent of the hard
labor required in these huge building enterprises of Ramses II was forcibly
impressed upon me by visits in November, 1947, to the excavated sites of these
two store cities. Located toward the eastern end of Wadi Tumilat, the Land
of Goshen, just south of the canal that today runs from the Nile to the Suez Canal,

are the ruins of Tell el-Maskhutah, identified by Naville, Montet, and Lucas as Pithom.[32] Roaming the ruins, I noted the extensive structures covering an extremely wide area, built of large sun-dried bricks. Then from Ismailia at the extreme eastern end of the Land of Goshen I drove on a three-hour, precarious but fascinating journey through Fakus, far down into the watery delta of the Nile to Ṣan. In the Old Testament (Ps. 78:12) this is called the "field of Zoan" (Çō'an), the Greek name of which is Tanis. It is at the extreme northwestern end of the Land of Goshen (Gen. 47:6, 11). The recent excavations of Pierre Montet have conclusively established its identification as Pi-Raamses, the Raamses (Exod. 1:11) built, that is, rebuilt, by Ramses II.[33] For originally (ca. 1720 B.C.) it was the capital and fortress of "the foreign kings," the Hyksos, their outpost that looked toward western Asia. Ramses II renamed it for himself and made it his residence about 1300 B.C. He made it one of the marvels of Egypt. Archaeologists have uncovered there a vast walled city. Huge granite monuments of the pharaohs, and particularly of Ramses II, are there, and massive obelisks erected by him now lie broken upon the ground. As one moves among the impressive ruins, a material grandeur and magnificence breaks upon his amazed eyes, which could only have been created by the heavy toil of innumerable slaves. One does not wonder that in Israel the Exodus was ever viewed as something akin to Calvary in Christianity.

We are now better prepared to catch the mood of the oracle that the inspired prophet is about to speak. The real burden of this prophetic oracle is a call to an effective monotheism, the worship of the one true God. And who is this God of Israel? (a) He is the God of Moses, who by His great release delivered Israel from their forced labor upon the store cities, the palaces and temples of Egypt, who lifted the harsh burden from their shoulders and took the basket out of their hands. (b) He is the God who heard the cry of His people in their bondage and rescued them through the Exodus. In the thunders of Sinai, He answered his people by revealing to them His will (Exod. 19:19; 20:18). And at Meribath-Kadesh, which was for a generation before the invasion of Canaan the center of Moses' leadership, the Lord tested His people and taught them trustful reliance upon Himself (vs. 7). (c) He is the God who through the prophet now speaking is teaching Israel, who longs for His people to listen and heed. The heart of the oracle is verse 9. The God of Israel is the only God for them to worship. They must have nothing whatever to do with foreign deities. Thus the Lord speaks:

> 6 "I removed your shoulder from the burden:
>   Your hands were freed from the basket.

---

[32] Albright identifies it as Succoth, op. cit., p. 194, and considers Tell Retabeh as Pithom.
[33] Montet, Le drame d'Avaris: essai sur la pénétration des Sémites en Égypte.

7   You called out in trouble, and I rescued you;
     I answered you in the hiding place of thunder;
     I tried you by the waters of Meribah.
8   Hear, My people, and let Me admonish you;
     Israel, oh that you would listen to Me!
9   There shall not be among you a strange god,
     And you shall not worship a foreign god.
10   I am the Lord your God,
     Who brought you up from the land of Egypt."

There is a sharp change in the following verses. The prophetic voice continues. The Exodus is left behind. There is less of history and more of a lament. The prophet is more general in dealing with Israel's sin as he sweeps through the centuries of his life. But one root sin has been present and is still present, the failure to hear and heed the divine voice. Since the Israelites neither really listened to God's voice nor obeyed it, God gave their stubborn wills free rein; He cast them upon themselves and let them suffer the results of their own evil choices (vss. 11-12). Yet all the time God has longed and still longs to guide His people (vs. 13). If they will but seek His counsel and follow it, He will make them so strong that they will strike terror into the hearts of their enemies and will be enabled to hold them in submission (vss. 14-15). Moreover, they will be blessed materially as well as politically. Their ground will yield wheat of finest quality in great abundance, and the rocky soil of Palestine will become even what the Lord has pledged that it will be, "a land of olive oil and honey" (vs. 16). If they only will! We feel the prophetic appeal, lamenting, exhorting, and promising, as the prophet strives to move the congregation toward God.

11   "But My people did not listen to My voice,
     And Israel did not yield to Me.
12   So I cast them off into the stubbornness of their heart;
     They went on in their evil plans.
13   Oh that My people would listen to Me,
     That Israel would walk in My ways!
14   In an instant would I humble their enemies,
     And turn My hand against their adversaries.
15   Those who hate him [i.e., Israel] would come cringing to him,
     And terror of them [Israelites] would be forever.
16   And I would supply him with the finest of the wheat,
     And I would satisfy him with honey from the rock."

Ps. 95. HEAR GOD'S VOICE TODAY

Ps. 95 is an excellent illustration of a prophetic liturgy. The period from which it springs is likely about the middle of the fifth century B.C., such as is reflected in Trito-Isaiah (58:2-4). The first part of it is a beautiful and quite representative hymn of praise (vss. 1-7b). The procession of worshipers passes through the gate of the Temple into the outer court. Led by a precentor, the worshipers sing a summons to praise the Lord with song and worship cry, glorifying Him as the reliable Saviour. The note of joyous thanksgiving thrills the summons:

> 1 Come, let us sing unto the Lord;
>> Let us raise a shout to the Rock of our salvation.
> 2 Let us come before His presence with thanksgiving;
>> Let us raise a shout to Him with songs.

The twofold theme of the hymn is announced and is introduced by the characteristic word "for." It is God the Creator, and the Lord as the King of the gods. This combination is already familiar to us from the psalms of the Lord's enthronement. The Lord, great in character and rule, holds in His mighty hand both the earth's deep canyons and its highest summits, both the majestic sea and the land, freed since creation from chaotic inundation.

> 3 For the Lord is a great God,
>> And a King over all gods.
> 4 In His hand are the deep places of the earth;
>> The peaks of the mountains are His.
> 5 The sea is His; yes, He made it.
>> And His hands fashioned the dry land.

As is frequent in the hymns, there now comes a renewed summons to praise. But it is at the same time an invitation to the worshipers to enter from the outer into the inner court of the Temple, where together they prostrate themselves with their faces toward the most holy place.

> 6 Enter in; let us prostrate ourselves and bow down,
>> Let us kneel before our Maker.

The new and deepened theme emphasizes the Lord as Israel's ("our") God, and Israel as the flock which He shepherds:

> 7a For He is our God,
> 7b   And we are His people and the sheep of His shepherding.

Then suddenly comes a change in person. The hymn ceases, and a prophetic voice, either that of a cultic prophet or of a priest imbued with prophetic spirit, speaks in the Lord's name a prophetic oracle, a message of warning to the entire worshiping throng. The message of this prophetic portion is threefold. It has its roots in those great days when Moses was leading God's people through the wilderness and teaching them to rely upon God's mighty provision for their needs. The first thought is, Let Israel listen to what God is saying to him today. God not only had a will for the "today" ("this day," see Exod. 34:11; Deut. 4:40) of the time of Moses, but He is now speaking to the Israel of the psalmist's time as well.

> 7c Today! Oh that you would hear His voice!

Second, the message says, let not your heart be stubborn, insensitive, and unresponsive to God as was that of your fathers in the wilderness days at Meribah and at Massah. These are two famous watchwords out of Israel's past. The reference is to what happened at Meribath-Kadesh (see Exod. 17:2-7). The ancient legend tells why the name Meribah—the *rib* part means "strife"—was given to Kadesh. It was because of the strife which Moses had with the quarrelling, bickering, and faultfinding people whom he was leading. This sharp and untrusting criticism on their part revealed their lack of faith both in Moses and in God. The other name, Massah—coming from *nasah,* meaning "test"—was also given to the region, because Moses' followers did not trust that God would be true to His promises or faithful to His nature, as Moses had taught, but they put Him to the test, thus showing their doubt as to the reality and power of His presence among them. And this faithless, faultfinding spirit was all the more inexcusable because those who thus doubted had seen the mighty work of deliverance and release which the Lord had wrought for His people at the Exodus. Thus the prophetic voice continues:

> 8 "Harden not your heart, as at Meribah,
>   As in the day of Massah in the wilderness,
> 9 When your fathers put Me to the test;
>   They put Me to the proof, though they had seen My work."

The third thought in the oracle is a warning. To Israel of the psalmist's day the prophetic oracle says in effect, Beware of such error of heart and ignorance of God's ways as characterized your ancestors in the forty years of their wilderness wanderings (Exod. 16:35). For their lack of trust and their protesting spirit made the Lord feel abhorrence for them (Deut. 1:34-37). God at that time made a solemn oath to the effect that He would not permit that generation itself to enter their ultimate home and heritage in Canaan (Num. 14:22-23), where Israel was destined at length to "rest" in security (Deut. 12:9-10). For although Israel had experienced the great release and the Lord's marvelous provision, yet its spirit had been utterly insensitive to the ways of God.

> 10 "Forty years I felt a loathing
>   For that generation, and I said,
>   'A people erring in heart are they,
>   And they do not know My ways.'
> 11 So I swore in My anger
>   That they would not enter into My rest."

Suddenly and quite unexpectedly the psalm is at an end. The psalmist's generation and every succeeding one which has made use of these words is left facing that creative past and brooding upon the lessons it holds for their needs at the present hour.

4. LITURGY OF SUPPLICATION

A supplication is a humble, imploring entreaty. At its heart is great intensity of feeling. Our one example of a liturgical utterance of this sort is Ps. 121, which is an imploring entreaty for the help of God. It grants us a glimpse of the religious opportunity which the priest had at the great festivals as the mediator of divine help. It was his privilege to give direct spiritual guidance and comforting assurance to individual pilgrims who came to the Temple in great inner need and looked up to him in godly awe.

Ps. 121. TO THE HILLS I LIFT MINE EYES

This psalm is a liturgy of supplication created by the joining of a priestly answer to an individual lament. It was originally rendered antiphonally. The psalmist stands in great need of help. Earthly assistance is not enough. So he looks up to the mountains, all of them holy places. Always men have sought for divine help from the heights. Mountains have been viewed as meeting places with Deity because they constituted thresholds by which Deity could step down to earth. But to which mountain should he turn? The question is addressed by the individual worshiper to the officiating priest. And as it is a liturgical question it is asked only to be answered constructively and positively by the officiating servant of God. Probably Budde is right in maintaining that originally in verse 2 we should restore the second person, which gives the priestly response to the suppliant's question, and in verse 3 the first person—my feet, my keeper—this being the utterance of the suppliant himself. Thus the suppliant:

> 1 I lift up my eyes to the mountains:
> From whence will come my help?

The priest answers:

> 2 Thy help comes from the Lord,
> Maker of heaven and earth.

This priestly answer represents the very center of Israel's faith in the availability of divine help, sufficient for every human need. The helper of this needy Israelite worshiper is the mighty Creator of the world. This it is which the psalmist will emphasize.

The suppliant again speaks. He is clearly in danger. A single slip, one false step, might destroy him. Moreover, he needs divine shepherding care, the deep concern of One who is alert, on the watch, and who stays awake on his behalf, feeling responsible for him. So the suppliant prays:

> 3 May He not permit my foot to slip:
> May He not become drowsy who keeps me.

And with certainty comes the priest's answer, wherein the Lord is called by one of the noblest titles of Israel's God:

> 4 Surely the keeper of Israel
> Will neither drowse nor sleep.

In the rest of the psalm the priest speaks, and his words are athrill with the reality of the protecting God. Four times his reverent words "the Lord" fall from his lips, in ever deepening assurance as to what He can do and will do for His worshiper who stands in so great need. It is concrete picture language that the priest uses to portray spiritual blessings. His keeper, preserver, protector, and shade from the hot Palestinian sun is the Lord. There is also a distinctively Oriental quality here. The Palestinians view sunstroke as caused by the demon who is active at midday. Intermittent fever and lunacy are thought to come from the night demon. The New Testament word used of the epileptic boy of Matt. 17:15 is σεληνιάζεται—"he is moon-struck." From every kind of evil the Lord will protect him, holding his very life in His care. The tender words with which the priestly assurance closes—"thy going out and thy coming in"—are from the Deuteronomic blessing pronounced at Gerizim (Deut. 28:6). The words of comfort and assurance pour forth from the priest's lips:

> 5 The Lord is thy keeper:
>   The Lord is thy shade upon thy right hand.
> 6 By day the sun
>   Shall not smite thee,
>   Nor the moon by night.
> 7 The Lord will keep thee
>   From all evil;
>   He will keep thy soul.
> 8 The Lord will guard thy going out and thy coming in,
>   From now on, even forever.

Chapter VII

NATIONAL AND CONGREGATIONAL LAMENTS

THERE WERE VARIOUS KINDS OF PUBLIC CALAMITY IN ISRAEL AND JUDAH THAT WERE occasions for the calling of a public fast. At such an occasion the congregation of Israel would assemble in the Temple in the mood of lamentation and, attired in sackcloth, would pour out their souls in prayer and song to the Lord. In exilic and postexilic times there were the regularly recurring fasts which lamented the capture and destruction of Jerusalem by the Chaldeans and the removal of its citizens to Babylon (cf. Zech. 8:19). There were also recurring calamities, largely outside the people's control, which were major national and community catastrophes such as famine due to dearth or a plague of locusts, pestilence, and the invasion of cities by wild beasts attracted by the bodies of the unburied dead, both of these latter the by-products of war. There was also the threat of invasion by enemy powers, which brought throngs to the Temple to lament before the Lord, appealing for His help. There were times when Israel or Judah felt the harsh pagan heel of dominant occupying powers such as the haughty Persians and in hurt dignity lamented to God. There were other times, such as about 351 B.C., when to punish Jewish rebellion pagan Persian forces entered the sanctuary at Jerusalem, striking the religious sense of the loyal Jews into outraged wrath.

Two vivid and instructive pictures of a national or congregational lament are presented in the Old Testament outside the Psalter. The reported occasion of one, in the book of Joel, is a devastating plague of locusts. The priests are summoned to clothe themselves with sackcloth and to lie all night before the altar. They are directed to proclaim a fast, gathering the whole population—men, women, and children—to the Temple. The priests move in solemn procession between the porch and the altar, uttering their wailing cries and chanting a psalm of lament:

> Look with pity, O Lord, upon Thy people,
> And do not give up Thy property to disgrace,
> So that the nations would use a byword against them.
> Why should they say among the peoples,
> "Where is their God?" (2:17.)

And in response to this lament the Lord has pity on His people and answers, probably through a prophet, giving the worshiping congregation a consoling and reassuring oracle:

> Lo, I will send to you
> Grain and new wine and oil:
> And you shall be satisfied with it.
> And I will not make you any more
> A reproach among the nations. (2:19.)

The other comes from the Chronicler, writing about 300 B.C., who knows well the nature of a congregational lament in the Temple. Although he represents this one as having occurred in the ninth century B.C.—with King Jehoshaphat, in the role of priest, as its leader—he pictures it in the vivid descriptive terms of one who has often seen and has possibly participated in such a service in his own day. News of the threat of attack upon Judah by the Moabites and Ammonites causes the king to proclaim a fast throughout the nation. The people gather in the Temple before the new court to seek the Lord's help. King Jehoshaphat prays to God on their behalf, in a prayer which is in essence a lamentation, appealing for His help in their weakness and vast need. During his prayer Judean men, their wives and children, stand before the Lord (II Chron. 20:1-13).

Then, quite similarly to what we have observed in Joel 2:19, a Levite of the sons of Asaph is seized with the spirit of prophecy and in response to the congregational lament gives a prophetic oracle of steadying assurance in the name of the Lord:

> Fear not, and be not dismayed before this great crowd,
> For not yours is the battle, but God's! (II Chron. 20:15.)

There are several specific parts to a national or congregational lament: (a) a detailed description of the reason for the lament; (b) the characteristic lamenting questions, "How long?" and "Why?" (c) the appeal to what God has done for His people in His ancient covenant with them. Often, but not always, is included (d) an answering prophetic or priestly oracle of comfort and assurance, either actually given (cf. Pss. 12:5; 60:6-8) or inferred as having taken place in the living worship, although not itself included as a part of the psalm.[1] The basic purpose at the heart of a lament is to persuade God to see the desperate need of His people, and by arguments and passionate appeals to move Him to intervene on their behalf. These psalms are 9–10; 12; 36; 44; 58; 60; 74; 77; 79; 80; 90; 94:1-15; 108; 137.

Pss. 9–10. ARISE: FORGET NOT THE OPPRESSED

Pss. 9 and 10 originally formed a single psalm, as is the case in the Greek translation of the Old Testament. Moreover, Ps. 10 has no title of its own, and the two psalms taken together form an acrostic poem, although in this instance an incomplete one. The model of this type of poetic form is probably to be found in Babylonia. The predominant features of the psalm lead us to classify it primarily as a congregational lament (see Ps. 10:1-18), coming probably from the later Persian period, when the various definite types of literary forms had begun to flow together and influence one another. The enemies (Ps. 10:1-11) are the Persian overlords, who are making life bitter for the Jews.

---

[1] See Ps. 58, pp. 231-32, where we may infer that an oracle was pronounced between vss. 9 and 10; likewise Ps. 79, p. 243, between vss. 12 and 13.

The psalm opens with a song of individual thanksgiving for the wonderful deeds of the Lord which the psalmist has experienced, and which lead him to exultation and praise (9:1-4). Such a worship setting for the rendering of this part becomes plain at verse 13. His introductory words are aglow with joy:

> א　1　I will praise Thee, O Lord, with all my heart;
> 　　　I will recount all Thy wonderful acts.
> 　　2　I will rejoice and exult in Thee;
> 　　　I will sing praise to Thy name, Most High.

The psalmist has just experienced a wonderful release. He was falsely accused by enemies. His case was brought before God at the sanctuary, and from His righteous throne the Lord vindicated His servant before the eyes of his humiliated and rejected foes. The statement of this forms the chief part of his song of thanks and gives the reason for his gratitude.

> ב　3　Because my enemies have been turned back,
> 　　　They stumbled and vanished before Thy presence.
> 　　4　For Thou hast maintained my right and my plea;
> 　　　Thou dost sit on the throne, judging righteously.

This thought of God as Judge forms the transition to the next major section (vss. 5-16), which is primarily an eschatological hymn.[2] In such hymns the distress of the present is relieved by the certainty of the ultimate triumph of the Lord over the pagan nations and over all the wickedness perpetrated by those who are enemies of His people and of His rule. God will blot out their fame, their armaments, their cities, even their memory. They will perish, but He will remain on His throne as the righteous Judge of the world. The oppressed have in Him a stronghold and a dependable defender. A half choir sings:

> ג　5　Thou dost rebuke nations and dost destroy wickedness;
> 　　　Their name Thou dost blot out forever.
> 　　6　The enemies are consumed; they are desolations forever;
> 　　　Their cities Thou hast broken down; memory of them has perished.
> ה　7　They have perished, but the Lord abides:
> 　　　He hath set up His throne for judgment,
> 　　8　And He will judge the world in righteousness
> 　　　And govern peoples in equity.
> ו　9　So the Lord shall be a retreat for the oppressed,
> 　　　A stronghold in times of distress.
> 　　10　And those who know Thy name shall trust in Thee,
> 　　　For Thou wilt not abandon those who seek Thee, O Lord.

The eschatological hymn suddenly and unexpectedly bursts into a choir hymn of brief compass (vss. 11-12). It summons the worshipers to praise the Lord, whose throne is in Zion. The theme of the praise is that God has avenged the

---

[2] Vss. 13-14 are not a part of this eschatalogical hymn, but give the psalmist's personal testimony, which concludes the song of personal thanksgiving (vss. 1-4) with which the psalm opened.

blood of His servants, which the pagan world power caused to flow. In harmony with the eschatological standpoint of the larger hymn, of which this brief choir hymn of praise is a part, the divine retribution is yet to come but is so sure that it is spoken of as though it has already been expressed. It is likely that in the actual rendering of the psalm this brief choir hymn would be sung by the other half choir. Thus the second half of the choir breaks forth into a hymn of praise.

> ז   11   Sing to the Lord, who sits enthroned in Zion;
>   Declare among the nations His deeds.
>   12   For He has avenged their blood; He has remembered their desire;
>   He has not forgotten the cry of the poor.

The song of individual thanksgiving, begun in verses 1-4, is taken up again (vss. 13-14), and light is now thrown upon the psalm's worship setting. The singer is in the Temple in Zion in the presence of the worshiping congregation and is recounting the story of his distress, from which he has been so wondrously delivered. Very simply he tells how the Lord has restored him from imminent death. He addresses himself first to the congregation as he gives his testimony (vs. 13), then to his God, in praise for what He has done for him. The story is succinctly given:

> ח   13   The Lord was gracious to me; He saw my affliction,
>   Raising me up from the gates of death
>   14   So that I might recount all Thy praises.
>   In the gates of the daughter of Zion I will exult in Thy salvation.

The psalmist now returns to the eschatological hymn (vss. 5-16), which the testimony in the above song of personal thanksgiving (vss. 13-14) has interrupted. He represents what history still waits to see accomplished as having already occurred. He fastens upon the avenging, retributive deeds of the Lord, which the choir hymn of praise (vss. 11-12) has celebrated, as representing an expression of God's activity in executing judgment. There is a quality in the retribution of God that acts upon the nations like a boomerang. The enemy nations dug a pit for Judah. They hid a net to entrap the Lord's people. But into that pit they will themselves fall! In that net they, not the Judeans, will be ensnared! Here is an expression of the justice of God that brings upon the perpetrators of evil the retribution of their own deeds. This conception of the divine judgment is found frequently in the Psalter. Both parts of the choir now join in singing the certainty of God's ultimate triumph over evil, which forms the climax of this eschatological hymn.

> ט   15   The nations have sunk down into the pit which they made;
>   In their net which they hid, their own foot has got caught.
>   16   It is known that the Lord executes judgment.
>   The wicked is ensnared in the work of his own hands.

Then come the wish (vs. 17) and petition (vss. 20, 18-19) characteristic of a lament. We are now back in the atmosphere of conflict between the Judean community and the godless nations. The Lord's people are called "the needy . . . , the afflicted." Let God terrorize the nations who do not take God into account! Let their plans come to nought! Let them hear the death sentence from the mouth of the Judge! But let God remember the long-deferred hope of His sorely tried people:

> ′ 17 May the wicked go down to Sheol, where they belong,[a]
>   All nations which forget God.
>   20 Put terror upon them, O Lord;
>   Let the nations know they are but men.
> ⊃ 18 For not forever will the needy be forgotten,
>   Not forever will the hope of the afflicted perish.
>   19 Arise, O Lord; let not man prevail;
>   Let the nations be judged before Thee!

We now come to the part of the psalm (10:1-18) which determines its primary nature as a congregational lament. All else in the psalm is preliminary to this. The psalmist here describes in considerable detail the practices of the godless within the nation. The times are hard for the members of the Lord's congregation who are pursued by the arrogant wicked and ensnared in their schemes. They are boastful and haughty. They live without God, yet they prosper in material ways. In strong consciousness of superiority they boast of their security and their freedom from anxiety. But their speech is laden with deceit and harm. Their acts are full of treachery. They are bent upon the destruction of the innocent; they lie in wait for them like a lion in the thicket to drag off his prey. One feels here that by "the poor" is meant those who depend upon God. Their oppressors are the godless. And the result is that the Lord's disheartened people begin to doubt that God sees or cares. He seems so aloof; His people have no awareness of His presence. The lament opens with a characteristic lamenting word, "why," which is addressed unto God.

> ⑨ 1 Why, O Lord, dost Thou stand afar off?
>   Why dost Thou conceal Thyself in times of trouble?
>   2 The wicked in his arrogance hotly pursues the poor;
>   May he be caught in the schemes which he has concocted.
>   3 For he extols his wickedness,
>   His soul's desire,
>   And glorifies unjust gain.
> ⒜ 4 The wicked disdains the Lord in the haughtiness of his countenance.
>   "He avenges not; there is no God," [he says].
>   All his schemes [prosper].
>   5 He brings his course to successful issue at all times;
>   Far removed from him are Thy laws.
>   As for his foes, he snorts at them.

─────────

[a] Cf. Ehrlich, op. cit., p. 19, for force of shûbh.

6   He says in his heart, "I shall not slip;
        From generation to generation my steps shall not draw down a curse."

 פ   7   His mouth is full of deceit and injury;
        Under his tongue are oppression and trouble.

8   He sits in a lurking place to murder,
        In the secret places to slay the innocent.

ע   His eyes spy out the unfortunate;

9   He lies in wait in concealment like a lion in a thicket,
        To seize the unfortunate one, dragging him into his net.

10   The innocent one is crushed, is prostrated;
        The unfortunate one falls into his plots.

11   He says in his heart, "God has forgotten;
        He has hidden His face so He does not see."

The situation is so desperate that the psalmist calls for the intervention of God. Let Him arise in His power to help His oppressed people against the contemptuous godless who in their innermost thoughts have no fear of divine vengeance. But God sees what is going on—the suffering of the unfortunate and helpless. And He knows that they have no one but Him to help them. His innocent people commit their fate to Him. In eager, passionate petition the psalmist cries unto the Lord to break the power of these evil men and bring upon them the divine vengeance, which they cannot escape. We note in this portion two terms characteristic of the congregational lament, the summons "arise" and the impatient "why?"

ק   12   Arise, O Lord; forget not the oppressed;
        Cease not to care for the afflicted.

13   Why let the wicked spurn God,
        Who says in his heart, "He cannot exact vengeance"?

ר   14   Thou seest trouble and provocation,
        For Thou lookest upon the unfortunate and orphan:
            He commits it to Thee; it is in Thy hand to give.
            Thou art his helper.[4]

ש   15   Break the arm of the wicked and shatter it!
        Avenge his wickedness; let him not escape!

In the closing part of the psalm (vss. 16-18) there is expressed the certainty that God will answer. The tense is the prophetic perfect—"the pagans have perished"; the Lord has heard. It is so sure, in the psalmist's faith, that it is spoken of as having already occurred. It is likely that this sharp change from passionate petition in desperate need to calm assurance rests upon the pronouncement of a prophetic oracle at this point in the actual Temple worship, which brings confidence to the congregation. This should take place between the rendering of verses 12-15 and 16-18. The tone of the closing section is in harmony with the prophetic manner of speech. In verse 16 we have a single reference to the ritual of the Lord's enthronement, which makes it likely that this psalm

[4] I follow here Gunkel's reconstruction of the text, *Die Psalmen*, p. 39.

would be rendered in connection with that annually recurring ceremony. The psalmist is assured that the time will come when the pagans, now so powerful, will be no more in the land. For the Lord has heard the appeal for His aid from the lips of His helpless and innocent people. He will manifest His power in their behalf as King and Judge. He will not only achieve justice for them, but will also make it impossible for any human being again to bring such tyranny and terror into the land.

> 16 The Lord is become King forever and aye;
>   The pagans have perished from His land.
> ♪ 17 Thou hast heard the desire of the afflicted, O Lord;
>   Thou dost confirm their heart; Thou dost incline Thine ear
> 18 To accomplish justice for the orphan and the oppressed,
>   So that no mortal from the earth can again terrorize.

Ps. 12. NOW WILL I ARISE

Ps. 12 is a solemn liturgy prepared for a regularly recurring service of petition. It is a lament of the public congregation and is closely akin to Ps. 14 (=53). It opens with a characteristic cry to the Lord for help (vs. 2); then in lamenting tones it describes the situation that brings the cry to the lips. Piety and faithfulness have vanished from the whole earth. Lies and flattery prevail in human relations. The congregation sings:

> 1 Help, O Lord; for piety has come to an end;
>   For faithfulness has vanished from the sons of men.
> 2 Lies they tell, each to his neighbor;
>   With flattering lips they speak heart to heart.

We are in Jerusalem in postexilic times. Since the national laments of the Psalter are almost all of a political nature, we are to think of the small colony of the Lord's people as in great inner distress, sighing under the oppression on all sides of ill-disposed neighbors and suffering primarily from their offensive speech.

We can easily imagine the proud Judeans in this "occupied area," where now enemy foreigners, probably the Chaldeans, are the ruling class. We can also realize how the proud attitude of the Jews toward them will itself tend to arouse bitter verbal clashes and provoke their foreign overlords to deceitful and insincere utterances. It leads to a strong imprecation against them from the poor and needy of the congregation because of their presumptuous and heartless words.

> 3 May the Lord cut off all hypocritical lips,
>   And every tongue which speaks insolently;
> 4 Who say, "By our tongue we will show our power!
>   Our lips are our own: who is lord over us?"

To the Lord's humiliated and hurt people the officiating priest now speaks an assuaging oracle of comfort. It is a single voice uttering the assurance that God

has seen the violence his poor have suffered. He has heard their groans of
distress. Now He will go into action to answer the congregation's cry for help.
He will speak and act as the champion and protector of His people.

> 5   Because of violence done the poor, because of the groaning of the needy,
>   Now will I arise, saith the Lord.
>   I will put them in safety, which they pant for.

To this comforting, steadying word from God the congregation lifts a hymn
of thanksgiving praising the words of God, even such words as have just been
uttered in this oracle. Here is a classic expression of appreciation for the message
of God as it has been received in public worship across the centuries. God's message is refined silver, completely refined gold. The Lord's congregation cannot
escape the encounters they are bound to have as long as they are closely surrounded on every side by this godless class of men in the land. But though they
act wickedly and talk insolently, God, seeing them for what they are, will protect His people from the ruin they would bring. Such is the appreciative answer
of the congregation to the words of the Lord.

> 6   The words of the Lord are words
>   Pure as silver seven times refined.
> 7   Thou, O Lord, wilt keep us from ruin; [5]
>   Thou wilt guard us from this worthless and unjust class.
> 8   Though on every side the wicked in the land talk proudly,
>   Thou lookest down upon [these] sons of men as [though they were]
>   a worm.

Ps. 36. OLD TESTAMENT MYSTICISM AT ITS BEST

Ps. 36 is a congregational prayer of lament which includes a hymnlike celebration of God's character and of what He does for "the sons of men" who worship Him in the Temple. The psalm is alive with the experience of congregational worship, and the psalmist clearly feels himself to be a part of that worshiping fellowship. He speaks of it as "those who know Thee" and "the upright
in heart" (vs. 10), and in the only place where he speaks of himself the context reveals his own sense of relationship to the larger group (vss. 10-11).
Moreover, he has a profoundly spiritual view of the ritual of public sacrifice
(vs. 8). The problem which gives rise to the psalm is the presence in the Judean
community of a bold group of godless men who are trampling down the righteous
and causing some of the Lord's congregation to waver in their loyalty.

The psalm opens with words which the psalmist represents as being spoken
to the inner soul of wicked men by "Transgression," conceived of as a personified evil spirit. The psalmist makes use of the oracle, a literary form which
belongs to prophetic utterance, in such manner as to introduce the element of
surprise. He represents "Transgression" as a demon who whispers to the inner

---

[5] Reading *mibbeliyya'al,* from vs. 6, and following Gunkel's reconstruction of vs. 8.

minds of evil men that God has no concern as to whether or not men fear Him. Yes, more, when God looks at men who hate Him, He lets His eyes slip lightly over their evil, finding no iniquity in them!

> 1   Transgression whispers to the wicked in his innermost heart:
>   "In the sight of His eyes there *is* no fear of God;
> 2   But He lets His eyes pass over him
>   So as not to find the iniquity of the one who hates Him." [6]

Then the psalmist turns upon the men who have listened to this sinister "revelation," this demonic "whisper" of "Transgression," and he utters against their words and deeds the judgment of his morally aroused soul. Shrewd as that demonic whisper may seem to be, its revelation, if accepted and heeded, will bring only trouble and disillusionment. He who accepts such teaching ceases to live wisely or to act aright. To such a one, night ceases to be the time for wholesome sleep, but is rather an opportunity for scheming up deeds harmful to others. And day is but the time for such action as represents the direct antithesis of what is good wherein evil is not rejected at all but rather embraced. Thus the psalmist criticizes the wicked man whom the demon Transgression has lured into practical atheism:

> 3   The words of his mouth are trouble and disillusionment;
>   He ceases to do wisely, to act right.
> 4   He schemes up harm upon his bed;
>   He takes his stand on a course of action that is not good;
>   Evil he does not reject.

Suddenly we are transported from the demon Transgression and the conduct which he inspires to the lofty, merciful, faithful, righteous, and just God! In the spiritual elevation of a hymn of praise the character of the Lord is proclaimed (vss. 5-7a). We feel the sinister background of evil, against which, in striking antithesis, is set the great and sovereign Goodness. As high as one can conceive, as deep as one can imagine, the Saviour of beasts and men is the Lord, precious in mercy!

> 5   O Lord, unto heaven reaches Thy mercy,
>   Thy faithfulness unto the clouds.
> 6   Thy righteousness is like the mountains of God;
>   Thy rule is as the great abyss.
>   Man and beast Thou savest;
> 7a   O Lord, how precious is Thy lovingkindness!

In such words the psalmist is dealing with a universe, no small section of which is bereft of God's presence. We are reminded of David's words to God in Browning's "Saul" in the climactic lines which acknowledge God's infinite presence everywhere in the universe:

---

[6] I follow here Gunkel's convincing reconstruction of the text.

So shall crown Thee the topmost, ineffablest, uttermost crown—
And Thy love fill infinitude wholly, nor leave up nor down
One spot for the creature to stand in!

The psalmist, continuing his hymn, reaches a noble climax as he deals with what this great God, Saviour of man and beasts, does for "the sons of men." There is a wonderful universalism here. He is thinking of worship, not merely on the part of Israel, but of all mankind. And he contemplates the Temple as existing, not merely for Israel, but, as the great disciple of Deutero-Isaiah's universalism taught, as "a house of prayer for all the peoples" (Isa. 56:7). He pictures humanity coming to the Lord in His Temple, finding there protection, even as do chickens under their mother's wings, and experiencing satisfaction of their material needs in the eating and drinking at the sacrificial feasts. But likewise do they find there in the true bliss of worship the satisfaction of their spiritual hungering and thirsting for righteousness. Our psalmist is a mystic and speaks out of his own profound experience of worship. The physical and material are for him primarily symbols of the spiritual. He finds that to worship God in the Temple is to drink from what Jeremiah has called "the fountain of living waters" (2:13). The worship of God gives him new life, spiritual life quickened by living water from holy springs. He finds too that worship illumines his problems and his daily walk with a light never seen on land or sea. It is that moral and spiritual light which has its fountain source in God, who Himself "is Light, and in whom there is no darkness at all." This is Old Testament mysticism at its best. Yet the psalmist's own experience is here enriched by his participation in the social fellowship of the congregation.

7b To Thee come the sons of men;
  In the shadow of Thy wings they take refuge.
8 They take their fill of the fatness of Thy house;
  And of the river of Thy delights Thou lettest them drink.
9 For with Thee is the fountain of life:
  In Thy light shall we see light.

The psalmist closes with the petition that God's lovingkindness and righteousness may be continued to His loyal worshipers. He utters the wish that he may be protected from the ruthlessness of his enemies and from uncertainty and wavering due to the pressure of the wicked.

10 Continue Thy lovingkindness to those who know Thee,
  And Thy righteousness to the upright in heart.
11 Let not the foot of pride trample me down,
  Nor the hand of the wicked make me waver.

Then there is a sudden change of tense to the perfect of certainty. He is sure that his prayer will be answered. It is likely that in the living worship an oracle of assurance was uttered by the priest immediately following the rendering of the petition in verses 10-11.[7] The oracle does not appear in the psalm, but from the sharp change of mood from lament to certainty it may reasonably be inferred that the oracle had been spoken. Thus the psalm closes in this assurance that the psalmist's enemies will be destroyed.

> 12   The evildoers shall be destroyed; they shall fall!
> They shall be thrust down and be unable to arise!

Ps. 44. LET GOD ARISE TO HELP US

Ps. 44 is a national lament. Many interpreters view it, along with Pss. 74, 79, and 83, as originating in the Maccabean period when the Hellenizing Syrian Antiochus IV (Epiphanes, *ca.* 167 B.C.) set in motion an intense persecution of the recalcitrant Jews who refused to espouse the Hellenistic cause. But recent authorities—Gunkel, Mowinckel, Schmidt, Oesterley—are at one in the belief that the whole book of Psalms was substantially complete by about 200 B.C., as is evidenced by the prologue of Ecclesiasticus and by what the author of Ecclesiasticus says about "David," meaning the book of Psalms (47:8-10). All this implies that the book of Psalms was already then part of the third of the recognized bodies of authoritative Hebrew literature, the Writings.

Moreover, verses 5, 17-18, and 22 of this psalm imply unanimity of loyalty to God on the part of the resisting Jewish community. This is inconsistent with the clear evidence of I Macc. 1:15, which states that many Jews under the influence of the Hellenizers "forsook the holy covenant, and joined themselves to the Gentiles, and sold themselves to do evil." Then too, the persecution which the Jews are suffering in this psalm is not of the huge proportions which characterized that of the Maccabean period.

Our knowledge from the time of Ezra (397 B.C.) to Alexander the Great (331 B.C.) in Judean history is very meager, but the psalm writers were acquainted with much history that has not come down to us. It is possible that this psalm belongs to this period. It is indeed likely that the persecution here implied is that which followed the putting down in 351 B.C. by Artaxerxes III (Ochus) of a three-year general uprising on the part of Phoenicia, Egypt, and all Syria, in which the Jews lined up with the revolutionaries. The Jews were then persecuted and thousands taken as captives to Babylonia and to Hyrcania on the Caspian Sea.[8] Jericho was destroyed, and most likely near-by Jerusalem was molested.

We learn from the Talmud that in Maccabean times until John Hyrcanus, verse 23a of our psalm—"Arise! Why dost Thou sleep"—was sung by the Levites. At that time Ps. 44 was already a part of the Bible.[9]

---

[7] Cf. Küchler, "Das priesterliche Orakel in Israel und Juda," in *Abhandlungen zur semitischen Religionskunde und Sprachwissenschaft.*

[8] See Guthe, *Geschichte des Volkes Israels,* p. 291; and Josephus *Contra Apionem* I. 194, who quotes Hecataeus of Abdera (306-283 B.C.) ; cf. also Oesterley, *The Psalms,* I, 67-73.

[9] *Sota* 48a. Cf. Gunkel, *Die Psalmen,* p. 187.

The psalmist begins with an appeal to Israel's history. In a form similar to a hymn he describes the Lord's deeds in the past (vss. 1-3). Knowledge of this was transmitted to his generation by the fathers through oral narration. The psalmist unrolls before his people the ancient events of the conquest of the peoples of Canaan by the Israelites and their settlement in the land, yet interprets this as achieved, not by Israel's military prowess, but by the might and the illumination of God, who was pleased with his people.

1   O God, with our ears we have heard;
     Our fathers have recounted to us
     The work Thou didst perform in their days,
     Which Thy hand didst do in days of yore.
2   How Thou didst uproot and plant nations;
     Thou hewest down nations and dost transplant them.
3   For not by their own sword did they take possession of the land,
     Nor did their own arms give them victory,
     But Thy right hand and Thy strong arm,
     And the light of Thy face, for Thou wast pleased with them.

What God did in this classic epoch of Israel, when it became a people with a homeland and a mission, becomes the basis of Israel's present confidence that God will help His people now. God is—that is, has been and remains—Israel's King and still sends victory to His people. In Israel's present weakness of military resources he trusts solely in God for deliverance from humiliation at the hands of his enemies, who are motivated by hate. Upon the Lord, he calls for help, even as he thrusts at his foes. It is by His help, granted in answer to his prayers, that Israel will be enabled to triumph over them. Nor will he glory in his own valor because of this, but in God, upon whom he calls. In this section the first person singular alternates with the first person plural. It is uttered by the leader of the congregation, who in such cases speaks in a representative capacity.[10]

4   Thou art my King and my God,
     Who commandest the victory of Jacob.
5   By Thee will we thrust at our enemies;
     In Thy name will we tread down our opponents.
6   For not in my bow do I trust,
     And my sword will not save me,
7   But Thou dost deliver us from our distress;
     And those who hate us, Thou dost put to shame.
8   In God we will make our boast all the day,
     And in Thy name we will give thanks forever.

Then begins the lament itself, and we now see that this recall of the past and the utterance of confidence that the Lord will help his people but throw into poignant contrast the painful humiliation being suffered by them in the

---

[10] Cf. Balla, *op. cit.*, pp. 106 ff.

present. They are spurned by God; their arms are disgraced before plundering enemies, who are more than a match for them. They are dispersed among the small peoples roundabout, who now make them, the once-proud Israelites, the butt of derisive insults that cut them to the quick. They feel that God has let them down, has sold out His people "cheap," to the lowest bidder. The leader continues to speak in a representative capacity (vs. 15). We feel the force of the strong, restrictive word "Yet," with which this vivid contrast to what has just been said is introduced.

9 Yet Thou hast spurned and humiliated us,
   And goest not forth with our armies.
10 Thou dost hurl us back before our adversaries;
   And those who hate us have plundered to their heart's desire.
11 Thou dost deliver us up like sheep to be slaughtered,
   And hast scattered us among the nations.
12 Thou dost sell Thy people cheap,
   And Thou madst no profit by the proceeds from them.
13 We are become a butt of insult to our neighbors,
   A target of scorn and derision to those around us.
14 Thou dost make us an object of satire among the nations,
   So that people shake their head over us.
15 All the day long my humiliation is vividly present to me,
   And Thou coverest my face with shame,
16 Before the voice of reproacher and blasphemer,
   Before the countenance of enemy and avenger.

Why has such distress come about? "Why?" It is the most characteristic question of the national lament. The psalmist makes no admission that the Lord's people have sinned. They evidently are not burdened with a sense of guilt. They do not acknowledge that in any sense they deserve what they are suffering. Rather do they assert their faithfulness. They have not been renegades from God unto the worship of other gods. Yet to all appearances the Lord has dealt with His people as He maltreated and trampled the monstrous and evil dragon. The reference is to the Semitic mythology of creation. Yes, more, denying them His light He has overwhelmed them with the abysmal darkness that belonged to that monster's reign.[11] The Lord, who knows the innermost being of men, must surely know the basic loyalty of His people. Indeed, so pleads the psalmist to God, we suffer because of Thee. The enmity that is tracking us down and slaughtering us like sheep marked for killing stems from our loyalty to Thee. We sense from the background for such words how the pretentious claims of the Hebrew religion made the people of the Lord odious to the other nations. But we feel the intensity and the inevitableness of their fiery "why?"

17 All this hath come upon us, but we have not forgotten Thee,
   Nor have we dealt falsely with Thy covenant.

---

[11] Cf. Gen. 1:2, "And darkness was upon the face of the deep [tehôm]."

18 We have not turned our heart back,
   Nor has our step swerved from Thy path,
19 Although Thou hast crushed *us* instead of the dragon
   And hast overwhelmed *us* with deep darkness.
20 If we had forgotten the name of our God
   Or had spread out our hand to a foreign god,
21 Would not God have found this out?
   For He knows the secrets of the heart.
22 Rather [12] on Thy account are we killed every day;
   We are thought of as a flock for slaughter.

The psalm comes to its climax in the impetuous petition to God. The "why" of the lament recurs (vss. 23-24). But the characteristic mood is expressed by the verbs "Arise! . . . Awake! . . . Arise!" Why does the Lord hide His face and ignore the suffering and misery of His people? Let Him awake as from a sleep. Let Him arise to protect them! As they pray, the congregation lie prone upon the ground (Deut. 9:18; Isa. 29:4; Jer. 14:2; Judith 4:11), in the attitude of humiliation before God. In spite of their earlier vaunted loyalty as the ground of their entreaty, their ultimate appeal, with which the psalm ends, is to God's own character, His mercy. We catch the overtones of importunity in the passionate appeal for help.

23 Arise! Why dost Thou sleep?
   Awake! Spurn us not forever!
24 Why dost Thou conceal Thy face;
   Why forgettest Thou our distress and our oppression?
25 For our soul sinks down to the dust:
   Our body cleaves to the earth.
26 Arise, for help [13] to us!
   And ransom us for Thy mercy's sake!

Ps. 58. THE MISCARRIAGE OF JUSTICE IN THE EARTH

Ps. 58 is a congregational lament over tyranny which is suffered by human beings. As is the case in Ps. 82, it opens with an address imaginatively given to the highest foreign divinities whose puppets and willing instruments are the pagan rulers who are spreading corruption in the earth (vss. 1-2). The psalmist is deeply stirred by the miscarriage of justice in the entire world. He addresses these pagan beings in a rhetorical question, which is uttered in ironical tones. The psalmist scoffs at the thought that such "judges" may be the fountain of any "justice," for their reign in the earth only smooths the way to oppression. Cries the psalmist:

1 You gods, do you truly speak what is right?
   Do you judge in equity the sons of men?
2 No, all of you judge corruptly in the land;
   Your hands smooth the way to oppression!

---

[12] Ehrlich, *op. cit.*, p. 99, has rightly sensed the force of *kî* here as *viel mehr*.
[13] Accusative of intention; cf. Gesenius-Kautzsch, *op. cit.*, sec. 90g.

So of the evil men who are the servants of such divinities the psalmist now speaks, of men who are wicked and liars from their birth. They are malicious men. They are like a venomous serpent which, deaf to the soothing murmur of the conjurer, discharges its deadly poison.

> 3 The wicked are degenerate, renegades from birth:
> From the very womb they speak lies.
> 4 Their venom is like a serpent,
> Like a deaf adder with its ear stopped up,
> 5 Which does not listen to the whispering murmur of the magicians,
> Those skilled in binding charms.

Upon these ungodly men the psalmist pronounces a sevenfold curse. This is spoken in a characteristic Semitic vein and represents a full and complete malediction, such as will influence God and lead Him to intervention with intent to destroy. Moreover, as is often the case in such a lament, these curses are increased in potency by examples of dreadful destruction: (a) the breaking of the strong jaw teeth of a lion; (b) the rapid vanishing of the prized and needed rain; (c) the withering of grass on the way; (d) the apparent vanishing of a snail as it disappears and closes up in its shell; (e) a miscarriage that never saw the light (cf. Job 3:16); (f) the cutting down of brambles; and (g) the milkweed tossed away by the wind. We feel here the psalmist's keenly observant eye, utilizing to a moral purpose common things perfectly familiar and strikingly pertinent. The curse had its definite place in the ritual of ancient Israel (cf. Num. 5:21-31; Deut. 27:14-26). Its aim was to remind God of His power and to strengthen the confidence of the supplicant. On the other hand, it was to do damage, to bring about destruction, to hamper and destroy life.[14] So in deep moral earnestness he attempts by appeal to God to draw down His curse upon these wicked men.

> 6 O God, break their teeth in their mouth:
> Break down, as of lions, their jaw teeth!
> 7 Let them vanish like water which runs off;
> Let them be dried up like grass on the way,
> 8 Like snails that close up and disappear,
> Like a woman's miscarriage that beholds not the sun.
> 9 Before they grow up may He cut them down like a thorn bush;
> May He whirl them away like milkweed in a storm!

Then comes a sudden change in the psalm. From sharp, passionate malediction we come to the mood of calm certainty that God, the righteous Judge, will take vengeance upon these pagan instruments of heathen divinities. We feel the fierce barbaric realism of the victor's exultation (vs. 10b). Their destruction will bring joy to the righteous and will strengthen their faith that the whole earth is in the hands of a just God. We are to infer that between verse 9 and

---

[14] Cf. Gunkel, *Einleitung*, pp. 131, 304.

verse 10 an oracle has been uttered in the worship by a priest or man of God, which brings to the humble congregation the answer of God to the wish and prayers of the lament. So in the certainty of faith that God will intervene to take vengeance upon the wicked, the psalm comes to its triumphant close.

> 10   The righteous will rejoice when he sees [God's] vengeance;
>   He will bathe his feet in the blood of the wicked!
> 11   And men will say, "Surely there is a reward [15] for the righteous;
>   Surely there is a God who judges in the earth!"

Ps. 60. LIVING VALIANTLY IN NATIONAL CRISIS

Ps. 60 is a national lament rendered at a festival just before the breakup and flight of the Judeans after the Chaldean destruction of the Judean state in 587 B.C.[16] The psalm was rendered in the hope of securing God's help in the midst of the desperate situation of His people.

It opens with a solemn lament (vss. 1-5). The congregation feels itself humiliated and under the interdict of God. He has rejected His people. In vivid metaphor, the defeat at Chaldean hands has been like an earthquake which left the land breached and fissured. God has handed to his people the cup of awful calamity, which they have drunk to its dregs. They pray for restoration and healing and for some place to which they can flee from the ruthless enemy. As the Lord's "people . . . , those who fear" Him, even "His beloved ones," they appeal to Him for deliverance.

> 1   O God, Thou hast rejected us; Thou hast broken out upon us;
>   Thou hast been angry; restore us!
> 2   Thou didst make the earth to quake; Thou didst split it open;
>   Heal its fissures, for it is shaking!
> 3   Thou hast made Thy people experience hard things:
>   Thou hast made us drink wine that caused reeling.
> 4   Give to those who fear Thee a refuge
>   To which to flee from before the bow.
> 5   That Thy beloved ones may be delivered,
>   Extend Thy right hand and answer us.

At this point in the rendition of the psalm a priest, skilled in the technique and acquainted with the content of existing oracles for the public worship, brings to the Lord's lamenting and humiliated people a consoling oracle.[17] It was not created for the moment but was already in existence and probably originally dated from a time just after the fall of the great power, Assyria (612 B.C.), had awakened fantastic political hopes in Judah for regaining by a reunited Israel [18] the extent of territory over which King David had once ruled. The whole oracle imitates a victory song and in bold strokes describes the triumphant march of the

---

[15] Literally, "fruit."
[17] Cf. Küchler, op. cit., p. 298.

[16] Cf. Gunkel, Die Psalmen, p. 258.
[18] Cf. Gunkel, Die Psalmen, p. 258.

Lord as, like a mighty, giant warrior, He regains on behalf of His people the territory which He first covenanted to give them, but the dominion of which has passed into other hands.

The important ancient Israelite city of Shechem, which is later to become the chief seat of the hybrid Samaritan community, is one of the "cities of Samaria" which Sargon II captured in 721 B.C., and where he settled foreign colonists (II Kings 17:24). The Valley of Succoth is the valley of the Jabbok River—east of the Jordan with Succoth at its head—some ten miles northeast of the point where the Jabbok reaches the Jordan. It also is in Assyrian hands. Gilead is in the possession of the Ammonites (Jer. 49:1). Manasseh and Ephraim, which once composed the heart of the northern kingdom of Israel, have been conquered by Assyria (721 B.C.). Judah has just been conquered by the Chaldeans. The oracle asserts in passionate nationalistic exultation that Shechem and the Valley of Succoth shall again become the Lord's possession, for Him to divide and portion out among His people. Gilead and Manasseh shall likewise once more be His. The oracle also is convinced that north and south, Ephraim and Judah, will become again one kingdom. Ephraim will provide the very defense of the realm, and Judah will be the nucleus—capital and ruler, "the staff" in the Lord's hand —of gathered and restored Israel. But still more, Israel, thus become unified, strong, and dominant, will reach out to conquer and add to its territory its one-time vassals and long-time enemies Moab and Edom. We feel the intense Israelite nationalism and implied derogatory aspersions in the oracle—the Sea of Moab, i.e., the Dead Sea, a mere washpot for the Lord's feet; Edom fit only for his sandals! But the throwing of the sandals was at the same time the striking symbol of the Lord's taking possession of His property.[19] The oracle represents God as gloating in triumph over Philistia, which will come again under Israel's power, even as it had in the golden age of King David.

This oracle is used verbatim in another national lament, Ps. 108:7-9. It was intended to awaken hope and courage and is here given as the word of God to His broken and distressed people.

> 6 God spoke in His sanctuary:
>   "I will exult; I will portion out Shechem;
>   I will measure [for conquest] the valley of Succoth!
> 7   Mine is Gilead, and Mine Manasseh;
>   Ephraim is My helmet;
>   Judah is My commander's staff.
> 8 The Sea of Moab is My washpot;
>   Upon Edom I cast My sandal;
>   Over Philistia will I shout in triumph!"

The psalm returns, in verses 9-11, to the solemn mood of lament. The psalmist begins with a wish for a safe escape from the overwhelming chaos of Jerusalem

---

[19] Cf. Boaz buying property of Naomi, Ruth 4:8-9.

to the protection of a walled city in Edom. He views Edom, not as an enemy
country, but as a place of asylum where many Judeans at that very time are
seeking and finding protection from the ruthless ravaging Chaldeans, who are
mopping up Jerusalem (Jer. 40:11). The "me" in verse 9 represents the leader
of an expedition of Judean refugees from Chaldean violence. He longs, on behalf of his people, for the protection of a fortified city, probably Petra, the
ancient capital of Edom.[20] He has no hope for safety through the protection of the
remnant of the Judean army, for the Lord has spurned the fighting forces of His
people. If help comes at all, it must come not from men but from God.

> 9 Who will conduct me unto the fortress?
>   Who will lead me to Edom?
> 10 Hast not Thou, O God, spurned us
>   And goest not forth with our armies?
> 11 Give to us help before the enemy,
>   For futile is deliverance through men!

There is another sudden change in mood in the closing verse of the psalm.
We move from longing wish and eager petition to the certainty of God's favorable response. It is likely that such sudden turn from inner stress to peaceful
certainty is due to the comforting influence of another oracle. This does not
appear in the text of the psalm, but at this point in the psalm's rendition it
will be spoken by the priest. It gives assurance to the congregation of God's intervention to help His harrassed and troubled people.[21]

> 12 In God we shall do valiantly,
>   And He will tread down our enemies.

Ps. 74. REMEMBER THY CONGREGATION

Ps. 74 is a congregational lament intended for a fast to bewail the destruction,
plundering, and burning of the sanctuary at pagan hands. This had taken place
so long before the psalmist wrote that the resulting ruins were called by him
"perpetual desolations." When the psalm was written, Jews were still suffering
the humiliation of slander and abuse at the hands of their persecutors, who
were representatives of a world kingdom. It is likely that the psalm, which
seems to show the influence of the Priestly Code (vs. 20), had its origin in the
period between Ezra and Alexander the Great. Most likely it came into being
in connection with the quelling by the Persian Artaxerxes III (Ochus) of the
widespread insurrection against him that broke out in 351 B.C., into which the
Jewish people had been drawn.

The congregation pour out their lament to the Lord. They feel that as His
"flock" they belong to Him, for has He not acquired them? He redeemed His people so that they became His own property, here called poetically the "tribe" pos-

---

sessed by Him, and He took up His abode in the Temple on the hill of Zion. But the Lord now is angry with His people and has spurned them, seemingly forever. "Why this harsh treatment?" the psalmist cries and asks Him to hasten, like a giant in majestic stride, to the protection of His sanctuary, which now for so long a time has been lying in ruins.

> 1 Why, O God, hast Thou forever spurned [us]?
>   Why dost Thy anger smoke against the flock which Thou dost pasture?
> 2 Remember Thy congregation which Thou didst acquire of old;
>   Forget not Thy property, Mount Zion, wherein Thou hast dwelt.
> 3 Lift up Thy steps toward the perpetual desolations;
>   The enemy hath damaged everything in the sanctuary.

In lamenting words the psalmist pictures what has happened. The holy place of the Temple, where only praise and prayer should be heard, has been desecrated by the crude roar of soldiers, unhindered in their destructive orgy by any pious inhibitions as they hew down the precious woodwork of the Temple, just as though wielding axes in a forest thicket. They strike down with hatchets and axes the delicate engravings, then set fire to the sanctuary, profanely destroying the Lord's holy dwelling. The psalmist interprets the reckless purpose that inflates the soul of these utterly irreverent pagan destroyers as being to exterminate all sacred places in the earth.[22]

> 4 Thy enemies have roared in the midst of Thy meeting place;
>   They have carried out the inclination of their lust.
> 5 They hew down like those who bring in foliage,
>   Like those who swing axes in the thicket of the forest.
> 6 And now Thy engraved work they have hammered all together;
>   With hatchet and axe they strike them down.[23]
> 7 They have set Thy sanctuary on fire;
>   They have profaned to the ground the place where Thy name dwells.
> 8 They have said in their heart, "Their holy place we will altogether efface.
>   We will burn all the sanctuaries of Deity in the earth."

The most serious consequence of the plundering of the sanctuary is that the congregation is deprived of the comforting or guiding oracles from God. It was the Israelite custom in the songs of national lament, after the song had ended, that the voice of the priest or prophet was heard pronouncing the answer of the Lord to the suppliant congregation. It was, as Gunkel says, all the more shattering and a sure indication of the divine anger when the oracle failed.[24] It is accordingly a solemn consideration in this lament when we are told that the

---

[22] Cf. Dan. 11:37, where just such purpose is likewise later attributed to Antiochus IV (Epiphanes).
[23] In vss. 5 and 6; see Gunkel's reconstruction of the Hebrew text.
[24] *Einleitung*, p. 137.

plundering of the Temple has deprived the congregation of the prophetic oracle. Here is indeed the great privation.[25]

> 9 Signs [26] for us we do not see; no longer is there a prophet;
>   And there is no one among us who knows how long!

The closing expression of verse 9, the "how long" of impatience, like the "why" of despair with which the psalm opens, is a decisive mark of the lament, and it is to this lamenting note that the psalmist still clings. The taunts of the enemy with their blasphemy of the Lord seem well-nigh unbearable. Instead of striking down His adversaries with His mighty right hand, God seems to withdraw it into His bosom and hold it there, restraining Himself from action.

> 10 How long, O God, will the adversary taunt [us]?
>   Will the enemy defame Thy name forever?
> 11 Why dost Thou turn Thy hand back,
>   And restrain Thy right hand in Thy bosom?

In his distress at the seeming inaction of God the psalmist turns for hope and assurance to primeval times, when the Lord in combat with the awful monsters of chaos showed His hand, defeated these gigantic powers, and created the world. It is in the psalmist's thought that the evil enemy of the present is comparable to that primeval dragon. So he gives us an Israelite version of the classic Babylonian myth of creation. In it the Lord has displaced Marduk; Tiamat, monstrous dragon of the deep, and Kingu, her consort, and their helpers do not appear, but the powerful beings they represent glimmer through the Hebrew words for the sea, the many-headed dragon of the deep, and the monster Leviathan. These beings were mastered and destroyed by God, just as Marduk defeated the dragon Tiamat, her monstrous consort Kingu, and their helpers. The mighty dragon, frustrated and killed by the Lord, became mere grub for the jackals, the howling things of the desert. Says the psalmist in this classic way, God is still in control, however great and powerful the adversary may seem to be. He is now as of old, King, still achieving victory, still creating triumph out of seeming defeat. So the psalmist sings:

> 12 But Thou, O God, art our King of old,
>   Achieving victory in the midst of the earth.
> 13 Thou didst split the sea in Thy strength;
>   Thou didst break the heads of the dragon upon the waters;
> 14 Thou didst crush in pieces the heads of Leviathan;
>   Thou didst give him as food, as grub for the jackals.

Then the dragon, which had held everything in chaos, having been destroyed, the Lord created the earth and introduced the new order of the world. First of all came His regulation of the once terror-striking torrents. Those destructive

---

[25] Cf. Mowinckel, *op. cit.*, I, 97.   [26] Or tokens, assurances.

waters were transformed into fountains. The overwhelming streams were bound, and dry land made its appearance, freed from destructive inundation.

> 15   Thou didst cleave out fountain and torrent;
> Thou didst dry up inexhaustible streams.

Then were created the luminaries making day and night. The zones of the earth were marked out, regions where it is hot and areas where it is cold; and the seasons, winter and summer, were established.

> 16   Thine is the day; Thine also the night:
> Thou didst establish the moon and the sun;
> 17   Thou didst fix all the zones of the earth;
> Winter and summer, Thou didst devise them.

In this magnificent passage we see that in spite of the monotheistic trend in Israel, which tended to shy away from mythological concepts, the great Hebrew poets, including the psalmists and the authors of Deutero-Isaiah and of the book of Job, [27] made use of this wonderful material. But they made its broad outlines, its living action, and its brilliant colors serve the very interests of monotheism. Through it, even as in this instance, they exalted the triumphant might of the Lord as the One who even at times of His people's deepest humiliation is still able, is still a God of infinite resourcefulness. He does not succumb to any crisis, but can and will still triumph over those who would thwart Him.

It is this mighty, ancient work of God—His creation of the world—that in this closing section the psalmist bids God to "remember." But there is deep pathos in his words. The psalmist here makes implicit reference to the priestly story (Gen. 6:12-13), which explains that it was when God saw the awful "corruption" to which His creation had fallen that He got into action, utterly destroyed that corrupt generation, but wondrously saved the righteous, Noah and his sons. Let Him again look and become concerned over the corruption that is *now* oppressing His creatures! Let Him see that for them, His oppressed and needy people, the earth has again become but a "field for violence!" Let God again intervene to protect them and to change their lot from despair to praise! Let the never-to-be-forgotten, insolent threats of the pagan victors, *His* slanderers, *His* enemies, arouse Him to action! The climax of the whole psalm is this passionate petition that the Lord will arise!

> 18   Remember this, the enemy slanders;
> Yes, an unprincipled people insult Thy name!
> 19   Surrender not to mischief the soul that acknowledges Thee;
> The life of Thy humble one do not ever forget!
> 20   Look at Thy creatures, for they are full of corruption,
> For the earth is fields of violence!

---

[27] Isa. 51:9-11; Job 26:12-13. I am here indebted to Gunkel's profound insight into the significance of this mythological material, first presented in his epochal book *Schöpfung und Chaos.*

21 Let the oppressed not be turned back humiliated;
    Let the poor and needy praise Thy name.
22 Arise, O God, plead Thy cause!
    Remember Thy insult from the senseless!
23 Forget not the threat of Thy adversaries;
    The raging of Thy enemies, becoming ever louder.[28]

Ps. 77. A GOD WHO DOETH WONDERS

Ps. 77 is one of the few psalms which came from the northern kingdom of Israel. The most likely date for it is between 733 and 721 B.C., when the north Israelite kingdom, so strong under Jeroboam II, had been struck a blow from which it never recovered, although it still continued to exist as a kingdom. The psalm is a national lament in which the personal note of lamentation which thrills it through verse 15 is ennobled by the solemn dignity of a great national concern. It would be at home in the first instance in the worship at the sanctuary of Bethel after the campaign into the west (733-732 B.C.) of Tiglath-pileser III of Assyria, which left the kingdom of Israel decimated and Damascus utterly destroyed. After the fall of Samaria in 721 B.C. along with other Israelite psalms this psalm was taken up into the later Judean hymnbook. It would there be rendered at the Jerusalem Temple in times of depression of the nation or of the religious congregation.

The psalmist opens with a lament. Ordinarily the cause of the distress in a lament is physical suffering, or an unsettling consciousness of sin, or the aggressive enmity of dangerous foes, personal or national. But in this psalm the suffering is that of the earnest thinker whose mind is restlessly seeking an explanation of a problem. Out of his deep distress even as he complains to God he stretches out his hand to Him in murmuring prayer. Sleep has vanished from his eyelids. In the dead of night, wide-awake and unable to rest, his mind ranges over the ancient past of his people. But the more he meditates, the more alarmed he becomes.

1 I cry aloud unto God;
   I cry to God that He will listen to me.
2 In the day of my distress I seek Him;
   I spread out [29] my hands.
   In the night my tears flow without ceasing;
   My soul refuses to be comforted.
3 If I remember God, I murmur:
   I complain, and my spirit faints.
4 Thou hast seized the eyelids of my eyes:
   I am disturbed, and I cannot rest.
5 I think upon the days of old;
   The years of antiquity I remember.

[28] Ehrlich, *op. cit.*, p. 123, rightly senses the fire of this verse.
[29] Cf. Ps. 143:6 and supply, with Gunkel, *pērasti.*

6 I meditate in the night in my heart:
   I ponder and search my spirit.

The psalmist has not yet told us what his problem is, but his lamenting words
have prepared us for it, and his very withholding has sharpened our curiosity.
What is it that so disturbs him? Now he speaks it forth. He feels that the springs
of God's compassion have been shut up. Yet not God's compassion to him as
an individual, but to his people. His lament began as the pouring forth of the
distress of his own soul, but now we see it is rather the lament of his nation,
uttered through him as one who feels keenly and with insight the woe of his
people.

How great the contrast of the present with those glorious days of old when
Israel found favor in the Lord's eyes, and when His compassion flowed forth
toward them! The psalmist is a north Israelite. To him Israel includes not
Judah but Jacob and Joseph, the northern kingdom. Accordingly it is most
likely that his psalm has as its specific background those tragic days in 733-732
B.C., when the Assyrian monarch "came and captured Ijon, Abel–beth Maacah,
Janoah, Kedesh, Hazor, Gilead, and Galilee, all the land of Naphtali, and
carried the inhabitants captive to Assyria" (II Kings 15:29), leaving the kingdom
of Israel but a mere torso of what it once was. Laments the psalmist:

7 Will the Lord spurn forever,
   And never again be favorable?
8 Has His mercy ceased forever?
   Has His faithfulness come to an end for all generations?
9 Has God forgotten to be gracious?
   Or has He in anger shut up His compassion?

As the psalmist raises such questions, contrasting the present distress of his
people with past glory, his mind comes to rest upon God. The opening words
of verse 10, "Then I said," point to the entrance into his mind of new spiritual
discernment,[30] a new conviction grounded in faith. By use of strong rhetorical
questions he gives expression to his belief that God's right hand, the hand of
action, has not weakened, nor has the purpose of His deeds on behalf of His
people changed. Then he turns at verse 11 to the Lord, speaking no longer
of Him but addressing Him directly and in words that have changed from lament
to prayer. The psalmist's prayer is in the form of a meditative hymn in which
he celebrates the attributes of God—His holiness and incomparable greatness—
and then moves on to the praise of His deeds. In the present, God still does
marvelous things which will demonstrate to the nations and to His own people,
Israel, His strength. The psalmist must have thought of proud Assyria itself
as one of those nations. He redeemed His people from Egyptian bondage, and
He will yet redeem them from their present distress. By "the sons of Jacob and

[30] So, suggestively, Nowack.

Joseph" he means, as did Amos (7:2; 5:6, 15; 6:6), the northern kingdom of Israel.

10　Then I said: Has it become weak,
　　　Has the right hand of the Most High changed?
11　I will remember Thy deeds,[31] O Lord,
　　　That Thy wonders are majestic from of old.
12　And I will meditate upon all Thy deeds,
　　　And Thy acts will I ponder.
13　O God, in holiness is Thy way:
　　　Who is a great God like our God?
14　Thou art a God who doeth wonders;
　　　Thou makest known among the nations Thy strength.
15　Thou redeemest Thy people with Thy right arm,
　　　The sons of Jacob and Joseph.

Already by implication the psalmist has touched upon God's mighty redemptive act in Israel's history when the Joseph tribes were led out of Egypt by Moses and Aaron (vs. 15). It was that momentous act which really began the national history of Israel. Accordingly it is by a quite natural transition that this psalmist, with his strong and brooding interest in "the days of old," moves, at verse 16, for his climax into a magnificent hymn full of fire and energy. It describes— with features enriched by primitive Israelite mythology and untouched as yet by eighth-century prophetic thought—the awesome, yes, fearsome manifestation of the Lord's presence then with His people. The psalmist's purpose is clear. Through this brilliant ending to his psalm he will say to worshiping Israel in its hour of deep dejection that the God of Israel's ancient and glorious past is still leading His people through waters that threaten to engulf them and will still provide "shepherds" like unto Moses and Aaron. Gunkel, noting the mythological features of these verses, suggests the possibility that the psalmist may have at hand an ancient poem which has already ornamented with such mythological features the Israelite saga of the Red Sea.[32] It is clearly not the Yahwist's account of events that he is following, because, like the Elohist's version of the saga (Exod. 4:14-16, 27-31), the psalmist gives a significant place to Aaron, who is entirely absent from the Yahwist's story. Yet Aaron here has no such exclusively priestly mission as distinguishes him in the Priestly Code. It would be expected that this Israelite psalmist would be most dependent upon the Elohist, whose account had its origin in the north. He gives us an imaginative, poetic version of the treasured story.

At that epochal event the waters of the Sea of Reeds drew back, writhing in terror-struck awe before the Lord's self-manifestation! Similarly all nature was perturbed. The clouds expressed their response in a heavy downpour of rain, and the sky roared in terrific peals of thunder, which accompanied the forked,

[31] Following Gunkel and Schlögl in rendering "Thy deeds" as parallel to "Thy wonders."
[32] Die Psalmen, p. 334. Similar features are in Ps. 114:3-6 and Ps. 18:7-15.

streaked lightning. Then the thunder subsided into continued grumbling, like the rumble of the divine chariot wheels, while the flashes of lightning lit up the world. The fear-struck land trembled in earthquake. The Lord's chariot made a way through the great and threatening waters, on which path Moses and Aaron, as the Lord's servants, led His precious flock through the sea, yet no visible traces of the presence of God were left behind.

> 16 The waters saw Thee, O God;
>   The waters saw Thee and writhed;
>   Yes, the deeps were perturbed.
> 17 The masses of cloud poured out water;
>   The sky gave forth its voice;
>   Yes, Thy arrows darted hither and thither.
> 18 The sound of Thy thunder was like the [chariot wheels];
>   Thy lightning flashes illumined the world;
>   The earth saw and shook!
> 19 Through the sea was Thy way, O Lord,
>   And Thy path through great waters,
>   But traces of Thee were not perceived.
> 20 Thou didst lead Thy people like a flock,
>   By the hand of Moses and Aaron.

Ps. 79. LET GOD INTERVENE FOR HIS PEOPLE

Ps. 79 is a national lament of the congregation of the Lord, which has as its background an attack upon the Temple by a pagan military force. It is likely that the aim of the attack, as earlier Judean history from King Rehoboam's time suggests, was to plunder the Temple of its treasures [33] and it was in the attempt to defend it from such violence that many Jews lost their lives. From the angle of the pagan invaders such Judean resistance would be viewed as insubordination and would be summarily dealt with. We are probably in the time between Ezra and Alexander the Great, and the opportunity for such a raid will be the battles of the Persian world empire against the rebellious Egyptians. It was probably the same incident as that to which Joel 3:4 ff. refers, according to which Tyrian and Philistine traders carried away Temple treasure from Jerusalem to their own sanctuaries and sold Jewish prisoners to the Greeks [34] as slaves. The citation of verses 2 and 3 of this psalm in I Macc. 7:17 indicates that these words are already cited as sacred scripture, which precludes a Maccabean origin for the psalm.[35]

The psalm opens with a lament. Heathen feet have defiled the Lord's Temple. Moreover the city of Jerusalem itself has been made a heap of ruins. Jewish dead, the Lord's servants, lie unburied. The psalmist and his people feel keenly the disgrace because honorable burial has been denied to the Jewish casualties.

---

[33] Cf. I Kings 14:25-26, Shishak's (Sheshonq's) plunder of the Temple.
[34] Cf. Guthe, Geschichte des Volkes Israels, p. 309.
[35] So Gunkel, Die Psalmen, p. 350.

The corpses are the carrion of vultures and beasts. Blood has flowed like water in Jerusalem and its environs. And worst of all, the small neighboring kingdoms scoff in derision at the fate of the Jews. We sense here the proud self-consciousness of Judaism, which felt itself to be the Lord's chosen people. Thus runs the lament:

1 O God, pagans have come into Thy property;
   They have defiled Thy holy Temple;
      They have made of Jerusalem a heap of ruins.
2 They have given the corpses of Thy servants
   As food to the birds of heaven,
      The flesh of Thy loyal ones to the beasts of the earth.
3 They have poured out their blood like water
   In the parts roundabout Jerusalem, with no one burying them.
4 We have become a butt of scorn to our neighbors.
   An object of derision and scoffing to those roundabout us.

The lament issues in passionate appeals to the Lord, which begin with the impatient question characteristic of the lament "How long?" The psalmist feels that his people are under the interdict of God. The Lord is angry with them; it is His burning indignation that the community is experiencing. But why is the Lord's own people the object of such wrath? Why not rather the pagan plunderers who know nothing about Him and do not serve Him? And they deserve it, for they are the ones who have devoured Israel, even as wild animals devour prey, and it is they who have devastated the home of the Lord's people. He uses "Jacob," the classic name of honor for Israel.

The psalm moves on to another basis of appeal (vs. 8). The psalmist implies that although earlier generations because of their iniquities have deserved the Lord's wrath, the Israel of the present, which has maintained the service of the Temple, does not. And indeed, if the Lord should hold them responsible for the sins of the former generations, His people are not now strong enough to bear the punishment. So the psalmist throws them upon God's mercy. If there is sin for which God is holding His people responsible, He in His sovereignty can provide atonement for them and their sins, which they cannot themselves provide.[36] Yet deeper goes his appeal (vs. 9) as he grounds his petition in God's very nature. God has proved Himself in the past to be Israel's Saviour. His own honor is now at stake. His very reputation hangs in the balance. For Israel's neighbors, seeing what is happening, are saying in derision, "Where is their God? Why doesn't He come to their protection?" So the psalmist prays that the nations, both those who are perpetrating the destruction and those who are with satisfaction looking on, may be shown conclusively that the Lord avenges the shed blood of His servants. And may this intervention of God take place in the sight of us who are experiencing these horrors, the psalmist prays, before our eyes! Still another appeal he makes (vs. 11). The heathen destroyers have thrown recalcitrant

[36] Cf. Brown, Driver, Briggs, *op. cit.*, p. 497, 2b.

Jews into prison. May God hear their cries of distress from their prison bars. Some of them have been condemned to death. May they be set free by the hand of God, for no human hand can emancipate them. The final appeal (vs. 12) is simply the insistence that the insults which have made raw the sensitive spirits of the Jewish sufferers are really direct insults to God, such as should call forth His sevenfold vengeance. This alone is consonant with the divine honor and likewise befits the scale of the crimes. Thus the petition with its varied inducement for the Lord's intervention pours forth from the psalmist's soul:

5 How long, O Lord? Wilt Thou be angry forever?
      [How long] will Thy anger burn like fire?
6 Pour out Thy wrath upon the pagans,
      Who know Thee not,
   And upon the kingdoms
      Who do not call upon Thy name.
7 For they have devoured Jacob,
      And have devastated his abode.
8 Remember not to our disadvantage former iniquities;
      Let Thy mercies come speedily to meet us,
      For we are brought very low.
9 Help us, O God of our salvation,
      Because of Thy honor.
   And save us and atone for our sins,
      For Thy name's sake.
10 Why do the nations say,
      "Where is their God?"
   Let be known among the nations, before our eyes,
      The vengeance for the poured-out blood of Thy servants!
11 Let come before Thy countenance the prisoner's cry of distress!
      As accords with the greatness of Thine arm, set free
         Those condemned to death!
12 And pay back to our neighbors sevenfold into their bosom
      Their insults with which they have insulted Thee, O Lord!

The psalm closes, as is frequent in the national lament, with the certainty of the Lord's favorable answer, and with the vow that His people, generation after generation, will praise Him. The psalmist uses here a tender and beloved descriptive phrase for the congregation of God, "the sheep of Thy pasture." It is likely that, in the actual rendering of the psalm, immediately after verse 12 an oracle of comforting assurance was uttered by the priest. This would account for the utter change of mood from lament to praise which is so evident in the vow that follows:

13 And we, Thy people and the sheep of Thy pasture,
      Shall praise Thee forever.
   From generation to generation
      We will rehearse Thy praise.

Gunkel finely says, "So the song of lament which began so full of despair, ends in the tone of jubilant assurance: the suppliants have struggled up from the depths of anguish, yes, of despair, to the lofty heights of assurance that the Lord lives and helps, a beautiful example of every genuine prayer." [37]

Ps. 80. LORD OF HOSTS, RESTORE US

Ps. 80 is a psalm of national lament. It is significant in that it is one of the very few psalms which had their origin in the northern kingdom of Israel.[38] The psalmist has in mind the northern tribes, the "sons" of Joseph, Ephraim, and Manasseh, and the beloved "brother" of Joseph, Benjamin. These three tribes represent the very heart of the northern kingdom. The earliest day from which the psalm could come is 721 B.C., when the northern kingdom fell, for the psalmist clearly looks back to this as a catastrophe, and as representing what is to him the inexplicable judgment of God. In these psalms whose place of origin is in the north we cannot discover any difference in spirit from those which originated in the Judean kingdom, and this it was which made it possible for such psalms to be taken up into the predominantly Judean Psalter.

The refrain, which appears four times (vss. 3, 7, 14a, 19), represents that part of the psalm which, in the living worship, was rendered by the congregation. The lament itself would be uttered by a spokesman of the congregation, as the lament of II Chr. 20:5-13 suggests. The psalm moreover is characterized by a striking literary richness in that it contains three remarkable elements: (a) It presents a clever play upon the word Benjamin (vs. 17), a feature which also guarantees the authenticity of the reference to that tribe in verse 1. (b) It includes a remarkable allegory intermingled with its meaning in a form which appealed greatly to the Israelite literary genius. (c) It has a feelingful and impressive refrain.

The lament begins with an appeal which in its praise features partakes of the qualities of a hymn, for the Lord is addressed with ancient titles of honor. He is Israel's shepherd (Gen. 49:24), tender of the flock of Joseph. The expression "Who art enthroned above the cherubim" is also an ancient title (II Sam. 6:2) of the Lord and implies the presence of the ark, His processional symbol. In that glorious classical antiquity to which the kingdom of Israel had as great a claim as the existing kingdom of Judah, God manifested Himself in majesty to His people (cf. Judg. 5:4; Deut. 33:2). So the psalmist prays, Let Him now manifest Himself in shining glory to Ephraim, Benjamin, and Manasseh, and along with His self-disclosure may He bring them strength and help. Once that psalmist's Israel was vigorous and fruitful (cf. Gen. 49:22-27; Deut. 33:12-17), but, alas, since its fall as a political entity it is but a fragile remnant of what it once was. The psalmist looks back certainly through decades, possibly through centuries,

---

[37] *Einleitung,* p. 133.
[38] So Gunkel, *Die Psalmen,* p. 353. The other psalms are 45, 77, 89, and 133.

that have elapsed and prays for the restoration of its lost splendor and for the saving favor of God. The appeal merges into the lament of the congregational refrain.

> 1 Shepherd of Israel, give ear!
>   Tender of the flock of Joseph,
>   Who art enthroned above the cherubim, shine forth!
>   Before Ephraim, Benjamin, and Manasseh,
> 2 Lay bare Thy strength
>   And come to help us!

The congregation responds in the first refrain:

> 3 O Lord of hosts, restore us,
>   And cause Thy face to shine, that we may be saved.

The lament proper, already foreshadowed in the refrain, begins at verse 4 with the characteristic question, "How long?" The Israelite remnant, the escaped exiles who—partly in 733 B.C. and in greater numbers in 721 B.C.—had been carried as captives from Samaria, feel themselves to be under the disciplining hand of God. For decades tears have been their meat and drink. They have been and are the butt of carping criticism and derision from the nations among whom the exiles have settled (cf. II Kings 15:29; 17:4-6). So the psalmist breathes a sigh of impatience. How long must they endure it? How long will God demand such punishment from those of His people who have escaped the sword?

> 4 O Lord of hosts, how long
>   Wilt Thou exact penitence of the escaped of Thy people?
> 5 Thou hast made us eat bread of tears;
>   Yes, Thou hast caused us to drink tears in full measure.
> 6 Thou makest us a target of carping criticism [39] to our neighbors,
>   And our enemies deride us.

The congregational refrain here stands out in bold relief from such sad experiences and in contrast to them.

> 7 O Lord of hosts, restore us;
>   And cause Thy face to shine, that we may be saved.

From the distress of the present the psalmist turns in sharp and heart-relieving contrast to the wonderful early history of his people. In ideal terms and in pictures of Palestinian charm he portrays the beautiful past. The purpose of this feature, quite characteristic of the lament, is to present inducements that will move God to intervene to help His people, and it is addressed directly to Him. The psalmist makes use of allegory and builds his thought around Canaan's most exquisite natural product, the grape. The Lord brought a vine out of Egypt

---

[39] Cf. Ehrlich, *op. cit.*, p. 195, who renders the Hebrew word *mādhón* by the German word *Mäkelei*, explaining that the Hebrew word means, not "a bone of contention," but "an object of critical comments."

into Canaan. He cleared away the obstacles from the soil which would have hindered its growth, then planted it. It took root and grew marvelously until it filled the land. It became so great that its shadow covered mountains, and its branches were comparable to great cedars. It kept on growing, its branches spreading until they reached the Mediterranean Sea on the west and the Euphrates on the east. As Gunkel says, "such enormous exaggeration was pleasing to Israelite taste." [40]

But God broke down the protecting walls of the vineyard, so that all passers-by plucked grapes from it; wild boars from the Jordan jungles overran and ravished it; and wild animals of the fields stripped it. Why did God so expose His people? Now the vine represents Israel brought out by the Lord at the Exodus into Canaan. At Israel's conquest God drove out the Canaanites, and His people settled down in the land, became a nation, and grew until they mastered the whole territory and under David and Solomon became a great nation, achieving the (ideal) boundaries of Israel (Josh. 1:3; Deut. 11:24), the Euphrates and the Mediterranean Sea. But the northern kingdom was overthrown. "Why," the psalmist asks, "did the Lord break it down?" For Israel's fall as a nation opened its territory to be plundered by the small surrounding nations and to be overrun by wild animals. We note in this section how the allegory and its meaning are woven together, a literary feature in which Israel excelled (cf. Judg. 9:7-21; Isa. 5:1-7; Ezek. 16; 17; 19; 23).

> 8 A vine Thou didst bring out of Egypt;
> 　　Thou didst cast out nations and plant it.
> 9 Thou didst clear away before it;
> 　　Its shoots took root,
> 　　　And it filled the land.
> 10 Mountains were covered with its shadow,
> 　　And its boughs were cedars of God.
> 11 It shot out its branches to the sea,
> 　　And to the river its shoots.
> 12 Why didst Thou break down its walls,
> 　　So that all who pass by the way pluck from it?
> 13 The wild boars from the thicket ravish it,
> 　　And the beasts of the field strip it.

How naturally at this point comes the refrain, uttered by the worshiping congregation, with its longing for restoration and for the return and saving help of the Lord's approving grace!

> 14a O Lord of hosts, restore us;
> 　　And cause Thy face to shine, that we may be saved.

The lament began in petition, and to petition it now returns. The allegory continues. Let the Lord from high heaven look down with concern upon this

---

[40] *Die Psalmen*, p. 354.

vine (Israel) which He has planted with His strong right hand. There are those who are burning it down, who are cutting it away (Assyria and the small neighboring peoples). Rebuke them so that they will perish! But, the psalmist continues, upon "the man of Thy right hand," whom God has made strong for Himself, let His right hand still rest in life-restoring power. There is a skillful play on the word Benjamin, "son of [God's] right hand," which here stands for the nation, the northern kingdom Israel.

The mood of petition rises into the certainty of God's response. The psalm comes to its climax in a vow that when that hoped-for consummation has become reality, Israel will [41] call upon the Lord and will not turn back from loyalty to Him.

> 14b Look down from heaven and see this vine,
> 15a   And raise up what Thy right hand didst plant.[42]
> 16 Let those who have burned it in fire, who have cut it down,
>   Perish at the rebuke of Thy mouth!
> 17 Let Thy hand be upon "the man of Thy right hand,"
>   The son of man whom Thou madest strong for Thyself.
> 18b Give us life, and on Thy name we will call,
> 18a   And will not backslide from Thee.

The psalm ends in a final chanting of the refrain by the congregation, full of the mood of hope:

> 19 O Lord of hosts, restore us,
>   And cause Thy face to shine, that we may be saved.

Ps. 83. WITH OUR BACKS TO THE WALL

Ps. 83 is a national lament which dates from the period between Nehemiah (*ca.* 444 B.C.) and Alexander the Great (*ca.* 331 B.C.). It opens with a desperate cry to God from His tormented and suffering people. God seems so passive, so silent!

> 1 O God, keep not quiet:
>   Be not silent, and be not undisturbed, O God.

The choir now pours out the lament of the worshipers before Him. We are in a period when the Jewish community of the restoration after the Chaldean exile was being gravely threatened by the pushing into its territory of vigorous neighboring peoples. Those mentioned with particular prominence are "the sons of Lot" (vs. 8), that is, the nations Moab and Ammon, and along with them Edom. At various times each of these three nations was subjected by Israel as long as the Israelite and Judean kingdoms existed. And after the final debacle of Judah (587 B.C.), these and other peoples tried to force their way into the

---

[41] The tense is voluntative. Gesenius-Kautzsch, *op. cit.*, sec. 72t; Driver, *Hebrew Tenses*, sec. 44.
[42] Omit vs. 15b as a variant to 17b.

territory which Israel and Judah formerly held.[43] This is definitely evidenced for
Edom and Ammon and is to be inferred for the Phoenicians and Philistines,
as Joel 3:4 implies. As Nehemiah's memoirs clearly attest, these nations sharply
opposed the restoration of the Jews, which the Persian empire had fostered.

Moreover, from the late sixth century and the fifth century B.C. the tribes
which had their seat on the borders of the wilderness had been encroaching upon
Jewish territory, having themselves been shoved forward by Arab tribes which
were penetrating north in a wave of migration into the sown land. For a time
those Arab tribes made confederates of these nations which bordered on the
newly reclaimed Judean domain and at length subjected and absorbed them.
The Arab tribes here mentioned are the Ishmaelites, a great north Arabian tribe
(Gen. 25:13); and, closely related to them, the Hagarites (I Chr. 5:10; 11:38);
Amalek, the ancient Bedouin tribe, which was still going strong as late as around
650 B.C. (Deut. 25:17-19); Gebal, an Arab tribe in the neighborhood of Petra;[44]
Ashshur, a north Arabian tribe (Gen. 25:3). All of these supported Moab and
Ammon with auxiliaries. These nations and tribes to the southeast and east,
and the Tyrians and Philistines to the northwest and west, of the Jewish community were in vigorous movement against it, allied together with the common
purpose of annihilating the Jews. All the craftiness and vigor of the Bedouin
Arab was in their plans, and they were a unit in their purpose to destroy. Thus
the psalm laments: But not merely enemies of the Lord's people are they. They
are the Lord's own enemies!

> 2 For lo, Thy enemies are in tumult;
> And those who hate Thee have lifted up their head.
> 3 Against Thy people they craftily plot,
> And conspire against Thy treasure.
> 4 "Come, let us annihilate them from being a nation,
> So the name of Israel will no longer be remembered."
> 5 For they determine unanimous counsel,
> And against Thee make a covenant;
> 6 The tents of Edom and Moab;
> Ishmaelites and Hagarites;
> 7 Gebal, and Ammon, and Amalek;
> Philistia, with the inhabitants of Tyre;
> 8 Ashshur also has joined himself with them;
> They are the arm of the sons of Lot.

From lament the psalm then moves into solemn petition (vss. 9-18). In passionate wish the psalmist longs that a curse may fall upon these nations and
tribes that are bent upon the annihilation of the Lord's restored people. It is
considered effective in such a wish to cite notable incidents in the past of men

---

[43] This began indeed even before 587 B.C. with Moab and Ammon (II Kings 24:2), but was
pursued with vigor after that date, which marked the political destruction of Judah (Ezek.
35:10; 36:5 for Edom; Jer. 49:1-2 for Ammon).

[44] Cf. Eusebius *Onomasticon*. 151, line 5; 211, line 4.

who were done to their death by the curse of God, asking that a similar curse fall upon the present offenders.[45] The psalmist recalls the destruction of Sisera, the commander of the Canaanite forces, at the hands of Jael, the Kenite woman, after he had been defeated at the River Kishon, in the plain of Esdraelon, by the Israelite tribes under Deborah and Barak. This was a severe blow indeed to Jabin, Canaanite city-king of Hazor, whom at length Israel destroyed (Judg. 5:19-27; 4:1-24). The psalmist brings to mind the great decimation of the Midianites by the Manassite Gideon and his forces, encamped by the spring Harod (Judg. 7:1), and he recalls the slaying by Gideon's army of the two Midianite princes Oreb and Zeeb (Judg. 7:25). Let the Lord do to the nobles and princes of the nations and tribes, now bent upon dispossessing Judah of her pastures, as He did in those days of old to earlier invading nomads and their leaders! It is felt that by thus bringing the accursed one in contact with the names of famous curse-laden individuals of the past, he will become infected with just such a curse as destroyed them.[46] So in passionate, colorful words, alive with classic references to that idealized past when the Lord's hand was manifest in His people's life, the psalmist calls down the curse of God upon the foes of His people.

9 Do to them as to Sisera,
    As to Jabin at the river Kishon;
10 As Midian was exterminated at the spring Harod;
    They became but dung on the ground!
11 Make their nobles like Oreb,
    And like Zeeb, all their princes.
12 Who say, "Let us possess for ourselves
    The pastures of the Lord our God."

Similarly the assembling in his petition of various vivid pictures of destruction is viewed by the psalmist as making yet more overwhelming the annihilating force of God's curse, which is now being passionately sought, upon His people's enemies. The pictures used are familiar, vivid, and impressive—a whirl of dust, chaff driven by the wind, a forest fire setting mountains aflame, a terrifying storm wind blowing all before it, a humiliating and consuming sense of shame. But there is one loophole left—and here we feel the realism of the psalmist. He prays (vs. 16) that these enemies, bent on dispossessing the Lord's people, may come to feel such disgrace, such dishonor, as will lead them to seek peace with God and be forgiven. At any rate, the ultimate aim of the curse upon these enemies of God's people, as the psalmist cherishes it in his heart, is the exaltation of the Lord as sole God of the earth, "the Most High." So the petition continues to its climax:

13 My God, make them like a whirl of dust,
    Like chaff before the wind.

[45] Cf. Gunkel, *Einleitung*, p. 308.   [46] *Ibid.*, p. 307.

14 As fire consumes a forest,
   As a flame sets mountains ablaze,
15 So mayst Thou pursue them with Thy storm wind,
   And with Thy hurricane terrify them.
16 Fill their countenance with disgrace,
   That they may seek their peace with Thee, O Lord.
17 May they be ashamed and dismayed forever,
   And may they be abashed and simultaneously perish,
18 That they may know that Thou alone,
   The Most High, art over all the earth.

Ps. 90. GOD, OUR ETERNAL HOME

Ps. 90 is a prayer of lamentation intended for a regularly recurring service of penitence of the Jewish congregation.

Schmidt has suggestively pictured the probable worship setting of this psalm. The day of prayer has been called. The throngs clothed in sackcloth, appropriate to a fast, press through the gates of the Temple court. The kind of worship setting implied is well pictured in Judith 4:9-12.

And every man of Israel cried to God with great earnestness, and with great earnestness did they humble their souls. They, and their wives, and their babes, . . . and every sojourner and hireling and servant. . . , put sackcloth upon their loins. And every man and woman of Israel, and the little children, and the inhabitants of Jerusalem, fell before the Temple, and cast ashes upon their heads, and spread out their sackcloth before the Lord; and they put sackcloth about the altar: and they cried to the God of Israel earnestly with one consent.

The priests are similarly pictured in Joel 1:13, where the summons to a fast is addressed to them:

Gird yourselves with sackcloth and mourn, O priests;
Wail, O ministers of the altar!
Come, spend the night in sackcloth, O ministers of my God!

The throng lies praying in the dust. Then one among them, probably a priest, an old man with gray hair, arises and utters the prayer of lamentation on behalf of them all.

It is definitely a congregational psalm. But in later times the form of the individual psalms was carried over into the congregational psalms, an evidence of growing interest in the individual, which increased with the fall of the state.

The psalmist's first solemn words express the mood of trust. They portray the Lord as one in whom His people have had their dwelling, their abiding spiritual home, and protecting shelter from generation to generation across the long centuries of Israel's existence. We feel the congregational note in the "our" and "we," which, as becomes clear at verses 13 and 16, mean the servants of the Lord. In verse 2 there is an echo of a myth, already archaic even for the Israelite poet, according to which the mountains were said to be "born" out of the womb of Mother Earth, a myth to which the author of the book of Job also refers (15:7). Before the mountains were born and before the fruit-bearing world had been travailed into being, God was and, as far into the distant future as the human mind can conceive, will be.

But though God is our home and though He is eternal, we, His servants, are but temporal, and our lifelong abode in His protecting shelter is but brief. For man, molded, as the oldest Hebrew story of creation said, out of the dust of the ground (Gen. 2:7), eventually will hear God's voice saying, "Return! Come back to that from which you have been fashioned." And this voice comes not merely to Israel but to all human beings. The psalmist feels keenly that the great contrast between God and man is that between eternity and finitude. We fragile children of today think of a millennium as a vast epoch. But the eternal God looks back upon a past millennium as though it were but yesterday.

1 Lord, Thou hast been our dwelling
    Generation after generation.
2 Before the mountains had been born,
    Before the earth and the fruitful world had been travailed into being,
    Even from everlasting to everlasting Thou art God.
3 Thou turnest man back to dust,
    And sayest, "Return, children of men."
4a For a thousand years in Thine eyes
4b   Are but as yesterday when it hath passed.

To what may man's brief life be compared? God has appointed for him a time of living comparable to a swiftly passing watch of the night. And when this brief interval of life is over, man lapses into sleep, the sleep of death. Again, to use another figure, man's brief life is like grass, which thrives luxuriously in the morning only to wither by eventide under the harsh Oriental sun. But why this brevity of man's life? Why vanishes he so swiftly from the scene? The psalmist speaks here for the congregation and gives utterance to a deep sense of sin. He feels upon his people the constant disciplining pressure of God's wrath because of their sins, those of which they know and those hidden even to their perpetrators. Day after day is lived and draws to its close under the wrath of God, and the years of every individual's life come to a solemn end, comparable to a great sigh from a heavy heart.

4c But a watch in the night Thou dost appoint;
5a   When they are relieved, they fall into sleep.[47]
5b-6a As the grass, which in the morning flourishes,
6b   At evening withers and dries up,
7 So we perish because of Thine anger,
    And before Thy wrath we wither and fall.
8 Thou dost set our iniquities before Thee,
    Our hidden sins in front of Thy face.

[47] I follow Gunkel's reconstruction of the text, beginning with 4c.

9 For every one of our days draws to an end under Thy wrath;
　 Our years come to completion like a sigh.

At best our life expectancy spans but seventy years, and if one should live,
due to exceptional vigor of life, to the age of eighty years, most of his years
would be full of sorrow and trouble, and then his soul would fly away. This
conception that the souls of the dead are like birds is an echo of antique thought.
The solemn theme, which like a minor fugue runs through this and the previous
section (vss. 7, 9, 11), is the wrath of God that lies heavy on the individual
souls of the congregation. It reaches its climax in a rhetorical question. Thus
keenly conscious of the pressure of God's anger, the psalmist asks, "Who knows
how to meet it?" Feeling the harshness of God's wrath, how shall the obedient
servant of God adjust himself to it? And to this rhetorical question he gives
answer. He still feels the fetters, not of any arbitrary action on God's part, and
not of sins on the part of individuals, but of the universal sinfulness of humanity,
and so of the congregation. Yet he does not complain, but through words of
humble submission finds his way back to God's heart and to trust.[48] So to God,
the great Teacher, the psalmist prays that He may teach His people to pay
earnest heed to the brevity of life and therefore to each passing day, and that
from the sum total of their experience they may bring in the good harvest of
a wise heart.

10　The number of our years—their acme is seventy years,
　　Or if through greatest strength eighty years—
　　Most of them [49] are trouble and sorrow,
　　For they pass swiftly, and we fly away.
11　Who knows how to meet Thy strong anger,
　　And, as fear of Thee demands, Thy harsh wrath? [50]
12　So teach us to count our days
　　That we may bring in a heart of wisdom.

The last part of the psalm (vss. 13-17) is not, as Gunkel thinks, a separate
psalm. The elevated, noble style is singularly similar to the rest of the psalm.
Schmidt says: "The alternation of dull acquiescence and shining confidence, of
deep melancholy and noble exertion of the will, correspond to the nature of
the human heart and leave behind the impression of real experience." [51] This
portion moves even more definitely in characteristic features of the congregational lament, in petitions and in wishes. In the petition (a) we meet the appeal
to God that He turn from wrath to mercy, and the characteristic lamenting
question "How long?" How long must His people suffer under His wrath?

---

[48] Cf. Kittel, *Die Psalmen*, p. 300.　　　　　[49] Reading *rubbām*, with Halévy.
[50] Construing *ûkheyirʾāthekhā* as "and as fear of Thee," continuing in both members of the sentence the force of "who knows," and following the interpretation of Ehrlich, *op. cit.*, p. 219,
which makes the word not repetitious (vs. 7) but climactic.
[51] *Die Psalmen*, p. 171.

How long until He turns to them in compassion? Yet the petition for the turn of fortunes is not concerned with the nation as such, but is individualizing for the members of the congregation. (*b*) Again comes the request that He satisfy His people with His mercy, which, though undeserved, might fill the days yet left of life's fleeting errand with happiness proportionate to the long days, yes, years, of misfortune which they had experienced. As Quell suggests, in verse 14 there is probably an allusion to a morning sacrifice in the worship or at least a reminiscence of the custom of the morning sacrifice.[52]

In the wishes which form a continuation of the petitions comes (*a*) the desire that God's servants may see with their own eyes the mighty deeds of the Lord as He moves now in compassion toward them, and that the oncoming generation may experience God's innermost being, His "glory." (*b*) Again comes the longing that the beauty of the Lord, His pleasantness, His graciousness, may rest upon the congregation. (*c*) There is the practical request of the serious person, who has work to do in the days yet remaining to him, that God may promote the work that his hands find to do.

13   **Turn, O Lord! How long?**
      And have compassion upon Thy servants!
14   **Oh satisfy us in the morning with Thy mercy,**
      That we may be glad and rejoice all our days.
15   **Make us glad according to the days Thou hast afflicted us,**
      According to the years during which we have seen evil.
16   **Let Thy deeds be seen by Thy servants,**
      And Thy glory by their children.
17   **And let the beauty of the Lord be upon us;**
      And promote the work of our hands.

Gunkel remarks that the whole psalm "is of indescribable majesty and power: bowing down under the hand of the powerful God and filled with the seriousness of the confession of sin, the psalmist nevertheless looks up trustingly to God, who in His day will save Israel."[53]

Ps. 94:1-15. [54] THE DISCIPLINE OF THE GREAT TEACHER

Ps. 94:1-15 is primarily a congregational lament. It opens with an imploring cry for help to the "God of vengeance, . . . Judge of the earth," that He will manifest Himself in shining splendor (Deut. 33:2) and in judgment upon the proud.

1   **O Lord, Thou God of vengeance,**
      Thou requiting God, shine forth!
2   **Rise up, O Judge of the earth:**
      Deal out retribution upon the proud.

[52] *Op. cit.*, p. 88.   [53] *Die Psalmen*, p. 399.
[54] For Ps. 94:16-23 see "Prayers of the Falsely Accused Seeking Vindication," p. 339.

Then comes the lament, itself marked by the opening question "How long?" and describing the activities of certain arrogant and irreverent, evil men. Those whose activities the psalmist describes are property owners who have fallen away from the worship of God and use their power to exploit the poor. They exult in triumph over their victims, belching out arrogant, boastful words. They crush the Lord's people, mistreating their property, and even murdering the helpless in Israelite society. Nor do they fear any punishment, for they boast that God neither sees nor cares what they do. The emphasis (vs. 5) upon "Thy people, . . . Thy property" aims at arousing God so that He will intervene

3   How long, O Lord, will the wicked,
     How long will the wicked triumph?
4   They belch forth and speak arrogantly;
     All evildoers boast.
5   Thy people, O Lord, they crush,
     And Thy property they mishandle.
6   Widow and orphan they kill;
     The resident alien and poor they murder.
7   And they say: "The Lord does not see it;
     The God of Jacob does not discern it."

The next part of the psalm (vss. 8-11) is a sermon to these practical atheists, full of indignation. They have boldly asserted that the Lord does not discern what they do. The psalmist, using the same term, challenges them, calling them too dullhearted and foolish to discern how futile and empty of meaning are their reckless words. We feel here the influence of the wisdom poetry in Israel, with its appeal to the understanding. The content of the sermon, which is in verses 9-11, argues from what God has done and does to what God knows. God, who can create an ear and an eye, must be able to hear and to see. The great God, who can instruct nations, knows how to reprove them. God is the great Teacher of men. Must He not have knowledge? You are saying God does not discern, but the psalmist says He well discerns that the thoughts which you in your superiority consciousness express about Him are utterly empty of truth.

8   Discern, O stupid-hearted among the people;
     And fools, when will you comprehend?
9   He who planted the ear, can He not hear?
     Or who formed the eye, can He not see?
10   He who instructs nations, can He not reprove them?
     Is the teacher of men without knowledge?
11   The Lord knows the thoughts of men,
     That they are futile!

From the godless, arrogant men the psalmist turns to those who heed the instruction and accept the discipline of the great Teacher. One of the surest marks of Hebrew wisdom is the utterance of blessing such as opens this section of the psalm. The psalmist starts with the thought already uttered in verse 10, that the Lord is the great Teacher. His textbook is His law. This indicates the period in Judaism after the introduction of the priestly law by Ezra (*ca.* 397 B.C.). The purpose of this instruction which the law affords is the moral discipline of the psalmist's life. This will give him tranquillity in evil times, for he will be divinely protected until evil is dealt the deathblow. But what is the content of the Lord's teaching which gives the psalmist such poise and assurance? The law teaches him that the Lord will never surrender His people. They are His property. He will never forsake or abandon them. The reference here is to the great belief that God is a covenant God, who keeps faith with His people, uttered first in the introduction to the Deuteronomic Code (7:6-11), then applied powerfully in Samuel's reputed words to Israel (I Sam. 12:22). And it teaches the psalmist that God will reward the righteous person in accordance with his just dessert, and that the issue of an upright heart will be happiness. This teaching of individual retribution goes back in origin to Ezek. 18:4, 20.

> 12 Blessed is the man whom Thou dost discipline, O Lord,
>   Whom Thou dost teach from Thy law,
> 13 To cause quietness for him in evil days
>   Until the pit is dug for the wicked;
> 14 That the Lord will not forsake His people,
>   Nor will He abandon His property,
> 15 That unto the righteous He shall return what is due him,
>   And a happy outcome to all who are upright in heart.

Ps. 108. A PRAYER FOR HELP AGAINST THE ENEMY

Ps. 108 in its present form is a national lament. It is made up entirely, however, from two portions of earlier psalms. Verses 7-13 have been taken bodily from verses 6-12 of Ps. 60, which is itself a national lament. Likewise verses 1-5 come from verses 7-11 of Ps. 57, which was originally a prayer of one falsely-accused seeking vindication by passing a night in the sanctuary. The predominant mood of the resulting psalm is lamentation, as especially verses 10-12 show. Our psalmist evidently chose Ps. 60 as the basic one from which he worked, but he rejected as being inappropriate to his purpose the solemn lamentation of verses 1-4—which must have been originally inspired by some terrible national disaster—and substituted a song of personal thanksgiving, which he took from Ps. 57:7-11. However, the mechanical nature of his work is shown in that the petition of verse 6 (Ps. 108), properly in its place in Ps. 60:5, where it follows a lament, now occupies a most inappropriate place, between a song of thanksgiving and an oracle.[55] The resulting psalm dates from the latest period of Israelite psalmody.

In calling attention to the presence of this identical section in two separate psalms (60 and 108), Mowinckel is probably right in suggesting that verses 7-9

---

[55] So Gunkel, *Die Psalmen*, p. 475.

were one of the already existing oracles in fixed form and thus were available to the officiating leader of worship as a part of the Temple's liturgical repertoire.[56] For the interpretation, see Ps. 60 and Ps. 57.

Ps. 137. "IF I FORGET THEE, O JERUSALEM!"

Ps. 137 is a congregational lament composed most likely by one who was in Babylonia among the exiles, for the mood of actual participation in the experience thrills the opening words with deep feeling. And familiarity with Babylonian landscape and scenery is apparent in his reference to the streams of Babylon and to the poplars, although the "rock" of verse 9 is not characteristic of Babylonia. The poet looks back probably from just before the Persian mastery of Babylon (538 B.C.). He is not in Babylon when he writes, as he speaks of it, not as here, but "there." Yet he is far from Jerusalem. The psalm clearly comes from the Diaspora but was created for the celebration of the fast of the ninth of Ab, which according to rabbinical tradition recalled the destruction of the Temple at the fall of Jerusalem.[57]

The psalm opens with a poetic narrative of an episode that took place early in the Chaldean captivity. We get the impression from verse 3 that the exiles do not as yet enjoy the measure of freedom they are to be granted by the Chaldean overlords, but feel themselves chafing under their captors' crude and unsympathetic demands. The exiles are sad of heart. We find them seated on the ground, which is the custom in the East for those who are in grief or great affliction. The scene is set beside one of the numerous streams that are the land's most characteristic mark, for through it flow the great Tigris and Euphrates rivers, and the many and characteristic canals are the main feature of Babylonia's unique system of irrigation. The exiles are a long distance from their beloved homeland, far removed from Zion, its holy Temple and its familiar worship, its prayers and rituals, its hymns, songs, and laments. We see the beautiful and stately poplar trees, a famed feature of the Babylonian landscape. How sick at heart and depressed the exiles are, when from afar they think about Zion and all for which that precious word stands! The Temple musicians have lugged along into exile their beloved instruments, but it is no time for music! Hang up your harps on the poplars! There is no place here for melody. The lamenting story begins:

> 1 Beside the streams of Babylon,
>   There we sat down; we also wept
>   When we remembered Zion.
> 2 Upon poplars, in its midst,
>   We hung up our harps.

---

[56] *Op. cit.*, II, 117, note 1. He considers the oracle as continuing throughout vss. 7-13. However, vss. 10-13 are clearly not oracular but are part of the lament itself. The compiler of this psalm had Ps. 60 before him in its present form.

[57] Cf. Moore, *Judaism in the First Centuries of the Christian Era*, II, 65.

Their Chaldean overlords now give them a request amounting practically to a command. They know well the fame of Judean music. (Still in our day the Jews are among the greatest musicians.) But particularly do they know of the famous Temple hymns and songs and possibly of that unique group, within the whole repertoire of Temple music, which celebrate Zion as the great pilgrimage goal of every Jew whether at home or abroad, "the songs of Zion." So for sake of their own amusement these very officers, who entered their Zion sanctuary with pagan tread and plundered and burned it, now call out to their captives: "Sing us a Zion song!"

> 3 For there our captors asked us for songs,
>   Yes, those who plundered us,
>   For something [58] joyful.
>   "Sing us one of the songs of Zion!"

The answer takes us out of the realm of historical narrative and into the mood of deep lament. Here are pagan enemies whose irreverent feet have contaminated Zion—who have razed it to the ground, who have pillaged and destroyed the Lord's Temple—now having the effrontery and the cruelty to ask the exiles to sing them a Temple song in that pagan land. It is no time for singing; besides, a Zion song should be sung only in the Lord's Temple, which now stands in ruins, the place He chose for His dwelling. We feel the deep pathos of the lament (vs. 4), which is introduced by one of the characteristic words for this type of life setting:

> 4 How can we sing a song of the Lord on foreign soil?

There then bursts forth from the psalmist's spirit a love for Jerusalem and all for which it stands. It is the homeland of his soul for this man of the Diaspora. He can express his love for it only in a solemn imprecation upon himself in case he should ever forget this dearest city of the world. Let his right hand lose its power! Let his tongue become dumb! Higher than any other conceivable thing of joy to him is Jerusalem. To sing a Zion song for the amusement of cruel captors in a foreign and pagan land would mean that he had turned traitor to Jerusalem and so would deserve God's curse. To Jerusalem he utters his self-imprecation:

> 5 If I forget thee, O Jerusalem,
>   Let my right hand deny its service. [59]
> 6 Let my tongue cleave to the roof of my mouth,
>   If I remember thee not;
>   If I do not exalt Jerusalem
>   Above my chief joy!

---

[58] With Ehrlicn, *op. cit.*, p. 356, placing *dibhrê* before *simḥāh*.
[59] Following Cheyne, *The Book of Psalms*, p. 404.

In words likewise quite frequently found in the congregational lament he utters a revengeful wish against Edom. That little nation most closely related to Israel (cf. Gen. 25:23-26; Gen. 32:28, Jacob is Israel; Gen. 36:8, Esau is Edom) turned against the Judeans at the Chaldean crisis in Jerusalem (Ezek. 25:12; 35:5) and aided the Chaldeans (Obad. 10-11) at that breakup of her national life. Let the Lord never forget Edom's treachery!

> 7 Remember, O Lord, the Edomites,
> The day of Jerusalem,
> Who said, "Lay it bare, lay it bare,
> Unto its very foundations."

Then with intense passion the psalmist turns to Babylon, capital of the world empire, destroyer of Judah, and to him the very epitome of evil. Happy that nation which pays Babylon back in its own coin! We feel how grief (vss. 1-2) is followed by revenge (vs. 7), and revenge by hate (vss. 8-9). How far below the love of Christ is the temper of these words! The closing picture is one of horror, but it helps us to see the extremes to which a pious Jew of the times might go. Let that nation count itself blessed which will ruthlessly put to cruel and violent death the children of Babylon! There are three forms which the imprecation of verses 5-9 takes. The first (vss. 5-6) is a conditional wish, the second (vs. 7) a petition to the Lord, and the third (vss. 8-9) the blessing of that nation which will destroy the Chaldeans.[60] Cries the psalmist:

> 8 Daughter of Babylon, you violent destroyer,
> Happy is he who repays you
> According to your dealing which you dealt us.
> 8 Happy is he who seizes your children
> And dashes them to pieces upon the rock!

[60] Gunkel, *Die Psalmen*, p. 580.

Chapter VIII

PSALMS CONCERNING THE KING

THE HEBREW KING, LIKE THE KINGS OF BABYLONIA AND EGYPT, HELD A PLACE OF unique distinction in the nation. He was considered to have prerogatives and powers that were more than human. He was the channel through whom the blessings of God were mediated to his people. We have already dealt with six psalms that have to do with the reigning Hebrew monarch so far as his relation to the ceremonies of the Hebrew New Year is concerned.

But there were many other occasions when the Hebrew king had a distinctive place in the public worship, or when the affairs of their monarch were of central concern to the worshipers in the Temple, whether the king was present or not. The king's interest in the national worship of the Lord, as revealed in the authentic sources for King David (II Sam. 6) and King Solomon (I Kings 6), exercised a normative influence upon succeeding monarchs. The Temple of Solomon, originally a private chapel for the king and court, gradually grew in national prestige until through the Deuteronomic reform it became the one legitimate sanctuary for public worship in Judah. It must have been a thrilling occasion whenever the king was present in the Temple worship.

In these psalms which concern the king one worship occasion is a thanksgiving service for a royal victory (Ps. 18). Two psalms are public intercessions for the victory of the king's army just before a military expedition (Pss. 20 and 144:1-11). Yet another worship setting is the marriage of a king (Ps. 45). Two of the king's psalms are personal laments. In one of these (Ps. 61) the king is ill. In the other, ill and beset by enemies, the king seeks a revelation from God in the Temple during the night watches (Ps. 63). And one of them is a national lament after the king suffers a great military reverse (Ps. 89).

Ps. 18. HE DREW ME OUT OF GREAT WATERS

Ps. 18 is a psalm of a reigning king of the line of David, sung at a thanksgiving celebration for victory (cf. Ps. 20:6). The court singer lays this song in the mouth of his ruler. It is likely, as Kittel and Gunkel maintain, that the monarch concerned is Josiah.

The introduction is in the form of a hymn. The Lord has accomplished a mighty act, which is viewed by the poet as of great moment.

> 1 I will exalt Thee, O Lord, my strength,
>   My crag and my fastness and my shelter;
> 2 My God, my rock, in whom I seek refuge;
>   My shield and the horn of my salvation.

The chief part of the psalm, a portion which is always present in a song of

personal thanksgiving, is the story of what has happened to the singer. First
he puts it all before us in summary fashion.

> 3   From those who were mad against me, I cried, O Lord,
>   And from my enemies I was saved.[1]

Then he describes with vivid imaginative detail how he was at the very gates
of death. It was as though the roaring sea of the underworld, the realm of the
dead, had already taken him into its power. He felt as though he were already
assailed by the streams of destruction. It seemed to him that death had snared
him and bound him as its captive.

> 4   The breakers of the sea had surrounded me,
>   And the rivers of destruction had assailed me.
> 5   The cords of Sheol encircled me;
>   The snares of death confronted me.

From his desperate situation he appealed to God, who heard the king and
answered him.

> 6   In my straits I cried unto the Lord;
>   Yes, to my God I cried out for help.
>   And from His holy Temple He heard my voice;
>   Yes, my cry came to His ears.

Then God came! The psalmist in vivid and elaborate description pictures the
awesome God, manifesting His fierce wrath against the king's enemies as He
comes in mighty power to rescue His loyal servant from his desperate distress.
In earthquake, volcanic fire, and storm wind—the three most sinister outbreaks
of nature in which the ancients ever saw the anger of God—He comes! We see
the dark, water-filled clouds that cover His visage as He majestically rides in
His divine chariot, hurtling through the skies. We see His weapons—lightning,
hail, and molten lava—against the king's enemies. We hear from His chariot
the thunder of the angry voice of the Most High, which cows the mighty deep
of the underworld, drives it back, and lays bare the very foundations of the
world. "Such sudden withdrawal of the sea belongs to the most sinister phenomena in connection with volcanic eruption." [2] This is magnificent poetry,
athrill with the atmosphere of the primitive. The Lord is the master of the
underworld. Its storming waters that reach out to draw the king into their
power withdraw at God's approach. And from those threatening floods the
Lord draws the king into the freedom of a roomy place, from awful peril into
glad release.

> 7   Then the earth shook and quaked,
>   And the foundations of the hills trembled.

---

[1] The imperfects are, as Gunkel has rightly seen, poetic aorists.
[2] So Gunkel, *Die Psalmen*, p. 64. Cf. Gressmann, *Mose und seine Zeit*, p. 119, where his view
is best stated.

8   Smoke rose up in His nostrils,
    And fire devoured from His mouth.

9   He bent the heavens and came down,
    A cloud was under His feet.

10   He rode upon a cherub and flew,
    And darted swiftly on the wings of the wind.

11   He made darkness His secret place,
    Thick clouds His covering.

12   Out of the brightness before Him issued forth
    Hailstones and coals of fire.

13   The Lord thundered from the heavens;
    Yes, the Most High gave forth His voice.

14   And He sent out His arrows and scattered them,
    And lightning flashed and confused them.

15   Then the channels of the sea became visible;
    Yes, the foundations of the earth were laid bare
  At Thy rebuke, O Lord,
    At the hot breath of Thy wrath.

16   He reached down from on high and grasped me;
    He drew me out of great waters.

17   He delivered me from my strong enemies,
    From those who hated me, for they were too strong for me.

18   He came to meet me in the day of my distress,
    And the Lord became my support.

19   And He brought me out to a roomy place;
    He rescued me, for He took pleasure in me.

The next section of the psalm rests on the basic principle of the Deuteronomic law that good fortune manifests the direct approval of God, just as misfortune indicates the Lord's punishment. The psalmist tells why God thus helped and helps him. It is because he has observed the ways of the Lord and has kept himself from doing evil.

20   The Lord dealt with me in accordance with my righteousness;
    In proportion to the cleanness of my hands He repaid me.

21   For I have kept the ways of the Lord,
    And have not sinned against my God.

22   For all His laws are before me,
    And as for His statutes I turn not aside from them;

23   I was blameless before Him,
    And have kept myself from iniquity.

24   So the Lord paid me back in accordance with my righteousness,
    In accordance with the cleanness of my hands in His eyes.

Such basing of the Lord's help in the king's own character leads the psalmist to bear a more general testimony to the way God deals with men. From God's dealing with his own life he concludes how God deals with men in general. He now speaks directly to God:

25   With the merciful Thou showest Thyself merciful;
     With the blameless Thou dealest in integrity.
26   But with the tyrant Thou actest tyrannically,
     And with the perverted Thou workest craftily.
27   And a humble people Thou dost help,
     But the eyes of the proud Thou dost humiliate.

This leads the psalmist back to God and his own life, and the first section of the psalm ends in his striking testimony that with God present the darkness on his way becomes light. He achieves courage, experiences the unwonted vigor of youth, and enjoys the divine protection.

28   For Thou art my lamp, O Lord;
     My God, Thou dost enlighten my darkness.
29   For by Thee I can leap over barriers,
     And by my God I can scale walls.[3]
30   As for God, His character[4] is perfect;
     A shield is He to all who seek refuge in Him.

It is customary, as here, for the song of thanksgiving to be composed of two parallel parts, and the second begins at verse 31. It is in this part of the psalm, and indeed at its climax (vs. 50), that we learn that the speaker is the reigning Judean king himself, of the lineage of David. What is only suggested in verses 17-19 becomes clear in this section, that the rescue for which the psalmist thanks God is from the power of enemies. And as was already dimly suggested in verse 29, the psalm has to do with a successful military expedition of the king.

This second and parallel part of the psalm begins, as is often the case in hymns, with a rhetorical question. In general terms it glorifies the Lord.

31   For who is God other than the Lord?
     And who is a rock except our God?

With this introduction the psalmist tells the story of his experience, beginning with the way God prepared him for battle. He strengthened him physically, disciplined his skill and prowess, and protected and steadied him. Joining his thought to "our God" (vs. 31), the opening words of the second cycle of the psalm, he continues:

32   The God who girdest me with strength,
     So that I leaped along my way safe and sound;
33   Who settest my feet secure like hinds' [feet]:
     And makest me stand firm on heights;
34   Who teachest my hands to fight,
     And layest the bow in my arms.
35   And Thou dost give the shield of salvation,
     And Thy discipline makest me strong.[5]

[3] I am indebted here to Buttenwieser, who rightly understands the passage.
[4] For *darkhô*, cf. Brown, Driver, Briggs, *op. cit.*, 6a (p. 203).
[5] Reading with Gunkel, *theghabberēni*.

36 Thou makest room for my steps,
   And my ankles do not slip.

Then comes the vivid description of the victorious battle (vss. 37-42), for which struggle God has prepared him. The king here stands for his whole army as he pursues his enemies to annihilate them utterly. He was girded for the battle by God, who is with him and opposed to his foes.

37 Let me pursue my enemies and annihilate them,
   And not return until their finish.
38 Let me finish them so they cannot arise:
   Let them fall under my feet.
39 So Thou didst gird me with strength for the battle,
   And madest my adversaries bow down under me.
40 Yes, as for my enemies, Thou givest me their back;
   And as for those hating me, Thou didst annihilate them.
41 They look about, but there is no savior;
   Unto the Lord, but He answers them not.
42 So I pulverized them like the dust of the earth;
   I crushed them like mire of the streets.

The monarch through his triumph has become chief of the nations. In awe strange people come to pay obeisance to him. The diffuse features of the delineation arise from the fact that the psalmist is not working from direct observation. His words are colored with features that are familiar in such royal celebrations, as the king says:

43 And Thou didst deliver me from myriads of warrior folk:
   Thou puttest me at the head of [the] nations:
   And people I have not known serve me.
44a Upon hearsay they are obedient to me;
   Foreigners are led to me,
45   And come quaking out of their fastnesses.

The psalm, which thus soars up in two parallel parts, likewise comes to its close in two portions. One is in the form of a hymn which glorifies the Lord as the psalmist's exalted Saviour from his adversaries and the destroyer of them:

46 The Lord lives, and blessed is my Rock;
   Yes, exalted is the God of my salvation.
47 God is the one who repaid vengeance for me;
   Who laid nations prostrate under me;
48 Who saved me from my angry enemies;
   Who lifted me up from my adversaries,
   And snatched me from violent men.

The other closing portion is in the form of a song of thanksgiving, where the king speaks of himself in the third person (vss. 49-50). It is the Judean king who here utters his praise for God's manifestation to him of His saving power.

49 Therefore I will praise Thee among the nations;
     Yes, unto Thy name let me sing;
50 Who conferred great help upon His king,
     And wrought kindness to His anointed,
     To David and his descendants forever.

Ps. 20. GOD SAVE THE KING!

Ps. 20 is a king's psalm, a king's liturgy. The occasion of such a psalm is a day of prayer for the king before an engagement in war, and it is preceded by a sacrifice (cf. I Kings 8:44-45; also I Sam. 7:9; 13:9-12; II Chr. 20:4 ff.).

It opens with a prayer for the king (vss. 1-5) that in the time of national crisis the Lord will receive his sacrifices and offerings favorably and from his sanctuary in Zion will send him help for the accomplishment of his aims. And the prayer concludes with a vow of a song of thanksgiving (cf. Ps. 144:9), in case victory is granted.

1 May the Lord answer thee in the day of trouble;
    May the name of the God of Jacob set thee securely on high.
2 May He send thee help from His sanctuary,
    And sustain thee from Mount Zion.
3 May He remember all thy meal offerings,
    And find thy burnt offerings acceptable.
4 May He give thee according to thy heart,
    And may He accomplish all thy purposes.
5 We will give a ringing cry of joy over thy victory,
    And in the name of our God we will exult.

Then comes a significant moment in the rendition of the psalm. A single voice of a prophetic person who has been stirred by a sense of revelation from God speaks forth to the congregation a divine word of assurance and, at the same time (vs. 7), of implied exhortation (vss. 6-8). We feel here the influence of Hosea, "Thou didst trust in thy chariotry" (10:13), and of Isaiah, "The Egyptians are men and not God; their horses flesh and not spirit" (31:3; cf. also I Sam. 17:45; II Chr. 14:11; 20:17).

6 Now I know for sure
    That the Lord saves His anointed;
    He answers him from His holy heavens
    By the might of victory from His right hand;
7 Some [trust] in chariots and some in horses,
    But we through the name of our God are strong.
8 They shall stumble and fall;
    But we shall arise and be restored.

The closing verse is a popular cry sung by the choir and the assembled congregation.

9 O Lord, save the king:
    And answer us in the day when we cry!

Ps. 45. THE MARRIAGE OF A KING

Ps. 45 is a song for a king, composed by a court poet who writes out of deep veneration and heartfelt enthusiasm for his young monarch. The unique element in the psalm is the supreme moment for which it was written—when the young monarch takes unto himself a wife.

As the psalm opens, the poet is moved to the depths of his being by a noble theme. Under inspiration he has composed a poem which he has dedicated to his king. His heart is "astir," and just as a skilled scribe writes dexterously and easily, so his tongue is the ready instrument of his devoted soul, pouring forth its thoughts and feelings:

> 1   My heart is astir with a good matter;
>   I am about to speak my poem concerning the king:
>   My tongue is as the pen of a skilled writer.

He sees his young king, surpassingly handsome; he listens to the words that come from his mouth and is convinced that the king stands uniquely under the blessing of God.

> 2   Thou art the fairest of human beings;
>   Grace hath been poured into thy lips:
>   Therefore [I say] God hath blessed thee forever.

He celebrates first the king's capacities as warrior. The supreme responsibility of a monarch is to go out before his people and fight their battles (I Sam. 8:20). The king's prowess as a future warrior is imagined as he stands armed in glittering weapons, ready to fight on behalf of his people for honor and right. His strong right hand will attack the enemy with sharpened arrows, and their morale will fail. The poet thus challenges his young monarch to the fray.

> 3   Gird on thy sword upon thy thigh, oh warrior;
> 4   In thy majesty and thy splendor be successful; mount and ride,
>   For the cause of truth and for the sake of righteousness:
>   And formidably lengthen [6] out thy right hand!
> 5   Thy sharp arrows will terrify the nations;
>   The courage of the enemies of the king will fall.

Not only is the king a warrior; he must also rule and judge. The royal throne stands for established authority of government, with a continuity which, in the anticipation of the poet, embraces not only the past but centuries to come. The scepter stands for the personal authority of the reigning monarch. He alone can carry it. It is a straight staff and in its very form suggests the ideal uprightness of the legitimate ruler who "hates the evil, and loves the good, and establishes justice in the gate." We have here a glimpse into the primitive thought of

---

[6] Following Perles, *Analekten zur Textkritik des Alten Testaments*, II, 57.

Israel, and indeed of the ancient East, in which the king is the point of unity
where God and the nation meet. Mowinckel puts it:

He is the channel through which the divine blessing flows into the nation. The
purpose of primitive religion is to bring divine power, the personal, power-producing
deity Himself, into the midst of the community to vitalize it. The king in Israel is the
divinely chosen and divinely anointed representative of the people. Through him
God shares Himself with His people.[7]

Thus the power of the king is something more than merely human. So here the
king is called God (Elohim), but we rightly render the term, with Kittel, "thou
divine one." The monarch's garments waft the famed aroma of the precious
anointing oil as the king stands before the poet.

> 6 Thy throne, thou divine one, is forever and aye:
>   An upright scepter is the scepter of thy kingdom.
> 7 Thou hast loved righteousness and hated wickedness:
>   Therefore the Lord thy God hath chosen [8] thee;
>   He hath anointed thee [9] with the oil of gladness;
> 8a   Myrrh of aloes perfumes thy garments.

Thus far the monarch as king has been the poet's theme. But now he lets us
see the particular features within the general picture. It is the king at the holy
moment when he is about to take unto himself a bride. She is a Tyrian princess.
Can it be that the young king is Ahab and the Tyrian princess Jezebel? No
doubt for some days already she has been in Samaria, the capital of the northern
kingdom. She is now brought to the youthful monarch, accompanied by her
young women attendants. The whole ceremony is lifted into beauty by the
music of gifted Israelite musicians playing on the lovely harps embellished in
ivory. The artistic elegance of the decorative ivories found by archaeologists in
Ahab's palace at Samaria gives to us the touch of vivid reality in the scene. To
the great throne room, where stands the waiting king, they usher her. The
queen-to-be enters, "a daughter of kings," and moves to the right of the young
king,[10] while her attendants bring as a bridal dowry gold from Ophir.

> 8b From instruments of ivory, harps make thee happy.
> 9   A daughter of kings takes her place to meet thee; [11]
>   The queen [to-be] at thy right hand, with gold of Ophir.

Then comes something quite unexpected and most impressive. The queen-to-
be stands at the ruler's side, lovely beyond words in the eyes of the king. Then
the king's gifted servant, our poet, aged in experience, and with love for his
young monarch and for his bride in his soul, is moved to speak to her both a

---

[7] *Op. cit.*, II, 301-2.   [8] Reading *behārekhā*.
[9] With Gunkel, setting *meshāhakhā* in the second member of the verse.
[10] Ehrlich notes that *niçebhā* does not here mean "stands," but "takes her place."
[11] Reading with Budde, *liqrā'thekhā;* cf. Exod. 5:20.

warning and an exhortation. She is the daughter of a king, and rich traditions are hers. The love of ancient Tyre is in her soul. Is the elderly, deeply religious poet afraid of what she might bring into Israel from that foreign environment? The story of Jezebel and her fanatical introduction of the worship of Melkarth, the Tyrian Baal, into Israel gives point to the need for the poet's warning. She must forget her own people and the palace and court of her royal father. She must now face toward Israel, her new people, and her husband, who from this moment is her lord and king.

> 10   Hear, daughter, and incline thine ear:
>   Forget thy people and the house of thy father:
> 11   The king has desire for thy beauty,
>   For he is thy master.

The poet in more gratifying mood now reminds her that as queen she will share with her king in the receiving of fealty and tribute which will pour in from all the rich nations of the world. The situation in which such songs are sung, with the accustomed glorification of the king, and the influence of the court style of Babylonia and Assyria account for such ostentatious exaggeration. World dominion Israel never had in actuality; but in the psalms of the king, Israel loved to play with such ideas.[12] Famed and wealthy Tyre, the great mercantile mart of the ancient world, here called "the daughter of Tyre," will be among the cities that will bring tribute unto her and unto her royal husband.

> 12   So may the daughter of Tyre bow down to thee
>   With a gift,
>   May all the rich of the nations
>   Entreat thy favor.
> 13   May they honor thee with corals plaited with gold.

From the bride the poet turns to the virgins who are attending her, and who enter the room behind her, true comrades from her own country who are thrilled to be present. We see the many-colored garments. We sense the universal mood of joy. We hear them lift the wedding song.

> 14   Clothed in variegated garments are the virgins behind her,
>   Her attendants who conduct her to the king;
> 15   They bear [her] [13] along with mirth
>   And with jubilation, into the palace.

The psalm comes to its climax in a promise which is in the form of a blessing. Marriage is one of the great focal moments in Israelite life, fraught with sacred meaning. Mowinckel has shown how the purpose of the cultic rites of a wedding is to acquire blessings essential to the propagation of the race, above all the blessings of fecundity, of childbearing: "The transmitting of the blessing is a religious act and is bound up with cultic rights." Rebekah left her father's house

---

[12] Cf. Gunkel, *Einleitung*, p. 160.   [13] Cf. Mowinckel, *op. cit.*, III, 100.

to be married to Isaac with just such a blessing (Gen. 24:60). Ruth became the wife of Boaz with a similar blessing (Ruth 4:11). The blessing mediated the power to be fruitful. And it is this blessing which makes the poem a psalm. Mowinckel says, "The psalm is written in the prophetic style; it seeks a religious foundation of the ceremonies and pronounces the blessing of the Lord upon the righteous king." [14]

Instead of looking backward at his royal ancestry, the king is to look forward to his posterity. The sons of this marriage are to share with him dominion in all the world. We sense again the Oriental exaggeration which colors such thoughts.

> 16   Instead of thy fathers shall arise thy sons;
>   Thou shalt make them princes in all the world.

The closing verse, as the opening, gives us a glimpse into the poet's soul and his pure love for his monarch. He has been dealing with a noble theme and he has done his best. He believes that his poem will be influential in holding the name of his beloved monarch in undying memory across the generations, with the result that nations will praise him forever.

> 17   I will keep thy name in remembrance in all generations:
>   Therefore nations shall praise thee forever and aye.

Ps. 61. THE KING'S SHELTER IN GOD

Ps. 61 is the lament of a king. Most likely he is ill, for he feels himself to be at "the ends of the earth." This phrase does not imply simply geographical distance from Jerusalem and the Temple. Rather does it refer to the entrance to the chasm of the underworld, the realm of the dead. He is beset by enemies. All in all, the king's spirit is low, and he feels insecure. With a cry for help, for a sure hold upon life, he appeals to God.

> 1   Hear, O God, my cry;
>   Give attention to my prayer,
> 2   From the ends of the earth
>   To thee I cry,
>   Since my heart is faint.
>   Lift me up upon a rock and make me secure.

He bases his petition upon the fact of his trust in God. This is frequently the case in the individual lament.[15] The tense of the verb he uses ("Thou art") is "the perfect of experience," [16] which suggests what God has been in the king's experience in the past and continues to be in the present. And to express this vividly he uses two related thoughts: God is his shelter, his protection, and God is his tower of refuge. Moreover he longs for the cleansing in the Temple which

---

[14] *Op. cit.*, III, 96.   [15] Cf. Gunkel, *Einleitung*, pp. 150, 233-34.
[16] Cf. Gesenius-Kautzsch, *op. cit.*, sec. 106*k*.

will guarantee the healing of his sickness.[17] The Temple means to him shelter in the shadow of God's wings. This picture of protection has its psychological origin in the mother bird's protection of her young. It is applied in Israel to the wings of the cherubim over the mercy seat of the ark, above which God communes with his priest (cf. I Kings 6:23-28; Exod. 25:18-22). In tender spiritual meaning it is here applied to God's protection of the individual worshiper in the sanctuary. It is a phrase of cultic poetry, such as "to seek God's face," or "to see God's face." [18]

> 3 For Thou art a refuge for me,
>   A tower of protection from before the enemy;
> 4 I would dwell in Thy tent forever:
>   I would take shelter in the shadow of Thy wings.

The psalmist is certain of God's favorable response, and to express it he makes use of a tense of the verb called "the perfect of certainty." This implies that God's favorable response is so certain to him that in his imagination it has already been given.[19] In his distress he vowed that in case his petition was answered, his voice would resound with God's praise. Moreover, his words refer implicitly to the prayer by the congregation of the Lord on his behalf, by "those who fear Thy name."

> 5 For Thou, O God, wilt give heed to my vows:
>   Thou wilt respond to the request of those who fear Thy name.

Then that request follows. It is not the king praying for himself, but it is the intercession of the congregation for the king, sung by the priestly choir. The burden of the prayer is that God will wondrously prolong the king's life and rule, and that lovingkindness and truth, like guardian angels, may attend him. The extravagant exaggeration and high-flown style in which these petitions are clothed come in part from the exalted nature of the occasion when the beloved monarch is at the center of attention, and in part from the influence of the royal court style of utterance upon the Israelite king psalms, which the Israelites derived from Babylonia and Egypt through Canaan.[20] Thus the prayer proceeds:

> 6 Mayst Thou add days to the days of the king;
>   May his years be as days, from generation to generation.
> 7 May he sit enthroned forever before God:
>   May lovingkindness and truth guard him.

Although the lament of an individual may close with the certainty of God's response, there often follows, as is likewise the case in Babylonian laments, a

[17] Cf. Mowinckel, *op. cit.*, VI, 48.
[18] Cf. Widengren, *The Accadian and Hebrew Psalms of Lamentation as Religious Documents*, pp. 252-53.
[19] Cf. Gesenius-Kautzsch, *op. cit.*, sec. 106n.
[20] Cf. Gunkel, *Einleitung*, sec. 5, especially nos. 5, 6, 13, and 21.

particular part of the psalm—the vow. In Babylonian psalms it follows directly upon the petition and was always considered as very effective in the persuasion of deity. But in Israelite laments the vow follows the certainty of God's response and so becomes an outburst of the feeling of thankfulness.[21] So it is here. There is intensity of devotion in the king's words as he declares his intention to pay his vows, not only once—for that will not suffice for the praise in his soul— but day after day!

> 8 So I will praise Thy name forever,
> As the payment of my vows day by day!

Ps. 63. THE THIRST OF A KINGLY SOUL FOR GOD

Ps. 63 is a prayer of lamentation written in the name of the king and for his use in the king's Temple at Jerusalem. My interpretation in the order of verses follows the suggestions of Gunkel and Schmidt, who restore what was likely the original arrangement of the psalm. It is one of the most deeply spiritual psalms of the Psalter. Sensitive to this religious quality, Oesterley maintains that "the earnest yearning for God, and the insight into communion with Him on the part of a truly good man, as these are set forth in the Psalm, are unrivaled in the Psalter." [22]

The psalmist is beset by enemies who are seeking his life. He is ill;[23] his physical being—"my body"—is faint, burning up as though with fever. As one sick and in distress, longing for the purification which will guarantee his cure, he comes to the Temple. But far greater than his desire to live is his longing for God. His soul is athirst; his physical need and his spiritual hunger together cry out for God as parched ground silently cries out for rain. As he sings, he is already in the sanctuary, eager to see and yearning to experience the power and the glory of God.

> 1 O God, eagerly do I seek Thee:
> My soul thirsts for Thee;
> My body faints for Thee,
> Like land dry and faint for water.
> 2 So I long for Thee in Thy sanctuary,
> To see Thy power and Thy glory.

It is in the Temple that his longing for God finds satisfaction. Many an unknown before Isaiah underwent experiences in the Temple similar to his when he "saw the Lord," although such experiences differed largely in form and in degree. In such hours God became more real to them and took them into His power.[24] So it is here. When the psalmist speaks of naming God upon his bed

---

[21] Ibid., no. 24, pp. 247-48. [22] The Psalms, II, 307.

[23] Mowinckel rightly interprets vs. 1 as having no reference whatever to the geographical location of the suppliant, but as implying his illness, op. cit., VI, 28, 46, 48.

[24] Ibid., VI, 95.

(vs. 6), we have an allusion to the cultic invocation of the Lord's name. This is one of the lamentations "which were occasionally rendered in the Temple at night to the accompaniment of stringed music."[25] Moreover, the Hebrews felt that in sleep the soul was freed from the body and so could soar into spiritual regions and commune with God. Through dreams the soul was influenced by God and led in the direction desired by Him.[26]

So meditating in the Temple at night as he lies near the ark and the sheltering wings of the cherubim, the king calls upon God and feels himself clinging close to Him, nesting in the shadow of God's wings and aware of His sustaining protection.

> 6 When I name Thee upon my bed,
>   When in the night watches I meditate [27] upon Thee—
> 7 Aye, Thou art my help,
>   And in the shadow of Thy wings I nest,[28]
> 8 My soul clings to Thee;
>   Thy right hand holds me up.

The next part of the psalm (vss. 4, 5, 3) is a little song of thanksgiving, complete in itself. The king, strong in the sense of security already felt in the Temple, sings in anticipation his thanksgiving for the Lord's answer to his prayer. He vows to praise God throughout his life, lifting up his hands to Him, not in the mood of appeal, but in a glad gesture of grateful joy. Thus to sing with his own lips songs of joy in praise of his God will satisfy his spiritual nature as truly as fat, the finest food, stills his physical hunger. To him the spiritual blessing of God's lovingkindness is of greater value even than life itself. This "noteworthy utterance of religious inwardness," as Gunkel calls it, is the theme of this little song of thanksgiving and is introduced by the characteristic word "for," which likewise most frequently ushers in the theme of a hymn. The psalmist's words thus uttered are the more significant when we sense how precious life appears to him at the present moment when he is in grave danger. Full of confidence, he sings:

> 4 So I will praise Thee as long as I live:
>   In Thy name I will lift up my hands;
> 5 Just as fat satisfies my appetite,
>   In songs of joy my mouth shall utter praise.
> 3 For better is Thy lovingkindness than life;
>   My lips shall praise Thee!

[25] Widengren, op. cit., pp. 26-27, 319.
[26] Cf. Hamilton, Incubation or the Cure of Disease in Pagan Temples and Christian Churches, pp. 1-2; Pedersen, op. cit., p. 134.
[27] The imperfect suggests that the action is just taking place, Gesenius-Kautzsch, op. cit., sec. 106 l.
[28] Reading with Halévy, Recherches Bibliques, III, 239.

Such words, as Staerk finely says, can only be

psychologically grasped. . . . It is the intimate personal experience of a pious soul which has its religious center in the Temple worship that speaks forth here out of the fulness of its experience of God. But this very perception is enough to guarantee to the psalm its great meaning as a witness for the spirituality of the religion of ancient Israel. It deserves to be placed side by side with the words of the prophets concerning the moral holiness of God.[29]

In sharp contrast to the deep spiritual quality of this section of the psalm comes the passionate wish that misfortune may fall upon those who are perpetrating evil upon the king. As is usually the case in the utterance of such longings, God is not mentioned at all, for such wishes take the form of curses which operate from themselves and need no other force.[30] When once spoken, a curse has independent power over which its utterer has no more influence. Pedersen says:

Just as a man may utter the blessing into the soul of another, thus he can also utter the curse into it. . . . It is as a poisonous, consuming substance that destroys and undermines, so that the soul falls to pieces and its strength is exhausted. . . . Therefore the striking power of the curse is particularly strong when it coincides with sin and injustice. . . . The strength of the word [of imprecation] was increased by its being spoken from the holy place in front of the altar.[31]

These imprecations uttered by the king seek the banishment of his lying enemies to the most gruesome place in the underworld, the realm of the dead. He prays that they may meet their death on the field of battle or by execution, and that their dead bodies may become the prey of jackals, who assemble "in troops on the battlefield to feast on the slain."[32] Thus the destructive influence of his enemies will be stopped at its source!

> 9 But as for those who seek my life,
>   May they go into the lowest depths of the earth!
> 10 May they fall into the power of the sword;
>   May they become the portion for jackals;
> 11c So [33] will the mouth of liars be stopped up!

The close of the psalm (vs. 11ab) is the most characteristic element in it, the prayer of the congregation for the king, sung by the priestly choir. This verse is not, as Gunkel argues, an addition to the original psalm adapting an individual poem for use in the king's temple, but is, as Mowinckel rightly sees, an authentic and original part of the psalm. It is related to the imprecation which immediately precedes it by a sharp contrast introduced by the adversative "but." The choir prays that the king may find joy in God, and that his loyal subjects who swear by him may glory, not in self-confident boasting, but on the ground of the king, his character, and his rule. In Israel men swore by God and the king (cf. I Sam.

---

[29] *Op. cit. (Lyrik)*, p. 219.
[31] *Op. cit.*, pp. 437, 441-42.
[33] Reading *kēn*, with Schmidt.

[30] Cf. Gunkel, *Einleitung*, secs. 6:15, p. 228; 8:14, p. 304.
[32] So Tristram, *The Natural History of the Bible*, p. 110.

25:26; II Sam. 11:11; 15:21) or by either alone (cf. I Sam. 17:55, by the king; I Sam. 14:45, by God). He who swears by the king puts "the whole of the substance and strength of his soul into the words he speaks" and throws himself entirely into his cause, which is the character and worth of the monarch.[34] Such is the burden of the prayer:

> 11ab But may the king rejoice in God;
> May everyone who swears by him glory!

Gunkel maintains that Pss. 61 and 63 were originally purely private songs which later were adapted for use in the worship of the king's temple at Jerusalem. Accordingly he considers the intercessions for the king (61:6-7 and 63:11) as later insertions into, or additions to, the original. Mowinckel, with vigor and insight, rightly opposes this. He argues that the temple in Jerusalem in the entire pre-exilic period was above all the sanctuary of the king, who at all worship celebrations played a prominent role. Without doubt the Temple ritual was richly provided with songs and prayers which were intended for the king and his house and were delivered by kings, or in their name, at different occasions, whether of distress or of joy. It was certainly the case in Babylonia and Assyria that the psalms were originally designated for the king and the nobles, and a large number of the psalms, including those concerning sickness, appear as prayers of the king and often contain the name of the particular monarch. Mowinckel maintains accordingly that these psalms are "prayers which were written in the name of the king." The "I" of these prayers is precisely the king himself.[35] Widengren, who likewise opposes Gunkel's view that there once existed in Israel religious poetry severed from any relationship with the cult, agrees with Mowinckel that Gunkel's view grows out of an inadequate appreciation of the spiritual content of the cult and on the whole believes that Gunkel-Begrich undervalue the importance of the cult as a factor of religion.[36]

Ps. 89. WHERE ARE THY EARLIER MERCIES?

Ps. 89 is a national lamentation uttered by or in the name of a reigning king of Judah. In its present form the psalm owes its origin to a great military reverse in which the reigning Judean king suffered a crushing defeat. The lament itself is concentrated in the last thirteen verses of the psalm (38-51).

The poet who composed this lament in the name of his reigning monarch made use of two other sources which already existed and were available in the psalm material of the Temple liturgy. One was a hymn which had as its primary theme the celebration of the might and supremacy of the Lord as Creator and Ruler of the world (vss. 5-18). This he prefaced with a hymnic introduction (vss. 1-2). This hymn is one of the very few examples from the northern

---

[34] Cf. Pedersen, *op. cit.*, p. 407.   [35] *Op. cit.*, VI, 24, 74.
[36] See the searching criticism in Widengren, *op. cit.*, pp. 29-31.

kingdom of Israel preserved in the Psalter. It was written at a time when the northern kingdom occupied a place of distinction and prosperity, probably during the reign of Jeroboam II, and must have been written before 721 B.C. It might well have been one of the "songs" which, at the time of the fall of the northern kingdom, were in the psalm repertoire of the temple of Bethel, the king's sanctuary, to which the prophet Amos refers (5:23).

The other existing source of which the author of this psalm availed himself was a prophetic oracle to the Judean king (vss. 19-37). There existed in the Temple repertoire many such oracles glorifying the royal house. In the Temple worship it would be uttered by a prophet or by a priest in the name of the Lord as God's message to the reigning king. To it verses 3-4 originally belonged as introduction and have been placed there in my interpretation. These two sections were arranged so as to build the groundwork for what was the real burden of the psalmist's soul. Thus the poet partly created and partly constructed his lament of the king.

The hymn (vss. 1-2 and 5-18) is sung as a solo by a gifted individual. First comes the introduction in which he announces as the theme the merciful deeds of God throughout the generations. These gracious acts have their fountain source in the Lord's mercy and faithfulness.

> 1 Of Thy mercies, O Lord, let me sing forever:
>   To generation after generation let me declare
>   Thy faithfulness with my mouth,
> 2 For Thy mercy is eternal;
>   It is built like the heavens:
>   Thy faithfulness is established even as are they.

Then comes the hymn itself (vss. 5-18), which represents the praise of the Lord as being sung by the heavenly choir of divine beings. These holy ones, which are worshiped by the pagan nations as gods, are here conceived as a heavenly assembly worshiping the Lord.

> 5 The heavens praise Thy wonders, O Lord;
>   Yes, the congregation of the divine beings, Thy faithfulness.

In imagination the psalmist beholds these pagan deities assembled before the one God of all the earth, the incomparable Lord of hosts. Here is a beloved theme of Israelite hymns that expresses the objectivity of Israelite religion—its deep enthusiasm for the incomparable God,[37] whose genius is expressed in His character of mercy and faithfulness.

> 6 For who in the sky is comparable to the Lord?
>   Who among the celestial beings can be likened to God,
> 7 To God, awe-inspiring in the council of divine beings?
>   Great is He and terror-striking to all around Him;
> 8 O Lord of hosts, who is like Thee?
>   Thy strength and Thy terror are roundabout Thee.

[37] Cf. Gunkel, *Einleitung*, sec. 2:11, 44; pp. 38, 65-66.

The next portion of the hymn takes us into a theme frequently present in the oldest hymns of Israel, the mighty deeds of the Lord at the creation of the world. It tells how He mastered the defiant, chaotic waters which were roaring against Him and stilled them; how He crushed the terrible dragon of the primeval watery deep as an unclean, arrogant, and abusive monster which had challenged His lordship. In alliance with this monster were other enemies (vs. 10) of the Lord, whom the poet of Job calls the "helpers" of Rahab (9:13). This monster of the primeval sea is an evil being. The inundation caused by the sea destroyed all life. But the might of the Lord broke the rule of this dragon and proved God to be the mightiest of divine beings and therefore feared by the rest of them. By this triumph He proved His power, but also His mercy and His faithfulness. Israel always interpreted this defeat of the primeval dragon as the mighty God "working salvation" in the earth. By this great act He opened the way to the establishment of the present order of the world, of which the cardinal points of direction, north and south, are symbols. So let the worshipers at Mount Tabor and Mount Hermon, the chief sanctuaries for the worship of the Lord in the poet's home region of northern Israel, sing to the Lord! His exalted and victorious arm now rules, and His reign has its foundations in His character of righteousness and justice. Mercy and truth are personified as ministering servants to their King.

9 Thou abidest ruler over the raging of the sea:
   The roaring of its billows, Thou stillest them.
10 Thou didst crush Rahab like one pierced;
   With Thy strong right arm Thou didst scatter Thine enemies.
11 Thine are the heavens, yes, Thine the earth:
   The world and that which fills it;
   Thou hast established them.[38]
12 North and south, Thou didst create them:
   Let Tabor and Hermon sing to Thy name!
13 Thou hast a right arm, and Thou hast strength:
   Thy hand is strong; Thy right hand is uplifted.
14 Righteousness and justice are the foundation of Thy throne:
   Mercy and truth go before Thy face.

An indirect way of praising God is the utterance of blessing upon the worshipers who claim such a God as theirs.[39] His loyal ones learned the characteristic festal shout, the beloved joyous cry as they receive their God. They learned this sacred cry in the worship of the congregation at the great feasts. They walk in the spiritual light that radiates from God's face and find their joy-spring in His nature, His righteous character. For they have God to thank for their prestige

[38] For vss. 9-11 see pp. 74-75 in the discussion of Ps. 93.
[39] Cf. Gunkel, *Einleitung*, sec. 2:32; p. 55.

and dignity as a people. Indeed the king of Israel, the shield of his people, is himself under the guidance and protection of the Lord.

> 15   Blessed are the people who know the festal shout,
>   Who walk in the light of Thy face, O Lord.
> 16   In Thy name they rejoice all the day,
>   And in Thy righteousness they shout for joy.
> 17   For Thou art the prestige [40] of our strength,
>   And by Thy favor Thou dost lift up our honor.
> 18   For our shield [i.e., our monarch] belongs to the Lord;
>   To the Holy One of Israel our king belongs.

A very important part of this psalm is the prophetic oracle it contains in verses 3-4, 19-37. It is addressed to David, but we do not have here an oracle from the time of David. The author of the psalm is more a compiler than actual author and has taken into his own work older poems—one, as we have seen, a hymn; and the other, one of the existing prophetic oracles which were composed and proclaimed for the glorification of the house of David. With this oracle we are now concerned. It is built around the promise reported in II Sam. 7, which Nathan uttered to David. It is a promise not to David as an individual, but to David as he lives on in his house—his descendants, his royal successors on the throne. It is a promise to the reigning king of the Davidic royal line. The poet here has use for such an oracle and makes it a part of his psalm.[41]

In verse 3 the psalmist introduces his oracle by calling to mind that God, through the prophet Nathan, made a covenant with David himself (II Sam. 7:5-17).

> 3   Thou didst make a covenant with Thy chosen one;
>   Thou didst swear unto David Thy servant.

Then in verse 4 he represents God as giving the content of that oracle which Nathan had then mediated to King David (especially II Sam. 7:11-13).

> 4   "Forever will I establish thy descendants
>   And will build thy throne from age to age."

At this point (vs. 19) our psalmist introduces the already existing oracle, which now becomes his message to the present reigning monarch of the Davidic line. This oracle has to do first (vss. 19-27) with King David himself. Verse 19, "at that time," points back to verse 3 and refers to the time when the Lord's revelation concerning David was made to him, "Thy godly one," through the prophet Nathan. Thus it tells the story: God anointed valiant David, chosen from the people, to be king of Israel and made him strong and secure in his rule. No enemy would ever act the creditor against him. The Lord would strike down David's adversaries but would be with him, bringing to him success and giving

---

40 Cf. Ehrlich, *op. cit.*, pp. 213, 292.
41 Mowinckel, *op. cit.*, III, 35-36; cf. Gunkel, *Die Psalmen*, p. 392.

him dominion over the Mediterranean border of Palestine and over regions of the Euphrates and Nile. Such a concept that calls David the Lord's "first-born" and the highest of earthly rulers is frequently found in the kingdoms of the ancient Orient. Since his Father is the God of the whole world, David, His first-born son, has the right to claim world dominion.[42] These are primitive conceptions which were greatly modified by the ethical teaching of prophecy, yet lived on in the folk soul of Israel.

> 19 At that time Thou didst speak in vision
>   To Thy godly one, and didst say:
>   "I have set a crown upon a valiant one;
>   I have exalted one chosen from the people.
> 20 I found David, My servant;
>   I anointed him with oil as My holy one;
> 21 Him whom My hand establishes,
>   Yes, whom My right arm makes strong.
> 22 No enemy shall make exactions of him;
>   No unjust man shall afflict him.
> 23 But I will crush before him his adversaries,
>   And I will smite those who hate him.
> 24 My loyalty and My kindness is with him,
>   And through My name his might shall increase.
> 25 I will place his hand on the sea,
>   And his right hand upon the rivers.
> 26 He shall call unto Me, 'Thou art my Father,
>   My God, and the rock of my salvation.'
> 27 Yes, I shall make him the first-born,
>   The highest among the kings of the earth!"

Then the oracle moves in transition from David himself to the house of David, the kings of the Davidic line. Beyond David's own time the Lord will keep His love for him and the covenant made with him[43] by continuing it to his descendants, the kings of the house of David. If his royal successors turn aside from obedience to the Lord's law, He will punish them. But under all circumstances He will continue to deal with them in lovingkindness and in faithfulness, holding inviolate His covenant, keeping His solemn oath that the Davidic dynasty shall endure as long as sun, moon, and heavens last.

> 28 "Aye, forever I will keep My love for him,
>   And My covenant inviolate with him.
> 29 And I will establish his posterity forever,
>   And his throne like the waters of heaven.
> 30 If his sons forsake My law,
>   If they walk not in My judgments,

[42] Cf. *ibid.*, II, 303.
[43] Cf. Isa. 55:3, "I will make an everlasting covenant with you, even the sure mercies of David."

31 If they profane My statutes,
       And do not keep My commandments,
32 I will punish their transgression with a rod,
       And their iniquity with a blow;
33 But my lovingkindness I will not remove from him,
       Nor will I play false to my faithfulness;
34 I will not dishonor My covenant,
       Nor change the utterance of My lips,
35 Once I swore by My holiness:
       Surely I will not lie to David:
36 His descendants will continue forever,
       And his throne as the sun before Me;
37 He shall endure forever like the moon,
       And shall last as long as the heavens."

Then comes the main part of the psalm, for which the earlier portions serve but as groundwork. This is the national lament for the king, who here stands as the representative of the people. The glorious past in creation and in history has already been unrolled. Then God's mighty hand showed itself, and He pledged Himself to abide permanently with His people and their monarchs of David's line, to be true to His oath, and to keep the pledge of His covenant. How hopeful and promising then (vs. 19)! How desperately different now! For God has turned in fury against the Davidic king. City walls have been broken down, the Judean fortresses destroyed. The nation has been plundered and disgraced. The monarch has met a severe military reverse, and his throne stands discredited. How youthful and hopeful once was the house of David; how senile and feeble it has now become! Thus the king laments:

38 But Thou hast spurned and rejected,
       Hast become furious toward Thine anointed one.
39 Thou hast abhorred the covenant of Thy servant:
       Thou hast disgraced his crown to the dust.
40 Thou hast broken down all his walls:
       Thou hast laid his fortified cities in ruins.
41 All who pass by plunder him:
       He is the butt of scorn to his neighbors.
42 Thou hast exalted the right hand of his adversaries;
       Thou hast made all his enemies rejoice;
43 Aye, Thou didst turn back his sword in defeat,
       And didst not support him in the battle.
44 Thou hast broken the staff of his majesty,
       And hast hurled his throne to the earth.
45 Thou hast shortened the days of his youth
       Thou hast covered him with gray hair of old age.

The lament rises in intensity to passionate petition. We feel the mood of impatience in the characteristic phrase of the lament, "How long?" How long will God deal in anger toward His king? The monarch stresses before God his frailty and transience. He appeals to the former mercies which the Lord swore He would continue to the Davidic house. The king appeals to God because of his own loss of face before other peoples which he has experienced, suggesting that his enemies are likewise God's!

46 How long, O Lord, wilt Thou hide Thyself?
     How long will Thy wrath burn like fire?
47 Remember how transient I ever am;
     Didst Thou create the sons of men for nought?
48 What man lives who will not see death?
     Who can save his life from the power of Sheol?
49 Where are Thy earlier mercies,
     Which in Thy faithfulness Thou didst swear to David?
50 Remember [44] the insult of Thy servant;
     Now I bear in my bosom disgrace from the nations,
51 With which Thine enemies have taunted [me], O Lord,
     With which they have followed, mocking, upon the heels of Thy anointed one.

The earliest time when this lament could have originated seems to be about 701 B.C. Then Sennacherib's campaign left Judah a desolation, with forty-six of its fortified cities captured and destroyed by fire and its soil devoured by aliens (Isa. 1:7). It would seem appropriate in the mouth of Hezekiah. But there is little doubt that this lament was often used even in the restored cult of the Temple after the restoration from exile. For the custom of rendering psalms in the public worship of the second Temple, wherein the Davidic prince himself participated, we have evidence from a time as late as the third century B.C. Then a great fast was envisaged in Jerusalem wherein "the clan of the house of David" would have its own separate and distinctive share in the worship (Zech. 12:12).

Ps. 144:1-11.[45] A GOD WHO GIVES VICTORY TO KINGS

Ps. 144:1-11, which originally made up a separate poem, is a king's psalm which would be sung by the king or for him just before a military expedition took place. It is a king's lament and dates from the late years of the Judean kingdom. The Aramaic words found in the psalm, in light of the clear evidence in verse 10 that a king is speaking, are not necessarily a mark of postexilic date. Gunkel says, "As early as the pre-exilic time poets have occasionally ornamented their productions with Aramaic words unless such Aramaisms owe their origin to the copyists." [46]

The psalm opens with a song of thanksgiving to the Lord, to whose teaching the king attributes his skill as a warrior. Through military terms which come from the experience of his campaigns he describes what the Lord has meant

---

[44] Omitting "Lord," with Mowinckel.
[45] For Ps. 144:12-15 see "Songs of Trust and of Wisdom."
[46] *Die Psalmen*, p. 606; see vs. 1, *qerābh* (for war), and vs. 11, *peçēnî* (snatch me away).

and means to his life. God is as strong and dependable as a rock. He is to the king a mighty warrior girded for action; He is his fortress; He is like a mountain citadel or fastness; He delivers him from grave peril; He shields and protects him from harm; He is the one to whom he goes aside for refuge. But not only does God thus help the king in defensive ways. In such offensives as he must wage against his foes He lays enemy nations prostrate before the victorious march of the king.

> 1 Blessed be the Lord, my rock,
>   Who teaches my hands for war,
>   My fingers for battle.
> 2 The Lord is my strength and my fortress,
>   My stronghold, my deliverer,
>   My shield, and in Him I seek refuge,
>   Who lays nations prostrate under me.

Over against so mighty a Being, the incomparable Lord, how unworthy is man of God's slightest interest! How utterly undeserving are mere human beings of His least consideration. The king is thinking of himself and of his insignificance in God's sight. How insubstantial, how transient, his life! It is like breath, like the mere shadow that one casts as he moves. The mood is clearly lamentation. What claim has such a being, even though a king, upon the concern and resources of God?

> 3 O Lord, what is man, that Thou takest note of him;
>   Yes, the son of man, that Thou thinkest about him?
> 4 Man is like a breath!
>   His days like a shadow moving along!

Yet the very knowledge of the king's unworthiness puts great intensity into the most important part of the psalm, his appeal, in dire need, from his own insubstantial being to the majestic and powerful God. Thus the above words form the transition to his petition (vss. 5-8).

We sense the indebtedness of this poet to the far greater poem of Ps. 18, whose author with superb poetic power pictures the Lord doing what the psalmist here prays for Him to do. The king is in extreme physical danger. Already in imaginative anticipation he hears the mighty, terrifying floods of the underworld that threaten to engulf him and sweep him into the realm of the dead. He fears the power of foreign enemies and the skill of their swords. But the thing that puts intensity into his prayer is the accusation that his enemies' words are lies, for they stand guilty of a breach of treaty (vs. 8). So he prays for the Lord to pierce the heavens. In wishful imagination he sees the heavens bend as the Lord breaks through. He employs the familiar primitive conceptions to describe what would accompany the self-disclosure of the Lord as He manifests His presence: volcanic eruption with the mountains belching their smoke, storm with lightning flashing and striking so as to scatter and rout the enemy. Then let the Lord reach down His mighty hand and draw the king out of his peril of imminent death at the armed hand of evil foes!

> 5   O Lord, bend Thy heavens and come down:
>   Touch the mountains so that they will smoke.
> 6   Let lightning flash and scatter them;
>   Send forth Thy arrows and confuse them.
> 7   Stretch forth Thy hand from on high;
>   Draw me from great waters.
> 10c-11a From the evil sword snatch me away,[47]
> 11b   And deliver me from the power of foreigners,
> 8a=11c Whose mouths speak deception,
> 8b=11d And whose oath is perjury.[48]

Victory has not yet come to the king, but the certainty that his petition will be granted is great. In his enthusiasm he already begins in anticipation his song of thanksgiving which he will sing after his deliverance has been accomplished. For the new and wonderful release anticipated, only a new song can give adequate thanks to the Lord! The theme of his song of thanks is introduced here by the clause "who gives." It is the royal victory whereby the reigning king, of the house and lineage of David and accordingly called "David," is delivered from his enemies.

So in anticipation of deliverance he sings:

> 9   O God, I will sing to Thee a new song:
>   With a ten-stringed lyre I will play to Thee,
> 10a Who gives victory to kings,
> 10b   Who delivers David, his servant.

[47] Following Gunkel's reconstruction of original text; cf. vss. 10c and 11.
[48] Cf. Ehrlich, op. cit., p. 380. They are disloyal allies who have broken their agreement and brought on war against Israel.

Chapter IX

THE SONGS OF PERSONAL THANKSGIVING

AMONG THE MOST ATTRACTIVE OF THE PSALMS ARE THE SONGS OF PERSONAL THANKS-giving (Ps. 23; 30; 32; 34; 40:1-11; 66; 92; 107; 116; 138; 146). These songs are a vital part of the payment of vows in Israel and are rightly understood only in relation to it. The importance of the vow in Judaism is evidenced by the fact that two whole tractates of the Talmud, Nedarim and Nazir, are devoted to it.

A vow represents something which, as McFadyen rightly says, "goes beyond the normal demands of religion." [1] It is voluntary; it does not have to be made, but it starts in the will of the individual who makes it. When made, however, it is obligatory that it be carried out. The attitude of Jephthah's daughter as regards her father's vow is an accurate illustration of how the Israelites felt. She says, "My father, thou hast opened thy mouth unto the Lord: do unto me according to that which hath proceeded out of thy mouth." (Judg. 11:36.) A vow may be simple, the pure expression of pious zeal or religious devotion, or it may be conditional, as in the case of Hannah, who thus prays to God: "If Thou wilt indeed look on the affliction of thy handmaid and . . . wilt give unto thy handmaid a man child, then I will give him unto the Lord." (I Sam. 1:11.) Having been made, the vow is viewed as influential with God, as laying hold on divine power. The motive of the vow is indeed just this, to secure the help of God.

When the hoped-for release or blessing has come, the one who made the vow goes to the sanctuary with his sacrificial offering to pay it and to render his thanks to the Lord. This he does always in the presence of the worshiping congregation, who also participate in the enjoyment of the feast provided by the peace offering. It is for him a high moment. He tells the story of his distress, of his prayer, and of his release, and acknowledges in deep gratitude the saving help of God.

It is probable that there was a great service at the autumnal New Year festival when vows made under various kinds of stress were paid, the participants being arranged in groups with each group proceeding as a unit. Ps. 107 is a case in point, as will be seen. Yet the payment of the vows was not limited to this service and could be made at any time, but particularly at the great pilgrimage festivals of Passover, Harvest, and Tabernacles.

Two things are important to note in this group of psalms. It is here that we are at the very fountains of Christian testimony. We see that the story of what God wrought in these lives has created classic forms of Christian witness which are still influential today. A second thing of great importance is the social rootage

---

[1] "Vows (Hebrew)," in Hastings, *Encyclopaedia of Religion and Ethics*, XII, 654.

of individual piety. Here is a moment in public worship when the individual, be he a man of prominence and importance or be he a "simple" man in Israel, is at the center of attention. All eyes are upon him as he tells his story, or as his story is told for him, with one such psalm as these the vehicle of utterance. But always he views himself a part of the congregation. It is not merely an acknowledgment to God that he is making, but a testimony to the congregation and in its presence. Thus was the individual buttressed and strengthened by the group. But likewise thus was the whole congregation enriched by the soul experience of an individual worshiper. The congregation is quickened and inspired by the concrete blessing that has flowed from God's bounty into one individual life.

Ps. 23. THE LORD IS MY SHEPHERD AND MY HOST

Ps. 23, universally the most beloved psalm in the entire Psalter, is a psalm of individual thanksgiving rendered in connection with the presentation at the Temple of a thank offering.[2] In verses 4-5 are mentioned the concrete experiences which gave rise to the psalm. The psalmist suffered a severe illness, from which he has been brought back to health. And he was hard pressed by dangerous enemies and has triumphed over them. The psalmist is a poet, one of the best. He takes two of the characteristic and universal figures of Israelite society, the shepherd and the host, and through these familiar features of Oriental life interprets the meaning God has for him.

First of all, the Lord is his Shepherd who provides for his wants. Ezekiel from the early years of the Chaldean exile had given the finest portrait of the Lord conceived as Shepherd of the people Israel to be found in the Old Testament. At a time when the dispersed and exiled people desperately needed the gathering care and healing skill of a shepherd, through that prophet the Lord had offered Himself to the exiles in unforgettable words: "I myself will be the Shepherd of my sheep, and I will cause them to lie down, saith the Lord God. I will seek that which was lost, and will bring back that which was driven away, and will bind up that which was broken, and will strengthen that which was sick." (Ezek. 34:15-16.) But our psalmist does not say the Lord is Israel's Shepherd, but the Lord is *his* Shepherd. For himself as an individual he claims the shepherding care of God, a claim made vivid and gripping by his familiarity with the figure in Judah of the shepherd, "on some high moor, across which at night the hyenas howl, . . . sleepless, farsighted, weather-beaten, armed, leaning on his staff, and looking out over his scattered sheep, every one of them on his heart." [3] The Lord is his Shepherd; he is the Lord's sheep. The Lord knows where to lead His sheep to those fresh shoots of green grass where they love to graze and rest. He knows where the cool water of the rushing mountain wadies is col-

[2] Cf. Mowinckel, *op. cit.*, I, 125-26.
[3] Smith, *The Historical Geography of the Holy Land*, pp. 311-12.

lected at the base of the hills in quiet pools where they can drink and be refreshed. Thus He restores the life and energy of His sheep.

1 The Lord is my Shepherd; I shall not lack.
2   In pastures of fresh green grass He lets me lie down.
   Along quiet waters He leads me.
3a He brings back my life.

Second, the Lord is his Shepherd who guides and guards him. He *guides* His sheep in right tracks, in ways that are safe and secure. And the psalmist here lays hold of a thought, likewise expressed by Ezekiel, wherein God asserts to scattered Israel that what He achieves on behalf of His people He does "for His name's sake," not according to your evil ways nor "according to your corrupt doings." What God does for His sheep in guiding them aright is not done to reward His people, but it is the expression of His own character; it is an indication that He could not be true to His own name and do otherwise. He is jealous of His name and is concerned that the nations shall know Israel's God for what He *is* by seeing what on behalf of His own people He *does*. "For His name's sake" is, accordingly, one of the most profoundly significant expressions in the entire Psalter.

Again, the Lord is the psalmist's Shepherd *Guardian*. Toward eventide the sheep must be led through gorges, so characteristic of Canaan, which by early afternoon lie in deep, dark shadows where wild animals lurk and where danger to the sheep may be imminent. The safe way is not easy to discern; the right path is not clearly marked. But the Shepherd knows the "right tracks" for the feet of His sheep and is prepared for every crisis. Thrust into His belt is His club, "a straight stick tipped with a heavy ball of bitumen, hard as rock." [4] And in His hand is a staff for support or protection. His sheep are secure.

It is likely that the reference to walking in the valley of the deep shadow is an implicit, figurative reference to the psalmist's own dangerous illness. Mowinckel says, "The poet had actually been near unto death; his foot had already stood in the valley of the shadow of death." [5] Moreover, as we shall see, he had been hard pressed by enemies. It is in just such concrete experiences that the psalm originated. In life's vicissitudes he learned the precious lessons of God's protection and restorative power, and through the pictures of shepherd and sheep brings them home to a pastoral people.

3b He leads me in right tracks
   For His name's sake.
4 Yes, when I walk in the valley of the deep shadow,
   I fear no evil;
   For Thou art with me;
     Thy club and Thy staff,
     They comfort me.

[4] Such as is used in Mesopotamia today; cf. Peters, *The Psalms as Liturgies*, p. 152.
[5] *Op. cit.*, I, 126.

The figure changes. We leave behind us the pictures of the Lord as Shepherd, and a new, yet as truly Oriental, picture in the vivid imagination of the psalmist takes its place. The Lord is his Host, and he is a guest in God's house. The psalmist is hard pressed by enemies, but the Lord has permitted him to triumph over them. Before their very eyes God lays out a meal on the table made ready for him! While they look on, frustrated and defeated in their evil purpose, the psalmist experiences protection, refreshment, and honor at the gracious hand of his God, who honors him by anointing his head with oil as he sits at meat, and hands him a cup filled to the brim—and abundance is in reserve. It is here in verse 5 that the deeper meaning for the psalmist's life clearly shines through the pictures. The psalmist is in the Temple, God's "house." The reference is to the joyous festal meal of the thank offering, in which the psalmist, restored to health from severe illness and saved from the onslaught of enemies, pays his thanks, feasts in unmingled joy, and bears his testimony of gratitude to his Host for what He has done for him.[6]

> 5 Thou arrangest before me a table
>   In the very presence of my enemies:
>   Thou dost anoint my head with oil;
>   My cup is brimful.

The psalmist brings his poem to a climax by what is a distinctive part of a psalm of personal thanksgiving, his testimony. He has already experienced the goodness and the lovingkindness of God, as evidenced by his restoration from illness as well as by protection from evil-intentioned enemies. And in the Temple, the house of the Lord, he has enjoyed the hospitality of his divine Host, as in deep gratitude he participated in festal thanksgiving in the sacrificial meal. His testimony looks toward the future. Such goodness and lovingkindness which have pursued him will continue as long as he lives—this is his faith. And wherever he is, the true home of his soul,[7] his real habitation, will be in the Temple.

> 6 Surely goodness and lovingkindness shall pursue me
>   All the days of my life,
>   And I will dwell in the house of the Lord
>   To the length of days.

Such warm affection for the Temple is akin to that felt by the deep soul of the elderly Anna at the time of the infancy of Jesus, she "who departed not from the Temple, worshiping with fastings and supplications night and day" (Luke 2:37). And as Schmidt has sensitively noted, the psalm helps us see what spiritual riches a worshiper in ancient Israel could derive from the services of the Temple.[8]

---

[6] *Ibid.*, I, 126.
[7] Jerome finely renders the clause in the Vulgate, *et habitabo* (and I shall have my habitation).
[8] *Die Psalmen*, p. 41.

Ps. 30. FROM LAMENTING WAIL TO DANCING DELIGHT

Ps. 30 is a song of personal thanksgiving from one who knew the experience of recovery from a dangerous illness. He sang it in the Temple in the presence of the worshiping congregation. The psalm was already in existence in the Maccabean times, for then it was used, as the title says, as a "song for the [feast of] consecration of the Temple," which festival dates from 165 B.C. The originally individual experience of a soul released from imminent death was thus ingeniously reinterpreted in a manner characteristic of that time, so as to be viewed as the experience of the Jewish congregation marvelously saved from destruction. Torczyner conjectures that this part of the title is to be rightly understood as the subscription of Ps. 29, where it would be much more appropriate.[9] The experience is without question intensely personal and pours out of the innermost soul of a gifted poet.

The psalmist opens by singing an individual hymn of praise unto the Lord. In brief, summary fashion he gives as the reason for his praise that God has brought him out of his distress, thus frustrating the rejoicing of enemies, who hoped for his death. In joy he sings:

> 1 I will extol Thee, O Lord, for Thou hast drawn me up,
>   And hast not let my enemies rejoice over me.

With this as an introduction he now narrates what is never lacking in a psalm of individual thanksgiving, a somewhat more detailed story of his experience. He was dangerously ill.[10] In familiar Oriental hyperbole he felt himself already in Sheol, in the deepest depths of the earth, the land of the dead. From such depths of distress he cried to the Lord, who answered him, bringing him up, healing his sickness, and saving his life.

> 2 O Lord, my God, I cried to Thee, and Thou didst heal me.
> 3 O Lord, Thou didst bring up my life from Sheol;
>   Thou didst preserve me alive from among those going down to the grave.

In the joy of his release he summons the listening congregation, as though it were a choir, to sing to the Lord along with him a hymn of thanks. It is that deep quality in God's nature which had most impressed the prophet Isaiah that likewise stirs the soul of the psalmist, the Lord's holiness. From out of that holiness of His being God deals with His loyal ones, both in anger and in favor. The lot His followers must expect is weeping as well as joy. Tears the psalmist has himself known all too well. For in his critical illness he felt himself under the shadow of God's wrath. His experience of wondrous release, however, has

---

[9] See *Zeitschrift der Deutschen Morgenländischen Gesellschaft*, LXVI (1912), 402.
[10] Cf. Mowinckel, *op. cit.*, I, 163; so we must infer.

convinced him that far more persistent is God's favor than His anger. Always His loyal ones may be sure that morning cries of joy will follow evening tears of pain. This is the precious truth that his experience deposited in his soul. The obligation is strong upon him to share this confession of his own faith with others. So he sings a little hymn of praise. His own restoration is itself deserving of congregational praise.

> 4 Sing to the Lord, you, His loyal ones,
>   And give thanks as you remember His holiness.
> 5 For though a moment passes in His anger,
>   Life persists in His favor.
>   In the evening there may be weeping,
>   But in the morning a ringing cry of joy!

It is often characteristic of the songs of individual thanksgiving that after the story of release has been told once, it is retold with enriched description of various aspects of the total experience, and this results in two cycles in the psalm. This indeed accords with human nature generally, which in an account of recovery from illness tends to cover the ground anew from a somewhat different angle. So here the psalmist, in a fresh beginning, goes back in memory to the time before his illness came upon him.

He had been in good health and had felt perfectly secure in the Lord's favor, as though he were standing upon high mountains above danger. He could almost believe that he would never experience misfortune and distress.[11] Then like a bolt from the blue God had withdrawn His protection from him, and taken unawares he had been thrown into dismay. True to the viewpoint of his time, he thinks some sin must have been responsible for his change of fortune. He does not tell us why God turned from him, but his words clearly imply that as he looks back upon the experience, he feels that he had forgotten his earlier utter dependence upon God and had become worldly-proud. But the deepest pain in it all is that he had lost the sense of the divine presence. The Lord had hidden His face.

> 6 But I—I had said in my health,
>   I shall never come to grief.[12]
> 7 O Lord, by Thy favor I had been made to stand
>   On protecting mountains.
>   Thou didst hide Thy face;
>   I was dismayed.

In his dismay he cried unto God, entreating His help. And in order to help his hearers to understand the wonder of his release, he recalls his lamenting appeal at the time, by which he hoped to move the mind of God. (The same

---

[11] So *Ibid.*, I, 163, and note 2; Mowinckel rightly understands the force of *bheshalwi*.
[12] Literally, "slip, totter"; the term suggests the opposite of security.

appeal appears in Pss. 6:4*b*-5; 88:10*b*; 115:17.) The psalmist is poetically gifted, and here is implied a vow on his part to declare to the congregation of worshipers, in case he is restored to health, the trustworthiness of the Lord, who comes to the help of His servants. In case God should permit him to die, and his body, now sick unto death, should thus be reduced to dust, it could not then praise the Lord. Never could he declare what the Lord had done for him and could do for others. What would the Lord therefore gain by refusing His saving help? But if God should restore him, He would gain one more who would utter His praise, yes, one who could create a song of thanksgiving and as a good witness exalt the dependableness of God. Gunkel suggestively says: "Such great value did that age place upon the devout song and this poet upon his own skill!" [13] So he prays that the Lord will hear, show Himself gracious, and help.

8 To Thee, O Lord, I cried; [14]
    My God, I implored:
9 What profit is there in my blood
    If I go down to the grave?
    Can dust continue to praise Thee?
    Can it declare Thy reliableness?
10 Hear, O Lord, and be gracious to me:
    My God, be my helper.

And the Lord heard his cry! How great was his release! From lamenting wail to dancing delight—the dancing here being a part of his worship, in which others would participate. From the dull garb of sackcloth to the bright girdle of festal joy! Yes, the Lord restored him so that in his innermost soul [15] his poetic muse might not be hushed, and he might forever sing praise to Him! In deep gratitude he acknowledges his deliverance, addressing himself, not to men, but to God:

11 Thou hast turned my wailing into dancing;
    Thou hast removed my sackcloth and girded me with festal gladness,
12 In order that my soul may sing to Thee and not keep silent.
    O Lord, my God, forever will I praise Thee!

Ps. 32. THE GLAD CONSCIOUSNESS OF GOD'S FORGIVENESS

Ps. 32 is a song of individual thanksgiving which is saturated with the characteristic teachings and literary forms of Hebrew wisdom. The mixture of various typical literary forms—such as blessing, the lamenting narrative of experience, admonition, address, general observation of the law of retribution, and hymn—found in this psalm indicates a date when the various literary forms had begun to mingle and enrich each other, and so later than 500 B.C. It is thus an expression of the Judaism of the restoration and dates probably from a time when the

---

[13] *Die Psalmen*, p. 128.
[14] The imperfect verbs are in the poetic aorist tense; see *ibid.*, p. 129.
[15] Literally "my liver," here a name for the soul; cf. Pedersen, *op. cit.*, p. 174.

Priestly Code had heightened the consciousness of sin in the congregation of the Lord. As Staerk points out, it is the lyrical transcription of the devout proverb:

> Whoever conceals his transgressions will not prosper,
> But he who acknowledges and abandons them will be shown compassion.
> (Prov. 28:13.)

Its theme is expressed in the classic New Testament utterance:

> If we say that we have no sin, we deceive ourselves, and the truth is not in us.
> If we confess our sins, He is faithful and righteous to forgive us our sins,
> And to cleanse us from all unrighteousness. (I John 1:8-9.)

The psalm opens with a confession of the psalmist's faith, based on the very experience which the poet is about to narrate. It is expressed in a type of utterance that has been influenced by Israelite wisdom poetry, the pronouncement of a blessing. It is really an exclamation and is thrilled with the psalmist's own profound experience of forgiveness. The psalm is penetrated through and through with the regretful admission of what sin had been in his life. He had trespassed, had rebelled against God. He had sinned, had missed the way and fallen into mistake. He had done iniquity, had erred from the right path, and thus had become guilty. But how profound and spiritually sensitive was his experience of forgiveness! The blame incurred by his rebellious spirit was lifted off, taken away from his soul, forgiven. The mistake he had made by missing the right way was covered over by God, who thus put it out of His sight. The guilt he had incurred by erring from the right path no longer lay as a charge held against him by God. The psalmist now has the glad consciousness that in his innermost soul there is no treachery, nothing deceitful, but only open sincerity. His soul is athrill with an experience of the forgiving grace of God!

> 1 Oh the happiness of him whose trespass is forgiven,
>   Whose sin is covered!
> 2 Oh the happiness of the man against whom the Lord
>   Does not charge iniquity,
>   And in whose spirit there is no deceit!

With so spiritually rich an introduction the psalmist now tells his experience. He had at the beginning kept glumly silent, confessing nothing of his sin to God but rather concealing his rebellious spirit and acts. But as a consequence of his hidden, unconfessed sin his physical body had been in distress all day long. By day and by night he had felt inwardly the divine disapproval, as though God had harshly laid His hand upon him to punish him. His life had lost its vitality and joy. At length, however, the burden of undeclared sin became so unbearable that he determined to confess it unto the Lord and was graciously forgiven and, so we may infer, restored to health.

> 3 While I kept silent, my bones were worn out
>   With my cries of distress all day long.

4 For day and night Thy hand
  Lay heavy upon me:
My life sap was changed
  As in the drought of summer.
5 My sin I did not declare [16] unto Thee,
  But my iniquity I hid.
I said to the Lord,
  "I will confess as to my sin."
And Thou didst pardon
  My iniquity and my sin!

The psalmist again speaks as one familiar with the characteristic admonitions and teaching of the wisdom poetry—toward which trend he seems to be definitely inclined—and with fine imagination counsels the devout members of the congregation to turn to God when life's destructive floodwaters are rising (vss. 6-7). In imagination he hears the roar of the threatening flood of life's experiences, but he who turns to God will be hid from destruction or surrounded as with protecting shields.

We must keep in mind in reading such words that the psalmist lived under the teaching which dominated the religious thought of his day. It may be expressed in two propositons: (a) The sinner is punished, the righteous man rewarded and protected by God. (b) Whenever one suffers misfortune, the cause is sin, either open and apparent or hidden and secret. It was the great author of the book of Job who eventually showed up the ethical limitations of such teaching.

In verses 8-9 the psalmist addresses especially the youth of the congregation and in so doing speaks exactly as a sage would do. He knows from experience the bitterness of an unrepentant and stubborn heart, and how youths need to have their almost limitless energies curbed, lest like unbridled horses or unhaltered dumb mules they bring destruction.

6 Because of this, let every devout man
    Pray to Thee:
  In a time of distress,
    At the flood of many waters,
      They shall not reach him.
7 Thou art a hiding place for him;
    Thou dost protect him;
  With shields of deliverance
    Thou dost surround him.
8 I will teach thee and enlighten thee
    In the way which thou shouldst go:
      I will lay counsel upon thee, my son.
9 Be not like a horse,
    Like a mule without understanding,

[16] The verb is in the imperfect, *tempus historicum*.

Whose overflowing energy [17] has to be curbed
By bridle and halter,
So as not to come near thee.

The psalmist adds to his counsel to youth another general observation that likewise roots in his own personal experience as to the protection which God in His lovingkindness gives to those who put their confidence in Him. He brings his psalm to a close, as is often the case in songs of individual thanksgiving,[18] with a joyous invitation to the congregation, similar to the introduction of a hymn, to rejoice with him and sing the Lord's praise:

> 10   Many are the troubles of the wicked;
>   But he who trusts in the Lord—
>   Lovingkindness surrounds him.
> 11   Rejoice in the Lord and exult, ye righteous!
>   And sing, all ye upright in heart!

Ps. 34. TASTE AND SEE THAT THE LORD IS GOOD

Ps. 34 is a psalm of personal thanksgiving. In literary form it is an acrostic and has been profoundly influenced by the Israelite wisdom poetry, dating probably from the late Persian period. The note of firsthand personal experience is strong in the psalm, and it is this which gives the psalmist the authority to teach others.

He begins with an introduction in hymnic form (vss. 2-4), in which he expresses his own purpose to praise the Lord continually in the congregation of God's humble people. They will listen sympathetically and rejoice. He also invites others to join him in exalting the repute of the Lord.

> א   1   I will bless the Lord at all times:
>   Continually will His praise be in my mouth.
> ב   2   My soul will glory in the Lord:
>   The meek will hear and rejoice.
> ג   3   Oh magnify the Lord with me,
>   And let us exalt His name together.

There follows what is always a completely dependable indication of a song of personal thanksgiving—the narrative of what has happened to the psalmist to call forth such thankfulness. He concentrates in a single verse the three customary parts of such an autobiographical account, his distress, his cry to God, and his deliverance.[19]

> ד   4   I sought the Lord, and He answered me,
>   And from all my dreads He saved me.

---

[17] Cf. Mowinckel, *op. cit.*, I, 52-53, *überströmende Lebenskraft*.
[18] Gunkel, *Einleitung*, p. 267.   [19] Cf. *ibid.*, p. 269.

Then comes the spiritual content of the psalmist's song of thanksgiving, what he has learned out of his own experience. We can readily picture the situation. Before the worshiping congregation stands a poor man, an ordinary, fairly representative Israelite. He, simple person that he is, called in great stress to the Lord, and his prayer for deliverance was answered. He feels keenly that he is a living example of just what God can do and is ready to do for all. Let them look at him in their need and have their souls made radiant with joy at the clear evidence of God's help and at the hope that they too may be similarly lifted out of the sense of shame with which their misfortunes have filled them. Around the one who looks in reverent dependence to God for help is encamped His angel to protect and deliver him. The figure is taken from warfare, but Elisha is in the psalmist's mind (II Kings 6:14-17). Let him learn by experience, tasting for himself the goodness of the Lord, perceiving for himself the happiness that trustful dependence upon Him brings. So the psalmist summarizes his appeal. Let the members of the congregation of the Lord's holy people revere Him, for then they will lack nothing, but the godless rich will experience want and hunger.

ה   5   **Look unto me and so be radiant!**
           And let not your faces be ashamed!

ז   6   **This poor man called, and the Lord heard**
           And delivered him from all his troubles.

ח   7   **The angel of the Lord encamps**
           Roundabout those who fear Him, and rescues them.

ט   8   **Taste and see that the Lord is good:**
           Oh the happiness of the man who trusts in Him!

י   9   **Fear the Lord, you, His holy ones,**
           For nothing is lacking to those who fear Him.

כ   10   **The rich will be hungry and in want,**
           But those who seek Him shall not lack any good thing.

At verse 11 the psalm passes completely into the characteristic poetry of Hebrew wisdom and becomes a didactic poem. The psalmist speaks now, no longer as a member of the Lord's congregation, but as a teacher, made such by his experience, speaking to his intellectual "sons." The subject which he introduces is religion, "the fear of the Lord." And he opens his instruction with a question.

ל   11   **Come, sons, listen to me;**
           I will teach you the fear of the Lord.

מ   12   **Who is the man who delights in life,**
           Who loves to experience good days?

His answer (vss. 13-14) is not a direct one, but is in the form of an admonition. In effect he says, If you would find joy in life, be careful of what you *say;* see that no deceitful word falls from your lips. And again, if you would enjoy good days, be careful of what you *do;* turn aside from evil and pursue the line of conduct that will lead to peaceful relations with others. Thus runs his answer.

ב   13   Guard thy tongue from evil,
          And thy lips from speaking deceit.
ס   14   Depart from evil, and do good;
          Seek peace and pursue it.

The next verses (15-21) have as their main unifying theme the divine retribution, a very prominent subject of Hebrew wisdom—how the Lord repays good
and evil conduct. God is opposed to evildoers and will wipe out any memory of
them. But His eyes and ears are sensitively responsive to the need of the righteous, and He delivers them when in trouble. He is near the brokenhearted and
saves the contrite. Though his miseries be many, the Lord rescues him from all
of them, preserving his body intact. Evil, viewed as a personified spirit, will kill
the evildoers, and the Lord will hold guilty those who hate righteous men.

ם   16   The face of the Lord is against the evildoers,
          To cut off memory of them from the earth.[20]
ע   15   The eyes of the Lord are [turned] toward the righteous,
          And His ears are [open] to their cry for help.
צ   17   They cry, and the Lord hears
          And delivers them from all their troubles.
ק   18   Near is the Lord to the brokenhearted,
          And the crushed in spirit He saves.
ר   19   Many are the miseries of the righteous,
          But from all of them the Lord delivers him.
ש   20   The Lord guards all his bones:
          Not one of them will be broken.
ת   21   Evil kills the ungodly,
          And those who hate the righteous will be held guilty.

The closing verse falls outside the acrostic, exactly as in the similar acrostic,
Ps. 25. Yet it is needed, as it gives the complement of the thought expressed in
verse 21. While Evil, like a powerful demon, kills the godless, and while those
who hate the righteous are held guilty by God,

     22   The Lord redeems the soul of His servants,
          And none are held guilty who seek refuge in Him.

This verse and the corresponding verse in Ps. 25 begin with the same Hebrew
word: Redeems (pôdheh) the Lord (34:22) ; Redeem (pedhēh), O God (25:22).
Lagarde, Cheyne, and Schmidt are possibly right in the view that in these two
acrostic psalms we have two poems from the same pen, and that the author,
Pedaiah, or some such name, in each instance is suggested in the first word of
the closing verse. This psalm of individual thanksgiving follows naturally upon
Ps. 25, which is a psalm of individual lament that was adapted to congregational

_____

[20] The order demands the placing of the פ verse before the ע verse, and this is the actual
order of the acrostic poems in Lam. 2, 3, and 4; and in the acrostic poem Prov. 31, as given
in the Septuagint.

use by the verse that contains the author's signature. The two taken together thus give the total experience of this wisdom-inspired poet.

Ps. 40:1-11. I HAVE COME TO DO THY WILL, O GOD

Ps. 40:1-11, which was originally independent of the rest of the psalm,[21] is a song of personal thanksgiving. It is distinguished by the advanced conception of spiritual worship that it contains.

The psalm opens with the most essential part of a song of personal thanksgiving, the narrative of the experience that has made the psalmist thankful. In such psalms it is not the minor deliverances for which the poet is grateful. A celebration such as this springs from one of the great experiences of his life, that of a wonderful release. He tells it briefly, yet with color such as is characteristic of an Oriental's description. He was close to death, so near that in his vivid imagination he was already in the realm of the dead. That abode is here pictured as the underworld, a great cistern, the bottom of which was miry, slippery clay where no foothold was certain or secure. From that miry depth he cried to the Lord, waiting upon Him in the steadfast faith that He would help. And from His lofty dwelling God, like a gracious father bending down to hear his child's voice, heeded his prayer. He restored the psalmist to health, lifting him, as it were, to the security of a rock.

> 1 I waited steadfastly upon the Lord,
>   And he bent down to me his ear
>   And heard my cry.
> 2 He brought me up out of the pit of Sheol,
>   From the miry clay,
>   And lifted up my feet upon a rock,
>   Making my steps secure.

The psalmist is himself a real poet, and the experience in all its freshness and wonder has put a new song in his soul. The song has already been sung in the living worship of the Temple—he sang his praise song in the presence of the worshipers even as he vowed in the dark hour of peril that he would do. The members of the worshiping congregation, who looked on and participated in that high hour, also experienced through it new impulses of faith which deepened their confidence in the Lord.

> 3 And He put a new song in my mouth,
>   A song of praise to our God:
>   Many have seen and feared,
>   And have trusted in the Lord.

That new song is a hymn of praise which the psalmist's own experience of

---

[21] With vss. 13-17 of Ps. 40, Ps. 70 is practically identical, and there the words are best preserved. The psalmist who was responsible for vss. 13-17 made use of Ps. 70, but under a profound sense of sin has prefixed vs. 12, which, however, is foreign to the rest of the verses.

God's wonderful acts led him to create. It praises God indirectly, in the form of a blessing upon the person who makes God the basis of his confidence. What the psalmist himself experienced at the Lord's hands is taken into the larger thought of God's purposes "unto us," that is, unto Israel, which the worshiping congregation represents. When tempted to turn to arrogant foreign gods for help or to pagan priests who give false oracles in their name, he remained loyal to the Lord.

> 4 Oh the happiness of the man who makes
>   The Lord his trust,
>   And does not turn to the arrogant ones [deities]
>   Or to those who fall away to lies.
> 5 Many things Thou hast done unto us;
>   Thy wonderful acts, O Lord,
>   And Thy purposes toward us—
>   None can compare with Thee.
>   If I would declare and tell [them],
>   They are too numerous to count.

Ordinarily when one had so great an experience of release and restoration in Israel he would come to the Temple and sacrifice whole burnt offerings and peace offerings in the fulfillment of vows made while in distress. But this psalmist has drunk deeply at the springs of prophecy (Amos 5:21-24; Hos. 6:6; Isa. 1:11-17; Mic. 6:6-8; Jer. 7:21-23; 31:31-34). His ear has not been closed to this prophetic teaching. He learned that what God desired was not sacrifice and offering but to do justly, to love kindness, and to walk humbly. He learned, as Jeremiah had taught (7:23), to listen to the Lord's voice, and to walk consistently with His commands. The psalmist absorbed into his innermost heart the thought placed in the mouth of Samuel, who had taught that

> To obey is better than sacrifice,
>   And to hearken than the fat of rams. (I Sam. 15:22.)

"The roll of the book" in which he finds God's will prescribed for him is the priestly law, and the psalmist is living under that law in Judaism, which gives large place to ritualistic and sacrificial requirements. But he read his law with prophetic eyes, and the trend of his deepest spirit is away from sacrifice and toward inner spiritual religion, such as Jeremiah had interpreted, wherein God's law is written on the heart. We must remember that sacrifice is but one part, although indeed traditionally the main part, of the Temple worship. Nowhere does this psalmist absolutely reject sacrifice, but no longer does he look upon it as something which is pleasing to God or desired by Him. He sees more profoundly into the heart of God and into the nature of His requirements than the sacrificial system could reach. We see here a most significant shifting of appreciation of individual elements in the public worship and a deepening grasp of inner spiritual religion.[22] But the presence of such words in a psalm intended for

[22] Cf. Mowinckel, *op. cit.*, VI, 51; also Ps. 50.

rendering in the public worship also is an illustration of the fact that the Temple worship, as Robinson has finely said, "like all ritual, was really a framework of different values experienced by the differing worshipers." [23] Out of this deep spiritual insight the psalmist gives his testimony:

> 6 In sacrifice and meal offering Thou hast no delight;
>   My ear Thou hast not stopped up.
>   Burnt offering and sin offering Thou dost not ask.
> 7 Then I said, "Lo, I am come;
>   In the roll of the book it is prescribed for me;
> 8 I delight to do Thy will, O my God,
>   And Thy law is within my heart."

While the psalmist mentions no actual sacrifice of thanksgiving, he feels both the obligation and the impulse to testify before the congregation of the Lord's worshipers as to what he experienced from the righteousness, faithfulness, and saving power of God. He gives evidence of the transparent nature of his own heart as he makes this pronouncement and emphasizes the fact that he has now fulfilled his obligation to tell the story in the presence of the great congregation of worshipers. And he utters the trustful wish and confident expectation that always in the future he will continue to be the recipient of the kindness and guardianship of God.

> 9 I have heralded Thy mercy and truth
>   In the great congregation;
>   Lo, I silenced not my lips,
>   Thou knowest.
> 10 Thy righteousness I have not concealed
>   Within my heart.
>   Of Thy faithfulness and Thy help
>   I have spoken out, concealing it not.
> 11 Thou, O Lord, will not restrain
>   Thy compassion from me.
>   Thy mercy and Thy truth
>   Will continually guard me.

Ps. 66. I WILL TELL WHAT GOD HAS DONE FOR MY SOUL

Ps. 66 is a psalm of personal thanksgiving. It is a liturgy for a private sacrifice in fulfillment of a vow.[24] It is divided into three parts. The first (vss. 1-7) is a choir hymn; the second (vss. 8-12) is a hymn of national thanksgiving; and the third (vss. 13-20), the most distinctive part, is a song of personal thanksgiving. This last and most important part of the psalm is primarily concerned with a single individual and presents an individual religious experience. It is, however, rooted in the social worship of the congregation and achieves both

---

[23] In Simpson, ed., *The Psalmists*, p. 62.   [24] Cf. Quell, *op. cit.*, p. 133.

dignity and force through the national and congregational background against which it is presented.

The psalm opens with a choir hymn of praise, rendered antiphonally by two half choirs. The first half choir sings an elaborate introduction (vss. 1-4), which, sweeping through the inhabited world, invites all the earth to *shout* in obeisance to God, to *sing* of His fame, to *speak* forth His glorious praise, to *acknowledge* His awesome work, and to *worship* Him, whom even His enemies, humbled by His superior strength, will adulate.

1 Raise a shout to God, all the earth:
2 Sing the honor of His name:
   Speak of the glory of His praise.
3 Say to God, "How fearful are Thy deeds!
   Because of the greatness of Thy strength,
   Thine enemies will come cringing to Thee.
4 Let all the earth worship Thee,
   And sing to Thee; let them praise Thy name!"

The second half choir responds, summoning all the earth to see and hear about the awesome deeds of God. It mentions in particular Israel's passing through the Sea of Reeds at the Exodus and his crossing the Jordan at the invasion of Canaan. It also celebrates the Lord as ruler over the nations, watching out for the least attempt at rebellion against Him.

5 Come, and see the works of God,
   Awe-inspiring in deeds to the sons of men,
6 Turning the sea into dry land.
   They crossed the river on foot:
   Hear, and let us rejoice in Him,
7 Who ruleth in His strength forever;
   His eyes keep watch over the nations,
   So the rebellious cannot ever rise up.

At verse 8 the psalm moves into a hymn of national thanksgiving. The psalmist is so thrilled with what the Lord has wrought for His people across the centuries that he imaginatively draws the nations into the great circle of those whom he summons to sing a praise song to God. They are called to praise Him and proclaim Him as the One who kept His people alive and held them steady in days of great stress.

8 Bless our God, O peoples,
   And sound out the voice of His praise song,
9 Who has established our soul in life,
   And has not let our feet slip.

The pre-eminent theme of this hymn of thanksgiving—introduced, as often, by the word "for"—is God's discipline of His people across the centuries and its issue in their respite and relief. The psalmist's words (vss. 10, 12) are largely reminiscent of the great exilic theologian, Deutero-Isaiah (40–55), whose moving poetry presented a vivid spiritual interpretation of Israel's suffering: his refinement through affliction and God's renewed choice of Israel *in* the very affliction experienced.[25]

> 10 For Thou didst choose us, O God:
>   Thou didst refine us as silver is refined.
> 11 Thou didst bring us into the siege;
>   Thou didst put our loins in distress.
> 12 Thou didst let men ride over our heads;
>   We went through fire and water,
>   And Thou didst bring us out into freedom.[26]

Thus far all in the psalm is preliminary to what follows. But all is necessary for an adequate picture of it. For in the midst of the congregation at worship verses 13-20 are rendered, which describe the payment by an individual worshiper of a vow that came from his lips when he was in great distress. So following directly upon the choir hymn of congregational praise and thanksgiving comes the song of personal thanksgiving from the lips of the host of the feast himself. There in the inner court of the Temple, with throngs of worshipers around him, stands this individual worshiper, most likely a wealthy man and one of the leaders of the congregation. He has come bringing with him sacrificial animals as a whole burnt offering to the Lord, and as a peace offering for the sacrificial feast in which probably the whole congregation will share. The choir is now silent as all eyes are concentrated on him. He speaks and addresses himself to the Lord.

> 13 I am come to Thy house with whole burnt offerings;
>   I would pay Thee my vows,
> 14 Which my lips uttered,
>   And my mouth spoke in my trouble.
> 15 I offer up to Thee whole offerings of fatlings,
>   With sweet smoke of rams;
>   I offer a young bull along with goats.

As already noted (vs. 14), he has been in great distress, and now we learn the circumstances, for he is about to give the chief part of his song of personal thanksgiving—a portion which is never wanting, and which is a sure mark of this type of psalm—the story of the experience of him who is paying the vow, told by himself to the guests of the celebration,[27] in this case most likely the whole congregation. So he tells his experience to his fellow worshipers, how he was in the power of those who hated him, cried out unto God, and was rescued from them

---

[25] For vs. 10, see Isa. 48:10, "I have refined thee like silver; I have chosen thee in the furnace of affliction"; vs. 12*a*, see Isa. 51:23*b*, "And you have made your back like the ground, like a street for those to pass over"; vs. 12*b*, see Isa. 43:2, "When you pass through the waters, I will be with you. . . . When you walk in fire, you shall not be burned."

[26] Literally "relief."   [27] Cf. Gunkel, *Einleitung*, p. 268.

and saved from harm at their hands. This is a greatly loved part of the whole ritual and a concentration point of attention to all present. The psalmist says:

> 16 Come, listen, and I will recount,
>   All you who fear God,
>   What He has done for my soul.
> 17 I cried aloud to him,
>   And I was raised up from under my enemies.[28]

In memory (cf. Ps. 116:10-11) he goes back to those bitter hours of peril and recalls words that he then spoke inwardly to himself, words of doubt. All the more wonderful becomes his experience of release, thus heightened by contrast, and his personal narrative rises in mood at the very close into a little hymn of praise which is introduced, as is frequently the case in the psalms, [29] by a passive formula, "blessed."

> 18 As for me, I said in my heart,
>   "The Lord will not hear me!"
> 19 But, in fact, God *did* hear!
>   He gave attention to the voice of my prayer!
> 20 Blessed be God,
>   Who has not turned aside
>   My prayer or His mercy from me.

Ps. 92. FLOURISHING, FRUITFUL LIVES

Ps. 92 is a song of individual thanksgiving. The psalmist was probably ill and because of that fact had experienced all the more the slandering aspersions of opponents, who were enemies of the Lord as well as of himself. But it was given him to see his own vindication before them and the severe way in which they were called to account.[30] He experienced a rite of cleansing and healing which follows the regulations of the Priestly Code, an indication that the psalm probably dates from a time not earlier than about 400 B.C.

This song of individual thanksgiving has been greatly influenced in style by the hymn, since both types of psalms have the predominant mood of praise. Instead of saying "Let us give thanks and sing" or "I will give thanks and sing," our psalmist with the influence of the reflective temper in Judaism says, "It is good to give thanks . . . , to sing . . . , to declare." As is often the case with a hymn, instruments of music are named—the ten-stringed harp, the lute, and the lyre. Verse 3 seems to point to some connection of the psalm with the morning and evening sacrifice. The theme or ground of the praise is introduced, just as in a hymn, by the word "for" (vs. 5). And the theme of the praise is the deeds of God, the works of His hands, which express His lovingkindness and His faithfulness.

---

[28] So following Wellhausen, *The Psalms*, p. 64. [29] Cf. Gunkel, *Einleitung*, p. 40.
[30] Cf. Schmidt, *Die Psalmen*, p. 174.

1   It is good to give thanks unto the Lord
    And to sing to Thy name, O Most High;
2   To declare in the morning Thy lovingkindness,
    And Thy faithfulness in the nights,
3   With the ten-stringed harp and with the lute,
    With resounding music on the zither.
4   For Thou hast made me glad with Thy deeds;
    Of the work of Thy hands let me sing.

All this is but introductory to the main part of the psalm (vss. 5-15), which opens with a characteristic rhetorical question. Through verse 9 the psalmist continues in contemplation of the great deeds and deep thoughts of the Lord. A dull-hearted man, ignorant of God and His ways, cannot understand such deeds and thoughts which permit the wicked to flourish. The truth is that God lets the godless thrive only to destroy them utterly. That such management of mankind whereby the wicked are permitted to flourish and the righteous left to pine away, can be called wisdom, only their contrasted fate at the end reveals. The dull-hearted man, with no understanding of God, does not think in terms of the outcome of conduct. But God is the exalted Lord, whose dominion over life, both the evil and the good, is not limited to today but is forever. And a firm principle of His eternal dominion is that evildoers, who seem so united and strong, will in the end be divided and destroyed.

5   How great are Thy deeds, O Lord!
    How exceedingly deep are Thy thoughts!
6   A dumb man does not know;
    A dullard does not understand this:
7   That when the godless sprout like herbage,
    And all doers of evil bloom,
8   It is only to be exterminated forever.[31]
    But Thou art exalted eternally.
9   For, lo, Thine enemies will perish;
    All evildoers will be dispersed.

In contrast to what will be the fate of the godless, the psalmist turns to the thought of the flourishing of the righteous (vss. 10-15). And at once we are in the mood characteristic of the song of personal thanksgiving for what the psalmist has himself experienced. He feels strong, exultant in joy and triumph, like a wild ox proudly brandishing its horns. He was ill, but in the Temple he has been anointed with oil by the officiating priest (Lev. 14:15-18) in accordance with the ritual for the sick and unclean. He has been healed. The enemies of the Lord (vs. 9) are likewise the psalmist's enemies (vs. 11). In and with his deliverance from distress he can now behold with satisfaction the discomfiture of his enemies, who have been insidiously watching and waiting for his downfall.[32]

[31] Literally, "[It happens so only] for their being exterminated forever."
[32] Cf. Mowinckel, *op. cit.,* I, 129.

10 But Thou hast exalted my horn like a wild ox;
   Thou hast poured upon me fresh oil.
11 And my eye hath gloated over those lying in wait for me;
   My ears rejoice over [33] the evildoers.

The psalm closes with attractive pictures of the fate of the righteous, which the psalmist knows in his own experience. The righteous are like date palms, beautiful, fruitful, and abundant. I am here reminded of a journey up the Shatt-al-Arab from the head of the Persian Gulf to Basra, where I saw many thousands of flourishing date palms on both sides of the river, reaching far inland, the greatest date palm region in the world. Again, the righteous are like the majestic, strong cedars of Lebanon. Our psalmist thinks of such wonderful trees, far less frequently found even than olive and cypress trees, as being planted in the Temple courts. There they continue to grow, under the care of Temple servants, blooming and budding, vigorous and fruitful still in their old age.[34] Just so shall the righteous be, still fresh, beautiful, and fruitful, even in their maturity. And their lips will continue to proclaim God's uprightness and the irreproachableness of His character.

12 The righteous sprouts like a date palm;
   Like a cedar in the Lebanon, he grows.
13 Those planted in the house of the Lord
   Bear buds in the courts of our God.
14 They shall still bear fruit in old age;
   Vigorous and green shall they be,
15 To declare that the Lord is upright,
   My Rock, with no wrong in Him.

Ps. 107. THE PAYMENT OF VOWS OF THANKSGIVING

Ps. 107 is a liturgy of individual thanksgiving. It is composed of two parts: The first (vss. 1-32) is a liturgy for a service in the Temple where individuals rendered their vows in groups. The second (vss. 33-43) is a choir hymn, less brilliant, less concrete. It was probably added later as a meditative, searching close to the earlier richly human and colorful part of the psalm. The first part was intended for rendering in connection with the great service for the presentation of votive offerings which took place at the autumnal New Year festival. The people who in various kinds of distress had made vows unto the Lord and had experienced His saving help then came to the Temple with their sacrificial offerings to pay their vows. Schmidt has shown that they were first arranged in groups according to the nature of their affliction and relief; and as each group of "the redeemed of the Lord" came forward, the priestly choir sang the portion of the psalm which was appropriate for that group; then their sacrifice was pre-

---

[33] Reading *tismaḥnāh,* with Grimme; cf. Gunkel, *Die Psalmen,* p. 410.
[34] The cedars of Lebanon, which I saw near the village of Besharré, Lebanon, are computed to be from four to five thousand years old.

sented. The time is that of the Jewish Diaspora, when from all parts of the world the Jewish pilgrims came to the Temple. Moreover, at the time the psalm was composed, the Jews were participants in seafaring commerce.

It must have been a magnificent and moving spectacle to see these throngs of worshipers gathered from the ends of the earth. They are arranged in order, under careful and experienced priestly direction, for this high moment of individual and group thanksgiving. There they stand in the inner court of the Temple, where was stationed the altar of burnt offering. They are grouped according to the nature of the distress from which they have been rescued. They are there in obedience to the law of the freewill, votive offering as given in Lev. 7:11-18 and 22:17-25.

The officiating priest appears on the steps of the palisade of the inner court and chants to the throng:

1 Give thanks to the Lord, for He is good;

And the throng cries out the beloved response:

For His lovingkindness endures forever.

Again the priest:

2 Let the redeemed of the Lord declare [it],
    Whom He has redeemed from the power of affliction,
3 And has gathered them from the lands,
    From east and west, north and south.

Then group by group they come forward. The priestly choir sings the story of the particular distress and relief experienced by each, in turn. For each group, first, the nature of the distress is vividly pictured (vss. 4-5, 10-12, 17-18, 23-27); second, the story of their cry of need to God and their deliverance by Him in His own way is told (vss. 6, 13, 19, 28); and third, a classic longing is expressed that men should recognize, accept, and be thankful for the proffered goodness of God (vss. 8, 15, 21, 31).

The first group of those redeemed come forward. They are pilgrims who lost their way in the Judean wilderness. Their caravan could not find an inhabited city where they would meet with welcome and sustenance. Hungry, thirsty, faint of soul, they cried to the Lord for help. He rescued them and set them on the right trail. How great should be their thanks! How wonderful His specific response to human need! In their behalf the choir sings:

4 Wanderers in the desert wilderness
    Could not find the way to an inhabited city.
5 Hungry, likewise thirsty,
    Their soul in them fainted.
6 Then they cried to the Lord in their trouble;
    He rescued them from their distresses.

7 Yes, He led them in the right way,
    So that they came to an inhabited city.
8 Let them give thanks to the Lord for His lovingkindness
    And His wonderful deeds to the sons of men!
9 For He satisfies the thirsty soul,
    And the hungry soul He fills with good.

This group moves forward to the altar of sacrifice, and the second group takes its place. Again the choir sings. These are former prisoners who were bound in iron fetters, for they had rebelled against God's commandments and had spurned His counsel. In misery of confinement and in the loneliness of neglect they cried out to the Lord. He brought them out of the dungeon and snapped their bonds. Yes, God it is who breaks in pieces bronze gates and hews down iron bars to set His people free!

10 Those dwelling in darkness and deep shadow,
     Prisoners in fetters of iron,
11 For they had rebelled against the words of God,
     And spurned the counsel of the Most High;
12 So their heart was humbled in misery;
     They stumbled, and there was no one to help.
13 Then they cried to the Lord in their trouble;
     He saved them from their distresses.
14 He brought them out of darkness and deep shadow,
     And snapped their bonds.
15 Let them give thanks to the Lord for His lovingkindness,
     And His wonderful deeds to the sons of men.
16 For He shivers gates of bronze to pieces,
     And hews down bars of iron.

As the second group moves on to the altar, its place is taken by the third group. This is the largest group of all, those who were sick unto death, whose condition was all the more poignant because they considered it to be the direct result of their own sin. They lost all appetite, and death seemed near at hand. In their dire distress they cried to the Lord. He sent forth, as an angel of healing, His mighty word of command, and they were restored to health as from the very edge of the grave. How joyful should be their cry of thanksgiving! Thus sings the choir:

17 The sick because of their sinful way,
     And on account of their iniquities, are afflicted.
18 Their appetite abhors all food;
     And they approach to the very gates of death.
19 Then they cried to the Lord in their trouble;
     He saved them from their distresses.
20 He sends out His word so as to heal them,
     And saves them out of the pitfall of their life.
21 Let them give thanks to the Lord for His lovingkindness,
     And His wonderful deeds to the sons of men.

22 Yes, let them offer sacrifices of thanksgiving
     And recount His deeds with a ringing cry!

As the third group passes on to the altar, the last group comes forward. They
are seafaring men who have been wondrously saved from shipwreck in violent
storm. The sea was ferociously tempestuous, and they were staggering about,
desperately seasick and at their wit's end. They cried out to God in their help-
lessness. He stilled the storm, silenced the noisy waves, and guided the ship to
its destined harbor. These mariners should praise the Lord not only in the
Temple, but also in public assemblies where sit the elders of Israel! Thus sings
the choir:

23 Those who go down to the sea in ships,
     Who do business in great waters;
24 They see the deeds of the Lord
     And His wonders in the deep.
25 He commanded, and the storm wind
     Was roused up,
         And it whipped up the waves.
26 They rose up to the heavens
     And went down to the deeps;
         Their soul melted away in distress.
27 They staggered in a circle like a drunk man,
     And they were at their wit's end.
28 Then they cried to the Lord in their trouble,
     And He brought them out of their distresses.
29 He stilled the storm to a whisper,
     And the waves of the deep became silent.
30 Then they rejoiced that they were quiet,
     And He guided them to their desired haven.
31 Let them give thanks to the Lord for His lovingkindness,
     And His wonderful deeds to the sons of men.
32 Yes, let them exalt Him in the assemblies of the nation
     And praise Him in the seat of elders.

The second half of this liturgy of thanksgiving (vss. 33-43) is a choir hymn.
The theme of it is the Lord's dealings with mankind in discipline and in mercy.
Each verse has to do, not with any one specific episode, but with what the Lord
is continually doing. Rivers are made a wilderness, springs turned into dry
ground. Fertile land, because of the evil of those who live there, gives no yield.
On the other hand He makes the wilderness into a refreshing water pool. Hungry
men can joyously dwell there and establish a city, their labor blessed with fruit-
age both in the fields and in the herds. But let them sin, and God reduces them,
transforming their lot into that of homeless wanderers. The trustful and humble,
however, both themselves and their descendants, He makes secure. As a consequence the upright rejoice, but the unjust are effectively silenced. The hymn
ends with a practical admonition of Hebrew wisdom. Let the truly wise, noting
all this, be discerningly receptive of divine blessings! The abstract, general nature

of this hymn provides a thoughtful, calm conclusion to the far more vivid and richly human quality of the liturgy of individual thanksgiving. Moreover, we sense in this section a characteristic note that marks the harvest New Year festival, the longing for new rain. We feel the calm, detached mood of the poet as the hymn proceeds, and the psalmist brings the whole liturgy to its close with an utterance characteristic of Hebrew wisdom.

33   He turns rivers into a wilderness,
        And springs of water into thirsty ground;
34   Fruitful land He makes barren,
        Because of the evil of those dwelling in it.
35   He turns the wilderness into water pools,
        And parched ground into a water fount.
36   He makes the hungry dwell there,
        So they establish an inhabited city.
37   Then they sow fields and plant vineyards,
        And they reap a harvest.
38   So He blesses them, and they multiply greatly,
        Nor does He decrease their cattle.
40   He pours contempt upon nobles,
        And makes them wander in the waste with no way.
39   So they were diminished and reduced,
        From pressure of adversity and sorrow.
41   But He sets the needy on high without affliction
        And gives them families like a flock.
42   The upright see and rejoice,
        And all injustice shuts its mouth.
43   Who is wise, let him observe this
        And show himself discernful of the mercies of the Lord.

Ps. 116. I WAS LOW, AND HE SAVED ME

Ps. 116 is a psalm of personal thanksgiving. It is composed of the two most characteristic features in such a psalm, the story of the psalmist's own experience, giving the circumstances that occasioned his thanksgiving (vss. 1-11), and the account of the payment of the vow which he had made in the hour of his deep distress (vss. 12-19).

The worship setting of the psalm is reasonably clear. The worshiping congregation is present in the Temple at Jerusalem. But we are at a moment in the worship and at a type of worship occasion where an individual who has experienced a great release holds the center of attention. For the time being the congregation is in the background, and all eyes are focused upon this individual man. In such a form of religious expression as has created a vital pattern of Christian testimony, in accents of gratitude, he briefly summarizes his experience. His soul is athrill with love for God, because God graciously heard him when out of great need he prayed to Him.

1 I love the Lord, for He heard
      The voice of my entreaty.
2 Because he bent down his ear to me
      In the day that I kept crying.

He was so very ill that the end of his life seemed certain and imminent. With Oriental vividness of imagination the psalmist describes how death already had begun to bind him and take him into its power. Already Sheol, the realm of the departed, had, as it were, trapped him into its network. He was in deep distress. Repeatedly he prayed to the Lord for deliverance, appealing to Him as a loyal worshiper.

3 The cords of death surrounded me,
      And the nets of Sheol had fallen upon me:
         I experienced trouble and sorrow.
4 I kept calling upon the name of the Lord:
      "Ah! Lord! deliver my soul!
16a   For I am thy servant!"

And the Lord heard his cry and restored him to health. His recovery was to him a truly wonderful experience. He was stirred to the depths of his being by it. For one thing, he considered it an expression of the gracious, righteous, and compassionate nature of God, whom both he and his fellow members of the congregation worshiped. The psalmist is evidently not one of the great in Israel, for his recovery from his low physical condition is proof to him that God is watchful over even the simple individuals in the nation. The psalmist had experienced a threefold deliverance: from imminent death to life, from sorrow to joy, and from insecurity to stability. How his soul thrills as he tells the story to the congregation; then suddenly addressing his own soul, he bids it return to its true resting place, the God who had thus dealt so graciously with him in his hour of dire need. How priceless seems to him the gift of life, even the power to walk about in God's world and in His very presence!

5 Gracious is the Lord, and righteous;
      Yes, our God is compassionate.
6 The keeper of the simple-minded is the Lord:
      I was low, and He saved me.
7 Return, my soul, to thy rest,
      For the Lord has dealt well with you.
8 For He delivered my soul from death,
      My eyes from tears,
         My feet from stumbling.
9 I will walk about before the Lord
      In the land of the living!

It is painful now for the psalmist to recall the dark hours when his life seemed to be slipping away, for his affliction was very severe. He was inwardly agitated. Evidently his illness, as in the case of Job, led men whom he trusted to accuse him of faults, viewed by them as the real cause of his low condition. At any rate, he now realizes that in those hours of extreme weakness he held a warped view of life and uttered unworthy and untrue judgments of men in general, and, no doubt, of some in particular. He sees it all in better perspective now, but then—

> 10 I believed when I spoke:
>   I was greatly afflicted:
> 11 I said in my agitation,
>   "All men lie!"

Then there unfold before our eyes the high moments of his worship experience, the payment of the vows which he made in those dark hours of weakness, uncertainty, and inner distress. For in ancient Israel a vow is a very significant spiritual act and is of great importance in religion. It is, as Moore has succinctly explained, "a voluntary obligation solemnly assumed toward God to do something not otherwise required, but believed to be acceptable or influential with Him." [35] When a vow had been made, it must be paid, as the Deuteronomic law (23:21, 23) explicitly requires: "When you make a vow to the Lord your God, you must pay it without delay; for the Lord your God definitely requires it of you, and you would incur guilt. . . . A spoken promise you must be careful to observe in the way that you promised the Lord your God, seeing that it was a voluntary promise that you made." The psalmist vowed that if the Lord should restore him to health, he would go to the Temple, testify before the worshipers as to what God had done for him, and offer the appropriate sacrifice of thanksgiving. With a lift of feeling he opens the narrative of the payment of his vow with a rhetorical question:

> 12 How can I repay the Lord
>   For all His benefits to me?

There are particular ritual requirements in the payment of the vow, which the psalmist now meticulously performs. First is the libation of the drink offering of wine, "the cup of salvation," which was the regular accompaniment of animal sacrifice.[36] He lifts his cup, calls on the name of the Lord, then pours the wine out before the altar. The second thing is his grateful acknowledgment directly to the Lord, but before the congregation, that God loosened the cords of death which seemed to be binding him into its power. God, counting him His servant, the godly son of a godly mother—the Lord's "handmaid"—did not let him die! Simple a man as he knows himself to be, he had his soul signally marked by God as being of value to Him. To the Lord every devout life is precious. It is of cost to Him when a good man dies. There is in the psalmist's words a quiet, awed dignity that rises from this sense that even he is of worth to God. The third

---

[35] "Vow" in Canney, *Encyclopedia of Religions,* p. 379.
[36] Cf. Macalister, "Sacrifice (Semitic)," in Hastings, *Encyclopaedia of Religion and Ethics,* XI, 35a; see Exod. 29:40; Deut. 32:38.

thing is his thank offering, the most important act of all. Again just as with the libation, he calls upon the name of the Lord, then offers his sacrifice of thanksgiving. Accompanying these ritual acts are his words:

13 I lift up the cup of salvation,
    And call upon the name of the Lord.
15 Costly in the eyes of the Lord
    Is the dying of His saints.
16 Ah, Lord, I am Thy servant,
    The son of Thy handmaid.
    Thou hast loosed my bonds!
17 To Thee I offer a sacrifice of thanksgiving
    And call upon the name of the Lord.

When he was in distress he vowed, but now these vows he has paid in the presence of the congregation of God's people. He is in the most sacred place in which he has ever been, the inner court of the Lord's Temple in the city of Jerusalem, and it is to this city that he speaks directly in the closing line. His words rise to a climax of feeling.

18 My vows I pay to the Lord,
    In the presence of all His people,
19 In the courts of the house of the Lord,
    In the midst of thee, O Jerusalem!

We sense the thrilling emotional lift at the very end of the psalm as his fellow worshipers, who have shared with him this high hour of thanksgiving, raise with warm enthusiasm and spiritual sympathy the familiar cry of praise:

Hallelujah!

Ps. 138. THE LORD ACTS FOR ME

Ps. 138 is a spirited psalm of individual thanksgiving on the part of a simple, private man in the congregation. It is uttered in the Temple court, which resounds with the beloved worship cry, "O Lord, Thy mercy endureth forever" (vs. 8). Unique in this psalm is the place given to the individual in the presence of gods and of kings of the earth. The psalmist's own experience of rescue and release at God's hands becomes a gospel even to earthly monarchs. It dates from the postexilic period sometime after 500 B.C., when the intermingling of the various literary types in the psalms began to take place.

The psalm begins with an elaborate introduction. With a full heart of praise the psalmist addresses his God, prostrating himself in the Temple court, his face turned toward the most holy place, where the Lord dwells. Distinctive in this psalm is the residue from polytheism which appears in verse 1. He thinks, in a fashion quite familiar in Babylonia and Egypt, of an assembly of the gods. But of all those divine beings which the imagination of the psalmist pictures as present, there is but One to whom he pours out his soul; the gods are but witnesses of his praise song to the Lord. Such grandiose type of utterance on the lips of a private man in Judaism was originally at home in kings' songs, which were very popular in Israel, and from that source have found their way into private poems.[37] Before this great and superior Being he bows in praise because in a most remarkable way the Lord answered his cry. Beyond any expectation based on what he had previously heard of God, the Lord strengthened his soul.

Thrilled with the impulse to praise, he sings:

1   I thank Thee, O Lord, with all my heart:
    In the presence of the gods, I praise Thee.
2   I bow down before Thy holy Temple,
    And I praise Thy name because of Thy lovingkindness.
    For Thou hast magnified Thy truth above all report of Thee.
3   In the day when I called Thou didst answer me;
    Thou didst increase strength in my soul.

Hymns early influenced the songs of personal thanksgiving, and sometimes, as here, a hymn may stand in the middle of the individual's praise, for verses 4-6 are a hymn. All the kings of the earth are summoned to praise the Lord because they have heard what the Lord spoke to the psalmist's soul. We can judge how great an experience of the kindness of God has been enjoyed when this private person pictures even pagan kings, because of what God has done to him, talking about the Lord and His ways! The Lord is "lofty" in His exalted majesty, yet— how wonderful in the poet's experience—He sees with consideration and concern "the lowly." For it is to the lowly in the community that the psalmist himself belongs. But the singer's haughty enemies God also sees from His lofty throne in the heavens. Their plots are not hidden from His eyes.

Such an idea, that the experience of this lowly man may influence kings, is likewise originally at home in kings' songs and from there has found its way into the thought and expression of the common man. So the psalmist summons the monarchs of the earth to share in his praise:

4   Let all the kings of the earth praise Thee,
    For they have heard the words of Thy mouth.
5   And let them talk about the ways of the Lord,
    For great is the fame of the Lord.
6   For though the Lord is lofty, yet He sees the lowly,
    And the proud He knows from afar.

The psalm ends with a confession of faith that roots in the psalmist's wonderful release. The exact nature of the distress from which he was delivered is not told us. But that it was caused by enemies whom he characterizes as "the proud," the closing verses reveal. We know only that God spoke to him words of comfort and strength, which in the very presence of oppressive enemies strengthened

[37] Cf. Gunkel, *Einleitung*, p. 147.

and saved him. In verses 7-8 is expressed the spiritual deposit of the psalmist's whole experience.[38] He is faced toward the future. Oppression may still be his lot; enemies may continue to threaten his life; but he is in the care of God's strong right hand, for the Lord will go into action in his behalf. In the closing lines he speaks to the Lord in glad faith that His lovingkindness endures forever, and in the fervent petition that God will never abandon him. And he views his own life, thus wondrously saved, as "the work of Thy hands!"

> 7 Though I walk in the midst of distress,
>   Thou leadest me, in spite of [39] the anger of my enemies.
>   Thou reachest out Thy hand, and Thy right hand saves me.
> 8 The Lord acts for me:
>   O Lord, Thy mercy endures forever;
>   Abandon not the work of Thy hands!

Ps. 139. THE GOD-EXAMINED LIFE

Socrates used to say that the unexamined life is not worth the living, and he gave his whole career to the examination of men's minds. Ps. 139 takes us beyond such mere human scrutiny into the imaginative sphere of the God-examined life. It is one of the most spiritually profound psalms of the Psalter. It is the awed utterance of individual thanksgiving (see vs. 14ab) on the part of one of the noblest thinkers of Israel. It comes out of the late period of classical Judaism when the sages of Hebrew wisdom flourished. The psalmist has close relationship in intellectual and spiritual sympathy with the author of the book of Job. There is a wonderful note of universality in the psalm that lifts it above mere Israelite nationalism; hence we do the psalmist no violence when we include ourselves as we explore with him the God-examined life.

First, the psalmist turns the searchlight of God upon our lives (vss. 1-6), and in its light we note five things: (a) God *sees* us as His perfect knowledge shows us up. (b) God *knows* us. We feel here the influence of Jeremiah, who experienced God as proving his heart, visiting him, and trying him (17:10). And we are aware of the influence of another psalmist, whose God searches out and knows the secrets of the heart (44:21). Thus our lives are understood, comprehended, and encompassed. Moreover, God knows the ordinary habitual daily acts of our lives, sitting down, standing up, the paths we take, all our ways, all our habits (vs. 3). (c) God is our wise teacher. He understands the dim aims we feel within us which lead us on into the unexplored future. Like the dominie in *Beside the Bonnie Brier Bush*, who could "scent a scholar in the egg" and prophesy latinity of a boy who looked fit only to be a cowherd, God understands what we have in us and the import of what we are trying to say and do. There is not a word we are trying to utter but God understands what we mean. (d) God's presence

---

[38] Cf. *ibid.,* p. 272.   [39] Brown, Driver, Briggs, *op. cit.,* p. 754, II, 1, f (f).

surrounds us. He is before us and behind us (Isa. 52:12b). He is round about us like Jerusalem's encircling mountains (Ps. 125:2). (e) God's hand is upon each of us, like in Browning's "Saul" King Saul's hand was upon young David's head as he looked into the young musician's eyes, which looked back into his troubled monarch's face with unutterable reverence and affection. Such knowledge, says the psalmist, is unfathomably great. We have no instruments of thought to comprehend it.

1   O Lord, Thou searchest me and knowest me.
2   Thou knowest my sitting down and my standing up;
    Thou dost fathom my purposes for the far future.[40]
3   The way I go, and the bed where I lie, Thou dost trace out,
    And Thou knowest intimately all my ways.
4   Indeed, there is not a word in my tongue,
    But lo, Thou knowest it entirely.
5   Behind and in front Thou hast besieged me,
    And hast laid Thy hand upon me.
6   Too wonderful for me is such knowledge,
    Unattainably high; I cannot reach it!

Second, the psalmist glories in God's inescapable presence (vss. 7-12). Can he go any place where God is not? To the peak of heaven's height? To the deepest recess of Sheol, where dwell the dead? Can he escape God's presence by speeding with the wings of light, flying, as it were, with the sun across the heavens until it dips at sunset into the sea and then, as the Egyptians taught, speeds at night through the world of the dead?

How close to life in our era seem such words now! Hurtling at vast speed through the air in jet-propulsion planes, can we escape God? Can we evade Him in the swiftest submarine? Can we hide from God in the darkness? Can God's eyes find us when all is black? One feels in such words the accent of spiritual experience every bit as real as the thoughts to which they gave rise in Francis Thompson's "The Hound of Heaven."

7   Whither can I go from Thy spirit?
    Yes, whither can I flee from Thy presence?
8   If I should ascend into heaven, Thou art there:
    And if I should spread my bed in Sheol, lo, Thou art there.
9   If I should take the wings of dawn
    And settle down in the outermost bound of the sea,
10   Even there would Thy hand seize me,
    And Thy right hand grasp me.
11   Though I should say, "Surely darkness shall cover me,
    And night shall close in about me,"
12   Even darkness does not become too dark for Thee,
    But night shines like day:
        The darkness as the light.

[40] See Ehrlich, op. cit., p. 361, and note, p. 426. He has caught the true force of this passage.

Third, the psalmist comes closer home and in holy awe contemplates the divine creative process that brought his own life into being. To him it all seems truly wonderful. He first thinks of his inner being, the seat of his emotions and affections, as the work of the divine Creator. Then he contemplates the nine-months period during which his body was taking shape—being "woven together," he calls it—in his mother's womb. His words remind us forcibly of Job's similar description (10:8-12). God knew him then and saw his bodily frame when thus he was being skillfully fashioned in the womb. Yet more, God's eyes saw the deeds that he would do, and in marvelous foreknowledge set them down in His book of life with his days all accounted for. So he cries:

> 14a I will give thanks to Thee, because Thou art awe-inspiring:
> 14b　　Thou art wonderful: wonderful are Thy works.
> 13　For Thou didst create my affections:
> 　　　Thou didst weave me together in the womb of my mother,
> 14c　　And my soul Thou didst know from then on.
> 15　My bodily frame was not hidden from Thee
> 　　　When I was made in the secret place,
> 　　　When I was skillfully wrought
> 　　　In the remotest recesses of the womb.[41]
> 16　Thine eyes saw my deeds:
> 　　　Yes, they were all in Thy book.
> 　　　My days were written down; they were counted,
> 　　　And not one among them was missing.

Fourth, the psalmist presents God as the divine Thinker. How priceless to him are the separate thoughts of God and how vast in their totality—more than the sand of the sea! Brooding on God's thoughts, so much loftier than men's thoughts (Isa. 55:9), he falls asleep; but when he awakes, *at once* the precious realization of the Lord's knowledge of him, His inescapable presence, and His loving informed concern for him as his Creator, sweeps over him in immediate awareness—he is with God!

> 17　How precious to me are Thy thoughts, O God!
> 　　　How great is the sum of them!
> 18　If I should count them, they would be more numerous than grains
> 　　　of sand:
> 　　　When I awake, I am still with Thee.

The keen insight of Buttenwieser has shown that verses 19-22, which in content, style, and cadence are radically different and mar the poetic unity and lofty thought of the psalm, have been misplaced here and rightly belong elsewhere— verses 19-20 after Ps. 140:11 and verses 21-22 after Ps. 141:4.

Finally, the psalm closes with a noble prayer in which the psalmist not only affirms but seeks and welcomes for his own life the scrutiny, knowledge, testing,

---

[41] "In the lowest parts of the earth" is a "chaste correction" for this original rendering, so Halévy, *op. cit.*, p. 350.

insight, and leadership of God. **Five** great verbs gather up his heartfelt prayer: "examine" me, "know" me, "test" me, "see" me (as to whether or not there is deceit in me), and "lead" me in the eternal way.

> 23   Examine me, O God, and know my heart:
>   Test me, and know my thoughts;
> 24   And see whether there be in me any deceitful way;
>   And lead me in the way everlasting.

Ps. 146. I WILL SING WHILE I HAVE MY BEING

Ps. 146 is a song of personal thanksgiving. The psalmist has experienced richly at the hands of God. He tells us all too little of just what has happened to him. But the most personal part of the psalm, in which we best feel the warmth of his spirit, shows us that he has been signally blest of God in such a way as to make him thankful as long as he lives.

He has come to Zion, to the worshiping congregation of the Temple. And there, in the presence of the congregation, in a general summons he calls his fellow worshipers to praise.

> 1a **Praise ye the Lord!**

Then in a wonderful utterance of devout, personal thankfulness he summons his own soul to praise, in words and mood very similar to those of the great poet who wrote Ps. 103. He also expresses the deep intent of his spirit to praise God as long as his physical being persists.

> 1b **Praise the Lord, O my soul.**
> 2   I will praise the Lord while I live.
>   I will sing to my God while my existence continues.

He seems loath to tell exactly what he has experienced that so fills his heart with singing joy. But from verses 3-4, which are a counsel expressed in the temper of the Hebrew sages, we may infer that a preliminary element in his experience has been a shattering disillusionment. He evidently put confidence in some man of high rank in society who failed him in a crisis and gave him no help when he had a right to expect it. The experience leads the psalmist to counsel against trust in man in general, even though he be a man of noble rank. Even at his best, man is a mere mortal who, as the most ancient account of creation said (Gen. 3:19), is made of dust and returns to dust, his heart purposes perishing with him. So out of such painful experience he speaks, first negatively:

> 3   **Do not trust in princes,**
>   Nor in a human being, who cannot give help.
> 4   **His spirit goes forth; he returns to his dust;**
>   In that day his purposes perish.

Then continuing in the method of the Hebrew sages and speaking generally, yet addressing the Lord's people, he counsels the congregation in positive terms which also root in his experience. Over against the failure of men to help him in the crisis, he directs them to turn, even as he has done, to dependence upon and trust in the living God. We hear the great historic phrases roll from his lips—the God of Jacob, maker of heaven and earth.

We see that this psalmist is also imbued with a prophetic faith. He has deep concern, comparable to that of the eighth-century prophets, for the oppressed in the Jewish community. The hungry, the prisoner, the blind, those whom disease, distress, or other trouble has humbled to the dust, the resident alien who has few rights but great needs, the helpless widow and the orphan, always the prey of exploiting forces—all of these lie heavy on his heart. Does he know the great words of Isa. 61:1? It is likely that he does. While he does not say so, it is probable that he too is such a one as these. Yet the thing that makes him thankful is that deep in the heart of his God, as he now knows, there is loving solicitude for just these, His poor and needy children who are so ruthlessly pushed about and exploited by godless men. So our sage psalmist exults in God.

> 5 Oh the happiness of him who has as his helper the God of Jacob,
>   Whose hope is based upon the Lord his God:
> 6 Who made heaven and earth,
>   The sea and all that is in them;
> 7 Who discharges firmness to the unjust;
>   Who accomplishes righteousness for the oppressed;
>   Who gives bread to the hungry;
>   Who sets the prisoners free.
> 8 The Lord opens the eyes of the blind;
>   The Lord raises up those who are humiliated.
>   The Lord loves the righteous;
> 9a   The Lord protects the resident aliens;
> 9b The orphan and widow he restores.

In contrast to this merciful kindness of God, in one brief sentence the psalmist reveals the reverse side of the Lord's compassionate nature. The wicked seems so strong and secure in his ways. But God is the kind of Being who frustrates wickedness and brings to disaster the evil man's way of life.

> 9c   But the way of the wicked He subverts.

The psalm draws to its close with a strong wish, fervently expressed to the congregation. May this just and compassionate God, whose help the psalmist has experienced, by all future generations be enthroned as King—not only in his own heart, but in all the hearts of Zion, the Lord's loyal and worshiping fellowship.

> 10 Let the Lord rule forever,
>   Thy God, O Zion, for generation after generation.

And the congregation responds with the cultic cry,

> Hallelujah!

Chapter X

PRAYERS OF THE FALSELY ACCUSED

ONE OF THE PERSISTENT PROBLEMS OF SOCIETY IS FOR AN ACCUSED MAN AND AN accuser to secure justice. This is one of the gravest issues of our time and becomes more complex and more difficult of solution as society develops. Ancient Israel early developed a simple system designed for the securing of justice. The Elohist's story of Moses, which is the most psychologically brilliant and most adequate of all the early traditions of which Moses is the center, sets the beginnings of it at Kadesh. Moses is pictured as sitting to judge the people from morning until evening. When a matter of dispute arises among the people whom he has led as far as the wilderness, the parties concerned come to Moses, who judges between man and man and informs them of the divine laws. Jethro, Moses' father-in-law, seeing how wearing this is both upon the long waiting line of people and upon Moses, encourages him to appoint able and responsible men who cannot be bribed and organize them in a system of judicial administration. Moses places officials over thousands, hundreds, fifties, and tens, who will at set times judge the ordinary matters, but those that cannot so easily be settled, the difficult disputes, are to be brought to him. In such cases he is to be the mediator of the divine decision. Says Jethro:

> Be thou for the people to Godward,
> And bring thou the causes unto God. (Exod. 18:19.)

Driver is right in maintaining that there is here a kernel of historicity which sets us at the beginnings of those precedents which are the origins of Israelite law. And it is clearly understood that some cases can be settled only by some one who is recognized as mediating the incisive truth and judgment of God.

The Deuteronomic law recognizes this same distinction. In the historical introduction to the Deuteronomic Code it is stated that when a dispute is too difficult for the appointed judges, the matter must be brought unto God: "The cause that is too hard for you, ye shall bring unto me, and I will hear it" (1:17b), that is, it shall be brought to the sanctuary, which in the Deuteronomist's thought was the Jerusalem Temple.

The Code of the Covenant, which was probably contemporary with Solomon in date, provides that in any trespass against another's property where the placing of the guilt is uncertain, the cause of both accuser and accused shall come before God, and he whom God condemns must make double restitution (Exod. 22:9). This means that the decision must be made and the sentence given at the sanctuary with the presiding priest acting as judge.

The fact that such matters were to be decided and judgment given at the Temple is implied in the prayer of the dedication of the Temple by King Solomon. Suppose a man accused by his neighbor of some crime solemnly affirms his innocence, yet in the regular avenues of justice his guilt or innocence cannot be proved. Then he is under obligation to go to the Temple and before the altar of the Lord solemnly swear to his innocence. The Lord is to hear and judge, condemning the wicked and bringing punishment upon him, and pronouncing the righteous one guiltless and ordering whatever redress shall be forthcoming to him (I Kings 8:31-32). Clearly the officiating priest at the Temple in such an instance is the mediator and instrument of the divine judgment.

Exactly how this decision was arrived at we are not told, but the fact that it was done in this way remains, and out of this practice and in connection with it there grew up a considerably large group of psalms which are properly viewed as prayers of the falsely accused. Upon this group of psalms Schmidt has thrown great light in his brochure on the prayers of the falsely accused,[1] and to it I am greatly indebted.

There are two groups of these prayers. The first is the prayers of the falsely accused seeking vindication. The second is the prayers of the falsely accused seeking vindication by spending a night in the sanctuary. The first group includes Pss. 7; 11; 25; 26; 27:7-14; 31:1-8; 42–43; 52; 54; 55:1–18b, 22; 55:18c–21, 23; 56; 64; 70; 94:16-23; 120; 140; 141; 142.

1. Prayers of the Falsely Accused Seeking Vindication

Ps. 7. VINDICATION BY THE SEARCHER OF HEARTS

In Ps. 7 we clearly have the oath of one who has been accused. When at verse 3 the psalmist says, "If I have done this," an accusation lodged against the one praying is presupposed, and in verse 4b the nature of the accusation appears. He was accused of a crime against property. He stands charged with theft, yes, more, with breach of confidence in relation to a fellow countryman. The accused has been brought to the Temple and there takes upon himself an oath of innocency (I Kings 8:31b). Before his God he calls down upon himself a curse in case he is guilty of the accusation. In the Temple, where such matters are settled (I Kings 8:31), solemnly affirming his innocence he seeks the protection of the Lord through the priestly decision that he is not guilty.

1 O Lord, my God, in Thee I seek shelter;
  Save me from my pursuer and deliver me,
2 Lest he rend my body like a lion,
  Tearing it to pieces, with no one to snatch it away.
3 O Lord, my God, if I have done this,
  If there is property in my hands through dishonesty,

---

[1] *Das Gebet der Angeklagten in den Psalmen. Beihefte zur Zeitschrift für die alttestamentliche Wissenschaft,* 49.

4   If I have done evil to my familiar friend,
   If I have plundered him bare who without reason is hostile to me,
5   Let my enemy pursue my soul and overtake it,
   And trample my life to the earth,
   And lay my dignity in the dust.

This vigorous curse, to be executed upon himself in case he is pronounced guilty, is followed by a passionate prayer which the accused lifts to God. We feel the majesty of God as the psalmist has experienced Him, a God who is the all-knowing Judge of men and of nations. In awe he pictures the Lord, the righteous Judge of the world in this court of judgment, supreme likewise over all other imaginable divine beings. And this mighty and awesome Being, Lord over gods and men, because of even one unjustified accusation will arise in defense of the accused. Such is the psalmist's faith. He will vindicate the essential righteousness of His loyal servant, the psalmist, who stands now in desperate need of defense. Let the Lord arise in His righteous wrath against those whose harsh hostility is without cause! So he prays:

6   Rise up, O Lord, in Thine anger;
   Arise on account of my adversaries;
   Awake, my God; command judgment.
8a   O Lord, judge the nations:
7   With the assembly of divine beings surround Thyself,
   And over it take Thy seat on high.
8b   Vindicate me, O Lord, in accordance with my righteousness,
   And according to the integrity which I have.

The accused knows the integrity of his own heart (vs. 8b), but he also knows the very nature of God. For he has drunk at the deep springs of the pure soul of Jeremiah (for 9b see Jer. 11:20; 17:10; 20:12). His prayer continues, combined with the expression of his trust:

9   Pray, may the evil of the godless come to an end,
   But let righteousness show itself confirmed.
   Yes, He who examines the hearts and the affections
   Is a righteous God.
10   God is my shield about me;
   He is the Saviour of the upright in heart.
11   God is a righteous judge,
   Yes, a God who denounces every day.

The tone of the following verses (12-16) moves into the mood of a calm, meditative monologue, which implies the psalmist's certainty that his prayer for deliverance will be answered. How finely and completely does he express a thought which is uniquely characteristic of Semitic [2] feeling! He who commits evil against another will inevitably experience the boomerang of his deed. The evil comes back upon him to destroy him, its perpetrator.

[2] Cf. also Harper, *The Code of Hammurabi King of Babylon*, sec. 2, p. 11.

12 Yes, for himself he sharpens his sword;
        He bends and fixes his bow.
13 For himself he prepares deadly weapons,
        [For himself] he makes his arrows fiery darts.
14 Lo, he writhes in travail with wickedness;
        He has conceived evil; he gives birth to fraud.
15 A pit he has dug, has dug it deep;
        And he has fallen into the pit which he made.
16 His evil turns back upon his own head.
        And his violent dealing comes down upon his own scalp.

This calm certainty rises to a climax in a brief but glad song of thanksgiving, which implies that his confidence in his deliverance has been justified and his prayer answered. He looks back in deep gratitude to God for his righteous vindication.

17 I give thanks to the Lord as His righteousness deserves;
        I praise the name of the Lord, the Most High.

Ps. 11. SHOULD SUCH A MAN AS I FLEE?

The psalmist is in a moment of tense crisis. Certain enemies, defamers and calumniators of his character, are concocting hostile schemes that are threatening his very life. Some of his friends, concerned for his safety, urge him to flee into the mountains. We shall see with what calm faith he meets their timid fears.

But he is aware of something far more serious than his own critical situation, for this psalmist is a community-minded man. The leadership of the community is corrupt. The moral foundations of Judean society have been thrown down. As the prophet Amos said concerning the leaders of Israel in his day, they have

turned judgment to gall
And cast down righteousness to the earth. (5:7.)

Under such conditions what is a righteous man to do? The psalmist has something to say as to his own personal faith and for the spiritual heartening of the community.

He opens with a brief expression of his personal faith, along with a gentle remonstrance to his counseling friends because of their fearful anxiety as to his life.

1 In the Lord I seek refuge.
        How can you say to me,
            "Flee to the mountains like a bird,
2 For lo, the wicked are bending the bow;
        They have fixed the arrow on the bowstring
            To shoot in treachery the upright in heart!"

He views this unjustified threat upon his life by his accusers as but a symptom of a deep moral lack in the total Judean community. In such a period when the seriousness of the times calls for men of moral leadership and vision, the leaders are corrupt, and the foundations of the social order are insecure. As though in lamenting dialogue with his own soul, he cries:

> 3 When the established foundations are thrown down,
>   What should the righteous do?

The psalmist has an answer to his deploring question, for he is a man of great faith. Indeed his whole psalm is a deep utterance of faith. The scene of the ensuing words is clearly the Temple, where the Lord dwells although His throne is in the skies (cf. Ps. 103:19). Perfectly sure of his innocency of any charge, he goes to the Temple, where the Lord, the righteous Judge and a lover of righteousness, will vindicate him. There he contemplates the righteous Being, who views from His lofty height the world and its inhabitants, with discriminating eyes, testing the hearts of all men, righteous and wicked alike, and meting out to each his due. The psalmist's chief accuser he calls the lover of violence. Upon him the Lord will send His burning, life-destroying desert wind and the erupting volcanic fire which destroys all human beings. By such symbolic pictures of awful destruction the psalmist describes the cup of the Lord's judgment, which evil men must drink to its dregs. But likewise from the Lord alone comes vindication for the righteous, even such as the psalmist will himself experience. For only the righteous will "behold his face." This expression is rich in spiritual content, for it means to be aware of God's nearness and to experience the joy of His fellowship and vindication. In a strangely tangled time of moral upheaval the righteous should resort to God in His Temple. Thus over against the secret machinations of his wicked enemies, in the face of which he feels so powerless, his heart turns to God:

> 4 The Lord is in His holy Temple;
>   The Lord has his throne in the heavens:
>   His eyes behold the world;
>   His eyelids examine the sons of men.
> 5 The Lord tests the righteous and the wicked,
>   And His soul hates the one who loves violence.
> 6 He will rain upon the wicked, fiery coals and brimstone.
>   And a raging hot wind will be the portion of their cup.
> 7 For righteous is the Lord, who loves righteousness;
>   The upright shall behold His face.

Ps. 25. THE HUNGER FOR INTIMACY WITH GOD

Ps. 25 is the lament of an individual. The consciousness of the congregation of the Temple—as revealed in the expressions "the humble" (vs. 9), "those who keep His covenant" (vs. 10*b*), and "those who fear Him" (vs. 14)—is strong in the psalm and shows that the author is himself joined to the Lord's worshipers. The petition for instruction (vs. 5) and the indication that the influence of the wisdom poetry with its method of question and answer has penetrated into the lament (vss. 12-14) show that it is of relatively late date, probably from not earlier than the late Persian period.

The psalm is an acrostic, and it is this fact which accounts for its lack of sharp thought divisions. The author is somewhat bound by the restrictions which such a form of poetic expression necessarily place upon him. Yet in spite of such limitations we feel ourselves in this psalm to be face to face with a poet of quite distinctive personality.[3] This is particularly true as regards his consciousness of sin, which reveals a deep inwardness of spirit. Lagarde has made the conjecture that the opening word *pedhēh* of the last verse, which lies outside the acrostic, gives an indication as to the author of the psalm, standing for some such name as Pedaiah (II Kings 23:36; I Chr. 27:20).[4] As we have already seen, the similar Ps. 34, which is the counterpart of this one, has a like indication, the first word of the last verse (*pôdheh*) coming from the same root, and the verse likewise standing outside the acrostic. It is a reasonable conjecture that these two psalms come from the same person and that this implied indication of authorship with its purpose of immortalizing the composer is an evidence of a growing individualism in Judaism. However, the poet has hidden this signature in a short and fervent prayer for the liberation of his people Israel from its distresses.

The psalmist, burdened with the memory of the sins of his youth, lifts up his soul unto the Lord in earnest petitions. His distress of spirit is deepened by the scornful laugh of deceitful enemies, and he prays for vindication before them. There is a deep inwardness of soul in this man. He pleads that God will deal with his life, not on the basis of what he deserves, but out of His lovingkindness and loyalty to him, out of His compassionate goodness, which he already has richly experienced. The psalmist's eyes look up to the Lord as to the great Teacher, Leader, and Saviour of his life. His mood of trust and expectancy is felt in the opening words:

א 1 Upon Thee, O Lord, I wait;
   I lift up my soul to my God.

ב 2 In Thee do I trust; let me not feel shame;
   Let not my enemies laugh scornfully at me.

ג 3 Yes, none who wait for Thee shall be ashamed;
   Those who act treacherously shall come off empty.

ד 4 Thy ways, O Lord, let me know,
   And teach me Thy path.

ה 5 Lead me in Thy truth;
   For Thou art the God of my salvation,

ו   And for Thee I wait all the day.

ז 6 Remember Thy compassion, O Lord;
   And Thy mercies, that they are from of old.

ח 7 Remember not the sins of my youth:
   In accordance with Thy mercy, remember Thou me.

[3] Cf. Schmidt, *Die Psalmen*, p. 46. [4] *Symmicta*, I, 107.

From lamentation his mood turns to praise, and in the spirit of a hymn the psalmist celebrates God as the righteous Lord of all those who are faithful to His covenant. By this he means His loyal congregation of the good and upright in character, who are also, in economic status, the humble and needy.

   ט   8   Good and upright is the Lord,
              Who teaches those who are erring the way.
   י   9   He leads the humble in what is right for him;
              He instructs the needy as to His way.
   כ   10   All His paths are mercy and truth
              To those who keep His covenant and His charges.

At the very center of the psalm (vs. 11) comes a simple yet profound confession of sin and a petition for pardon which is grounded in the very nature of God. Conscious of how great is his sin and pleading, as in verse 7, no virtue of his own, in true Protestant fashion, the psalmist throws himself upon the mercy of God. He appeals to what God is in His innermost being, what God feels in terms of responsibility to His own covenant people.

   ל   11   **For the sake of Thy name, O Lord,**
              Pardon[5] Thou my iniquity, for it is great.

The influence of the literature of Hebrew wisdom, with its method of question and answer characteristic of the sages and its emphasis upon God's retribution, is apparent in verses 12-14. God rewards the man who reverences Him by teaching him to choose the right way, by permitting him to experience throughout his own life the goodness of God, and by granting to his descendants what the Palestinian peasant most desired, permanent hold upon the land. Intimacy with God is the reward of reverencing Him and opens the way for the Lord to impart the meaning and blessings of His covenant.

   מ   12   Who[6] is the man that fears the Lord?
              He will teach him the way he should choose.
   נ   13   He himself shall abide in goodness,
              And his descendants shall inherit the land.
   ס   14   Intimacy with the Lord have those who fear Him;
              He is ready to teach[7] them His covenant.

Back to the predominant mood of lament the psalmist now returns. In loneliness and need, still surrounded by many enemies who are hating him without cause, he turns the eyes of his soul to the Lord, who alone can deliver him from his stress. In petitions which breathe the spirit of trust he prays for God to pay

---

[5] The tense of the verb "pardon" (consecutive perfect) here follows what forms a "ground or condition of a new development" (Davidson, *op. cit.*, sec. 56) expressed in a causal clause, which here means, "Because of Thy nature, pardon thou . . ." (Gesenius-Kautzsch, *op. cit.*, sec. 112 *mm*).

[6] "Who" is here emphatic, cf. Brown, Driver, Briggs, *op. cit.*, p. 261.

[7] "To teach" is an emphatic infinitive, Buttenwieser, *op. cit.*, p. 810.

heed to him, to take note of the nature and extent of his trouble. Then comes the major request of his distressed soul, his petition for forgiveness, his innermost spiritual need. Although deepest, it is not his sole need. Still in peril at enemy hands, he prays for rescue and protection. Thinking, in the mood of personification, of two noble character qualities of which he now stands in need, integrity and uprightness, he prays for their protecting presence in his life.

ע 15 My eyes are continually toward the Lord,
  For He will bring out my feet from the net.

פ 16 Turn to me and show me favor,
  For alone and needy am I.

צ 17 Remove far the sorrows of my heart:
  Bring me out of my distress.

ק 19 Confront my enemies, for they are many:
  With groundless hatred they hate me.

ר 18 Give attention to my affliction and my trouble,
  And pardon all my sins.

ש 20 Guard my life and rescue me:
  Let me not be ashamed, for I seek refuge in Thee;

ת 21 Let integrity and uprightness guard me,
  For I wait upon Thee, O Lord.

As the psalmist, in a sense, "signs off," leaving, as we have noted, an indication of his authorship, he hides his personal signature in a fervent prayer for the redemption of his people as a whole from their distresses. Through this prayer his primarily individual lament becomes of representative congregational value.

22 Redeem Israel, O God,
  From all his distresses!

Ps. 26. THE LOVE OF GOD'S HOUSE AND ITS RITUALS

The psalmist stands accused of guilt. His accusers are so fierce that he fears sudden death at their hands. He is confident in his innermost being that he is innocent. To the Temple he goes and petitions God for justice, solemnly protesting that his manner of life makes him innocent of any charge. His opening words are a petition to the Lord, in which is mingled his declaration of innocence.

1 Bring forth justice for me, O Lord;
  For, as for me, I walk in innocence.

2 Test me, O Lord, and prove me;
  Pure [8] are my affections and my heart.

3 For Thy mercy is before my eyes,
  And I walk up and down in Thy truth.

What his manner of life has been he now describes, but negatively. With worthless, vicious men he has had nothing whatsoever to do. He shuns all groups of evildoers and has no companionship with them at all.

[8] With Ehrlich, *op. cit.*, p. 55, reading *çerûphāh* (purified, refined).

4　**I do not sit down with worthless men,**
　　Nor do I associate with vicious men.
5　**I hate the getting together of evildoers,**
　　And I have no fellowship with the godless.

Then occurs an interesting bit of ritual. The psalmist ceremonially washes his hands, as a solemn declaration on the part of one accused that he is innocent. The psalmist's prayer is his oath before God, his solemn attestation that he is guiltless (cf. Deut. 21:6; Ps. 73:13; Matt. 27:24). And as he performs this ceremonial act, he intones the words:

6a　**I wash my hands in innocency.**

His passionate petition follows immediately upon his oath.[9] Let him not suddenly and horribly die! The psalmist shares the common Semitic feeling that God brings, not only vindication to the innocent, but severe retribution upon the guilty. He speaks his petition before God with his eye upon his accusers—sinners, murderers, evil schemers, bribers, he calls them. In his eyes they stand already doomed. He will have no participation in their company or in their fate. Over against their way of life he affirms, even as at the beginning, his innocency and cries to God for gracious consideration and release.

9　**Snatch not my soul away along with sinners,**
　　Nor my life together with murderers,
10　**In whose hands is an evil scheme,**
　　And whose right hand is filled with a bribe.
11　**But as for me, I go my way in innocence:**
　　Release me, O Lord, and be gracious to me.

The close of the psalm (vss. 12, 6b-8) is prepared for the psalmist's use as a song of personal thanksgiving at the payment of his vow in the event that his prayer is answered. We learned from Ps. 22:22 that the payment of such personal vows took place within the framework of a great festival, most likely at the close of the harvest and New Year festival. Those who in various kinds of distress vowed to present unto the Lord their thank offerings in case He proffered them deliverance, assemble in the forecourt of the Temple and are arranged in groups according to the nature of the distress from which they were rescued. There stands the psalmist—such is the picture—"in a level place," that is, he has been helped; the mountain of trouble has, as it were, been scaled. The hard climb has been successfully made. "But," says Schmidt, "it is a poetic elegance that an outer reality corresponds to the picture: when one had climbed the steep temple mount with his votive offering he then stands in the outer court 'on a level place!' " [10]

[9] So Schmidt, who calls attention to Pss. 7 (vss. 6-8 after 3-5) and 17 (vss. 6-9 after 3-5) and rearranges vss. 6b-8, placing this section after vs. 12.
[10] Die Psalmen, p. 48.

From the outer court the throng of votive worshipers ascends the steps to the inner forecourt, where stands the great altar of burnt offering. Parts of the ceremony are a procession around this altar (cf. Ps. 118:27), the prayer of acknowledgment—in which the story of the release is told by a representative from each group—the shouts of thanksgiving, and finally the sacrifice itself with the joyous sacrificial repast to which all present in the Temple are invited (cf. Ps. 22:26). Sings the psalmist:

> 12 My foot stands in a level place;
> In the groups will I adore Thee, O Lord.
> 6b I will go in solemn procession about Thine altar,
> 7 To sound aloud the song [11] of thanksgiving,
> And to recount all Thy wonderful deeds.

How sensitive to all this is the psalmist! How he loves the sanctuary, where in awesome splendor, yet hid from the eyes of man, *dwells* his God! What a lofty issue to his soul-burdened distress is his enthusiastic testimony!

> 8 I love the house where Thou dwellest,
> The place where Thy glory abides!

Ps. 27:7-14. WAIT FOR THE LORD; BE STRONG

In Ps. 27:7-14 the psalmist is in deep distress. He is falsely accused and is beset by harsh opponents. They are slandering his reputation and are determined to do him violence, possibly even unto death (vs. 13). False witnesses are ready to help bring this about (vs. 12c). He stands before the court of justice in the Temple.

We have to do here with a lawsuit, and the defendant is before the court.[12] In bitterness of heart and in loneliness and extremity of need he turns in passionate eagerness to God, longing to see God's face turned toward him in approval and justification.

> 7 Hear, O Lord, my voice,
> In the day when I cry:
> Be gracious to me, and answer me, my God,
> For bitter is my heart.
> 8 Thy face, O Lord, I seek!
> 9a Hide [it] not from me.
> 9b Thrust not Thy servant away in anger:
> Thou art my help.

A poignant element in his desperate situation is that even his parents have abandoned him. Will God forsake him also? Earnestly he prays:

[11] Literally "the voice of the thank offering."
[12] So Bertholet, *Die Heilige Schrift des Alten Testaments*, II, 149.

9c Leave me not, forsake me not,
   Thou God of my salvation!
10 Since my father and my mother have abandoned me,
   May the Lord take me up! [13]

Now he appeals for the leadership of God. His way has been dangerous and rough. He prays that God may guide him in His way, the way of righteousness and of truth, in His path that is level and straight. If he may go forth in happiness and security, how great will be his vindication before his violent accusers!

11 Shew me Thy way, O Lord;
   And lead me in a level path,
   Because of my slanderers.
12 Give me not up to the hatred of my opponents:
   For false witnesses have risen up against me,
   And they breathe out violence at me.
13 So that I did not believe that I would experience
   The goodness of God in the land of the living.

At length comes the solution of the psalmist's case. The priest, addressing the harassed, accused petitioner, utters an encouraging and heartening word as the answer to his urgent prayer:

14 Wait for the Lord:
   Be strong! May He give thy heart assurance!
   Yes, wait for the Lord!

Ps. 31:1-8. THOU HAST SET ME AT LIBERTY

The psalmist is in great distress. He has been caught in the net laid for him by his enemies. These enemies have nothing to do with God, but they *cling to* what the psalmist calls "worthless vanities," a designation which he utters with reproach, for their enmity has called into action demonic powers and has resulted in depriving the psalmist of his freedom. He feels the shame in which his situation has placed him. Time is of prime importance, and relief, if it comes at all, must come swiftly. In his deep distress he cries out to the Lord for help and speedy deliverance:

1 In Thee, O Lord, do I seek refuge;
  Let me never be ashamed:
  By Thy righteousness deliver me and rescue me.
2 Bow down to me Thine ear;
  Speedily snatch me away, O Lord.
  Be to me a rock of refuge,
  A fortified house to save me.

The purpose of such a lament is to appeal to God, to touch His heart and move Him to action, so now the psalmist states the basic ground which may

---

[13] "Take up, care for," Brown, Driver, Briggs, *op. cit.*, p. 62.

induce the Lord to proffer His help. It is His trust in God as His refuge. Into God's hand he commits himself (vss. 3-5). It is fitting to recall that according to Luke's narrative (23:46) Jesus quoted vs. 5a as his final word spoken from the cross.

> 3   For my rock and my fortress art Thou:
>   So for Thy name's sake, lead me and guide me;
> 4   Bring me out of the net which they have concealed for me.
>   For Thou art my refuge, O God;
> 5a Into Thy hand I commit my spirit.

Suddenly a change comes in the psalm. Between verses 5a and 5b-8 we must assume that the prayed-for and longed-for help has come, and now the psalmist lifts his heart in a song of thanksgiving (vss. 5b-8). He has been set free, and this psalm was created for use of the suppliant to express both his lament and his thanksgiving. His case having been judged, he has had his freedom restored by the Lord. Deeply stirred he sings his gratitude:

> 5b Thou hast redeemed me, O God of truth.
> 6   Thou hatest those who cling to false vanities;
>   But I have put my trust in the Lord.
> 7   I will exult and rejoice in Thy lovingkindness;
>   Thou who didst see my trouble:
>   Who didst know the distress of my soul,
> 8   And didst not deliver me into the hand of the enemy;
>   Thou hast set me at liberty! [14]

Pss. 42–43. WHY ART THOU CAST DOWN?

Pss. 42 and 43 originally composed one psalm. Ps. 43 has no title of its own. The content and wording of the two are clearly similar (cf. 42:9b and 43:2b), and Ps. 43 has the refrain which appears twice in Ps. 42. The psalm is a lamentation or one who has been hurled into deep despair and believes himself to be so near death that he can already hear the watercourses of the underworld, the world of the dead (42:7). His enemies are oppressing him. Their loveless voices taunt him, and one of them, a man of deceit and iniquity, has with evil intent spoken lies against him.

The psalmist has one desire which is indeed a passionate longing, to come as he has done of yore to the Temple, there to see God, and there be helped by God.

The first part of the psalm is in the mood of a meditation. It opens with a vivid picture taken from the animal world. It is the dry season of the year. The wadies of the tableland of Palestine are arid, and one fountain after another has run dry. We see a hind with parched tongue standing between the rocks, panting for water. It is to the sensitive soul of our poet-psalmist a picture of his

---

[14] So rightly Moffatt; literally "Thou hast set my feet in a roomy place."

spiritual thirst to "see the face of God," that is, to worship in His Temple (42:1-2) :

> 1   As the hind pants for the water channels,
>   So pants my soul for Thee, O God.
> 2   My soul thirsts for God, for the living God:
>   When shall I come and see the face of God?

The first hint of his problem comes at 42:3. He is in the midst of the taunting, insulting voices of enemies, men who feel that they have him in their power, who humiliate him by pointing to his God-forsaken condition. The situation is not one which has just now arisen. Already many a day and many a night he has experienced their humiliating remarks over the seeming neglect he has suffered at the hands of his God. It has caused him bitter tears:

> 3   My tears have been bread for me by day and by night,
>   While they say to me all day long, "Where is thy God?"

Then the psalmist lifts the curtain from his past experience, and we see who he was and what he was. He was a musician, a player upon the harp (43:4) , and no doubt, in part because of this, he had formerly been a leader of pilgrims to the holy place. Many a pilgrimage had he made to the Temple on the great holy days when all Israel observed its appointed festivals, and when the Temple was thronged with a vast multitude in holiday mood and in festal attire.

How poignant now are such glorious memories! How they stir him to the depths of his being!

> 4   These things I would remember and would pour out
>   My soul within me;
>   How I passed along to the sanctuary;
>   [How] I led them in procession to the house of God,
>   With voice of rejoicing and thanksgiving,
>   The clamor of those celebrating a festival.

But how different from these joyous memories is the present mood of his spirit. In a refrain which will occur again and yet again he lets us peer into his depressed and despondent soul. The emphasis of the refrain this first time is upon the depression of his soul, although he speaks to it confidence and hope.

> 5   *Why art thou cast down, O my soul?*
>   *And why dost thou murmur within me?*
>   *Wait thou for God; for I shall yet praise Him,*
>   *Who is the help of my countenance, and my God.*

The psalmist is far from the Temple. Indeed he tells us just where he is, at the sources of the Jordan, the many-peaked Mount Hermon and Mount Mizar.[15] And he is in the constant presence of enemies who taunt him, whose heartless words crush his spirit. He stands in grave peril of his life, so much so that in

---

[15] Probably a mountain near Banias, a half mile high; so Dalman, *Palästinajahrbuch*, V (1909) , 101.

vivid Oriental imagination he seems to hear already the water floods of the underworld, the realm of the dead, sweeping in upon him,[16] drawing him into their power. His great inner need leads him to remember God.

> 6 My soul is cast down within me; therefore I remember Thee.
>   From the sources of the Jordan and Hermon, from Mount Mizar,
> 7 Deep calleth unto deep, at the noise of its cataracts;
>   All its waves and its billows are gone over me.

In the fear that death is imminent, the psalmist day after day and night by night prays unto the Lord for help and waits expectantly for it to come, although God seems to have given him over into his enemies' power to face—all day and day after day—their crushing taunts.

> 8 During the day I wait for the Lord, and for his mercy in the night.
>   A complaint [17] is with me, a prayer, to the God of my life.
> 9 I say to God, my Rock, "Why hast Thou forgotten me?
>   Why must I go mourning under the oppression of the enemy?"
> 10 Like a torment in my bones my enemies taunt me
>   When all day long they say to me, "Where is thy God?"

His spirit is still profoundly depressed, but the deep darkness of the soul's abandonment has been penetrated by a growing spiritual confidence. The emphasis of the now-repeated refrain falls upon the sentence that expresses this emerging certainty, *"I shall yet praise Him!"*

> Why art thou cast down, O my soul?
>   And why dost thou murmur within me?
> Wait thou for God; *for I shall yet praise Him,*
>   Who is the help of my countenance, and my God.

The last section of the psalm opens with the clearest indication we have of its life setting, "Vindicate me, and defend my cause against the hostile people, O God." The psalmist is many miles distant from the Temple, the place where his case may be judged and where he may be vindicated before his hostile enemies. The treachery and injustice of their persistent oppression make him feel spurned by God. If only he can be brought to the place where God dwells, the holy altar of the Temple! Thus his specific longing for the Temple rises to its deepest intensity. With vivid imagination he prays that God will send out to him His light and truth, which, like two angelic messengers, will come to him in his crisis of need and gently lead him to the Temple hill. And now he is certain that his prayer will be heard and that he will be vindicated by God. So, as is characteristic of the lament, his prayer ends, not in the mood of per-

[16] Cf. Gunkel, *Einleitung,* p. 186, who calls attention to this theme in the individual laments, Ps. 69:2, 15; Jonah 2:3.

[17] Reading *siḥāh,* with Graetz, *Kritischer Commentar zu den Psalmen.*

suasion, but in the bubbling up of a feeling of thanks.[18] It is the expression of the certainty of his faith. (43:1-4) :

1 Vindicate me, and defend my cause against the hostile people, O God!
    Deliver me from deceitful and unjust men,
2 For Thou art the God who protects me: why dost Thou spurn me?
    Why must I go mourning under the oppression of the enemy?
3 Send out Thy light and Thy truth; let them lead me.
    Let them bring me to Thy holy hill and to Thy dwellings.
4 That I may come to thy altar, O God, to God my joy;
    That I may exult and praise Thee on the harp, O Lord, my God!

The mood of the refrain, now rendered for the third time, reaches its climax. The emphasis this time is upon God, the certainty of His help, and the sublime confidence that waiting for Him will not be in vain:

5 Why art thou cast down, O my soul?
    And why dost thou murmur within me?
    Wait thou for God; for I shall yet praise Him,
    Who is the help of my countenance, and my God.

Ps. 52. LIKE AN OLIVE TREE IN THE COURTS OF THE LORD

Ps. 52 is the lament of an individual who as a member of the community of the righteous feels himself assailed by a powerful enemy. The utterance of his resentment begins in the form of a prophetic address, as though he were speaking directly to the enemy whom he is condemning. The psalm takes us into a period of party strife in the Jerusalem community between the worldly-minded and the godly. The enemy is most likely some man of prominence and wealth who is the leader of the worldly-minded, while the psalmist is the leader of the godly. The central conflict between these two classes is over how God requites the godly and the ungodly man, a question which is dealt with here in verses 5-7. Such indications point to a postexilic date for the psalm.

The psalmist's words open with an arresting question addressed to an ungodly man. The one to whom he speaks is a powerful, boastful evildoer, and the psalmist accosts him in the name of the community of the righteous, the congregation of the Lord. The thing which he particularly condemns is what the man has been saying, his treacherous, malicious, spiteful speech. His words are utterly false and are motivated by an evil heart, the utterance and outflow of a purpose to deceive, sinister in their intention, and terribly destructive in their influence.

1 Why do you boast of evil,
    O man, against the godly all the day?
2 You plot engulfing ruin;
    Your tongue is like a sharpened razor, working treachery!

[18] Cf. Gunkel, *Einleitung*, pp. 248-49.

3   You love evil rather than good,
     Falsehood rather than righteousness.
4   You love all who speak destructive words,
     You deceitful tongue!

The psalmist then utters a dreadful curse against this enemy (vs. 5), but God is the subject of the action contemplated.[19] This is followed by an earnest wish as regards the righteous (vs. 6) that, seeing what the curse has accomplished, they may fear the Lord's power and laugh in derision over the destroyed enemy. To portray the destruction intended by the curse, the psalmist uses four vigorous pictures: may the enemy because of his ruinous words be broken down like the dismantling of a fortress, shoveled up like broken fragments of pottery, swept out like dirt from a tent, and uprooted from human existence! When this curse has taken effect, and the righteous, the Lord's congregation, see its work, the destruction of the enemy will be for them an arresting illustration of what happens when a man trusts for his protection, not in God's power, but in the violence of his own ruinous speech and acts. Verse 7 gives the scorning, derisive words of the Lord's people over the enemy's destruction. To the evil man the psalmist says:

5   So may God, on His part, break you down forever;
     May He shovel you up, and sweep you away from the tent,
     And uproot you from the land of the living!
6   Then may the righteous see and fear,
     And scoff [derisively] over him, [saying],
7   "Behold the man who does not make
     God his protection,
     But trusts in the abundance of his riches,
     And takes refuge in the ruin he brings about!"

In vivid contrast to this wicked man and all for which he stands, the psalmist thinks of the people in God's loyal congregation and of himself merely as a representative of them. He compares the godly man, in simile, to a green olive tree in the courts of the Temple. There is here an implied contrast between the frustrated enemy uprooted from human life and the flourishing olive tree rooted in the Temple court, gray-green, beautiful, and fruit-bearing (cf. the similar picture in Ps. 92:13-14). The psalmist, with lamentation still present in his spirit, is yet joyously sure that *his* life roots in the protection of God's lovingkindness. In the opening words of verse 8 "But I," we feel the contrast between the godly man such as the psalmist represents and "the man who does not make God his protection" (vs. 7). Thus he sings:

8   But I—I am like a verdant olive tree in the house of God.
     I trust in the lovingkindness of God forever and aye.

[19] Only a few laments make God the subject of the wished-for action; cf. Gunkel, *Einleitung*, p. 227.

It is usual for a lament to close in the wish that at some future time the psalmist, his lament having been turned to gratitude, may sing a song of personal thanksgiving to the Lord, in the presence of the worshiping congregation, for what God will have done for him. It is on just such a note of hope that this lament closes.

> 9 I will thank Thee, O Lord, forever, that Thou hast done it!
>   And I will proclaim Thy name, that it is good, in the presence of
>   Thy loyal ones.

Ps. 54. IT IS GOD WHO UPHOLDS MY SOUL

Ps. 54 is the lamenting prayer of one who has been falsely accused. He has come to the Temple to secure his own vindication and to pray that his insolent and formidable accusers may themselves be destroyed by God.

The psalm opens with a petition to the Lord that his prayer may be heard, that the righteous God may vindicate him and by His name deliver him:

> 1 O God, by Thy name deliver me,
>   And in Thy might vindicate me.
> 2 O God, hear my prayer;
>   Give ear to the words of my mouth.

To call upon the "name" of the Lord refers to the utterance of the Lord's name in divine worship. Those who call upon His name are His worshipers. Those who do not call upon His name do not worship Him.[20] Moreover His name implies His nature, His character.

Then comes the lament itself (vs. 3), which portrays how the psalmist's very life is sought by insolent, formidable, and godless enemies.

> 3 For insolent men have risen up against me;
>   Yes, formidable enemies seek my life:
>   They do not set God before them.

But the psalmist is not alone. He has faith in the supporting presence of his God, and at the same time with thirst for revenge he longs for the destruction of his enemies. With characteristic Semitic feeling he hopes that their evil may "come back upon" themselves.

> 4 Lo, God is my helper:
>   The Lord is one who upholds my soul.
> 5 May the evil come back upon my adversaries:
>   Annihilate them in Thine anger,[21] O Lord!

We understand the close of the psalm (vss. 6-7) when we see that its background is that of the songs of personal thanksgiving, where those who have

---

[20] See Ps. 79:6; also the suggestive views of Pfister, "Kultus," in Pauly-Wissowa, *Real Encyclopädie der klassischen Altertumswissenschaft,* XXII, col. 2155.

[21] Reading with Ehrlich, *op. cit., baḥamāthekhā.*

peculiar cause for gratitude bring their offering to the Temple and in the presence of the congregation give their testimonies as to what the Lord has done. Our psalmist is now certain of vindication at God's hands. As though in anticipation of this longed-for experience, he hears the glad festal chorale of the Temple, "for it is good." The Lord will deliver him from all his present distress, and he will gloat in triumph over his enemies. The tense of the verb suggests certainty.

> 6 I will offer to Thee a freewill offering:
>   I will give thanks to Thy name, for it is good.
> 7 For from all distress He has saved me,
>   And my eye will gloat over my enemies.

Ps. 55:1-18*b*, 22. CAST THY BURDEN UPON THE LORD

The psalmist opens with an eager plea to God that his prayer may be heard.

> 1 Hear, O God, my prayer:
>   Do not hide Thyself utterly:
> 2a Incline to me and answer me.

In a lamentation of anxiety and terror he describes his situation and its cause. Wicked men are showing him enmity and are driving him to distraction with their accusations. His is a sensitive nature, and he lingers upon his shuddering fear of death, which seems to him near at hand. Thus he describes his situation:

> 2b   I am humiliated by my trouble;
> 2c-3 Yes, I am driven to distraction by the voice of the enemy,
>   By the outcry of the wicked,
>   For they hurl wickedness against me,
>   And they cherish animosity toward me in anger.
> 4 My heart in my bosom is in anguish,
>   And the terrors of death have fallen upon me:
> 5 Fear and trembling come upon me,
>   And shuddering covers me.

He longs to escape from their defaming accusations, for all day long he experiences a perpetual torrent of abuse. He cries:

> 6 Oh that I had wings like a dove,
>   That I might fly away and settle down!
> 7 Lo, I would flee far away;
>   I would lodge in the wilderness.
> 8 I would hasten to a place where I might escape
>   From the tempest,
> 9a From the destructive storm of their throat,
>   [From] the canal of their tongue!

There are concrete details in the psalm. He is in a city of inner upheaval where the "guardians" of her walls are violence and strife, and where misery is in her heart. The city can be only Jerusalem. We are in the troubled epoch when Palestine was overrun by Ptolemy (312 B.C.). Jerusalem was conquered, and many people because of the disturbed conditions in Palestine migrated to Egypt and Phoenicia.[22] The psalmist gives us vivid glimpses of the demoralized conditions that existed there, a situation which heightened his own personal anguish.

> 9b **For I have to experience violence all the day**
>   **And strife in the city.**
> 10 **By day and night they walk around upon its walls,**
>   **And trouble and sorrow are in its heart.**
> 11 **Engulfing ruin is in the midst of it,**
>   **And oppression and deceit depart not from its public square.**

Then the psalmist confides an element in the situation that lends peculiar poignancy to his problem. If his accusers were merely his enemies, he could protect himself against them. But the fact is that the very leader of them, "my enemy" he calls him, was formerly of equal status with himself, and indeed his close friend, with whom he enjoyed intimate fellowship in the Temple worship.

> 12 **For if only my enemy had abused me,**
>   **I could have borne it;**
>   **If only one who hated me had dealt treacherously with me,**
>   **I could have shut myself from him.**

Suddenly turning to this man himself, he addresses him with a feeling of deep injustice.

> 13 **But you are my equal,**
>   **My friend, and my intimate!**
> 14 **We used to have sweet intimacy together**
>   **In the house of God.**

From the cry of outraged friendship the intensity of his feelings finds relief in passionate imprecations. He will bring down upon his accusers the stern judgment of God. He will have fear and death overtake them, indeed, a death in which the element of fear will be intensely real! So he cries,

> 14c **May they walk about in quaking!**
> 15   **May death come deceitfully upon them!**
>   **May they go down alive to Sheol!**
>   **May they pass away in their terror!**

Such words, which are so often found in the psalms, were originally spoken by the officiating priest in the name of the innocent worshiper and were a regular part of the ritual to bring the innocent sufferer out of the power of the torrent of evil which proceeded from the mouth of the enemy.[23]

[22] Cf. Buttenwieser, *op. cit.*, pp. 706-8; also Hecataeus of Abdera, who is quoted by Josephus *Contra Apionem* I. 209 ff.

[23] Cf. Mowinckel, *op. cit.*, V, 93.

From such passionate imprecation against men, in sharp contrast of mood he turns to God, longing to be heard of Him and answered by Him. Morning, noon, and night he utters his lamenting prayer to his Redeemer.

> 16 But as for me, I cry to God;
>   May He save me!
> 17 Evening and morning and noonday
>   I lament and murmur;
> 18a May He hear my voice; may He ransom
> 18b My soul and put it in peace.[24]

Then comes the climax of the psalm, the promise to the worshiper, quite similar to an oracle and uttered by the priest.[25] It is a counsel of the assurance of faith, a summons to trust in God's sustaining, steadying, undergirding help.

> 22 Cast thy burden upon the Lord, and He will sustain thee.
>   He will never let the righteous slip.

Ps. 55:18c-21, 23. SMOOTH SPEECH WITH A SWORD IN THE HEART

The remainder of this psalm (vss. 18c-21, 23) composes a fragment of another personal lament. The situation is similar to that implied in Ps. 120. The psalmist is evidently in contact with Edomite tribes of northern Arabia, among them Ishmael and Jalam. With these "wild sons of the steppe" [26] the psalmist has made a covenant, but they are ignoring such an agreement, for they fear neither God nor men. The psalmist is in grave peril, which he describes:

> 18c For there draw near me shooters of the bow
>   Who have become my opponents.
> 19 Ishmael and Jalam,
>   And dwellers in the east, all of them,
>   Who regard no alliance,
>   And who fear not God,
> 20 Have put forth their hand against their covenant friend; [27]
>   They have violated their covenant.

But what makes the poet's situation all the more critical is the fact that these godless nomads are deceitful, hiding their treacherous aims in smooth and friendly speech.

> 21 Smoother than butter is their mouth,
>   But a sword is in their heart:
>   Softer than oil are their words,
>   But they are drawn swords.

[24] Cf. Gesenius-Kautzsch, op. cit., sec. 119 gg.
[25] Cf. Mowinckel, op. cit., I, 154.   [26] Gunkel, Die Psalmen, p. 239.
[27] So reading with Briggs. The verbs are singular, for the two tribes, Ishmael and Jalam, are viewed as a unit in treachery, but the meaning is clearly plural and has been so rendered here.

The poet is confident that such treachery will be punished by the Lord, and his psalm ends in the certainty of divine vengeance upon these deceitful and murderous sons of the east through their violent and premature death. His own heart rests in his confidence of God's help.

> 23 But Thou, O God, wilt bring them down
>   To the pit of the grave;
>   Men of blood and treachery
>   Will not live out half their days:
>   But as for me, I trust in Thee.

Ps. 56. PUT MY TEARS IN THY BOTTLE

Ps. 56 is a prayer of one who has been falsely accused. He is beset by enemies who thirst for his blood and who are violently oppressing him. All that the psalmist has to say in his crisis he directs to his God, who, as he is confident, will help him.

> 1 Be gracious to me, O God;
>   For men pant after me:
>   All the day they violently oppress me;
> 2 Those who insidiously watch me pant after me all the day,
>   For many are fighting against me.
> 3 Lift me up in the day that I cry;
>   I trust in Thee.

He renews his lament, picturing his scheming, evil-bent antagonists as they lie in wait to entrap him.

> 5 All day long they debate, they consult;
>   All their schemes are against me.
> 6a For evil they lie in wait; [28] they spy;
> 6b Lo, they slyly watch my footprints.

The poet is filled with the strong Semitic passion of retribution. He would have the Lord weigh out unto his persecutors a punishment commensurate with their wily treachery toward him. For his own soul he asks a blessing proportioned to his sleepless tossings and his briny tears. His rest-bereft nights, let God note down in His book! His bitter tears, let God treasure up in His bottle! The most significant part of any lament is the petition, such as the psalmist now pours forth. It is the very core of this type of psalm, for it is the endeavor of the psalmist to secure the desired blessing from God.[29] We feel this strongly here. Moreover, his petition shows us that he has absorbed the cult language so familiar in the national laments, for he speaks of his enemies in verse 7 as nations, even as was done in the king's psalms when king and people were the butt of national

[28] Best meaning for yāgûrû is "lie in wait"; cf. Gunkel, *lauern.*
[29] Cf. Gunkel, *Einleitung*, p. 218, sec. 6:12.

aggression. Such speech, seemingly inappropriate on the lips of an ordinary man, thus has its origin in the model given in the earlier stirring and majestic king's poetry.[30] We feel his passionate intensity as he seeks help from his God. He alone can help the poet, can save his life.

> 6c As they have lain in wait for my life,
> 7a   Weigh out to them on the basis of [their] iniquity!
> 7b   In anger, lay prostrate the nations, O God.
> 9a Then let my enemies turn back
> 9b   In the day when I cry.
> 8a Cause my tossings to come into thy accounting;
> 8b   Put my tears in Thy bottle, O God.

"In the day when I cry." The psalmist thinks here (vs. 9b; note also vs. 3a) of the day of decision when the judicial sentence will be pronounced by the priest, and the poet will be justified in the congregation and before his scheming enemies. He thinks of his "case"[31] (vs. 10) as being in the hands of a God who hears his cry.

The second part of the psalm (vss. 9c-13) shows that the psalmist's confidence has been justified. It is a song of personal thanksgiving. In his deep distress, when his very life was imperiled, he vowed unto God that in case he was delivered from his distress, he would render unto the Lord a thank offering. His confidence has been justified. His prayer has been answered. In the consciousness, newly achieved, of his right so to do, he stands in the Lord's congregation with his thank offering. His problem has been settled. He does not tell the story of how his situation was resolved, but simply rejoices over his "case," by which he means his distress, and the way the Lord has brought him through it to release. With a heart deeply stirred by gratitude he cries:

> 9c This I know, that God is for me!
> 10   In God will I rejoice over my case.
> 11 In God I trust; I will not fear,
>   What can man do to me?
> 12 Upon me, O God, are vows;
>   I will render thank offerings to Thee.
> 13 For Thou hast delivered my life from death;
>   Thou hast withheld my feet from stumbling,
>   That I might walk before the face of God
>   In the light of life forever.

Ps. 64. THE BOOMERANG OF MALICIOUS SPEECH

Ps. 64 is a short and fervent prayer from one who belongs in the circle of the righteous and upright in heart, loyal members of God's worshiping congregation. He is for some reason beset by malicious and crafty enemies who are menacing

---

[30] *Ibid.*, p. 148, sec. 5:9.   [31] Read with Schmidt, *debhārî* (my case).

his very life. As is usual in such a lament, his psalm opens with an appeal to God, a cry for help:

> 1 Hear, O God, my voice as I complain:
>   Guard my life from the menace of the enemy.
> 2 Hide me from the secret counsel of evil men;
>   From the vehemence of doers of wickedness.

Vividly he laments over their evil schemes and especially over their speech. Mowinckel, calling attention to the psalmist's emphasis upon the bitter, base, and destructive words flying like deadly poisoned arrows to their mark, maintains that the psalmist has in view something more realistic, more sinister, and more deadly than the psychological pain caused merely by enemies' bitter words. Their crafty words are the spells of sorcerers, who are the perpetrators of black magic.[32] Their tongues are like whetted swords; their speech is barbed like poisoned arrows. In sureness of aim and in unexpected suddenness their malicious words strike the innocent in the hiding places to which they have fled, yet the evildoers themselves remain to their victims unseen. Thus he describes them:

> 3 Who have whetted their tongue like a sword,
>   Who have polished bitter words like arrows,
> 4 To shoot into the hiding places of the innocent:
>   Suddenly they shoot, but are not detected.
> 5a They use their strength for evil things;
> 5b   They dig to lay snares.

And the psalmist lets us listen to the triumphant exclamations which these crafty schemers utter. They are supremely confident of their own safety and of the inability of their victims to ferret out their dastardly plots.

> 5c And they say, "Who can see us,
> 6   And search out our secrets?
>   The disguise has succeeded;
>   Our mind is unfathomable; [33]
>   And our heart is deep!"

Over against these godless and malicious plotters and in scornful opposition stands the psalmist, and he pronounces his wish upon them in the spirit of just requital. Intentionally he uses the very words by which he described their evil deeds to portray the wrath of God coming upon them. Just when they are jubilant in the apparent success of their secret schemes, may the Lord's arrows meet them, just as suddenly and unexpectedly as was their onslaught upon the innocent! May their own defaming and ruinous speech, which trapped their victims, come back upon them, causing their fall! May they whose schemes were hidden and secret be destroyed before the jeering eyes of men! So he cries:

---

[32] *Op. cit.*, I, 16; see similarly Schmidt, *Die Psalmen,* p. 120.
[33] Reading with Bauer, *nô'āsh.*

7 But may God shoot at them with His arrow,
   So that their slaughter will come suddenly.
8 May the mischief of their tongue cause them to stumble:
   May everyone who sees them wag the head in derision.

As is usual in the lamentation, a wish stands at the close of the psalm. It is a striking fact that the psalmist's wish does not limit itself to his friends or to the congregation of the Lord, but embraces all mankind. It is his strong desire that even those who do not hail God as their Lord may nonetheless be impressed by His dealings. May the ruin of these godless schemers, accomplished before the eyes of mankind, cause all humanity to note and ponder the mighty works of God. But from all the world thus impressed by God's requital upon wicked men, the psalmist turns to the "righteous" and the "upright in heart," the congregation of the Lord. May they not merely be impressed, but may they rejoice and glory in their God! Yea more, may they take refuge in Him from all such malicious speech or magic spells. Thus he utters his wish:

9 May all humanity fear,
   And declare the deed of God;
     And may they ponder His work.
10 May the righteous rejoice in the Lord and seek refuge in him,
   And may all the upright in heart glory!

Ps. 70. LORD, HASTEN HERE FOR ME

Ps. 70 is a prayer of one falsely accused by malicious enemies who are gloating over his misfortune. The psalmist begins with one of the customary ways of opening a lament, an invocation of God. Then he introduces at once, not the lament itself, but because of the intensity of the need his petition for help, which is the most significant part of a lamentation.[34] Cries the psalmist:

1 Be pleased, O Lord, to save me;
   Hasten to help me.

Petition, wish, and lament now intermingle until the psalmist has found peace. He expresses a passionate wish that His enemies, who are seeking his life and are taking malicious pleasure in his dire distress, may be frustrated and degraded:

2 May they be ashamed and disgraced,
   Those who are seeking my life:
  May they be turned back and humiliated,
   Who are taking delight in my misfortune.
3 May they be appalled because of their disgrace,
   Who are saying, "Aha! Aha!"

The psalmist feels keenly the solidarity of the righteous community of those who worship the Lord, who exult and rejoice in their God. His own rescue

---

[34] Cf. Gunkel, *Einleitung*, pp. 212, 218, 241.

from the schemes of his enemies and his vindication before them would strengthen the *esprit de corps* of the whole religious community. Indeed Staerk is probably right when he says that "the immediate aim and purpose of the suppliant's deliverance in the full view of his enemies is the inner exaltation of the whole community of the godly." [35] Thus the psalmist's wish turns toward the congregation when he prays:

> 4 May they exult and rejoice in Thee,
>   All who seek Thee;
>   And may they continually say,
>   Who love Thy salvation,
>   "Let the Lord be exalted!"

From this sincere longing for the dignity and health of the worshiping community the psalmist reverts to his own crucial need. We feel the poignancy of the words "as for me" in his closing appeal to the Lord for immediate help:

> 5 But as for me, I am poor and needy;
>   O Lord, hasten here for me:
>   My helper [36] and my deliverer art Thou;
>   O Lord, do not delay!

With this psalm, Ps. 40:13-17 is almost identical. By prefixing to it verse 12 a later writer with a deep sense of sin made use of Ps. 70. But the intense consciousness of sin in that verse is foreign to the rest of the prayer. The original psalm is best preserved in Ps. 70.

Ps. 94:16-23. EXPERIENCING THE COMFORT OF GOD

In Ps. 94:16-23 the psalmist is experiencing the false accusation of evil enemies who without law are framing up mischief against him, condemning him, an innocent man, as guilty. He has had many crises in his life when he stood in danger of death. And out of deep spiritual experience he knows God.

His lament begins in the depths of loneliness and need from which he utters a burning query. It is a reproachful question, but at the same time an indirect petition. The subject matter is lament; the form is petition.[37]

> 16 Who will rise up for me against the wicked,
>   [Who] will take his stand on my side against the evildoers?

In his deep distress he resorts to his past experience. Had God not been his helper in crisis after crisis, he would long ago have descended to the world of the dead, to the realm of silence. Frequently in times of great uncertainty when he could find no secure foothold and felt weak and alone he experienced the undergirding lovingkindness of God. His inner turmoil of anxious thoughts often was stilled by soul-quieting divine comfort. Such recall of experiences

---

[35] *Op. cit.*, III, 1, 136.   [36] So read with Duhm.   [37] Cf. Gunkel, *Einleitung*, p. 230.

in which he had received spiritual help is characteristic of the lament wherein
the suppliant is fighting for assurance.[38] So now he answers his own lamenting
question:

> 17 Unless the Lord had been my help,
>   My soul would already have taken up its dwelling in the realm of
>   silence.
> 18 When I said, "My foot has slipped,"
>   Thy mercy, O Lord, has repeatedly sustained me.
> 19 In the strife of my disquieting thoughts in my bosom,
>   Thy comforts have delighted my soul.

From this steadying recall of deep spiritual experience in sharp contrast the
psalmist turns back to his present prevailing mood of lament, in which he
vividly describes his accusers:

> 20 Truly they make common cause who conceal their base desires,
>   Who without law frame up evil;
> 21 They lie in wait for the life of the righteous,
>   And condemn as guilty the blameless and innocent.

Then suddenly the mood of the psalm changes definitely from lament to
certainty. The psalmist is sure of the blessing of the Lord's protection. His
consciousness of refuge in God is overwhelming. It is likely that between verses
21 and 22 in the actual rendition of the psalm in Israelite worship a priestly oracle
is pronounced assuring the suppliant of the protection of the Lord and mediating
to him the certainty that his enemies will be destroyed.[39] In victorious assurance
the psalmist cries:

> 22 But the Lord is for me a refuge;
>   Yes, my God is my sheltering rock.
> 23 And He will repay to them their wickedness;
>   Yes, because of their evil the Lord will annihilate them!

Ps. 120. LIVING IN AN ANTAGONISTIC ENVIRONMENT

The psalmist is far away from his home, living among the Bedouins of the
northern edge of the Syrian Arabian desert. The tribes of Qedar and Massa particularly are referred to, and both are listed in Gen. 25:13-14 as descendants of
Ishmael.[40] The sons of Qedar were famous as warlike archers (Isa. 21:17). The
psalmist himself is a man of peaceful bearing, but his life is being made bitter
by the contentious temper and warlike spirit of these ferocious Bedouins, who
treat him with suspicion and deceit and hurl at him false aspersions and accusations. The whole psalm breathes the atmosphere of lament. It opens with a
cry to the Lord from the psalmist's inner distress, a cry that he might be saved
from betrayal at his enemies' hands.

---

[38] Cf. *ibid.*, p. 236.   [39] Cf. Küchler, *op. cit.*
[40] Cf. similarly Ishmael and Jalam in reconstructed text of Ps. 55:19; see p. 334.

> 1 To the Lord in my distress
>   I cry, that he would answer me.
> 2 "O Lord, save my soul
>   From lying lips!"

Instead of continuing his petition asking the Lord to render unto these lying lips His just retribution, the psalmist in unexpected and original fashion addresses the traitorous tongues themselves. What does such treacherous, lying speech deserve from God? It pierces into the psalmist's sensitive soul like sharp arrows, like burning coals in human flesh.

> 3 What shall be given thee;
>   Yea, what added to thee,
>   Thou traitrous tongue?

And he answers his own question. As they have done, may it be done to them! May an enemy tribe come against the Qedarites and the Massa-ites with the sharp arrows of warriors, yes, even *fiery* arrows. He uses here the figure of broom charcoal, which makes a hot fire and retains it for a long time, to suggest fierce and endless strife.[41] Thus may the Lord's retribution be visited on them!

> 4 Sharpened arrows of war,
>   And with them live coals of broom!

Then comes his lament itself, which breathes profound discontent. We sense that of which he feels deprived in being so far from Zion and among unsympathetic neighbors. It is an ancient lament of the tragedy of modern Jewry in Europe and the Middle East today. And it is in this part of the psalm that we learn that he is sojourning among the wild sons of the steppe, who are classically characterized as living with their "hand against everyone, and everyone's hand against" them (Gen. 16:12). We sense poignantly how this son of Zion, trained in the love of peace and truth, feels his soul imprisoned in an utterly pagan and sharply antagonistic environment. Feel the heart burden of his sigh as he laments!

> 5 Woe to me that I am a stranger in Massa,
>   That I stay with the tents of Qedar!
> 6 Long enough has my soul stayed
>   With those who hate peace.
> 7 As for me, I speak peace and truth,
>   But as for them—they are for war!

Ps. 140. A RIGHTEOUS CAUSE MAINTAINED BY GOD

Ps. 140 is the lamenting prayer of one who is accused by fierce enemies, whose antagonism is chiefly shown by the defaming words which issue from their mouths. The tongues of these "men of violence" are like serpents' tongues

---

[41] Cf. Buttenwieser, *op. cit.*, p. 773.

emitting poison. Their evil hearts concoct secret schemes against him and keep stirring up war. They are set to trap him, to get him enmeshed in their net.

After a crisp distress cry unto the Lord for rescue and protection (vss. 1, 4ab) he vividly pictures his heartless foes in action.

> 1   Rescue me, O Lord, from evil men;
>   Guard me from men of violence,
> 2   Who have hatched up evil in their heart,
>   Who keep stirring up war all day long.
> 3   They whet their tongues like a serpent;
>   Viper's venom is under their lips.
> 4   Protect me, O Lord, from the hands of the wicked;
>   Guard me from men of violence,
>   Who scheme how to trip up my steps.
> 5   The proud conceal a trap for me,
>   And the arrogant spread out a net for my feet;
>   Beside the way they have set baits for me.

In this hour of grave need the psalmist gives an utterance of believing faith in the Lord, his God. He believes that God is able to save him. And this steadying faith he grounds in his past experience. Confidence wells up in his soul, because in times past whenever his life was a battleground of contending forces, God's strong hand protected him. The terms he uses (vs. 7b) describe what God has done and ever again does. In such believing confidence he appeals to God to hear him now.

> 6   I have said to the Lord, my God art Thou:
>   Listen, O Lord, to the voice of my entreaty.
> 7   O Lord God, Thou art my saving strength,
>   Thou dost cover my head in the day of battle.

And he lifts a passionate petition that the evil plots of his enemies may be frustrated:

> 8   Permit not the [evil] desire of those who long after me:
>   Let the wickedness they have devised against me not succeed!

This passionate petition to the Lord that He bring to nought the schemes of his accusers leads to the utterance of a solemn curse upon them. Here is a primitive, Semitic conception that roots in magic. There was thought to be terrific power in a curse, and there were methods by which it could be robbed of its power. It was possible to dispose of a curse by turning it back upon those who had pronounced it.[42] This is what we have here. With passionate feeling the psalmist utters, not a prayer to the Lord—note the third person in verse 10— but a countercurse upon his enemies (vss. 9-10), with the aim of bringing back upon them the maledictions which have poured upon him like poison from their

---

[42] Illustrations are Gen. 27:29; Num. 24:9. See for this view Hempel, "Die israelitischen Anschauungen von Segen und Fluch im Lichte altorientalischen Parallelen," *Zeitschrift der Deutschen Morganländischen Gesellschaft*, LXXIX, pp. 37-38.

lips. His hot curse passes (vs. 11) into the mood of calm reflection, and he maintains that such slanderers have no stability in life, for evil tracks down its perpetrator for certain punishment. This issues in a passionate wish that God will destroy the wicked, murderous, and rebellious men.[43]

> 9   Let not those who flout me lift up their heads on every side.
>   Let the mischief of their lips overwhelm them;
> 10 May He rain upon them coals of fire;
>   May He cast them into pits so they cannot rise.
> 11 The slanderer cannot endure in the earth;
>   As for the violent man, evil shall hunt him down with thrust upon
>   thrust.
> 139:19 Oh that Thou wouldst slay the wicked, O God,
>   And that the murderous men would vanish,
> 20 Who rebel treacherously against Thee,
>   Who rise up against Thee to no good purpose.

We must infer that the ceremony in the living worship by which the psalmist is vindicated before God and man and pronounced innocent now takes place. The closing words are his acknowledgment of this from a heart thrilled with thanksgiving. His words are alive with present spiritual experience and with the message which his experience has, not only for himself, but for the whole congregation of the humble, poor, righteous, and upright.

> 12 I know that the Lord maintains
>   The cause of the humble, the right of the poor.
> 13 Surely the righteous will give thanks to Thy name;
>   The upright shall abide in Thy presence.

Ps. 141. THE LURE OF THINGS AND THE HIGH CALL OF GOD

The psalmist is a young man with the interests and inclinations of flaming youth battling for mastery in his breast. He feels the lure of *things,* the material interests of the godless and their luxuries. But in the will and aim of his life he knows the call of goodness and of God. He is in great need, and he is in the Temple. It is at the evening hour, the sacred hour of the cereal offering (Exod. 29:41; Num. 28:4-5) when prayer was the order of worship (I Kings 18:36; Ezra 9:5). To this spiritually minded psalmist his prayer is as incense, the lifting up of his hands to the most holy place as an evening offering. We feel that he has advanced beyond the necessity of sacrifice to truly spiritual religion.

The psalm begins with a cry to God for help:

> 1   O Lord, I call to Thee; pay attention to me;
>   Give ear to my voice, when I cry to Thee.
> 2   Let my prayer be esteemed as incense before Thee,
>   The uplifting of my hands as an evening offering.

---

[43] So Ps. 139:19-20, which, as the keen insight of Buttenwieser, *op. cit.,* p. 739, has shown, should be restored to Ps. 140 after vs. 11.

In his petition which follows, the psalmist's delicate situation becomes clear. He is a sorely tempted youth. He feels a strong impulse both to speak words inconsistent with his faith in God and to do deeds which he knows are evil. He prays:

> 3 Put, O Lord, a watch upon my mouth,
>   And a guard at the door of my lips;
> 4a Let not my heart incline to evil matters,
> 4b   To practice deeds of wickedness.

But stronger than his inclination to resort with evil men and share their luxuries is his will to do right. He turns from these godless trends and associations, the lure of which he has felt. For deep down in his soul there is a loathing for those who loathe God. God's enemies are also his. Yet more significantly, to those who are the righteous and the loyal he looks with admiration and respect. He is eager to follow *their* counsels, yes, ready even to submit to their severe rebuke and discipline, accepting it in trustful humility and resignation. So he continues, giving earnest expression to the sincere desire of his soul:

> 4c I would not sit with evildoers,
>   Nor would I eat of their dainties.
> 139:21 Do not I hate those, O Lord, who hate Thee, [44]
>   And feel a loathing for those who loathe Thee?
> 22 With complete hatred I hate them;
>   They have become enemies of mine!
> 5   If the righteous smite me, if the godly rebuke me,
>   It is the best oil; my head will not refuse it.

The psalmist strengthens his petition, not only by this statement of the sincere desire of his soul to accept discipline at the hands of the Lord's congregation, but by illustrating it from a stand he had formerly taken. There had been a time when the righteous community itself because of the stern exercise of their religious zeal upon him had fallen into the hands of the judges. He writes most likely from the Persian period, at a time when the Israelites were under foreign rule and even the internal affairs of their community were under strict supervision. Before that court the psalmist, instead of defending *himself,* had defended the righteous community on principle because of the very discipline he had suffered at their hands. His words spoken at that time by their selfless sincerity had moved these pagan judges. Thus the psalmist describes the stand he made in a particular instance on behalf of the righteous. He states it here in order to strengthen his claim upon God's help in the present moment.[45]

> 5c Yes, more, I even defended them [i.e., the righteous] in their misfortune.
>   They had resigned themselves to the stern hands of their judges.

[44] I follow the suggestion of Buttenwieser, *op. cit.,* pp. 735, 739, who restores these verses (139:21-22) to their original place.
[45] Cf. Gunkel, *Einleitung,* pp. 237-38.

> 6 They [i.e., the judges], however, lent an ear to my words, because
> they were gracious.
> 7b   Our defensive arguments penetrated to the deepest depth,
> 7a   Like something piercing and penetrating the earth.[46]

This is indeed a remarkable passage and reveals a man of unusual social outlook who is more concerned about the strict moral standards of the community and their enforcement than about any painful consequence this may have for his own life.

From that vivid memory when he thus acted on principle he turns to the Lord. His situation of the moment now becomes clear. He has been falsely accused by reckless, wanton men who have skillfully laid a trap for him. May they fall into their own trap, is his passionate wish. In his grave peril there is one source of protection for him. If that fails, all is lost. We feel the implied appeal to God in his recall of the episode just narrated. May this also move his God to help. His psalm thus ends upon the note with which it began.

> 8 Because [47] my eyes are on Thee, O Lord,
> [Because] I seek refuge in Thee, leave not my life unprotected.
> 9 Guard me from the hands of the braggarts who have laid a trap for me,
> And from the snares of evildoers.
> 10 Let the wicked fall into their own nets all at once,
> But may I escape calamity.

Ps. 142. NO ONE CARES FOR MY SOUL

Ps. 142 is a prayer uttered by one who has been falsely accused by persecutors. He is a prisoner in a dungeon (vs. 7a), where he has been held pending the determining in the Temple of the Lord as to whether or not he is guilty. Faint and in deep distress, he pours out his lament before the Lord (vs. 2), who knows his condition, that he is innocent of the charge against him.

> 1 Loudly I cry to the Lord;
> Loudly I implore His favor.
> 2 I pour out before Him my complaint;
> I declare before Him my distress.
> 3a When my spirit faints away,
> 3b   Thou knowest my condition.

His tricky persecutors are more than a match for him; and although the righteous congregation of the Lord believe in him (vs. 7c), yet they do not visit him, and he feels desperately neglected. Among the loneliest words in the Psalter is his lament: "No one cares for my soul."

---

[46] I am indebted to the penetrating insight of Ehrlich for the meaning of this passage.

[47] "Because" is connected with the following petition, its force carrying into the second line of the verse; see Ehrlich, *op. cit.*, p. 374.

> 3c **In the path in which I go,**
> 3d   **They have hidden a trap for me.**
> 4 **I look to the right, and to the left,**
>   **But no one pays attention to me.**
>   **There is no escape for me;**
>   **No one cares for my soul.**

In his loneliness and seeming lack of any human concern, from the neglect of men he cries straight to God, grounding the petition he soon will utter in an earnest expression of his trust in God.

> 5 **I cry to Thee, O Lord;**
>   **I said, "Thou art my refuge,**
>   **My portion in the land of the living."**

His petition follows. Emphasizing his weakness and inability to cope with his persecutors, he throws himself upon God for deliverance from them.

His petition moves into the solemn utterance of a vow that if God heeds his petition and rescues him from prison, he will praise Him in a song of thanksgiving, just such a song as other prisoners have sung in the Temple in gratitude for their release from prison (Ps. 107:10-16).

> 6 **Give attention to my cry,**
>   **For I am weak.**
>   **Deliver me from all who are persecuting me,**
>   **For they are too strong for me.**
> 7a **Bring out my life from the dungeon,**
> 7b   **So that I may praise Thy name.**

The psalm ends with a heartening thought. Although this prisoner feels lonely and bereft of any human concern, he now has been brought to the realization that the members of God's congregation of the righteous do care. They "wait" in prayerful eagerness and in hope for his release. Thus his own prayer is buttressed by the prayers of the faithful, and he is lifted out of his loneliness into the warmth of a gracious human concern.

> 7c **Yes! the righteous wait,**[48]
>   **That Thou mayest deal bountifully with me.**

2. Prayers of the Falsely Accused Spending a Night in the Sanctuary

A number of these prayers of the falsely accused include a reference, more or less clear, to the ancient rite of incubation, the practice of sleeping or at least passing the night in the place most likely to be in contact with the Deity. We recall the experience of Jacob at the ancient sanctuary at Bethel (Gen. 28:10-17) and that of King Solomon at Gibeon, the great high place (I Kings 3:4-15). It is

[48] Cf. the Aramaic *kātar* (wait, hope for).

implicit reference to such practice in Israel that Amos makes when he speaks of worshipers who "lay themselves down beside every altar upon clothes taken in pledge" (2:8). It was a way of consulting Deity in case of any grave difficulty or distress. The suppliant would offer sacrifices or perform rites intended to secure God's favor, then lie down to sleep awaiting a divine visitation. In sleep the soul was thought of as freed from the body, so as to be able to communicate with Deity. As Hamilton says, "Accordingly memories of what passed in sleep were to be cherished as divine visitations granted to the soul." The object was "to meet with the deity in sleep, ask questions, and receive answers." [49] These prayers are Pss. 3; 4; 5; 17; 27:1-6; 57; 59; 143.

Ps. 3. A NIGHT IN THE SANCTUARY OF GOD

Ps. 3 is a prayer of one who stands accused by many enemies, who have been rising up against him in increasing numbers. Their enmity has humiliated him and deprived him of his dignity. Through the mouths of these ungodly men there is pouring forth a flood of slandering accusations. He hears their infamous, antagonistic words coming at him from every side. Evidently the psalmist is suffering personal distress of some kind, most likely bodily illness, which leads them to blaspheme him as one cast off by God. It is not likely that their enmity is due to his physical misfortune, but it is heightened because of it.

One thing clear is that the psalmist craves from God the restoration of his dignity. God is for him the righteous Judge who alone can restore his honor, even as a judge lifts up the accused, if found innocent, from the ground where he has thrown himself before him. And this restoration of the psalmist's dignity by the righteous Judge of all the earth takes place at the Temple hill, where the psalmist utters his prayer and where the Lord answers from His most holy place.

The psalm begins with the lament. We note the mounting number of foes by which the psalmist is surrounded. We feel the continued taunting of these enemies that his case is hopeless, even to God!

> 1   **O Lord, how many have my foes become!**
>   **Many are rising up against me;**
> 2   **Many are saying concerning my life,**
>   **"There is no help for him from his God!"**

But the psalmist knows that he is not without help. He trusts in God, in what He has been and what He is, his Protector, the Upholder and the Restorer of his honor, the One who lifts him out of his humiliation to a sense of dignity and a consciousness of worth. He speaks from religious experience. When in peril or in any need, he cries unto God, nor does he cry in vain. The psalmist's

[49] *Op. cit.*, pp. 1-3.

words in verse 3, "But Thou," mark a contrast and introduce a new theme, a transition here from lament to confidence.

> 3 But Thou, O Lord, art a shield about me,
>   The defender of my dignity, and the one who lifts up my head.
> 4 If I cry aloud to the Lord,
>   He answers me from His holy hill.

His expression of trust continues. In times past, similarly burdened and in trouble, he came to the sanctuary. Before the Lord, who dwells in the most holy place, again and again he lay down and fell into a sleep which had brought him to waking consciousness in the wonderful awareness of being sustained by God. It is these past experiences that now lend him confidence. Should he indeed be set upon and surrounded by myriads of warriors, he would not be afraid. His opening words "as for me" stress the contrast between his own faith in God's help and the scoffing triumph-breathing words of his enemies that "there is no help for him from his God."

> 5 As for me, I lay down and slept; [50]
>   I awoke, for the Lord sustaineth me.
> 6 I will not be afraid of myriads of warring folk,
>   Who might set upon me from every side.

The climactic part of the psalm follows. It is the petition for God's present help. And it is followed by a type of statement which expresses the highest degree of certainty that one can reach. The psalmist in anticipation sees, as though it has already taken place, the utter disgrace of his accusing enemies and the divine retribution upon their insolent speech.

> 7 Arise, O Lord; save me, O my God:
>   For Thou wilt smite all my enemies upon the cheek; [51]
>   Thou wilt break the teeth of the ungodly.

The psalm has a liturgical conclusion, an utterance by the priest which emphasizes the Lord as the source of all salvation and asks for His blessing upon His people.

> 8 Salvation is God's affair:
>   May Thy blessing be upon Thy people!

It is an original part of the psalm. As Staerk says, "It summarizes powerfully the essential religious ideas of the psalm. The congregation of the godly is set alongside the praying psalmist. It feels itself to be, in contrast to the sinners, God's true people under the grace of the Lord." [52]

[50] The forms of the verbs suggest facts which have formerly taken place and are still of common occurrence; cf. Gesenius-Kautzsch, *op. cit.*, sec. 106k.

[51] Cf. I Kings 22:24.   [52] *Op. cit.* (*Lyrik*), p. 167.

Ps. 4. THE WONDERFUL KINDNESS OF GOD

In Ps. 4 the psalmist has to do with men who are bent upon what is utterly worthless (vs. 2*b*). Moreover, these men have attacked the psalmist's honor (vs. 2*a*). In his trouble he turns for relief to God, calling out to Him for help.

> 1 When I call, answer me, O God of my righteousness;
>> In trouble, procure for me freedom: [53]
>> Have mercy upon me, and hear my prayer.

He is convinced that there is no ground for his accusers to stand on. There is no basis whatever for their aspersions against him, yet only God can clear and relieve him, the God of his "righteousness," that is, the God who both knows his innocency and can make it apparent. He is in the Temple for this purpose, that he may be cleared of the false accusation. He turns to his accusers, prominent men of the community, but men of wrong motive, and earnestly appeals to them, protesting that there is nothing true in their accusations. He does not reprimand his accusers, but he witnesses before them as to the wonder of God's grace, which even now he is marvelously experiencing. God has revealed Himself to the psalmist in love and acceptance. There is tranquility in his own heart, as in calmness he asks his accusers to desist from their accusing words. However disposed to anger they may be toward him in their hearts, let them withhold themselves from the guilt of unjust dealing with him. However contentious they may feel, let them in silence keep their rancor to themselves. Moreover, it will be to their own advantage to do this, for they too, as well as he, must offer sacrifices. Let them do it, not in unbridled passion, but with good intention. So he cries to them:

> 2 You men, how long will you debase my dignity to humiliation?
>> [How long] will you love what is empty, will you seek what is false?
> 3 Know that the Lord has made His kindness wonderful to me!
>> The Lord hears when I cry to Him.
> 4 Although you may be angry in your heart, do not sin:
>> Though you are filled with rancor upon your bed, keep silent.
> 5   Offer sacrifices with clean hands, and trust in the Lord.

In contrast to his own priceless consciousness of inner joy—a spiritual happiness which is greater than the jubilation associated with a good grain and vintage harvest, and which is God's gift to his own soul (vs. 7)—he thinks of the vast numbers who have no such vivid awareness of the gracious consideration and blessing of God, yet long for it (vs. 6).

> 6 Many are saying, "Oh that we might experience what is good!
>> The Lord has concealed over us the light of His countenance."
> 7 Thou hast put joy in my heart,
>> More than at the time of harvest of corn and wine.

[53] Schmidt thus gives a free rendering, *Schaffe mir Freiheit.*

As he drops off into sleep, we can detect the trembling and longing expectation that the morning at the hour of his awakening will bring him the expected revelation from God,[54] so he prays:

> 8   In peace will I lay me down and at once drop off to sleep!
>   For Thou, O Lord, dost let me tarry in security.

Ps. 5. AWAITING A MORNING REVELATION

Ps. 5 is the prayer of one who has been falsely accused. In great need, yet in expectant confidence, he pays a visit to the Temple in the hope of being decisively vindicated by the Lord, who protects His own. He has arranged an omen sacrifice (*bōqer*), by means of which he hopes to secure from the Lord a "sign," a revelation assuring his innocence and vindicating him. The "omen sacrifice" is to be interpreted in the light of the *biqqōreth* (an "investigation"; note margin of A.S.V., "inquisition") of Lev. 19:20. The psalm opens with a prayer for such an assuring revelation:

> 1   Listen to my words, O Lord;
>   Understand my murmuring.
> 2*a* Pay heed to my loud cry for help,
> 2*b*   My King and my God;
> 3*a* In the morning Thou shalt hear my voice,
> 2*c*   For I pray to Thee.
> 3*b* An omen sacrifice I prepare unto Thee,
> 3*c*   And I watch expectantly for my sign.[55]

It is of course the task of the priest to transmute the expected oracle into a meaningful message of the Lord. Presumably it will bring the vindication of His accused servant and the great discomfiture of the psalmist's iniquitous, murderous, and deceitful enemies. The early morning after the night of expectant seeking is the hour of revelation when the Lord will thus make plain the psalmist's way.

Stirred by a believing trust in the lovingkindness of God, the suppliant feels that he has the right of a true worshiper, the right of a guest in the Lord's house. Peering into the suppliant's soul, we feel the contrast between the boastful, smooth speech and loose conduct of the psalmist's enemies and the sincere simplicity of his own reverence as he prostrates himself before God and asks Him to illuminate his peril-strewn way:

> 4   For Thou dost not delight in wickedness:
>   No guest of Thine can evil be!

[54] See Mowinckel for the rite of incubation, *op. cit.*, I, 155.
[55] Following Mowinckel, *op. cit.*, I, 147, in inserting *leôthi;* cf. Ps. 86:17:

> Perform in me a gracious sign,
>   So those who hate me may see and be ashamed.

Also cf. Ps. 74:9: "Signs for us we do not see"; and II Kings 16:10-15, where the bronze altar was used for priestly oracles "to inquire by" (*lebhaqqer*).

> 5 Boasters cannot hold their ground
>   Before Thine eyes.
>   Thou hatest all who do iniquity:
> 6   Those who speak lies,
>   The man who sheds blood and is treacherous,
>   Thou dost abhor, O Lord.
> 7 But as for me, in the abundance of Thy kindness
>   I come to Thy house:
>   I bow down before Thy holy Temple
>   In awe of Thee.
> 8 O Lord, lead me in Thy righteousness,
>   Because of my enemies;
>   Make plain my way before me.

Deep upon the psalmist's spirit are the wounds of his enemies' smooth but treacherous words. He prays for the Lord to declare his adversaries guilty and to bring to utter failure their schemes and criminal acts.

> 9 For not in their mouth is anything upright;
>   Their inner being is engulfing ruin;
>   Their throat is an open grave,
>   Though they are smooth with their tongue.
> 10 Declare them guilty, O God;
>   May their own counsels fell them.
>   Because of their numerous transgressions, banish them,
>   For they rebel against Thee.

It is likely that such prayers for divine vengeance and words of imprecation which have so large a place in the psalms of individual lamentation were originally *spoken* by the officiating priest. They formed a fixed part of the acts and words of the ritual for cleansing in connection with the sin offering presented by the sick and suffering. Their appearance in these psalms represents the influence which the priestly formulas of imprecation, as pronounced in the living worship, had upon the style and vocabulary of such religious utterance. It often strikes us as exaggerated, unreal, and inconsistent with loftier elements in the psalm.[56]

Then, as is frequently the case in lamentations,[57] immediately following this execration upon the enemy, and in sharp contrast to it, comes the psalmist's eager wish for the righteous:

> 11 But let all who seek refuge in Thee rejoice;
>   May they forever shout for joy.
>   And let those who love Thy name
>   Exult in Thee!

The psalm closes with the suppliant's certainty of God's answer. No more is the mood that of lamentation. Now it is deep and untroubled confidence.

---

[56] Cf. Mowinckel, *op. cit.*, V, 93.   [57] Gunkel, *Einleitung*, sec. 6:15, p. 228.

12   For Thou dost bless the righteous, O Lord;
     Thou dost cover him as with a shield;
     Thou dost crown him with favor.

Ps. 17. AWAKENING TO THE VINDICATION OF GOD

Ps. 17 is a prayer of an accused. The suppliant is bringing his cause before the Lord for His decision as to an accusation because his truthfulness has been challenged. He calls upon God to hear his prayer and prays that there may come to him a just verdict.

1   Hear, O Lord, a righteous cause; pay attention to my ringing cry:
    Give ear to my prayer, from lips that do not deceive.
2   From Thee emanates my verdict.
    Let Thine eyes see rightly.

Then comes the main part of the psalm, the solemn declaration of the psalmist's innocence of any evil of which he has been accused. He mentions particularly murder and robbery as the violation of God's commands of which he is not guilty. He seems to open his inner being to the scrutiny and testing of God. He is in the Temple, and through the night he waits before His God, who explores the heart.

3   If Thou dost examine my heart, dost search [me] in the night,
    If Thou dost put me to the test, Thou wilt not find any evil that I
       have done.
4   I have not transgressed Thy commandment concerning blood deeds;
    The word of Thy lips I have heeded.
5   My steps have held firmly in the paths of Thy commandments;
    In Thy tracks my footsteps waver not.

Thus sincerely convinced of his own innocence, in loyalty and faith the psalmist cries to God for shelter from his opponents, who are wicked men lying in wait for him, enemies who are seeking his life. Thus he utters his petition:

6   So I cry to Thee, for Thou dost answer me, O God;
    Bend down Thine ear to me; hear what I say!
7   Deal wondrously with Thy loyal one; save him who seeks shelter in Thee
    From [his] opponents, by Thy right hand.
8   Keep me, like [Thou keepest] the apple of Thine eye;
    Hide me in the shadow of Thy wings
9   From the face of wicked men who lie in wait for me,
    My enemies who are closing in against my life.

The psalmist is not troubled about the enduring protection of God. Rather is it a question of a decisive moment when that protection will be made manifest, when the accusation will be proved false.[58]

_____

[58] Cf. Schmidt, *Das Gebet der Angeklagten in den Psalmen*, p. 20.

Around him—closing in, eager to thrust him down to the ground, their hostile eyes upon him—are his enemies, poised like a lion before he leaps. Thus in lamenting words he describes them:

> 10 The door of their heart they have closed;
>   With their mouth they speak arrogantly.
> 11 They watch me; now they surround me;
>   They set their eyes to thrust me down to the ground.
> 12 They have plotted against me like a lion that longs to tear,
>   Yes, like a young lion that lies in a lurking place.

Beset by such undeserved enmity, he appeals unto God in a cry for divine vengeance which will pursue the enemies to the third generation. One of them particularly is singled out (vs. 13). The psalmist has in mind here that the Lord, in some decisive, momentary manner, will thus answer him, deliver, and vindicate him.

> 13 Arise, O Lord, confront him!
>   Bow him down! save my life from the wicked!
>   With Thy sword kill them, with Thy hand, O Lord!
> 14 Exterminate them from the world; tear them out of life!
>   With what Thou wilt spare *them*, let the body of their children be filled!
>   May *they* be satiated [with it] and still leave what yet remains to
>   *their* children!

The psalm closes with a remarkable conception. The psalmist knows that he is righteous and innocent of any charge. He is confident, not only that God will manifest his innocency, but that his vindication and assurance will be given him at a particular moment of intimate spiritual experience. In verse 3 the psalmist has in mind the spending of the night in the Temple under the examination of God. But in the morning, at the moment of awakening, he is confident that he will have God's answer, a vision of God, a sense of His reality, nearness, and His acceptance of him.

> 15 But as for me, in acknowledged righteousness I shall behold Thy face;
>   I shall be satisfied, upon awaking, with Thy presence.[59]

Ps. 27:1-6. BEHOLDING GOD'S BEAUTY IN THE MORNING!

The situation portrayed in Ps. 27:1-6 is that of an innocent man, a loyal worshiper of the Lord, and a man of great trust in Him. Certain enemies are laying traps for him, and they are hurling their false and slanderous accusations against him. These accusers are bold, daring, and wicked men. In Aramaic the phrase "to devour my flesh" is a familiar figure of speech for "accusation" (cf. Dan. 3:8). The poet is an Oriental. He uses pictures of the attack of an advancing army quite figuratively to describe his enemies' malicious accusations. He

---

[59] Literally "with Thy form," but clearly it is conceived here in a spiritual sense, the form representing the vivid sense of God's spiritual presence in vindication and acceptance.

knows, moreover, that in case the charges of his accusers are not sustained it will
go hard with them; "they shall stumble and fall" (vs. 2).

Out of profound spiritual certainty which is athrill with the psalmist's vital
fellowship with God he sings his song of trust, for God is to him illumination,
rescue, and security:

> 1 The Lord is my light and my salvation;
>   Of whom shall I be afraid?
>   The Lord is the protection of my life;
>   Of whom should I be in dread?
> 2 If the wicked should draw near against me
>   To devour my flesh,
>   My adversaries and my enemies, as for them,
>   They shall stumble and fall!
> 3 If an army should encamp against me,
>   My heart would not fear.
>   If battle should rise up against me,
>   In spite of this I would be in repose.

But the psalmist's day of trouble has come (vs. 5), for himself a day of crisis
and decision, and for his enemies a day of humiliation. The place of decision
for such matters, and the place where the Lord will vindicate him in his innocency, is the Temple. And to him the Temple is precious. Two words he uses
for the sanctuary, both alive with tender historical associations. It is a "booth"
which recalls the Lord's protecting presence with His people in the classic days
of their wilderness wanderings (Lev. 23:42-43). And he is within the hospitality
of God's "tent, tabernacle" ('ōhel), which recalls the sanctuary of the Lord
before the Temple was built. Here within the hospitable coverage of the Lord's
sanctuary the psalmist is spiritually aware of the protection of God, just as though
he is lifted up to the unassailable security of a towering rock beyond the reach
of malicious foes. Yet, reassuring as all this is, for this day of trouble it is not
enough. He has now one supreme desire in his soul. It is that in the morning
he may behold the beauty of the Lord in His Temple! The reference is to an
experience after a night in the sanctuary which proves the innocency of the
accused.[60] It is likely that sleep in the sanctuary plays an important role in such
an ordeal. In the morning comes the revelation of the Lord's will. It is a reference to the practice of incubation.

> 4 One thing I ask of the Lord;
>   For it I long:
>   To behold the beauty of the Lord
>   In the morning [61] in His Temple.[62]

[60] So Schmidt, Die Psalmen, p. 28. He cites an illustration of the part played by a night in
the sanctuary in determining guilt by divine revelation in Musil, Arabia Petraea, III, 318.
[61] Reading with Schmidt, babbōqēr for ûlebhaqqēr.
[62] The clause "my dwelling shall be in the house of the Lord all the days of my life" probably is an insertion into the psalm from Ps. 23:6.

> 5 Yes, He hides me in His *booth*,
>   In the day of trouble.
>   He shelters me within the cover of His *tent;*
>   He lifts me high upon a rock!

The psalm ends in a note of triumph. We are to infer that his answer has come. Vindicated, he stands in the presence of his foes. Joyously he utters a challenge to his own soul, and he vows that he will be among those groups who, in the grateful consciousness of release, will pay their thanks to the Lord in His sanctuary with music and song.

> 6 So now let my head be up
>   Above my enemies around me!
>   And I intend to offer in His sanctuary
>   Sacrifices with shout of joy!
>   I intend to sing and play to the Lord!

Ps. 57. I WILL AWAKEN THE DAWN

In Ps. 57 the psalmist feels himself to be in the gravest peril. Engulfing ruin stands at the door. Deadly enemies are panting after his life. He can compare them only with ravenous lions all set to spring upon the prey. Their slanderous words against him he likens to piercing weapons. Moreover, they maliciously set a trap for him. But his soul is alive with the certainty of his own innocence.

In his dark hour when there is no other place to go for help he turns to "the shadow of Thy wings." The reference is to the Temple, where from the sanctuary he can see in the most holy place the wings of the cherubim, above which sits enthroned the invisible God. In his grave crisis he prays unto the Lord:

> 1 Have mercy upon me, O God; have mercy upon me;
>   For in Thee my soul seeks refuge.
>   In the shadow of Thy wings let me hide
>   Until the engulfing ruin is passed.

The psalmist is certain that he is innocent of any charge. But his deliverance, exoneration, and the consequent humiliation of his enemy accusers can come only from God. At the strategic moment God will show His hand and rescue him. Trust and petition mingle as the psalmist continues:

> 2 I cry to God most high,
>   To God who deals bountifully with me;
> 3 May He send from heaven and save me
>   From the power of those who hate my soul!

He knows himself to be in deadly peril because of the falsity and the vituperous slander of their accusations. And he is convinced that their iniquitous and deadly dealings will come back upon themselves in destruction. In the midst of all this, with a calm confidence, the spiritual poise of which we feel, he lays himself down:

4   In the midst of lions, greedy for me,
        I lay myself down;
    Their teeth are spear and arrows,
        And their tongue a sharp sword.
6   As for the net they have set for my footsteps,
        Their own foot spreads itself in it.
    They have dug before me a pit,
        But they themselves have fallen into it! [63]

The second part of the psalm begins at verse 7 and is vitally related to the
first part. Between verse 4, where the psalmist says, "I lay myself down," and
verse 8, where in glad enthusiasm he says, "I will "awaken the dawn," there is a
definite connection. For while the first part of the psalm is full of lament, the
second is athrill with confidence. As Schmidt suggests, we may infer that in the
last hours of the night there took place something in his experience which
"averted the evil, tore the net and brought to light the innocency of the accused." [64] It is with the vibrant sense of spiritual release and a deep sense of
religious security that he summons the Temple musicians to accompany his
joyous song of praise:

7   Fixed is my heart, O God;
        Fixed is my heart:
            I will sing and praise Thee;
8   Awake, my soul;
        Awake, harp and zither;
            I will awaken the dawn!

Ps. 59. GOD CONFRONTS ME WITH HIS MERCY

In Ps. 59 the psalmist is being persecuted by harsh and bitter enemies—"evildoers" and "men of blood" he calls them. Yet it is not under their murderous
deeds that he is suffering, for the weapons of these enemies are not swords but
words of abuse and defamation. They have attacked him by accusations for which
there are no grounds. So he comes to the Temple, where he prays to be saved
from these accusers and to be placed beyond their reach by God. Passionate
and eager is his petition:

1   Save me from my enemies, O God;
        Put me out of reach of those rising up against me.
2   Rescue me from evildoers;
        And from men of blood save me.

In general terms he pictures his formidable accusers who, as it were, are lying
in ambush. Then they show their hand and charge him openly with wrongs of
which he is not guilty.

[63] Omit vs. 5, with Duhm and Cheyne, as disturbing the context.
[64] *Die Psalmen*, p. 110.

3   For lo, they lie in wait for my life;
        The formidable make attack upon me.
     Without any transgression or any sin of mine,
4   They make running attack and take their stand.

He renews his petition, using three verbs that are most characteristic of a lament:
"rouse . . . , awake . . . , spare not."

5   But as for Thee, O Lord of hosts,
        Rouse Thyself to confront them!
     Awake to punish all the nations!
     Spare not the treacherous wicked!

The word "nations," as is the case in Ps. 56:7b, is rightly seen as giving evidence of the influence exerted in this manner of speech by the king's psalms, where the enemy is the heathen nations.[65]

A description of his accusers in action follows. He gives an animated picture of them, comparing them particularly to vicious dogs, which in the Orient are, not as with us house pets, but howling night scavengers prowling about under cover of darkness.[66] Vividly he describes their accusing, defaming speech as dogs foaming at the mouth!

6=14 At evening they come again;
          They howl like dogs,
              And go about the city.
15a   They go wandering about for food;
15b   When not satisfied, they growl;
7   Lo, they foam at their mouth;
          Their lips are swords.

But bitter and treacherous as is the enmity of his false accusers, the psalmist himself has profound confidence that God will help him. At such calumny, comparable to the slander of proud pagans, the great God laughs in derision. And even now, although relief has not come, the psalmist finds refuge in God and feels himself confronted by His mercy. In due time he will stand vindicated before his would-be destroyers. Thus he gives words to his confidence:

8   But Thou, O Lord, dost laugh at them;
        Thou dost view all pagans with scorn.
9=17 My refuge! for Thee will I wait;
        For Thou, O God, art my retreat.[67]
10   My God confronts me with His mercy;
        God lets me gloat over those lying in wait for me.

The psalmist does not wish upon his enemies destruction and ruin, although he has in his heart no mercy for them. He wants them rather to be restrained

[65] Cf. Gunkel, *Einleitung*, sec. 5:9, p. 148.
[66] Cf. Meissner, *op. cit.*, I, 221. Vss. 6 and 14 are identical.
[67] Vss. 9 and 17 are identical.

from their arrogance and to become keenly aware that the Lord rules over His
people Israel in loving concern and holds the ends of the earth in regal control.
He wants them to be impressed by this, a result that will be far more significant
than their sudden punitive destruction. So his petition pours forth:

> 11a Kill them not, lest my people forget;
> 11b Withhold from them strength, and bring them down;
> 11c-12a Hold them back, O Lord, from the sin of their mouth,
>   The word of their lips,
> 12b That they may be restrained from their arrogance.
>   Let them be stopped from cursing and from lying.
> 13 Restrain their wrath; restrain [it] so that it be no more,
>   That they may know that God rules over Jacob
>   To the ends of the earth! [68]

The psalm closes with the vow to sing a song of thanksgiving. It is in the
form of a hymn, with the theme of praise introduced by the characteristic hymnic
word "for." Here it closes the lament, but in our psalm it is not intended, as is
the case in the Babylonian laments, to persuade God, but is rather the expression
of a feeling of deep thanksgiving which wells up from the psalmist's heart. Not
yet has release come. He expects deliverance from the violence of his accusers
through an experience between the evening and the morning. In the blessed
experience of joyous release which God will meditate to him during the night
he will lift in the morning a thankful cry of joy.

> 16 But I will sing of Thy protection,
>   And I will lift a ringing cry in the morning for Thy mercy.
>   For Thou art my refuge,
>   And a shelter in the day of my trouble.

Ps. 143. SATISFY ME IN THE MORNING WITH THY GRACE

Ps. 143 is the prayer of a man who has been falsely accused and is in danger
of the judicial sentence of death. He is convinced of his innocence, but even
while appealing to the Lord for justice he confesses that no one *can* be righteous
before God. This thought is something utterly his own and characteristic of
his deeply spiritual personality.

The psalmist addresses God with a cry for help, appealing to His righteousness, to His fidelity.

> 1 O Lord, hear my prayer;
>   Listen to my supplication;
>   In Thy fidelity answer me.
> 2 In Thy righteousness bring not Thy servant into judgment,
>   For no living being can be righteous before Thee.

[60] In this passage I follow the convincing reconstruction of the text suggested by Gunkel.

The lament itself follows. The accusation of his enemy—he singles out one among many—has thrown him into the darkness of the prison,[69] where his courage is now at an ebb, for his whole inner being has grown numb.

> 3 For an enemy pursues my soul
>   And crushes my life to the earth:
>   He makes me sit in darkness.
> 4 My spirit faints upon me; [70]
>   My heart within me is grown numb.

In his crucial need, while longing for the help of the righteous and faithful God, the psalmist resorts to meditation on what the Lord has done in the past. From the present distress he turns to the glorious days of old and meditates upon the mighty deeds of God, no doubt the wondrous marvels which He wrought in the release from Egypt. He thinks also of his own habitual attitude of dependence upon God, wherein he has implored, and *still implores*, His help. Like a thirsty land longing for rain, so is his thirst for God's help.

> 5 I remember the days of old;
>   I muse over all Thy deeds;
>   I meditate on the works of Thy hands.
> 6 I spread forth my hands to Thee:
>   My soul is like a thirsty land toward Thee.

Such utterance of trust, a religious attitude that is normal and persistent in this psalmist's life, is most frequently the ground upon which the petition of a lamentation is based.[71] His petition follows, rich in content but diffuse in nature. He appeals for God's swift response. Time is at a premium, for his life force is being rapidly exhausted. He longs to be noticed by God, who will then not let him descend to the grave, but will hold him in life. But far deeper than this, he longs for the spiritual illumination of God for light upon the way he should take. As God's trustful servant he prays that, following a night spent in preparation in the sanctuary,[72] there may come to him in the morning a soul-satisfying revelation of God's grace. Even more than deliverance from his falsely accusing enemies, he longs to know and do the will of God and to be led by God's good spirit in a level path. Thus he prays:

> 7 Hasten to answer me, O Lord,
>   For my life strength is exhausted;
>   Hide not Thy face from me,
>   And let me not be like those who go down to the grave.

---

[69] So Schmidt, *Die Psalmen,* p. 249.
[70] Cf. Brown, Driver, Briggs, *op. cit.,* p. 753 (II, 1*d*), which interprets the force of '*al.*
[71] Cf. Gunkel, *Einleitung,* p. 232.
[72] The implied reference here is probably to the rite of incubation; cf. also Pss. 3:5; 4:8; 5:3; 57:8; 59:16.

8 Satisfy me in the morning with Thy grace,
    For I trust in Thee.
  Make me know the way which I should go,
    For I lift up my soul to Thee.
9 Deliver me from my enemies, O Lord,
    For my confidence is in Thee.
10 Teach me to do what pleases Thee,
    For Thou art my God:
  May Thy good spirit lead me
    In a level path.

As his prayer draws to a close, it deepens in intensity (vss. 11-12). The psalmist appeals to the three profoundest elements in the character of God. The first is God's regard for His own name—for that which He is in His essential being. If God is true to Himself, He will not let the psalmist die. The second appeal is to God's mercy, out of which flows His compassionate sympathy for His children. It is on this that the psalmist bases his hope for release from his present trouble. The third appeal is to God's righteousness—to His righteous judgment which will express itself in the destruction of the psalmist's persecuting enemies, and to His righteous vindication which will approve him as God's loyal servant.

11 For the sake of Thy name, O Lord, let me live:
    In Thy mercy bring my life out of trouble.[78]
12 And in Thy righteousness exterminate my enemies;
    And destroy all who are harrassing my soul;
    For I am Thy servant.

[78] I follow Perles, who transposes "mercy" and "righteousness" in vss. 11 and 12, *Analekten zur Textkritik des Alten Testaments*, p. 114.

Chapter XI

PRAYERS OF THE SICK AND THE PENITENT

1. Prayers of the Falsely Accused and Ill

IN A LARGE GROUP OF PSALMS, WITH WHICH WE WILL NOW DEAL, THE PSALMIST IN each case is suffering first and foremost under false accusation, in a matter which was to be settled at the Temple. In addition to this cause of suffering, he is ill. Although his illness is not the primary cause of the accusation, it tends to make it more severe, since according to the generally accepted view, which his accusers also hold, the sick man already has one sharp count against him, the divine disapproval. This opens the way for greater ruthlessness toward him than his accusers would ordinarily show. Such a situation we find in the psalms which now follow: 13; 22; 28; 31:9-24; 35; 38; 41; 69; 71; 86; 102; 109:

Ps. 13. SINGING FORTH THE CERTAINTY OF DELIVERANCE

In Ps. 13 the psalmist has an affliction which he has already endured for a long time, and which has led him to feel that God had forgotten him, possibly forever. He is experiencing tormenting pain. It is probable that we should interpret verse 3 literally, and that this man is suffering a severe disease of the eyes, a type of physical malady which even today is prevalent in Palestine. His disease is increasing in severity and is threatening his very life.[1]

Yet almost more than by physical pain and suffering is he disturbed by the antagonism of an enemy who has risen up against him, an adversary who does not desire his restoration to health but gloats over the apparent fact that his situation is growing worse. No doubt the psalmist's physical condition was a factor leading to his being falsely accused by his enemy, although the nature of the accusation is not given.

The psalmist pours forth his lament in distress and in great impatience. Four times comes the characteristic lamenting question, "How long?" [2]

> 1 How long, O Lord, wilt Thou forget me forever?
> How long wilt Thou hide Thy face from me?
> 2 How long must I harbor pain in my soul,
> Suffering in my heart day and night?
> How long shall my enemy rise up against me?

His petition follows, uttered in three penetrating sentences, one coming fast upon the other—"Show regard to me; answer me . . . ; lighten me"—and each closely related to the feelingful lament.

[1] Cf. Schmidt, *Die Psalmen*, p. 22.
[2] Cf. also Pss. 74:10; 79:5; 89:46; Isa. 6:11; the first two are national laments; the third a king's lament; the last an individual lament uttered under influence of familiarity with cultic practice.

3 Show regard to me; answer me,
   O Lord, my God.
Lighten my eyes,
   So that I sleep not in death;
4 So that my enemy will not say,
   "I have prevailed over him";
So that my adversaries will not exult because I slip.

We note here that the mental pain caused him by the eagerness of his enemy to see him slip is greater even than his physical suffering. Moreover, he feels that his problem is likewise God's. If God lets him die, yes, if God even lets him slip, the cause of the Lord is weakened. His fall would be interpreted by his enemy as the collapse of religion.

The closing part of the psalm gives expression to the certainty that God will answer his petitions. Often a lamentation ends in that way. But here follows a vow that he will sing unto the Lord a song of thanksgiving. Yes, more, so certain is he that God will answer his prayer, and so deep is the stir of his spirit because of it, that he starts to sing his praise as though he were already delivered.[3] His vow is expressed in its simplest form, in the cohortative, which indicates the direction of the speaker's will, denoting self-encouragement, a resolution or a wish.[4]

5 But as for me, I trust in Thy mercy;
   My heart exults in Thy salvation.
6 Let me sing unto the Lord;
   For He has dealt bountifully with me.

Ps. 22. SOULS NOT YET ALIVE SHALL PRAISE HIM

This noble psalm is called the Passion psalm because Jesus made its opening verse the channel of expression for His own profound sense of loneliness when He was hanging on the cross. He quoted it in Aramaic, His mother tongue. The psalm is an individual lament. At the close (especially vs. 28) it has points of contact with the thought of Deutero-Isaiah, and is probably postexilic. It divides sharply into two parts, the first (vss. 1-21) being a lament of an individual because of illness (vss. 14-17). But his lament is likewise occasioned by enemies whose scoffing derision has been made the sharper and bolder because his illness points up to them conclusively that God has forsaken him. The second part (vss. 22-31) is a song of thanksgiving, sung in advance of his cure from illness, but under the conviction that the cure at God's hand is certain.

The first part, the lament proper, is interspersed with expressions of trust. It opens with a classic utterance of awful loneliness. Because of Jesus' quotation of these words at his crucifixion, they have a unique sacredness (Mark 15:34). The psalmist feels himself to be abandoned by God, but does not know why, for

---

[3] Cf. Gunkel, *Einleitung*, p. 248.   [4] Cf. Gesenius-Kautzsch, *op. cit.*, sec. 48e.

he is conscious of no sin. To his cry in the daytime no answer comes, and night brings his disturbed spirit no rest.

> 1   My God, my God, why hast Thou forsaken me?
>   Why stayest Thou far from my cry for help,
>   From the words of my call of distress?
> 2   I cry by day, but Thou dost not answer;
>   And by night, but I have no repose.

By this vivid and intense voicing of his incessant suffering he hopes to touch and move the heart of God. Then in his poignant desolation he resorts to his own faith, fed and fired as it has been by the marvelous story of his people's past. He speaks to God in a classic utterance of trust, picturing Him as King seated on his Temple throne, the recipient of the praise of worshiping Israel. The fathers of Israel trusted Him. To Him in their hours of strategic need they called and were delivered. Cannot so mighty a God be depended upon to help him?

> 3   But Thou sittest enthroned in the sanctuary,
>   The praise of Israel.
> 4   Our fathers trusted in Thee;
>   They trusted, and Thou didst deliver them;
> 5   They cried to Thee, and they escaped;
>   They trusted in Thee and were not ashamed.

But such help as the fathers experienced serves only to set in somber relief his own contrasted lot of misery. He knows no answer to his "why?" He is aware of no sin which can be the cause of his distress. He feels as mean as a worm, the target of the insult of the secular-minded men of this world, who scoff at piety and at every sincere worshiper of God. Their profane, undiscerning words cut him to the quick. The psalmist has been a well-known devotee of the Lord and claims still to be, but look at what it has brought him! In the same breath these men of the world deride him and scoff at his God. And in irony they utter a mocking challenge: Let the God in whom he claims to trust deliver the darling of His delight! Thus he resumes his lament:

> 6   But as for me, I am a worm, and no man,
>   A butt of men's insult, and despised by the people.
> 7   All who see me hold me in derision;
>   They open their mouths [insultingly] wide; they [mockingly] wag
>   their heads, saying,
> 8   "He has cast himself on the Lord; let Him deliver him!
>   Let Him rescue him, for He delights in him!"

Such biting scorn from men drives the psalmist back upon God. In tender words of trust he acknowledges that from his very birth God has been his refuge, so now in his loneliness he pours forth to the Lord a petition for His presence and help. We meet here an indication of the enmity which he is experiencing, and before which he feels helpless.

> 9 For Thou hast been my refuge from the womb,
>   Making me secure on my mother's breasts;
> 10 Upon Thee I was cast from the womb;
>   From the womb of my mother Thou art my God.
> 11 Be not far distant from me,
>   For an enemy has drawn near me,
>   And there is no one to help.

In the next part of the first major section of the psalm (vss. 12-21) we are again in the mood of lament. First, in vivid and vigorous figures of speech the psalmist describes his enemies. Like a gang of hunters with their dogs closing in upon a wild, hunted thing, so his enemies close in upon him. Like the powerful and dangerous bulls from Bashan's rich cattle country across the Jordan, they surround him. They spring upon him like roaring, ravenous lions.

> 16a For many dogs surround me:
> 16b   A gang of evildoers closes in upon me.
> 12 Strong steers encircle me;
>   Bulls of Bashan surround me.
> 13 His jaws open wide against me,
>   A roaring and ravenous lion.

Second, in the clearest glimpses as yet granted us we see the psalmist's pitiable mental and physical condition. He has no heart to stand up against such enmity. His physical body is disintegrating. His mouth is parched and dry from fever. He is so emaciated that his ribs stick out. And his enemies gloat over his weakening physique.

> 14 My soul is poured out like water,
>   And all my bones are loosed from one another;
>   My heart is become like wax,
>   And melts away in my inner being.
> 15a My mouth is dry as a potsherd,
> 15b   And my tongue sticks to my gums;
> 17 I can count all my bones;
>   They gloat over me.

Third, in imagination he foresees his death. In vivid Oriental exaggeration he pictures his relatives and friends as having already bound his hands and feet for burial. Already they have laid him in the grave, in the dust (cf. Job 17:16; 21: 26) of the underworld; already in anticipation they have divided up among them by lot the clothing he will leave behind.

> 16c They have bound my hands and my feet,
> 15c   And in the dust of death have they laid me.
> 18 They have divided up my garments among them;
>   Yes, for my clothing they have cast lots.

As was the case in the first part of the psalm (vs. 11), so here (vss. 19-21) this lament rises to its climax in a passionate petition for the Lord to come to help and save him. We sense how the previous lament is summed up. "From the sword" (vs. 20) is but an exaggerated metaphor for peril of death. Dogs, lion, and wild ox suggest the ferocious temper of his enemies.

> 19 But as for Thee, O Lord, stay not far off;
> O my Help, make haste to assist me.
> 20 Snatch my life from the sword,
> My soul from the power of dogs.
> 21 Save me from the jaws of the lion,
> My poor soul from the horns of the wild ox!

As a high point of the whole psalm comes the final part (vss. 22-31), which is a psalm of thanksgiving. The vow is uttered in verse 22, and the psalm of thanksgiving is rendered in verses 23-26, in anticipation of the hoped-for deliverance. Very often the lament closes with such a vow of a song of thanksgiving. Not content, however, to utter by himself his thanks for the anticipated deliverance, the psalmist draws into his expression of gratitude ever greater circles, and his words rise into the exalted tones of the hymn [5] (vss. 27-31) with which the entire psalm closes. Thus vows the psalmist, using the cohortative with its expression of deep, personal emotion:

> 22 Then I will tell of Thy renown to my brethren:
> In the midst of the congregation will I praise Thee.

The praise song that he will then sing follows. There unrolls before our eyes the vivid scene in which such a psalm of thanksgiving is rendered. It is likely, as Küchler [6] has suggested, that between verses 21 and 22 a priestly oracle assuring deliverance has been given to the sufferer. In anticipation the psalmist stands in the great congregation of the Lord's worshipers, the "offspring of Jacob . . . , descendants of Israel." He has come to pay his vows with a peace offering and in a song of thanksgiving. His brethren (fellow Israelites) are there. He is one of a great congregation who fear the Lord and who seek Him. He invites them all to share in a bounteous sacrificial meal, his own peace offering. The poor are there. For once they may eat until they are satisfied. In his good fortune the devout all share. For the psalmist's rescue proves the mercy of God even to the poorest and lowliest of His people. Thus in anticipation he sings his thanksgiving song:

> 23 Praise Him, you who fear the Lord;
> Honor Him, all offspring of Jacob,
> And stand in awe of Him, all descendants of Israel.
> 24 For He has not disdained
> Nor detested to answer the poor.
> He has not hidden His face from me,
> But has listened to my cry to Him.

[5] Cf. Gunkel, *Einleitung*, pp. 248-49.   [6] *Op. cit.*, p. 300.

25 His faithfulness will be my praise song in the great congregation;
   I will pay my vows in the presence of those who fear Him.
26 The poor shall eat and be satisfied;
   Those who seek Him shall praise the Lord;
   May their hearts be revived forever!

Yet even this does not exhaust the psalmist's poetic rapture. His deliverance, not yet experienced but confidently hoped for, is so great a thing that it will awaken distant peoples, pagan nations, even the dead, yes, and those still unborn, who shall pass on to succeeding generations the story of what God has done for him! We feel here the exultant note of imaginative praise, such praise as will touch the whole world into resounding jubilation. We sense here also the throbbing religious feeling that brings imagination into the service of faith.

27 All the ends of the earth shall remember
   And turn to the Lord;
   And all the clans of the nations
   Shall worship before Him.
28 For the kingdom is the Lord's,
   And His dominion is over the nations.
29 Only before Him shall all who sleep in the earth bow down.
   Before Him shall all who go down to the dust kneel;
   Souls not yet alive shall honor His might;
30 And the generation to come shall tell about the Lord.
31   Yes, they shall declare His righteousness to a people yet to be born,
   That the Lord has done it!

Ps. 28. HELPED AND REJUVENATED BY GOD

The psalm is a supplication of a person who is ill, as we infer from verse 7. He is also suffering at the hands of false friends, who are secretly persecuting him. He is in the outer forecourt of the Temple. Lifting his hands in the gesture that is humanity's universal speech of supplication, he cries out to the Lord, urging Him not to deny response to one for whom death seems so near.

1 To Thee I cry, my Rock:
   Be not deaf to me,
   So as to be silent toward me while I become like
   Those gone down to the grave.
2 Hear the voice of my entreaties
   When I cry to Thee;
   Pay heed when I lift up my hands
   To Thy most holy place.

Hard upon his help cry follows his petition. He knows how the Lord will deal with his false friends, those evildoers whose bad intent belies their apparent friendliness. Passionately he asks God to give them what they deserve! Far more serious to him than their falsity is the fact that they give no attention to the works of the Lord, and as a consequence the psalmist hopes for their overthrow at God's hands by a retribution proportioned to their deeds.

> 3 Carry me not off with the ungodly,
>   And with those who do iniquity,
>   Who speak in friendliness with their neighbor,
>   While evil is in their heart!
> 4 Render to them, O Lord, in proportion to what they do;
>   Give to them what their evil deeds deserve.
>   Give them what accords with the work of their hands;
>   Pay back to them what they have dealt out.
> 5 For they pay no heed to the deeds of the Lord,
>   To the work of His hands.
>   Therefore may the Lord overthrow them
>   And build them not.

At this point in the actual rendering of the psalm, as verses 6-7 imply, there comes an oracle of healing, the Lord's response to the psalmist's prayer. This is mediated by the priest and comforts the psalmist, even before release comes, with the glowing assurance that the Lord has heard and will answer his petition.

So the psalm ends in a prayer of thanksgiving, which praises the Lord because the psalmist's supplication has been heard. Already rejuvenated in health and strength, he cries out:

> 6 Blessed be the Lord, for He has heard
>   The voice of my entreaties.
> 7 The Lord is my protection and my shield;
>   My heart trusts in Him.
>   I am helped, and my body is rejuvenated;
>   So from my heart I will praise Him.

To this psalm, purely individual in character, has been added an intercession for the nation and for the king, the Lord's anointed. This makes it practically certain that the psalm has its origin at a time when a king ruled over Judah. It begins with a confession of faith, then moves into a prayer on behalf of the whole congregation.

> 8 The Lord is the strength of His people;
>   Yes, a saving defense for His anointed is He.
> 9 Save Thy people and bless Thine inheritance!
>   Shepherd and carry them forever!

Ps. 31:9-24. MY TIMES ARE IN THY HAND

This psalm is a lament of an individual. The psalmist is ill; his strength is wasting away; great sighs shake his body; and his eyes have lost their sparkle. Consequently his friends and neighbors, viewing him as having been struck by the punishing hand of God, treat him with derision and avoid him.

He does not anticipate a natural death, but thinks it will come through the violence of enemies. This began after his illness had marked him in their eyes as "cast out" by God (vs. 22). This was their ground for insolent and lying charges which they hurled against him at the Temple.

The psalm opens with a cry for help:

> 9a Be gracious to me, O Lord, for it has gone hard with me.

He then proceeds to describe vividly his lamentable condition. Sorrow and sighing have taken their toll from his life span. His strength is gone. He compares his fragile hold upon life to that of a moth. Seeing his physical condition, his horrified friends and neighbors avoid him as one who is being punished by God. He stands before those who are ill-disposed to him, scoffed at and humiliated. His acquaintances flee from him when they see him. He has lost any importance as a person that he ever enjoyed; it is as though he were nonexistent; he feels like a damaged and useless vessel. He is touched to the quick when he sees groups of those who wish him ill whispering together. They are scheming to do away with him.

So he pours out his lament in bitter words:

> 9b   My eyes are dulled by grief,
> 10 For my life is wasting away in pain,
>   And my years in sighs.
>   My strength grows weak because of affliction,
>   And my bodily vigor [wastes away] like the moth.
> 11 I am become a butt of scorn
>   To all my adversaries,
>   And to my neighbors an object of derision,
>   Yes, a source of fear to my acquaintances:
>   Those who see me in the street
>   Flee from me.
> 12 I am forgotten as though dead, non-existent;
>   I am become like a spoiled vessel.
> 13 For I hear the whispering of many,
>   Terror on every side,
>   When they sit in secret conclave against me,
>   Plotting how to take my life.

Yet in the very midst of such physical and mental distress the psalmist has unseen spiritual resources, for he trusts his life and its *issues* to God. His mood grows ever more urgent. As he gives expression to this profound yet childlike trust in the consciousness that he is the Lord's servant, he prays earnestly (vss. 15, 16) for deliverance from the deadly schemes of his enemies. He seeks vindication in the presence of his foes and voices a solemn petition that the Lord will suddenly silence their lying accusations and send them to Sheol, the land of silence and of the dead. Thus in confident trust, in which petition and wish are mingled, he prays:

14 But as for me, upon Thee do I put my trust:
   I say, "My God are Thou;"
15 My times are in Thy hands; deliver me
   From the power of my enemies and my persecutors.
16 Let Thy face shine forth upon Thy servant;
   Save me in Thy mercy;
17 O Lord, let me not be ashamed, for I call to Thee:
   Let the godless be ashamed; let them be silenced to Sheol!
18 May their lying lips be struck dumb,
   Which are speaking insolently against the innocent one!

Then suddenly there is an utter change in the psalmist's spirit. Not only does he praise the goodness of God in beautiful words of general nature, but at verse 21 he says that God's wonderful kindness has been shown to him in the time of his distress. At this point in the living worship has come the utterance of a priestly oracle as the answer of God to his prayer.[7] Our own spirits respond to the wonder of the psalmist's release, as his psalm rises in exalted feeling to its climax (vs. 19-22). He begins to tell of the release in the lofty tone of a hymn, which in exclamatory fashion celebrates the inexhaustible goodness of the Lord. God holds this goodness in His storehouse, but releases it for His loyal worshipers, such as the psalmist, who has just experienced it (vss. 19, 21). His praise moves into the utterance of his own credo, his belief in the dependable shelter which the Lord in His faithfulness provides for His worshipers (vs. 20). The burning, light-giving core of his story is the succinct summary of the whole experience, told as the narrative of a thankful heart (vs. 21). His glad assurance of relief leads him to recall how he had so poignantly felt that God cast him out. But now he knows that God heard his entreating cry (vs. 22).

19 How great is Thy goodness, O Lord,
   Which Thou dost treasure up for those who fear Thee,
   Which Thou providest to those who seek refuge in Thee,
   In sight of the sons of men!
20 Thou dost shelter such with the covering of Thy wings.
   From the tissue of lies [8] of men,
   Thou dost hide them in Thy tabernacle,
   From the strife of tongues.
21 Blessed is the Lord,
   Who hath wondrously shown His kindness to me
   In a time of distress!
22 But as for me I had said in my alarm,
   "I am cast out from before Thine eyes."
   But surely Thou didst hear
    My loud supplications,
     When I cried to Thee for help!

[7] See Mowinckel, op. cit., I, 152.
[8] So Schmidt finely renders mērukhesê, literally "snares, bands."

In verses 23-24 the summons and warning of the priestly choir follow upon the vow of the suppliant who has been restored. This part lifts the individual psalmist's experience into the meaning it should have—and the warning as well —for the whole congregation. It emphasizes the just retribution of God, both in blessing and punishment, and summons the congregation of those who wait upon Him to do it with trustful and resolute hearts.

23 Love the Lord, all His loyal ones;
   The Lord stands guard over His faithful ones,
   And punishes the others
   Who act insolently.
24 Be strong, and make your heart firm,
   All you who wait for the Lord!

Ps. 35. SAY TO MY SOUL, "I AM THY SALVATION"

In Ps. 35 a judicial procedure is implied. Malicious and criminal witnesses have risen against the suppliant, testifiying that he is guilty of what he actually knows nothing about (vs. 11). Indeed they swear that they were eyewitnesses to his crime (vs. 21). They are seeking his life. Schmidt says: "In these ancient times justice was harsh and incalculable, and punishment by death quite customary, evidently at little provocation." [9]

The psalm opens with the suppliant's appeal to God as the righteous Judge. Ill [10] and falsely accused, he is on trial before the Lord. He pours out his petition to God to fight on his behalf against his accusers. Imaginatively he pictures God armed with weapons, taking his side against his persecutors! He cries:

1 Conduct my case, O Lord;
   Fight those who are fighting me:
2 Seize shield and buckler,
   And arise to help me!
3 Draw out the spear and battle-ax
   To confront those pursuing me!
   Say, O Lord, to my soul,
   "I am thy salvation."

In fashion quite characteristic of Hebrew thought he utters passionate wishes— not so strong as to be called curses—against those pursuing him. His words suggest how insecure, how insubstantial are these evil men who have accused him falsely. How vivid are his pictures of what he desires them to experience! Only an Oriental would say it thus:

4 Let those who are seeking my life
   Stand ashamed and humiliated:
   Let those who are plotting evil for me

[9] *Das Gebet der Angeklagten*, p. 37.
[10] So we infer from the suppliant's argument in vss. 13-14.

> Be driven backward and abashed.
> 5a Let them be as chaff before wind,
> 6b   And may Thy angel, O Lord, pursue them.
> 6a Let their way be slippery,
> 5b   And may Thy angel push them violently,
> 7 For they have laid their net for me without cause;
>   Yes, they have dug a pit for my soul.
> 8 But may their net which they have laid catch them;
>   Let them fall into the pit!

Conscious of his innocence, yet fully aware of the bodily peril at enemy hands in which he stands, he has such confidence that the Lord will rescue him that he vows unto God a song of thanksgiving. The psalmist stands under the influence of that stream of prophetic thought (cf. Pss. 40; 51; 69) which viewed a heartfelt song of thanks as more acceptable to God than a thank offering. Gradually the vow to sing a song of thanksgiving unto the Lord displaced the vow to sacrifice a thank offering unto Him.[11] Thus he vows:

> 9 But my soul shall rejoice in the Lord:
>   It shall exult in His help.
> 28 My tongue shall speak of Thy vindication,[12]
>   All the day in praise of Thee.
> 10 All my bodily members shall say,
>   "O Lord, who is like Thee,
>   Who rescues the poor from one too strong for him,
>   Yes, the poor and needy from one robbing him?"

The psalmist moves back to the theme of lament (vss. 11-16) and in great detail pictures his situation. His accusers present witnesses before the Lord's priest and falsely charge the accused with a crime of which he knows nothing. With a sense of stark injustice rankling in his soul he reveals an element in his situation that makes his unjust suffering at his accusers' hands all the more painful. They were formerly his friends. When they were sick, he suffered with them, prayed and fasted in their behalf as though they were his intimate friends or relatives. How different their unfeeling treatment of him; just as though he were a foreigner, they hurl at him profane insults!

> 11 They present witnesses supporting violence;
>   They ask me of that which I know not.
> 12 They pay me back evil for good;
>   They lie in wait for my life.
> 13 But *I* when *they* were sick put on sackcloth:
>   I castigated my soul;
>   My prayers kept returning to my lips.

---

[11] See Gunkel, *Einleitung*, p. 248.

[12] Such is the objective force of righteousness here. Vs. 28 rightly belongs with vs. 9, as Gunkel and Schmidt have seen.

14　As though for my friend, my brother, I went about
　　As one mourning for a mother, bowed down in black.
15　But when I stumble, they rejoice and flock together;
　　　They gather against me,
　　Like foreigners whom I do not know:
　　They hiss and keep not silent.
16　As the profane, they derisively mock:
　　　They gnash with their teeth.

Suddenly comes his petition, but introduced by the sure mark of lamentation, "How long?" [13] In the presence of these brutal enemies he feels as though he were faced with lions roaring as they leap upon their prey! Already he sees his enemies winking at each other, their eyes aglint with triumph.

17a　O Lord, how long wilt Thou look upon
19b　　Those who hate me without cause;
17b　Rescue my life from these roaring ones,
　　　My soul [14] from the lions!
19a　Let not my enemies, who wink their eyes,
　　　Rejoice in their fraud.

Again he lapses into the mood of lament, as was the case in verses 11-16. He is cut to the quick by their corrupt and baseless testimony. They have manufactured their accusation against him. It is groundless, yet they testify that they have seen him do that with which they have charged him.

20　For not of peace do they speak
　　　To the quiet in the land.
21　They devise treacherous words,
　　　And they fling open their mouth against me.
　　They say, "Aha! Aha!
　　　With our eyes we have seen it!"

From the irreverent, unfeeling, shameless accusers, so false and unrighteous, the psalmist turns unto God, the righteous Judge, in whose vindication of his innocence he has firm confidence. And there is intensity in his appeal. We feel the desperation of his need as he calls upon God to awake on his behalf and render His favorable decision. And he prays that when He vindicates His loyal servant, He may bring utter humiliation and disgrace upon his persecutors. Thus the psalmist cries:

22　But as for Thee, O Lord, be not silent;
　　　My Lord, be not far from me!
23　Rouse Thyself, and awake for my cause,
　　　My God, for my dispute.
24　See justice done me [15] according as thou art righteous, O Lord.

[13] Omit vs. 18 as an intrusive insertion.
[14] Literally "my only one"; cf. Ps. 22:20.
[15] This is the correct force of "judge me"; so rightly, Buttenwieser.

> Do not let them rejoice over me.
> 25 Let them not say in their heart,
> "Aha! we have what we desired!"
> Let them not say, "We have swallowed him up!"
> 26 Let those who are rejoicing in my misfortune
> Be disconcerted and simultaneously abashed!
> May those who are doing great evil against me
> Be clothed with shame and disgrace!

The psalm closes with a brief hymn of praise to God, which the members of the Lord's congregation, those who will take delight in the psalmist's vindication, are to sing upon his deliverance.

> 27 Let those who take delight in my vindication
> Sing and rejoice;
> And let them continually say,
> "May the Lord be magnified, who takes pleasure
> In the welfare of His servant!"

Ps. 38. LET NOT MY SIGHING BE HIDDEN FROM THEE

At the time when the superscriptions to the individual psalms were inserted, Ps. 38 was rendered as an accompaniment to the presentation of that portion of the cereal offering which, mingled with oil, was burned with incense upon the altar as a "memorial offering" (*'azkārāh*). Its purpose was to bring to the Lord's remembrance the distress of the sufferer.[16] We have here a lament of one suffering from an acute skin disease. He views his experience from a standpoint which, previous to the challenge it met in the book of Job, was one of the foundation pillars of Old Testament piety, that all suffering is punishment for sin. In his severe illness he sees the proof of his own wrongdoing. From his physical distress he cries out unto God:

> 1 O Lord, correct me not in Thy wrath,
> And chastise me not in Thine anger.

In figurative terms he vividly describes his physical condition. But the consciousness that he has sinned lies heavy upon his heart and sharpens the poignancy of his pain, for he is aware of the stern pressure of God's vindictive hand upon him.

> 2 For Thine arrows have penetrated into me,
> And Thy hand has come down hard upon me.
> 3 There is no soundness in my flesh because of Thine indignation,
> And no peace in my bones because of my sin.
> 4 For my iniquities have gone over my head:
> Like a heavy load they are too severe for me.
> 5 My wounds stink; they fester
> Because of my folly.

---

[16] Cf. Mowinckel, *op. cit.,* IV, 15-16.

6 I am bowed down; I am utterly prostrate:
   All the day I tramp along dark in mourning.
7 For my loins are full of burning,
   And there is no soundness in my flesh.
8 I am numbed and utterly crushed;
   My cry is louder than a lion's roar.
9 Lord, before Thee is all my lamentation,
   And my sighing is not hidden from Thee.
10 My heart palpitates; my strength has forsaken me;
   And the light of my eyes is gone.

The severity of his suffering is augmented by the conduct toward him of his intimate and trusted friends. His very condition has marked him out in their eyes as sinful before God. Those from whom he might normally expect sympathy stand aloof. He feels isolated and alone. But worse than that, deeming him under the punishing rod of God, his friends let their imaginations run riot as they deliberate over him and devise what he must have done to be reduced to such a condition (vss. 11-12). Over against them, keenly sensing their change in feeling toward him, yet at the same time turning a deaf ear to their false and baseless indictments, he looks expectantly to his God in certainty of His answering help.[17]

11 My friends approach me, aloof;
   And my neighbors stand at a distance.
12 They strike at [me]; they speak engulfing ruin;
   And they utter treachery all the day.
13 But I am as a deaf person who does not hear,
   And like a dumb person who does not open his mouth.
15 For I wait on Thee, O Lord;
   Thou wilt answer, my God.

Following this apologia for his bearing toward his revilers under persecution, he tells how he appealed to God with a threefold inducement: (a) God must not let him down in his delicate and treacherous situation (vss. 16-17). Those who are (now) his enemies have become many. With no adequate basis for their hostility they have flung him out as something abhorrent and are just waiting for calamity to claim him. (b) Again, the psalmist has confessed his sin (vs. 18). What it was he does not tell us, and indeed he does not reveal any deep-seated awareness of concrete sins that he has committed. Yet to the pious soul of his day no one could suffer as he is doing were his sin not considered great. Accordingly, feeling the load of it upon his soul (vss. 3-5) as he stands in anxious terror before God, he confesses that he has sinned and thus opens the way for his restoration to the favor of God. (c) Moreover, in spite of this burden of sin he knows that, compared with his treacherous enemies who are requiting good with evil, he has steadily pursued the good (vss. 19-20).

[17] Omitting vs. 14 as an explanatory variant.

16 I said, "So that they shall not rejoice over me,
>
> If my foot should slip; [so that] they shall not deride me,

17 For calamity lies just waiting for me to stumble,
>
> And my pain is continually present with me;

18 I confess my iniquity;
>
> I am anxious because of my sin."

19 And those hostile to me without cause are numerous;
>
> Yes, those who wrongfully hate me are many.

20 Those who return evil for good
>
> Accuse me because I pursue the good.
>
> Yes, they flung me out, me the loved one, like an abhorred carcass.

This threefold inducement likewise provides to some extent the motivation of his final petition. Yet while he thus appeals to God on the basis of his own conduct under undeserved persecution, this is not the real ground of his confidence. "This rests in God alone, in His will to help." [18] So the psalmist's lament reaches its climax in a passionate petition for God's presence and succor.

21 Forsake me not, O Lord;
>
> My God, be not far distant from me.

22 Hasten to my help,
>
> O Lord, my salvation!

Ps. 41. I KNOW THOU ART MINDFUL OF ME

This psalm springs out of the deep spiritual experience of a poor and needy worshiper of the Lord who, when languishing upon his bed of illness, enjoyed a wonderful release. It begins in a song of thanksgiving. Deeply moved by his gratitude, the psalmist cries:

1 Oh the happiness of him who takes account of God, though poor and needy:
>
> In the day of distress the Lord will deliver him.

2 He keeps him and preserves him alive in the land,
>
> And does not give him up to the desire of his enemies.

3 The Lord supports him upon his bed of languishing:
>
> All his pain He turns into strength.

Suddenly the singer transports us back to that dark hour of pain and crisis which drove him to God. Now we see that something far more than his illness stirred him to prayer. That illness was the occasion of a false accusation on the part of one who, once his friend, had become his deceitful enemy. In the Orient it is considered a duty on the part of the friends of a sick man to pay him a visit.[19] So this smooth-tongued friend while visiting him made a pretense of comforting him. Then the friend went out and broadcasted falsehoods concocted against the psalmist, whispered with others about him, and thus poured out infamous

---

[18] Schmidt, *Die Psalmen*, p. 73.   [19] Meissner, *op. cit.*, II, 318.

gossip to those who were only too ready to believe the worst. His sickness was pointed to as an indication that because of some sin God marked him out for punishment, yes, for death. In that crisis hour he poured out to God his lament:

> 4 But as for me, I said, "O Lord, be gracious to me:
>   Heal my body, for I seek refuge in Thee."
> 5 My enemy speaks evil against me, [saying],
>   "When will he die and his name perish!"
> 6 But when he comes to see me, he speaks deceitful consolation;
>   He assembles lies; he publishes them abroad.
> 7 All who hate me whisper together against me;
>   They concoct evil against me.
> 8 An infernal thing they pour out against me, [saying]:
>   "From where he now lies he will never rise again!"
> 9 Even an intimate friend, in whom I trusted,
>   Who ate at my table, is bigmouthed against me.

In his dire distress the suppliant pours out his passionate appeal for vindication. And, driven by his outraged consciousness of innocence, he even prays for the opportunity to wreak vengeance upon his false accusers.

> 10 But, O Lord, be Thou gracious to me and lift me up,
>   That I may pay them back.

It is no perfect prayer, for vengeance belongs to God. Yet it comes from an outraged soul who feels that he is being dealt with in rank injustice, so we can understand his bitter mood, even though we may not approve it.

Wonderful indeed is God's answer to His humble worshiper in that dark hour. To him there comes the deep inner assurance of the Lord's mindful care and of his future vindication and approval before the very eyes of his enemy. He is dear to God. It is from this profound inner spiritual experience of God that he utters his confession of faith in God's care and abiding support:

> 11 By this I know that Thou art mindful of me,
>   That my enemy shall not shout in triumph over me.
> 12 Yes, as for me, Thou dost support me in my integrity
>   And dost set me before Thee forever.

It is little wonder that so great an experience has caused the psalmist to begin with a burst of thankfulness.

Verse 13 is not part of this psalm, but is a doxology which closes the first book of the Psalter:

> 13 Blessed be the Lord, God of Israel,
>   From everlasting even to everlasting!
>   Amen and amen.

Ps. 69. LET THY HELP SET ME SAFELY ON HIGH

In Ps. 69 the suppliant has been accused of theft by men who are persecuting him. But he is innocent, and we feel the outraged justice in his soul as in bitter irony he cries:

> What I did not rob,
> This am I to restore! (vs. 4.)

He is charged with guilt. He prays the Lord that He will vindicate his innocence, that He will redeem his life, and that He will set him free (vs. 18). He knows the seriousness of his situation. "The knife of an accuser who can bring upon him the punishment of death is at his throat."[20] But the distress of his situation is augmented by his illness. Already God has smitten him—such is his own interpretation of his pain. And this makes all the more bitter the persecution he is suffering. Says he:

> But I am weak and in pain:
> For they persecute him whom Thou hast smitten;
> Yes, they increase the pain of him who was pierced by Thee. (vss. 29a, 26.)

It is to be inferred that his accuser sees in this illness God's indication that he is guilty. The psalmist himself believes that some guilt, some folly, is in question. His very condition is for him sufficient evidence of it. But he is just as sure that it is not the sin of theft, that with which he has been charged. Moreover, the psalmist is well aware that before his illness his zeal for the Lord made him the butt of derision from his godless enemies. It was his illness, however, that gave them the welcomed opportunity to accuse him of guilt.

Death seems near. Already, in his vivid Oriental imagination, his feet are in the slippery, miry clay of Sheol, the land of the dead, which is flooded by the "waters . . . , the stream" of the underworld (Ps. 124:4). It is a suggestive picture also of his psychological insecurity. He cries to God in his crisis (vs. 1a), then pours out his lament before Him (vss. 1b-4).

> 1 Help me, O God, for waters
>   Are come up to my neck.
> 2 I sink down in deep mire,
>   And there is no foothold.
>   I am come into deep waters,
>   And the stream sweeps me off.

The reason for his insecurity soon becomes clear. He is beset by enemies, numerous and full of hate, who are accusing him of robbery. His voice is wearied from calling unto God; his spirit is tired from hope of help deferred; and in lamenting mood he maintains his innocency of the accusation.

> 3 I am weary from crying;
>   My throat is parched:
>   My eyes are exhausted
>   By waiting for my God.

[20] Schmidt, *Das Gebet der Angeklagten*, p. 33.

4 More than the hairs of my head
  Are those who hate me without reason:
  More in number than my bones
  Are those who are wrongfully my enemies
  What I did not rob,
  This am I to restore!

He admits that he has done wrong, and that God is aware of it. But there is a strong sense of social responsibility in his guilt, for he thinks first of the Lord's community of loyal worshipers—"those who wait on Thee"—of which he feels himself a part, and prays that his life may not bring disgrace upon them nor lead them to be ashamed of him. The psalmist is clearly a leader in the congregation.

5 O God, Thou knowest my sin;
  Yes, my wrongdoings are not hidden from Thee.
6 May those who wait on Thee not be ashamed of me,
  O Lord of hosts.
  And may those who seek Thee not be disgraced by me,
  O God of Israel.

Back to the mood of lament the psalmist turns, and we are informed of the humiliation he is now suffering. His religious acts of devotion, his scrupulous attention to religious rites, and his zeal for the Temple and its services are being derided as insincere. His name is bandied about both in the gossip of the elders in the gate and in the taunt songs of drunkards. Sharp and deep is his own conviction that his sufferings are really in behalf of God, borne because of his loyalty to God and his people. So he cries:

7 For on behalf of Thee, I endure insult;
  Humiliation covers my face.
8 I am estranged from my brothers;
  Yes, I am as a foreigner to my mother's sons,
9 For the zeal of Thy house has consumed me,
  And the taunts of those who despise Thee have fallen on me.
10 Though I have humbled my soul with fasting,
   It has become a disgrace to me.
11 Though I have made sackcloth my raiment,
   I have become to them a butt of derision.
12 Those sitting in the gate talk against me,
   And I am a taunt of those who drink strong drink.

His lament turns to petition. It is eager and intense, for the time is short. He feels, as at the beginning, that the stream of death and the mire of the underworld are at the point of swallowing him up. He appeals to God, to His mercy, His compassion, and His faithfulness. Only in God has he hope. Only He can rescue, redeem, and free him. So the psalmist cries to God to answer him, speedily to redeem and ransom him, to set him free.

13 But as for me, my prayer comes to Thee
    In an acceptable time, O God;
    Answer me in the greatness of Thy mercy
    With Thy faithful help.
14 Save me from the mire; let me not sink down;
    Lift me up from the deep waters.
15 Let not the stream [of death] sweep me off,
    And let not the deep swallow me up.
    Let not the pit shut its mouth over me.
16 Answer me, O Lord, in Thy merciful goodness.
    Turn to me in Thy great compassion.
17 Hide not Thy face from Thy servant;
    For I am in trouble; hasten to answer me!
18 Draw near my life to redeem it:
    Ransom me because of my enemies.

In the next verses (19-21) he deals with these enemies. Vividly he describes their insulting taunts, not one of them proffering sympathy. His very life is imperiled by the food and drink they give him. He laments to God. We feel the great sensitiveness of his spiritual nature.

19 Thou knowest my insult;
    All my adversaries are in Thy sight.
20 Their taunt breaks my heart;
    Yes, my shame and my humiliation are incurable.
    I look for one to show sympathy, but there is none;
    I look for comforters but find them not.
21 But they put poison in my food,
    And they make me drink vinegar for my thirst.

His lament moves to a lower moral level, from description of his accusers and persecutors to terrible curses upon them. Here is hot emotion fired by the strong Semitic feeling that evil is self-destructive, that injustice comes back in retribution upon its perpetrator. The psalmist calls down upon them execrations proportioned to what he has experienced at their hands.

22 Let their table, spread out, become a trap,
    And their sacrificial feasts a snare.
23 Let their eyes go blind, so they cannot see;
    And make their thighs continually totter.
24 Pour out upon them Thine indignation;
    Yes, let Thy hot anger overtake them.
25 Let their dwelling be desolated;
    Let there be no inhabitant in their tents.
26 For they persecute him whom Thou hast smitten;
    Yes, they increase the pain of him who was pierced by Thee.
27 Give them iniquity for iniquity;
    Let them not experience Thy vindication.
28 Let them be blotted out of the book of life;
    Let them not be listed with the righteous.

Back to his own physical condition of weakness and pain he turns for a moment and cries out to God for rescue and vindication:

> 29 But I am weak and in pain:
>   Let Thy help, O God, set me safely on high.

Suddenly the tone of the psalm changes from lament and petition to a song of thanksgiving. At this point in the worship occurs the priestly oracle, assuring to the suppliant God's answer to his prayer. This is responsible for his sudden turn in mood.[21] In deep spiritual certainty and in profound gratitude he lifts his song of thanksgiving. His simple song of gratitude is, he thinks, more acceptable to God than animal sacrifice. We are conscious here of a development in thought that was influenced by the great prophets from Amos through Jeremiah (cf. Amos 5:21-24; Hos. 6:6; Isa. 1:11-17; Mic. 6:6-8; Jer. 7:21-23), but also by developing psalmody.

> 30 I will praise the name of God in a song;
>   I will extol him with a song of thanks.
> 31 And it will be more pleasing to the Lord than an ox,
>   Than a horned bullock with cloven hoofs.

The psalmist is in the congregation of the Lord's worshipers. To them he turns. He gives his heartfelt testimony as to what God has done for him in lifting his soul into certainty.

> 32 See it, you humble ones, and rejoice:
>   You who seek Him, let your hearts live.
> 33 For the Lord hears the needy,
>   And does not disdain his loyal ones.

His praise song leads into a hymn, which brings the psalm to its close. The wonder of God's dealing with his own life leads the psalmist to the certainty of God's eventual deliverance of Zion from its distress and the restoration of the Judean cities in abiding stability across the generations. Clearly we are here in the fifth century B.C.

> 34 Let heaven and earth praise Him,
>   The seas and every creeping thing in them.
> 35 For God will deliver Zion
>   And will rebuild the cities of Judah.
> 36   And they shall dwell there and take possession of it;
>   The descendants of His servants shall inherit it;
>   And those who love His name shall abide in it.

Ps. 71. I HAVE SEEN GOD'S HAND THROUGH A LIFETIME

The situation of the psalmist in Ps. 71 is clear. He is an elderly man who has experienced God's help throughout a lifetime. He has been in many and grave

---

[21] Cf. Küchler, *op. cit.*, p. 285; Gunkel, *Einleitung*, p. 246; and Jer. 15:15-21, where we have such an oracle (vss. 19-21) after a lamenting prayer (vss. 15-18).

troubles and is now suffering under an illness that is threatening his life. Moreover, he feels the shame of his condition and considers it an indication that God's wrath rests on him. But more, his life is in the power of godless enemies, ruthless and unjust, men who are lying in wait for him and conspiring against him, as against one who has been abandoned by his God. The psalm is composed of three parts, each containing eight verses.

In the first part of the psalm (vss. 1-8) the theme of trust and confidence in God predominates, and it closes with a shout of joy. The psalmist turns to the Lord for refuge from his sense of shame and insecurity and from the power of his ruthless and unjust foes. In his great need he depends upon the righteousness of God, which is to him the real fountain of his confidence. God has been his support throughout his life, yes, even before his birth, while his body was being fashioned in the womb of his mother. And in spite of his present great need he gives constant praise unto God. Thus he expresses his trust:

1   In Thee, O Lord, I seek refuge:
    Let me never be ashamed.
2   In Thy righteousness deliver me and make me secure:
    Bend down Thy ear unto me
      And help me.
3   Be to me a rock of refuge,
    A mighty fortress to save me,
      For Thou art my crag and my stronghold.
4   My God, rescue me from the hand of the godless,
    From the power of the unjust and ruthless.
5   For Thou art my hope, O Lord,
    My confidence from my youth, O God.
6   Upon Thee have I been supported from the womb;
    From the body of my mother Thou hast been my refuge:
      My praise song is continually of Thee.
7   I am as a solemn portent to many,
    But Thou art my strong refuge.
8   My mouth is filled with Thy praise,
    With Thy renown all the day.

In the second part of the psalm (vss. 9-16) the mood of lamentation prevails, but at its close comes a larger and fuller song of jubilation (vss. 14-16). The psalmist is old; his strength is far gone. His enemies lie in ambush to seize him, and we can hear their exulting words as they glory in the thought that even God has abandoned him. But the psalmist prays to the Lord for help, urging Him to bring chagrin and humiliation upon his enemies. In a vow of thanksgiving over the anticipated relief from God, he pledges himself to add his praise to all other praises of the Lord. He will tell the story of His mighty acts and righteous deeds, for God has taken account of his sad state, and blessings received at His hand "baffle description." Thus he laments and entreats his God:

9　Fling me not away in the time of old age;
　　　Forsake me not when my strength is spent.
10　For my enemies lie in wait for me,
　　　And those who keep watching my soul conspire together.
11　"God has abandoned him," [they say;]
　　　"Pursue and lay hold on him,
　　　　For there is no one to rescue him."
12　O God, be not far from me;
　　　O my God, hasten to help me.
13　Let the accusers of my life be ashamed;
　　　Let them wrap themselves with disgrace and insult.
14　But, as for me, I will hope continually
　　　And will add to all Thy praises.
15　My mouth will recount Thy righteousness,
　　　All the day Thy deliverance,
　　　　Though I know that they baffle description.[22]
16　I will pour forth the mighty acts of the Lord;
　　　I will make mention of Thy righteous deeds, Thine alone.

A song of thanksgiving in hymnic form makes up the third section of the psalm (vss. 17-24). And here we see that this aged man is a skilled poet, one who from youth to old age has been taught of God how to declare effectively the wonderful deeds of the Lord's mighty arm. He has much within his soul still to utter and longs for life that he may have the chance to declare God's might and his righteous character to the coming generations. In a moving retrospect he tells of his long life, during which he has experienced the grace of God. From troubles multitudinous and severe, wherein he was so near the gates of death that he could hear in imagination the floods of the underworld, he was repeatedly released and restored. How great was his deliverance! And now *again* he is confident of God's answer to his prayer, so he will thank the Holy One with song and music and will utter the story of God's vindication of him before his humiliated foes. Thus he sings:

17　O God, Thou hast taught me from my youth,
　　　And until now I declare Thy wondrous deeds.
18　Yes, and even until old age and hoary hair;
　　　O God, forsake me not,
　　　Until I declare Thine arm to all the generations to come,
18d-19　Thy might and Thy righteousness unto the height,
　　　Because Thou hast done great things;
　　　　O God, who is like Thee?
20　Thou hast caused me to experience many and grave troubles;
　　　Thou wilt restore me to life;
　　　And from the floods of the underworld
　　　　Thou wilt bring me up again;
21　　Thou makest my redemption great.

[22] So Buttenwieser suggestively translates, basing it on the Septuagint, πραγματίας.

22 In return I will thank Thee on a harp
    For Thy faithfulness, O God;
    I will sing to Thee with lyre,
    Thou Holy One of Israel.

23 My lips will give a ringing cry,
    And my soul, which Thou didst redeem;

24 Also my tongue all the day
    Shall speak of Thy vindication,
    That they are ashamed, that they are abashed,
    Who seek my disaster.

Ps. 86. PERFORM IN ME A GRACIOUS SIGN

Ps. 86 is a lament of a devout and lowly worshiper of the Lord. He is one of the congregation who "call upon" Him and is the son of a pious woman in Israel (vs. 16c). He implies that he has committed transgression, yet he is not oppressed by the burden of unpardoned sin, because from experience he knows the merciful forgiveness of God. Day after day and all through the days he has kept crying unto God to gladden his burdened soul (vs. 4), to answer his earnest prayers (vs. 6). But now this continuous sorrow has come to its climax in the day of his trouble (vs. 7).

1 Incline Thine ear, O Lord, answer me,
   For poor and needy am I.

2 Guard my soul, for I am loyal:
   Save Thy servant who trusts in Thee.

3 Be gracious to me, O Lord; Thou art my God,
   For to Thee I cry all the day.

4 Gladden the soul of Thy servant, O Lord,
   For to Thee I lift my soul.

5 For Thou, Lord, art good and forgiving,
   And rich in mercy to all who cry to Thee.

6 Listen, O Lord, to my prayer;
   Give heed to the voice of my supplications.

7 In the day of my trouble I cry to Thee,
   For Thou dost answer me.

In verses 14-17, which, as Schmidt has shown,[23] originally followed verses 1-7, we learn yet more concretely the nature of the psalmist's trouble. His life is in grave peril at the hand of enemies, insolent and terrifying, who have risen up against him and have falsely accused him. They are godless (vs. 14c) and ruthless (vs. 14b). His peril is real.

In the day of his trouble, that is, the day when their enmity has reached a crisis he turns unto God and seeks His protection. He prays that God may give him a sign (*'ôth*), some favorable omen, whether by dream[24] or by a priestly

[23] *Die Psalmen*, p. 162.
[24] Cf. Jastrow, *Die Religion Babyloniens und Assyriens*, II, 95.

oracle, by which he will be vindicated and will receive the assurance of God's help and protection. Thus he pours out his lament unto God:

> 14 O God, insolent men have risen up against me;
> A pack of terrorizers seek my life,
> But they have not set Thee before them.
> 15 But Thou art a God compassionate and gracious,
> Slow to get angry, and of great mercy and faithfulness.
> 16b Give Thy protection to Thy servant,
> 16c And help the son of Thy handmaid.
> 16a Turn to me, and be gracious to me.
> 17 Perform in me a gracious sign,
> So those who hate me may see and be ashamed,
> For Thou, O Lord, dost help me and comfort me.

He has great certainty that God, in response to his prayer of importunity in the Temple, will give him his sign which will vindicate him and humiliate his enemies. This assurance leads the psalmist into a hymn of praise of this God (vss. 8-10), whose mighty deeds will *at length* win even all nations unto Himself. This is a unique theme in the psalm, inspired by the assurance of the psalmist's own confidence. It gives expression to the high enthusiasm of faith in God's ultimate triumph in the whole world. Sings the psalmist:

> 8 There is none like Thee among the gods, O Lord,
> And none like Thy deeds which Thou doest.
> 9 All nations will come,
> And prostrate themselves before Thee,
> And glorify Thy name, O Lord.
> 10 For Thou art great, One who does marvels:
> Thou alone art God!

The psalm ends in a song of personal thanksgiving (vss. 12-13) for what the psalmist has himself experienced. The transition to this song of thanks is the beautiful prayer of verse 11:

> 11 Show me Thy way, that I may walk in Thy truth,
> That my heart may rejoice to revere Thy name.

The tone of the thanksgiving and the change from prayerful and hopeful expectation to certainty leads us to infer that the "sign" for which he prayed has been granted him. So in a glad song of release he sings forth his thanksgiving unto God:

> 12 I will give Thee thanks, O God, with my whole heart,
> And I will glorify Thy name forever.
> 13 For Thy mercy is great toward me,
> And Thou hast snatched my soul from the deep realm [25] of death.

[25] Literally "from the lowest Sheol."

Ps. 102 is a psalm of one who is ill, and its superscription accurately describes its use. It is "a prayer to be used by an unfortunate person when he is in distress and pours out his lament before the Lord." [26] The one offering the prayer is desperately sick, emaciated, and near unto death. He cries out to God in his distress:

> 1 O Lord, hear my prayer;
>   Let my cry come to Thee.
> 2 Turn not away Thy face;
>   Give attention in the day of my distress:
>   Incline Thine ear to me;
>   In the day when I cry, hasten to answer me.

He describes his ailment vividly and in considerable detail. It is, as Ehrlich has noted, of an intestinal nature. It gives the psalmist acute pain which forces moans and groans from his lips. He has no appetite and is steadily losing weight. He cannot sleep and spends the long night in lonely lamentation.

> 3 For my inwards have wasted away like a cloud,
>   And my bones burn like a hearth.
> 4 My heart is withered like the grass;
>   I have grown thin, not eating my food.
> 5 I am weary of the sound of my groaning:
>   My skin cleaves to my bones.
> 6 I am like a pelican of the wilderness;
>   I am like an owl in the ruins.
> 7 I am wakeful, and I lament all alone,
>   Like a solitary bird on the roof.

His physical pain is augmented by two things. He is being taunted by enemies in whose eyes he is already as good as dead, so that they use his name as an example when they wish to lay upon someone a curse to bring about that person's sudden death.[27] So what little food he consumes he eats in tears, his body the while being covered with ashes. As his life energy gradually oozes out, he feels that God has cast him off in wrath.

> 8   All the day my enemies taunt me;
>   Those who make a fool of me curse by me.
> 9   For I eat ashes with my food,
>   And I mix tears with my drink,
> 10 Because of Thine indignation and Thy wrath,
>   For Thou hast picked me up and cast me off.
> 11 My days decline like a shadow,
>   And as for me, I wither like grass.

Often in the psalms of lament the psalmist is accustomed to recall the nature and the deeds of God in order to raise himself up from his depression, and such

---

[26] Cf. Mowinckel, *op. cit.*, I, 166.   [27] Cf. Schmidt, *Die Psalmen*, p. 184.

words, as here, take the form of a hymn of praise to God. When his life seems so fragile and insecure, from the poignancy of his own personal suffering "he flees to the majestic past of his nation" [28] and finds in the God of that noble history something steadying and reassuring:

12 But Thou dwellest forever,
    And Thy throne unto the future ages.

In his uncertainty as to his own immediate future the psalmist comforts himself with the certainty held in prophetic faith. He does not pray for God to intervene. He says God *will* arise—it is a strong prophetic word—and show to Zion, the community of the faithful, His favor. Nor does he say the time of prophetic hope is now at hand. It is to him, as to the prophets, still in the future. But to him, as to them, it is *certain*. He *will come* to Zion's help because His true servants love her very stones! And when He comes and restores the community of the faithful, rebuilds Zion and establishes anew His residence in her midst, it will be in response to the prayers and supplications of the destitute. It will attract the attention of the nations and kings of the earth! The psalmist's own generation will not experience it, but future generations will. So he sings his hymn of hope unto God:

13 Thou wilt arise, wilt have compassion on Zion,
    For the time will come to show her favor,
14 For Thy servants take pleasure in her stones,
    And toward her ruins they direct [their] compassion.
15 The nations shall see Thy fame, O Lord,
    And all the kings of the earth Thy glory.
16 For the Lord will rebuild Zion;
    He will appear in her midst in His glory.
17 He will turn to the prayer of the destitute,
    And will not scorn their supplication.
18 This is written for the generation to come,
    And a people yet to be created [29] shall praise the Lord.

The words that follow (vss. 19-22) are the theme of this hymn of praise imaginatively put into the mouth of that privileged future generation. The Lord, who aloft in the heavens had seemed so far from His suffering people, now looks down upon the earth, hears the groans of the prisoners unjustly incarcerated, and sets them free! The effect of this mighty emancipation will be that the nations and kingdoms of the world will gather in Jerusalem to praise the Lord and recount what He has done.

19 For the Lord looks down from His holy height;
    From the heavens He looks upon the earth

[28] Cf. Gunkel, *Einleitung*, p. 258.
[29] Cf. Gesenius-Kautzsch, *op. cit.*, sec. 116e, where the niphal participle is equivalent to the Latin gerundive.

20   To hear the groaning of the prisoner;
       To set free those condemned to die;
21   So that men may recount the fame of the Lord in Zion
       And his praise in Jerusalem
22   When the nations assemble themselves together,
       And the kingdoms, to serve the Lord.

From such steadying and inspiring thoughts the psalmist now comes back to his own fragile hold upon life. He longs to live, yet he seems sure that his life span is limited, for he knows the nature of his disease. So in passionate petition he prays that his life be not taken away when only half of it has been lived.

23a   My strength has been brought low, so that it cannot last; [30]
23b-24a   The brevity of my days has been imparted to me.
24b   Take me not away at the half of my days!

Again his thoughts move from brief, intense lament over the untimely death awaiting him to the contrasted eternity of God. Through beautiful words of hymnic tones the short span of his own days is contrasted with the eternity of God. It is the same contrast that we have noted at verse 12, where the psalmist's own transience turns him for refuge to the permanence and security of God, except that here the idea of the eternity of God is developed with noble thoughts spoken in majestic tones:

24c   Thou, whose years embrace the generations [31]
25   Of old, Thou didst establish the earth,
       And the heavens are the work of Thy hands.
26   They shall perish, but Thou shalt abide;
       They shall all wear out like a garment;
       Thou wilt change them like a garment, and they shall pass away.
27   But Thou art, and Thy years have no end.

Just as the earlier hymn of comfort based upon the optimism of prophecy looked ahead in imagination to the future generation which would experience the intervention of God, so the psalmist ends with the similar contemplation of that generation yet to come. Then the descendants of the Lord's present servants will experience a life not brief but of settled permanence, not a fragile and uncertain existence but one secure and established.

28   The children of Thy servants shall settle permanently,
       And their descendants shall be established before Thee.

Thus we see in this great psalm a unified and artistic whole. Starting in lamentation and petition, it moves into a brief hymn celebrating the Lord's eternity and into a prediction of the certain ultimate redemption of the community of the faithful, which is actually to be experienced only by the future

[30] I follow here Gunkel's reconstruction of vss. 23-24b, chiefly on basis of the Septuagint.
[31] Cf. Brown, Driver, Briggs, op. cit., p. 190, dôr, "apparently including both past and future."

generation. Starting again in lamentation and petition (vs. 23), it moves into a noble hymn of the Lord's eternity, climaxing in the glorious experience which awaits the future generation.

Moreover, this psalm teaches us how the Temple worship sought to lift the mind of the individual from immersion in his own personal lot to contemplation of life as a whole, and from his own uncertain foothold in life to the sureness and dependability of God. Such a psalm would likewise have its own intent and mission in teaching the Israelite sufferer that his life and his lot had solidarity with the lot of God's people as a whole, and therefore the attitude he took in facing his own misfortune was socially important.

Only men who knew at firsthand the experience of sickness and tried to see it in the divine light could have written such psalms. They must have written them in order to help people in similar dire and desperate need to lay hold upon the help of the living God.

Ps. 109. THEY WRONGFULLY OPPOSE ME, BUT I PRAY

The psalmist, who, as verse 1 implies—"O God, whom I praise"—is accustomed to come into the sanctuary along with the worshiping throng, is now there for a quite different purpose. He has been compelled to come and has come alone. He has been accused by godless and ruthless men with whom he has dealt from a heart of love. The accusations being hurled at him are groundless. His accusers have returned to him evil for good. All he can do is to pray. So from this tense situation, and in deep need, he cries unto God:

1 O God, whom I praise, keep not silent,
2   For they have opened mouths full of malice against me.
   They have spoken against me with lying tongues
3   And have surrounded me with words of hate.
   Yes, they fight with me for no reason;
4   In return for my love they oppose me,
        But I pray! [32]
5 They have paid back evil for good,
   And hate for my love.

Yet his petition does not follow at once, for his soul is too heavy with these harsh charges and accusations of his opponents. So before he takes upon himself in the presence of God the oath in which he swears to his innocence (vs. 20) he has the right to call upon God in his own behalf.

Verses 6-19, as Schmidt has clearly shown,[33] are not a part of the psalmist's own prayer, but a recitation by him of the charges which have been preferred against him. What he quotes are the charges uttered by a number of men who have in view the fate of one man—himself. And there is no need of intro-

[32] Reading with Schmidt, 'ethpallelāh.   [33] Das Gebet der Angeklagten, p. 41.

ducing them with "so my accusers say," because the liveliness of gesticulation with which an Oriental accustomed to graphic presentation speaks would make any such introduction or explanation quite superfluous.[34] The psalmist gives these charges in detail, quoting both the monstrous accusations and the presumptuous curses his enemies have uttered against him, not just now in the Temple, but also before their clash with him reached this climax. The accuser, who here represents all his opponents, stands at the right side of the altar (cf. Zech. 3:1). Poignant indeed it is to hear from the psalmist's own lips the powerful curses being hurled against him. The climax of their indictment is given at verse 16, where the psalmist quotes their charge that he persecuted a poor and needy man who already had heart trouble, so as to bring on his death. He did this, so the charge goes on to state, by black magic. He drew down a curse on this poor man. And his accuser—the psalmist is still quoting—begs the Lord to strike down our psalmist by turning the curse back upon him (vss. 17a, 18), thus causing the dissolution of his soul! So the accusers long that the decision which our psalmist now awaits at the sanctuary may be, "Guilty" (vs. 7). If such guilt is proved, then the other horrors mentioned will naturally follow, for the dissolution of soul he would have perpetrated upon another will come back in terrible destructive power upon himself. There will then follow loss of position and premature and violent death, making his wife a widow and his children orphans to be driven from pillar to post without protection and with no mercy shown them. His hard-earned property will be gobbled up by greedy creditors and plundered by conscienceless strangers. No posterity will perpetuate his memory, nor will the iniquity of his parents ever be forgotten by God. The charges are mingled with curses as the accuser states them. The psalmist's accusers have said:

6   "May he be visited with evil:
     May an accuser stand at his right hand.
7   When he stands at the bar of judgment, may he come off as wicked
     And let his sentence be, 'Guilty.'
8   May his days be few,
     And let another take his office.
9   May his children become orphans,
     And his wife a widow.
10 May his children go roving about and beg,
     And let them be driven out from their own wreckage.
11 May the creditor search for all that belongs to him,
     And may strangers plunder what he has wearisomely gained.
12 May there be no one to continue mercy:
     And may there be no one to show compassion to his orphans.
13 May his posterity be cut off;
     May his name be wiped out in one generation.

[34] Schmidt, *Die Psalmen,* p. 4.

14 May the iniquity of his father be remembered,
   And may the sin of his mother not be obliterated.
15 May they [i.e., their sins] be continually before the Lord,
   But may the memory of him in the earth be cut off,
16 Because he remembered not to do kindness,
   But persecuted a needy and poor man,
   And one broken in heart unto death.
17 He loved the curse; now may it befall *him;*
   He took no delight in blessing, so may *it* [i.e., blessing] keep far
   distant.
18 Yes, he drew on a curse as though it were a garment;
   May it penetrate into him like water,
   And into his members like oil.
19 May it be like a robe in which he enwraps himself,
   And as a girdle which he continually puts on."

The recitation of the curses of the psalmist's accusers has now come to an
end. In deep passion the accused suppliant calls down upon his enemies the
very curses they would bind upon him!

20 May *that* be the punishment of those who hate me,
   Of those who speak evil against me!

Then follows his prayer, for which, as we have seen, he has already prepared
the way (vs. 4).

We now learn how serious the whole matter is to the psalmist. His own life
is at stake. Everything rests upon the decision reached at the sanctuary (cf. vs.
7). He knows, moreover, that he is free of any guilt. The investigation pro-
ceedings at the sanctuary he feels must have as their issue the decision of his
full innocence. The psalmist, himself "poor and needy," even as the one who
died, has sought by strenuous fasting, so severe that it has made him haggard
and thin, to arouse the attention and even the sympathy of the Lord. His
accusers, to be sure, have pointed to his thus weakened condition as evidence
of his guilt! The psalmist has done his utmost. Everything now depends upon
God. So he pours forth his lamenting supplication:

21 But as for Thee, O Lord God,
   Deal with me for the sake of Thy name.
   Save me, in accordance with the goodness of Thy mercy.
22 For I am poor and needy,
   And my heart writhes within me.
23 Like a shadow as it extends, I am gone;
   I am stormed along like a locust and am no more.
24 My knees totter from fasting;
   My flesh is grown lean from lack of fatness.
25 I have become the butt of their insult:
   They see me and shake their head.

His lamenting words now move on into eager petition (vss. 26-29). He asks that God in His mercy may save him by showing his accusers clearly that the dead man was not hurried to the grave by black magic, which, acting within his body and gnawing the substance of his soul,[35] would have brought about its dissolution. Rather let God show that the poor and needy man died a natural death, that the Lord Himself has done it, and no violent human hand (vs. 27). Yes, let the Lord vindicate the psalmist in the presence of his accusers, clear him of all guilt, and fill his accusers with shame and disgrace! His prayer rises in its intensity to a cry for help:

> 26 Help me, O Lord, my God;
> Save me in accordance with the greatness of Thy mercy.
> 27 Let them know that this is Thy hand,
> That Thou, Lord, hast done it.
> 28 Let them curse, but do Thou bless;
> Let my opponents be ashamed, but let Thy servant rejoice.
> 29 May my accusers be clothed in disgrace,
> And may they wrap themselves in their shame as with a mantle.

The psalm ends in a vow of thanksgiving based on his confidence that the Lord will rescue him in his crisis. In case the prayed-for deliverance comes— the Lord's acquittal of the charges for which the psalmist stands accused—he will render his vow at the sanctuary among the worshipers of the Lord in a song of individual thanksgiving.

> 30 I will give thanks to the Lord with my mouth;
> I will praise Him in the midst of many.
> 31 For He stands at the right hand of the needy
> To save him from the opponents of his soul.

2. PRAYERS OF THE SICK

Many psalms of the Psalter grew out of the experience of illness. Hebrew thought in large measure accepted the dogma that viewed sickness and suffering of any sort—material, physical, intellectual, or spiritual—as the punishment of God. To be sure, the brilliant author of the book of Job grappled with that dogma and showed it up in its great limitations. Yet the theory that considered sin the cause of physical suffering was so definite and so comprehensible that its throttle hold upon biblical thought never was entirely loosened and still today has a strong grip upon human life generally.

Occasionally these psalms mention those who are enemies to the psalmist— 6:8, 10; 39:8; 62:3-4. But in most cases it is an enmity, or antagonism, or heart-lessness which is more subjective than objective. It is not portrayed with con-

[35] Cf. Pedersen, op. cit., p. 452.

crete details and psychological exposition of the enemies' aims. The most absorbing fact is the experience of sickness itself. These psalms are 6, 39, 62, 88.

Ps. 6. THE LORD HAS HEARD THE SOUND OF MY WEEPING

Among the universal experiences of humanity which find their mirror in the psalms is sickness. What gives poignancy and urgency to these psalms is the fact that sickness was generally viewed as the retribution of God upon the sinner. In Ps. 6 the psalmist, physically weak, even worn-out, feels himself to be suffering under the rebuking and chastening rod of God's anger.

Moreover, the pain of his illness is heightened by the fact that he has enemies, "doers of iniquity" he calls them, who are taking malicious satisfaction in his suffering (vss. 8, 10). They also, evidently in delight, view it as punishment from God. He longs for vindication before them.

In his physical and spiritual misery he cries out his lamenting petition:

1 O Lord, do not rebuke me in Thine anger,
And do not chasten me in Thy wrath.
2 Be gracious to me, for I am weak;
Heal me, for my bones are dried up.
3 My soul is greatly disturbed:
And Thou, O Lord, how long?

This petition for the moderation of his suffering is followed by a second, in which he offers the Lord an inducement to interpose on his behalf and save his life. First, he grounds his appeal in the lovingkindness of God. For God to save his life is consistent with His own nature.

4 Turn, O Lord; save my life:
Deliver me, for Thy lovingkindness' sake.

But his inducement now goes further. He utters a childlike thought which ascribes human feelings to God, and which finds frequent place in the Psalter (Pss. 30:9; 88:10; 115:17; see also Isa. 38:18). The psalmist considers himself a singer who presents to God beautiful songs, and he is therefore of value to Him, even as is a minstrel to a king whom he praises and celebrates. If the psalmist should die, so he pleads, no such praise songs from him would be forthcoming out of Sheol, the land of the dead.

5 For there is no remembrance of Thee in death:
In Sheol, who can give Thee thanks?

Back to lament he turns and now describes, in vivid detail but colored by characteristic Oriental exaggeration, his physical and mental suffering:

6 I am weary from groaning;
I complain [36] every night upon my bed;
I drench my couch with my tears.

---

[36] Reading ' āsiḥāh.

> 7 My eyes have become dull from grief;
>   I am enfeebled because of my distress.

Suddenly there comes a change of mood in the psalm. Lament is replaced by certainty that the psalmist has been heard and his petition answered by the Lord. Something has clearly happened which has lifted his heart. Either he has received like a lightning flash an inner revelation or in some more external way the certainty of having been heard and accepted by God has become his. The latter is probably the case. We are to infer that at this point in the rendition of the psalm in public worship the priestly rites of expiation were performed, and the suppliant's acceptance by God was uttered in a priestly oracle. While these rites formed no part of the psalm, they were a definite part of the total worship experience in which it was rendered in the Temple. In the actual worship the closing verses would follow these priestly rites and oracle. No longer does the psalmist lament. In triumphant certainty he rebukes his malicious enemies who gloried in his distress, for his prayer has been answered.

> 8 Turn away from me, all you doers of iniquity,
>   For the Lord has heard the sound of my weeping.
> 9 The Lord has heard my supplication;
>   He has received my prayer.
> 10 All my enemies shall be greatly dismayed:
>   They shall turn; they shall suddenly be ashamed.

Ps. 39. TURN AWAY THY GAZE FROM ME

Psalm 39 is designated in its superscription by a term which implies that it is a "confession." [37] It is an acknowledgment of iniquity and an expression of utter dependence upon God. The psalmist in the mood of silent resignation takes for granted that sin is the cause of his sickness.

He begins by telling that in a tense situation he kept himself in control. He experienced a severe illness, the cause of which he considered a blow from God. Death seemed near. He bore his illness in silent resignation, although he was severely tempted to give vent to complaining and rebellious words:

> 1 I said, "Let me guard my words,
>   So as not to sin with my tongue: .
>   Let me put a muzzle on my mouth,
>   On account of the wicked before me."
> 2 I was silent, resigned;
>   I refrained from speaking rashly;
>   Yet my soul was stirred up;
> 3a My heart grew hot within me,
> 3b   In my musing a fire burned.

[37] See Mowinckel, *op. cit.*, IV, 16-17, who interprets *lîdhûthûn* in this manner rather than as a proper name, Jeduthun, identified for the most part with Ethan.

Eventually, however, he has to speak, for his struggle was like fire in his bones which must out. In ill-tempered words he then pours forth his lament.

> 3c I spoke with my tongue:
> 4 "I make known to Thee, O Lord, my end,
>   And the limit of my days, what it is:
>   Thou knowest how transient I am.
> 5a Lo, mere handbreadths long hast Thou constituted my days;
>   And my life span is as nothing before Thee."

He is rebellious as he feels his life slipping away and God seemingly unconcerned about it. He feels so transient; his hold upon life is so fragile. Then swiftly his thought moves from his own frail life to the brevity of human existence generally. He sees no purpose in life. Man's existence is mere appearance, not reality. All earning and amassing of wealth on man's part is futile. Man seems especially frustrated when God disciplines him because of his sin and consumes his treasured possessions like a moth destroys clothing. The psalmist continues:

> 5b "Surely for nothing every man takes his stand;
> 6   Surely in mere semblance does man walk about;
>   Surely to no purpose he heaps up wealth
>   And knows not who will gather it.
> 11   Through rebuke because of iniquity,
>   Thou dost discipline man,
>   And consume, like a moth, his treasure:
>   But a mere nothing is every man."

From such general pessimistic observations and such brooding, as in God's presence, upon the seeming futility of all human existence he turns back to his own life. But now his mood has changed. That benumbing judgment of his own futility has vanished. The sense of life as a purposeless, meaningless existence drops off like a garment. For one thing, the psalmist now has hope in God, the expectation that God will hear his cry and will do something to help him. If he has no right to full citizenship in human life, he is at least a "sojourner," a resident alien, and shares with his Hebrew fathers, who were "sojourners in the land of promise . . . , dwelling in tents," the sojourner's right to the Lord's protection. He claims his guest right at the hand of God!

> 7 But now upon what rests my hope, O Lord?
>   As for my hope, it is in Thee.
> 12c For a guest am I with Thee,
> 12d   A sojourner like all my fathers.
> 12a Hear my prayer, O Lord;
> 12b   Give ear to my tears; be not deaf!

The psalmist closes with earnest petitions. He is clear that his suffering has come from a hostile God, and he accepts it as such in the mood of pious resignation. But he appeals to God to save him from the humiliation of being the butt of the scornful comment of fools who are violating his personality and his honor. He alleges his silent resignation, his uncomplaining endurance of God's hostile hand upon him (vs. 9), as an inducement for God to turn from enmity against him to mercy. He prays for relief from consuming pain, but most of all, like the sufferer Job before him, longs for release from the disapproving and seemingly heartless gaze of God. This is keeping his spirit in the slough of despond, even as his life hastens toward its close.

8   Save me from all who are transgressing against me;
     Make me not the butt of the scorn of fools.
9   I am silent; I will not open my mouth,
     For Thou hast done this.
10   Turn from me Thy stroke;
     I am consumed by the hostility of Thy hand.
13   Turn Thy gaze away from me, and let me show a smile
     Before I go and be no more.

Ps. 62. MY SOUL IS SILENCE, WAITING ALL HUSHED FOR GOD

Ps. 62 is the prayer of a sufferer from a severe illness. The psalm properly opens at verse 3 with an outraged and indignant lament.[38] The psalmist first addresses his opponents who are hurling threats at him and attacking him. In his weakened physical condition he feels like a pushed-in wall. Then suddenly (vs. 4a) he speaks, not unto, but of, these deceitful enemies whose smooth words hide the hateful intent of their hearts.

3a   How long will you threaten a man,
3b   Will you run, all of you, upon him
3c   [Who is] like a bent wall?
4a   Yes, they plot deceptions;
4b   They run [upon me] to thrust me down
3d   Like a pushed-in battlement.
4c   They bless with their mouth so as to deceive,
     But in their heart they curse.

Contrasting with this indignant lament there comes just as unexpectedly a clear note of trust (vss. 5-7). The psalmist faces the fierce threats of the enemy with the calm confidence that God will save and protect him. Here is one of the profoundest expressions of confident, trustful waiting upon God to be found in the entire Psalter:

5   Only upon the Lord, my soul waits in calm stillness,
     For my expectation stems from Him.
6   He alone is my rock and my salvation,
     My refuge; I shall not swerve.

---

[38] Vss. 1-2 are a variant to vss. 5-6, where they are properly in place.

7   My salvation and my dignity are based upon **God**;
        My protecting rock is He.

Taught as he has been by past experience, now in his hour of great need
the psalmist waits for God's help with inner calm and trustful expectancy.
In the present crisis God is his only hope. From Him alone comes protection,
steadiness of spirit, and a basis of confidence. What he now says is couched
in a form of speech that is most familiar in the utterances of Hebrew wisdom.
He ventures indirectly to set forth his own spiritual attitude as an example for
the Lord's congregation, even while he identifies himself with that worshiping
fellowship. Thus he counsels the congregation:

8   Seek refuge in God!
        Trust in Him, all the congregation of the people;
    Pour out your heart before Him;
        God is a refuge for us.

We note here particularly well how this instructional type of speech, so familiar in the wisdom literature and so characteristic of its style, has its anchorage
in the public worship.[39]

Something still more striking follows. Such help from the recall of the psalmist's past experience now receives the buttress of his present worship. We have
to do here with a liturgical act, a rite of expiation performed by the officiating
priest. And it is accompanied by an oracle of assurance [40] which teaches the
superiority of God's strength over the craftiness or material wealth of godless
men. The content of the oracle as well as the indication of its oracular nature
is given in verses 11-12. Godless men with their crafty distortions seem so powerful. Material wealth promises great protection. But the sole source of real protection upon which mere man can depend is to be found in God, who is not
only merciful but just in His dealings with humanity, proportioning a man's
lot to his conduct.

9   Humanity is only a puff of wind:
        The sons of men are a lie.
    In the scales they are altogether
        Lighter than breath.
10 Trust not in distortion,
        And put no futile hope in craftiness.
    As for riches, when it increases
        Be not deceived in your heart.
11 Once God spoke,
        Twice, that which I heard,
        That might belongs to God.
12 And with the Lord is mercy;
        For Thou rewardest man in accordance with his work.

[39] Cf. Quell, *op. cit.*, p. 128.   [40] Cf. Mowinckel, *op. cit.*, I, 153-54.

Ps. 88. THE CRY OF A SICK MAN FOR ATTENTION AND HEALING

Ps. 88 is a psalm of a sick man who feels that he is near the door of death. The designation in the superscription, "for self-abasement," implies the penitential and expiatory rites in connection with which the psalm is rendered. The superscription also suggests that it has to do with sickness. It is further called a *maskil,* a term which means that it embodies a meaningful, potent, blessing-bringing knowledge which originates in divine revelation.[41] To his physical suffering is added the excruciating mental pain that his friends are estranged from him and his acquaintances have forgotten him.

The psalm opens with a cry that humbly seeks the ear of God.

> 1 My God, I cry for help in the daytime;
>   My cry in the night comes before Thee.
> 2 My prayer comes into Thy presence:
>   Bend down Thine ear to my cry.

In a soul-stirring lament (vss. 3-9) he bares his soul to God. It is heavy with trouble, for recovery is viewed as hopeless, and death seems near. He feels forgotten of God as though he is among the profane dead who are denied honorable burial. In his vivid Oriental imagination he feels himself already in the world of the dead. More poignant than this is the belief that he is suffering under the wrath of God, who has sent upon him calamity after calamity like successive breakers of the sea. As a consequence his friends shun him, viewing him as under God's interdict and thus unclean. Shut away from divine and human fellowship, he finds that the joy of life is gone. Thus he laments:

> 3 For my soul is full of troubles,
>   And my life has arrived at Sheol.
> 4 I am thought of along with those going down to the grave;
>   I have become like a man without help.
> 5 I am forgotten as are the dead:
>   Like the dishonored, deprived of the grave,
>   Whom Thou rememberest no more;
>   Yes, they are cut off from Thy hand.
> 6 Thou hast laid me in the pit of the nether world,
>   In the dark regions of the shadow of death.
> 7 Thy wrath rests upon me,
>   And with all Thy breakers Thou dost afflict me.
> 8 Thou hast removed my acquaintances far from me;
>   Thou hast made me a horror to them;
>   I am shut up, and I cannot go out.
> 9 My eye languishes because of my affliction.
>   I cry to Thee, O Lord, every day;
>   I spread out my hands unto Thee.

[41] Cf. *ibid.,* IV, 6, 15, 33.

Just as in Ps. 6, this psalmist seeks in childlike fashion to move God to bring about his recovery from his illness. In effect he argues, "If Thou shouldst let me die, I would descend to Sheol, the dark abode of the dead, among disembodied spirits or 'shades,' where Thy presence cannot come and Thy righteous acts are unknown."

> 10　Is it to the dead Thou doest wonders?
> 　　Do shades arise and praise Thee?
> 11　Is Thy lovingkindness recounted in the grave,
> 　　Thy faithfulness in the kingdom of the dead?
> 12　Are Thy wonders known in the darkness,
> 　　Or Thy righteousness in the land of oblivion?

The psalmist ends in a lament full of intense entreaty to his God, who seems to have hidden His face so as not to see what is taking place. Distressed, wearied, and exhausted, pommeled by outburst after outburst of the fury of the Lord—their force hurled upon him like submerging billows—shunned by acquaintances and friends, in his loneliness he cries out to God. Morning after morning as a suppliant he implores Him:

> 13　But as for me, to Thee I cry;
> 　　Yes, in the morning I come to meet Thee with my prayer.
> 14　Why dost Thou spurn my life?
> 　　Why dost Thou hide Thy face from me?
> 15　I am distressed and weary from my youth:
> 　　I have had to bear Thy terrors so that I am exhausted.
> 16　Thy gusts of anger have passed over me;
> 　　Thy alarms have annihilated me.
> 17　They have surrounded me like water all the day:
> 　　They have closed on me together.
> 18　Thou hast removed far from me lover and friend;
> 　　My acquaintances have forgotten me.

Such a sincere outpouring originating in the soul of an articulate sufferer reminds us of the cries of physical and spiritual anguish from the deep heart of Job. It is not hard to believe that such a psalm was created to be a vehicle of expression for inarticulate souls who in similar desperate physical and spiritual need came to the Temple seeking from God expiation, cleansing, and restoration.

3. Prayers of Penitence

Two of the most loved of the psalms, 51 and 130, have as their profoundest theme penitence. They are prayers that reveal a unique sensitiveness to the experience of sin and the spiritual realities of cleansing and forgiveness. It is likely that in the rendering of such psalms as these the rituals that have to do with ceremonial and ethical cleansing would be employed and in the case of

Ps. 51 part of the psalm almost certainly was rendered in connection with the ritual ceremony itself.

Ps. 51. THE CRY OF A SOUL FOR CLEANSING AND PARDON

Ps. 51, the most heart-searching of all the penitential psalms, is an individual lament because of sin. No psalm of the Psalter has so profound and varied a concept of sin as this. And we can readily penetrate through the great words of the psalm to ritual acts in the living worship which the words originally accompanied. The psalmist is ill and longs to be healed. Yet far profounder than that physical longing is his passionate desire for forgiveness, because he views his physical condition as the result of the Lord's punishment for his sin.

The psalmist's prayer begins with a cry to the Lord for cleansing and pardon. Three different terms are used for sin, which lead us into the deeps of spiritual sensitiveness. The first is "transgression" (*pesha'*), the sin of conscious rebellion, the act which violates a known standard; the second is "iniquity" (*'āwôn*), the sin of error; and the third is the "sin" (*haṭṭā'th*) of missing an aimed-at mark. And these three vivid terms he uses for forgiveness: The first, "blot out" (*māhāh*)—wipe off or efface—is used also for the ritual act performed by the priest of washing off into the water curses which he had written on a tablet (Num 5:23). The second term, "wash" (*kābhaṣ*)—tread out—roots in the familiar Oriental method of washing garments by thorough-going treading (Exod. 19:10). The third, "declare me clean" (*ṭāhēr*), is a ceremonial term used in the ritual in which the priest pronounces the worshiper clean (Lev. 13:6).

Thus the psalmist cries:

1 Be merciful to me, O God, in accordance with Thy mercy;
   In proportion to Thy compassion blot out my transgressions.
2 Wash me thoroughly from my iniquity,
   And declare me clean of my sin.

As though to give adequate grounds to the Lord for answering such a longing prayer, he confesses his sin. The psalmist is a deep and noble soul in Israel. He is not conscious of having committed sin against men, even though men who see his condition may judge him guilty of such sin. Yet who can count himself guiltless before the all-seeing eyes of God? His heart had not been completely right with God. Therefore he believes God is justified and blameless in sentencing him to suffer. In thus acknowledging the divine justification the psalmist at the same time makes implicit appeal to God's mercy.

3 For I acknowledge my transgression,
   And my sin I am continually confessing.
4 Against Thee, Thee alone, have I sinned
   And done what is evil in Thine eyes,
   So that Thou art right in Thy sentence;
   Thou art free from fault in all Thy judgment.

Yet deeper he goes in his appeal to the just God. The psalmist shares with all mankind proneness to sin. He is aware of weakness toward the good, that tendency toward error, that consciousness of being inadequate, which is characteristic of all human beings. To what is *human* he belongs, having been conceived in *human* passion and born in *human* agony. How can any such one be a complete creature before God? [42] For he shares the view of the law that procreation and birth are unclean. He cries out:

> 5 Lo, I was brought forth in iniquity,
>   And in sin my mother conceived me.

Mowinckel [43] has shown the most likely interpretation of verse 6, which now follows. At this point in the rendition of the psalm, through certain technical, cultic means of divine instruction a revelation is given to the suppliant as to that which has made him unclean before God. This revelation is under the administration of the priest. To the suppliant, who feels himself to be unclean, the priest reveals whether or not the Lord wills to be gracious to him, to cleanse him, and to heal his sickness. The revelation in this instance is favorable to him. The terms translated in the American Standard Version "in the inward parts" and "in the hidden part" rightly understood are the technical designations of such means of revelation, and the verse has the significance of a trust motif which forms the foundation of the petition that follows. Moved deeply by this profound revelation of God's truth and of His unsearchable wisdom, the psalmist cries:

> 6 Lo, I have searched [44] out truth by inward [communication],
>   And in hidden [revelation] Thou dost teach me wisdom.

There follows a prayer for cleansing from sin, for restoration from his broken health to joyous physical vitality, and for God's gracious forgiveness of his sins. We are to think here of ritual acts, accompanying or following the prayer, as being performed by the priest, in which hyssop, a shrublike herb with redolent leaves, will be dipped in water ritually prepared for ceremonial cleansing, then the water sprinkled upon the suppliant (Num. 19:18) as he prays:

> 7 Cleanse me with hyssop that I may be clean;
>   Wash me that I may be whiter than snow.
> 8 Satisfy me with exultation and gladness;
>   Let the bones which Thou hast crushed rejoice.
> 9 Hide Thy face from my sins,
>   And blot out all my iniquities.

The prayer continues, and in petitions unique in the Psalter. It is a prayer for inner renewal and breathes the deepest thoughts of Jeremiah and Ezekiel,

---

[42] Cf. Gunkel, *Die Psalmen*, p. 223.   [43] *Op. cit.*, I, 143.
[44] Reading, with Gunkel, *ḥāphastî*, instead of *ḥāphaçtā*.

who of all the prophets were the most interested in the inner life (Jer. 31:33; Ezek. 36:26-27). But to our psalmist a clean heart can come only as the "creation" of God. In his prayer he makes use of the very term ($b^e r \bar{a}$ ', create) employed by the priestly account of creation, which describes how God in the beginning *created* ($b \bar{a} r \bar{a}$') the heavens and the earth (Gen. 1:1–2:4a). Moreover, just as Ezekiel promised that God would put His spirit within His people and thus cause them to walk steadfastly in His statutes and to keep His ordinances, so the psalmist prays that God may not fling him away in disgust, counting him as of no value, and that God's spirit may not be withdrawn from his inner life. And he further prays that the joyous consciousness of the Lord's saving presence may be restored to him, and that God may imbue him with a spirit of willingness. It is one of the deepest prayers of religion that here is addressed to God:

> 10 Create a clean heart in me, O God,
>   And renew within me a steadfast spirit.
> 11 Cast me not out from Thy presence,
>   And take not Thy holy spirit from me.
> 12 Bring back to me the exultation of Thy salvation,
>   And sustain me with a willing spirit.

At the end of the prayer comes the vow. It is the unconditional determination of his soul: may God keep him from such silence [45] as death would impose upon him, so that he may become a teacher of others, to turn sinning men into the right path. Then he will sing of the Lord's faithfulness to him. So may God thus permit His praise to pour forth through his eager lips!

> 13 I will teach transgressors Thy ways,
>   And sinners shall turn back to Thee.
> 14 Deliver me from silence, O God:
>   My tongue shall sing of Thy faithfulness.
> 15 O Lord, open Thou my lips,
>   And my mouth shall declare Thy praise.

The psalmist shows another clear indication of the profound influence upon him of the prophets in his attitude toward sacrifice. He is at one with Amos (5:21-22), Hosea (6:6), Isaiah (1:10-17), Micah (6:6-8), and Jeremiah (7:21-23) in his rejection of animal sacrifice as a rite that is pleasing to God. He has achieved a deeply spiritual conception of religion. It is not sacrifice that God desires, but a heart free from pride and rebellion.

> 16 For Thou hast no pleasure in sacrifice;
>   And if I had brought a whole burnt offering, Thou wouldst not
>   have been pleased with it.
> 17 My sacrifice is a broken spirit;
>   A crushed heart Thou dost not despise.

[45] Cf. Ps. 94:17; 115:17. The reference is to the silence of Sheol, the realm of the dead.

The last two verses of the psalm form a later supplement and come from a less spiritually minded poet. He looks longingly forward to the time when, with the worshiping community of Zion restored and the walls of Jerusalem rebuilt, the appropriate sacrifices may again be presented upon the Temple altar and win God's hearty approval. This supplement dates from before Nehemiah's time (445 B.C.). Thus the psalmist prays to God:

> 18 Do good in Thy favor to Zion:
>   Build the walls of Jerusalem.
> 19 Then wilt Thou take pleasure in right offerings;
>   Then will they offer bullocks upon Thine altar!

Ps. 130. OUT OF THE DEEPS I CRY TO THEE

Ps. 130 is an individual lament in the form of a prayer of penitence. As such a prayer it is truly a classic, and its opening verse has been a vehicle of utterance for the soul's profoundest distress across the long centuries of human experience. The very fact that the deeps are not more concretely described than they are has made the words applicable to all serious suffering, whether it be physical, mental, or spiritual, in the lowest moods of life's darkest hours. It is with this cry from the depths to God that this psalm opens. It is an urgent appeal to One who seems far away, whose ear seems inattentive to the psalmist's distress cry:

> 1 Out of the depths have I called to Thee, O Lord.
> 2 Lord, hear my voice:
>   Let Thine ears be attentive
>   To the voice of my supplications.

Little does he tell as to the nature of his distress. But one thing now becomes clear. He is conscious of iniquity. He stands before God with a deep sense of sin. Yet the poignancy of that conviction of sin is softened by two thoughts. If God holds in His mind the iniquity of human beings generally, who can possibly stand in innocence and approval before Him? The second thought, yet more positive and influential in his present need, is that it is characteristic of God to forgive, and that such pardon, undeserved by men as it is, springs solely from God's merciful compassion. It is this quality in God, the grace of His forgiveness, that is supremely influential in leading His worshipers to reverent dependence.

> 3 If Thou shouldst hold iniquity in mind,
>   O Lord, who could stand?
> 4 But forgiveness is with Thee;
>   Wherefore [46] Thou art revered!

Mowinckel, remarking on the force of the clause "Thou art feared," suggestively says: "In the word 'fear' the poet expresses the entire fulness of his re-

---

[46] See also Buttenwieser, who rightly understands the Hebrew word *lema'an*.

ligion: his anguish over sin; his thankfulness, love, trust in God; his awe before Him, the Holy One, who manifests Himself as holy in forgiveness and grace, inasmuch as pardon is precisely the removal of the sin and uncleanness." [47]

Thus it is upon this forgiving God, whom the psalmist holds in awe, that he now waits, eagerly seeking His assuring word that will pronounce him forgiven and longing for His presence, just as night watchmen long for the release of dawn. The psalmist is familiar with the great words of Deutero-Isaiah (40: 31): "They that wait for the Lord shall renew their strength."

> 5 I wait eagerly for the Lord with my soul,
>   And for His word I hope.
> 6 My soul waits eagerly for the Lord,
>   More eagerly than watchmen for the morning.

In the close of the psalm the psalmist becomes teacher, and out of the richness of his own experience in waiting not in vain for the Lord he calls upon Israel, the worshiping congregation of which he is a part, likewise to wait upon Him who in His mercy will redeem His people from the results of their sins.

> 7 Let Israel wait for the Lord,
>   For with the Lord is mercy and manifold [48] redemption.
> 8 And He will redeem Israel
>   From all his iniquities.

[47] Op. cit., II, 130.
[48] So rightly Ehrlich, op. cit., p. 342, "vielerlei Wege der Erlösung."

Chapter XII

SONGS OF TRUST AND OF WISDOM

1. SONGS OF TRUST

UTTERANCES OF TRUST ARE FOUND IN ALL THE GROUPS OF PSALMS, FOR TRUST IN God is one of the foundation elements in Hebrew religion. As a constituent of Hebrew religious life it appears first in the Old Testament in the Elohist's great epic story, where of Abraham it is said,

> And he believed in God;[1]
> And He reckoned it to him as righteousness. (Gen. 15:6.)

It was to a large extent due to the teaching and example of the prophet Isaiah that trust became central in Hebrew religion, a place of distinction which it occupies in New Testament religious thought and life as well. Isaiah under-stood clearly the two elements in faith, belief and trust. To the timid and frightened young King Ahaz of Judah, Isaiah said,

> If you will not have faith
> Surely you cannot have staith [i.e., steadiness]. (7:9.)

Faith here means steadying belief in the presence, power, and help of the invisible God for the nation and the individual. Some twenty years later when the popular trend in Judah was for alliance with Egypt, Isaiah called Judah back to her primary covenant alliance with God in the great words:

> In returning and rest shall you be saved:
> In quietness and confidence shall be your strength. (30:15.)

Faith here means an unperturbed confidence in the presence, interest, and help of God, such as shows itself in quietness and calm of soul on the part of the nation's leaders and its people.

While very many psalms of the Psalter breathe such belief and confidence, their setting in worship is such as to give them their distinctive classification elsewhere. But Pss. 16, 91, and 131 present a trilogy of trust such as give rich, and at the same time varied, expression to this most important aspect of religious experience.

Viewed purely from the standpoint of the kind of worship setting in which this trust glows in warmth and power, this trilogy reveals great variety. Ps. 16 partakes of features of the lament of the individual (vss. 1-4), yet has its closest association with the songs of personal thanksgiving, as seen both in this psalmist's glad personal testimony (vss. 7-8) and in his magnificent credo of confidence in God (vss. 9-11). Ps. 91 partakes of characteristic features of

---

[1] Reading, with Buhl, *wayya'amēn bē'lōhīm.*

Hebrew wisdom (vss. 1-13), and at its close through its priestly oracle takes on the features of a psalm liturgy. Ps. 131 in its present form is a New Year prayer which has its worship background in the expectancy of the Lord's annual coming anew to His people in power. Yet compared with the inner quality of religious experience in these psalms such marks are superficial. For in this trilogy the distinctive thing that outweighs all else in determining their classification is their thrilling note of intimate, confident, and believing trust in God on the part of the individual soul. From this point of view they are unrivaled in the Psalter.

Ps. 16. THE PRACTICE OF THE PRESENCE OF GOD

Ps. 16 is a song of trust from a devout and deeply spiritual soul. The psalmist is in danger of death, a situation which causes him great concern, and he seeks earnestly and indeed trustfully the protection of God (vss. 1-2). It would seem that he is among Arabs who are putting pressure upon him to participate in their pagan rites, to call upon their gods by name, and to pour out to them libations of blood (vss. 3-4).

The psalm opens with a petition for protection, a request which is undergirded by the habit of his soul—trustful dependence upon God. For him life's supreme good is God.

> 1   Protect me, O God, for I take refuge in Thee.
> 2   I say, Thou art my good.

But not all in his environment share his faith. Indeed, he is of the Diaspora, and around him everywhere are impulses to the worship of heathen deities, "sacred beings" which for him do not even exist, and whose rites of worship are utterly abhorrent. For he is a loyal worshiper of the Lord and has kept the law that forbids even the mention of the name of other gods (Exod. 23:13).[2]

> 3   Good for nothing are all the *sacred beings*,
>   Yes, the *powers* in whom I have no pleasure.
> 4   Those who are pleased with them
>   Increase their own grief, make their ways evil.
>   Not will *I* pour out libations of blood to them;
>   Not will *I* take their names upon my lips.

But this psalmist's religion is not characterized primarily by negations. He has a great stake in God, the chief good of his life. So in vivid pictures he now tells what he has experienced at God's hands. Just as the sheik of a clan divides to the heads of the families their allotted portions of land, some of it favored and well-watered, so God takes and casts the psalmist's lot, which secures as his share in life an area pleasant and beautiful. The psalmist accepts

---

[2] I follow Gunkel's brilliant reconstruction of the text in vss. 3-4, which makes the psalmist's meaning clear.

his lot in life as his divinely appointed portion direct from the hand of God. He drinks of the cup that God has handed to him, which overflows with blessings.

> 5 O Lord, Thou dost appoint my portion and my cup:
>   Thou dost grasp my lot.
> 6 The measuring lines have allotted to me pleasant places;
>   Yes, my heritage is beautiful for me.

A second picture of what God does for him follows. God counsels him and in the silent watches of the night disciplines his innermost soul. Praise wells up in the psalmist's heart as he sings:

> 7 I will bless the Lord who counsels me;
>   Yes, in the nights He warns my inner being.

In still a third picture the psalmist tells how he responds to this divine provision and persistent discipline of his life. It is by the practice at all times of the presence of God. The Lord set in front of him means that in all his ways he takes God into account. The Lord at his right hand implies that he is kept safe and protected from falling by God's ever-present help.

> 8 I have set the Lord always in front of me:
>   Since He is at my right hand, I shall not slip.

The psalm rises at its close to the mood of glowing joy. There is joy in the psalmist's heart, a lift in his soul, and a sense of restful security in his physical being as he ceases speaking *about* God and pours out his soul *to* Him. He is in the hands of God, who counts him as one of His loyal ones. God will not give him up to Sheol, the land of the dead, but on the contrary will show him the path which leads to life, and, quite concretely, which will eventually lead him also to the Temple, where the Lord dwells. To see His face, that is, to worship in His Temple [3]—this will mean that his cup of joy is full. Forever will God's right hand, protecting and providing, bring delight to his soul. So in triumphant gladness he concludes:

> 9 Therefore my heart rejoices, and my soul exults;
>   Yes, my body lies down in security.
> 10 For Thou wilt not give up my soul to Sheol;
>   Thou wilt not let Thy godly one see the grave.
> 11 Thou dost show me the path of life:
>   Thou dost satisfy me with joy in Thy presence:
>   Delights are in Thy right hand forever.

Ps. 91. THE PROTECTION OF THE MAN WHO TRUSTS IN GOD

Ps. 91 is a noble song of faith, full of fire and energy. It holds the individual person in the center of attention. "The most beautiful treasure of the poetry

---

[3] Cf. Quell, *op. cit.*, p. 120.

of the psalms is the inner personal relation of the devout man to his God," and this psalm comprises "a powerful, yea, an unsurpassed expression of individualism."[4] Kittel, placing it alongside of Ps. 46 as "the second noble song of faith in the Psalter," says that "like that psalm it has become for the congregation of all times, in a thousand hard situations and in all kinds of perils, the faithful companion of those in sore trial." [5] One theme runs through the entire psalm, the marvelous protection enjoyed by him who trusts in God.

There are spiritual limitations in the thought of the psalm which we of later times cannot ignore. There is, for example, a hardheartedness in the poet which condemns sinners to death with no feeling of compassion over their fate. Indeed he counts it the Lord's blessing upon him that he is permitted to gaze upon the destruction of the wicked, himself unharmed. However, seen from his point of view it is this calamity upon them which confirms his faith in the divine government of the world, for he views the outer lot of men as the immediate and necessary result of their character. Moreover, the on-going, living faith of the congregation of God in temple, synagogue, and church, while clinging to verse 7 as to a household treasure of faith, has tended to ignore verse 8.[6]

Another limitation which we feel is that the psalmist makes no differentiation between God's protection of a man's soul and His protection of his body. To the psalmist the idea of the immortality of the soul is not yet present. But as we use this beloved psalm, we are aware that a growing piety, both in Judaism and in Christianity, has spiritualized the words of the psalm, lifting them out of such accidental limitations in thought, and has shown the psalm's very spiritual vitality in so doing. Thus it has become, and continues to be, a classic utterance of an exuberant faith that overcomes the world. And, as Gunkel remarks, "it is in just this exuberance that the beauty of the poem consists." [7]

The first major part of the psalm (vss. 1-13) is in the form of a wisdom poem and deals with the subject most characteristic of the wisdom psalms, that of retribution. While its form is that of a wisdom poem, it was rendered in the worship of the Temple as a blessing pronounced by the priest upon the laity.[8] This dominant theme of retribution shows that the psalm comes from a period when Hebrew wisdom had brought this subject into the center of attention. Thus the psalm must date after the time of Ezekiel. The theme of the psalm is expressed in the first two verses, the Lord the shelter and the protection of the godly:

> 1   Oh the happiness of the one who dwells in the secret place of the Most
>   High,
>   Who abides in the shade of the Almighty!

[4] Gunkel, *Die Psalmen,* pp. 403, 405.   [5] *Die Psalmen,* p. 302.
[6] See the suggestive words of Kittel, *ibid.,* p. 304.
[7] *Die Psalmen,* p. 405.   [8] Gunkel, *Einleitung,* p. 394.

2 Who says to the Lord, "My refuge and my stronghold,
        My God, in whom I trust."

Four pictures are here painted. God is to such a godly soul a secret place where he may hide. He is the shade from the burning heat, a shelter, and a fortress. And two distinguished ancient names for God are used, pre-Israelite in their origin—*Elyôn* (Most High) and *Shaddai* (Almighty). Yet most impressive of all and rich in personal meaning is his simple, feelingful expression, "My God."

In verses 3-13 the psalmist gives the grounds upon which the above theme rests, and this portion of the psalm is in two parts (vss. 3-8 and 9-13). The first part, through pictures very familiar in Oriental life, describes the perils to which men are daily exposed, perils wherein death threatens—the trap of the wild-bird catcher and the pitfall that brings the unsuspecting wild animal to its ruin. The righteous man is hidden from danger as is the young of an eagle under its mother's protective wings. But more, the man who trusts in God is protected from the most sinister and inexplicable of horrors (vss. 5-6). Here the psalmist reveals the influence upon his thought of Babylonian demonology. First is the terror by night, the night demon. At night, it is held, there is a triad of demons who "rush about . . . , seeking what harm they can do to people." They are spoken of as flying; one of them, who inflamed evil passions, produced sleeplessness, and caused nightmare, is spoken of as "flitting in through a window after a man." [9] "The arrow that flies by day" is the demon that causes sunstroke. The "pestilence" demon is like "the angel of the Lord," who in the night, so the account reports, slew 185,000 in the camp of the Assyrians (II Kings 19:35). The "plague" demon is that which "devastates at midday"; the hot Oriental sun with its destructive power easily accounts for this belief. In pestilence or in plague, when thousands, even tens of thousands fall right and left, says the psalmist, there stands the man who trusts in God, calm and protected, but seeing with his own eyes the awful evidences of the divine retribution. Let us hear his own words:

3 For He will snatch you
        From before the trap of the birdcatcher,
        And from before the pit of destruction.
4 With His pinions shall He cover you,
        And under His wings you shall find refuge:
        As shield and wall [10] is His faithfulness.
5 You need not be afraid of the terror by night,
        Nor of the arrow that flies by day,
6 Nor of the pestilence that stalks in the darkness,
        Nor of the plague which devastates at midday.

[9] Oesterley, *A Fresh Approach to the Psalms*, p. 284.
[10] So Kittel, from the Syrian meaning. The word is *sōhērāh*, an enclosing wall.

> 7 Though a thousand should fall at your side,
>   And ten thousand at your right hand,
>   It shall not draw near you.
> 8 Surely with your eyes shall you look
>   And shall see the retribution of the wicked.

While verses 3-8, as we have noted, describe the perils, the second part of this section (vss. 9-13) describes the help which God makes available to the one who trusts in Him. While the wicked fall, in contrast the man who trusts in God has Him as his shelter, his refuge. He is under the guardianship of angels. He may walk the rough stony trails of Palestine without contracting foot wounds. Gunkel suggests that the psalmist has evidently seen the familiar illustrations on seal cylinders and on reliefs, widely distributed in the ancient East, wherein the god Marduk is portrayed as standing with his foot upon the conquered monster Tiamat. Similarly in Egypt, in reliefs or in figurines worn as charms around the neck, the deity is often pictured as holding a lion, serpents, and scorpion by the tail and as treading on crocodiles and lions. Such charms betray the hope that the wearer too may thus triumph over these vicious enemies in the animal world. Similarly the righteous man experiences, not only God's help, but God's power to make him victorious over these deadly perils. So the psalmist continues:

> 9 For as for you, the Lord is your shelter;
>   You have made the Most High your refuge.
> 10 Evil shall not be sent to you,
>   Nor will a stroke draw near your tent.
> 11 For He will give His angels charge of you,
>   To guard you in all your ways.
> 12 They will bear you up, upon wings,
>   So that you shall not strike your foot against a stone.
> 13 You may tread upon lion and cobra;
>   Young lion and serpent you can crush under foot.

Then unexpectedly comes a change in person, which introduces the second major part of the whole psalm (vss. 14-16). This is rightly understood as a priestly oracle having its place in the framework of the worship and uttered in the name of God by the officiating priest. It follows upon the sermon-like assurance of the protection of God and justifies and confirms it.[11] God himself utters through His priest the assurance of which His loyal worshiper stands in need. Security, response, relief, honor, long life, and salvation in its fullest meaning—all this will come to the man who knows God's name (cf. Ps. 20:7) and puts his trust in Him (cf. Ps. 9:10). Thus the priest, speaking in the name of the Lord, mediates the divine blessing:

[11] See the suggestive and illuminating article by Küchler, *op. cit.*, p. 299.

14 "Since he has attached his love to Me,
 I will bring him into security:
 I will set him [securely] on high,
 For he knows My name.
15 He shall call upon Me, and I will answer him;
 I will be with him in trouble:
16 With length of days I will satisfy him,
 And let him drink his fill of My salvation."

Ps. 131. I HAVE COMPOSED AND QUIETED MY SOUL

Ps. 131 in essence is a song of trust, but with a strong background of the spirit of lament. It is an intensely individual psalm in its origin, as verses 1-2 clearly show. But in its present form the utterance of an individual soul has been transformed into a congregational prayer by the addition of verse 3.

The psalmist, speaking directly to God, renounces any arrogance, pride, or pretentiousness in his spirit. He lays no claim to great things and aspires to nothing beyond his own abilities.

1 O Lord, my heart is not presumptuous,
  And my eyes are not haughty;
  And I do not move among pretentious matters,
  Nor in things too wonderful for me.

Yet not always was it so. There was a time when he was proud and ambitious, when he pretended to be what he was not, and when he overreached himself. But now it is different.

The psalmist has come to an inner calm and poise of soul. He has arrived there, partly, to be sure, by renunciation of his selfish, ambitious aims, and certainly in some measure by the sternest self-discipline, but chiefly by the change of center in his life from self to God. No longer does he make his selfish demand upon God, like a sucking babe pressing urgently and demandingly upon its mother's breast. But he rejoices in God's fellowship, just as a weaned child is satisfied with the near presence of its mother, not so much for what she has as for what she is. Not *things* from God will now satisfy him, but only God Himself. We feel the vivid and striking contrast between the once and the now, emphasized by the adversative "but" in verse 2 as he says:

2 But I have composed and quieted my soul;
  Like a weaned child with its mother,
  So is my soul weaned within me.

We feel the wonderful inner peace of intimate fellowship with God which has become the psalmist's experience.

This strikingly individual lament has been given a fresh interpretation and applied to the congregation of Israel. As its title shows, it is one of the psalms connected with the great procession (*hamma'alôth*) which forms one of the most important parts of the autumnal New Year festival. Thus viewing the congregation as a great "I," this intensely individual lament is carried over to the wider social unit and made the corporate expression of the congregation by the addition of verse 3, which is an indirect prayer, more a sigh of the spirit than a prayer.[12]

> 3 Wait, Israel, for the Lord,
>   From now even forever!

All the more significant does this prayer become when we remember that the New Year festival emphasized the "coming" of the Lord in power to His people. In its present form the psalm would be at home in the ritual for that festival.

2. SONGS TINGED WITH THE TEMPER OF HEBREW WISDOM

The literature of the sages or wise men in Israel—Proverbs, Job, Ecclesiastes—developed relatively late, but its roots are in the popular wisdom which first appeared in Egypt and Babylonia as early as 3000 B.C. This popular wisdom, expressing itself in folk sayings, maxims, riddles, and parables, was largely practical and secular. The wise men were the humanists in Israel, and everything human was their province. Much of this popular wisdom we still find in the literature of the Hebrew sages, but Hebrew wisdom tended to become increasingly spiritual, and certainly it reaches us at length from men who were deeply religious, although only occasionally does their religion reveal anything akin to mystical fellowship with God.

By the time of Jeremiah (626-586 B.C.) it was popularly recognized that the sages of Israel with their characteristic "counsel" of wisdom formed a class alongside of the priests with their "torah" and the prophets with their "word" of the Lord (Jer. 18:18). They were teachers of youth, and there were distinct schools of them, as is clearly indicated in the Wisdom of Jesus ben Sirach, who about 180 B.C. had a school in Jerusalem.[13] While there are elements in Proverbs and in Job that are pre-exilic,[14] the books of Old Testament wisdom all come from a time after the Exile.

The wisdom trend in the psalms has two major emphases. The first is the problem of retribution. It is the problem of problems to the sages. How does God deal with men who sin? What is the relation between a man's lot in life and his character? Three psalms grapple with this problem—37, 49, and 73.

The second emphasis of the wisdom trend in the psalms is closely related to this, yet is more positive and constructive in its nature. It is the reward of virtue. It embodies a strong conviction that happiness and prosperity, success in business and in the bringing up of a family, are founded in the fear of the

---

[12] Mowinckel, *op. cit.*, I, 164-65.
[13] Cf. Pfeiffer, "The Growth of Old Testament Religion," in *Shane Quarterly*, VIII (1947), 20.
[14] See Leslie, *Poetry and Wisdom*, pp. 95, 127.

Lord. These psalms are 112; 127; 128; 133; 144:12-15; and, especially appropriate for the opening of the Psalter, Ps. 1.

The wisdom psalms would be rendered in those Temple services where instruction in the good life, and particularly instruction of youth, would have the right of way. There were times in postexilic Judaism when for the religious man the going was hard, when religious living seemed futile and fruitless, and when the secular-minded man in his easy material security seemed to invalidate the claims of religion. At such times the note of triumphant religious experience in these psalms would render a great service in the congregation of the Temple. The most appropriate setting for them would be in connection with the great pilgrimage festivals, and more particularly the Festival of Tabernacles and the New Year. Themes expressed in these psalms are the following: the issues of life (Pss. 1, 37, 49, 73, 112), thanksgiving for the increase of the soil and for fecundity in the family (Pss. 127, 128), the renewal of the covenant bond between the Lord and His people and between fellow Israelites (Ps. 133), and social well-being viewed as a community ideal or as the result of a change of fortunes brought about by the Lord (Ps. 144:12-15). However, the unique thing in all these psalms, which determines their present classfiication, is that they are all tinged with the temper and the interests that are characteristic of Hebrew wisdom.

Ps. 37. THE COUNSEL OF AN ELDERLY SAGE TO YOUTH

Ps. 37, both in form and in subject matter, is a wisdom psalm. In form it is an acrostic poem with two whole lines given to each letter of the alphabet, but only the first line in each case beginning with the pertinent letter. Its subject matter is the problem of divine retribution, which theme held the central place in Old Testament wisdom. It deals with the problem of theodicy, the vindication of the justice of God in permitting natural and moral evil. The point of view of the author is approximately that of Eliphaz, Bildad, and Zophar of the book of Job. The psalm dates probably from the fourth century B.C., after Ezekiel (Ezek. 18), after the Priestly Code had become Judaism's rule of life (vs. 31), but before the author of the book of Job (ca. 350 B.C.) in vigorous intellectual independence grappled with the problem. Eventually such wisdom teaching, which was greatly loved by the Israelite laity, was taken up by the priests and singers and made part of the cult, although exactly at what type of occasion in the worship such psalms were rendered we cannot say.[15] The sage whose words are here retained is an Israelite whose wisdom is profoundly impregnated with the worship of the Lord. Moreover, he is an elderly man and is addressing youth.

The psalm opens (vss. 1-11) with a series of admonitions in which warning, reproof, counsel, and promise meet and mingle. The tempers against which he

[15] Cf. Gunkel, *Einleitung*, p. 394.

warns are those of hot indignation of spirit toward evildoers and vexatious envy at their fortune in life. He reproves youths for allowing themselves to get disturbed when they see men of evil practices who appear to be getting along so well. He counsels them to trust in the Lord, nurturing their spirits on the fact of His faithfulness, throwing upon Him their problems in the spirit of trustful resignation and confident expectation. And he exhorts them to keep their self-control. He assures them that the prosperity of the wicked will not long continue, and that the evildoers will be destroyed, for they have no permanence. The land now in evil hands is destined to be possessed by the righteous meek who, awaiting God's own time, will at length with thrilling delight come into possession of it as their rightful inheritance. Says the sage:

א 1 Heat not yourself in vexation over evildoers;
        Be not envious of those who do injustice.
    2 For they shall quickly languish like green herbage,
        And fade like the greenness of grass.
ב 3 Trust in the Lord, and do good;
        Dwell in the land, and feed in security.
    4 And take exquisite delight in the Lord,
        And He will bestow upon you your heart's requests.
ג 5 Roll off upon the Lord your course of life,
        And depend upon Him and He will do [it].
    6 Then He will cause your righteousness to go forth like the light,
        And your justice as the midday.
ד 7 Be resigned to the Lord, and wait longingly for Him:
        Heat not yourself in vexation over one who succeeds well,
        Over a man who does evil deeds,
  14c   Causing the poor and needy to fall.
ה 8 Refrain from anger, and abandon wrath:
        Do not heat up yourself so as only to do evil.
    9 For those who do evil shall be cut off,
        But those who wait for the Lord shall inherit the land.
ו 10 For yet a little time and the godless shall not be:
        Yes, you will diligently consider his place, but he shall not be.
    11 But the meek shall inherit the land,
        And shall take enjoyment in abundant prosperity.

The next part of the psalm (vss. 12-24) has to do with the contrasted lot of the wicked and the righteous. As for the wicked, his day of destruction will come. The psalmist does not seem to view God as directly bringing this about. God sees it, awaits it, knows that it will happen, and so laughs at the now-confident wicked. But the destruction of the wicked comes about in a form and manner that expresses physical necessity.[16] The psalmist is convinced that wickedness in its very nature is suicidal. It brings its perpetrator to his own destruction (vs. 15). There is something in the universe that destroys the

---

[16] Mowinckel, op. cit., I, 4, note 2.

weapons of the ungodly. And, vice versa, there is something in righteousness that wickedness cannot touch. The little which the righteous man possesses comes ultimately to more than the vast possessions of wicked men. The Lord sustains in loving solicitude and in rewarding prosperity the whole career of the righteous. Indeed, since the land is destined to be in the possession of those who are blessed of God, the wicked will be reduced to borrowing, but will be unable to pay back, while the righteous, having enough and to spare, will graciously give. Nor will the righteous ever be dispossessed; even in famine they will have plenty. But the wicked will perish, and their children will become beggars. The Lord's enemies, flaming ovens though they now seem to be, will die down to mere smoke. All that a righteous man does is made possible by the Lord, who takes joy in keeping him steady. Even if he falls, the force of his fall will be broken because God has not let go of him.

ז 12 The wicked schemes up evil against the righteous
       And gnashes his teeth against him.
   13 The Lord laughs at him,
       For He sees that his day is coming.
ח 14a The wicked draw their sword
   14b And bend their bow;
   15 Their sword goes into their own heart,
       And their bows are broken.
ט 16 Better is the little of the righteous
       Than great wealth of the wicked.
   17 For the arms of the wicked shall be broken:
       But the Lord sustains the righteous.
י 18 He cares for the life of the innocent,
       And their property continues forever.
   19 They will not be dispossessed in hard times,
       But in days of famine they shall have their fill.
כ 20a But the wicked perish,
   25c And their offspring seek for bread.
   20b The enemies of the Lord, like the fire of ovens,
   20c Are consumed; they vanish as smoke.
ל 21 The wicked has to borrow and cannot pay back,
       But the righteous is gracious and gives.
   22 For those blessed of Him shall inherit the earth,
       But those cursed of Him shall be cut off.
מ 23 From the Lord come the steps of a man;
       He establishes him in whose way He takes delight.
   24 If he falls, he is not hurled headlong:
       For the Lord supports his hand.

The instruction of this sage-psalmist is based on personal observation. He is now an elderly man and can look back across the years to his boyhood. Throughout his life he has never witnessed a righteous person uncared for, but on the contrary he has seen how gracious and generous the righteous man is to others and how the very remembrance of him is a blessing. He now calls upon what life has taught him, as he says,

> **ר** 25*a* A lad have I been; moreover, I am become old;
>   25*b*   But I have not seen a righteous man forsaken.
>   26   All day long he is gracious and lends,
>   And remembrance of him is a blessing.

So on the basis of all that he has said, in truly prophetic fashion (vss. 27-34) he now summons youths to forsake evil and pursue what is good. This alone will lead to security such as the Lord, the just and faithful, will assure. For while the unrighteous and their descendants are headed for destruction, the righteous will inherit the land and dwell permanently in it. The wise and just speech of the righteous and the steadiness of his conduct are due to the fact that he obeys God's law, which he treasures in his heart. If a righteous man should be in danger at the hand of one who is secretly trying to murder him, God will see to it that he escapes, and if he should be unjustly accused, God will pronounce him innocent. So the psalmist counsels youths to live in God's way. They will then be blessed of the Lord and will be permitted to see with their own eyes the destruction of the wicked. We see clearly in this section that the ideal of piety which our psalmist has is life under the law.

> **ס** 27   Turn from evil and do good,
>   And dwell in the land.
>   28*a* For the Lord loves justice
>   28*b*   And does not forsake His loyal ones;
> **ע** 28*c* The unrighteous will be destroyed forever,
>   28*d*   And the descendants of the wicked will be cut off.
>   29   The righteous shall inherit the land
>   And shall dwell forever upon it.
> **פ** 30   The mouth of the righteous utters wisdom,
>   And his tongue speaks justice.
>   31   The law of his God is in his heart,
>   And his footsteps do not slip.
> **צ** 32   The wicked spies upon the righteous
>   And seeks to kill him.
>   33   The Lord will not leave him in his hand,
>   Nor will He condemn him as guilty when he is judged.
> **ק** 34*a* Wait for the Lord, and keep His way;
>   40*b*   He will bring you into security from the wicked,
>   34*b* And He will exalt you to inherit the land.
>   34*c*   You will gaze at the destruction of the wicked.

Again, as in verses 25-26, our sage-psalmist reaches back into his own personal observation (vss. 35-36) and draws from it the lesson (vss. 37-40) that the prosperity experienced by a wicked man is a very transient thing, for his life will come to an end in destruction. Moreover, although the righteous man may suffer for a time, he will end his life in peace, for the Lord will deliver those who in their trouble seek His protection. Thus the psalmist reports:

ר 35 I have seen a wicked man jubilant,
   Exalting himself like a cedar of Lebanon.
36 Then I passed by, and lo, he was not:
   And I sought for him, but he could not be found.
ש 37 Keep integrity, and aim at uprightness;
   For the final lot of [that] man is peace.
38 But transgressors will be destroyed together;
   The future of the wicked is destruction.
ת 39 Deliverance of the righteous comes from the Lord,
   Their protection in time of trouble.
40a Yes, the Lord will help them and deliver them
40c From evildoers, for they seek refuge in Him.

Ps. 49. AN INTIMATION OF IMMORTALITY

Ps. 49 is a wisdom psalm which deals with the knottiest problem of Hebrew wisdom, the adjustment of the balance between personal character and outward lot. The psalmist has brooded earnestly over this central problem of evil and has come to conclusions to which he attaches great worth. He is himself gripped by what he has to say, and as he opens his psalm, he seeks to arrest the attention of all mankind of all nations, the inhabitants of the world, both the rank and file of men and the nobility. He has a bit of wisdom to utter, the findings of his own brooding mind over the "riddle" of life—a didactic "poem" which is the literary product of his own grapple with the problem. He sings the musings of his heart to the accompaniment of the harp and views music as itself an aid to insight and solution.

1 Hear this, all peoples;
   Give ear, all inhabitants of the world,
2 Both common people and nobility,
   The rich together with the poor.
3 My mouth will utter wisdom,
   And the musing of my heart will be understanding.
4 Incline your ears to a poem;
   I will solve my riddle upon the harp.

The riddle with which the psalmist has been wrestling is now concretely stated and in vivid terms. He speaks here as a teacher to his students. He sees them awed at wealth and strongly attracted by the indulgences in which these material-bound men engage. "Why do you permit yourselves thus to be duped?" the psalmist asks. "Why do you look with awed envy upon carousing wine drinkers, men whose happiness depends upon their material resources, and who boast over the extent of their wealth?"

> 5 Why do you gape at carousing men,
>   Enviously looking at the footsteps of winebibbers,[17]
> 6 Who trust in their wealth
>   And boast over the abundance of their riches?

These men who thus attract you are wealthy. They can buy whatever they want, but they cannot buy their way out of the solemn experience of death. Wealthy men, accustomed as they are to ransoming themselves out of punishment, cannot thus extricate themselves from the common lot of men. The psalmist here begins to express the findings of his own earnest grapple with the problem.

> 7 But man cannot buy himself off at all;
>   He cannot give to God a ransom price for himself,
> 8-9a That he might continue to eternity and live forever,
>   9b So that he need never see the grave.

Learned men and fools are alike in this: both go to their graves, which remain their dwellings for all succeeding generations. Their names, to be sure, live on, for the farms which they leave to others continue to be called by their names. But they themselves perish, and their wealth passes into other hands. Even the richest man becomes poor at death. Moreover, because of their wealth such men during their lifetime are held in honor by others. Yet if they lack moral discernment, they are no better than dumb beasts and are doomed to the same end. This is particularly the case with those who though blind to moral discernment possess silver and gold. But it is likewise the case with those who, whether or not possessing it, consider material wealth as something essential to their happiness.

> 10a For see, wise men die;
> 10b   Fools and intelligent alike perish.
> 11 Their graves are their houses forever,
>   Their dwellings generation after generation.
>   They have given their names to their lands,
> 10c   And they have left their wealth to others.
> 12 But man in honor, yet without discernment,
>   Is like beasts that are dumb.
> 13 Such is the way of those who have silver;
>   Such the end of those who take pleasure in gold.

The psalmist pictures these wealth possessors and money lovers descending penniless to the grave, their flesh there subject to the universal lot of decay. Gruesomely he portrays the humiliation of these once so secure, whose wealth had "shepherded" them. Now, however, they are shepherded only by death-dealing processes of disintegration; their once handsome bodies now have been reduced to mere dung.

[17] See Gunkel's reconstruction of the text of this line.

14 They sink down and descend to Sheol;
    Death shepherds them like sheep:
    Their flesh becomes rotten, and their form decays:
    Their body fertilizes Sheol.[18]

Sheol, the land of the dead, is the common experience of mankind, so the psalmist has maintained. He has just now vividly pictured what happens to the life that is wealth-centered when death shepherds it in Sheol. But is that the lot of the righteous as well? How about the man who *has* moral discernment and lives by it? Here it is that our author takes a leap of faith. The psalmist, who is just such a man, is aware in his own life of a relationship to God that death cannot end. This is the unique Hebrew approach to faith in immortality, which is here shadowed forth. No man can buy his way out of the experience of death. But from the realm of the dead, God can take His own. Only profound religious experience, vital fellowship of the believing, trusting soul with God can inspire such a thought. So our psalmist sings:

15 But God will ransom my soul
    From the power of Sheol, for He will take me.

In the close of the psalm we are in the same atmosphere as in verses 6-12. The psalmist, warning against envy of the rich, emphasizes once more the fact as regards wealth—that "you can't take it with you." Though the man who depends upon his wealth may congratulate himself because of his prosperity, all to which he who lacks moral discernment can look forward is the unillumined darkness of Sheol.

16 Look not [in envy] when a man becomes rich,
    When he increases the wealth of his house,
17 For he will not take any of it when he dies;
    His wealth will not go down after him.
18 Although he blesses his soul when alive
    And praises it because it goes well with it,
19 He must go to the dwelling place of his fathers;
    Never will he see the light.
20 Man, who like the ox does not discern,
    Is like the beasts that are dumb.

Ps. 73. THE PLACE OF WORSHIP IN THE SOLUTION OF LIFE'S PROBLEMS

The psalmist opens his psalm with the conclusion to which the whole struggle of his soul—soon to be described—finally brought him. To the upright, whatever the appearances may be, God is good!

1 Nothing but good is God to the upright,
    Is God to the pure in heart.

---

[18] For this difficult passage I accept Gunkel's illuminating reconstruction of the text, which has been influenced by Ehrlich, Budde, Graetz, Duhm, and Gressmann.

Ah, but the struggle—how real it was, how painful even in memory! At one time his inner tension was so great that he came near to deviating from his upright way. The pressure was so severe that he almost departed from his accustomed calm. And what caused it? Jealousy. When he saw how well-to-do, how prosperous the godless were, jealousy embittered his soul, especially (vs. 13) when he compared their situation with his own condition. Thus he reports:

> 2 But as for me, my feet had almost deviated,
> My steps had almost been made to slip.
> 3 For I was jealous at the wealth of the boasters;
> I was heated up at the prosperity of the ungodly.

He sees how free from trouble they are. They appear to be favorites of fortune, well-fed and protected from calamity such as men generally suffer. And how proud they are! He pictures them holding up their arrogant heads. Their pride sticks out like a gleaming necklace. They wear gorgeous garments, but they have been bought with blood money wrested violently from the oppressed classes. Their hearts have lost their feeling for humanity, and their minds are drugged with dissipation and drunkenness.

> 4 For they have no pangs;
> Full and fat is their belly.
> 5 They have no share in the travail of men,
> And they are not stricken along with men in general.
> 6 Therefore pride serves as a necklace for them;
> They put on for themselves [each] a garment of violence.
> 7 Their iniquity proceeds from an unfeeling heart;
> Drunkenness overcomes their mind.

Then the psalmist describes them as they talk in deep corruption, uttering crookedness as though they were giving an oracle, indeed as though they were God in heaven, their proud tongues expatiating on anything and everything! How vividly the psalmist pictures these loquacious, bold, and impudent "oracles" who speak with such a convincing show of authority. And the tragedy is that the Lord's simple people are duped by this show of wisdom. They turn to them, obsequiously drinking in what they say and absorbing especially their secular spirit, and then on their own part the simple people give open expression to the practical atheism they have thus imbibed.

> 8 Profound is their evil speech:
> Oppressive slander they speak from the height;
> 9 They set their mouth in the heavens,
> And their tongue walks about in the earth!
> 10 Therefore my people turn to them,
> And water in abundance is drained by them.
> 11 So *they* say, "How does God know?"
> And "Is there knowledge in the Most High?"

The psalmist closes his description of the appearance and speech of the wicked by a summary statement which suggests their freedom from misfortune and their mounting wealth.

> 12 Lo, such are the wicked,
> And the unjust, who are carefree, increase in wealth.

The psalmist now makes all the more vivid his description of the godless well to do by contrasting his own frustration. He kept his life clean, lived free from iniquity, and gave open testimony of this through the ritual washing of his hands. He had every reason to look for good fortune from the hand of God, but instead he experienced severe physical suffering which lasted throughout the day and broke out afresh morning after morning:

> 13 Surely in vain have I kept my heart pure
> And washed my hands in innocency;
> 14 Yes, I was stricken all day long,
> And I was chastened afresh every morning.

Yet in spite of his inner turmoil of spirit, his bitter feeling of God's injustice, he did not give utterance to his complaints and doubts among the members of the Lord's congregation, the Lord's children. He would then have felt himself to be a traitor among his people. Rather he kept his doubts to himself.

> 15 If I had said, "I will speak like this,"
> Lo, I would have dealt treacherously with the congregation[19] of
> Thy children.

Thus far the psalmist has dealt with his grave problem, one that was too big for him, which troubled him to the depths of his being. Now he tells the wonderful story of how he triumphed over his great distress. Brooding upon his problem, he found it only became increasingly severe to him until at length it drove him to the Temple. The narrative becomes psychologically luminous as he describes how the worship of the Temple brought him step by step from darkness into light. The first step toward the light was taken when the worship in the sanctuary lifted his mind to final issues. He had been thinking in terms of the present. In the Temple he began to think of final outcomes (vs. 17). He began to see life more under the aspect of eternity. Viewed from the angle of the present, those godless, untroubled rich were firmly established and secure. But viewed in terms of outcomes, of life under the administration of God, their feet are actually standing on slippery places where their foothold on reality is anything but firm. They have fallen into deceptions. Appearance is not reality. His mind now becomes extremely sensitive to their imminent destruction. They are living in the dream world of *seeming* security (vs. 20). But there will be a

---

[19] Literally "generation," but here representing the righteous as a class; cf. Brown, Driver, Briggs, *op. cit.*, pp. 190, 3.

solemn and sudden awakening when they will despise their false security, know-
ing it for the cheap delusion that it is. So the psalmist reports:

> 16 When I considered how I might understand this,
>   It was a burden in my eyes,
> 17 Until I went into the sanctuary of God,
>   [Until] I discerned their final lot.
> 18 Surely Thou dost put their feet in slippery places.
>   Thou dost make them fall into deceptions;
> 19 How suddenly they come to destruction!
>   They cease; they are finished by trouble!
> 20 As a dream of one awakening does not exist,
>   Upon rousing oneself its empty form is disdained.

His mind reverts to the bitter experience of his heart's unspeakable distress
when his problem was most acute, when there seemed to be no such thing as
justice in the retribution of God, no moral fairness in the lot dealt out by Him
to men. But now he sees his problem in a new light. And he realizes as he looks
back upon the fierce spiritual struggle of his soul that he then was ignorant
in mind and dull in heart, more like a dumb beast than a thinking human
being:

> 21 For my heart was embittered,
>   And I was pierced to the core of my being;
> 22 Yes, I was a dullard, ignorant;
>   Like a beast was I before Thee.

Now, however, in worship the psalmist has lost his fretfulness, irritation, and
peevishness. In the first two words of verse 23, "nevertheless I," [20] there is
implied a contrast between the life of the ungodly and his own life. The
ungodly is doomed to speedy destruction, but his own life is held continually
in the enduring grasp of God. But "nevertheless" has also a wider reference.
It is as though the psalmist should say "for all that, in spite of" all the doubts
and laments which before drove him almost to the loss of his faith, now in the
very experience of worship he has won the confidence that his life is in the
intimate and precious comradeship of God. God does not and will not leave
him, but guides him in the difficult hours of decision, and finally will take him
into honor, into splendor. Kittel finely says: "That is the glorious fruit and the
gleaming goal of the present fellowship with God." [21]

> 23 Nevertheless I am continually with Thee:
>   Thou dost grasp me by my right hand.
> 24 Thou dost guide me by Thy counsel
>   And afterward wilt receive me in honor.

The psalmist feels himself to be a loyal member of the worshiping community, the "pure in heart" (vs. 1). He definitely counts himself as belonging

[20] Kittel suggestively entitles this psalm "the great nevertheless" (*das grosse Dennoch*).
[21] *Die Psalmen*, p. 247.

to "the congregation of Thy children" (vs. 15). He participates in the Temple rituals designed to mediate the spiritual cleansing of God (vs. 13). Nor in his highest moments does he renounce that relationship. Yet he goes his own individual way and certainly, by his deep spiritual experience of being held in the grasp of God and by the certainty that in the end he will be received in honor at God's hands, advances the faith of Israel *toward* immortality. Such a psalm teaches us that the Hebrew conception of God grew, by reflection, to be sure, but yet more by enthusiasm, by deep emotion, by rich spiritual experience.[22] The psalmist rises to his spiritual climax in one of the noblest and profoundest utterances of the Psalter, and indeed of the faith of Israel. God is his soul's supreme good. And, as Oesterley finely says, this psalmist "is certain that a material event like the dissolution of the body is powerless to break the love-forged links of the soul." [23] If he has fellowship with God, he has all that his soul truly wants; every other desire fades into insignificance before it.

> 25   Whom have I in heaven save Thee?
>   And besides Thee I have no desire on earth.
> 26   My flesh and my heart waste away,
>   But God is my portion forever.

The last two verses of the psalm summarize it, placing before us the picture of God's annihilation of the ungodly, and also of His protection of those who draw near to Him. We feel in the psalmist's closing words an implicit appeal to the congregation for loyalty at a time when desertion of the comradeship, guidance, and protection which religion affords is rife. And we see how the spirit of testimony is alive in the psalmist's soul. He has the strong impulse to tell the story of his inner spiritual struggle and triumph in the most sacred place of which he can conceive.

> 27   For lo, those who depart from Thee shall perish;
>   Thou dost annihilate everyone who is disloyal to Thee.
> 28   But as for me, to draw near [24] God is good for me:
>   I have made the Lord my refuge,
>   So I can tell of all Thy wonderful works,
>   In the gates of the daughter of Zion.[25]

Ps. 112. TRUST IN GOD AS A STEADYING POWER

Ps. 112 is an alphabetic psalm which has been strongly influenced by the wisdom poetry. It deals with the virtue and reward of the righteous, and in two places (vss. 1 and 5) gives blessings, both of which are characteristic of the

[22] Kittel, *Die Psalmen*, p. 243.

[23] *The Psalms*, II, 344. Cf. Knudson, *The Religious Teaching of the Old Testament*, p. 402: "Such perfect communion with God manifestly could not brook the thought of its own cessation."

[24] Cf. Brown, Driver, Briggs, *op. cit.*, p. 898, where Cheyne renders *qirebhath 'elōhîm* as "approach to God."

[25] So read with the Septuagint.

wisdom type of utterance. The period from which this psalm comes is a time
when the priest, the prophet, and the sage formed the very pillars of Judean
life. Such wise men or sages were not interested in a worldly, secular wisdom,
but in a kind of counsel that rooted in religion, that is, in the requirements of
the worship of the Lord. It is possible that this psalm, so strongly influenced by
the style of Israelite wisdom poetry, was composed for the Temple worship [26]
in connection with the psalms of blessing and cursing. Its alphabetic form,
which belongs largely to the wisdom literature or to that which has been influenced by it, could indicate a relatively late date. Moreover, its interest, not
in agriculture but in commerce, and the central importance it gives to the law
would indicate a time after the Priestly Code had been introduced, so probably
not earlier than the fourth century B.C. This psalm was best adapted to those
services in the Temple where instruction of the worshipers of the Lord in
right conduct, and especially instruction of the youth, would have central
emphasis. The alphabetic arrangement of precepts would be advantageous as a
memory device. Such instruction in conduct was clearly the purpose of the
psalm.

Its sentences are relatively unrelated to one another and are arranged, not
in strict logical sequence, but like a string of pearls. However, we can discern
some order, as the interpretation will show. We get here a good picture of the
kind of person a true worshiper of God should be.

The opening verse is an exclamation and sounds the psalmist's keynote of
the good life, joyous obedience to the priestly law.

> א   1   **Oh the happiness of the man who fears the Lord,**
> ב   **Who greatly delights in His commandment!**

Certain rewards inevitably come as the result of such obedience: his descendants will be well-to-do [27] in the land (vs. 2a); that class of men which he
represents will be prospered (vs. 2b); he will become wealthy (vs. 3a); his
righteousness in its social expression will have no interruption (vs. 3b); upon
his hours of darkness God's light will break (vs. 4a).

> ג   2   **His descendants will be well-to-do in the land:**
> ד   **The race of the upright will be blessed.**
> ה   3   **Wealth and riches are in his house,**
> ו   **And his righteousness [28] will continue forever.**
> ז   4a **Light breaks forth in the darkness for the upright.**

The psalmist then characterizes the righteous man as to his spirit and conduct (vss. 4b-6). The righteous man is gracious and merciful (vs. 4b); he has a
lively, practical concern for and participation in the weal and woe of his people's

[26] Cf. Mowinckel, *op. cit.*, VI, 33.   [27] Cf. Ehrlich, *op. cit.*, p. 283.

[28] "Righteousness" here has the meaning of "charity," righteousness expressing itself in deeds
of love, this very wealth guaranteeing its steady flow"; cf. *ibid.*, p. 284.

lot [29] (vs. 5a); he is just in the conduct of his affairs (vs. 5b); he has dependable stability (vs. 6a); and as a consequence he will always be remembered (vs. 6b).

ח	4b	Gracious and merciful is the righteous man;
ט	5	Happy is the man who shows favor and lends,
י		Who maintains his affairs with justice,
כ	6	For the righteous shall never be moved;
ל		He will be remembered forever.

The innermost sustaining faith in the Lord, how it manifests itself in the community life, and how it is rewarded, now brings the psalm to its climax (vss. 7-8). Such a righteous man lives above fear of evil tidings (vs. 7a); his innermost soul is fixed trustfully in the care of God (vs. 7b); his heart supported by the Lord, is not afraid in the presence of adversaries (vs. 8a); and such divine upholding sustains him until the very hour when he witnesses their fall (vs. 8b). His inner faith issues in outer service to the needy, and his benevolence is unceasing (vs. 9b); such inner faith and social conduct bring their reward in a life that steadily increases in dignity and honor (vs. 9c).

מ	7	He is not afraid of bad news;
		His heart is established, entrusted to the Lord.
ם	8	Sustained in his heart, he will not be afraid,
ע		Until he sees in triumph [30] his [fallen] enemies.
פ	9	He disperses plentifully to the needy;
צ		His righteousness [31] continues forever:
ק		His dignity towers up in honor.

Over against such a life of nobility, social vision, and community recognition the psalmist paints in colors of vivid contrast the fate of the wicked. He thinks of the wicked as observing in disappointed, helpless futility the happiness, stability, and growing honor of the righteous. The evil man's indignation is aroused (vs. 10a); he grinds his teeth in frustrated rage and melts away (vs. 10b), for it is a characteristic Israelite idea that evil has no permanence, no enduring hold upon reality. So the wicked man's expectation will come to nought (vs. 10c). The treatment of the wicked in three short lines in contrast to the nineteen devoted to the righteous gives an impressive close to the psalm.

ר	10	The wicked sees and is indignant;
ש		He gnashes his teeth and melts away:
ת		The hope of the wicked comes to nought.

Ps. 127. THE FOLLY OF LEAVING GOD OUT OF ACCOUNT

Ps. 127 had its origin in two general maxims of Hebrew wisdom which at first had no reference to the Temple and its worship. Both are definitely re-

[29] Cf. Gunkel, *Einleitung*, p. 298.   [30] Cf. Gesenius-Kautzsch, *op. cit.*, sec. 164f.
[31] In the sense of charity, benevolence.

ligious, however, with the Lord at the center of attention. The first (vss. 1-2) stresses the folly of any person's building a house without seeking the Lord's blessing, or of guarding a city without God's help. Hard toil for a bare liveli-hood—continuing from early morning to late evening with but little time out at noon for a hurried meal—without taking God into account not only fails of its aim but even brings harm upon the toiler.[32] All that he gains by such feverish industry, God gives to His loved ones while they sleep!

> 1   Unless the Lord build the house,
>   In vain do the builders labor on it:
>   Unless the Lord guard the city,
>   In vain does the watchman keep guard.
> 2   In vain do you get up early to work,
>   Sitting down late to rest,[33]
>   Eating bread gained by mere toil;
>   So much He gives to His loved ones in sleep!

The sage is here stressing with freshness and originality what another sage with Oriental overstatement had urged:

> The blessing of the Lord makes rich,
>   And toil adds nothing to it. (Prov. 10:22.)

Such words by no means counsel against industry, nor are they a brief for idleness. The sage is rather pleading for an orientation toward toil on the part of the industrious Palestinian farmer, who trustfully takes God into account in all his labor, depending upon His presence, interest, and help. It fosters the attitude of living but a day at a time with no anxious care as to the morrow. The conception is basically the same as that of Jesus in the Sermon on the Mount (Matt. 6:25-34). The thought of the sage sounds "a tone from another world, a wholesome antidote to the anxiety of our restless lives." [34]

The second utterance of Hebrew wisdom in this psalm is likewise distinctively religious and characteristically Oriental, as true to Eastern thinking and feeling today as ever. The greatest desire of a Hebrew husband is that his marriage may be blessed with sons. He may have passed down to him as an inheritance from his ancestors his home and his wealth. But whether or not he has children, and more especially sons, depends upon the blessing of God. Sons are the reward of piety. The sage thinks of sons of a husband's youthful vigor as arrows in a warrior's hands. Fortunate indeed is he who has many of them in his quiver ready for use when a fight is on with his enemies! But the sage here thinks not of an actual fight with weapons but of the fight for justice at the

---

[32] See Mowinckel, op. cit., I, 55, for penetrating insight into the significance of the term rendered "in vain" (vs. 1).

[33] Cf. Isa. 5:11; the words mean "rise up to work" and "cessation" from it; cf. Ehrlich, op. cit., p. 336.

[34] Cf. Gunkel, Die Psalmen, p. 554.

city gates, where justice is administered. Even there justice often miscarries. The poor are robbed because they are powerless to protect themselves against such thwarting of justice. The needy are crushed in the gate (Prov. 22:22). The innocent are often oppressed, and the poor are thrust aside from their lawful right (Amos 5:12). It strengthens a good man's cause if at his side stand stalwart sons, able to fight and ready at the drop of a hat! The sage's word is presented with a characteristic introduction of a Hebrew maxim.[35]

> 3 Lo, sons are the inheritance assigned by the Lord;
>   The offspring of the womb is His reward.
> 4 Like arrows in the hand of a warrior,
>   So are the sons of a man's youth.
> 5 Happy the warrior
>   Who has his quiver
>   Full of them:
>   He will not be ashamed when he speaks
>   With enemies in the gate.

Mowinckel is probably right in maintaining that these two utterances of Hebrew wisdom, which were not originally composed for use in worship, were united into this psalm and connected with the Feast of Booths. This fall festival was, as we have seen, the festival of the consecration of the Temple (1 Kings 8:2), even as it was the festival which celebrated the Lord's abiding presence in the midst of His people.[36] As the New Year festival it also emphasized the Lord as the dispenser in the coming year, both of fruitfulness in agriculture and of fecundity in the family. These themes were thus given a new interpretation in this psalm. The first part of the psalm celebrated Jerusalem as the city on Mount Zion which could not be moved and in the psalmist's thought the city of God. In the second the congregation calls that man happy upon whom many sons were bestowed by the Lord as the dispenser of life.

Ps. 128. A PICTURE OF HOME LIFE UNDER THE BLESSING OF GOD

Ps. 128 is a wisdom psalm. It has as its characteristic introduction an utterance of blessing and is dominated throughout by the distinctive Hebrew teaching as regards retribution. But it is also a psalm that is definitely related to the public worship in Judaism. The psalm originated after the fall of the Judean state, in postexilic times when the Jewish community knew all too well the impoverishment from the exorbitant taxes demanded by Persia, the empire of occupation, and from oppressive Jewish landlords such as we learn about in Nehemiah's memoirs (5:1-13).

The setting of the psalm in worship is in connection with the Festival of Booths, the New Year festival of Israel with its emphasis upon Zion's good fortune (vs. 6), and the blessing of fecundity in the life of the family, blessings

---

[35] Cf. Gunkel, *Einleitung*, p. 391.   [36] *Op. cit.*, VI, 4, 36; II, 5, 168-70; cf. Pss. 125:1; 46:5.

which were sought in the public worship, [37] and particularly during that season of the Temple year.

The psalm opens with a general utterance of blessing upon everyone who fears the Lord and walks in His ways. The verbal forms suggest the unbroken continuity of atttiude on the part of the worshiper, and the mood of the words is best rendered as an exclamation.

> 1 Oh the happiness of everyone who fears the Lord,
>   Who walks in His ways!

Well enough did the hard-beset postexilic Jewish community in Palestine know the experience of being so impoverished by taxes levied by the occupying empire, and by exorbitant interest exactions of indifferent landlords, that although they planted their vineyards, others might eat the fruit which the Jews had husbanded (Isa. 65:21-22; 62:8-9). Fortunate indeed would be the community when it could enjoy the fruit of its own labor.

> 2 When the product of thy hands thou canst eat,
>   Oh thy happiness and thy prosperity!

From the general picture of God-fearing people and the glimpse of the happy peasant farmer the psalmist comes closer home as he deals with the Palestinian family in a representative peasant home. It is one of the priceless pictures of family life in the Psalter, and indeed in the entire Old Testament. The wife's first duty, in the Israelite view of family life, was to give her husband children, thus "assisting him in creating a 'house' and in upholding him within his family." The Orient is at one in this still today, that children, and primarily male children, represent the longing of a woman's soul. Through bearing her husband male children a wife perpetuates her husband's family.[38] So our psalmist pictures the wife as the one who in the inner part of the house, the place of privacy, bears her children, and the picture implies that she waits upon her husband and her sons as they sit at meat around the table. How appropriate and pertinent are the similes here employed for a Palestinian peasant home! The wife is a vine which bears fruit. These children are like the clusters of delicious grapes that prove the vitality of the vine. This is implied, not stated. But the other simile is clearly painted. See these boys seated around that Palestinian table. Count them, for they are numerous, and they will stay there long enough and still enough to be counted! We see the stalwart peasant father at the head of the table, like an olive tree. And grouped around him we see his boys, not as "chips off the old block," as our wooden idiom might suggest, but as olive shoots from the parent tree! The psalmist gives each his place, woman and man, in the rearing of a "house." The words are addressed in the singular to the representative Israelite head of his household, who ever in

---

[37] *Ibid.*, II, 5, 166, 170, 180; VI, 33.   [38] Cf. Pedersen, *op. cit.*, p. 70.

Israelite opinion held the place of prime importance among the Lord's worshipers.

> 3 Thy wife is like a fruit-bearing vine
>   In the innermost part of thy house;
>   Thy sons are olive shoots
>   Around thy table.
> 4 Lo, a man is blessed
>   Who fears the Lord.

It is a happy, co-operative, and godly Jewish home which is here pictured,
and this very psalm has played its own influential part in the creation of that
noble family life for which Judaism is justly famous.

The closing part of the psalm is the utterance of the priestly blessing. From
Zion, where the Lord dwells and where annually He was re-enthroned, proceeds God's blessing, first to His worshiping congregation, then to His people
everywhere. The priest is here represented as the mediator of something precious
to the present generation, the blessing of the Lord, which will mean the longed-
for good fortune of Jerusalem, the well-being of the holy city, not to be looked
upon as a spectacle, but to be enjoyed as a participant. But more, just as those
fine boys of the Palestinian home sit there as representatives of the new generation, so the psalmist's thought sweeps into its compass both them and their
children yet to be. For the deepest interest of this psalmist is not a single
Palestinian home nor the continuity of one strong family, but Israel, the whole
people of the Lord. As Pedersen reminds us, "apart from the family the totality
which has the strongest hold upon the Israelites is that of the people." [39] It is an
indication of the nobility of this "people of the book" that in the enjoyment of
family happiness the Israelite never forgot his longing for the welfare of Israel.

Thus the priest, still preserving the second person singular as is the case in
the great Aaronic benediction (Num. 6:24-26), utters the Lord's blessing upon
the congregation.

> 5 May the Lord bless thee from Zion,
>   [His holy place,] [40]
>   That Thou mayst see Jerusalem in good fortune
>   All the days of thy life:
> 6 And that thou mayest see the children of thy children.
>   Peace be upon Israel!

Ps. 133. THE PROBLEM OF LIVING TOGETHER

Ps. 133 is a wisdom psalm, beginning as it does with a characteristic word
that introduces a wisdom utterance, and giving vivid comparisons of one thing
with another, likewise a strong feature of the wisdom literature. It deals with
a great and persistent problem, as crucial in our day as in the era of the post-

---

[39] *Ibid.*, p. 275.   [40] Budde thus supplies the lacking line.

exilic congregation, from which period the psalm sprang—the problem of community, of living together. It comes from a time when the Priestly Code had become the foundation of the social and religious life of postexilic Judaism, when, accordingly, there was an Aaronic high priesthood at the head of the community. This dates the psalm not before the early fourth century B.C.

The psalm paints with freshness and rare beauty the ancient Israelite ideal of community, which goes back to the covenant formed at Sinai between the Lord and the Israelites, "out of which covenant," as Pedersen says, "grew the whole fabric of their existence." [41] "This covenant ideal viewed the nature of Israelite community as being reciprocal brotherhood, rooting in God, each one in his own place, the one giving of his blessing to the other." [42] The annual ceremonies of the New Year had as one major aim the renewal and deepening of this mutual covenant bond, primarily between the Lord and His congregation, but also between the individual Israelites. This annual cultic renewal of the covenant brought to the participating worshipers an increase of strength and religious emotion which joined them together as links in a chain of brotherhood. Moreover, this renewal of the bond of brotherhood between Israelites was not merely a result of the religious celebration. It was also interpreted in the psalms themselves as a necessary prerequisite for the full blessing of peace and harmony which God desired the celebration to bring. That which gave rise to such a psalm as this, with its exaltation of brotherly love, would be the great lack of such love in the social life of Israel. It was created in order to emphasize to the brothers of the Lord's worshiping community the common duty of holding together and of helping one another, the lack of which would result in the withholding of the divine blessing. [43]

The psalm opens with an exclamation as to the delight experienced when the "brothers," the Lord's worshiping community, dwell intimately together in harmony.

> 1 Lo, how good and how delightful it is,
>   For brothers to dwell intimately [44] together.

To describe this deep spiritual reality of brotherly love the psalmist gives us two vivid comparisons. The spirit of brotherhood—and here the psalmist joins together a chain of pictures, one suggesting the other, in order to explain this strangely intangible yet marvelous thing—is like colorless, costly anointing oil, of rich quality and delightful odor, poured upon the head of one who deserves it (cf. Matt. 26:7), which trickles gently and slowly down upon the beard. The figure of the beard in turn suggests the beard of Aaron—that is, the beard of the high priest, which must not be cut (Lev. 21:5), a thing of dignity and rare beauty, well kept and highly prized—which beautiful symbol

---

[41] Op. cit., p. 18.   [42] Mowinckel, op. cit., I, 118.   [43] Ibid., II, 168.

[44] The last two Hebrew words joined together add to the concept of togetherness that of intimacy; cf. Ehrlich, op. cit., p. 347.

of manly honor flowed down over the edge of his priestly robe. The flowing down of the oil and of the beard suggests another picture of something coming softly and fruitfully down from the heights, not now heights of dignity, but of physical elevation. The psalmist thinks of the towering mountain range of Hermon, snow-capped, surrounded by clouds, and drenched with the creative, life-giving dews which flow gently down to the otherwise arid hill country roundabout it, that bring life wheresoever they come. Such are pictures of the spirit of brotherhood. The brotherly spirit, fragrant, precious, and honorable, noble, beautiful, and dignified, life-giving, restoring, and refreshing is a divine blessing forever wherever it is found.

> 2 It is like costly oil upon the head,
> Which flows down upon the beard;
> Like Aaron's beard, which flows down
> Upon the edge of his robe;
> 3 Like the dew of Hermon,
> Which falls down upon the arid [45] hill country.

The psalm comes to an arresting close, in which everything thus far expressed rises to an appealing and challenging climax to the worshipers. We sense how it must have searched the innermost spirit of the congregation, touching with sharp warning any unbrotherly elements or attitudes in the worshiping fellowship. Only "there," it implies, where the spirit of brotherhood prevails, are the conditions met for the blessing of spiritual vitality to be poured out by God in bounteous, never-ending stream.

> 4 For there hath the Lord commanded the blessing,
> Life forevermore!

This psalm reminds us forcibly of the noble utterance in the first epistle of John:

> No one who does not do right is of God,
> Nor anyone who does not love his brother. . . .
> We know that we have passed out of death into life,
> Because we love the brethren. (3:10b, 14.)

Ps. 144:12-15. OH THE HAPPINESS OF THE PEOPLE WHOSE GOD IS THE LORD!

Ps. 144:12-15 forms an independent psalm and was originally unrelated to what precedes it. It is strongly tinged with the interests of Hebrew wisdom, and especially with that strain of teaching by the sages which springs from the Deuteronomic doctrine of reward. This doctrine exerted a strong influence while the Judean kingdom was still intact, and profoundly affected Hebrew wisdom

---

[45] Reading, with Schmidt, çiyyāh (arid), instead of çiyyôn, which is impossible here geographically.

from the religious angle.[46] It is a vivid, colorful poem and may belong to a
fairly early time.[47] Its similarity in tone to I Kings 10:8-9 leads me to date it
very close to 621 B.C., when the Deuteronomic reform inaugurated under Josiah
had raised high hopes for Judah. Its most likely place in the later postexilic
worship of Judaism would be at the New Year festival, when the psalm would
express, not so much a situation which existed in Judah, as that longed-for
sense of social well-being which the turn of fortunes might bring from the Lord's
hand.

The psalmist pictures the Judean young men as the newly-driven pillars of
a tower, straight, sturdy, and strong. The young women are compared to the
carved corner columns of a palace, shapely and beautiful. The granaries are
bursting with all kinds of grain. The fields are covered with flocks rich in
increase. The regiments of soldiers are not marching off to war, nor do they
send out their scouts ahead to search for water, but they are free to turn their
energies to the agricultural and pastoral phases of community life. No wailing
for slain soldiers is heard in the streets. And most significant of all, the people
recognize the Lord as the giver of these blessings, and worship Him with loyal
hearts.

The whole psalm is a prolonged exclamation of joy.[48]

12 Oh our happiness! [49]
      Our sons are like newly-driven tower pillars: [50]
    Our daughters are like corner columns,
      Carved after the pattern of a palace.
13 Our granaries are full to overflowing,
      A granary for every kind of [grain].[51]
    Our sheep bear thousands,
      Ten thousands in our meadows;
14 Our regiments [52] are peacefully occupied,[53]
      No vanguard,[54] and no army marching out,
        And no cries of lamentation in our streets.
15 Oh the happiness of the people for whom it is so!
      Oh the happiness of the people whose God is the Lord!

[46] Cf. Pfeiffer, *Introduction to the Old Testament*, pp. 655 ff.
[47] Gunkel, *Die Psalmen*, p. 608.
[48] I am indebted for the understanding of these difficult verses to the illuminating textual
study of Ehrlich, *op. cit.*, pp. 380 ff, whose insight into the psalmist's meaning is profound.
[49] So read with Graetz, *op. cit.*, II, 684.
[50] Reading *kineti'ê migdālim,* with Ehrlich, *op. cit.*, p. 380.
[51] Reading *mezān'el zān, zān* being Aramaic and meaning "kind," *ibid.*
[52] Reading *'alāphênû, ibid.*
[53] Literally, "burdened," construed in the spirit of Isa. 2:4 (Mic. 4:3), "military weapons
transformed into agricultural implements."
[54] The word is *pereç,* construed as coming from the Arabic root designating a messenger
sent ahead for water; so, "vanguard"; cf. Mic. 2:13.

Ps. 1. LIFE'S TWO WAYS

Ps. 1 is a wisdom psalm which combines the two characteristic interests of postexilic Judaism, the trend toward legalism and the teaching concerning retribution. This latter problem, as Paulsen has said, is "the first great fundamental truth to which reflection on moral things has led all nations." [55] The psalm has a strong pedagogical interest which comes to focus in the congregation of the Lord. And the trend in the psalm toward the law and its study points to a time of origin after around 397 B.C., when the priestly law was introduced to the restored community in Jerusalem and Judah. Such a psalm would be appropriate in the congregation whenever the pedagogical interest which centered in the law was being stressed, and this, at least in later Judaism, would be at the Festival of Weeks (Harvest or Pentecost), which celebrated the giving of the law at Sinai.

The psalm itself has no superscription and was intended to be an introduction to the book of Psalms as a whole. How pertinent, then, is its portrayal of the two ways of life which are with such variety and sharpness differentiated in the Psalter!

The psalmist first describes negatively the man who walks life's good way, that is, by what he does not do. He refuses to walk as the morally loose, criminal element in society counsel him to do, or to stand where those congregate who have missed life's true goal, or to sit as a willing crony among those who scoff at goodness. Then the psalmist turns to positive description and depicts the good man in terms of what he does. He delights in religion and meditates upon the Lord's requirements as enjoined in the law, brooding over them by day and in the wakeful hours of night.

> 1   Oh the happiness of the man who walks not
>   In accordance with the counsel of the ungodly,
>   Who does not take his stand in the way of sinners,
>   And does not sit in the seat of scoffers,
> 2   But finds his delight in the fear of the Lord,
>   And in His law meditates day and night.

Such a person grows as a tree grows when, its roots having been moistened by a water stream, it bears fruit in season, according to the law of its being, its leaves keeping perennially fresh. Likewise such a person brings to a successful issue everything he undertakes to do.

> 3   Then he will be like a tree planted by streams of water,
>   Which bears its fruit in season;
>   Its leaves, moreover, do not wither;
>   And everything which he does he makes prosper.

[55] In Gunkel, *Die Psalmen*, p. 1.

The psalmist is indebted both to Jeremiah (17:5-8) and to Ezekiel (47:12) for his comparison of a good man to a growing tree.

Turning to the other side of the picture, the psalmist now describes the morally loose, the evildoers. How vivid the contrast which he paints! For the wicked compare with the good as wind-driven chaff compares with a securely rooted tree. We note here a characteristic Hebrew idea that in goodness there is permanence: it has hold upon reality. In evil there is nothing substantial. As a consequence the evildoer will not be able to stand up before the sifting forces of the Lord's judgment.[56] Sinners will not have what it takes to come through the purging discipline of God into membership in the congregation of God's righteous worshipers. For what happens to the righteous is of concern to God, but any hope which the wicked man has is futile.

> 4 Not so [is it with] the evildoer, not so;
>   But he is like the chaff which the wind pursues.
> 5 Therefore the evildoer will not endure in the judgment,
>   Nor will sinners endure in the congregation of the righteous.
> 6 Because the Lord cares about what becomes of the righteous,
>   But the hope of the wicked will vanish.

[56] This psalmist is familiar with Mal. 3:1-3 and 4:1. Cf. also Isa. 33:14-16.

BIBLIOGRAPHY

Albright, W. F. *From the Stone Age to Christianity*. Baltimore: Johns Hopkins University Press, 1940.

————. *Archaeology and the Religion of Israel*. Baltimore: Johns Hopkins University Press, 1942.

Alt, A. *Die Ursprünge des israelitischen Rechts*. Berichte über die Verhandlungen der Sächsischen Akademie der Wissenschaften zu Leipzig, Philologisch-historische Klasse. Vol. 86. Leipzig: Hirzel, 1934.

Balla, E. *Das Ich der Psalmen*. Göttingen: Vandenhoeck und Ruprecht, 1912.

Barton, G. A. *Archaeology and the Bible*. 7th ed. Philadelphia: American Sunday School Union, 1937.

Bertholet, A., in E. Kautzsch-Bertholet, *Die heilige Schrift des Alten Testaments*. Vols. I-II. 4th ed. Tübingen: Mohr, 1922-23.

Blackman, A. M. "The Myth and Ritual Pattern in Egypt," in S. H. Hooke, ed., *Myth and Ritual*.

————. "The Psalms in the Light of Egyptian Research," in D. C. Simpson, ed., *The Psalmists*.

Bornhäuser, Hans. "Sukka,' 'in Beer and Holtzmann, *Die Mischna, II Seder, 6 Traktat*. Berlin: Töpelmann, 1935.

Breasted, J. H. *The Development of Religion and Thought in Ancient Egypt*. New York: Charles Scribner's Sons, 1912.

Briggs, C. A., and Briggs, Emilie G. *A Critical and Exegetical Commentary on the Psalms*. Vols. I-II. New York: Charles Scribner's Sons, 1906-7.

Brown, Francis; Driver, S. R.; and Briggs, C. A. *A Hebrew and English Lexicon of the Old Testament*. Boston: Houghton Mifflin Co., 1907.

Buhl, F. "Liber Psalmorum," in Kittel, *Biblia Hebraica*. 3rd ed.

Buttenwieser, Moses. *The Psalms: Chronologically Treated with a New Translation*. Chicago: University of Chicago Press, 1938.

Charles, R. H., ed. *The Apocrypha and Pseudepigrapha of the Old Testament in English*. Vols. I-II. Oxford: The Clarendon Press, 1913.

Cheyne, T. K. *The Book of Psalms*. London: Kegan Paul, Trench & Co., 1888.

————. *The Origin and Religious Contents of the Psalter*. London: Bampton, 1891.

Cooke, G. A. *A Text-Book of North-Semitic Inscriptions*. Oxford: The Clarendon Press, 1903.

Cumming, C. G. *The Assyrian and the Hebrew Hymns of Praise*. New York: Columbia University Press, 1934.

Dalman, G. "Zu Psalm 42:7, 8," in *Palästinajahrbuch*, V (1909).

Danby, Herbert. *The Mishnah*. London: Oxford University Press, 1933.

Davidson, A. B. *Hebrew Syntax*. 3rd ed. Edinburgh: T. & T. Clark, 1902.

Davies, T. Witton. *The Psalms LXXIII-CL* (The New Century Bible). New York: Oxford University Press, n. d.

Davison, W. T. *The Psalms I-LXXII* (The New Century Bible). New York: Oxford University Press, n. d.

Dibelius, M. *Die Lade Jahves*. Göttingen: Vanderhoeck und Ruprecht, 1906.

Driver, G. R. "The Psalms in the Light of Babylonian Research," in Simpson, ed., *The Psalmists*.

Driver, S. R. *Hebrew Tenses*. 3rd ed. Oxford: The Clarendon Press, 1892.

————. *Studies in the Psalms*. London: Hodder & Stoughton, 1915.

Duhm, B. *Die Psalmen* (Marti's "Kurzer Hand-Commentar zum Alten Testament"). Tübingen: Mohr, 1899.

Ehrlich, Arnold B. *Die Psalmen*. Berlin: Poppelauer, 1905.

Elbogen, Ismar. *Der jüdische Gottesdienst in seiner geschichtlichen Entwicklung*. 2nd ed. Frankfurt a/M: Kaufmann, 1924.

Erman, A. *A Handbook of Egyptian Religion*, trans. by A. S. Griffith. London: Constable, 1907.

————. *Die Religion der Ägypter*. Berlin: DeGruyter, 1934.

————. *The Literature of the Ancient Egyptians*, trans. by A. M. Blackman. London: Methuen, 1927.

Eusebius *Chronicon*. Vols. I and II, ed. by A. Schoene. Berlin, 1866.

————. *Onomasticon*, ed. by Larsow and Parthey. Berlin, 1862.

Faw, Chalmer E. *Royal Motifs in the Hebrew Psalter*. Chicago: University of Chicago Libraries, 1939.

Fiebig, P. "Rosch ha-schana," in Beer and Holtzmann, *Die Mischna, Seder II, Traktat 8*. Berlin: Töpelmann, 1935.

Gadd, C. J. "The Myth and Ritual Pattern in Babylonia," in Hooke, ed., *Myth and Ritual*.

Gesenius-Kautzsch. *Hebrew Grammar*, trans. by A. E. Cowley. 2nd ed. Oxford: The Clarendon Press, 1910.

Graetz, H. *Kritischer Commentar zu den Psalmen*. Vols. I-II. Breslau: Schottlaender, 1882-83.

Gray, G. B. *Sacrifice in the Old Testament*. Oxford: The Clarendon Press, 1925.

Gressmann, H. *Altorientalische Texte zum Alten Testament*. Berlin: DeGruyter, 1926.

————. *Mose und seine Zeit*. Göttingen: Vandenhoeck und Ruprecht, 1913.

Gross, Morris. *Blessing and Cursing in the Psalms*. Chicago: University of Chicago Libraries, 1937.

Gunkel, H. *Ausgewählte Psalmen*. 3rd ed. Göttingen: Vandenhoeck und Ruprecht, 1905.

————. "Die israelitsche Literatur," in P. Hinneberg, ed., *Die Kultur der Gegenwart*, Teil I, Abteilung VII: *Die orientalischen Literaturen*. Berlin and Leipzig: Teubner, 1906.

————. *Die Psalmen übersetzt und erklärt* (Göttinger Hand Kommentar zum Alten Testament). Göttingen: Vandenhoeck und Ruprecht, 1926.

————. *Einleitung in den Psalmen* (Part II by J. Begrich). Göttingen: Vandenhoeck und Ruprecht, 1927, 1933.

————. *Schöpfung und Chaos in Urzeit und Endzeit*. 2nd ed. Göttingen: Vandenhoeck und Ruprecht, 1921.

————. "The Poetry of the Psalms: Its Literary History and Its Application to the Dating of the Psalms," in D. C. Simpson, ed., *Old Testament Essays*. London: Oxford University Press, 1927.

————. *What Remains of the Old Testament*, trans. by A. K. Dallas. London: Allen & Unwin, 1928.

Guthe, H. "Ausgrabungen bei Jerusalem," in *Zeitschrift des Deutschen Palästina-Vereins*. Vol. V. Leipzig, 1882.

————. *Geschichte des Volkes Israels*. 3rd ed. Tübingen: Mohr, 1914.

Halévy, J. *Recherches bibliques, notes pour l'interpretation des Psaumes*. Tome III. Paris: Leroux, 1905.

Hamilton, Mary. *Incubation or the Cure of Disease in Pagan Temples and Christian Churches*. London: Henderson, 1906.

Harper, R. F. *The Code of Hammurabi King of Babylon*. 2nd ed. Chicago: University of Chicago Press, 1904.

Hempel, J. "Die israelitischen Anschauungen von Segen und Fluch im Lichte altorientalischen Parallelen," in *Zeitschrift der Deutschen Morganländischen Gesellschaft*, LXXIX (1925).

Herrmann, J. *Hebräische Wörterbuch zu den Psalmen*. Berlin: Töpelmann, 1937.

Hooke, S. H., ed. *Essays on the Myth and Ritual of the Hebrews in Relation to the Culture Pattern of the Ancient East.* London: Oxford University Press, 1933.

————. *The Labyrinth.* London: Oxford University Press, 1935.

————. *The Origins of Early Semitic Ritual.* London: Oxford University Press, 1938.

Humbert, Paul. "La relation de Genèse 1 et du Psaume 104 avec la liturgie du nouvel-an israélite," in *Revue d'histoire et de philosophie religieuses.* Strasbourg University, 1935.

James, Fleming. *Thirty Psalmists.* New York: G. P. Putnam's Sons, 1938.

Jastrow, Morris. *Die Religion Babyloniens und Assyriens.* Vols. I-II. Giessen: Töpelmann, 1905-12.

Johnson, Aubrey R. *The Cultic Prophet in Ancient Israel.* Cardiff: University of Wales, 1944.

————. "The Prophet in Israelite Worship," in *The Expository Times,* XLVII (1936) .

————. "The Role of the King in the Jerusalem Cultus," in Hooke, ed., *The Labyrinth.*

Juynboll, T. W. "Pilgrimage (Arabian and Muhammadan) ," in Hastings, *Encyclopaedia of Religion and Ethics,* Vol. X.

Kautzsch, E., in Kautzsch-Bertholet, *Die Heilige Schrift des Alten Testaments.* Vols. I-II. 4th ed. Tübingen: Mohr, 1922-23.

Keet, C. C. *The Liturgical Study of the Psalter.* London: Allen & Unwin, 1926.

Ker, John. *The Psalms in History and Biography.* Edinburgh: Elliot, 1887.

Kirkpatrick, A. F. *The Psalms* (The Cambridge Bible for Schools and Colleges) . Cambridge University, 1901-4.

Kittel, Rudolf., ed. *Biblia Hebraica.* 3rd ed. Stuttgart: Priv. Württ. Bibelanstalt, 1937.

————. *Die Psalmen übersezt und erklärt* (Sellin's "Kommentar zum Alten Testament") . 5th and 6th ed. Leipzig: Dcichert-Scholl, 1929.

Knudson, Albert C. *The Religious Teaching of the Old Testament.* New York: Abingdon-Cokesbury Press, 1918.

Küchler, F. "Das priesterliche Orakel in Israel und Juda," in *Abhandlungen zur semitischen Religionskunde und Sprachwissenschaft,* W. W. Graften von Baudissin überreicht. *Beihefte zur Zeitschrift für die Alttestamentliche Wissenschaft,* 33. Giessen: Töpelmann, 1918.

Lagarde, P. *Symmicta.* Vols. I-II. Göttingen: Dieterich, 1877-80.

Langdon, Stephen. *Babylonian Menologies and the Semitic Calendars.* London: Oxford University Press, 1935.

————. "Semitic Mythology," in *Mythology of All Races.* Vol. V. Boston: Marshall Jones Co., 1931.

————. *Sumerian and Babylonian Psalms.* Paris: Geuthner, 1909.

————. *The Babylonian Epic of Creation.* Oxford: The Clarendon Press, 1924.

Leslie, Elmer A. "Introduction to the Psalms" and "Commentary on Psalms 1-72," in *Abingdon Bible Commentary.* New York: Abingdon-Cokesbury Press, 1929.

————. *Old Testament Religion, in the Light of its Canaanite Background.* New York: Abingdon-Cokesbury Press, 1936.

————. *Poetry and Wisdom,* "A Guide for Bible Readers." New York and Nashville: Abingdon-Cokesbury Press, 1945.

Macalister, R. A. S. "Sacrifice (Semitic) ," in Hastings, *Encyclopaedia of Religion and Ethics.* Vol. XI.

McFadyen, J. E. *The Psalms in Modern Speech.* Boston: Pilgrim Press, 1916.

————. "Vows (Hebrew) ," in Hastings, *Encyclopaedia of Religion and Ethics,* Vol. XII.

Meissner, B. *Babylonien und Assyrien.* Vols. I-II. Heidelberg: Winters, 1920.

Moffatt, James. *The Old Testament: A New Translation.* Garden City: Doubleday & Co.

Montet, Pierre. *Le drame d'Avaris: essai sur la pénétration des Sémites en Égypte.* Paris: Geuthner, 1941.

Moore, George Foot. *History of Religions.* Vol. II. New York: Charles Scribner's Sons, 1919.

————. *Judaism in the First Centuries of the Christian Era.* Vols. I-III. Cambridge: Harvard University Press, 1932.

————. "Vows," in M .A. Canney, *Encyclopedia of Religion.* London: Adam and Charles Black, 1903.

Mowinckel, Sigmund. *Psalmenstudien.* Kristiania: Dybwad, 1921-24.

   Vol. I. *'Awen und die individuellen Klagepsalmen.*

   Vol. II. *Das Thronbesteigungsfest Jahwehs und der Ursprung der Eschatologie.*

   Vol. III. *Kultprophetie und prophetische Psalmen.*

   Vol. IV. *Die technischen Termini in den Psalmenüberschriften.*

   Vol. V. *Segen und Fluch in Israels Kult und Psalmdichtung.*

   Vol. VI. *Die Psalmdichter.*

Muilenburg, James. "Psalm 47," in *Journal of Biblical Literature,* LXIII (1944), 235-56.

Musil, A. *Arabia Petraea.* Vol. III. Wien: Hölder, 1908.

Oesterley, W. O. E. *A Fresh Approach to the Psalms.* New York: Charles Scribner's Sons, 1937.

————. "Early Hebrew Festivals," in Hooke, ed., *Myth and Ritual.*

————. *The Psalms, Book III, Book IV.* London: Society for the Promoting of Christian Knowledge, 1933.

————. *The Psalms Translated with Text-Critical and Exegetical Notes.* Vols. I-II. London: Society for Promoting Christian Knowledge, 1939.

———— and Robinson, T. H. *Hebrew Religion, Its Origin and Development.* 2nd ed. New York: The Macmillan Co., 1937.

———— and Robinson, T. H. *History of Israel.* Vol. II. Oxford: The Clarendon Press, 1932.

Pallis, S. A. *The Babylonian Akitu Festival.* Copenhagen: Host & Son, 1926.

Patton, J. H. *Canaanite Parallels in the Book of Psalms.* Baltimore: Johns Hopkins University Press, 1944.

Pedersen, J. *Israel, Its Life and Culture.* Vols. I-II. London: Milford, 1926.

Perles, F. *Analekten zur Textkritik des Alten Testaments.* München: Ackermann, 1895. New series, Leipzig: Engle, 1922.

Peters, J. P. *The Psalms as Liturgies.* New York: G. P. Putnam's Sons, 1922.

Pfeiffer, R. H. *Introduction to the Old Testament.* New York: Harper & Bros., 1941.

————. "The Growth of Old Testament Religion." *Shane Quarterly,* VIII (1947), 7-31.

Pfister, F. "Kultus," in Pauly-Wissowa, *Real Encyclopädie der klassischen Altertumswissenschaft.* Vol. XXII. Stuttgart: Metzler.

Popper, W. "Pilgrimage (Hebrew and Jewish)," in Hastings, *Encyclopaedia of Religion and Ethics.* Vol. X.

Quell, Gottfried. *Das kultische Problem der Psalmen.* Berlin: Kohlhammer, 1926.

Rahlfs, Alfred. *Septuaginta.* Vol. II. Stuttgart: Priv. Württ. Bibelanstalt, 1935.

Robinson, H. W., ed., *Record and Revelation.* Oxford: The Clarendon Press, 1938.

Rodkinson, Michael. *New Edition of the Babylonian Talmud.* Vol. VII, "Tractate Sukkah." Boston: New Talmud Publishing Co., 1896.

Schechter, S. *Some Aspects of Rabbinic Theology.* New York: The Macmillan Co., 1909.

Schmidt, H. *Das Gebet der Angeklagten in den Psalmen. Beihefte zur Zeitschrift für die alttestamentliche Wissenschaft,* 49. Giessen: Töpelmann, 1928.

————. *Die Psalmen* (Eissfeldt's "Handbuch zum Alten Testament"). Tübingen: Mohr, 1934.

Schürer, Emil. *A History of the Jewish People in the Time of Jesus Christ.* First Division, Vols. I-II; Second Division, Vols. I-III. New York: Charles Scribner's Sons, 1891.

Sellers, O. R. "Musical Instruments in Israel," in *The Biblical Archaeologist,* IV (1941).

Sethe, Kurt. *Dramatische Texte zu altägyptischen Mysterienspielen.* Vol. I. Leipzig: Hinrichs, 1928.

Simpson, D. C., ed. *The Psalmists.* New York: Oxford University Press, 1926.

Smith, G. A. *The Historical Geography of the Holy Land.* Garden City: Doubleday & Co., 1919.

Snaith, Norman H. *Studies in the Psalter.* London: Epworth Press, 1934.

Speiser, Ephraim A. *Mesopotamian Origins.* Philadelphia: University of Pennsylvania Press, 1930.

Staerk, W. *Die Schriften des Alten Testaments.* 3 Abteilung, Band I (*Lyrik*), 2nd ed. Göttingen: Vandenhoeck und Ruprecht, 1920.

Strack, H. L., and Billerbeck, P. *Kommentar zum Neuen Testament aus Talmud und Midrasch.* Vol. IV, Part I. München: Beck, 1928.

Stummer, F. *Sumerisch-akkadische Parallelen zur Aufbau alttestamentlicher Psalmen.* Paderborn: Schöning, 1922.

Swete, H. B. *The Old Testament in Greek According to the Septuagint.* Vol. II. Cambridge: Cambridge University Press, 1891.

Thackery, H. St. John. *The Septuagint and Jewish Worship, a Study in Origins.* London: Oxford University Press, 1921.

The Holy Scriptures, According to the Masoretic Text. Philadelphia: Jewish Publication Society, 1917.

Thureau-Dangin, François. "Le rituel des fêtes du nouvel an à Babylone," in *Rituels Accadiens.* Paris: Leroux, 1921.

Torczyner, H., in *Zeitschrift der Deutschen Morgenländischen Gesellschaft,* LXVI (1912).

Tristram, H. B. *The Natural History of the Bible.* 3rd ed. London: Society for Promoting Christian Knowledge, 1873.

Volz, Paul. *Das Neujahrfest* (Laubhüttenfest). Tübingen: Mohr, 1912.

Walker, Rollin O. *The Modern Message of the Psalms.* New York: Abingdon-Cokesbury Press, 1936.

Welch, Adam C. *The Psalter in Life, Worship, and History.* Oxford: The Clarendon Press, 1926.

Wellhausen, Julius. "The Psalms," in P. Haupt, *Sacred Books of the Old Testament.* New York: Dodd, Mead, & Co.; 1898.

Widengren, George. *The Accadian and Hebrew Psalms of Lamentation as Religious Documents.* Stockholm: Bokforlags Aktiebolaget Thule, Uppsala, 1937.

Zimmern, H. "Babylonische Hymnen und Gebete," in *Der Alte Orient,* VII (1905).

_____. "Das babylonische Neujahrfest," in *Der Alte Orient,* XXV (1926).

_____. Über Alter und Herkunftsort des babylonischen Neujahrsfestrituals," in *Zeitschrift für Assyriologie,* XXXIV (1922).

INDEX TO BIBLICAL REFERENCES

Apocrypha